(6.) Entra
how w
Street and C
(7.) Delivery.
either front

office

Cross Section
Main
Shopping District —

store floor +3

ing & Storage —

traffic.

100'
— Stores fronts at most N'

Some 4' or more above street level.
arking below eye level from road
level of road — So parked machine
very of goods below build
window.

tures of autos into parking space.

The Writings of Clare

*Published in cooperation with
the Center for American Places,
Harrisonburg, Virginia*

The Writings of

CLARENCE S. STEIN

Architect of the Planned Community

Edited by KERMIT CARLYLE PARSONS

The Johns Hopkins University Press

Baltimore & London

This book has been brought to publication with the generous assistance of the Graham Foundation of Chicago and the Aline MacMahon Stein Endowment Fund of the College of Architecture, Art, and Planning at Cornell University.

9 8 7 6 5 4 3 2 1

The Johns Hopkins University Press
2715 North Charles Street
Baltimore, Maryland 21218-4363
The Johns Hopkins Press Ltd., London
www.press.jhu.edu

711.45
WRI

Title page illustration: Clarence Stein, in his late fifties, relaxing at A Thousand Years, his summer retreat.

Library of Congress Cataloging-in-Publication Data will be found at the end of this book.

A catalog record for this book is available from the British Library.

ISBN 0-8018-5756-2

In memory of Aline MacMahon Stein

Contents

Acknowledgments   ix

Editorial Policy   xiii

Introduction   xvii

Abbreviations   xxxv

1   Early Education in New York and Paris, 1903–1911   1

2   Home Again: Architect and Civic Reformer, 1911–1919   75

3   Regional Planning, Community Architecture, and Collaboration,
     1920–1929   103

4   Years of Success and Stress, 1930–1935   173

5   Time of Troubles, 1936–1939   359

6   The War and Postwar Planning, 1940–1949   399

7   Fulfillment and Recognition, 1950–1959   501

8   Satisfaction, 1960–1968   595

Appendixes

   A. Chronology   649

   B. Architectural, Planning, and Housing Projects   655

   C. Biographical Sketches   660

Bibliography

   Works by Clarence S. Stein   681

   Works about Clarence S. Stein   685

Index   689

Picture Credits   717

Acknowledgments

Two architects' wives were partners in this enterprise, making exceptional contributions to this book. The late Aline MacMahon Stein's determination to bring her husband's ideas to a larger readership added immeasurably to the editor's commitment to his work; she also contributed materially to the book's production. My wife, Janice Parsons, has contributed her hard work and endless patience to my efforts to understand Clarence Stein and his contribution to architecture and city and regional planning. She has left her mark on every page of this book. Clarence has been a member of our household for over a dozen years.

Much generous help and stimulation has come from many members of the architectural and city and regional planning intellectual community at Cornell and elsewhere: the University of Maryland, Massachusetts Institute of Technology, the University of Pennsylvania, and the University of California at Berkeley. My close friends and colleagues have contributed many hours to help me understand Stein's lifework, character, and influence on city building. First among many such friends are Eugenie Birch and Georgia Davis, who have provided encouragement, asked tough questions, edited my work at various stages of development, and helped me select letters that best convey, interpret, and evaluate Stein's contributions to city and regional planning. Professors Larry Gerckens of Ohio State University, Donald Krueckeberg of Rutgers University, Daniel Schaffer of the University of Tennessee, and Arnold Alanen of the University of Wisconsin–Madison provided their enormously valuable judgments about the organization and content of the book and most especially about the editor's selection of letters. These four scholars represent a de facto editorial board for the project and the publisher.

My Cornell colleagues Pierre Clavel, John Reps, and Michael Tomlan went out of their way to read and comment on the manuscripts of several articles about Stein, his projects, and his associates written during the editing of his papers. Helpful comments and criticism of my work on Stein and his associates were provided by Christopher Silver of Richmond, Virginia; Gorän Sidenbladh of Stockholm, Sweden; Gordon Cherry of Birmingham, England; and Mervyn Miller of Letchworth, England. Professors Gerhardt Fehl of Aachen, Germany, Hans Mammen of Arhüs, Denmark, and Francesco Dalco of Venice, Italy, also provided valuable encouragement and help. Julian Whittlesey's close reading of and comments on my early papers on Stein provided many invaluable insights into his character, his stubbornness, and his perceptions of the future.

I am greatly in debt to several dozen part-time research assistants, mostly graduate students at Cornell, who over the last decade or so helped organize and identify selections from the Stein Papers and transcribe the manuscript letters from the large collection of Stein Papers at Cornell. First among these was Ann Boyer Cotton, who organized and helped catalog much of the material during the first stages of the work. Matt O'Brien, Robert McCullough, Lane Addinazzio, Todd MacCain, Will Dunham, Adrienne Cowden, Evelyn Baker, Jennifer Hanna, Bret Garwood, Ted Gravsted-Nordbrock, and Kristen Larsen, to name only a few, are memorable among these scholar-helpers. I am also thankful for the skillful work of Bill Staffeld, who has, over the years, provided excellent photographic images for my articles about Clarence Stein and for this volume.

In this kind of collection, the most basic information is provided by archivists. Dr. Herbert Finch is by far the most important contributor to the collection and preservation of Clarence Stein's papers. He and my Cornell colleague, Professor Barclay Jones, founded the Cornell City and Regional Planning Archives. Finch personally acquired the C. S. Stein Papers. I am very grateful to him for this and his ever-smiling help. He and his colleagues, especially Nancy Dean, Elaine Engst, now the Cornell archivist, and H. Thomas Hickerson, have provided wonderful support in the preparation of this book, including the very thorough catalog of the Stein Papers. I am also grateful to the archivists of the University of California at Berkeley (Catherine Bauer Papers), the University of Pennsylvania (Lewis Mumford Papers), and Dartmouth College (MacKaye Family Papers). They have provided access to important sources for Stein's letters and related materials. The Housing Affairs Papers of the Rockefeller Brothers at the Rockefeller Institute, the Performing Arts Collection of the New York Public Library, the Archives of the Ethical Culture Society of New York, the Prints and Photograph Division of the Library of Congress, and the Manuscripts Division of the National Archives also yielded valuable information about Stein's life and career.

Over the years my research and writing have been much aided by the exceptional skills of many producers of computer-processed manuscripts. I am thankful for outstanding work by John Parsons during the early stages of production and by Nancy Hutter throughout my research and writing about Clarence Stein.

The research and travel during the start-up work on the selection of papers from various collections was made possible by an individual grant from the National Endowment for the Arts from 1984 to 1989. Publication of this volume became a real possibility when George F. Thompson, president of the Center for American Places, decided to work with me in 1991. His judgment and skill as an editor and his ideas about reorganizing and supplementing this volume were essential in bringing it to publication. Working as a consultant to the Johns Hopkins University Press, Thompson brought his good judgment and talents, as well as those of several readers and the book's editorial board of Schaffer, Krueckeberg, Gerckens, and Alanen, to bear on problems of earlier drafts.

At the Johns Hopkins University Press, Linda Forlifer's copy editing produced many improvements in the text; production editor Juliana McCarthy shepherded the book through the Press; and Omega Clay saw to it that the book's complex elements were set within a clear and beautiful design.

I am, of course, finally responsible for the choice of letters and other unpublished papers to include and the decisions about whether and how to annotate them. If not for the support of all of the above, however, I would still be reading Stein's letters and thinking that others should have a chance to sample part of the record of this pioneering community architect.

Editorial Policy

This single volume of selected correspondence and unpublished papers and sketches is designed to provide better access to the most interesting letters, unpublished essays, articles, and speeches of the innovative and influential American architect, Clarence S. Stein. Stein was noted for his interest in and design of housing and shared spaces that promoted equity and community values. These extensively annotated documents, presented in chronological order, have been selected from the large collection of his papers preserved in the Cornell University Archives and from the collections of friends and associates with whom he corresponded. They are published with bibliographic and biographical data to elucidate both the personal context within which Stein wrote them and the events, organizations, persons, and places he mentions.

These documents were selected to provide insights into Stein's personal development, his times, his associates, his architectural work, and his thoughts. Some reveal his early education, professional training, and experience of urban life in America and Europe. Others provide an understanding of the social, political, and architectural events on which Stein comments in his letters, speeches, and other papers; finally, some documents show his thinking about architectural and urban design issues, many of which are as relevant today as when he lived. The documents reveal his reactions to the quality of his environment and to problems of the natural and urban world he observed and to which his skills as a community-oriented architect were directed. My intention was, first of all, to give readers access to some materials that document the development of Stein's character, interests, and talents; second, I wanted to provide a sense of context—the people Stein worked with and observed and the organizations within which he thought and worked. Third, I selected letters and unpublished papers to provide an intimate personal idea of Stein's urban design values and the human values from which his innovations in community design grew.

The selection is limited by the large number of letters and papers written by Stein and by the fact that only some have been preserved. For example, the documents are not entirely representative of the time when he produced his most valued designs (Sunnyside, Radburn, and Chatham Village) because many of the business records of his New York office were destroyed when it was closed in the mid-1950s. Most of the letters dealing with his work during that period are from other collections or were brought home by Stein before the office was closed. Fortunately, Stein wrote often and at length to his parents from Paris in 1905–12 and to his wife, Aline MacMahon, during the 1930s and 1940s, when she was in Los Angeles making films and he was in New York designing communities. Stein's extensive correspondence with Lewis Mumford, Benton MacKaye, and Catherine Bauer provides a clear sense of his ideas on many issues and a good understanding of his relationships with his friends.

In preparing these documents for publication, I have not always provided the complete text. This is especially true for letters that include lengthy discussions about travel plans, schedules, and comments on the activities and foibles of mutual family friends and relatives. Where such passages have been deleted, they are marked with ellipses [. . .].

Stein's many letters to his parents and his wife sometimes include more detail than we need or want to know about places he is visiting, the everyday activities sociologists call *pattern maintenance,* and people he is working with. Representative passages of such texts should suffice to illuminate the texture of his everyday life. Correspondence about the day-to-day events, achievements, and disappointments of his wife's career in Hollywood films was similarly limited, while keeping in the printed text many passages giving a sense of how these two artist-professionals from different fields, architecture and acting, shared their lives and supported each other's struggles.

Clarence Stein's education at the Ethical Culture Workingman's School prepared him well for his work as an architect and his productive efforts in social and political reform, but he seems not to have learned much about grammar and spelling. We do not know whether the improvement of both in later writing is the result of learning or of the help of capable secretaries and editors. Many of the later easier-to-read typed manuscripts, letters, and texts probably benefited from both. I have silently corrected his documents, using standard American spelling, capitalization, and hyphenation, making complete sentences out of phrases, removing many long dashes between phrases, paragraphing less erratically, and adjusting punctuation for clarity. This was especially necessary in many long and interesting letters to Aline, which were often more like spoken phrases. Any text that was underlined in the original document is rendered here in italic type.

The letters, especially those written to Aline, frequently included sketches in the text or on separate pages; some of these are reproduced. Some of Stein's architectural and planning sketches and presentation drawings have also been included. Only a sample of his more formal presentation drawings and photographs of his architectural projects are published here to provide a visual context for some of his writing about architectural and planning matters. Numerous other publications—journal articles, books, and his own monograph, *Toward New Towns for America*—provide many readily available images of his designs. Most of the drawings and photographs selected for inclusion here were chosen to provide images of Stein, his family, and his associates, or they are reproduced from drawings directly executed in manuscript letters.

These letters and other papers are presented in chronological order, except for a few later autobiographical pieces, which are included in the time period they describe. A chronology of the main events of Stein's life, a list of projects, and biographical notes about most of the people mentioned in the texts are provided as appendixes. The bibliography includes Stein's published articles and articles about his work.

All manuscript material and drawings included in this volume, unless otherwise noted, are in the Clarence S. Stein Papers (Collection 3600) in the Cornell University Archives, which are housed in the Carl A. Kroch Library Rare and Manuscript Collections, Ithaca, New York.

Introduction

From time to time in every field of work, someone strikes out in a new direction, inventing new and clearly better ways to deal with the problems of the work at hand. Sometimes these innovations are in response to changes in opportunities or problems (e.g., changes in technology or stress in a society caused by conflict or growth). Some innovators seem to be especially well prepared for the task by unusual combinations of creative skills, values, and personality. In the profession of architecture and the emerging field of city planning during the second quarter of the twentieth century, Clarence Samuel Stein was such an innovator.

The ideals, community designs, ideas, projects, and writing of this American architect and planner are part of the intellectual and ideological roots of the modern American city and the regional planning profession. Stein, a New York City–reared, École des Beaux Arts–trained architect of more or less independent means, devoted much of his long life to improving the quality of community architecture and community life. He was awarded the Gold Medal of the American Institute of Architects in 1955 for his extraordinary contribution to community design and was recognized by the American Institute of Planners in 1962 as one of nine "pioneers of American planning."

Stein grew up during the last decades of the Progressive Era. He participated in its social reform politics and idealism and sought to extend his version of the good life to the less fortunate by working to eliminate residential blight; build affordable, high-quality housing; reduce urban congestion; and respond to the opportunities and problems of the automobile in the city. He was particularly effective in designing residential areas that included accessible green open space and improved the distribution of and access to essential community services and facilities.

As an architect, Stein is best known for his invention of new urban forms for residential settlement, including his housing designs with Henry Wright at Sunnyside (Long Island), Radburn (New Jersey), and Chatham Village (Pittsburgh); his designs for Phipps Garden apartments in Queens and Hillside Homes in the Bronx; and his influence on the program and design of Rexford Tugwell's Greenbelt Towns in the mid-1930s. In the United States these designs have demonstrated for more than six decades the power of attractive, safe, well-planned residential environments and the values that hold residents to life in such environments. Stein's designs also influenced major examples of excellence in post–World War II urban and suburban residential design in Great Britain, Scandinavia, France, and other European countries.

As a planner, Stein and his associates, Benton MacKaye and Lewis Mumford, produced innovative approaches to open space planning, wilderness preservation, and related new human settlement patterns for dispersing urban populations in a system of variously sized communities. They called this new pattern of metropolitan regional form the "regional city." They also defined a new form of connections between these communities, which they called the "townless highway."

Although the solutions to the problems of urban form that Stein proposed and convincingly demonstrated in his projects have not found universal acceptance in the United States, particularly in the area of moderate income or affordable housing for which they were intended, the community descendants of Radburn can be seen today in a number of residential area plans for affluent upper- and middle-income suburban communities and, on a large scale, in some more diverse New Towns, including Irvine (California), Reston (Virginia), Columbia (Maryland),[1] and most recently Woodlands (Texas).

In city and regional planning, Stein's writing and his conception, organization, and leadership of the Regional Planning Association of America (RPAA) provided several models for thinking about the settlement patterns of urban regions and about policies for shaping the decentralization of the Western metropolis.[2] Urban

1. Eugenie L. Birch, "Radburn and the American Planning Movement: The Persistence of an Idea," *Journal of the American Planning Association* 46 (October 1980): 424–39.

2. For the intellectual history of the RPAA, see Roy Lubove, *Community Planning in the '20s: The Contribution of the Regional Planning Association of America* (Pittsburgh: Pittsburgh Univ. Press, 1963); Carl Sussman, *The Fourth Migration* (Cambridge: MIT Press, 1979); Francesco Dal Co, "From Parks to Gardens," in *The American City, from the Civil War to the New Deal,* ed. Giorgio Cuicci, Francesco Dal Co, Mario Marrieri, and Elia and Manifredo Tafuri (Cambridge: MIT Press, 1979); Kermit C. Parsons, "Collaborative Genius: The Regional Planning Association of America," *Journal of the American Planning Association* 60 (autumn 1994): 462–82; Edward K. Spann, *Designing Modern America: The Regional Planning Association of America and Its Members* (Columbus: Ohio State Univ. Press, 1996).

social historians, including Roy Lubove, Carl Sussman, and Francesco Dal Co, have noted the great influence on the evolution of city planning and housing thought of the ideas of Stein and the first RPAA members, including Lewis Mumford, Benton MacKaye, Henry Wright, Alexander Bing, Stuart Chase, Frederick Ackerman, Robert Kohn, Charles Whitaker, and Edith Elmer Wood. Later, Charles Ascher, Catherine Bauer, Henry Churchill, and Albert Mayer joined them in developing major elements of the ideology and practice of city and regional planning in America after 1925. The RPAA's critical analysis of the modern metropolis published in 1925 and Stein's and Wright's 1926 proposals for a plan for New York state are major landmarks in modern thinking about urban regions.[3]

From 1923 to 1933 the RPAA functioned as a policy research and discussion group that spread its ideas by extensive publication and tested them by shaping innovative communities. Its members, especially Stein, Wright, Bing, and MacKaye, conceived and built projects that embody many of the ideas developed in RPAA discussion and writing. MacKaye's Appalachian Trail and Stein's, Wright's, and Bing's Radburn are the best-known products of the RPAA's genius. But the group, never larger than a dozen or so active members, was so integrated in its writing, teaching, and action that it is difficult to give sole attribution of many of its specific ideas to specific members. It is clear from his unpublished letters and papers that Clarence Stein first conceived such a group,[4] did most of the work needed to keep it functioning, and was its most active and effective member when it came to implementing its concepts in tangible policy documents, community designs, and projects. The success of the group was limited because many of its ideas were too radical even for adoption by Franklin Roosevelt's early New Deal, but, as Francesco Dal Co's investigations suggest, the work of this group of "idealistic intellectuals [contained] a model and a wealth of insights [that] would become part of [the New Deal's] far more complex ideology."[5]

For over forty years, Stein and his RPAA colleagues made important contributions to North American ideas about urban design, architecture, affordable housing, and urban policy. The writing and teaching of Mumford and Bauer, as well as the major urban planning projects of Stein and Wright, influenced the thinking of a generation of city and regional planners. Stein's ideas and projects in affordable housing, socially and environmentally responsible urban development, and shaping the growth of our sprawling metropolitan regions into systems of cities are set forth in his classic 1950s book, *Toward New Towns for America*. They are still relevant to our thinking about the critical problems of American urban development.

3. *Survey Graphic* (Regional Planning Number) 54, no. 5 (1925); Henry Wright and Clarence Stein, "Report of the New York State Commission of Housing and Regional Planning" (1926).

4. C. S. Stein, "Notes on the Establishment of a City Planning Atelier," c. 1922, Clarence Stein Papers, Cornell University Archives (CSP/CUA).

5. Dal Co, "From Parks to Gardens."

Stein called himself a *community architect* because he saw the need for architects to be concerned with not only the design of buildings and their decoration but also the design of whole communities. He argued that community design should satisfy human needs that could be met only by the total environment: the housing of people according to their economic, social, and physical needs, in relation to their place of work, where they shop, where their children play and go to school, libraries, day care, and health centers—all of those community activities that are essential parts of everyday life. And among essential human needs he included access to elements of the natural environment, more than just the light and air that earlier tenement house reformers had advocated and the large parks and picturesque, natural subdivisions that Olmsted and his nineteenth-century associates had designed. Stein proposed the incorporation of trees, parks, open space, cul-de-sac streets, and safety restrictions for traffic in residential areas in totally new patterns of urban layout, which came to be known as the *Radburn Plan* after the community in which it was first used.

The clients Stein served were not the rich, but rather were lower- and middle-income families and the working poor who had been priced out of the housing market and were crowded into the tenements of cities that were changing and expanding around them. He was one of the first "advocacy planners" who worked in New York City's Chelsea district as early as 1917, when changes stemming from railroad investment and increased port activity were threatening the neighborhood. He exhorted Chelsea's residents to get involved in city-building decision making before outsiders decided their future. He tried to apply his skills and professional expertise by working with people in the neighborhood to encourage and guide the city's response to change. On open land, where there were no residents with whom to work, he designed and developed communities such as Sunnyside, Radburn, one of the Greenbelt Towns (Greenbelt, Maryland), and Kitimat based on RPAA deliberations backed up by careful studies of needs.

What was the life experience of this talented, creative, orderly, quiet, yet stubborn man who helped invent modern city and regional planning? Clarence Stein has no biography or autobiography,[6] but there is in the Cornell University Archives a veritable archival treasure trove,[7] some fifty boxes of his letters, drafts of papers, published and unpublished articles, books, sketches, and planning studies that fur-

6. Stein did not take on the job of writing an autobiography. From time to time he collected materials for one. He assembled a notebook of biographical data and wrote brief sketches of special periods of his life. "Home Again," a two page document, is about his return to New York from Paris in late 1911. He was usually careful to date drafts of his papers, especially the latter ones, but he did no sustained biographical writing.

7. Stein's papers are located in the Cornell University Library Archives, where they are part of a special collection of papers of American planners and planning organizations.

nish insight into the mind and character of the man who styled himself a "community architect."

Stein began early in life to acquire the values that led to his interest in architecture, housing design, urban development, and city and regional planning. He was born in Rochester, New York, in June 1882, the third of six children of Rose Rosenblatt Stein and Leo Stein, a successful casket manufacturer and the grandson of an immigrant German cabinetmaker. The family moved to New York City in 1890, and Rose enrolled Clarence in Felix Adler's Ethical Culture Society's Workingman's School on West Fifty-fourth Street as one of the few paying students. For the next eight years, until he was sixteen, Stein's visual imagination, sense of social responsibility, and inquiring intellect were shaped by the methods and tenets of Felix Adler's innovative school. Its curriculum followed the pioneering work of Friederich Froebel, whose ideas about the kindergarten influenced the entire primary educational program of the Workingman's School. Here, activities, art, and play were essential parts of the learning process.[8] The school's teachers included John Lovejoy Elliott, who, like Adler, was committed to the new methods of teaching and to the progressive reform movement in New York City politics. Elliott involved his students in studies of the life and politics of the city and in the activities of the Hudson Guild Settlement House in the Chelsea neighborhood. This unusual education helped to produce a young man who was very attuned to observing, analyzing, and criticizing the city around him. He was critical of the bad qualities of the urban environment, felt strongly about social injustice, and decried urban congestion.

Stein left the Workingman's School in 1898, most likely because of a traumatic experience that left him "nearly blind."[9] After several years of recovery in Jacksonville, Florida, Clarence, like his brothers William and Herbert, went to work in his father's casket-manufacturing business. Stein did not take to his father's business or to the study of architecture at Columbia University in 1903 and 1904. Then, acting upon the stimulus of a tour of Europe with his father in the summer of 1903, he left New York for Paris in the summer of 1905 to study interior decoration and soon "all of architecture."[10] His life in Paris, perhaps at that time one of the most cosmopolitan cities in the Western world, and his study of architecture at the demanding École des Beaux Arts under the tutelage of Victor Laloux, were for twenty-

8. For a brief history of the New York City Workingman's School, see Howard Radest, *Toward Common Ground: The Story of the Ethical Societies in the United States* (Garden City, N.Y.: Feldston Press, 1987), 42–44.

9. Recollection of his brother, William, in a letter of 12 June 1967 to Clarence: "Seventy years ago you went to Furgotta (?) in Jacksonville nearly blind" (CSP/CUA). Aline MacMahon Stein, interview by editor in New York City, October 1986: Aline recalled the injury suffered, a blow to Clarence's head, and that he was sent to Florida to recuperate from partial blindness.

10. Stein's papers in the Cornell University Archives include several hundred letters written to his parents and other family members about his life and education in Paris.

three-year-old Stein not only a rigorous education but also an urban apotheosis. Taken together they were a powerful educational experience, which provided an expanded understanding of the possibilities of city life. Both the school and Paris had profound influences on his career in architecture, his cultural interests, and his imaginative ideas about the relationship of people to their communities. His letters to his family from these years recount the difficulties, the joys, and the wonders of a young American in Paris and a firsthand account of student life at the École.

Shortly after his return from Europe in 1912 at the age of thirty, Stein joined the office of Bertram Grosvenor Goodhue, who was well established as a major force in American architecture. There Stein plunged into the design problems of the San Diego World's Fair and its buildings; a large copper mining town in southern New Mexico; houses and a country club in Santa Barbara, California; a major church, St. Bartholomew's, in New York City; and military bases in southern California during the period before World War I. He worked on large projects with big ideas and a great variety of architectural problems. Biographical material filed by Henry Churchill as part of Stein's nomination for the Gold Medal of the American Institute of Architects (AIA) refers to him as Goodhue's "chief designer." After 1919 he continued to evolve in his own architectural practice following Goodhue's example with powerful, picturesque composition and appropriate and disciplined use of color and ornament. But Stein had a second, parallel vocation. From 1912 to 1918 he was active (as he had been earlier) in the New York Ethical Culture Society's civic reform efforts and tenement house reform. He became active in the Hudson Guild Settlement House's movement in the Chelsea Association for Planning and Action and in the City Planning Committee of the Ethical Culture Society's City Club.

As U.S. involvement in World War I became imminent, Clarence Stein was caught up in a desire to join the fighting. Underweight and thirty-five, he managed to secure a commission as a lieutenant in the Army Corps of Engineers to fight the war, as he wrote later, in the hills of Virginia. Service during the war was a turning point in Stein's career. At war's end he did not return to Goodhue's office. He began to integrate his professional practice of architecture with his personal interest in political, environmental, and social reform. While he continued to work as an architect, he increased his attention to work in urban planning, housing, and New York State housing policy. Just after World War I, his letters to the editor of the *Journal of the American Institute of Architects,* Charles Whitaker, provide a brief glimpse of his thinking about housing reform and regional planning and about the importance of a major role for state government in housing for the poor and "near poor." Through his friends in the Ethical Culture Society, Stein became involved in New York City politics and campaigned for Al Smith, who in 1919 appointed him chairman of the Housing Committee of the Reconstruction Commission of New York State. In the summer of 1921, Stein began his collaboration with Benton MacKaye on MacKaye's idea for the Appalachian Trail.[11] This work on the problems of city housing and the promise of the wilderness trail shaped the most creative and productive period of Stein's career.

In a note that seems to have been written late in the summer of 1922 during his voyage back from a tour of European housing and New Towns, he outlined a "Plan for a City Planning Atelier,"[12] which would meet for dinner "every second week," after which the members would discuss a variety of topics and work on projects. Stein suggested that the members of such a group should include architects, engineers, landscape architects, sociologists, economists, city officials, union leaders, and writers. Its purpose would be the "study of man's physical environment as it was influenced by social, economic, and aesthetic needs, and the technical means of creating new environments serving these needs—with special emphasis on America and the future."

Stein's proposals for subjects for the group's discussion and projects were broad in scope: study of the history of the plan of New York City, as well as current planning of the Port Authority and other local city-planning issues. These subjects were to be balanced by consideration of the "possibility of" developing satellite cities, studies of the plans of other cities, of housing legislation, and of the "underlying economic principles" of and "social influences" on city development. The group's research was to consider the application of planning at all levels, "rural, regional and national," and they also were to consider, Stein thought, "what type of Garden City will fit the needs of America." His visits with Ebenezer Howard in England and to his prototype Garden Cities at Letchworth and Welwyn in 1922 were clearly a source of inspiration. It is equally clear that the study group he proposed was a product of his experience in Dr. Elliott's civic clubs at the Hudson Guild Settlement House, in Laloux's atelier at the École des Beaux Arts, and in design collaboration in Goodhue's office.

Early in 1923 Stein organized the first meeting of the study group. At first, members chose the name Garden Cities and Regional Planning Association of America. Later, under the influence of Patrick Geddes, the theorist and Scottish regional planner who was Mumford's mentor, they changed the organization's name to the Regional Planning Association of America (RPAA). With Stein as their convenor and Alexander Bing as their president, this small band formulated what some of their contemporaries during the following decade considered very radical ideas about housing policy, community design, and regional planning.

---

11. Benton MacKaye, "An Appalachian Trail: A Project in Regional Planning," *Journal of the American Institute of Architects* 9, no. 10 (1921); C. S. Stein to Benton MacKaye, 19 December 1921, MacKaye Family Papers, Dartmouth College Archives (MFP/DCA).

12. Stein, "Notes on a City Planning Atelier."

Several RPAA members, including Frederick Ackerman, Henry Wright, Benton MacKaye, and Lewis Mumford, worked directly with Stein during the early and mid-1920s, when he was chairman of the American Institute of Architects' Community Design Committee and served as associate editor of the *Journal of the American Institute of Architects*. Stein, now with the assistance of the RPAA, continued to help implement Benton's idea for the Appalachian Trail in an active program of trail building. Another set of RPAA members' articles, in a special "Regional Planning Number" of *Survey Graphic* magazine of May 1925, were published to coincide with the New York meetings of the International Federation for Housing and Town Planning. Mumford wrote two articles and edited the issue. Stein's contribution, "Dinosaur Cities," was an indictment of the waste and human suffering that characterizes the worst parts of large American cities. He argued that large cities were breaking down and becoming obsolete because congestion and high land costs had caused overcrowding, slums, and the collapse of transportation systems. "Beyond a certain point, more transportation routes mean more congestion." This insight was not fully accepted by transportation policy makers and planners until the 1970s. The RPAA also railed against the conventional city planning of the day. For example, Mumford's attack on Thomas Adams's concepts for the Regional Plan Association's Plan of New York and Environs grew out of discussions of the group and received its staunch backing.[13]

The RPAA's influence on urban development was advanced through its members' skillful and prolific writing, but equally important were the efforts of several of its members to provide examples of their theories in action. Two such examples were the large-scale housing developments Stein and his associates built at Sunnyside in Queens and at Radburn, New Jersey, in 1924 and 1928. In these projects, Stein, Henry Wright, and Alexander Bing rethought the basic social and environmental needs, as well as the financing and physical layout, of the American urban residential community; in so doing, they created new urban forms.[14]

To execute these residential design experiments, Bing organized the limited-dividend City Housing Corporation (CHC) to acquire and develop land. He successfully interested philanthropic investors, including V. E. Macy, John D. Rockefeller, and Robert Simon. Bing invented financial instruments that would attract philanthropic capital and mortgage loans that allowed families of moderate income to

---

13. Lewis Mumford, "The Plan of New York (I & II)," *New Republic* (15 and 22 June 1932). For discussions of Mumford's criticism and Adams's response, see Michael Simpson, *Thomas Adams and the Modern Planning Movement* (Oxford: Alexandrian Press, 1985), 153–58; and David A. Johnson, *Planning the Great Metropolis: The 1929 Regional Plan of New York and Its Environs* (London: E. and F. N. Spon, 1996), 185–94.

14. Daniel Schaffer, *Garden Cities for America: The Radburn Experience* (Philadelphia: Temple Univ. Press, 1982); K. C. Parsons, "Collaborative Genius: The Regional Planning Association of America," *American Journal of the American Planning Association* 60, no. 4 (1994).

own or rent the housing that would be constructed. His corporation was organized under the pioneering New York State housing legislation that Stein had championed as chairman of Governor Al Smith's Commission of Housing and Regional Planning.

Stein and Wright served as the company's principal town planners and architects. In Sunnyside Gardens they experimented with the central organization of blocks. They created common green space at the center of each block and developed a system of legal covenants that established community joint responsibility for these commons. At Sunnyside they also acquired the management skills needed for large-scale urban development enterprises and pioneered long term, low-interest home loans and mortgage guarantees. This enabled people who otherwise could not have been approved for home purchase loans to secure them. The Sunnyside development, which housed twelve hundred families, was so successful that the CHC moved quickly to acquire land for a more extensive experimental New Town development in New Jersey.[15]

The design for the New Town of Radburn, New Jersey, was even more innovative than Sunnyside. Radburn was Stein's prototype adaptation to America of Ebenezer Howard's Garden City concept. The CHC initiated the project in 1927, when it began to acquire almost two square miles of land in the borough of Fairlawn in Bergan County, New Jersey, sixteen miles from Manhattan. At Radburn, Stein and Wright created what Stein termed a "revolution in planning" to deal for the first time, he wrote later, with the problem of "how to live with the auto." The typical urban or suburban residential block was replaced by a "superblock." Access to single, duplex, and triplex houses for motor vehicles was provided on cul-de-sac lanes penetrating from the superblock's perimeter roads. Row houses and apartments were part of the housing mix. A complete pedestrian circulation system for the interiors of the superblocks provided children with access to recreation and schools protected from the noise and danger of automobile traffic. This continuous interior footpath and park system also gave a focus for outdoor living and affected the room arrangements in the houses. For example, the principal living areas of the houses were oriented toward the green space and away from the streets. The green spaces and walkways of each superblock were connected to adjacent superblocks and the town center, schools, and recreation facilities by underpasses and overpasses, thus forming a continuous footpath and open space system for the use of the entire community. Planning for Radburn got under way in 1927.

A year later, at the age of forty-six and after an extended courtship, Clarence Stein married the sloe-eyed and versatile Aline MacMahon, a Broadway actress. She

15. Clarence Stein, *Toward New Towns for America* (Liverpool: Univ. Press of Liverpool, 1951); Kermit C. Parsons, "Financing Affordable Housing: Lessons from Alexander Bing's Innovations at Sunnyside and Radburn in the 1920s" (paper presented at the Annual Conference of the Association of Collegiate Schools of Planning, Tempe, Ariz., 6 November 1994).

was a Barnard College graduate with an Irish father and a Russian-Jewish mother. At twenty-eight, Aline had already achieved critical acclaim in the Broadway production of one of Eugene O'Neill's early plays, *Beyond the Horizon*.[16] When they were married, Aline had been appearing in *Artists and Models, Paris Style,* under contract with the Schubert organization, and she took occasional leave to perform in the *Grand Street Follies* at the Henry Street Settlement Playhouse.

Then, in the late 1920s, just when the RPAA's writing was reaching its most biting critical sharpness and the projects of Stein, Wright, and Bing at Sunnyside and Radburn were reaching a peak of recognition, the national economy collapsed. The subsequent steep decline of the housing market between 1929 and 1932 eventually bankrupted the City Housing Corporation. Bing was forced to end construction in 1932 and end the Radburn experiment in 1937.

Radburn's declining home sales, Sunnyside's well-publicized financial troubles, and the ultimate failure of the CHC with great losses to Al Bing did not dissuade Stein from trying to build on the lessons that had been learned. He was a somewhat perplexed and dismayed observer of the effects of the Depression. But, like many of his colleagues in the RPAA, he thought a revolution was at hand—that capitalism could not and perhaps should not survive. For Stein personally, the revolution was to take place in the design of communities and urban regions as he and the RPAA worked to influence FDR's New Deal policies.

Stein's dozen years of leadership in the RPAA and his lifelong influence on his friends and associates are of equal and possibly more lasting value than his projects. He was a strong leader, though he seemed at times somewhat shy and retiring, polite, quiet, unobtrusive, and deferential. His character was that of a diminutive, sophisticated, streetwise, city politician, well dressed and well versed in the politics of Al Smith's crowd of urban reformers. Like Al Smith, he bridged the gap between the well-to-do Fifth Avenue civic reformers and the working people of the Chelsea district and the lower East Side. He, more than any of his colleagues in the RPAA, was a political person, an outgoing, persistent advocate of reform in housing and of strong state and national intervention in the urban development process. He had a well-developed sense of the political problems of achieving his ideals. As Radburn continued to receive national and international notice, Stein emerged as a national leader in housing and planning policy.

Lewis Mumford's biographer Donald Miller comments on Clarence's "camouflaged" leadership qualities in a sketch that seems to be based on an interview with Mumford.[17] "[Clarence Stein's] physical appearance," he writes, "disguised his con-

---

16. *Beyond the Horizon,* the fourth of O'Neill's full-length plays, opened early in February 1920 to critical acclaim, including Alexander Woolcott's "The Coming of Eugene O'Neill" in the *New York Times. Beyond the Horizon* won the first of O'Neill's four Pulitzer Prizes in 1920.

17. Donald L. Miller, *Lewis Mumford: A Life* (New York: Weidenfeld and Nicholson, 1989), 193.

siderable talents for leadership." He was slight, thin, even frail looking. Miller speculates that, "perhaps to compensate for his frail appearance, he smoked large black cigars, talking out of the side of his mouth as he chewed the end of his cigar." Of course, this cigar smoking may also have been part of his lifestyle, his lifelong enjoyment of good food, fine wines, and stimulating conversation. Miller reports (speaking for Mumford, for the biographer never met Stein) that Clarence "could be steel-willed and decisive, but . . . never inflexible or dogmatic . . . a modest man, withdrawn, but congenial." He could be tough, but he had a sweet nature. These contrasting personal characteristics are reported by others and documented in Stein's own letters, especially those written to his wife, Aline, from the early 1930s onward.

The first half of the 1930s is the most completely documented period of Clarence Stein's career. In 1931 Aline accepted a leading role in the West Coast company of Moss Hart's Broadway comedy success *Once in a Lifetime*. The role provided a "showcase" for Aline's talents, and Warner Brothers soon offered her a screen test, which marked the start of her long career in films. Clarence and Aline were separated for long periods while she was in Hollywood beginning her career in the film industry. They corresponded daily, and sometimes Stein wrote two letters a day. Many of their letters have been preserved. They provide an appealing human record of the excitement and frustration of their work, the pain of their separation, and the pleasures and accomplishments of their professional and social lives, as well as an interesting account of social, cultural, and economic change in New York City and the nation during the Depression.

The projects Stein completed and designed in the early 1930s include his most famous: the completion of Radburn (New Jersey), the planning with Henry Wright of Chatham Village (Pittsburgh), his design for the Phipps Garden Apartments at Sunnyside (Long Island) in 1931, and Hillside Homes (1932–35), a very large, influential, medium-density housing development in the Bronx. In 1935 Stein participated as a consultant and design review team member in FDR's innovative Greenbelt Towns program led by Rexford Tugwell.

Stein's letters to Aline and his close friends Mumford and MacKaye during the early 1930s provide many open, uninhibited reactions to the people he met and worked with and their ideas. He comments on such political figures as Franklin D. Roosevelt, Fiorello LaGuardia, Nathan Straus, Robert Kohn, Harold Ickes, and Gerard Swope, as well as on people from his professional and social life, including Eliel Saarinen, Charles Whitaker, Raymond Hood, Harold Shreve, Diego Rivera, e. e. cummings, Moss Hart, Aline Bernstein, Lee Simonson, Lewis Mumford, Catherine Bauer, Frederick Ackerman, and Archibald MacLeish.

He also wrote much about his travels, as one might expect from from someone who worked hard to keep intact one of the first transcontinental marriages. The Steins' long rail trips early in this period (writing while en route) gave way to short daytime-only air travel and Clarence's first coast-to-coast airline trip in an amazing sixteen hours with two stops. His excited descriptions of the views of the American landscape and cities from the air are no doubt typical of the initial amazed reaction of early airline travelers.

During the mid-1930s the activities of the RPAA slowed down as its members dispersed, and their meetings almost ceased during World War II. But the group resumed its policy discussions in 1948 as the Regional Development Council of America (RDCA) and expressed its views on major national policy issues in housing and regional development. Lewis Mumford, Stein, Benton MacKaye, Stuart Chase, and Albert Mayer, a World War II recruit to the group, continued to write for major national periodicals (*Fortune, Architectural Forum, Nation,* and *New Republic,* among others). Stein's letters report on these activities, the members' mutual criticism of each others' work, and their collaboration on integrated presentations of ideas and projects, such as the 1939 documentary *The City.*

Meanwhile, the Radburn idea slowly began to shape American residential design. In 1935 Stein had a determining influence on the Greenbelt Towns program and especially on the major elements of the design of Greenbelt, Maryland. He accomplished this by participation in design review sessions for the first Greenbelt Town. After one meeting, he wrote to Aline that he was pleased and "terrified" by the deference of Greenbelt's designers and by the willingness of the project's architects and planners to make changes he suggested in their plans.[18]

Late in 1935 Stein, disappointed that he was not commissioned to design one of the Greenbelt Towns, and Aline, frustrated by losing the lead role in the film of Pearl Buck's *The Good Earth,* took a four-month trip around the world. They spent long periods in Bali and in Peking, China, and returned refreshed. For Clarence, however, there was the difficulty of not having any architectural or planning work of consequence.

In late 1936 and early 1937, Stein suffered the first in a series of episodes of the illness that was then termed a *nervous breakdown.*[19] Although he was more or less incapacitated by several long periods of this illness before, during, and immediately after World War II, Stein managed to contribute effectively to the formulation of

18. Clarence S. Stein to his wife, 24 and 29 October 1935, CSP/CUA.

19. Stein's letters to Aline and Lewis Mumford from Silver Hill Sanitarium in Connecticut in 1937 and from a ranch in Arizona, where he went to recover in 1942, document some of the trauma of these episodes of depression. They may have followed manic phases of his mental state during his most productive years in the 1920s and early 1930s. There is some evidence that Stein's illness was manic depressive. Accounts of his moods are also found in his and Aline's correspondence. Aline M. Stein to Benton MacKaye, 22 February 1937 (MFP/DCA). Kay Redfield Jamison argues in her recent books, *Touched with Fire* (New York: Free Press, 1993) and *An Unquiet Mind* (New York: Alfred A. Knopf, 1996), that great artists' aesthetic sensibilities and their intensity and creative force are often related to manic-depressive illness.

U.S. defense housing policy in 1941 and to wartime community building and facilities policy from 1942 to 1944. He designed several high-quality "defense" housing projects in Pittsburgh in the early 1940s. During the war years Clarence and Aline spent increasing amounts of time together, but he was frustrated in his main purpose in life. True, the urban planning and architectural design innovations he had introduced at Sunnyside, Radburn, Chatham Village, Hillside Homes, and Baldwin Hills Village were incorporated in his wartime consulting and housing projects. However, he yearned to participate in making possible totally new patterns of urban development after the war.

By mid-1947 Stein had made a remarkable recovery from his illness. He actively lobbied Congress and the Truman administration to prevent the sell-off by the federal government to private developers of the three FDR Greenbelt Towns. They were, Stein thought, ideal models for the dispersed and decentralized regional system of cities that he and fellow RPAA members envisioned. He worked with Catherine Bauer and his Republican friend, Ernest Bohn, "the father of public housing" and Director of the Cleveland Metropolitan Housing Authority,[20] in lobbying efforts that were partially successful. His most significant success was at Greenbelt, Maryland, which was sold to a Veterans Cooperative and whose greenbelt was incorporated into regional parks.[21]

But the most important achievement of Stein's late 1940s recovery of productivity and influence was his response to Lewis Mumford's urging that he "write about the main achievements of his life's work in community architecture." With the encouragement and support of Mumford and Gordon Stephenson, the editor of the British planning journal *Town Planning Review,* he wrote three long, clear, persuasive, and well-illustrated articles about Sunnyside, Radburn, Chatham Village, Phipps Garden Apartments, Hillside Homes, the Greenbelt Towns, and Baldwin Hills Village. He wrote about their objectives, his design process, and the building of these communities, as well as the meaning of their designs to possible future American urban development patterns. These articles were well received in England, Sweden, and North America. Many planners and architects, faced with rehousing Europe after the war and catching up with housing demand in the United States and Europe, were seeking just these kinds of ideas for and examples of socially and environmentally responsible, humane, efficient, beautiful, and safe urban residential development projects. The purpose, the agenda, and the reality of these examples of Stein's "revolution in planning" were now presented together for the

20. Larry Gerckens, "Some Preliminary Notes on the Life of Ernest John Bohn of Cleveland, the Father of American Public Housing: The Foundation Years 1920–1924" (paper presented to the 24th Annual Conference of the Association of Collegiate Schools of Planning, Chicago, 23 October 1982).

21. K. C. Parsons, "Clarence Stein and the Greenbelt Towns, Settling for Less," *Journal of the American Institute of Planners,* Spring 1990.

first time in a major planning journal and, soon after, in 1951, were published in book form as *Toward New Towns for America*[22]

Stein's correspondence with Catherine Bauer and Paul Oppermann in California and Carl Feiss and Tracy Auger in Washington, D.C., in the 1950s reveals both the breadth of Stein's vision and the limitations of local and national urban planning policy as he sought almost single-handedly and from a distance to implement the regional planning ideas of the RPAA. He utilized every opportunity and every contact to propose New Towns as an organizing mechanism to influence the quality and balanced mix of uses and open space in future regional development.

Stein's letters of the 1950s to Catherine Bauer and Tracy Augur record his efforts to take advantage of unique opportunities to influence the shape and quality of future development in two particularly important and naturally beautiful regions of the country. First, he saw in the large land estate left to Stanford University by Governor Stanford an opportunity for planned development of a broad range of land uses in the path of the urban expansion of the San Francisco Bay Area. In 1950 he recommended that the university take the lead in developing a new community. At almost the same time Tracy Auger, former Tennessee Valley Authority (TVA) planner now assigned to the federal government's General Services Administration (GSA), asked Stein's help in preparing a plan for the dispersal of a dozen federal employee office centers in the Washington metropolitan region. Truman feared an atomic bomb attack by the Soviet Union on the capital. Stein reasoned that, if essential offices related to "war making" were to be dispersed north and west of the District of Columbia, so should be their employees' housing and related services. Stein proposed an arc of planned New Towns in the Maryland and Virginia countryside.[23] In 1951, Congress did not approve funds for the GSA's employment centers. It is remarkable that the locations of Washington suburban federal employment centers and New Towns, such as Reston, Columbia, and Gaithersburg, built later are essentially similar to the Augur and Stein proposals of 1950. The Washington-Baltimore metropolitan region's so-called edge cities also embody a weak echo of Auger's and Stein's dispersion plans.

More tangible evidence of the urban development consequences of Clarence Stein's conceptual thinking, leadership, and organizational ability are to be found in his correspondence with Albert Mayer and his associate, Julian Whittlesey, on two important new communities of the 1950s: Chandigarh in East Punjab, India, a new

22. *Toward New Towns for America* was published in 1951 by the Liverpool University Press using the *Town Planning Review* plates. It has subsequently been reprinted in revised editions by Reinhold Press (1957) and MIT Press (1966).

23. K. C. Parsons, "Shaping the Regional City, 1950–1990: The Plans of Tracy Augur and Clarence Stein for Dispersing Federal Workers from Washington, D.C.," in *Proceedings of the Third National Conference on American Planning History* (Cincinnati: Society for American City and Regional Planning History, 1989), 649–91.

provincial capital, and Kitimat, British Columbia, a New Town generated by the smelter operations of the Aluminum Company of Canada (ALCAN). The high points of Stein's "second career" as a consultant, writer, and urban statesman in the 1950s were his role as director of planning for the Canadian New Town of Kitimat and his influence on community building in India, Great Britain, and Sweden.[24]

Throughout the last decades of his life, Stein continued to write to his old friends, Catherine Bauer, Benton MacKaye, and Lewis Mumford, and his circle of correspondents continued to grow. Letters to many of these new correspondents were selected for inclusion in this volume: to Karl Belser, planner of the ambitious and admired open-space preservation effort in San Jose, California; Paul Opper-mann, director of planning in San Francisco; Edmund Bacon, director of planning in Philadelphia; Benjamin Kizer, an attorney active in regional planning in the Pacific Northwest; Chloethiel Woodward Smith, who was designing a residential district for Washington, D.C.,'s southwest redevelopment project; Carl Feiss, a key figure in federal urban development policy; Frederic J. Osborn in England; Göran Sidenbladh and Yngve Larsson in Sweden; and Arieh Sharon and Arthur Glikson, key planners and regional planning theorists in Israel.

Both the number of correspondents and the range of Stein's interests are staggering. For example, he gave time to planning and architectural education at Berkeley, where his friends the Wursters were setting up the School of Environmental Design, and at the Massachusetts Institute of Technology (MIT), Columbia, Cornell, and North Carolina. He was concerned about the imminent demise of the *British Town Planning Review*, the only international publication of its kind at the time, and corresponded to secure funds in North America to support its continuation. In the twenty years from 1948 to 1968, his New York City apartment was the East Coast hub for many transatlantic visitors engaged in significant architectural and town planning activity. By means of his extensive correspondence and professional contacts, he helped move them around the country so that their ideas and experience might gain further currency.

Occasionally the letters included in this volume are not about architecture or planning, but rather serve to establish the social and cultural milieu of the Steins: letters about close friends in the theater, for example, who are part of other stories, or letters that highlight their concern for the plight of Jewish refugees under German oppression and genocide, or comments that provide historical insight to political issues in which they were involved, such as the Hollywood blacklist. Stein's letters and notes, especially those written to Benton MacKaye and Lewis Mumford,

24. Norma Evenson, *Chandigarh* (Berkeley: Univ. of California Press, 1966); K. C. Parsons, "American Influence on Stockholm's Post World War II Suburban Expansion," *Planning History* 14, no. 1 (1992); K. C. Parsons, "British and American Community Design: Clarence Stein's Manhattan Transfers—1924–1974," *Planning Perspectives* 7 (1992): 181–209.

continue well into the early 1970s, when Clarence Stein entered his ninth decade. These documents deal mainly with personal matters. Although his death did not occur until 1975, his lifelong concern with urban and architectural issues came to a quiet close in the late 1960s.

Stein's letters reveal his ideas and motives, his high ethical standards, and his strong personal character: his analytical skill, his stubbornness, his humility, and the importance to him of friendship and collaboration, as well as a single-minded focus on the development and dissemination of ideas and concepts aimed at social and aesthetic objectives. He used his talents, his political and organizing skills, his ability to judge men and ideas, and above all his intellect, energy, and optimism to bring about change. He was a good steward of his superior resources, and he lived life fully, enjoying good food, good friends, stimulating conversation, and beautiful environments, whether urban or bucolic.

Stein was above all not antiurban, as some critics, including Jane Jacobs, have argued. He loved cities in general and New York, Paris, and Venice in particular, but he found some of New York's qualities reprehensible. He hated the squalor of its slums, its tenement housing, the overcrowding of its commercial districts, its noise, and its traffic congestion. While he hated New York's bad qualities, he loved its people, its architectural drama, its skyline, its cultural riches, and its many special places. New York's theaters, museums, film palaces, concert and opera halls, art exhibitions, parks, art galleries, clubs, lecture halls, libraries, restaurants, and educational institutions were all part of the city's *urban equipment,* a term that he used regularly and that he insisted be part of the future "regional city" he envisioned.

Whatever the subject of Clarence Stein's precise observations on cities and his pleasure in them, aesthetic sensibilities were important aspects of his life. This is obvious in his rapturous descriptions in letters to Aline about the skyline, the landscape, and the sunrises and sunsets seen from the Steins' apartment perched above Central Park. Stein's pleasure in the visual world was noted by others. Sir Frederic Osborn wrote to Lewis Mumford that he had "noted in [Stein] the ecstasy that essentially urban architectural effects gave him—quite as acute, I think, as that of the aesthetes who edit the magazines. But, like Unwin,[25] he is pulled two ways, having sympathy with less sophisticated pleasure in simple surroundings, and perhaps he is more sensitive to natural beauty than Unwin."

The importance of Clarence Stein's work to community design and city and regional planning ideology is reflected in praise for his design projects, especially Radburn and Hillside Homes, and in his book *Toward New Towns for America.* However, his correspondence and unpublished essays reveal much about his char-

25. Frederic J. Osborn to Lewis Mumford, 25 October 1958, *Correspondence of Lewis Mumford and Frederic J. Osborn* (Cambridge: MIT Press, 1968); Marvin Miller, *Unwin: Garden Cities and Town Planning* (Leicester: Leicester Univ. Press, 1992).

acter, ethics, social values, joy in life, thoughts about urban issues, and great intellectual and personal contribution to society. These documents also reveal the importance of his close friends and of his great love, Aline MacMahon Stein, to his accomplishments. All are best understood by reading his letters. They reveal a man of strong purpose, whose stubborn character and aesthetic sensibilities were balanced by his sense of humor, his gentleness, and his determination to build humane cities.

AEC	Atomic Energy Commission
AIA	American Institute of Architects
AIP	American Institute of Planners
ALCAN	Aluminum Company of Canada
AMS	Aline MacMahon Stein
ASPO	American Society of Planning Officials
ATC	Appalachian Trail Club
CHC	City Housing Corporation
CHF	Cooperative Housing Foundation
CHPC	Citizen's Housing and Planning Committee
CIO	Congress of Industrial Organizations
CIT	California Institute of Technology
CSP/CUA	Clarence Stein Papers, Cornell University Archives
CSS	Clarence S. Stein
CUNY	City University of New York
FHA	Federal Housing Administration
FPHA	Federal Public Housing Administration
FWA	Federal Works Administration
GSA	General Services Administration
HHFA	Housing and Home Finance Agency
HUD	Department of Housing and Urban Development

IFHTP	International Federation for Housing and Town Planning
JAIA	*Journal of the American Institute of Architects*
JAPA	*Journal of the American Planning Association*
MFP/DCA	MacKaye Family Papers, Dartmouth College Archives
MIT	Massachusetts Institute of Technology
MOMA	Museum of Modern Art
NAHO	National Association of Housing Officials
NRA	National Recovery Act
NRPB	Natural Resources Planning Board
NYCHA	New York City Housing Authority
PBA	Public Buildings Administration
PHA	Public Housing Administration
PUD	planned unit development
PWA	Public Works Administration
RA	Resettlement Administration
RDCA	Regional Development Council of America
RFC	Reconstruction Finance Corporation
RIBA	Royal Institute of British Architects
RPA	Regional Planning Association
RPAA	Regional Planning Association of America
TPR	*Town Planning Review*
TVA	Tennessee Valley Authority
ULI	Urban Land Institute
USHA	U.S. Housing Administration
WPA	Works Progress Administration
WS	Wilderness Society

The Writings of Clarence S. Stein

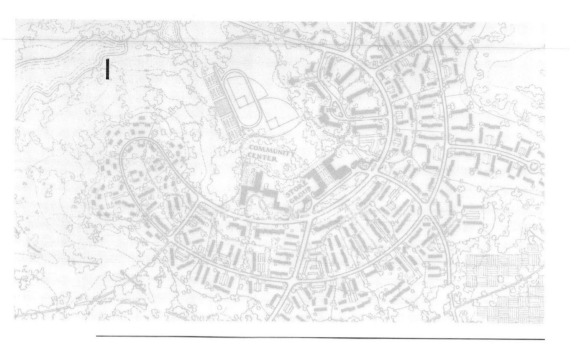

Early Education in New York and Paris
1903–1911

Clarence Samuel Stein's childhood was spent in an industrious and loving German Jewish family, in an innovative urban school, and in the exciting, intense urban scene of the Upper West Side and Chelsea of turn-of-the-century New York City. After the Stein family first moved from Rochester, New York, in 1890, they lived in the northern section of the Chelsea district in the lower 30s near Eighth Avenue. Clarence's father, Leo Stein, a vice president of the National Casket Company and manager of their New Jersey manufacturing facility, commuted to work on the Eighth Avenue el and the Hoboken ferry. Leo provided well for Rose Stein and their five children.[1] Clarence Stein's mother, Rose, had lived in New York as a young girl before she married Leo, and she had been an early member of the Ethical Culture Society. Felix Adler, its founder, had stayed with the Steins when he visited Rochester. Their move to New York provided an unusual educational opportunity for the Stein children. To meet the costs of the Workingman's School, established for the poor in 1878, the society had decided to admit a few tuition-paying pupils. Clarence's mother enrolled him and his sister Gertrude in 1890.

The Ethical Culture Society emphasized education as a primary method for achieving societal change, including the transformation of the working class. It first opened a free kindergarten for New York City children of the poor and within a few

1. The Steins' second child, Clara, born in January 1881, died at age sixteen months in May 1882. Clarence was born on 19 June 1882.

years expanded it to a full primary school. The curriculum of the Workingman's School was based on the European educational ideas of Johann Pestalozzi and Friedrich Froebel, which were brought to the United States by Felix Adler. These ideas influenced the kindergarten, the full elementary school, and later the entire Fieldston School of the Ethical Culture Society. Academic subjects were taught through activities including play, hand work, drawing, weaving, shop work, and building with maple blocks and colored sticks that were elements of larger geometric forms, which introduced arithmetic and geometric concepts.[2] These methods followed the concepts of Froebel, the inventor of the kindergarten.

Froebel had been influenced by the ideas of Johann Pestalozzi, an earlier reformer, who used concrete objects to encourage observation and reasoning.[3] In Adler's school, Clarence Stein received Froebel's "gifts" at the same age as Frank Lloyd Wright, whose mother brought them to him in Boston in 1876.[4] Clarence's talents for dealing with color, form, and space were obviously shaped by these direct approaches to early childhood education. At the Workingman's School, Felix Adler's and John Elliott's concerns about moral corruption and the deterioration of the urban environment, especially the living conditions of the poor, encouraged Stein's deep interest in cities, urban reform politics, and neighborhood life. Clarence's most important teacher, John Elliott, incorporated Froebel's approach to learning by using direct experience of the material world to get at concepts. Stein's formulation of his occupation as a "Community Architect" must also have grown from his direct study of Froebel's gifts provided by Adler and designed to develop his aesthetic sensibilities.

As a schoolboy, Clarence Stein also became familiar with the streets, apartments and tenements, subways, elevated trains, and neighborhoods from the Upper West Side of Manhattan to Chelsea in the West 20s and 30s. From his family's Manhattan Avenue apartment at West 112th Street, opposite Morningside Park, "Subway Stein" traveled to school in Chelsea under Eighth Avenue and above Eighth and Ninth Avenues on the Ninth Avenue el. In 1898 Clarence left the Workingman's School. This was probably the result of a head injury that caused almost total loss of vision. Stein was sent to Florida for two years, where he recovered his vision. When he returned to New York, Clarence worked with Elliott's boys' clubs in Chelsea during those post–Workingman's School years when others were in high school. His visits "to other lands" in Manhattan were all integral parts of Clarence's "city learning." These visits included a trip with his father to Bleeker Street, the Bowery, and

2. Kate Douglas Wiggan and Nora Archibald Smith, *Froebel's Gifts* (Boston, 1895).

3. Diane Ravich, *The Great School Wars* (New York: Basic Books, 1988), 10.

4. Frank Lloyd Wright, *An Autobiography*, 2d ed. (New York: Duell, Sloan and Pierce, 1943), 13–14. Wright describes the importance of Froebel's gifts to architectural sensibilities. Wright attributed much to this aspect of his early education.

Al Smith's lower East Side neighborhood, described in a 1904 letter to his mother.[5]

Clarence's grandfather had been a cabinetmaker and, in the family tradition, Clarence worked in his father's casket factory for a few years after he had recovered his eyesight in 1900. At twenty, in 1902–3, he grew restless. Lewis Mumford later speculated that Clarence decided that he wanted to design and decorate spaces for the living rather than the dead. Stein enrolled to study architecture at Columbia University in 1903–4. His older brother William and younger brother Herbert continued to work in the factory. But Columbia was not right for Clarence. In the summer of 1903, he and his father had traveled together to Europe, where Clarence learned about the École des Beaux Arts in Paris. His father soon decided (no doubt with strong support from his mother) that Clarence could go to Paris to study "interior decoration," which he did in the summer of 1905.

The young man reveled in the vitality of Paris, in the sophisticated and civilized behavior of its citizens, in their theaters, museums, and parks, and in the glorious landscapes of the French countryside. He read widely and observed carefully. Stein's six years in Paris had an undoubted influence on his understanding of the values of cities and city folks and on his ideas about city design. He roamed Paris's streets, admired its urbanity, and enjoyed the beauty and utility of its parks and community spaces, boulevards, and streets, and he wrote regularly to his parents and siblings of his experiences. A small selection from more than two hundred surviving letters from Paris form the bulk of the following section.

As soon as the wonder and strangeness of his initial immersion in Paris was over, Clarence Stein began to observe and systematically report to his family on the places and people of the city and on his student world. He joined a preparatory atelier in August 1905, started French language lessons, and settled into temporary digs at 13 rue Jacob on the left bank near the École. In December he took the entrance exam for the first time, not expecting to pass, but to get some experience with its content and to measure himself. The following year Stein transferred to the atelier of Umbdenstock, an Alsatian architectural design master. Under his tutelage Clarence flourished. Stein wrote extensively about the fellowship of student life with the American, English, and German students in the boisterous but always hard-working atelier. Later, when Clarence moved to an apartment at 42 rue Jacob, they shared evening meals at the restaurant Pres aux Clerces, or "the Pres," as they called it. Its food, Clarence reported, was of "a forgettable quality, which permitted [him] to turn his attention to the conversation."[6]

5. C. S. Stein to his mother, 3 June 1904, includes a detailed description of these ethnic districts of Little Italy, Mulberry Bend, and the densest parts of the Lower East Side. It provides a sense of Stein's growing ability to observe and evaluate urban living conditions.

6. For an account of the place, see Stein's letter (document 17) to his mother of 20 April 1906.

The discipline of the École and Stein's separate studies of mathematics, language, history, and drawing were broken by long cycling tours to visit and sketch the architectural monuments of France at Versailles, the châteaus of the Loire valley, and French cathedrals and towns. In 1906 Henry Klaber, one of Clarence's friends from the Ethical Culture school in New York, arrived in Paris to study architecture. Klaber and Stein took a sixth-floor apartment together at 46 rue Jacob. During recess periods they cycled to sketch in the provinces. Many of these architectural sketches have been preserved, as are Stein's sketches from study tours to England, Germany, Switzerland, Italy, and Spain.

It was difficult for Americans to gain admission to the École des Beaux Arts because of its small quota of foreigners, but Stein persisted and gained a high level of competence in architectural design. At first, he had no French and he had no high school diploma. Was this the reason the Columbia School of Architecture was not open to him as a degree candidate? Perhaps, but the École had no such prerequisite. One had only to pass the entrance examinations in drawing, mathematics, descriptive geometry, architectural history and theory, and, of course, architectural design. École applicants who had a traditional secondary school and college preparation, including languages (especially those who had completed a four-year course of study in one of the dozen or so architectural schools in the United States), had little or no difficulty passing the entrance tests. Partly because few places were available for non-French students, Clarence found the exams quite a challenge. But he demonstrated his lifelong capacity for hard work and his determination, which bordered on stubbornness. After two and a half years of study, he passed the exams and became an "élève de l'École des Beaux Arts" in December 1907, two years after his arrival in Paris.

In January 1908, Stein was formally admitted to the École, where he took his architectural problems in the Atelier Laloux,[7] a favorite of American architectural students in Paris. Stein returned home only once while he was a student at the École des Beaux Arts, but his parents, his sisters, and his New York teachers, Felix Adler and John Elliott, visited him several times during his stay in Europe. Clarence's studies progressed steadily, if not brilliantly. He received high marks on projects, but to achieve the *diplôme* would have required many more years than he was willing to invest.

As his years in Paris drew to a close, two New Yorkers who had come to Paris to study art and architecture became Clarence's close friends. Ely Jacques Kahn, who had studied the full four-year course in architecture at Columbia University, entered the École in 1909. He and Clarence traveled together in Germany, Switzerland, Italy, and Spain during Stein's last two student years. Artist and set designer

7. Arthur Drexler, *Architecture of the École des Beaux Arts* (New York: Museum of Modern Art, 1977), 459ff. Laloux's most famous project was the Gare du Quay d'Orsay in Paris (1898–1900).

Lee Simonson, whom Clarence had met as a student at the Ethical Culture Society's school in New York, began to study art in Paris in 1909. Simonson's studies in Paris provided a foundation for his successful career as a Broadway stage-set designer, which also brought him into close contact with Clarence Stein after they returned to New York just before the start of World War I.

In 1912 Stein decided that his education (two years of preparation and four years as a student) had prepared him well enough to enter the practice of architecture. The wisdom of this decision was confirmed by a family friend, Robert Kohn, who had preceded Clarence by ten years in the study of architecture in Paris and with whom Clarence would later associate in architectural practice. Kohn advised that Clarence not work for the *diplôme* and that his experience with several of the École's large, complex architectural design problems had already given him an excellent foundation for a career in architecture.

Clarence's Stein letters from Paris provide a firsthand account of an American architectural student at the École and convey his experience of Paris districts, parks, boulevards, and suburbs. The style of these letters is sometimes difficult. Clarence had not developed very good writing skills. He had not learned accurate spelling, clear sentence structure, or composition—but he was practicing. His letters to his family include very detailed accounts of Parisian places, people, and institutions. These sometimes tedious letters were a consequence of his conscious decision to practice descriptive writing skills in his letters home. The letters were, as he indicates in one to his brother Herb, a self-conscious, formal effort to achieve a literary style.

It is surprising that Clarence gave no hint of the artistic ferment in Paris at this time. He and his fellow École students seem to have lived in a compartment of Parisian life that had no openings to the scenes of unfolding Cubism. The young Pablo Picasso, Juan Gris, and Henri Matisse, for example, are not present in the art salons Clarence frequented. At least he did not mention them. Of course, the well-developed and rigorous system of the École required strict attention to formal method: long hours at the sketching easel and laborious hours over the drawing board, training the eye and hand to shape architectural form and ornament with classical proportion and above all with the power of well-organized, clearly structured plans. The school's emphasis was on developing compositional skills, using well-developed ideas based on traditional forms, and not on artistic innovation that responded to modern technical means or societal change. When the modern movement came to New York in the late 1920s and early 1930s, it came as a surprise to Clarence Stein.

Stein's letter-essays from Paris of the very early 1900s record the view of a somewhat naive and charming American of the city and of the apparatus of the École, its students and teachers, and their simple everyday life and pleasures. The record is special because it was written by a maturing young man with unusual talents of observation and description that had been developed and nurtured by the theory of learning from life and place inherent in the teaching methods of Felix Adler's Workingman's School. Clarence's mental and ethical life in New York had taught him to understand at a simple level the complex relationships among the life and values of Parisians, their architecture, and the urban matrix. He loved Paris's great parks and the boulevards that sliced through the streets of a medieval city with still-intact walls, and he loved the Baroque culture that infused Paris's art and music.

Paris came as a revelation to Clarence Stein, and he reveled in it as an urban delight. Could he, he wondered, bring to New York City some of its qualities, the pleasure of its formal beauty, its vital urban life, its easy access to nature? Reading these letters, one cannot doubt the influence of Stein's European experience, especially that of Paris, on his lifelong efforts to conceive and build the good city.

1   To his mother

Roma   June 20, 1903

Dear Mamma:

When one has seen the ruins of ancient Rome, the churches and palaces of the last fifteen hundred years, one is not through with "The Eternal City"—one might be eternally at it and then hardly finish. There is still the Rome of today. There are broad avenues and stores with large glass windows that might remind one a bit of Paris, if one had seen the modern city of modern cities. There are the parks, where stand the statues or busts of the great men of modern Italy. Here, as almost everywhere else in the parks of the large cities, is a large monument to Garibaldi. In the evening the band plays in one of the squares—plays modern tunes at the base of a column erected in the days of Marcus Aurelius. The crowds that fill the space around the bands or sit at little tables before the restaurants or wineries have probably forgotten that there were ever emperors at Rome. And so [Rome] is . . . not the most modern but still a modern city built among the ruins of the City of many ages. . . .

Clarence

2   To his mother

July 3, 1904

Dear Mamma:

Last evening Papa, Herbert, and I traveled to many foreign lands without setting our feet off the island of Manhattan. We visited Naples (or little Italy, the Ghetto, if it may be called so), Chinatown, a German beer hall, and the home of the American tough, the Bowery. We did all this between half-past five and nine-thirty.

We met at the Astor House. We walked past the City Hall, which is in a horrible mourning on account of the "Slocum" disaster. Then we passed along Park Row. After you have left the large newspaper building and the Brooklyn Bridge behind, you come on what seems a part of the Bowery. The elevated railroad's structure darkens the street. The sidewalks are crowded mainly with men—and they mostly a pretty tough lot. On either side are shops—many of them pawnbrokers—with saloons in great quantities. A good many of the men show that the latter are used not infrequently. But you can see for yourself by looking through the ever-swinging doors into the dark rooms with the long bars, on each of which is set many of the largest schooners in the city!

We turned down Banter Street. On either hand are clothing shops, with a good part of the ware hung outside—clothing of all kinds, military as well as civilian. In front of the shops stand the "pullers-in," in shirtsleeves many of them. It is not necessary to read the signs of the proprietors to know that they are Jews. About the only other way in which other nationalities are represented [is] by the ownership of the saloons. But there are plenty of these. The "puller-in"—his duty is, you know, to pull into the shop anyone whom he can get hold of. The part of the man inside is to cajole the victim into becoming a customer. They did not get us inside, though some of them tried to. One particularly strenuous one told us, "I don't want you to buy; I just want to you to see." But we could see enough from without.

It did not take us long to reach Little Italy. But first we passed through Mulberry Bend Park, a small, irregularly shaped plot of grass covered with many benches and crossed by a number of paved paths. Therein was a crowd of men, women, and children—mainly Italian. At one end is a handsome bandstand. Anything that can be called architecture is noticeable in this district. Most of the buildings are perfectly plain brick structures of five or six or sometimes fewer stories, with a cornice above and a number of iron balconies on each story. . . . The chief form of decoration [is] clothing, hung out to dry at almost every floor, with sometimes here and there a pan as a point of emphasis.

We passed through a street as crowded as those of Naples. And the crowd was of much the same quality as those of Naples. There were shops on either hand and by the sidewalk a row of pushcarts, vending many things eatable, as well as wearable. For more than an hour or so, we passed through streets inhabited by Jews. There were Jews of every age. There were old men in their Sabbath costumes, long coats and high hats some; most of them bearded. It was they more than the younger men [who] stood around the temples. We saw two or three temples. Through the windows of one, a second-story room on one of the business streets, we could see the old rabbi facing a small congregation of old men, all hatted and all seated and moving backwards and forwards, seemingly as they repeated some prayer or catechism. In front of the larger temples stood crowds of the old men arguing with hands and tongues. There were younger men—a good many of them at the shops or the many pushcarts which line some but not all the streets through which we went. In most are rows of tall tenements. And here are the children, watched over some of them by their mothers. There are hordes of children. They crowd the sidewalks and the roads. What a place . . . to grow up in!

But there are rays of light even in this darkness. One is the outdoor gymnasium and playgrounds in Hamilton Fish Park. Another is, or will be before long, the summer gymnasiums and playrooms which will be open in the splendid school buildings. These buildings in their architecture set up ideals for the neighborhood, well worth follow[ing]—but so far not followed. Everywhere is the same monotonous, plain brick wall. Not everywhere, to be true; there are a few buildings that look something like our uptown apartments. A foreign appearance is given to these structures by their Hebrew signs.

We took dinner at a good and inexpensive restaurant on Grand St. Then we walked down the Bowery. The sidewalks were crowded with men—tough-looking characters most of them—strong-looking brutes. There was [a] brainless, careless look in their faces. They seemed to have but one desire, to get drunk. Most of them had succeeded. . . . [One] reeled up to a young fellow and with one blow knocked him down. In a moment the other was up and had felled him and was pounding him. A crowd rushed toward them and in a moment was surging backwards and forwards—such is the Bowery. . . .

Love from
Clarence

---

3 To his parents

Paris   July 4, 1905

Dear Folks:

This is Paris. There is too much. I must think, try to comprehend it somewhat, before I try to describe it. It is strange, different, yet not so strange or different that I have not been able to begin to get accustomed to it.

The Latin Quarter, in which I am living, [is] just tall apartments, but such queer folks that walk around among them, many of them Americans. In fact, there are almost too many Americans for one to get used to the French language. I will try to get away from them presently. Just now it prevents my feeling homesick. . . . The first American we met was Maurice Stern, a friend of Weiss, who was at the railroad station and took us to [the] Grand Hotel des Écoles, 15 rue Delambre. (Do not send my mail here.) The hotel is all right, nice and clean and cheap, but I probably will move to more "French" parts before long.

Sunday, I visited another American, a Mr. Foulds, to whom Levi gave me an introduction. I wanted to find out about the Beaux Arts examinations. He told me the first of them had taken place on the day before . . . , but it does not make very much difference. I could not have passed. I just wanted to see what they were like. I do not know

just what I am going to do now, but will decide in a few days. I saw Herbert Baer later on Sunday. He suggested a good man to work under. I will see Baer again to-morrow. . . .

Love to you all,
Clarence

---

4   To his parents

Paris   July 10, 1905

Dear Folks:

The latter part of the week I was kept fairly busy helping Monsieur Figarol. I told you in my last letter, did I not, that he asked me to assist him in finishing some drawings. After lunch at his mother's apartment we went to the atelier at which he works. The problems in design, which is the principal work of the school, are given out at the school, but the drawings are made at the atelier to which the student belongs.[1] There are a number of these ateliers—a number of students band together to hire a studio. Each atelier has a master, a practicing architect, who comes two or three times a week to criticize the work of the students. The ateliers have been long in existence and have numerous customs that are matters of tradition. There are always the "anciens" and "nouveaux," the older and newer students. The latter must do service, for three to six months; they must keep the place in order, run errands for the "anciens," and, when required, help them with their work.

Figarol is an "ancien" of the Atelier Lambert, which is situated on the Cité, or Island. We walked up many stories of old stairs, so old that the wooden coverings had worn away, showing the bare bricks beneath, and then, after unlocking a heavy door, up a still narrower stairway to the attic. It is a good-sized, barnlike room, filled with many working tables. One whole side is made up almost entirely of windows. Above them is a row of the portraits of the members of the atelier, cut out of black paper and pasted on white. At other parts of the room are posters, a few rough sketches, large sheets of paper covered with French scribbling, and a couple of dust-covered casts; besides, there was a large pile of old lumber, high up among the rafters of the ceiling.

Not a particularly inspiring place. Yet they do turn out work there. They do it even though there is a constant uproar. They act like a crowd of young boys, though many of them have great beards, and almost none are without at least a mustache. There is always a great hubbub of voices: one or two singing the same line over and over again, others making jokes and telling stories in a loud voice, always a loud voice that carries round the place and back again. Then there is much rushing and chasing about. They used their small supply of English words on me; almost everyone seemed to have some. "How do you do, des morning; very well I thank you" (all in a slow, drawn-out tone) was the favorite expression. I was called "Meester American" or "Figarol's neger" (nigger, which is what they seem to call nouveaux who do service for some special anciens).

I worked at the atelier Wednesday afternoon, Thursday, Friday, and part of Saturday morning, inking Figarol's work. It was interesting. Besides learning a bit about how they do their work, I saw something of how an atelier runs.

Outside of that my time has been mainly spent in "catching on" to the methods of running things here. I am getting acquainted with people, American students and one or two French-speaking men, and I took lunch with the Figarols again Friday. As to my work, I am not yet settled. I have been looking for an architect who, Levi says, will be a good instructor. At last, I found his address this morning but will not be able to see him until Wednesday. I think it better to take my time about starting than to make a false start. I expect to start studying French tomorrow or the next day.

I have moved to a hotel near the Seine and near the school. Good light and all that. But it is after 7 P.M. and I am hungry.

Love to all from,
Clarence

1. The large ateliers were private schools of architecture, not professional offices. Their architect teachers (called *patrons*) maintained their offices elsewhere and visited the ateliers perhaps three times a week. Their purpose was exclusively teaching. They might enroll thirty to eighty students.

---

5   To his parents

Paris, Hotel d'Angleterre, 42 Rue Jacob   July 14, 1905

Dear Folks:

Last time I wrote you I had just moved. I am quite used to this abode. The hotel is well situated, within two blocks of the École. I wonder if it will ever be my school. The École is just across the narrow Seine from the Louvre; then behind, about two streets away, is the Boulevard St. German, where one may eat at innumerable places and near which one may buy innumerable things; then the Luxembourg Gallery and the delightful gardens of the same name. I like to go there evenings and sit under the big trees. The Luxembourg is near the Pantheon, as the Louvre is near the Garden of the Tuilleries, which leads one to the Place de la Concorde soon, an endless chain of beauties all linked together by great avenues of trees.

But I was talking about the Hotel d'Angleterre. I am on the second floor, that is, two above the ground. My room faces a small court planted with a few little trees. But until that room is unoccupied, I am in a larger one facing the narrow rue Jacob. The place is a bit old-fashioned, but so are most of the less expensive hotels—no electricity, no gas in the rooms. One takes a candle downstairs and with its light finds his way upstairs and to bed. Everything is clean and comfortable, so I am not complaining.

Yet I may not stay here very long. I will probably study under a M. Bruel,[1] who lives way over at another part of the town, the other side of the Trocadero. If I work at his atelier, I may find it inconvenient to live so far away. But I will not start with him until the end of the month, as he is going to take a vacation until then.

Meanwhile I am going to put in most of my time seeing Paris and its surroundings. But it is not merely a matter of sight-seeing. I can put the time into study, very important study, of some of the best examples of interior decorating. Yesterday, for example, I spent about four hours making quick sketches and examining just a few rooms of the immense palace of Fontainbleau. . . .

Clarence

1. Apparently Clarence decided not to join the atelier of Bruel, but rather that of Chifflot, in which many Americans of this era worked to prepare themselves for the examinations of the École des Beaux Arts.

---

6   To his parents

22 rue Jacob, Paris   July 23–25, 1905

Dear Folks:

I am getting used to Paris. That which seemed strange at first is now the thing of everyday; before long I will probably notice only that which is extraordinary, which is not characteristic. Before I get to that state I want to try to give you a general impression of this place. . . .

First, there is the driver of your open carriage—red faced and red vested with a long blue frock coat with gilt buttons and on his head a shiny high hat. In a moment he makes his way through a maze of carriages under the railroad shed and you are in the streets, streets just full of other strange folks. You will notice the bits of color first, perhaps: the soldier in red and blue; the policeman (or whatever they call the guardians of the place) . . . in duller blue, sometimes with white trousers and always with a little sword dangling at his side; the working man fixing the road, the most picturesque of all with great baggy blue trousers and a large sash of red and blue. Most of the other costumes are duller. The common people here dress what Mamma would call "very sensibly." The children, even the boys, wear black aprons that show a little bare leg and below socks and shoes. There are men also in big aprons, the little shopkeepers or their assistants.

Both sides of the narrow street through which we are driving are lined with little shops: clean little places, particularly the butcher's and baker's stores, and neat, too.

There is the barber's shop with an old-fashioned shaving plate as sign, the stationer's and the tobacconist, at either of which [are] postals, illustrated postals, you find them everywhere.

Among the stores, say as numerous as our saloons, are the restaurants and cafes. These are the cheaper cafes, here on this narrow street, but like the grander ones of the boulevards they have lined the sidewalks with their tables, where there is room enough. The tables are little round affairs on which is a bottle of wine or glass of some syrup. A glassful is enough to last a Frenchman an hour or more as he sits and reads his paper or talks to his neighbors or just watches the passing crowd. . . .

Above these shops and cafes is a long wall with windows, three or four rows of windows in height. The wall is unbroken, otherwise, from one street to another. There are no vacant lots, excepting where they are cutting through to make a new boulevard.[1] Here and there is a bit of interesting carving, but as a whole there is merely a monotonous white or yellow stucco on soft stone—with bands of railing before the windows, big windows that almost come down to the floor within. . . .

Now, what am I doing? Well, I'm seeing things. One hour a day I study French under an elderly professor. From half past four to six-thirty generally I go to a sketch class. A nude model poses four times, twenty-five minutes at a time. It is fine practice at quick drawing. Sunday, the 16th, I visited Versailles; Monday, the Cathedral at St. Denis; Tuesday, Wednesday, and Thursday, the Louvre (it is endless); Friday, some other museums; Saturday, Versailles; Sunday, Château at Chantilly; Monday, Cathedral at Chartres. So you see, there is much to tell you in my future letters.

Yours fondly,

Clarence

1. Construction of the Paris boulevard system planned by Baron Haussmann in the 1850s continued over a seventy-year period. Some of these streets were still being cut through or laid out in the western part of the city in the 1920s.

---

7 To his father

Hotel d'Angleterre, 22 rue Jacob, Paris[1]   Friday, August 4, 1905

Dear Pop:

At last I have settled down to work. Last week it was officially announced that the examination for the Beaux Arts would take place in December. I have joined the preparatory atelier to which most of the American boys go. Problems very similar in character to those I had in college last year are given out weekly,[2] at present. Later they will be expected to be done in one day, as they are at the examination. I have also started to run through some French mathematics books with another fellow, so as to get on to their way of doing things. We will probably begin the serious study-ing at the beginning of September, when the regular mathematics instructor returns to the city.

As a whole, I think these months will be well spent, if only I get the training that I necessarily must in preparing. But that, of course, is not what I want. I want to get in the school. It is going to be a pretty hard pull. I am competing with men, most of whom have had more training than I, and precedent says that one must fail at least once before passing. Most of those who try do so. Well, I am going to do my best. I cannot do any more.

When the date of the examinations was settled, I gave up my idea of working for M. Bruel. I would like to take lessons in watercolor during this month from him. I saw him the other day about this. He asks a pretty steep price, so I am undecided what to do.

I am getting settled in other ways. I moved into my room at this hotel yesterday (you know I have been occupying temporary quarters here). It is a bit smaller than our room at home and looks a little crowded with all of the furniture in it. But it has two windows, is on a quiet courtyard, and has almost enough closet room to make Mamma happy. So I will probably stay here until I move into some apartment. The last item, but one, of the expenses is the one you would be most likely to ask me about. It is a book of four large volumes on the general subject of architecture. It is by the principal professor of that subject at the École.[3] I expect to make a good deal of use of it, as it is well illustrated and deals with most of the problems I am likely to have for some time. I have mentioned this partially because I want to know what you think of my buying architectural books. There are a good many of them that I could pick up as I go along, that will not only be valuable now but when I start work.

My love to all.

Remember me to George, John, Firth, Wetmore, and others at the factory.

Your fond son,
Clarence

1. In March 1906 Clarence moved to a seventh-floor apartment at 46 rue Jacob.

2. Stein studied at Columbia during the 1904–5 academic year. He refers to this in later letters, but there are no records for him at Columbia. He may have studied in the College of Architecture's special program for those without high school diplomas or in the summer session.

3. Stein is referring to Ernest Gaudet, *Elements and Theory of Architecture* (Paris, 1902).

CASH ACCOUNT

June 1905

		fr.
Started with—in cash—		1031.40
Spent—on Rotterdam	fr.	
Tips	25.25	
Stamps, etc.	1.40	
Total	26.65	
On hand July 1st		1003.75

July 1905

		fr.
Spent:		
R.R. Bologne to Paris	20.45	
Hotel des Écoles 9 days @ 3 fr.	27.00	
Meals (average 4.43 a day)	147.40	
Baths	5.00	
Art materials	11.45	
French lessons @ 2 fr.	36.00	
Sketch class @ .50	4.00	
Stamps	3.75	
General utilities (umbrella, lamp, pajamas, etc.)	34.60	
Books (Baedeker N. Fr., French books, etc.)	17.75	
Photos and postals	20.60	
Carriages	4.75	
Laundry	6.00	
Theaters, museums, etc.	17.00	
Excursions	35.20	
Book on architecture, 4 vol. (Gaudet, *Elements & Theory of Architecture*)	75.00	
General expenses	35.70	
Total	501.65	
On hand August 1st		502.10

8   To his sister Gertrude Stein[1]

Hotel d'Angleterre, 22 rue Jacob, Paris   August 11, 1905

Dear Gertrude:

There probably is no real need of writing to you individually, as you are under the necessity of reading my letters, anyhow. . . .

Work—yes, I am hard at it now. I have joined a preparatory atelier,[2] where they give us one architectural problem a week. I spend a good part of my time on it. I am up at five-thirty and work most of the morning, excepting during the time that I take my French lesson. I am beginning to speak straight for as much as a half a minute at a time with my instructor around. But when I want to make use of my knowledge—well, it's just like swimming when you are first learning. When the swimming teacher lets you go, you just go down. Splash! The Frenchies shrug their shoulders and look queer, and I get more rattled. It will come after a while—it just has to. Afternoons, I attempt a little work, but without much success. The tired feeling that grows naturally in this soil and a strong desire to get out and see generally get the better of me, and by five, or before, I drop math or design and go and see Paris—and sometimes sketch. . . . Paris is commencing to seem quite natural. Why, I caught myself reading a newspaper as I walked along yesterday through the street as though there was nothing to see, with the endless flow of ever-changing life about me and the buildings so varied that they also almost seem to change. And yet, of course, it is not home. It cannot ever be. As far as attraction goes, there is no comparing New York with Paris. Paris is the place to draw inspiration,[3] but when it comes to work, to giving what little you may have, then it's your business to go home. . . . To me, it is my strongest desire to try to help at least a little in making New York more what Paris is, but different, not a Parisian New York, but a finer, more beautiful New Yorkish New York. . . .

Well, I do not know whether you can make much meaning out of this, but if you can't, do not call me up. Phone is out of order and in three weeks I will perhaps have drowned all recollection in mathematical and architectural terms. But write, write often to . . .

Your fond brother,

Clarence

1. This is Clarence's sister, not directly related to the well-known art collector and author Gertrude Stein.

2. These schools prepared students for taking the entrance exams for the École des Beaux Arts.

3. From 1905 to 1911 Stein observed Paris and Parisians carefully and reported his observations in long letters to various members of his family. He perceived the life of Paris with analytical skill. For six years he admired her boulevards and great parks and enjoyed her theaters, concert halls, and art galleries. Even more, he admired, enjoyed, and learned about the ways the people of Paris

made these public spaces and places so much a part of their daily lives. He learned from Paris how to design and make effective use of green spaces, distinctive places, and public facilities. His early experience in Paris was the beginning of his lifelong absorption with the question of the supply, design, qualities, and use of what he called *community equipment.*

---

9   To his parents

22 rue Jacob, Paris   October 17, 1905

Dear Folks:

You want to know how I am doing, as usual, I suppose. As I have said, it is work most of the time. There is mathematics, charcoal drawing, and design.

Design: Up to last week we had one problem for each seven days. Hereafter, we will have, besides the regular weekly design, which we do in whatever spare time we have between what we give to our other studies, what is called an *esquisse* of twelve hours. We have just the same conditions and the same kind of work as we will at the most important examination, that in architecture. We are given a problem and allotted twelve hours to solve it and draw it. I will tell you of last Saturday, when we had our first twelve-hour esquisse.

At about eight-thirty in the morning, we received a printed copy of the program or problem, and we at once started our mental machines going. The design was to be the entrance and vestibule of a circus building. Gradually, our ideas began to formulate themselves and pencils began to move. There were forty to fifty (Frenchmen and Americans) in two large rooms. There must be about fifteen Americans at our atelier. The Frenchmen are a noisy crowd: work or no work, they must be continually prattling or singing. The Americans keep them pretty good company. There were generally one or two songs being sung or hummed at the top of everyone's voice. Besides, two Frenchmen were likely at any moment to break into a heated argument (their only way of fighting), which would not end until one or the other had come to the utmost limit of his vocabulary and had called the other every name under the sun that he was able to remember. Luckily, our knowledge of French is not perfect.

. . . Noontime came before we knew it—and one by one the different workers went out to lunch. I did not rush out for a few bites until half-past two, then how the afternoon sped on. Before long it was dark and we had the electric lights on. All too soon it was nine and time to stop.

It was a quarter of ten before we were seated at the table, taking our first good meal of the day—breakfast does not really count here, you know.

Love to you,

Clarence

10   To his parents

22 rue Jacob, Paris   November 14, 1905

Dear Folks:

. . .

Winter! One would hardly believe it had come, or almost come. It is not very cold here. It is disagreeable, though, so we have to wear an overcoat when we go out. In our room (sitting room or working room), we generally burn a stove. . . . One of the rules of the hotel—and [of] all hotels around here, in fact—is that you buy the coal from them. Of course, they charge you a good price. One of the advantages of rooming with other fellows, as I am doing, is that it lessens the expense of fuel for each of us.

Winter is almost here, yet it seems almost no time since the end of summer and the end of vacation. . . . Everyone took a vacation of some length. The tall, good-looking proprietor and head cook of our restaurant was away for two weeks or so, and, of course, everything went wrong. The steaks were no longer thick and juicy, and the assistant garçon drank too much of the house's good wine, but all is well now, and the proprietor is there again to shake our hands across the table and then to disappear into the kitchen, after changing his black jacket for a white apron, ready to send forth steaks like those of yore. They say his vacation was spent in Switzerland, but someone saw him on the other side of the river in the company of a young lady. After his return, of course, the garçons had to have their vacations, as well as did Madame. . . .

But that is all over and they are back to work again. Work—work in a sense, not work as the American knows it. Things go easier here. They do not chase wealth at such a rate that they are too worn out to use it when they have gained it. They take their pleasure easily and their work the same, and often they succeed in mingling the two. . . . Whatever their faults, the Frenchmen certainly have the sense to get a certain joy out of life. Life to them is more than business.

The desire to make [life] a thing of pleasure shows best, I think, in the way they have laid out their city and decorated it. But of that another time. . . .

Love to you all,
Clarence

11   To his parents

22 rue Jacob, Paris   November 28, 1905

Dear Folks:

Sunday morning was a joyful time; letters arrived from home. There was one from Mamma, one from Lillie, and the unabridged, combined effort of the Hudson Guild Library Theatrical Co. I did not get down until late that morning; it was very close to ten before I got dressed and ready for breakfast. You see, we had one of our twelve-hour designs on Saturday, which was not finished until half-past nine at night, and then after taking a bite we took a long walk up and down the Grand Boulevard. We got back and to bed about twelve, tired—well, I should say so. Sunday is supposed to be a full day, but Mayence got it into his head that it would be a brilliant thing to give us a mathematics examination on that day, so from ten to twelve we were to plug away at his place. It was quarter of ten when I got to the mail box downstairs and received my voluminous correspondence. . . .

I should have set right to work on my return to our rooms, preparing for Monday's mathematics, but the sun was shining, and one cannot tell just how long sunshine will last in Paris or when it will return, so I went out for a walk. I happened to pass by Notre Dame, so simply beautiful and so wonderfully attractive through its quaintness of carving and the way in which their carving has been massed together—[in] what shall I call it, the artistic way, the pleasing way, the masterly way in which the spots of carving have been made into one great whole of the facade; the three great doors surrounded by miniature saints and angels; the row of kings— stone kings across the whole length of the facade above; and then still higher the great rose window in the center and above that, on the two sides, the square towers. Age and weather has helped the masterly composer of the facade in welding [it] into a wonderful oneness.

I climbed to the top of one of the towers, after going within the church. One reaches the top in a dizzy condition, after much winding up a narrow, circular staircase. But the view was worth any amount of climbing. It was not of the kind one is supposed to climb great heights to get, in which case you can see so many miles. No, the distance was blanketed in clouds. The mist that told of days of rain, past and future, hung over the city and brought it all into one great mass—gray confines with deeper gray roadways winding in and out and about, and the more emphatic zigzag band of the Seine broken up into square patches by the gray bridge strings . . . .

After a short walk and a glance at some of the interior architecture of the Louvre, I returned home to study mathematics. Dinner—seven until eight or after. Then some more mathematics and bed. Sunday was over. . . .

Love to all the Steins. Remember me to the Cohens (Julius, Henry), and others.

Clarence

---

12 To his parents

"Les Charmettes," Barbizon (Foret de Fontainbleau)   December 15, 1905

Dear Folks:

To begin at the end of the story, I did not pass the examinations. Which explains my being here out in the country, thinking over my past battles and defeats and planning for future victories. . . . But of that later.

Now, a little more about the days of work, the days before the examination. Up to within a week of them, we continued turning out twelve-hour esquisses, or designs. They were work, good, hard work. But we succeeded in getting in a little amusement with them. The Frenchmen were generally able to make themselves comical, singing, shouting, and particularly when they would lose their tempers and flare up like a volcano, or more like a skyrocket, dying down just as quickly. We had our last twelve-hour design a week before the examinations and then a long week of waiting for the day of days. It was a week of rest for many—for us a week of work, but not hard work. We would stop now and then to talk it over: so-and-so's chance and how much the other fellow would get in freehand drawing. Everybody else was doing the same thing. It came nearest to being like the day before an election than anything I have seen. There was the question of who would win and, what was most important to us just then, what would the problem be. There were all sorts of guesses—it would be a baptistery, or a dome; no, a staircase. Anyhow, it would be something, and something we would not know until the day, so what was the use in bothering? . . .

And then finally it came: the day. It dawned like other days; no, not exactly, it commenced before it was light. We had to get up by lamplight to get over to the school at 7:30. The four hundred or more applicants were divided among the different rooms of the building. Until eight we were crowded together at the bottom of various stairways waiting for our names to be called. Even when one's name was read off, it was no easy thing to get through the crowd and up the stairs. The Frenchmen in front of me seemed to think I was trying to cheat them of something. They refused to make way. Well, I finally pushed through those who had not yet been called.

In a few moments I was settled in my loge trying to decipher the French of the program, or problem. The loges are the small divisions into which the rooms are divided, by wooden partitions, spaces just large enough for one man to work without being bothered by his neighbors and without being able to see his neighbor's work. At first, the guards make you stay in your own loge, but as the day passes they allow you to go around as you wish and see the other men's designs. That does not help you much. It is a question of pounding out the design all by yourself. So we worked, first thinking and then trying to put those thoughts in form on paper. My watch was in front of me and I could see the hours rushing ahead, racing with my design. And I worked, for those twelve [hours] meant six months—the six months that will pass before the next examinations. That was ringing in my head: six months, six months, six months, all centered on this one day. . . .

We had good light from the skylights above, and when this gave out the electric bulbs were lit. All of a sudden, for some unseen reason, these went out and all was blackness. What a howl went up! But not many minutes passed—candles were given out, and we were soon at it again. All too soon the guard called out, "Half an hour more." We were working for all that was in us. "Five minutes more." We quickened speed. And then, "Time is up, hand in your drawing." That ended the story.

We got our baggage together, washed up, and went over to the restaurant. Everyone there was talking it over. This was the only way to do it. Why did they not do this or that? . . . Dinner over, we took a walk and I discovered that, somehow or other, my legs were tired. Then it occurred [to me] that, although there had been a chair by my side all day, I had not [sat] down since early in the morning. So before long I returned home and, after a little reading, I turned in.

Then came the days of waiting for the returns, just like waiting for election returns. Most everyone just sat around and waited. We continued work on our studies, mathematics and drawing. Well, Wednesday afternoon we went around to the school to see the results, and there were many who were happy and many who were not. I celebrated by going to the theater that night, a thing I have not had the time to do for some months. And next day I packed my satchel, and here I am in Barbizon, home of the Barbizon School. . . .

> Love to all,
> Clarence

---

13   To his father

Barbizon   December 15, 1905

Dear Pop:
You have probably already received news, through my letter to the family, of my failure to pass the examinations. I would like to find some way (as my optimistic mother probably could) of showing how the results were for the best, but I cannot. . . . On the other hand, there is no use crying over spilled milk. Time is much better spent in looking forward.

Though I would, of course, a good deal rather have made the school, my time has not, as I have already told you, been at all wasted. I do not think I could have very much better used it, even if I had not expected to take the examinations. Mathematics and charcoal drawing have both been good training, though I might have taken them in a somewhat different form. Anyhow, they will come in useful at the next examination.

The design work I have done, I believe, is about as good practice as I could have had in that kind of work. We have not had time for a great deal of study on each design, but we have had an opportunity to gather a great many ideas. Since I started, we have had something like twenty problems, each taking up some other form of architectural design: fountains, monuments, interiors, exteriors, senate chambers, palaces, and park entrances—all sorts of things.

I was just trying to think what it was in which this work trained us. That is, what [are] the essentials one needs for architectural design? They are mainly three, I believe: first, a knowledge of motifs, of different forms that have been and can be used for design; second, the ability of thinking, reasoning; third, taste—the ability of choosing the best among the many motifs one has in mind. The last two take the place, almost entirely in practical design, of what is generally called "originality." The first, the knowledge of motifs, I got a smattering of at Columbia, but very little exact knowledge, very little that I could put down on paper without a reference book before me. My work here has given me much broader as well as more exact knowledge. But there is still much, very much, to be done along this line.

In the second, architectural reasoning, I had very little, almost no practice at Columbia. Here, I am just beginning to learn how to bring it into play. This ability of thinking out (of reasoning) seems to me to be the basis of the school's work here, that which gives it, or the best of it, its high standing.

The last, taste—there is certainly a hundred times the opportunity to cultivate it here than there is at home. I do not myself in any way see the results of the examination as a criterion of my ability. I have just as much faith in myself as I ever did. You have more than once asked me whether I thought I had ability, originality, etc. I told you that I had not done enough to judge. The same is true still. It is foolish for me to attempt to form an opinion even of myself without sufficient work to judge. But I can at least say that I have a certain faith in myself, however groundless it may be, that I think I am coming out all right.

In the examinations I did not fall down in any of these three that I have spoken of as the essentials of architecture design. At least, I do not think I was weak enough in any of them to have failed. The jury divides those who receive no mark into two groups: those who deserve none on account of their work and those who might have passed but for some error or neglect. I was placed in the latter class. On my drawing they wrote "Plan unfinished." In fact, the reason I did not at least pass in design was that I did not work quickly enough. Of this, speed, I spoke to you in my last letter. It is up to me to quicken my speed. . . . With a more certain knowledge of the work I am doing, I expect to be able to do this.

This, as well as better draftsmanship and a good many other things, I expect to get before the next examinations. Unless I decide differently, I will take those that will be given between the 18th of June and the 10th or so of July. Just how much of my time I will spend in preparation, I do not know. In fact, my exact plans for my future work will not be definitely decided until next week, when I return to Paris. I know, in a general way, what I want. It remains to be seen what I can get. I came out here to get a few days rest, or rather, change. I will probably return to Paris on Monday or before. Within a week I expect to be hard at work again. I will then let you know what my plans are. . . .[1]

Merry Christmas and Happy New Year.

Your fond son,

Clarence

1. Near the end of 1905, Stein's parents began to discuss the possibility of visiting him in Europe in the summer of 1906. He warned them that he expected to be working and sketching on his own travels and so could not spend the entire summer as an "escort."

14   To his parents

22 rue Jacob—Paris   January 30, 1906

Dear Folks:

Work has commenced in earnest. Daily program is generally: Up at 6 or there-abouts; breakfast at creamery; walk of about fifteen minutes through Luxembourg Gardens, etc.; 8 or 8:30 to 12 at an academy in the painter's district, drawing in charcoal from life; lunch; afternoon at the atelier; dinner; evening 8–10 at the library of decorative arts at the Louvre; bed 11 or so. Wednesday evenings there is a lecture at the atelier. Friday or Saturday I sometimes go to the theater. Sunday is no longer a day of rest. From 9 until 12 we are at the atelier taking a special course in watercolor work. In the afternoon I try to get around to the Louvre, and then I spend the rest of the day writing letters.

I have not told you of either of the studios to which I belong. First, [there is] Mr. Umbdenstock's, in architecture.[1] The Frenchmen there are not as numerous and are more refined than those that were at Chifflot's, this, perhaps partially, because the price is slightly higher. There are a number of Americans at the atelier; they hail from the west, most of them, Chicago and St. Louis. They have not the "go" of the Easterners, but they are good fellows. I have been spending a good part of my time with them. Until I started in with my charcoal drawing, I was with them at the atelier all day. We would take our lunch right there. A couple of us would go out to the bakery, the creamery, [or] the grocer shop and get bread, which we toasted over the atelier fire, cakes, jam or apples, butter, and a bottle of milk each. . . .

The life of the place is Umbdenstock. His ideas dominate the atelier. I would not want to work under him for more than six months or a year. He is too strong in his own views, so strong that he is likely to always force them on you and thus prevent your individual growth. At first, I was uncertain about coming here just on that account. But the more of his criticisms I have heard, the more enthusiastic I have become. He is a man of ideas, of independent ideas, of up-to-date ideas. He does not let the past restrict him. He would teach us to build for the present. What is best of all for us beginners, he does teach by both action and word. He will work for hours at a stretch, showing us how to do the work and talking all the time.

On Wednesday evening he gives us a lecture that sometimes lasts for two hours or more. He knows his audience and he keeps them interested, talking often to the individuals present, asking them if they understand. A number of the Americans are of German extraction, and he will explain, very often, as he goes along, to them in German. He is from Alsace-Lorraine but is in no way in character a German, as far as I can make out, unless perhaps it be in an ability to scientifically systematize art.[2] He speaks a couple of words of English, which he picked up while at the St. Louis Fair and which he tries to use to their fullest possibility. He is trying to teach the men that are here from the États-Unis, and who are not trying for the examinations, to make architecture that will be American. His idea is that there is a great likeness between Americans and Frenchmen in temperament. They are the "action people," as he says it in English, and their architecture would show it in its openness and force.

He has great ability as to ideas and to their expression, particularly in drawing, and he knows it. I never met a more positive man, a more self-satisfied man. He is full of conceit, or should I say of self-assurance. He will step back from a drawing he has made and say, "That is fine. That is the way to do it. Just look at that." He has the kind of "go" that would make a success in America. It is not the most refined or polished way perhaps, nor is his habit of trying to discredit other architectural instructors. He perhaps is not in every way a gentleman, as reckoned by the general standards, but he is individual, he is different—seems to me, a man of his strength is not weighed on the same scale as others. . . .

It is hard to write here, at the atelier Umbdenstock, as the Frenchmen are raising the mischief as usual downstairs. They do not [know] how to keep still. An American and Frenchman next to me are trying to teach each other the other's language with the assistance of the others present, and one or two are singing.

Love to you all. Regards to many.

Goodbye,
Clarence

1. A change in Clarence's place of study was prompted, perhaps, by his failure in his first try at the examinations.
2. Umbdenstock's atelier had been established in 1903. It was quite popular with German,

Swiss, and Australian students, as well as Americans and less affluent Frenchmen. It continued with partners of Umbdenstock's until 1940

---

15 To his father

22 rue Jacob, Paris   February 5, 1906

Dear Papa:

. . . I wanted to start this letter by telling you how much I appreciated your kindness in telling me to stay here until I felt that I had all the preparation needed. I will do so; that is, unless I find that I am not making the progress that I should. I cannot yet tell whether I have "the stuff" in me. If I have, I mean to take every opportunity to bring it out. You are perfectly right in saying that I will always be sorry if I do otherwise. I do not like the idea of starting in work at the age I will have to, but it is better to start in late than to come late at the end of the race. What my course of study here will be, I will be able to decide as I go along. Whether it will be best to go through school or not, I have not yet decided.[1] Anyhow, I will arrange matters so I can do so, after I get in. First thing is to get in. I expect to have the very best kind of chance of doing so . . . the next time but cannot reckon on making it as a sure thing. . . .

The scope of my work has grown in my mind very much, since I have been able to see more clearly what it is. I had the notion at first that I could learn how to design a few things, interiors and furniture and the like, and that was all that was necessary. But it is design that I must learn, design in all its applications, so that I may be able to apply the big principles to my work, the principles [that] are true in painting and sculpture and architecture and even music. There are a great many things I see that I have got to study even though they do not seem to directly apply. Of these, the principal is architectural design, that is, the design of buildings as a whole. Then there is the cultivation of an ability to draw and paint; for instance I think that the studied work I am now doing from the nude model is going to be of the utmost value to me, though I may never have to do more than suggest a figure in a drawing. . . . The ability . . . to draw with accuracy and [to] see and comprehend form and the movement of line I will use in a hundred ways. Even after two weeks, I have found that my other work has been helped. But the main thing is the cultivation of taste, and that comes slowly. In fact, one must take his time about the whole thing. If this kind of work is to be learned well, it must be taken without too much haste. It must be left to soak in.

For a man to make a success in any kind of design at home, it is going to be more and more necessary that he be thorough. The competition is constantly growing stronger. What is more, the taste of people and their expectation [are] constantly growing. The artistic age for America, I believe, is coming. The country is at the height of its prosperity. More people are coming over here every year, and they are going back to America filled with the ideas of past art. The strength of the artistic movement in America is best shown, I believe, in what is called "Municipal Art." City after city are working out schemes for the beautifying of their public places. People have been satisfied for a good part with the rehashing of old work. I believe that they are going to require something different. . . .

Love to the family.

Your fond son,
Clarence

1. As Clarence had noted in an earlier letter, not all students of architecture in Paris studied at the École. Many who did not aspire to do so or who could not pass the examinations found study in an atelier sufficient preparation for practice. Public examination as a requirement for the practice of architecture did not exist in the United States until the 1930s.

16   To his brother Herbert Stein

22 rue Jacob, Paris   February 24, 1906

Dear Herb:

After a long wait, a whole bunch of letters turned up this evening: one from Mamma, one from Will, yours of the 11th, and one from Hen Klaber,[1] written a few days later. . . . I am not homesick (not exactly), but I would like to see the old place just for a few hours, and take dinner down in the dining room, and talk things over there, and then perhaps hustle away to [the] theater. There are not any plays here like those on Broadway. I still keep up an old habit of reading the reviews of new plays in the *Times* and/or the ads. Once in a while I almost get to the point of trying to make up my mind whether or not to go. [The] other night in the Quartier Latin, I sat at a table near a crowd of New Yorkers of the fat-and-full species that eat big meals down in the tenderloin district and go to the theater each night after and before. They had enough champagne to set them singing, and finally they came to "Give my regards to Broadway/ Remember me to Herald Square/ Tell all the boys, etc." And although I do not know that I was ever particularly in love with Broadway excepting on a wintry night, when there is snow enough flying to hide its ugliness, I did feel a strong desire to hie myself thence straight forth.

It's darned lonesome here in a way, Herb. Although I know lots of fellows, I cannot say that I have really made any friends. I was very glad to hear from Hen in his letter that he was really coming. His being here will make a lot of difference to me. But I am glad I came over here alone and have been alone during the last eight months. It has broadened me a good deal. I have come in contact with people more than I ever did at home. I have learned better how to get along with others, how to be satisfied with less comfort than I would wish, so that there might be peace.

Yes, I have been broadened a great deal, in coming in contact with a different class of people [from] the few with whom I always associated at home, with Frenchmen as well as Americans. I never appreciated how I was bound in, how I was narrowing myself, going through the same routine day after day, week after week, almost year after year. Just because I was interested in a number of different things—my architectural work, the Sunday Evening Clubs, the Society, politics—I could not see my narrowness. I do not say that I have outgrown it now—perhaps I never will entirely. And yet, I feel that I breathe more freely, that I look at things a bit more broadly.

A trip over here may really do very little in turning the current of your life, and again it may mean as much to you as my trip did to me. If I had not taken it, I might have remained at the factory, a work that would always have been more or less unsatisfactory to me, instead of taking up this work that I believe I was built for. A trip here may have as much effect on your future, but even if it does not it will broaden you; it will in every way better fit you to conduct a newspaper. . . .

So long,
Clarence

1. Henry Klaber, a New York City friend of Stein's, came to study architecture in Paris in the spring of 1906. Their friendship grew as students of architecture in Paris and on sketching tours. It lasted their lifetimes. Klaber worked in New York and occasionally collaborated with Stein on civic projects from 1912 until the late 1920s, after which he joined Ernest Gruensfeldt in architectural practice in Chicago. Klaber wrote his sensible and sophisticated book, *Housing Design* (New York: Reinhold, 1954), after several decades of experience in federal housing agencies.

---

17 To his parents

46 rue Jacob, Paris[1]   April 10, 1906

Dear Folks:

"Chez nous"—46 rue Jacob—[is] just down the street from the Hotel "Dingleberry." You enter by the porte cochere, a covered passageway that leads you into the large court. The concierge is in the little room to the right—fat and smiling. What would we do without that concierge! She receives whatever "Bon Marche" or anyone else may send us and sees that [it is] put in our room. She orders our coal and wood and whatever else of the kind we may need. And, in fact, with the assistance of the maid, who is perhaps her daughter, she makes life livable at 46. She will tell you we are on the "sixième," which is what we would call the seventh floor in New York. Finally, you will reach the top of the last flight of stairs, that is, unless you get discouraged before and turn back. Pull the bell, and Hen or I will let you in.

. . . First comes the entrance vestibule, in which there is just room for the two of us to stand. One wall of it is mainly a window; the others [are] three doors. One of these gives entrance from the staircase, a second leads to the bedroom, while the third is the door of the clothes closet.

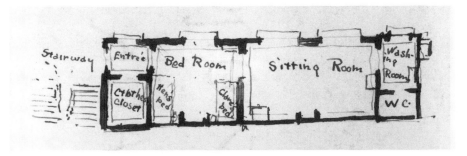

The clothes closet is as big as a hall bedroom. In it, each on its own hanger, are the various suits worn by the most honorable occupants of the apartments, also any other old thing they want to get out of the way.

Now we come to the bedroom, not the best place for a bedroom, between the entrance and the reception room, but we wanted to keep the big room with the two windows for working and lounging. All the rooms are well lit. Really, that is one of their greatest advantages. The windows are plentiful, . . . and they are all large, round-headed ones, what we call "French windows" at home; that is, they open like a double door and reach almost to the floor. . . . To the side you can see out over the rooftops (the old ones have fine deep green and red tiles) to the École des Beaux Arts. (You see, we keep our goal well in sight.) We were in the bedroom. Main decoration, without which no French living room would be finished—the mantelpiece. Then two beds; they are not large. There is also a small hanging bookcase in the room, which is already pretty well filled. . . .

Now, the sitting room, working room, parlor, loafing room, writing room, or what you will is somewhat larger. It is just full of light and air and whiteness. The wide dado and the ceiling, as in the bedroom, are a clean white. The wallpaper is of a light color, yellow with blue decoration. It is all as clean and nice as can be. Floors are of parquet and covered where necessary with rugs, which are in very good condition. . . . Sitting room furniture: a writing table, a bookcase containing our architectural library, chairs, two working stools, two chairs for ordinary use, and one easy chair. We need another of those that are made for lounging; we have to take life easy in turns now—if there were only Morris chairs growing hereabouts!

In front of the mantelpiece is the stove, the best one of the kind I have seen here. The last fellow who occupied the room kept it going all winter. He burned hard coal. We found keeping the fire going at the hotel a great nuisance. Here we will not have to bother about it, as the "bonne" will fill it up when necessary. The maid keeps things in general order [and] does it very well, as far as we have been able to see. She cleans up the room, makes our beds, gets us water, etc. Water is brought from the faucet in the court six stories down. Think of it! Nighttime we burn oil, not midnight oil at present. Days are getting long, so I am beginning to rise at six, which means generally going to bed at 10:30 or so. No water, no gas, but this is not New York, this is Paris. Paris of the Latin Quarter is a place to live if you want to appreciate the conveniences of home. . . . Plenty of water is brought up for us. We can make hot water whenever we wish on our oil stove. Why, we even can take a bath, and in fact we do every second day or so, in the rooms. Other times we go to the "Bains St. Germain," where one pays ten cents for a shower bath. . . .

Now how did we get our furniture? Most of it we bought from the fellow who last had the apartment. It is in that way that an apartment and its furnishings remain in the architectural family here for years. One man buys another man's beds and chairs and so on for just half of what the other fellow paid, and so it goes on down. . . .

Love from

Clarence

1. Clarence had continued to live at the Hotel d'Angleterre for the first nine months of his stay in Paris. On the arrival of Henry Klaber, they decided to rent an apartment just down the street.

---

18   To his mother

46 rue Jacob, Paris   April 20, 1906

Dear Mamma:

If there are any details of the management of our home of which I have not written you, which you would like to hear, let me know. I spoke in the last letter of how we bought our furniture and so on. What sheets and towels we needed we bought of about as cheap a quality as we could. If we find that the laundress does not ruin them too speedily, may get some good-quality linens to take home, if you wish. Bought one very good blanket for each bed. We change our sheet each week, and put the top one on the bottom. That is the correct system, is it not? I say "we"; it is really the "bonne" who does the job. She also keeps things in general order, brushes up the place and even our clothing if we leave them around.

You are always bothering about how we would keep alive if we were laid up in bed for a few days. Guess the concierge would cook enough for us if we wanted. She is good-natured—and only too willing to help along. She takes care of our mail and is in general our representative when we are away from the house, even paying our bills and not bothering us about them, but keeping account of them until the end of the month. But about being [sick]: prospects for the doctor or undertaker are not very rosy at 46 rue Jacob, sixième, sur la cour—too much air and sunshine. . . .

In the sitting room are hung framed pictures of Prof. Adler and Doctor Elliott, also some photographs of sculpture here: Venus, Flying Victory, and Rodin's work—Rodin is a wonder—to say nothing of a great big edition of the stars and stripes. Other pictures are expected to make their appearance before very long. Over on the bookcase is one lovely cast, a head, in the beautiful, soft ("dainty" I guess is the word) carving of the early Italian Renaissance. Best of all as decoration is a large array of books within the case. Their subject is architecture, and they are more than ornaments of the room. . . .

Although we are at home most every evening, we have taken off a couple of late to go to the theater. Monday a week ago we saw "Faust" again. This was the third time I heard it, twice here—and I am beginning to appreciate its beauty. It takes about that many times for an opera to "soak" in. Saturday we saw "Cyrano de Bergerac" with the great Coquelin as star—with the younger Coquelin and [a] well-chosen group of minor actors to assist. It is fine. The play you know from Macrafield's production. I think it is the greatest thing in the way of a play that has been written in the past century. That is as far as my knowledge or memory goes! There is not very much reason in the whole thing, or moral, or anything else perhaps, but it is all beautiful, and each act by itself is an artistic gem. Linked together they make a wonderful, dazzling jewel. And Coquelin—you should have seen him in the last act. There is another interest such plays as "Cyrano" have to us here. They depict the life and customs of the people that lived right here—and make so much more alive the dead buildings around us and so much more comprehensible the customs of the people.

It is Mr. Ries who took us to see "Cyrano," as well as treating us to dinner before. We received a letter from Hugo telling us that he was here. Called on him one night and took a walk with him along the boulevards and then the following night went to the theater with him.

. . . Last Sunday we took a boat down the crooked Seine to Saint-Cloud. We passed under the various and interesting bridges that span the river every few blocks and then out past the edges of civilization and the suburbs with their little houses spotted with colored tiles and past rows of trees. Sometimes [the trees were] planted in even rows along the edge of the stream, sometimes quite free and natural. [We] finally landed at the little village of Saint-Cloud. We made at once for the park. The Château d'Eau is the sight of the place. [It is] a large decorative fountain or artificial waterfall. Of course, we had to see it. And then we climbed up the hill behind and walked along the garden walks: first the formal ones, laid out in long, straight lines of statues and hedgelike trees, but much taller, and then on to the free paths that circle in among the woods.

And after that we lounged on the grass, just as everyone else was doing. What good times they were having. Everyone was there, rich and poor. A carriage drove up to let out my lady in all her Sunday splendor accompanied by her maid and two children dressed like dolls. While she read the children romped and played on the grass, enjoying themselves quite as much as the merry group not far away who hailed most likely from the "slums," if there are any slums here. These, like many others, had come out for the day, had brought their lunch . . . to eat on the grass, and were having the best kind of time. The park is free to all—walks, grass, and all. And the people do enjoy their freedoms and don't abuse them, I think. We found the same spirit at Versailles when we visited it the Sunday before.

I tell you people at home do not really know how to enjoy even their holidays. They work when they work, and they play when they play. They do not know how to loaf. These parks (Saint-Cloud, Versailles) were once for the king and his lords alone, and the people could stay outside and look through the railing. The revolution did do something for France, if it only gave to the people a place to rest and enjoy themselves.

But it is getting late: seven-thirty. I have been writing since six, and I must go out to breakfast and to work.

Much love to you and to the others from your fond son,

Clarence

---

19   To his parents

46 rue Jacob, Paris   Sunday, May 18, 1906

Dear Folks:

It is not the food that makes dinner worthwhile, it is the companionship of those that sit around the table with you. The eatables should be so good and simple that you can forget them. That which one gets at "our" restaurant, the Pres aux Clerces, certainly is up to that standard. And then there is no need of remembering what you have had to eat—one eats a "prix fixe." There is a little restaurant back by Boulevard Montparnasse at which I sometimes take lunch, where one must give a list of all one has, even down to the number of pieces of bread, to the patroness, who then calculates your bill on her slate. At the Pres we pay once every week or so. The food being of a forgettable quality, one can turn his attention to the conversation of his companions. . . .

There are a certain number of us who are regular customers at the Pres who can be found almost any evening at the table. Most of the other fellows, who are not keeping house or stopping at a pensione, drop in now and then to get a good solid meal. The most ancient member of our family is "Popsy," who sits over in the corner looking wise and saying nothing. He has been here two or three years and knows most everything about the place, or is supposed to. He is old in that way, not in the sense of years but that he has hidden, as do his friends, the Frenchies, under a well-pointed beard. My, how many years he lost in our estimation when the barber's scissors clipped away the hairs that [hide] his age, and let us see his round and boyish face. . . .

The other, "Wyck," who is as long and lanky as "Popsy" is small and solid, on the contrary never takes himself or anything else seriously. He has one of the finest senses of humor, but it is not on the surface. One is given at first to laughing at him, until you find his peculiarities are all his humor and the laugh is on you. He seems quite innocent of the world and its ways at first sight, a good product of the Jersey town from which he hails, but you soon learn that he is quite as worldly wise as anyone that has knocked around the Tenderloin and knows the "real New York" from top to bottom. He is an all-around New Yorker, a touch of the slickness and bright roughness of the Bowery, with all the quick polish of 23rd Street. . . .

We all have a calm manner of disregarding all the rules of syntax, grammar, and pronunciation of that great and beautiful language that is the pride of our French friends. But in that regard I think Biz deserves first mention. You ought to hear him butcher it. . . . Biz always confides in you, in everyone. Before a thought is quite formed in his brain, it is out of his mouth. . . . He takes everything seriously. He is perfectly German. His name, Biswanger, might tell you that if his characteristics did not suggest it. He has worked hard since his parents died when he was a young fellow. He earned his way through a special course at architectural college and since then has made enough in business by himself to come over here to see Europe. He is studying for the school. You ask him why; he says he does not want to get in; no, he just wants to see what it is like, so that no one can come to him after his return and say they are a "Beaux Arts" man and fool him by it. He is seeing Paris, and he will see the rest of Europe, so that no one will be able to fool him about it. Is that not characteristically human?

Quite the opposite type is my former roommate Murphy.[1] He just bubbles over with Irish humor. He is about the same age as Biz, twenty-seven, but his little pug nose makes him look much younger than does Biz's projecting Roman nose. Biz says Murph is the greatest man at argument; he can make you tell him all you know on the subject without giving you the slightest inkling as to his opinion. . . . He is careless throughout, but in his work, architectural, at least, he gets the effect.

Groben, his roommate, in his architecture is all neatness and carefulness. Every line is drawn just as it should be. He does very good work. He took a number of prizes in America and comes here on scholarship. He has no spark of genius. All that he has gained he has gained by hard plugging. As might be expected, his way of work is reflected in his ways away from work.

There are other more or less regular boarders at the Pres; there is C——, of "good" family and well read, who sees the humor of life to the full, enjoys it, and invites you to enjoy it with him. And there are many other Americans who drop in now and then. . . . The only other foreigner who sits at our table is a Dutchman who is not an architect, and so of course does not belong there. But he happened along, and he is fairly good company, and so he has stayed.

Clarence

1. Frederick V. Murphy was awarded the Diplôme École des Beaux Arts in 1909. He practiced architecture in Washington, D.C., and taught design at Catholic University from 1911 to 1938.

---

20   To his father

46 rue Jacob, Paris   June 23, 1906

Dear Papa:

Sad news again: I did not pass the examinations. That means another wait of six months, but not six months wasted. I will be able to keep myself busy enough and will probably make as much progress as if I were in the École, but that does not mean at all that I do not feel pretty bad about having missed out. It is not a matter of pride with me. It makes no difference to me what people think of my ability as long as I myself am satisfied with it, and then the fellows here understand very well that the examinations are no sort of accurate measure of a man's architectural ability. I do think my time could be spent to better advantage in the school, if only because there is stronger competition, but there is enough to be done outside.

One reason I feel so very sorry about my failure is the fact that I fear that you may take it as a basis of judgment of my ability. I do not think this would be entirely fair. Although a man is able to test himself fairly well by these examinations, I do not think that the mark he receives can be taken as a criterion of his ability because there are a good many things to be considered (not only architectural knowledge and reasoning but also speed, draftsmanship, etc.) and a lack in any of them may mean utter failure. To myself, the examination showed that I had made a great deal of progress since the last time I tried. I am satisfied with the progress, but, of course, not with the results.

It was up to me, of course, to prepare in such a way that I could not be caught up on any point. My draftsmanship more than anything else was lacking, and there I must put my attention.

I would not write this lengthy excuse or explanation to another; I am willing to be judged by what I do, but I want you to understand where I stand, or at least where I think I do, and I believe you are willing to take my word for it. I still have plenty of confidence in myself and only hope that you have likewise.

Plans for the future, I have hardly had time to formulate. In the first place I am going to take a good, long vacation and see something of France at the same time. I feel rather tired out, for my work has kept me hard at it through the past year. You need not mention this fact to Mamma, as it would probably result in much worrying and many letters of motherly advice. [I] will write to you again at the end of the month, with probably more or less definite plans of my future work.

Regards to all in the office.

Your fond son,

Clarence

21   To his parents

46 rue Jacob, Paris   July 8, 1906

Dear Folks:

It was a "Glorious Fourth" after all. You would not have believed *the* day had come. There was not a firecracker heard throughout Paree. Yes, it rained as it always does on the Fourth, and I suppose down in that district around the Opera, where at this season French is a foreign tongue, the Stars and Stripes could be seen on more than one building. But our celebration did not take place until late in the evening.

The report has gone forth that old grandma at the "Pres" was going to make some pie for the Americans on their Independence Day. . . . The proprietor treated us to three bottles of the fizzy stuff. He also had our part of the room redecorated with flags and with a little edition waving from the top of each pyramid of white napkins on the long table.

There were only eight of us, but we were able to take care of the champagne and the bottles ordered one after another by each member of the party. And after we had become quite joyful, we were able to make ourselves heard in song. First we sang every American popular tune or college air that any of us could remember. It was proposed that it might be appropriate to sing the American National Anthem, but no one knew it all. Queer, but there is hardly an American really knows the "Star-spangled Banner." . . .

After that came speeches—rather poor ones, but jolly. Biswanger spoke in German and then translated into English all about the meaning of the red and the white and the blue. "Biz" serious is funnier than anyone else's jokes. Popsy spoke on the changes that had come over the American settlement since his arrival and of the awful, awful "Harvard bunch." And everyone else took his whack at those aristocrats. So things moved along quite merrily, and champagne corks jumped, and glasses were filled again and again. . . .

I was going to leave here on a bicycle trip on Sunday but did not, for on Friday evening I received a note from Doctor Elliott announcing the arrival of "the head and tail of the Ethical Movement." Saturday morning I had breakfast with Professor Adler and the doctor. Then I visited with the latter, Notre Dame and Sainte Chapelle. Next day we (the two doctors and myself) spent the day at Versailles. We met Henry there in the afternoon. Yesterday, with the professor and with Doctor Elliott, I went to Fontainbleau and then by carriage through the woods to Barbizon. As you can believe, it has been a big treat for me to be with the professor and the doctor during these two days. I have seen things that I have seen again and again in a different light. It is from the historical point of view that the professor has looked at these things, although he has a strong appreciation of the beautiful.

He has a wonderful memory for history, in fact, for everything. He seems to know Paris through and through. Was I not turned stiff by such close proximity to the saint? Not a bit of it. The professor is just as human as any of them, most of the time anyhow, and quite as lovable when you know him. They leave for home next Friday. . . .

Love to you all,
Clarence

---

22 To his parents

Hotel du Château, Blois   August 9, 1906

Dear Folks:

We are still in Blois, as you see. We will probably be here for a few days more. We have been working steadily eight to ten hours a day sketching, but there is still an endless amount of detail of the château that is well worth drawing. I have been working mainly indoors, so I was not at all sorry to take a short spin on [my] bicycle this afternoon . . . to visit the Château of Chaumont, which is sixteen kilometers away. We got there in almost no time; the road along the riverside is as smooth and flat as can be. . . .

We first caught sight of the irregular skyline of its many roofs and towers from a distance. It looked big up there at the summit of a wooded hill, and its bigness was magnified by the fringe of little houses that bordered the river below. That little village with its little church had probably very much the same appearance in the old days when the battlements of the château above served a purpose, and the baron lived most snugly within his four strong walls, and the poor folks below paid homage for the protection these walls and the strong men behind them could give against some other strong barons downstream. And there is the whole story of the feudal system. . . .

Within the château we were permitted to visit those rooms not occupied by the family that now owns the place. They gave me the best idea I have yet been able to form of the living rooms of a wealthy family of the latter part of the Middle Ages. The walls at either side of the room were some ten feet thick, making immense window reveals. These are stone through the whole thickness, but they are covered with dull tapestries. The ceilings are heavily beamed. These beams are crudely painted with monograms and dates. The floors are tiled. They must have been cold in winter. We poor students refused to take a very good apartment just because it had a floor of that kind. At one end of each room is a big, heavy chimney. The furniture is dull and strong and was probably none too comfortable, though it was finely carved. Catherine de Médicis and Diana de Poitiers and princes and counts and bishops lived here, but for just solid comfort I think I would choose 292 Manhattan.[1] Mine for a Morris chair. . . .

So farewell,
Clarence

1. The Steins' apartment across Manhattan Avenue from Morningside Park at West 112th Street.

---

23   To his parents

Paris   September 19, 1906

Dear Folks:

From Rouen to Amiens I rode in one day. It is a seventy-two-mile run, but the roads are good, as they are everywhere in France. So, though my wheel was very well loaded with baggage, I had no trouble in making it. . . .

Of Amiens there is little to say. It was a disappointment in a sense, as all the cathedral towns of like type are destined to be after seeing Rouen. There is the cathedral, which, to me, had its own special architectural interest, of course. Then there are the boulevards, the "Palais de Justice," the "Hôtel de Ville," the theater, and the museum, as in all French cities of this size. Amiens is a factory town and is surrounded by a fringe of tall chimneys. Almost the entire population seems to work in the factories, and their youngsters are a ragged-looking lot. Their streets, along which the tenements are built, are not particularly sweet smelling. In fact, there was very little attractive about Amiens excepting its grand cathedral, so I shortened my stay there to a day. . . .

From Compiègne, a short ride [took me] through a beautifully kept forest to the little village which massed itself around the hill on which stands the mighty castle of Pierrefonds. It is impossible to comprehend the power and immensity of Pierrefonds from pictures or description. Outwardly, it consists of some eight or so gigantic towers with battlemented tops, connected by a massive wall with loopholes along its top. It is a fighter place through and through.

They entrusted the work of rebuilding to Viollet-le-Duc, who rejuvenated so many of the cathedrals. He was a wonderful man. He had studied the architecture and the life of the Middle Ages with such thoroughness that he could not only copy their work with accuracy, but [also] build, in their spirit, things they had never constructed. His was not the work of the free artist whose labor is to please himself and people of his kind. He was like the student who, after studying all the books and documents on a subject, writes down in his own way the results of his research. That student has a joy in expressing that which he [has] mastered. In Pierrefonds one feels that Viollet-le-Duc had that same joy. Much of the château is his own original work. Much is the rebuilding of the old château. . . . All of it, from the portcullis at the gate to the chapel, the courtyard with its forceful low arches, the rooms with their queer pictures of medieval hunting and home life, all has the powerful force of the barons of the medieval days. But it has a bit [of] the unreal, theatrical effect. It seems too good to be true.

If I had any suspicion that it was a grand hoax, it was dispelled when I saw the real ruins of a château of a period slightly earlier at Coucy. Its immense towers and long wall stand out wonderfully white at the top of the tall, green hill, as seen from across the valley. There are only ruins remaining, and yet with the assistance of the guide's explanations and after seeing Pierrefonds one could almost imagine this immense fortification back into reality. . . .

From up on top of the tall "donjon" tower, one could get an excellent view of the surrounding country. The fertile valleys are of just the same character as most of the farmland I had passed on my trip. It differs from our American country, lacking the breadth and ruggedness. Every bit of soil has been cultivated in them. There are woods, but they are in small patches and even they have a "cared for" look. The whole has the appearance of being polished down to its finest finish as part of man's civilization. That is, there is just the same kind of difference between our rough way of using the immense amount of land that we have and their cultivation as there is between the rugged life of our West and the culture and polish of their cities and all that surround them, the architecture and all else.

One other very noticeable difference in their country life . . . is the lack of farmhouses, in our sense. We came on some in the Loire district that looked like those in America, but very few in the North. People seemed to live together in the village. The only reason for their doing so that I can think of is that of habit—the habit that grew out of the need [for] protection in the Middle Ages. . . .

Love to you all from
Clarence

24   To his parents

46 rue Jacob, Paris   october 21, 1906

Dear Folks:

That you may know how I am spending my time, I will give you a short synopsis of the events (or lack of events) of last week. It is about the same story over and over again every seven days. Monday I got up at six, dressed, and had breakfast. The latter consists of about a pint of milk and two rolls. These are delivered at my door early each morning; price, six cents. With breakfast I have the *Times.* I try to do one each day. But of late Hughes's speeches have been so interesting and Hearst's so entertaining that I have been getting way behind.[1]

After eating I do a little studying and at eight go over to the atelier of M. Besson, where I take freehand drawing lessons. His studio is on the sixth floor, a large airy room with walls of a very architectural appearance and a big window that looks out over jolly backyards with trees and grass to the Louvre across the river. The subjects that we draw are rather uninteresting, but it is good training in exact work, and Besson, I think, is a first-rate instructor. I work at the atelier until dark, only taking off an hour or so at noon for lunch.

I take that meal at the cuterie. There are other "cuteries," but for us Americans this is the "cuterie." A good many of us go there as regularly as we conveniently can for one or two meals a day. One can order eggs in any form and milk, coffee, tea, or chocolate, also nice, and, if one is very extravagant, fruit. Lunch generally costs one franc to one franc twenty-five. The "cuterie" is clean, the food is good, one can meet the fellows there, and besides, they take the *Herald,* which, with all its failings, at least gives you a suggestion of what is happening at the west side of the Atlantic.

The evening meal we always take at the "Pres." . . . The bill of fare is much the same night after night, but so it is at home. The food is good, but, what is much more to the point, the company is good. Dinner and talk generally takes an hour or more. It is after eight by the time I get back to the room at 46.

Evening work is much the same every day, mathematics and a little architectural research. The math I do on a blackboard; . . . when not in use [it is covered] by the big American flag [and] forms the dominant feature of our sitting room. The decoration and appearance of our room has not greatly changed since I last wrote of it. There are a few more pictures on the wall: Professor Adler and Doctor Elliott and some views of architectural monuments and postal card photographs of statues. . . .

Tuesday I work all day at the architectural atelier and spend the evening and the following morning at home finishing up the design I had started. Wednesday afternoon, the "patron," M. Umbdenstock, criticizes our design. That is always entertaining. He is an excitable Frenchman who is full of talk and ideas.

Thursday: freehand drawing again and mathematics late in the afternoon. Friday, I spend another day drawing, but this time at the Louvre. Working there is so much more interesting; the subjects are better. I am trying to draw an exquisite little Roman affair, three figures supporting a something or other. They are the real models, not mere casts; besides, there is so much more to see when one rests for a minute: a room, rooms, just full of marvelous works of art. . . .

Saturday I worked at home on another architectural problem until the middle of the afternoon and then went to the atelier to receive a criticism.

Sunday morning I stayed home making up some accounts. After lunch we took one of the riverboats up as far as it would go, Henry and myself, of course. The weather was splendid, not even cold this Sunday, could not be better if [it was] made to order. After leaving the boat we took a good long walk, first through the woods of Vincennes, which is a park, perhaps more like [the] Bronx than any other park we have near New York. But it is more woods, more the same all the way through, and the roads are better. . . . Another walk through the woods and we arrived at a little suburban village, just like one I remember near New York, with a main street lined with shops along which runs a trolley-line and side streets with houses. But many of these latter were in the stuntiest kind of art nouveau.[2] Then we came to the Marne River. It was just lovely. . . .

Sunday evening I started this. And today, Monday—finish it.

With love from

Clarence

1. Charles Evans Hughes was nominated for the governorship of New York by the Republican party after his very successful investigation of New York life insurance companies. Hughes won the colorful and turbulent campaign over William Randolph Hearst by fifty-seven thousand votes and was reelected in 1908. His active involvement in progressive labor and welfare legislation attracted Clarence Stein to him.

2. There were some rather elaborate art nouveau houses in the western suburbs of Paris near the Bois de Vincennes.

---

25   To his parents

46 rue Jacob, Paris   Sunday, November 18, 1906

Dear Folks:

Henry and I have just arrived home from our regular Sunday afternoon walk. We were on the go for four hours and a half and are so glad to be back near our fire, comfortably seated one at either end of the table and both busily trying to think what to write next. It is raining again now. It just let up long enough to let us have our promenade. We crossed the river, passed up between the two wings of the Louvre and straight through the Tuilleries Gardens, where the little French kids were having a good time playing, as were the fountains. Then across the Place de la Concorde and past the house of the president of the Republic, or rather the joyful grille that separates the garden from the street, where the president may be quite as peaceful as he wishes. We continued through some of the "best" parts of the city, where one still finds private houses. Almost everywhere, apartments have taken their places. . . .

The fortifications (there really are fortifications all around the city) from the inside look merely like grass-covered mounds of earth.[1] Without is a straight stone wall and a deep ditch, the latter empty of water. We passed the octroi and were out of Paris. . . .

This place was quite in contrast to the respectable Parisian district we had just been passing through. It was of about the character of Second Ave. or lower Tenth or perhaps still more of Hoboken. In fact, it reminded me of them all, with its very American-like grocery stores, . . . drinking places that looked more like saloons than cafes, and long rows of uninteresting apartments. Its streets were crowded with working folks and their numerous offspring (numerous for this land).

It was surprising how many of the men were more or less drunk. One does not see so much of intoxication over here. I wonder if it is a result of the weekly rest law.

. . .

We were headed for the city hall, the tower of which we had sighted as we left Paris. Finally we reached it, a splendid big building that we enjoyed to our full from a comfortable bench in the park in front. The building is larger, I think, than our city hall and to me it seemed more pleasing. Funny that one should find such a pretentious piece of architecture as this in such a poor-looking town, but the French take more pride in the home of their city government (or, more exactly, their grand ballroom with offices connected) than we do in those buildings that stand for our principal government. How do they pay for it? I don't know. How do they pay for all their expensive government buildings, museums, parks, and their keep? The octroi helps, and so does the tax on everything you look at, or touch, or smell, or taste, just about everything but air.[2]

Nothing much happened last week outside of the regular routine.

Clarence

1. These walls were not removed in the construction of the Peripherique Boulevards until the 1930s and 1950s. Stein continued his study of Paris decades later when he returned for an extended stay in 1950, after which he wrote an article about Paris as a modern city, which, unfortunately, has not been published.

2. As late as 1995, the French policy of generous spending on Paris institutions, parks, street improvements, and so forth was seen as an important reason for huge taxes.

26   To his parents

Florence, Italy   May 6, 1907

Dear Folks:

It is lucky I tried to give you my impression of the brilliancy of Venice in my last letter. Since then, there have been a few clear days, which gave me an opportunity to climb the hills at either side of Florence and look down at such a picture, an endless circle of rolling hills, dotted with spots of white buildings, by ones and twos near the tops, and gradually growing more numerous as they approach the solid, red-tiled city with its old towers and, in the center of all, the great dome of the cathedral. It makes one feel bigger and better (I don't know why) to take in at one glance all of great Florence and the grander hills around her. It is all so simple, unpretentious, strong. Yes, Florence is the city for me. Venice is beautiful, it is bright, it is gay, and yet it is sad, it is so much pretense. Florence is real, virile, living.

But, nonetheless, Venice is a very pretty show, well worth seeing. And I was very sorry I had to leave. But what did I do there? It is true, I have said a good deal about impressions and color and such like but very little about how I spent my time at Venice.[1]

I put up the first night at a hotel. But the prices were too much for me, so the next day I went in search of a pensione. Everywhere I received the same answer—"no room." Apparently April is one of the favorite months for visiting Venice. [One of Stein's drawings made in Venice is illustration 16 on page 73.] Finally, I decided to take a furnished room and, after some search, I found one in an out-of-the way corner that was not so far from things, that is, the Piazza S. Marco, if you knew the way. It was cheap, and that was good. The room was clean and all I wanted. Meals I took at various restaurants. I found only a very few were good enough and not too expensive, and these grew very tiresome. Breakfast I took at a cafe. It is quite customary to do so here, unless one is stopping at the better class of hotel, and it costs about half what it does at a hotel.

I do remember very vividly a good many days of rain, how many I cannot say. Their number has probably been exaggerated in my mind on account of their disagreeableness. Rain in Venice just ties one down to the Place St. Mark's, for you do not want to paddle around in the narrow streets and what is the use of going out in a gondola if you cannot see anything. Until three you can visit the art gallery or the Doge's palace. My time, as I have said, was much given to the study of the latter building. From three on, there was little to do except walk around under the arcade that surrounds the piazza on three sides and look in at the windows filled with paintings, statues, mosaics, and other temptations to the visitor laden with gold, or else sit down at one of the cafes of the piazza and see what effect mental persuasion will have on the rain. These cafes are nice places to sit on a sunny day, when the band is playing in the square, and everyone is there taking his coffee or ice. . . . On a rainy day it is gloomy indoors. About the only amusement is trying to guess the nationality of the endless line of tourists promenading under the protection of the arcade outside.

The Venetians themselves do not promenade so much in the piazza. They take their evening walk, a good number of them anyhow, in the narrow, crooked street that connects the Piazza San Marco with the Rialto Bridge.

It was hardly necessary to say that this street is narrow and crooked. All Venetian streets are, with the exception perhaps of one, a new way, that is broad merely in contrast to the others. But it is not necessary to make the Venetian streets wide enough for two wagons to pass one another. In fact, it would be difficult to push even a little cart along the street, for one is constantly coming on a bridge, which generally means a few steps up at one side and down at the other. All traffic is carried on by boats, but the land thoroughfares are used in general by the Venetians in going from place to place.

One's idea of Venice is always of a canal city. One never thinks of the streets until one has visited the city. But they are, I think, more numerous. Although the houses of a good many of the wealthy are directly on the canals, the homes of most of the people are separated on the narrow paths or are on the narrow ways that run across the town. I did most of my traveling in Venice by land because gondolas cost too much. The layout of those streets is worse than any maze that was ever invented, but after a while I found a way to go from one place of interest to another, often a very roundabout way.

This was on the clear days, of course. There really were a good number of sunny ones. Then I visited the various sights—the churches, the museums—and rode up and down the Grand Canal or walked along the streets nearby, coming out wherever there was a chance to walk along the main waterway to study and admire the wonderful palaces that line it. With a little sketching and a good deal of sightseeing my twelve days at Venice passed altogether too quickly. . . .

Love to you all,
Clarence

1. Venice became, in time, one of Clarence's favorite cities. In the 1950s he wrote a long article on its admirable qualities as a pedestrian city, which was never published.

27   To his parents

46 rue Jacob, Paris   January 6, 1908

Dear Folks:

I certainly owe you a good big letter, or a number of them, but you have excused my neglect, I hope, or anyhow will when I tell you how busy I have been these last four or five weeks.

Yesterday it was all over. The results of the examinations were posted. Happiness regained. You can't imagine what an important event these exams are to us here. We have been speaking of them constantly for months past, and during these weeks that they have really been in progress we have talked, and thought, and dreamt of nothing else.[1] Everybody here is interested in the results, whether they have taken part in the fray or no. Mademoiselle Pres and old Mother Pres seemed as joyful at our success as anyone else. And even the concierge wanted to congratulate me, though how she had heard of my passing I can't say.

Well, to start at the beginning: When the suspense of waiting was put to an end by the Secretaire assuring me that I was a full-fledged élève d'École des Beaux Arts, I wasted no time in thanking him but went in search of somebody to help me celebrate. I picked up Johnny on the way along with a miscellaneous assortment of Frenchmen, Bulgarians, etc. We drank. Well, then, after returning to the school yard and spending an hour or so in congratulating and being congratulated, I went over to the other side of the river to send word to you.

Then after some rambling, I got back to the vestibule of the school, where a group of fellows of the same atelier as myself were gathered around the official list of men received. Some were glowing in their own success, and the others were trying to beam in the reflected light of their comrades. . . .

After dinner was the real celebration. It is the custom at the Pres for the successful candidates for the school to set up the drinks. Of course, nothing else than champagne would suffice for such an event. Ely Kahn[2] and I, who were the only ones of the Pres bunch to "make it," lived up to the best prestige. Everyone drank to their heart's content. We had invited our mathematics instructor to be present. You remember him, Pop, the long-haired gentleman that came up to see me one day when you were up in the room. He seemed to enjoy himself. By a special effort we all spoke French. It is hard at the Pres, and he did not seem to object to the fizz-water any more than did we. Well, afterward, Hen, Ely, another chap, and I took a long walk and ended up by doing a little shooting in a shooting gallery just to show each other that we could hold a gun. We really had not taken as much of the sparkling wine or other wines as this account would lead one to believe, or else we didn't know it. That ended our celebration.

We expect to continue it to some slight degree this evening by going to some show, probably "The Prince of Pilsen.". . .

Until Friday, farewell.

Clarence

1. It had been two and a half years since Clarence Stein had arrived in Paris to study interior decorating and two years since he had first taken the entrance examinations of the École des Beaux Arts. Considering the fact that he could have studied architecture at Columbia for no longer than one year, this period of study in Paris prior to passing the exams seems natural. Most French students took two years of preparation to gain admission to the school.

2. Kahn had arrived in Paris during the preceding summer after graduating from the four-year undergraduate program in architecture at Columbia. Kahn was fluent in French before his arrival. He and Stein became close friends and companions for summer sketching trips during the next four years.

---

28   To his parents

46 rue Jacob, Paris   Sunday, January 12, 1908

Dear Folks:

I told you in my last that I would write you about the examinations for the École des Beaux Arts. It is a rather long tale, and one I have told you at least in part before. But it is difficult to make one who is not here and taking them to understand this complicated system of examinations. There is a series of five examinations: in architecture, freehand drawing, modeling, mathematics, and history. One must have a passing mark in the first subject to be permitted to continue. After the modeling and drawing examinations, the standings of all the competitors are reckoned, and only the one hundred and twenty men or so of the highest standing have the privilege of finishing the examinations. Of these the 60 men with the highest standing are finally chosen to enter the school. Forty-five of this number are Frenchmen, the other fifteen foreigners. But all of these last-named must have a higher standing than the last of the natives. In reckoning the standing of the competitors, the marks in each subject are multiplied by a coefficient which varies according to the importance of the subject; one's mark in architecture is multiplied by fifteen, that in drawing ten, modeling by five, mathematics by ten, and history by one.

The architectural examination is of twelve hours' duration. It starts at eight o'clock in the morning. That means one must get up while it is still dark and dress by lamplight. It is cold these winter mornings. I don't know why, but it is a great deal harder to get up in the early morning here than it is at home. So as to be sure not to oversleep, one very carefully sets and winds his alarm clock the night before and then stays awake half the night for fear it won't go off. And when one does sleep, one dreams architecture and exams, exams and architecture.

The lamps are still lit along the streets when one finally gets downstairs; the blinds are down over the storefronts; no one is stirring except the bakery women, with their great blue aprons full of bread and a lamp in one hand, the "laiterie" boys with their hands full of clinking bottles, the scavengers emptying the contents of ash cans in search of odds and ends that may be reconstructed into something of use, and a few clerks. A few of us meet at the laiterie where we always get our morning chocolate. We find only one subject of conversation, that which has filled our minds for weeks past: the day's work, the examination. By the time we started for the school the sun had probably risen, but it was still dark; everything was enveloped in a beautiful blue fog.

The four to five hundred competitors that participate in the first examination are distributed in the various "loges" of the school. These "loges" are alcoves that line the sides of long hallways. Each man is supposed to have a separate alcove, where he can work undisturbed and without assistance, but there are not enough loges to accommodate all those who will take the examinations. For the couple of hundred that remain, tables are set up in one of the large exhibition rooms. I happened to be among these. There it was impossible for the guardians to keep the men at their places, so one was comparatively free to discuss the problem with his friends.

A half hour or so before the doors opened, a large crowd was gathered in front of the examination room, bags of instruments over shoulders, boards under arms. At eight we were admitted and there was a wild rush for places. In a few minutes the program was distributed. It told us that we were to design a part of a château like Versailles. We read, studied, sketched various schemes, and then finally started drawing out the idea we had decided upon as the best solution of the problem. . . . But then comes eight o'clock. All is over. The result of one's day's work is handed in, and again the racket breaks out. . . .

A good many of us Americans dine at the Pres. Of course, we have one topic of conversation—the problem, its proper solution, what we did, what we wished we had done, etc., etc.

It is a custom of long standing that the American architects shall meet at the American bar of the Pantheon cafe on the night of the architectural examination. There we gathered—not only those who were trying the examinations, but also a great many of the other members of our little colony. There are really only three occasions on which we all, or at least a good portion of us, get together. The semiyearly exams [are two, and the other] is at the yearly dinner.

We take the architectural examination on Monday. The results of the examination are not known until the following Friday. The time intervening was spent finishing our preparation for the examination in drawing. But even with this work it is impossible to keep one's conversation or thoughts from the results to be posted on Friday. They mean too much to us.

Fred Rosenblatt arrived Friday morning. So I was prevented from spending that day in nervously walking up and down in front of the school. It is noon or after before one of the guardians appears with the fateful list of the marks. He mounts on a bench and commences to read it. All who can, climb up behind him and try to see their standing or that of a friend to whom they afterward signal it. There is silence in the room while the first few names are read, but that does not last; there is a shout of joy as a man hears of his success or else some not-too-polite exclamations of sorrow, which, in the case of some of the younger boys, may be followed by weeping. I was not there when the results were read this time but came around later to find that the fairly good mark I had been expecting was not mine. I had received a mark but a very low one. The world seemed a very unhappy place.

But by evening I had made up my mind that there was still hope that good work in drawing might still pull me through. In fact, I almost made myself believe that I was as good as anyone in the school.

Monday morning I again had to rise at an unearthly hour to be at the school at 7:30, in time for the modeling examination, which commenced a half hour later. We are given eight hours in which to copy some antique composition. It is not overdifficult . . . to make the very incomplete copies we produce. But it is hard manual work, and we are good and tired by four o'clock.

Almost no one puts in more than a day or two of preparation for the modeling examination. The general opinion is that [it] is useless to attempt to become a finished modeler in the limited time that one could give to it, . . . and so the best thing to do is to just take chances. On the contrary, everyone prepares most thoroughly for drawing and depends on it to help put them in the school. I did. I knew that without a rather good mark in drawing I had no chance of getting up to the mathematics examination. So Tuesday morning I was there with "blood in my eye," as the saying goes.

When I reached the school at a little after seven, I found that quite a crowd had gathered. There are certain positions from which more effective drawings can be made, so everyone wants to be first in the hall. We whiled away the hour that intervened before the doors were opened by singing. We did work; anyhow, I did. I was on the job the whole eight hours, excepting five minutes for lunch.

Love to you all from,

Clarence

---

29   To his parents

46 rue Jacob, Paris   January 16, 1908

Dear Folks:

I will take up the tale of those examinations where I left off in my last letter and finish with the tiresome story.

The modeling and drawing examinations were on Monday and Tuesday. The results were not posted until Friday evening. The intervening time we spent trying to keep from worrying about our fate and in preparing for the mathematics examination. Friday came at last and dragged along. We went to the school again and again in the late afternoon, but the marks had not yet been posted. Finally, at about half past six, on returning, I found a great crowd around the bulletin board. Presently Henry fought his way out. "Well?" "All right, seven in drawing, eight in modeling." I was dancing around the court with some Frenchman or other. The marks were rather good; anyhow, good enough to take me up to the mathematics. Once that far, I felt I could make it.

One hundred and twenty-seven men were chosen to continue the examinations. Of these, a larger percent than usual were foreigners. There were twenty-four of these ahead of me, and of all of us only fifteen could be received. It was with the Americans, Swiss, Russians, etc., that I was to have the toughest fight. It was mathematics that would tell the tale.

The first of the math examinations was on the following Monday, a written test of two hours' duration. In the afternoon we had the written examinations in history, the principal difficulty of which for us Americans is putting our thoughts into understandable French. The following day we had to show our ability to make practical application of what we knew of descriptive geometry in making a mechanical drawing. For this we were allowed eight hours.

Then commenced final preparation for the most trying test of all, the oral examination in mathematics. The field covered is more or less simple: algebra, geometry, logarithms, descriptive geometry, and arithmetic, but one must know them perfectly, every bit of them. For one has but little chance to think or invent when one gets up to answer questions before a crowded amphitheater. So we plugged at that math all day long and far into the night, day after day. All the time the examination was going on at the school; some thirty men or so each day were being tortured by the math instructor. And the rest of us were there, when time permitted, to see the show. It is amusing enough from outside the rail. The men are called in alphabetic order. My name was luckily near the end, so I had plenty of time to study. It seemed that the professor would never come to the end of the list. Christmas Day came, and New Year's. I have very slight recollections of what happened excepting that I was studying math.

Oh, yes, we did see the New Year in: Hen, Ely, and a couple of other chaps and I. We heard a bully concert at the Rouge. . . . I had attended the Rouge about every second night of the week before. It does not take long, and it is a good rest. Afterward, New Year's eve, we went to a cafe and there greeted 1908 with as loud a racket as we could command. The Frenchies are not quite as demonstrative as the Broadway crowd on this occasion. They drink much, but that is about all. A man with a long horn would seem quite lost. The boulevards were rather dead, more so than usual.

The examinations: Finally my turn came. I walked down to the bottom of the amphitheater, signed my name, took a piece of chalk, and awaited my question. For a few minutes I was "fussed" but then luckily was able to forget that I was the center of attention of the crowd in the room behind. And so I pulled through the quarter of an hour ordeal more or less successfully.

Only one examination now remained, that in history. This one oral test has always been one of the greatest jokes here. It counts so much less than any of the others that almost no one spends more than a few hours in preparation for it. And so the answers that are given to the various questions are likely to be rather weird. The history professor is a good-hearted gentleman who hates to see anyone fail, so he kindly assists the student. For instance, he asks, "Who conquered the Gauls?" A blank look is the only answer. "Ju-Ju—," says the examiner. Still blankness. "Jul—" No light. "Julius—" The student looks as though he might be trying to think. "Julius Cae—" "Julius Caesar."

Light has dawned. "Oui, oui, oui, Julius Caesar," says the brilliant young man. And so the professor gradually answers his own questions. The Americans are particularly funny, at least the French find them so, for, besides being blessed with the Frenchman's lack of knowledge of history, he has his own original pronunciation and vocabulary.

History does not count much. But I needed every point I could get, so I "boned" up for a day and a half. Luck was with me, and I had as question "the Renaissance in Italy," the period of history which of all I find the most interesting. I received about as high a mark as is given in the subject, which helped greatly to put me into the school.

I have already written you what the results were and how we celebrated. As I had said, I felt sure that I would get a higher place than the forty-fifth (last) Frenchman. The only question was whether I could make up ten places ahead of me among the foreigners. I was fourteenth of these and, in order, was just after the twenty-fifth Frenchman.

So there you have the story.

That is all today,
Clarence

---

30 To his brother Herbert Stein[1]

46 rue Jacob, Paris   February 21, 1908

Dear Herb:

Some weeks ago I wrote you. I suppose the answer is on the way here, but I will not wait for it, as I want you to receive this before your birthday. Congratulations and best wishes for a successful year.

There has been plenty doing here. In fact, there is so much under way that I have time now to tell you but little of it. My first problem at the school "renders," that is to say, must be finished by next Saturday. That will keep me humping until then. So let there be no kick if you receive but scant news from Paree during the coming week. Monday last I joined one of the ateliers connected with the school. These ateliers are associations of men doing the problems of the École des Beaux Arts. Each one chooses as instructor some architect and is to a certain extent under his direction. But, for the main part, they are self-governing.

After the "patron" (the instructor) [Laloux] had approved of my reception as a member of the atelier, I was initiated.[2] I was stripped and painted from head to foot. Blue they chose to make me in front, red behind. I was quite a glorious sight. Nobody seemed to enjoy the sight particularly. They have initiated so many "nouveaux" of late that they seem to be kind of tired of the show, and so I was not bothered any too much but was left to dry off before the fire and get into my clothes.

Then we went around to a nearby cafe, but first they painted me a beautiful black moustache and reddened my cheeks and the end of my nose and stuck bits of plaster over it, on my head they placed a hat swiped from one of the guardians of the school, somewhat like that of the great Napoleon, but grander. And yet as we marched through the street no one seemed to pay any particular attention to me. Imagine going through the streets of New York in that condition.

They sent me around to the bakery shop to buy some cakes, and the bakery lady didn't even crack a smile when she saw my decorous head. Guess she is accustomed to that kind of sight. At the cafe at which the members of the atelier gathered to drink at my expense, I was made to sing a song. "John's Brown's Body" they asked me for, and I gave them what I could think of. And then I had to make a speech. After this I was told that I could now consider myself a member of the atelier Laloux and had better hie me to a bathhouse. This I did. They served me out two hot baths in quick succession, and I scrubbed for nigh on an hour before I got rid of my new red and blue covering.

The first week at the atelier one is on "service"; [one] must run errands and assist the "anciens" as they command. I will tell you more of what this "service" means another time. Let it suffice to say that it has kept me on the go since Monday.

Wednesday evening the atelier gave its yearly dinner to the patron. There were one hundred and thirty members and ex-members of the atelier at the table. The affair started quietly enough, but about the time the fish was served someone started throwing chunks of bread, and of course those at the other side of the room had to return them. This continued until the wine began to take effect, and then there was some more heavy play. A half-loaf of bread knocked over a bottle of wine and then all by itself one of the tables went smash-bang on to the floor with dishes, food, glasses, and everything, and madness prevailed. The old patron just sat back and laughed and enjoyed it with all the rest. He has been there himself. Some twenty, thirty years ago, he was a nouveau and then an ancien, and he understands all the tricks and jokes of the fellows. This is the great thing of the system, no professor ever becomes an old fogy.

We gave a play afterward. Scene: an atelier at the time of the Golden Age of Greece. You would not have known it but for the costumes. The actions and characters are those of the atelier today. There were very clever take-offs on the principal members of the atelier. The scenery and costumes were got up by the fellows. They were clever, as were the words. Music was by an orchestra of some ten of the boys. I took part dressed in flowing gown and bare legs forming, with the other nouveaux, part of the scenery and chorus. . . .

Clarence

1. The youngest of the Stein brothers, Herbert, continued to work in Pop Stein's casket business in New York.

2. The atelier Laloux was a special favorite for American students at the École, so much so that Laloux was made an honorary fellow of the American Institute of Architects in the 1920s. His studio was located in an elegant eighteenth-century house at 8 rue d'Assons. There, students' drawings were pinned on Louis XV wood-paneled walls. The atelier Laloux was large (seventy-two students in 1891).

---

31   To his parents

46 rue Jacob, Paris   March 10, 1908

Dear Folks:

This morning Mamma's letter of the first of the month arrived. During the past week I have also had notes from Papa and Herbert. All were very welcome.

I have been a member of the atelier Laloux for almost a month now and have not as yet told you of my experiences in connection with it. I have sufficiently explained what an architectural atelier is in my past letters, so I will go on to tell you of my reception four weeks ago. The atelier Laloux is situated in an old private house back in the quarter. The high-ceilinged rooms still bear some traces of their former decoration in the style of Louis XV, but the walls have been pretty well plastered over with posters, placards, and silhouette portraits of the great men of the atelier. There are a goodly number of rooms, all filled with tables, for a great many students work at the atelier Laloux.

Well, I walked into the atelier one fine day and was introduced by one of my friends to the "massier." The "massier" is the head or chief of the organization of students that run the atelier. His word is the final law. The "massier" introduced me to the "patron," or professor, when the latter made his appearance. After a few questions, M. Laloux said I was accepted as a student. When he had finished his criticisms and had departed, preparations were made to initiate me. How I was painted from head to foot and all that, I have written to Herbert and so will not repeat.

Now, the members of an atelier are divided into strongly marked classes. There are first the "anciens"—those that have belonged to the organization for two years or more. They form the oligarchy which rules and commands. Then there are the "minets" who have not yet reached the dignity of "ancien" but still are no longer "nouveaux." Last and least are the nouveaux.

During his first six months, a "nouveau" is "en service," that is to say, he is at the command of the older members of the atelier [and] must run their errands and help them when needed. He is required to be at the atelier one day a week for this purpose. It is this service that makes entering an atelier disagreeable to an American. The French boys are young when they become members and do not much mind it. It is like being an office boy. It must be put up with, that is all, and one might as well take it with a smile as otherwise. The theory that underlies it is not entirely wrong: the new member of the atelier should be kept in contact with the work going on; if he were left to do as he saw fit he would be at the atelier only when he had some work to do himself and would never gain by the experience of his elders; besides, there is a certain amount of labor to be done—mounting paper, buying materials, etc.—and the more experienced men do not want to be taken from their work for that purpose.

The "nouveau" not only gives, he receives quite as much in the way of assistance from the "anciens." These constantly criticize his work and show him how. The patrons correct in a broad way, but all the little tricks of the profession one gets from the "anciens." The first law of the atelier is that of mutual assistance.

I am sure I learned much more from the comrades of the atelier than from M. Laloux on my last "project," or problem. I told you how these designs render once every two months. This one, my first, was due at the school a week ago last Saturday. The week before was a busy one. The greater part of the work always remains to be done at the end. The patron constantly suggests some change so that, when it comes to finally putting the design on paper, one is kept day and night, or at least part of the night. Very often one "passes" the last night. One works straight through it. I did this last time. I have no desire of doing so again in a hurry. We went out at two in the morning, a few of us, in search of coffee and tramped all around the quarter before we found a bakery that was still doing business. The cafes close at two promptly. We were just too late. We had coffee and sandwiches and returned to the atelier. That was the last I had to eat until twelve hours afterward. One cannot very well start putting the washes of watercolor on one's drawing until the daylight appears, and so we had to wait until seven to start finishing our work. After that we were too busy to think of anything but work.

The designs must be submitted at the school promptly at two o'clock Saturday. From one on there was wild excitement at the atelier. Everyone was trying to get his drawings mounted and ready to send to the École. The paste-brushes were wanted everywhere at the same time. Everyone was shouting and running around. The whole atelier seemed to have gone mad. Finally, we had loaded all the drawings mounted into small carts (charettes). I, as last nouveau, was commanded to act as horse for the last charette. It was five minutes of two. A good steady walk will take you to the school in about ten minutes. I took it on the run. I was out of breath before I had gone far. That cartload was heavy. It seemed to be pulling me back, but I jogged along. A tram came along and almost ran us down, and we in turn came near to knocking down innumerable old men and children. It was two minutes of, on the clock of St. Germaine des Pres. One final spurt and we were at the school. Then the drawings had to be carried into the great hall. My, I was tired when it was all done. I felt like sitting down there on the stairs and dying, but instead I went and had a good big dinner. . . .

That's all from
Clarence

---

32   To his brother Herbert Stein

Washington Hotel, City Road, Chester [England]   August 13, 1908

Dear Herbert,

Day before yesterday we visited the so-called "model village" Bournville, just outside of Birmingham. It seems to be a more or less successful solution of the problem that so much worries you social reforming people, that is, how can we do away with the fearful overcrowding of our city tenements? So I thought you would want me to write you something about it.

The poor of the big cities here seem to be quite as badly off as at home, perhaps worse. The streets are full of ragged, dirty children, and plenty of the grown-ups are no better kept. I have, of course, seen nothing of their homes, but they seem to be crowded together in tenements facing on narrow lanes or alleyways.

Bournville is like a park.[1] The streets, as broad as there is any practical need of their being, are lined on either side with trees. In front of each house is a small, but generally very pretty garden. These, as well as the fruit trees in the yard behind, are planted before the house is ever let, so they have the initial care of a good gardener. The vegetable and fruit gardens that have been planted in these yards have proved very successful. The average value of the product per garden and per week being, according to the statistics, 1 shilling 11 pence (practically 50 cents). This seems enormous when one takes into consideration that the rent rates are only 5-1/2 to 12 shillings a week.

The houses, instead of being built in solid, monotonous rows, as they are in most workingmen's villages, are made for two to four families each. And then they are of an endless variety of design. I don't believe there are two houses that are exactly alike in the whole place. They are . . . pretty . . . too, almost every one of them, in plaster and half-timber and brick with vines and flowers growing about them. They are kept [clean]. . . . The children . . . looked as though they had been washed within the last twenty-four hours, and their clothes were not all holes and patches. In fact, as might be expected, they were in harmony with their surroundings. There is a library, baths, schools, and a meetinghouse. . . .

Now, as to how Bournville came into existence. It was created by Mr. George Cadbury, the former proprietor of the cocoa works, near the factory for which the village has been built. But it was not merely for the use of his own workmen that he started it. Less than half the inhabitants are employed by the Cadbury works. Almost as many come and go daily from Birmingham, four miles away. By the way, there is a special workingmen's rate for round trips on the street railroads of two pence (4 cents). The founder of the village gave it in charge of a board of trustees . . . with the exception of 28 of the houses, that had been sold. It was decided that it would be better to keep the rest, as directly as possible, under the guidance of this board.

There were, at the time of the publication of the little book from which I am getting most of this information, 586 houses with a population of over 2800. The trustees reckon on making four percent on the capital invested. This is done in great part to prove that it is possible to attain the same conditions elsewhere without any outward assistance. There is a great demand for all vacant houses.

There is much more I could tell you about Bournville, but [I] don't know just how much will interest you. I was quite enthusiastic about the place. In fact, I felt it to be the most inspiring thing I had seen in England. Utopian dreams can be made realities, if we only go about it in a practical, sane way.

I have seen a number of suggestions here for municipal improvement that may interest you, and I will write of them another time. Most particularly, there are urinals and toilets that would not shock New Yorkers. I am also trying to find out something about municipal management of street railroads.

Hen and I are having a bully good time. We are taking things easy, seeing a good deal, but having quite a loaf and a good deal of exercise at the same time. We have a busy winter before us and want to be in good condition for it.

I expect there will be a letter from you awaiting me at Liverpool. We have had our mail forwarded there.

How are things?

Clare

1. This model industrial village was built from 1879 through the turn of the century by the brothers Cadbury, chocolate manufacturers, principally but not exclusively for their workers. In 1879 the Messrs. Cadbury had moved their chocolate factory from Birmingham to a site at Bournville. They erected twenty-four cottages for their workmen. This became the nucleus of the village that they subsequently developed. In 1895 George Cadbury began work to transform it

into a "model village." And in 1900 he turned it over to a trust to manage. A 1901 meeting held by the British Garden Cities Association at Bournville was a turning point in the growth of the Garden City movement and its shift from the radical coalition that Ebenezer Howard meant it to be to a "thrifty" means by which corporate leaders and politicians could relieve urban congestion. See Dennis Hardy, *From Garden Cities to New Towns* (London: E. and F. N. Spon, 1991). By 1905 George Cadbury had purchased additional land and the 458-acre site contained about 450 houses. See W. Alexander Harvey, *The Model Village and Its Cottages* (London: B. T. Batsford; New York: Charles Scribner's Sons, 1906).

---

33 To his mother

46 rue Jacob, Paris   September 21, 1908

Dear Mamma:

Yesterday afternoon we had a tea. Guests were Mrs. Alexander and daughter Irma, Miss Laib (a cousin of Irma from Philadelphia), Miss Englehart, Ely Kahn, and Lee Simonson.[1] We all had the jolliest kind of time. Henry left some camp stools with the concierge to give to Mrs. Alexander and the girls, that they might rest on the way up our six floors. When we went to answer their ring at our doorbell, we found them all comfortably seated in our little hallway. Of course, they admired our sumptuous quarters and the original works of art that decorate them. . . .

I have met so few American girls in the last three years that the company of these three has been a perfect delight to me. They are so natural and so interesting. We (that is, Ely, Henry, and I) took them out to see Versailles on Saturday. We spent the whole day there. We didn't get back, in fact, until about quarter of eight. Through the palace in the morning and all over the Trianon and the Gardens in the afternoon. Between time we had lunch under an arbor, and we behaved like a most uncivilized lot of little children. [We] quite shocked the English family at the only other occupied table, I fear.

. . . I wish you would make your vacation plans just as though you had no such inconvenience as a son studying architecture, and then let us see if we can't arrange some way of seeing each other. I do hope that no plans of mine are going to prevent you and the girls taking a trip to Europe, if such has been arranged.

Much love to you and the rest from your affectionate son,

Clarence

1. Lee Simonson, with whom Stein had developed a friendship in the "Sunday Club," Dr. Elliott's young men's club of the Ethical Cultural Society, had come to Paris to study painting. They were lifelong friends. Simonson, who later became a very successful stage designer, was a frequent dinner guest of the Steins in New York City.

34   To his parents

46 rue Jacob, Paris   Friday, November 20, 1908

Dear Folks:

. . . Last week, as usual, I worked at the atelier, but not on our own design. I was "niggering" on the "diplôme" of one of the older men. The "diplôme" is what one calls the final series of drawings that one does in the school. Instead of giving the general idea of a building with three or four drawings, one is supposed to picture it from every possible point of view and to give details, just as one would if he were going to construct the affair. The drawings are much less academic and much more businesslike than those we generally turn out, and so I was glad of the opportunity to help. The man that was doing the "diplôme" was one of the most popular fellows in the atelier, so he had plenty of assistance. The crowd of "niggers" brought together in one of the rooms of the upper story of the atelier was a happy bunch, forever singing and guying each other. They were a miscellaneous crowd, representing many nations. Next to me worked a Bulgarian, behind were two Swiss—one

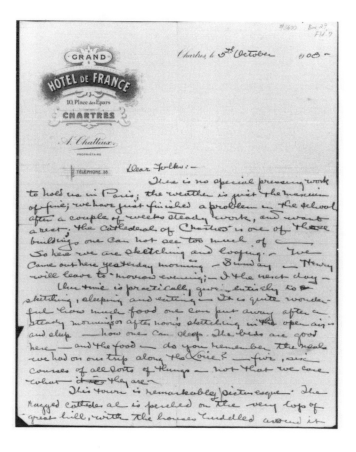

more or less a German, but of course he would not admit it. One can be anything in the atelier and be welcome, anything but a German. There were Frenchmen from various parts of the country, from the "Nord," the "Midi," from Paris. And there was even one Englishman, the only representative of France's ally that has as yet joined our atelier. . . .

A week ago Ely gave a tea at his new apartment. He is very nicely situated, way up toward the heavens in a house near the Odeon. His roommate is a Rochesterian and a former Columbia man. These teas are rather fool stunts. Along with getting the fire started and a half dozen other things, you don't get the tea brewed or the fudge made until six or so, and then there are the sandwiches and the various cakes to be tasted, and so dinner at seven has no chance at all. Of course, the girls were outnumbered three to one, but we had a good time.

Last night I dined with Lee Simonson up in his region, the painter's quarter. He comes down to eat at the Pres now and then. He is coming along very well with his work.

Love to all,

Clarence

---

35   To his brother William Stein

46 rue Jacob, Paris   December 20, 1908

Dear Will:

Yesterday we finished a problem at the school; tomorrow I start in with another with just ten days before it must be submitted, and that means work straight through day and night. There isn't going to be any Christmas, but what is the difference? It is all good fun. I don't know when I have worked harder, but I don't believe I have ever enjoyed life more thoroughly. It is good sport, the life of the atelier. There is a constant vein of good fellowship and good fun running through the work. There is always some joke being played, some song being sung, or some story going the round. Practically no one is in a bad humor. The crowd will not stand for it. . . .

I have been practically living at the atelier. Since my return from England, I go there every day and sometimes in the evenings. In fact, I am getting rather disgusted with myself; I can't get interested in anything else. When I go home after dinner, I fall asleep over anything heavier than *Life* or Thackeray's *Snobs*. [I] finally end by taking up some architecture book or jumping into my little cot. I really ought to call on people, go to museums, and a hundred things, I know, but there seems to be only one way to succeed and that is to keep on the job. And I am at last succeeding, of course, in a little way.

It has been a long pull. My first two and a half years of constant failure were more or less trying, but I think I have reached the point where I am beginning to reap the crop. The fact that I have mastered many things that seemed utterly difficult to me gives me confidence that I can, in time, accomplish all that I aim at. . . .

As ever,

Your "bud" Clare

---

36   To his parents

46 rue Jacob, Paris   February 14, 1909[1]

Dear Folks:

I did not write to you last week because, by the time my letter day came around on Friday, I was so deep in work, I did not want to take the time. Last week, you see, was one of the great weeks of the school year — the week of the Rougevin. Now, the Rougevin is one of the two big decorative problems of the year. The students of the first class are given just seven days to work it up. That means work day and night. Although I could not render the Rougevin, of course, as I am in the lower class, still I was naturally interested to see how the men carry on their work and at the end was able to give some help to some of the weaker men. So I spent most of my time at the atelier. Although the preliminary drawings are made at the atelier, the Rougevin must be rendered, that is, finally put on paper, "en loge" at the school. It was good fun helping at the final rush to finish Saturday afternoon.

But the real sport of the Rougevin is the procession that follows the rendering. Work must finish at dark. But long before that time the "nouveaux" have commenced to collect in the great court of the school with the floats that are to form the principal part of the procession. A good many of these "chares" are more or less clever. The subject of the Rougevin this year was a doorway to a pantheon, leading to the staircase of the crypt in which are buried the great leaders of the country. One atelier's float consisted of an immense coffin, while others thought it appropriate to represent a guillotine. In one of these, the knife was arranged so as to fall and cut off the head of a stuffed dummy whenever a string was pulled. Another cord pulled the knife up and the head back into place, and the show started over again.

By six, when darkness had fallen, the court was filled with a happy, shouting mob. In one corner a band, hired for the occasion, was playing various favorite atelier tunes. Some hundreds were chanting in time with the music or quite some other tune. A crowd was wildly dancing around in the center of the court. Firecrackers were being shot off, and colored lights threw out in strong black relief the architectural fragments that divide the court into two divisions. In the rear . . . the "nouveaux" were lighting the illumination of the "chares" and distributing lanterns to the wild and joyous mob around. The week's work was done; everyone was very dirty, their hands and faces blackened and colored by the carbon pencil or paints they had been using, and their clothing covered with the paste that should have stuck their drawings on to the mounts, but they were happy. And they raised as much rumpus as they wanted to, even though there were thirty or more policemen lined up near the gates. We were still in the school grounds and could do as we wished.

Then the procession lined up and marched around the court and then out into the quarter. First comes the band, then another set of noisemakers, a crowd of boys from one of the ateliers mounted on mules, and playing sweet discord. The rest of the ateliers were singing, but, as no two of them chose the same tune, it was hard to say what. It was just a mad racket. Each atelier marched behind its own "chare," which was pulled by the nouveaux. We march down the narrow rue des Beaux Arts, the rue Bonaparte, the Boulevarde St. Germaine, the rue d'École des Médicine, and then the Boulevard St. Michel, the old "Boul Mich," and everywhere there were crowds along the streets and in all the windows. . . .

The Rougevin procession destination is always the Pantheon. The last two blocks, up the hill straight along the rue Soufflot, is taken on a run, everyone goes at top speed trying to pull or push his "chare" ahead of all the others. Then, when the open space in front of the great colonnade of the Pantheon is reached, the great piles of wooden framework, covered with cloth or paper, are cut free from the carts and dropped in one great heap. In a moment this is flaming up toward the sky. Then everyone takes hands and dances around, until the policemen at last succeed in pushing the crowd back and permitting the attendants from the "marie" on the place to throw a few pails of water on the flames. It is always the same story, but it is always good fun.

There are no further developments as to the trip. In fact, there is nothing else worth reporting.

Clarence

1. In the Stein Papers at Cornell, there is a large gap (from mid-February 1909 to November 1910) in Stein's letters to his parents and family members. We can only speculate that the missing letters were lost in one of the many moves they made in over eighty years.

---

37 To his parents

46 rue Jacob, Paris   December 9, 1910

Dear Folks:

Henry reached your shores, so I judged from the papers, last Monday. I suppose he has already assured you that I am in sufficiently good health, etc., etc.

I have been working at home instead of at the atelier for the past two weeks. I am busy at a competition for a terra-cotta building, a hotel. The *Brick Builder,* an American architectural magazine, yearly gives prizes for the best design of a required building in terra-cotta. Another chap, Van Allen, and I, if we have time, expect to compete this year. He comes around evenings, and we work together. Otherwise, it is quite lonely.

Tuesday evening our atelier gave a dinner in honor of our patron, who was made a member of the Institute a while ago. This, as you know, is the final goal of all those who follow the arts and sciences here in France. On account of this being a very special occasion, we had our dinner in a first-class restaurant—that of the Palais d'Orsay Hotel. (The same was built by the patron.) There were a hundred and seventy or so of us present, most of us that are in the atelier at present, and former students from years back. These were elderly men. . . . Many of them have large practices and much honor and fame in their profession.

They were all there to honor their master. M. Laloux was all smiles. There is something fine in the attitude of instructor or, rather, that of master and student, here in the atelier, something we don't seem to have at home at all. M. Laloux has no children, and he has said that he looks upon his students as his children. He certainly acts that way. And he was proud of the size of his family the other night. . . .

I have been reading Bennett's *Old Wives Tales,* not because I find it particularly worthwhile, but because Herb told me to.

Love from
Clare

---

38   To his parents

46 rue Jacob, Paris   March 17, 1911

Dear Folks:

I have received the program of the Hudson Guild Library play produced under the direction of Hoibie. Sorry I could not be there. Regrets also on account of the Evening Club dinner. Is Herb running everything?

Life over here runs along in the same monotonous manner. For the last two weeks I have been working evenings with Ely at the home of a former member of his atelier, Guidetti. We have been helping him finish some competition drawings. Guidetti is married, and his young wife does her sewing in the same room in which we work. Conversation makes the evening pass very quickly. They are both very interesting. She has lived much in foreign parts: Spain, Italy, Greece. He is one of the foremost watercolorists here and has traveled a good deal.

Otherwise, socially, I had tea at Ely's Sunday and met Mrs. (Dr.) Bretauer, her sister, and her beauteous young daughter. The latter is studying at a school near Paris. Mrs. Bretauer inquired as to the health of Mamma, my sister (Gertrude, I suppose), etc., etc.

I had all sorts of difficulty getting together sufficient and proper clothing to be presentable. Most everything I own is in shreds. But patched suits suffice for work days, and most days are such. Finally, I found a summer suit (vintage of 1908) that does not look too worn, excepting in strong light. So I waited 'til 4:30 to make my appearance. I arrived just in time for tea, luckily in time, as Ely is short of cups and saucers, and I had brought along enough to complete his set.

Otherwise, work is the history of

Clarence

---

39 To his parents

46 rue Jacob, Paris   June 27, 1911

Dear Folks:

Here are many thanks for your congratulations. My birthday is already a long time ago, and of course I should have written sooner.

But last week was one of these very busy ones, the end of a project. How I did work! Up every morning at five, atelier at six, work until eight in the evening, dinner, a little walk, and then bed. The last night I did not get to bed at all. It is my last project, or perhaps I will be able to do just one more. But I have had enough. I do not mean at all that I have learned all I can from projects, not by any means. But I want to do real things.

My, but I am glad I am going home.

I have started to make my final preparations. I am trying first to throw away the less useful stuff, cutting out the poorer sketches from my sketchbooks, for instance. It is hard to do. Each drawing, even the scrawls, means something to you, reminds you of some event of your travels. So I have to go through the books again and again, each time clipping [them] down, smaller and smaller.

In the same way I am cutting all the useless stuff out of my architectural magazines. I have load enough in my books, without burdening myself with any more of other matters than necessary. I must have boxes made for my books, have them stored, etc., etc. Oh! there is much to be done. My furniture is practically all sold. By the 15th of July, I will have said goodbye to 46, and I will have but one home, but that is Home.

Love to everyone there, from

Clarence

40   To his parents

7 rue Corneille, Paris   July 17, 1911

Dear Folks:

Do you notice the address? I have just moved here, to Ely's place. 46 rue Jacob is no longer. The fact is, it really has not been the old 46 for a week past. It was then that I moved the books out. It was so barren after that, I hated to go back to it evenings and stayed away as much as possible days. The books, really much more than the pictures, made the place home. I boxed them, the books, downstairs because, once crated, they would have been almost too heavy to carry down. But there was lots of other packing to be done upstairs and so much to systematize. I could not take everything along with me, and yet it was so hard to throw away familiar things I had had for years and years.

Hardest of all was the task of throwing away old letters. There were hundreds of them divided into packages marked Mamma, Papa, Will, etc. I said, "Better throw them all away," but I put off doing it. Finally, last night I ran through, read some of them thoroughly, skipped through others, but I went through all of them and lived through much of the last five years. Six years, can it be six? Today I helped the young fellow that took most of my affairs carry them downstairs and then up to his rooms. This afternoon I moved.

But continue sending letters to 46 rue Jacob. The concierge has been kind enough to promise to forward them for me.

Love from,
Clarence

---

41   To his parents

147 via Frattina, Rome   August 20, 1911[1]

Dear Folks:

Tomorrow it will be two weeks that we are in Rome. We have seen most of the sights and have done a little sketching. We are now getting down to steady work. Yesterday we started making studies of some of the frescoes in the Museum of the Baths of Diocletian.

These museums are inhabited mainly by guardians, swarms of them. They have nothing to do all day but doze. They seem quite put out when your tramping through the museum disturbs them. It takes the sound of clinking cash to make them friendly. One franc bought the man that slumbers in the room where hangs our fresco, and we own him now for ever and ever (also, all the comforts that the museum may offer in the way of stools, etc.). These Roman frescoes are wonders. The Renaissance never outdid them.

In fact, has any age since theirs approached them in the arts? After each visit to the museums, we answer No. What sculpture! It is so strong and yet so delicate. And their architecture! What is the use, anyhow? Two thousand years ago they did what we can never hope to outdo. So we said last night, after we had finished a watercolor in the Forum, as we saw it all lit up by the most glorious light, a Roman sunset. And so we say every time we pass the Colosseum, or the Column of Trajan. Oh, what is the use?

Well, anyhow, we are going home in October to see. Until then, we will take in as much Roman inspiration as possible.

Clare . . .

1. Late in July 1911, Clarence Stein and Ely Jacques Kahn began a tour of southern Europe. After traveling, sketching, and painting in Italy and Spain, they returned to the United States in October 1911.

1. Mother Rose Rosenblatt Stein (1878).

2. Pop Leo Stein (1878).

3. Clarence Stein (c. 1884).

4. Kindergarten at the Ethical Culture School in the late nineteenth century.

5. Clarence clowning on a vacation trip. From the left: Clarence Stein, brother Herb, Pop Leo, brother Will, and grandfather Samuel Stein (c. 1896).

6. Clarence Stein at about twenty years of age (1902).

7. Charcoal sketches of Nürnberg from Clarence Stein's sketchbook (July 1907).

8. Clarence Stein at home at rue Jacob, Paris, France, when he was a student at the École de Beaux Arts (1908).

9. Clarence Stein sketching in Paris (c. 1908).

10. Marketplace in Verona, with column. Pencil sketch by C. S. Stein (April 1907).

11. Party in the studio of the atelier Umbdenstock. Written on the back of the photo in Stein's hand: "How C. S. and Henry spent their time in Paris" (1908). Stein is seen in profile in the upper row (second from right).

12. Victor Laloux, whose atelier Stein joined after he was admitted to the École in 1908.

13. Street scene in Rouen, France. Pencil sketch by C. S. Stein (c. 1908).

14. Half-timbered facade in Chester, England. Pencil sketch by C. S. Stein (1908).

15. Clarence Stein, his sister Lillie, his parents, Leo and Rose Stein, and his sister Gertrude during a family visit to Clarence in Europe (c. 1909).

16. Venice. Pencil sketch by C. S. Stein (c. 1909).

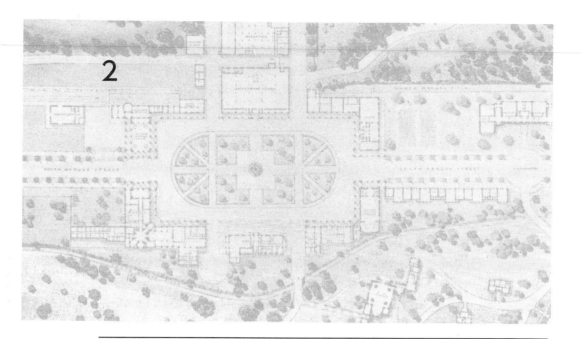

2

Home Again: Architect and Civic Reformer
1911–1919

Clarence Stein returned to New York City from Paris in the fall of 1911 to pursue work in architecture and to resume his participation in several political and social reform movements. The handful of letters by the thirty-year-old Stein written during the decade after he returned to New York tells us little about his early career in architecture. He lived with his family in their large apartment at 96th and Broadway on the upper West Side, and he thrived in the productive camraderie of Goodhue's office.[1] Years later he wrote a brief note on his early professional years, which is included in this selection from Stein's papers. Stein also retained copies of a few unpublished documents, some of which are included in this section. They provide some knowledge of his concerns about living conditions in New York and his early ideas about city planning and urban reform. These brief excerpts, a few letters, and unpublished notes, essays, and reports of Clarence Stein written from the age of twenty-nine to thirty-seven provide a glimpse of an earnest, ambitious, and talented young New York City professional man with a considerable commitment to environmental, social, and political reform.

The neophyte architect almost immediately secured a job in the New York office of Cram, Goodhue, and Ferguson, where he worked directly with Bertram Grosvenor Goodhue. The latter liked Stein's European travel sketches, especially those he

1. Richard Oliver, *Bertram Grosvenor Goodhue* (Cambridge: MIT Press, 1983), 154, 171, describes the high spirits that characterized this office.

did on his last trip to Spain with Ely Jacques Kahn. Goodhue put him to work on the overall plan for the San Diego World's Fair and the development of the design for the California Building, one of its major theme buildings.[2] With Goodhue, Stein also worked on plans for Tyrone, New Mexico (a model copper mining town for the Phelps Dodge Corporation), several large houses and a country club in Santa Barbara, California, St. Bartholomew's Church in New York, and World War I naval training bases in California. He worked on large-scale projects and major commissions that developed his talents and skills in the decorative arts (chiaroscuro sculpture on the California Building and decorative and color elements of the St. Bartholomew's design) and large-scale planning (Tyrone's layout and major buildings, open spaces, and circulation). These projects provided valuable experience in the design of large-scale multipurpose community environments and also made good use of his well-informed aesthetic skills in color, ornament, sculpture, and interior design.

The San Diego World's Fair (in contrast to the earlier Chicago and contemporary San Francisco fairs, which had embodied European and international architecture) placed great importance on the American experience, emphasizing the history and culture of the Southwest United States/Mexico region and especially its relationship to Native American civilization and Spanish-Colonial art and architecture. The Tyrone (New Mexico) New Town design gave Stein experience thinking through the needs of community life and problems of urban form, including the location and design of community buildings, churches, banks, shops, theaters, and open spaces, as well as the houses for company officials and the American and Mexican mine workers.[3]

Stein's experience working in Goodhue's office from 1911 to 1918 gave him an extraordinary range of opportunities to explore and expand his architectural talents and to develop the full range of his interests, from city planning to architectural ornament and color, from worker housing to urban design. He evolved from Goodhue's example a powerful, picturesque, personal style of composition and a vivid but disciplined use of color and ornament, and he developed from the management responsibilities implied by his alternative titles, "chief designer" or "chief draftsman,"[4] the skills necessary to organize the work process of a large office and coordinate the collaborative efforts of the architects, landscape architects, artists, engineers, and builders.

---

2. See Stein's essay, "A Triumph of the Spanish Colonial Style," in Bertram G. Goodhue, *The Architecture and the Gardens of the San Diego Exposition* (San Francisco: Paul Elder and Co., 1916).

3. "The New Mining Community of Tyrone, NM," *Architectural Review* 6 (April 1918): 159–62; "Tyrone Revisited," *Architectural Forum* (August 1966).

4. Henry Churchill's statement in the AIA Archives filed in connection with the award of the Gold Medal of the institute to Stein in 1956.

While he worked effectively in these years from apprenticeship to chief designer in Goodhue's office, Stein developed his knowledge of and skills in social and political reform outside the office. Independently and in work with John Elliott, he sought to improve the physical environment of New York City's working people and to promote greater social equity. In 1912 he began on his own to study city planning and to participate in the social reform activities of Felix Adler's disciple, John Lovejoy Elliott. He worked on community work in Elliott's "good government" clubs and in the development of the Hudson Guild's community organizations in the Chelsea district of Manhattan. The text of his 1915 speech to the City Club on city planning provides a sense of his efforts to learn more about this subject, as do the insights of his unpublished papers and his ideas about the Chelsea district and on a strategy for "abolishing the slums."

Stein seems to have developed independently the idea of "survey before plan" and of working directly with the people in the Chelsea community to understand the dynamic structure of change in their community before advocating solutions. He came to these ideas about cities and New Towns from his New York City neighborhood work with Elliott and from his study of that era's meager literature of city planning and housing. His methods may also have evolved from the spirit of learning through direct experience which he had acquired at the Workingman's School. Stein's formulation of regional survey and planning concepts were not as elegant as were Patrick Geddes's ideas. Stein's were rather pragmatic approaches to data collection, analysis, and physical planning for a New York City neighborhood.

Early in 1917 Stein, as a member of the city planning committee of the Ethical Culture Society's City Club, formulated several important ideas for neighborhood planning: that community physical change should be locally determined, that the use of surveys before planning was essential to good plans, that planners should use alternative ideas for change to select proposals, and that plans should include the possibility of architectural preservation and adaptive reuse of important buildings. Some of these ideas are developed in the documents in the following sections. Stein believed that "each neighborhood best understood its own needs [for] better and safer physical surroundings" and that it could "find a [better] solution than [could be found by] a central bureau."[5]

Stein's Chelsea report discusses the need for "taking hold" of the problems of making Chelsea a livable place for its workers, replacing the housing torn down for industrial development, preserving older houses, making the streets less dangerous for children, replacing its old school, and providing other needed community facilities, a "public bath and gymnasium, auditorium, . . . library and perhaps [a] neighborhood theater." His essay also exhorts the citizens of Chelsea: "It is a question of

5. C. S. Stein, "Neighborhood Planning in Chelsea," 19 April 1917, unpublished draft, CSP/CUA.

whether some outside selfish interest is going to plan Chelsea or whether you are going to do it." By the end of his first decade back in New York City, young Clarence Stein had already made considerable progress developing a community-based philosophy for city planning.

This budding planner also accepted the tenets of the Ethical Culture Society, though he was not a regular participant in their meetings. He believed in the society's goal of individual growth toward excellence, which was considered a function of furthering the "unlike excellence of others." His Workingman's School education had made him particularly sensitive to civic concerns. He believed in the society's social reform agenda (the Hudson Guild's Settlement House and the City Club) and in the possibilities of positive evolution of economic institutions. He also believed in political activism, in the need for individuals to act to reform government through community organization and politics. He participated fully in the agenda of the Progressive Era, working against corrupt machine politicians and for and with Al Smith, New York's "happy warrior," a reform movement politician of the Democratic Party. By 1919 Clarence found himself in a New York City primary election running as a candidate for vice president of the United States on the Independent ticket with Al Smith.

In 1918, before he entered the Army Corps of Engineers, Clarence Stein visited his architectural mentor, Robert D. Kohn, in Washington. He admired the work being done by Kohn and the Shipping Board staff to build housing for shipyard workers. Frederick Ackerman, another New York architect whom Stein knew, served on Kohn's staff. Ackerman had proposed an expanded program of federal construction of workers' housing after the war. Stein was surprised to discover that the whole "Ackerman Program" was to be accepted by the AIA Board and recommended to Congress.[6] Stein thought that a national housing program was premature and that the states should be the focus of governmental intervention in housing production. During his trip to Washington early in 1918, Stein also met with Charles Whitaker, the radical editor of the *Journal of the American Institute of Architects* (*JAIA*), and formed a long-lasting alliance as associate editor of the *JAIA*. His letter to Whitaker about a "regional survey of New York" provides a brief glimpse of his thinking about housing reform and regional planning.

6. C. S. Stein to Eleanor Manning, 10 September 1918, CSP/CUA. See also the articles on European housing by Charles Whitaker and Frederick Ackerman, "What Is a Home?" *Journal of the American Institute of Architects* (September 1917 to February 1918), reprinted in *The Housing Problem in War and in Peace* (Washington, D.C.: Octagon, 1918).

42   Autobiographical Note

1911[1]

"HOME AGAIN"

Returned from my prolonged stay in Europe with Eli Jacques Kahn, with whom I had taken many trips of discovery . . . , including the memorable one through Spain ending with the then-little-traveled Isle of Majorca. Then there was our journey to the Lowlands.

Our last night we had other things to think of. What chance had we of getting a job? Our studies at the Beaux Arts might be of help in an architectural office. . . . We didn't know. We were very uncertain then. We had much competition not only from the many who had studied and traveled as we had, but also from the unemployed draftsmen who had spent years in practical office work.

I had good luck. The first architect I visited was Bertram Grosvenor Goodhue, then a member of the architectural firm Cram, Goodhue, and Ferguson. They were noted particularly for their church work, inspired from the Gothic.

Mr. Goodhue, after a short period of questioning, looked at [the] sketchbooks . . . I had brought with me. I showed him a book or two of my drawings of English and French medieval churches and towns. He asked, "Is that all?" So I brought out my latest book, careful drawings made on my trip with Ely Jacques Kahn through Spain. "That's most interesting," Mr. Goodhue said. "I am about to start work on the design of the San Diego World's Fair." He proposed to do that in the style of the buildings left by the Spanish conquerors. "See if you can perhaps help on that." So I entered the architectural office of Bertram Goodhue, and there I stayed for some seven years.

Bertram Grosvenor Goodhue was a sensible boss. He gave his draftsmen just as much responsibility as they were capable of carrying. Before long, I found myself in charge of the design and production of drawings for the principal, dominant building of the proposed San Diego World's Fair and, ultimately, of the general layout of the fair.

Mr. Goodhue had made a splendid perspective of his conception of the central group of buildings and the bridge across the ravine, a tower and quay, a cathedral-like construction with colored tiles on [the] dome and [a] soaring tower, inspired by the early Spanish-American structures. It was up to me to see that it be developed and realized.[2]

This was followed by other work of the same general architectural style, Mexican colonial, which was the Spanish of the fifteenth to seventeenth centuries as carved in large part by the Mexican Indian. So the sculpture of the rich masses of carving that combined main entrance and east window . . .

1. The year only is given, with no month or date.

2. Stein's initials are in the "Drawn By" and "Checked By" boxes of the detailed drawings for the sculptural ornament of both the entrance and the tower windows of the California Building of the San Diego Fair. The building has been preserved in its original setting, along with the chapel in an adjacent building, for which Stein designed the reredos of the alter (San Diego Public Library: San Diego Fair Drawings).

---

43   Essay on city planning for the City Planning Committee of the City Club

January 16, 1915

We are city planning in New York as we have never done before. But are our plans going to be realized? We have commissions, committees, and proposed legislation without end, but are we going to really change the plan of New York? Not greatly, until we have educated the public to the vital need of city planning. We have got to put city planning in terms that every man can comprehend. At present, much valuable time is being spent in working out a system of districting for New York. But does anyone here think that New York is going to be zoned because [of] the few who know . . . that it must be zoned? If the real-estate people cannot be educated to the need of restricting all for the good of each, then the public as a whole must be educated. There is the same need of education in every phase of city planning. I speak not of education for the purpose of giving up knowledge or culture, but because education is the only means by which we can attain the ends for which this committee exists. Somebody must start and keep going this campaign of public education. I think it is the proper work of the City Planning Committee of New York's central civic organization, the City Club.

The education of the public can only be accomplished through a patient and steady campaign that must last through the years. The ideas cannot be crammed down people's throats. We must take the interest of the moment and show its relation to city planning. For instance, now that everyone is talking markets, now is the time to have an exhibit which will show the relation of the wholesale markets to the retail and the importance of proper transportation in the connection of the two. These phases, which Mayor Laynor's commission considered the essentials, have almost been forgotten in the grand hurrah about bringing the farmer and the purchaser together.

What are the means by which the public may be educated? There are lectures—lectures in the public night courses, at the Brooklyn Institute, at Columbia, at the settlements. There are exhibits—exhibits taking up some small phase of city planning and always connected with some matter of public interest. There are the movies and, of course, newspaper and magazine publicity, which must be properly fostered and guided. The American Institute of Architects is doing very able work of this kind through its committee of public information, of which Mr. Ackerman is chairman. There are many other means by which we can carry on this work—competitions, for instance. The City Club of Chicago has had two competitions: one, the planning of a district on the outskirts of Chicago; the other, the arrangement of a neighborhood center.

When I suggest that this committee undertake this work, I have no idea of our doing it single-handed. I am sure we will have no difficulty in getting the cooperation of not only the city's commission and in time the Department of Education, but [also] numerous organizations, clubs, and associations throughout the city. Our committee will serve merely as a guide. We will bring together various organizations that have common interests. We will find the men who can speak and write on city planning and bring them in touch with those that are ready to listen to them. We will see that exhibits are given the proper turn so that the public will come to gradually see how all that goes to make up a city is related [and] how it all forms part of a city plan.

---

44 Talk at a neighborhood meeting

April 19, 1917

"NEIGHBORHOOD PLANNING IN CHELSEA"

To some it many seem that you have chosen a poor time to start replanning Chelsea.[1] Our energies are strained, or soon will be, in preparing for a gigantic struggle. But it is in just such time of great changes and reorganizations that we are awakened to our weakness. Because we see in a more clear-sighted manner our defects at such a period as this, it is now that we should prepare to remove them. Soon after the beginning of the war, the city planners of England invited the architects who had been driven out of Belgium to come to Great Britain and to devote their time to the replanning of Belgium. And so, when the Germans have been driven back across their borders, the plans for a new Belgium will be ready. France, too, has been preparing plans for the future layout and improvements of its cities in the devastated north. At the same time the cities that have not been overrun by the Germans are cleaning up their slums, so that their soldiers may return to better environs. Before the war is over, a city planning law for all France will probably be passed. If these nations, which have borne the brunt of this struggle, could meantime consider the future layouts of their cities, is there any excuse for us to do otherwise?

But their cities have been wiped out of existence, you say, and they must be rebuilt. New York also, or most of it, every fifteen years or so is rebuilt. According to anyone's plans? No. Just as chance wills. That is, unless some big outside interest takes hold. But never does a neighborhood's destiny seem to be worked out by that neighborhood itself.

Here is an example in Chelsea. The West Side Improvement is to be approved; perhaps not this year, but soon. We cannot much longer have that railroad endangering the lives of the children of this part of the city, nor can we have the commerce of New York weakened through the use of an antiquated railroad system. Let us see what the proposed agreement will do for Chelsea. The agreement permits an elevated railroad parallel to 10th Avenue, 100 feet to the west of that avenue, with sidings not only into 10th and 11th Avenues, but also between 9th and 10th. This means that the [New York] Central [Railroad], or others, are going to, if they can, develop all the land between the 9th Avenue elevated and the river for industry. There will be nothing but factories and warehouses—a remarkable industrial development.

A few of your streets were saved for residential purposes by the efforts of the Chelsea Neighborhood Association when the zoning ordinance was passed last June. If the Central carries out its plan of development, these streets will go with the rest. The charming old residences will be swept away and will be replaced by big industrial plants. The zoning ordinance will not stand in the way.[2] The Board of Estimates may change the restrictions of this ordinance; in fact, it is practically certain to do so, if requested to by the greater part of the property owners of a block. When the time comes that these few streets are entirely surrounded by industry, the property owners most certainly will petition to have the restrictions lifted.

But we should not forget that the neighborhood as a whole, as well as the residents of a single block, have an interest in the rights and uses of that block. We are interdependent. Until a short time ago, we thought that an individual could develop his property as he thought best, without thought of the use his neighbor was going to make of his land. Experience has shown us that this does not work. The first builder robs his neighbor of light and air by covering all of his property and building up within the property lines as near the clouds as he wishes. And he, in his turn, is restricted of the proper use of his property when the owners of land at either side follow his example and make full use of their liberty. But even if all the owners of property and residents of a block were agreed as to the limitations they should set upon the use of their individual properties, there would be additional limitations that should be set upon them . . . so that their land should be of the maximum use to the neighborhood [and] also to themselves.[3]

Let us say that the [New York] Central [Railroad] makes a go of its improvement, and it will, a big go. That means that it will turn all Chelsea from 9th Avenue to the river over to industry. Great. There will be every facility for the easy handling of goods. Raw products will be delivered at the factory, and finished products will be taken away without expensive carting. This means that land will be very valuable for factory purposes. And then the Jersey railroads coming later will cross over the Central and turn blocks even further to the east over to factories and warehouses.

But industry needs workers as well as materials. If Chelsea is going to be a big industrial center, it must keep its workers here in Chelsea. It costs too much time, it costs too much money, it costs too much energy for workers to come from the East Side, from the Bronx, from Long Island City to work in Chelsea. They will find work nearer home more congenial and less wasteful. What is more, it is impossible to solve our transportation problem until we have worked out some arrangement of the city whereby the workers can be in walking distance of their work.[4]

Now the ideal system is that of the Garden City of Letchworth outside of London. Here is a city in the country with its own business and industries—a complete town, but one limited in area. It is surrounded by a belt of forest land, which limits the growth of the town. When it has reached these limits, other similar towns will be built beyond, but each with its woodland forever closed to the town and with strict limitation as to housing and crowding.

Now the time is coming when Garden Cities of this kind are going to be built around New York, and Chelsea will be asked what inducements it offers to workmen to man its industries. Chelsea is going to be rebuilt by the [New York] Central [Railroad] improvement. Now is the time to take hold of the problem of making it a livable place for its workers. What does this mean? First, better housing. . . . Chelsea Homes opposite Chelsea Park [are] pointing the way. There is an improved tenement that has been full since the day it was opened. And it is paying. Compare it with the old tenements. Many of these will go when the Central puts through the new improvement. Chelsea must replace them. The neighborhood planning committee should see that they are properly placed [and] are better than the tenements in any other part of the city.

Chelsea also has many rows of charming old houses. You must see that they are preserved where possible. . . . Where they are no longer used, they must be converted into some new use (studios, for instance).

But it is not sufficient to improve the residences of Chelsea. We must make it livable, particularly for the children. We must have playgrounds. Chelsea Park is not enough. Look at the way the streets are crowded with children. As industry increases the streets are going to be more and more dangerous. We must work out some scheme by which heavy trucks are limited to certain streets and others are used merely for delivery wagons. These will be comparatively safe for children to play in. The city is soon to appoint a traffic commission. Chelsea should try to formulate some scheme to suggest when the times comes. A neighborhood planning committee should also show the way to use vacant lots, roofs, and yards thrown into a common space for playgrounds.

Dr. Elliott has spoken of the neighborhood center that has already been started around Chelsea Park. You must see to it that this grows. You can only do so by having a committee that will not only plan, but [also] wait and watch for the day when its plans can be made a reality. There is a school in Chelsea Park (it is a very old school), and some day it will fall to pieces. It should not be rebuilt in the park. The space it covers is badly needed for additional playground space. If there is no committee watching and waiting, they will probably remove the school to some narrow street where it will be quite unrelated to its surroundings. Now, this new school belongs at the side of Chelsea Park. It should form the center of a group of public buildings that should be run as a single unit. At one side should be the public bath and gymnasium. These are already there. At the other side the auditorium and library, and perhaps the neighborhood theater. These buildings should be used by old as well as young; for clubs, social and political meetings, and voting places. Our modern school system requires a playground. If the school is moved elsewhere than on Chelsea Park, it will be necessary to lay out a new playground. These buildings will be the center of a group of public and semipublic buildings such as Dr. Elliott has described, which will be coordinated both in use and appearance. They will form a center which will be a symbol of the cooperative spirit of Chelsea, of the best that is in Chelsea.

The City Planning Committee of the City Club has long had the idea that city planning could not be done only from the municipal building. We have believed that each neighborhood best understood its own needs [for] better and saner physical surroundings and, if it was only awake to the necessity of physical change, could better find a solution than could a central bureau. Do not misunderstand me. There are a great many big problems that affect the city as a whole that can best be solved by a central office, but there are many details of these problems in which the advice of those who must live in new surroundings are invaluable. But this opinion must be formed by broad study and understanding. It has been our desire to offer our cooperation to committees in neighborhoods that are prepared to undertake this work. But first we wished to try out the idea with a neighborhood that we thought could make a go of the work.

We have come to Chelsea to offer our services because we believe that Chelsea is soon to have the biggest and most interesting problem in replanning in New York. The Central is going to remake Chelsea unless Chelsea takes it into its head to remake itself.

We have come to Chelsea because we believe that the spirit of cooperation is alive here, . . . because we believe that various organizations will pull together to make Chelsea more liveable.

We have come to offer our cooperation because of the charm of old Chelsea, which we hope to be permitted to help you in preserving.

Let us look at the matter clearly. The [New York] Central does things in a big way. It is going to make a big thing of this improvement. But it is going to do it in its own way. It is thinking of big industrial growth, but it may forget the homes of the workers. It may sweep them all away. If it does, Chelsea Park will be useless and might as well be covered with industrial plants; Chelsea Park and the baths and the Hudson Guild and all. Or they may push the homes to the east, none knows how far. And then the park will be useless where it is, and you will have to fight in the Board of Alderman again to create a new park elsewhere. And after many years perhaps you will get a new public bath, and so on.

It is a question of whether some outside selfish interest is going to plan Chelsea or whether you are going to do it. If you decide to undertake the task, we hope you will permit us to assist you, if we can in any way help you.

1. The nineteenth- and early twentieth-century lower West Side community of Chelsea was located between the Hudson River and Sixth Avenue from Fourteenth Street to Forty-second Street. By midcentury, the district of Manhattan known as Chelsea was smaller (say, from Twenty-second Street to Thirty-eighth).

2. New York City enacted the first "comprehensive" zoning ordinance for a large U.S. city in 1917. Edward M. Bassett, New York attorney and charter member of the American City Planning Institute, chaired the Commission on Building Districts and Restrictions, which drafted the legislation in 1916.

3. The term *limitations* is probably a reference to the use of restrictive covenants or deed restrictions, a device that Stein used in several later housing developments, most often to reserve common open space and establish community associations.

4. This is an early American statement of the community planning goal of establishing substantial numbers of work opportunities proximate to the homes of workers to reduce travel demand and therefore congestion in transport systems.

---

45 Essay for Dr. Elliott's class

May 13, 1917

"CITY PLANNING"

The City Planner is like the member of every other profession and trade. He must answer, in explaining his work, the two questions of why and how. It is always the temptation of one who is deep in his work to think and talk of the how of it, its technique, and to forget the why of it, its reason for being, its relation to the life of the community. Now, the why of medicine is the general health of the community, and its how is many books full of science, which most of us are not interested in. The why of the legal profession is justice, but the how of it, which the lawyer seems interested in, is the law that has been built upon the customs of the past. Every once in a while, with a jerk and sometimes with a revolution, we pull the law into relation with the life of today or what we think that life should be.

The City Planner, too, is very likely to become lost in technique. How wide should one make different kinds of streets? How high should different types of buildings be? How should the industrial part of a city be related to the residential? How far will a young child go to a playground?

But Why? I do not mean the little whys. A certain roadway should be 27 feet wide because we must allow 9 feet of room for automobiles going in each direction and the same for those which are parked at one side of the road. This is one of the little whys. But the big whys: Why do we all crowd together in cities? Why do we live all piled up one above the other when there is so much land stretching back behind us toward the Pacific? Why do we want to separate residences from factories? Why do we not all work in our homes, as did the people of the Middle Ages? Why do we want to group our municipal or neighborhood buildings together? Why do we want to make our city beautiful as well as healthful and useful? Why order? Why arrangement? Why beauty? Why a city?

Men came together in cities first for mutual protection. They stayed in the cities because of the enlarged social intercourse it gave them. Later they clung to the city because it simplified life, inasmuch as each family was not forced to do all forms of work. One family could concentrate its energy on making one sort of thing and could trade this for the products of its neighbors. Then came the age of machinery. Few could afford the means of manufacturing, and many came together to cooperate in manufacturing. Just as, in Rome, hordes of freedmen congregated in the tenements to be near their masters and the emperor on [whose bounty] they existed, just as in the Middle Ages the masses crowded together on narrow streets around the castles of their lords, who protected them from their enemies, so in the nineteenth century the workers crowded around the factories in tenements.

Look back through the past, and think of the why of these cities, the form of civilization that [made cities], and then think how well [the city's] arrangements, its every form expresses that civilization, its ideals, its habits. The grandeur of Rome, the Forum, the triumphal arches, the colossal bathing establishments, the tomb of Hadrian, the wonderful palaces of the Caesars of the Palatine, and the dungeons of the slaves, and the tenements. You could see them from the Palatine stretching way out in the plains behind the Colosseum. Tenements quite as awful as those of America. They are gone now. And when we visit Rome now, we see only the reminders of its ancient glory and beauty.

The medieval town clustered around the castle of the barons who controlled the destinies of the crowded houses on the streets below. Later came the guild halls, with a new life developed around them, but always crowded within the walls of the towns.

Each of these cities expressed in a more or less complicated way the life that flowed within it. But, more than that, to a great extent it made that life. The city is the mold in which we are formed. The ideals and habits of one generation are handed on to the next much more by the forms one sees about one than by spoken or written word. . . .

The city is the mold that forms us, but we can make that mold. People say, "City planning, that is all right for other places, but New York is made, we cannot change it." And yet every twenty years or so there is a new New York. The old buildings are gone, [and] new ones have replaced them. But the changes are changes of chance. A few manufacturers decide to move their businesses into a residential part of town. The people who live thereabouts move away to escape the noise and crowds. More business, and then industry. Greater crowds. The streets must be widened to hold all the vehicles and people. The material of the pavement must be changed. In this haphazard way the character of a neighborhood is altered. This particular kind of change is less likely since the zoning ordinance was passed last year. But practically all that is done to form this great mold, the City, is haphazard. We do nothing to radically remake it. This is mainly, I think, because we have not realized that it is [the city that] forms us and the lives of all those we know and because we do not seem to understand that we can remake this great mold. . . .

There is no attempt to relate these buildings, to group them so that they can co-operate in their work. The playground should serve as part of the school, [and] so should the gymnasium. Why should the library not be connected with the ed-ucational system? The neighborhood house takes the child when the school leaves him, but there is practically no cooperation between the two. Why should they not cooperate in the use of their auditorium as well as all their other facilities, not only for the children but for the grown-ups?

Think what an interesting group could be made of all these buildings, properly related and surrounded by trees in a small neighborhood park. Such a group would be a symbol of the best ideals of the neighborhood.

But I am trying to picture this mad jumble—New York, as it really is. Crowded tenements with no place for children to play, excepting on streets that are given over to traffic. All streets have the same uses. Most of us seem not to have been im-pressed by the fact that different streets can be used in different ways, that, where there are only homes, heavy traffic need not pass. Now that we have restricted fac-tories and stores to certain parts of the city, we can use our streets in different ways. . . .

A big factory is organized so that all goods are kept moving in a regular order and in one direction from the time they enter the factory as rough material until they leave as a finished product. So should the working part of a city be organized.

Our buildings are so high and so crowded that a great part of us work without proper light and air. We certainly have not crowded together in this way so that the factories and shops would be nearer the homes of the workers and buyers. Look at the crowded subways; everyone seems to be going to and from long distances un-derground to their work.

. . . [T]hings shall be different in the future; . . . man shall not work twelve hours and then go home to such surroundings as our tenements offer. We want him to have a shorter day's work. When he has it we must give him a city in which he can spend [his leisure] in a worthwhile manner. We must not permit the dark chimney of the factory to throw its shadow constantly over his home. And yet he must be close enough to his work so that he can walk to it. These are the problems of the city planner: to relate the elements of the city one to the other and to tie them together with streets and railways and waterways.

But what are our elements and where can they best be placed in the city plan?

. . .

Industry: We see factories belching out smoke, sometimes with disagreeable odors. We will place them where the wind will blow away from the city the smoke and odors. So the first thing we must consider is what are the prevailing winds? Then we must place these factories where we can most easily supply them with the raw materials they need and where the finished product can be taken away without too much trucking. Now it is cheaper to carry goods over water than over land. So our factories in New York we will naturally place near the water. And our freight railroads, too, for certain goods can more easily be brought in by rail. We will run directly into the factories. This is what the [New York] Central R.R. is doing in its proposed improvement. In Chicago the railroads run under the factories, and cars are switched off and taken by elevators up to the levels at which the raw goods are used. There will be great warehouses in which goods will be stored before and after they go through the factories or are sent to the stores to be sold. These, of course, should be near the water and the railroad and will be served directly by the railroads, as are the factories. A big factory is organized so that the goods are kept moving in a regular order and in one direction from the time they enter the factory as rough material until they leave as a finished product. So should the working part of a city be organized.

The goods, when made, must be passed on to the merchant to sell. First there is the wholesale merchant. He must serve not only the smaller dealer in town, but also the buyer from outside. Goods of a certain kind should all be sold in a limited area for the convenience of the buyer. In old cities the manufacturer and merchant worked in his home. The printing shop of Antwerp is an example. This meant that home life was interfered with. It meant that the whole family constantly lived in the atmosphere of work. In a big city it is essential that the big stores be not spread over the entire city. Fifth Avenue is well placed as a mercantile street. Perhaps it is more attractive than any retail street in the world.

Where shall we place our homes? I suppose there is not a one of us who would not prefer to have his in the country, with grass and trees about, up at the top of a hill, overlooking the water, with a chance of roughing it, with long tramps, and a swim in the lake or river. But we must work, and it is a nuisance to run and catch a train to go into the city. And then, if you want to go to the theater or concert, it is such a long trip home. Also, the traveling is expensive. In spite of all these objections, a great many people do live in the suburbs.

But if everyone lived out of town and came in to work, we would never have transportation facilities to take care of them. So our problem in laying out the residential part of the city is to place our homes in surroundings as near as possible like the country surroundings we desire to live in and at the same time have them near work and places where they can meet others for amusement or education. We must bring the country into the city or the city into the country.

How can we bring the country into the city? We can do so to a limited extent by increasing the number of parks and playgrounds; by using our backyards as common playgrounds; by lining our residential streets with trees, decreasing the paved portion of the road, and using the rest for playgrounds; by using our water edge, as much as industry will permit, for parks. All this will help, but it is not a solution. And the problem of combining city and country has been solved. The Garden City is the solution. Now, a Garden City is not a garden suburb. A garden suburb is an area near a city set aside for residential purposes only, in which the size and character of the homes, as well as the percentage of the land to be covered by building, is restricted. But there is no industry in such a suburb, and the inhabitants must be carried back and forth from the city where they work. This means much time wasted in the bad air of street cars. It means that ultimately the city's growth will reach the point where it will be impossible to increase our transit facilities sufficiently to handle the crowds. So the Garden City not only gives the ideal surroundings for living, as does the garden suburb, but it also contains the industries at which its inhabitants work.

The Garden City of Letchworth, England, is the result of a book called, first, *Tomorrow: A Peaceful Path to Real Reform*, published in 1898, and afterward, *Garden Cities of Tomorrow*, published in 1902. This book of Mr. Ebenezer Howard was his dream of a modern utopia. And his dream has at least partially been realized. By a Garden City he meant a place where homes could be near the country as well as industrial plants. He limited the size of his city by surrounding it by a belt of farmland, which is owned by the corporation and can never be used for any other purpose. By limiting the density of population to twelve families per acre, the ultimate population of the Garden City will be no more than 30,000 persons. It was Mr. Howard's idea that many other Garden Cities should be created, all with limited population, and each with its own industries, but always separated by the wide belt of open country. The first Garden City was Letchworth, which was started a couple of years after Mr. Howard's book, *Garden Cities of Tomorrow*, was published.

I have spoken of only a few elements of the city. I have not even spoken of the common buildings, the government buildings, the places of public entertainment. But I do hope that I have made you understand that our city forms us. What is quite as important [is that] we can make it. To do so, we must understand the life about us and how it fits into the mold. We must see the need of changing things. We must not be afraid to dream great dreams of radical changes. Our dreams, like those of Mr. Howard, may be realized.

46   To Charles Whitaker[1]

November 8, 1917

Dear Mr. Whitaker:

I was in Washington a week and a half ago and called you up at the Octagon. I was informed that you were still in the country. I hope, if you are going to pass through New York on your way back and you have not as yet returned to Washington, I will have the opportunity to see you. There is a great deal that I want to talk to you about.

As to your letter of August 21st, I am glad that you have decided to put off the matter of the model housing law for the time being. I have given this matter a great deal of thought, and I have, in fact, roughly written an article which I hope you may find worthwhile printing in the next number of the *Journal*.

The article deals with the subject of housing and reconstruction.[2] I take the side of housing legislation, for the reconstruction and afterward, by the states rather than by the national government, for the purpose of having diversified experiments. If possible I am going to try to knock this thing into shape in time to send it to you next Tuesday. Shall I forward it to Washington or to Brandon?

The reason I am troubling you about this thing during your vacation is that my time for thought and action in the field of town planning is growing very short. I have had the luck to get a commission in the engineers, and I am to report to camp on the 14th of this month.

I would very much like to talk over this matter with you before that time, if it is possible, or at least to get your criticism as to my ideas in the matter of after-war housing. I am afraid the article may be a bit rough in expression. I have a great deal to do in putting my things in order before leaving and have not all the time that I would wish to give this matter.

I will devote just as much as possible of the time that remains in starting a housing movement here in New York. I really think we are going to make a success of it. Mr. Purdy[3] is enthusiastic about the idea and is giving us his advice; you know how valuable that is. Our plan of campaign (of course, this is not for publication as yet) is as follows: We are going to try to induce the candidates for election during the campaign this fall, particularly Whitman and Smith,[4] who are running for governor, to favor the appointment of a commission by the next legislature to investigate the whole question of housing in New York State and what has been done elsewhere to solve problems of housing. Our first move in this direction is to get together a committee that can influence the candidates. Mr. Purdy has wisely suggested that as large a part as possible of this committee be composed of labor men and women. We are after the labor men now.

By the way, I understand that Mr. Henry Sterling, who, as you know, was secretary of the Massachusetts Homestead Commission, now represents the American Federation of Labor at Washington. I have this information from Mr. Andrews, secretary of the American Association of Labor Legislation. It might be very much worthwhile, unless you have already done so, if you got in touch with Mr. Sterling in Washington. You might induce him to lead the unions in the proper direction. It certainly would be very helpful for us if he could steer the labor people in New York in the right direction.

At the same time that his committee tries to get a commission appointed in Albany, it is my idea that the same committee carry on a campaign of education throughout the state. This can be done, it seems to me, by working not only among the unions, but among the Chambers of Commerce, City Clubs, etc., etc. Perhaps it will be better that this be done by another committee of experts, if such exists. These latter certainly should be preparing material for the commission.

I think it is much safer not to attempt to put forward any particular solution of the housing problem but to let the commission, influenced by the various organizations throughout the state which have had a certain amount of preliminary instruction in the problem, work out its own solution. This solution, in legislative form, Mr. Purdy thinks, should be broad enough not to hamper the permanent bureau or commission in facing new problems as they develop.

Please let me hear from you soon. I do hope I will have a chance to talk to you before I leave for camp.

Faithfully yours,
Clarence S. Stein

1. Charles Whitaker was the editor of the *Journal of the American Institute of Architects.* Stein's interests in housing reform and city planning led to a long working association with Whitaker. Stein was actively involved in the Community Planning Committee of the AIA and served for six years as associate editor of the journal. Through Whitaker, Stein met Frederick Ackerman, New York architect and housing designer for the U.S. Shipping Board during World War I; Benton MacKaye, who was developing the idea for the Appalachian Trail; Lewis Mumford, who was then writing on American architectural history for the journal; and Walter Behrendt, German architectural historian.

2. An article with this title was published in the journal of the AIA in October 1918.

3. Lawson Purdy, who was active in the New York Charity Organizations Society, was appointed, in 1917, vice chairman of the New York Zoning Commission. In the early 1920s he was a member of the group, headed by Charles Dyer Norton, called the Regional Plan Committee, which organized the preparation of the "Regional Plan for New York and Environs."

4. Al Smith, then a city reform politician, was a successful candidate for governor of New York in 1918.

47   To Eleanor Manning

September 10, 1918

Dear Miss Manning:

After all, I am afraid I am not going to see Boston with you this summer. I had hoped to be able to stop there on my way back from Maine, but my vacation was cut short by a call to go to Washington, and now there is but little hope of my getting to Boston before the war is over. I have had the luck to be appointed a first lieutenant in the engineers. I am to go to training camp for some months and then, I hope, across.

The last two times I was in Washington I saw a number of the housing people. Mr. Eidlitz seems to have built up a very good machine for carrying on the work. He, and all who are working with him, seem at last to have come around to a broad point of view as to policy. In fact, it seems that the whole Ackerman program is to be accepted.

Mr. Kohn and Mr. Ackerman, from all I can hear, are working very hard in Philadelphia to turn out housing. Just what the policy of the Shipping Board is going to be is difficult to find out. I suppose it would not greatly surprise anyone if ultimately the two bureaus were merged.

I had a long talk with Mr. Whitaker in Washington and he seemed very happy about the way everyone is accepting the ideas that were originally brought out by the *Journal*.

Personally, during the past month or so, I have been very much more interested in how we are to carry on governmental housing after the war. It seems to me that this work should be carried on by the states, rather than by the national government. We have had altogether too little experience to attempt to centralize this work without a great deal of experimenting. This experimenting can unquestionably be diversified more easily if it is carried on by a number of state commissions than if all governmental housing is directed from Washington. It seems to me that, if we are to have the machinery to carry on this work ready when peace comes, it is time that we were preparing legislation in the various states. Of course, Massachusetts had made a start, and I hope the other States will follow or go farther than has Massachusetts.

[Balance of letter missing]

48   To Charles Whitaker

September 20, 1918

My dear Mr. Whitaker:

I have been thinking a good deal, since I saw you, of the idea of a regional survey of New York. The thing must be undertaken, but I do not think it can be done now. A great difficulty, and of this I think I spoke to you, is the fact that a part of the essential work of such a survey is now being undertaken by the New York and New Jersey Port and Harbor Development Commission, which is making a survey of the port of New York, including both shipping and railroads. It will probably be a year or eighteen months before the results of their research are available. Until then, it seems hardly possible that anything really worthwhile in the way of a plan could be drawn for New York, unless their work was to be paralleled.

As I see it, there are four big divisions in a plan [and] survey of a large metropolitan region such as New York:

I. The tying up of the city with nearby regions, with the rest of the country and the rest of the world, by

　　1. waterways,

　　2. roads, and

　　3. railroads.

II. The tying together of these various elements and the different sections of the city and their better joining by

　　1. traffic roads,

　　2. transit lines, and

　　3. waterways.

III. The location and relation of industry, business, and residences—where they are located and why they are located there, and where they might be better located.

IV. The care of the population, how it is fed, the market problem, what is its recreation, and how is it housed and where, etc.

Of course, although all the other elements in reality exist for the fourth, a study of New York's city plan would lead one to quite a contrary opinion. But we must remember that New York is New York and her value in peace or in war depends on her harbor. It seems to me that, until some program has been made as to the unification of the port, it is useless to work out a plan for the city. What we must be prepared to prevent is the dropping of the plan as soon as the solution of certain of the principal difficulties of the organization and the handling of the port have been solved. We must be ready to undertake the bigger work of relating all parts of the plan and of making them serve the human element when the time comes.

It might be possible to carry on a parallel survey in regard to the highways. I understand that half of the freight brought into New York at present is carried by truck. Much has already been done since the beginning of the war to organize the trucking deliveries. This again is a problem that will have to be handled in connection with the general problem of the port. . . .

In order to find out exactly what were the housing conditions in New York, I suggested, back in June, that a housing and industrial survey be made. I am sending you a copy of a tentative program that I made up at that time. This work was never carried out. We learned that a similar survey of "available warehousing and industrial housing in New York City" was being made by the building industries of New York. Their report, of which you can secure a copy by writing to the Building Industries of New York at No. 50 East 42nd Street, New York City, shows how far behind of real needs we are in New York. The report, however, is anything but satisfactory. It does not seem to go deep enough into the problem.

Under the old administration, when Mr. John Murphy was head of the Tenement House Department, they kept yearly records of the vacancies in the so-called tenements. No such census seems to have been taken this year. The normal average of vacancies was 5.60 percent. This had dropped in 1917 to 3.66 percent, and there can be no question that during this past year this percentage has greatly decreased because there has been practically no building carried on. This means that the very poor are being forced back to the worst type of old style tenements. . . .

I have been rambling. I do wish that there would be some way in which to start a real survey of New York and to plan for its future. I have attempted one or two sectional surveys of Staten Island, the Newark Bay region, and the Chelsea district, and I know what a colossal task it would be to undertake the work in New York City. Until it can be done in the right way, it hardly seems worthwhile doing at all.

Faithfully yours,
Clarence S. Stein

---

49   Essay

September 20, 1918

"A SURVEY OF THE CHELSEA DISTRICT"

The tendency of our city planners has been to broaden the scope of their plans. We now speak of regional instead of city surveys and plans. We soon will be speaking of a national plan. At the same time, we should not forget that there are certain local problems, such as the individuality of a town or even a section of a town, which may be lost if we neglect to make, from time to time, more detailed surveys of their needs.

In New York we have many sections that have started as suburbs and ultimately, as the city grew, become part of the big scheme of the city. Such regions as old

Chelsea, however, have not entirely lost their old individuality. In this section of New York, bounded roughly by Fourteenth and Forty-second streets, Sixth Avenue, and the [Hudson] River, there are still many of the old Irish American habitants who have dwelt there for many generations. They have conventions and habits which change slowly. They live in Chelsea and they work in Chelsea. This characteristic of the Irish American population has been of great value to the factory owners in this region.

Conditions are changing in Chelsea. The railroads which run along the west shore plan to build up a great warehouse and factory region where there are now a few but antiquated factories, coal pockets, lumber and railroad yards all wasteful of space. At the same time, the needle work and other industries, which require many workers, are filling in and building up the factories between Fifth and Seventh avenues. Between these two long parallel zones, running north and south, there is a region of homes. Many of the delightful old houses of older Chelsea still remain. Crowded in with them are tenements, mostly of the old type.

As industry grows on the east and west, its tendency will be to gradually crowd toward this central region and ultimately to entirely crowd out the residences. This is Chelsea's problem. Shall it preserve a residential section from which its industries can recruit at least a part of the labor [needed], or shall it develop to the utmost its opportunities for industrial growth and depend on improved transit to supply it with workmen?

At the suggestion of the City Planning Committee of the City Club,[1] a committee was formed in Chelsea for the purpose of making an investigation to ascertain what would be the probable industrial growth of Chelsea and how workers might be secured for Chelsea's future. . . . Mr. Eugene Henry Klaber was chosen to carry on the preliminary survey. His very able report deals with factories, workers, population, and transit. He finds that, in the eastern zone between Sixth and Seventh avenues, the growth of industry has been rapid and . . . a large part of the buildings are fireproof or of a substantial character, and that, in the region along the river, there is an impression of an arrested development. Here, most of the buildings are old. There are very few large industries and much space which would be of great value for industrial purposes, if properly served by the railroads, is now given over to large railroad yards. The scarcity of new building operations is due probably to the uncertainty which existed for many years as to the proposed improvements of the New York Railroad Company.

Klaber believes that, even with the problems of the future more or less settled by a definite plan of railroad improvement, the growth of this region would probably be slow on account of the vast expense of building up the region with modern factories and warehouses. To build up the region between Tenth Avenue and [the] river he calculates might cost sixty-eight million dollars. The City Planning Committee of the City Club believes that, with proper harbor and railroad facilities, this portion of Chelsea, which is so well connected on the east with the shops and stores of New York, would be the most valuable industrial section not only in New York but in the whole country and that the question of expense of construction would not prevent its rapid growth.

On the basis of his investigation of factories of various types, Mr. Klaber calculates that about twelve percent of the workers employed in Chelsea live in that region. Those living outside he finds to be distributed about the various parts of the city in direct proportion to their accessibility to Chelsea by the present transit lines.

A large part of the population of Chelsea . . . are not employed in factories. These are the longshoremen and truckmen. According to the last census, there [were fewer] than one hundred and fifty thousand inhabitants in Chelsea. In ten years there had been a decrease of over twelve percent. Two improvements were responsible for the clearing out of almost ten thousand of the dwellers of this region. These improvements were the building of the Pennsylvania Station and of Chelsea Park. It is surprising, in the light of what London has done to rebuild districts that were cleared of old tenements, that the city at no time felt the responsibility of caring for the population that was swept out by these changes.

The fact is that there has been but little residential building in Chelsea for a long time. Many of the old houses have been turned into two- or three-family dwellings. Since the tenement house law was passed in 1900, there has been practically no building of tenements. Between the years of 1902 and 1916, there were 5,433 tenements built in Manhattan. Of these, only thirty-six were constructed in Chelsea, and a third of the latter were erected as philanthropic enterprises.[2] Mr. Klaber believes that this is due to the high price of land in Chelsea as compared with the residential sections of Brooklyn and the Bronx. The rental price per room in all but the poorest type of tenements . . . is higher than in most of the other regions in which tenements are to be found. Mr. Klaber further points out that, if houses for the workers of Chelsea are to be built in that region, there must be subsidies of some kind, either from the factory owners [or] philanthropic limited dividend corporations, or there must be government aid, either by direct financing or by loans to limited dividend corporations.

A chapter of the report is devoted to . . . interesting suggestions for the development of transit lines in such a way as to connect the Chelsea region with the subway lines and the branches of the Hudson Tubes, which might be continued at some future time through an additional tunnel so as to connect up the section west of Ninth Avenue with a large section of the Jersey shore.

Chelsea and the city must decide whether it is worthwhile, for the purpose of keeping a nucleus of its workers within easy reach of their work, to partially pay for the dwellings of these workers. It must be remembered that the time may come when America, as well as Great Britain, will boast of many Garden Cities where the workers may dwell in pleasant surroundings and in close touch with industry. When such a time comes, Chelsea may be hard put to induce workers to travel long distances back and forth each day from their places of employment.

The majority of the members of the City Planning Committee of the City Club, however, were of the opinion, after a careful study of Mr. Klaber's survey, that the economical and reasonable solution of this problem was to let industry grow to its full in this region and to depend on improved transit to supply it with workers. Nonetheless, for the time being, until the western section is built up with industry, Chelsea should preserve as much as possible its residential section.

1. The City Club, which still functions as a luncheon club on 33 West Forty-seventh Street, was organized around the turn of the century under the leadership of Felix Adler, John Elliott, and other reform movement members of the Ethical Culture Society.

2. These philanthropic dwelling units were the twelve model homes built by the Hudson Guild Settlement House as part of the efforts to improve living conditions in Chelsea.

---

50   Draft Report of the Housing Committee of the New York State Reconstruction Commission[1]

[c. 1919]

The housing committee believes that the only way to meet the present housing emergency is to build more houses at once. The plan which it proposes is based on the following assumptions:

1. Cost of building will not return to its prewar cost; for some years it will probably not greatly decrease.

2. Next winter the scarcity of houses in New York City will be so great and rents will be so high, unless houses are built this season, that labor will be turned away from this city and New York's business [and] industry will suffer.

3. Building at the present moment can be made to give a limited return on present average rentals, if

a. Cheap land within easy reach of existing industry can be used.
b. Building [can] be carried [out] on a large scale.
c. Expert services of those experienced in design, building, and management of the best types of economical dwellings be secured.
d. If the land be held long enough to secure the increased value brought about by its settlement, and if the regions devoted to shops, etc., be so arranged as to add as much as possible to the total value of the property.

Based on these premises, the following plan is suggested:

1. The Reconstruction Commission will form a housing corporation, financed by citizens interested in the welfare of New York. Additional stock or bonds in this corporation would be sold to the public at large.

2. The housing corporation would secure loans from insurance and banking organizations, individuals, and large charity corporations.

3. The corporation would buy a large tract of cheap land on one of the new subways and carry on building on a large scale. The housing corporation will utilize men experienced in handling housing on a large scale from the point of view of design, building, and management. On cheap land it will be possible to build apartments far less congested than existing apartments. Experienced builders and designers will be able, working on a large scale, to build a better type than much of existing housing in New York.

4. It is absolutely essential that no loans be issued except upon a basis of approved plans that will guarantee an immediate type of housing built economically and so planned as to guarantee against a repetition of the present housing conditions.

5. The interest on the bonds of the corporation would be limited to a small number, or a system of cooperative ownership might be developed in connection with the housing scheme to be carried out by the corporation. All tenants shall be stockholders. A portion of their rent would go toward paying for their stock. No tenant would hold stock beyond the value of the premises occupied by him. No lease would be terminated by the corporation without the consent of the leasee, except for violation of the terms of the lease. A stockholder would have proprietary right to his house or apartment but not to the land on which it is built. But he will not be tied to his property. A lease may be terminated at any time by the tenant, by giving thirty days notice. The corporation would then return to the stockholder the amount paid for his stock minus a fair amount for deterioration of the property.

1. Many of the most radical of the proposals outlined here were adopted in federal and state legislation, which provided for publicly financed or subsidized housing or nonprofit housing production. For example, leasing land for housing construction by a public or nonprofit organization has become an important means for reducing the land cost component of the cost of housing.

17. Stein (about thirty years old) at the drawing table in Bertram Good-hue's office (c. 1912).

18. View of Balboa Park from a balloon shows the California Building (top center) at the Panama-California Exposition, San Diego (1915). Stein participated in Goodhue's development of the overall plan for the large exposition.

19. The front facade of the California Building at the Panama-California Exposition, San Diego; Cram, Goodhue, and Ferguson (New York), 1911–15. Stein, working directly from Goodhue's sketches, developed in detail much of the chiaroscuro Spanish Colonial ornament of the theme buildings of the Exposition.

20. North side of the California Building in Balboa Park at the Panama-California Exposition, San Diego (1915). Stein supervised the development of Goodhue's design for this building, designed some of the color mosaics and sculptural ornament, and supervised the preparation of the construction drawings.

21. Plan of Tyrone, New Mexico (1917). Planning of this town gave Stein another opportunity to work at large scale. The Phelps-Dodge Copper Company provided a greater range of community facilities and services than had many earlier "company towns."

22. The Plaza at Tyrone, New Mexico (1918): office, shop, and bank building at right; railroad station and freight depot in center; department store and warehouses at left. This town gave Stein one of his first opportunities to work at a large scale. During his later years in the Goodhue office, Stein carried out some of the design development and supervision of Goodhue's southwestern projects, both large and small, in the new mining town of Tyrone, New Mexico, and in Santa Barbara, California.

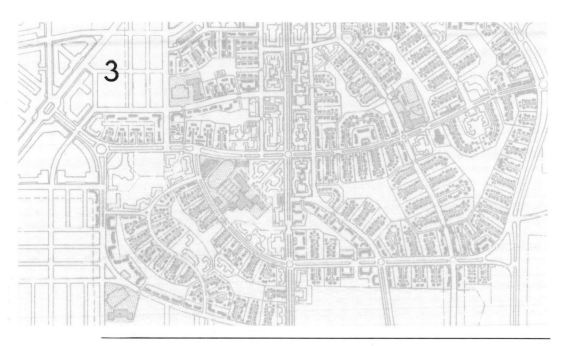

Regional Planning, Community Architecture, and Collaboration 1920–1929

As Clarence Stein's career opportunities unfolded just after World War I, it became apparent that integration of his architectural talents and his interests in large-scale community design and housing reform needed a new framework. He did not return to Goodhue's office. Stein's new central activity was an independent architectural practice in flexible and supportive association with Robert Kohn and Charles Butler. This provided opportunities to develop a conventional practice of architecture and to take on unconventional projects while expanding his associations with New York housing reformers and with collaborators from other fields of work.

We have only a small cache of unpublished letters and working documents from Clarence's hand during the 1920s, which was the period of his greatest professional achievement. The best sources for understanding the design process at Radburn, the records of his practice, were dispersed or destroyed when his association with Kohn and Butler ended in the mid-1950s. The story of Stein's important work in this decade is well covered in published articles and books. We provide here the supplementary evidence of a few letters, unpublished manuscripts, and drawings Stein brought home from his office and his letters to Lewis Mumford and Benton MacKaye from the collections of their papers at the University of Pennsylvania and Dartmouth College.

Stein's 1920s architecture had an enormous range: from "arts and crafts" buildings for the Hudson Guild Camp at Netcong, New Jersey, to participation with Kohn and Butler in the design of Temple Emanu-El, a major synagogue on upper

Park Avenue. With Kohn he also designed a number of buildings for the Fieldston School at Riverdale in New York City, an outgrowth of the Ethical Culture Society's Workingman's School. On his own, in addition to buildings in his large projects, he designed some individual houses, including the beautifully site-integrated Wasser House and other residential projects.

In 1919 he began to play a more active role in community and regional planning and a new role in New York State housing and planning policy. Stein began to serve under Governor Al Smith in a series of New York State appointments as chairman or secretary of committees and commissions charged with developing housing policies and regional planning policies and with securing the legislation needed to implement these policies. Stein believed firmly in the importance of the state government's role in housing and regional planning. His reports and speeches of the decade provide a record of these achievements. During the 1920s Clarence Stein did more than any other individual to put New York State in the forefront of state participation in the construction of housing for families with low and moderate incomes and to formulate a statewide land use and settlement planning process.

From 1921 to 1925, Stein served as chairman of the AIA committee on community planning and worked for Charles Whitaker as the associate editor for the *Journal of the American Institute of Architects* (*JAIA*). Stein became an important worker in Whitaker's effort to change the editorial policy of the journal, introducing more articles on architectural education, urban development, housing, and national urban policy.[1]

In 1921 Whitaker introduced Stein to Benton MacKaye at Whitaker's New Jersey farm, where MacKaye, a Harvard-educated forester, was recovering from the loss of his wife, Jessie MacKaye. Benton MacKaye was struggling with an article proposing the development of the Appalachian Trail. Stein and MacKaye, from their first meeting, became effective collaborators and warm friends. The growth of their productive friendship can be traced in Clarence Stein's letters to MacKaye, starting in the early 1920s, as they worked together to develop the political and organizational process by which the first parts and ultimately all of this remarkable 2,000-mile foot trail was built.

Early in 1923 Stein called the first meeting of his so-called atelier, a club of architects, economists, social reformers, community designers, urban critics, and writers,

---

1. George B. Ford, "Town Planning," *Journal of the American Institute of Architects* 5, no. 4 (1917); Thomas Adams, "The Need for Town Planning Legislation and Procedure for Control of Land as a Factor in House Building Development," ibid. 6, nos. 2, 3 (1918); Frederick L. Ackerman, "The Real Meaning of the Housing Problem," ibid. 6, no. 5 (1918); Clarence S. Stein, "Housing and Reconstruction," ibid. 6, no. 5 (1918); Clarence S. Stein, "The Housing Crisis in New York City," ibid. 7, no. 5 (1919); Henry Wright, "Shall We Community Plan?" ibid. 9, no. 12 (1921).

who ultimately named themselves the Regional Planning Association of America.[2] At first, this close circle of friends met in his office and at the City Club, where Stein was a member. The small band formulated what some of their contemporaries of the following decade considered very radical ideas about housing policy, community design, and regional planning.

Several RPAA members, including Frederick Ackerman, Henry Wright, Benton MacKaye, and Lewis Mumford, worked with Stein in the early 1920s in his task as chairman of the American Institute of Architects' Community Design Committee. MacKaye first seriously proposed the establishment of the Appalachian Trail in the pages of the *JAIA* in 1921.[3] Another set of RPAA members' articles were published in a special "Regional Planning Number" of *Survey Graphic* magazine in May 1925.[4] Mumford wrote two articles and edited the issue. Clarence Stein's contribution, "Dinosaur Cities," was an indictment of the waste and human suffering that characterizes the worst parts of large American cities. In it he argued that large cities were breaking down and becoming obsolete because of high land costs, which were causing overcrowding, slums, and the collapse of transportation systems. In early 1923, Stein began a productive ten-year association with Henry Wright, who joined him as an associate and whose role as collaborator and critic in their well-known projects was complementary to Stein's. In 1924 they studied British and Dutch housing, the New Town of Letchworth, Hampstead Garden Suburb, and other work of Raymond Unwin in England.

By the end of the decade, Stein, working with several of his RPAA associates, had achieved the best-known product of his integration of community architecture, housing policy, and regional planning: the conception, design, and partial construction of the New Town of Radburn, New Jersey. Radburn was the embodiment of Stein's most innovative concepts of community design as part of a metropolitan region-shaping process, and building it included a strategy for affordable housing. Radburn was, and is, the signal accomplishment of Stein and his associates in the RPAA, a product of five years of the RPAA's thought, discussion, pragmatic organization, and experimentation.

Clarence Stein brought A. M. Bing into the RPAA. Bing, a philanthropist and

2. Stein's note first suggesting the formation of such a group was written on several small pieces of the stationery of the United American Line. His brief list of possible members does not include Wright, MacKaye, or Mumford, although the Appalachian Trail is mentioned as a possible subject for discussion. Stein had floated MacKaye's trail idea in his community planning column in the *Journal of the American Institute of Architects*.

3. Benton MacKaye, "An Appalachian Trail: A Project in Regional Planning," *Journal of the American Institute of Architects* 9, no. 10 (1921).

4. Carl Sussman, *Planning the Fourth Migration: The Neglected Vision of the Regional Planning Association of America* (Cambridge: MIT Press, 1976), reprints these articles.

real estate developer, managed the financing, development, and building of RPAA projects through the City Housing Corporation. First, Stein, Wright, and Bing developed a prototype design for a new community for the south shore of Long Island. This prototype preceded the design and building of Sunnyside Gardens in Queens, the first large-scale housing community of the CHC. Construction on Sunnyside Gardens, designed by Stein and Henry Wright, started in 1923.

To execute these large-scale residential city-building experiments, Bing organized and managed the limited-dividend City Housing Corporation to acquire land and to build. Stein and Wright, in the design of Sunnyside, experimented with the central organization of blocks to create common green space at the center of each standard "NYC grid block." They also developed a system of deed restrictions that established community joint control of these commons. At Sunnyside, the CHC acquired the management skills needed for large-scale urban development enterprises. Charles Ascher, a young lawyer, was employed by the CHC to help develop the legal covenants for open-space management and a community association. Ascher soon became a "junior" member of the RPAA.[5] The success of Sunnyside, a community designed for white-collar, moderate-income workers, gave Bing and his associates in the CHC the assurance they needed to start assembling, in 1927, two square miles of land in Bergen County, New Jersey, for a New Town they called Radburn.

Stein's architectural and community planning skills were combined with Wright's site-design talent to invent and apply a totally new approach to community design, which Stein called "a revolution in planning." At Radburn the continuous independent pedestrian system provided children with access to recreation and schools protected from the noise and danger of automobile traffic. The footpath and open-space system also provided a focus for outdoor living and access to the central services of the community. This integrated approach to community planning, first stated at Sunnyside and fully developed at Radburn, was extended over the following decades to many Stein-Wright, Stein-only, and Stein consulting projects, including Chatham Village in Pittsburgh; Hillside Homes in the Bronx; the Greenbelt Towns; Baldwin Hills Village in Los Angeles; several Defense Housing projects in Washington, D.C., Pittsburgh, and Los Angeles; the Indian provincial capital of Chandigarh; and the New Town of Kitimat in British Columbia.

In their design process, Stein and Wright paid careful attention to comparative studies of costs of alternative residential area plans at various densities and with various relationships of buildings to circulation. This approach led to major economies in residential layout and to significant improvements in day-to-day living. Residents' associations to oversee common green space represented a new social

5. Miller, *Lewis Mumford*, 241, 263. Charles and Helen Ascher lived near the Mumfords at Sunnyside in the mid-1920s and early 1930s.

form. At Radburn the ownership of vacant, nonzoned, unplatted land allowed Stein and Wright to implement enough new ideas to attract national attention.[6] This innovation in residential planning was a major international influence in housing design.

New York City in the 1920s was a cauldron of intellectual ferment, rich in literary, artistic, and architectural innovation. At 56 West Forty-Fifth Street, Clarence Stein pondered over his drafting board and later discussed his ideas in the associates' office on the eighth floor. Meanwhile, Stein worked independently with Benton MacKaye to shape a strategy for building the Appalachian Trail, and Stein, Bing, Wright, and Ascher argued about how to shape Sunnyside and Radburn for family and community life.

During the same period, at lunch in the Algonquin Hotel on the south side of the same block of West Forty-Fourth Street (between Fifth and Sixth avenues), Alexander Woolcott and his pals (Dorothy Parker, Robert Benchley, and others) gathered at a round, white-clothed table and talked brilliantly about cultural life in New York City and life at large. The Algonquinites wrote about the emerging culture of New York City with perception, clarity, and wit.

On East Forty-fifth and East Forty-sixth, these disparate circles of close friends may have been vaguely aware of each other's ideas and work, but this is not likely. Stein was, of course, connected with the Broadway theater through his actress wife and may have read the Algonquin crowd's writing in *Vanity Fair* or the newspapers. If the Algonquinites had noticed Stein, they might have ignored him as they walked up Sixth Avenue after lunch. He was, after all, only a small, very thin, unassuming, well-dressed wraith with a friendly but very serious gaze. A contemporary of the Algonquin group, James Thurber might have drawn a cartoon of Stein as a nervous, shy observer of humanity, somewhat apprehensive about the riot of life in New York. But Thurber would have been wrong. Clarence Stein was a determined warrior who fought with drawing pencil, writing pen, and politics against the evils of urban life and invented new means and strategies for changing it for the better.

Individual members of both "clubs" alternated between enjoyment of the spectacle of New York culture and despair about the difficulties of achieving popular acceptance of their work. The members of each group worked hard at their trades and were recognized in them. Clarence Stein's regional planning group explored urban issues, produced increasingly satisfying designs for communities, and wrote earnestly about the urban past and future in important contemporary magazines: the *New Republic, Survey Graphic,* and the *New York Times.* Members of the Algonquin Club were both amused and amusing. They produced elegant poetry and prose

6. Eugenie L. Birch, "Radburn and the American Planning Movement: The Persistence of an Idea," *Journal of the American Planning Association* 46 (October 1980): 424–39; Daniel Schaffer, *Garden Cities for America: The Radburn Experience* (Philadelphia: Temple University Press, 1982).

published in popular newspapers, magazines, and books, and the world reacted with interest to their ideas and cultural views. But several of them, perhaps for personal reasons, became increasingly disaffected and alcoholic. The Regionalists were persistent and sober in their determination to change the way cities were built and to improve the effects of urban environments on people's lives.

These two clubs, which met regularly in the 1920s so near each other in Manhattan, developed unconnected parallel and contrasting reactions to the city and its culture. Both were products of a diverse and stimulating New York City as it became the world's cultural capital. Dorothy Parker was clever, detached, irreverent, and amused; Clarence Stein was serious, worried about ethical justice, and focused on poverty, slum housing, congestion, and the quality of architecture and urban design in America, as well as community design and patterns for more socially just and environmentally correct regional development. The Algonquin Club's sophisticated, literate humor and the RPAA's intense philosophical, social, and urban form analyses were probably examples of many such 1920s intellectual "clubs" of New York City.

The 1920s were Stein's most productive and creative years. Under his leadership the RPAA reacted to the evils they perceived in city development with radical programs and specific proposals for building utopian models of community. The members of the RPAA were always hopeful about the future of cities and determined to advance policy and legislative reforms that would change the priorities of society, redistribute wealth, help the poor, and restrain the greed of owners of slum property and despoilers of the natural environment. Most urban reformers and planners in the United States were trying to solve the housing problem through zoning and building code enforcement, but Stein and his colleagues focused on its context: the larger issues of the overall development patterns of urban regions, residential densities, the relationships between improvements in transportation and possible new systems of cities, the need to disperse industry and urban population, and the need to build affordable housing for moderate- and low-income families on vacant land before initiating large-scale slum clearance that would reduce the housing supply and increase rents.

A good example of the creativity of a subgroup of the RPAA working independently was the 1926 "Report of the New York State Commission of Housing and Regional Planning." Stein served as chairman of this commission from 1923 to 1926. The text and diagrams of the commission's final report are a brilliant analysis of the historic forces that shaped the patterns of New York State's urbanization in the valley belt stretching from New York City north up the Hudson River, westward up the Mohawk valley, and south of Lake Ontario to Buffalo. The commission's proposals for future urbanization patterns were based on the probable effects of the automobile, air transportation, and electric power on settlement patterns. Although the document was not an official state plan, it was the first logical and lucid presentation of a new system of cities, the "regional city" idea of the RPAA. It was also an early version of the modern concept of a linear city.

Patrick Geddes, the Scottish regional planner who visited New York in 1923 and April 1925, met the RPAA at the Hudson Guild's camp in Netcong, New Jersey. He, no doubt, influenced the method and concept developed in Stein's and Wright's 1926 New York State "Epoch III diagram, which called for each [geographic] part to serve its logical function in support of wholesome activity and good living."[7] From affordable housing policies to affordable and green communities in balanced regions, the formulations of Clarence Stein and his RPAA associates in the 1920s were major sources of new ideas for Western architecture and planning.

7. *Report of the New York State Commission of Housing and Regional Planning* (Albany, 1926).

51 Draft Report

March 22, 1920

"STATEMENT OF THE CITY PLANNING COMMITTEE OF THE CITY CLUB"[1]

The speculative builder, who in the past assumed the responsibility of supplying us with homes, has failed in this emergency. Other investments are more attractive. Without great increases in rentals, speculative building of houses will not pay for years to come. But the people of New York cannot be expected to live on the streets or herded together two or three families in an apartment merely because the building of theaters or loft building is better business. The poor of New York, half the population, [have] always lived in unwholesome, dark, leftover dwellings because it did not pay to build new homes. The only difference between the present and so-called normal times is that a large and more articulate part of the population is suffering. Temporary relief of taxation of buildings or mortgages will only help the speculating system that has created our slums.

The provision of adequate housing in decent surroundings for all the people is a public service. Until this is generally recognized, we cannot set up the necessary machinery either to meet the present menacing shortage or the shortage of decent homes for working people that has existed at all times. This cannot be attained without the use of every possible economy. Among the economies suggested by the Reconstruction Commission, which the lengthy study of the City Planning Committee of the City Club leads it to endorse, are the following:

Land: The increment of land value which results from the fact that individuals are crowded together should be preserved for the benefit of the community. It should not be wasted in speculation. The cost of land has always been a large factor in the cost of housing. Much of it might be saved if the community purchased and held large areas of land in the direction of its probable development. This land need not be built upon by the city or state, but might be let on long-term leases to tenants who would have every advantage of ownership except the right of selling the property.

Credit: The use of credit or money for housing purposes has been in the control of the heads of a few insurance and banking institutions. They have considered it their first duty to gain the largest possible return on the money held for their stockholders that the law would permit. As a result, at the present time, when money is most needed for housing purposes, it is impossible to borrow the necessary funds. The conditions on which money is offered by the lending institutions for housing purposes are such that most builders cannot afford to accept. Credit, based on the use of the peoples' earnings and savings, should be made available to meet the most pressing need of the people, sufficient decent homes. This report has already set forth the manner in which this is possible through the use of state credit.

To prevent a recurrence of the present rent difficulties, such loans should be made only on condition that rental costs shall be dependent on the actual cost of land and buildings.

Municipal Housing: Speculative building cannot, under the most favorable conditions, supply us with sufficient homes to meet the present emergency for many years to come. State loans cannot be made available until a constitutional amendment is passed. Meanwhile, the suffering in our cities for lack of houses will continue. The cities of the state should therefore have broad powers for dealing with the problem, even including the power to build and operate housing. Such authority has always been desirable for dealing with conflagrations or other sudden emergencies. The dangers in the present crisis are so grave that no city should be left without the power, where necessary, of protecting itself and its citizens.

1. Several leaders of the Ethical Culture Society helped establish the City Club, a reform institution in which they continued to be active in the 1920s. Felix Adler, the "leader" of the society, had studied the roles of municipal and state governments in Europe (Felix Adler Papers, Columbia University). The City Club also included some members of Al Smith's post–World War I Reconstruction Commission, of which Robert Moses and Clarence Stein were co-secretaries for government organization and housing, respectively.

52 Draft Report

March 22, 1920

"RECONSTRUCTION COMMISSION OF THE STATE OF NEW YORK"

Recommendations of the majority of its Housing Committee, presented to the Commission on March 22, 1920. Transmitted by Gov. Alfred E. Smith to the Legislature on March 26, 1920.

Plan A

1. It is recommended that a law be enacted requiring the appointment of local housing boards in communities having a population over 10,000, the members of such boards preferably to serve without pay, and for the appointment of a central State housing agency for coordinating local effort. The function of the central and local boards shall be:
   a. Aiding each locality in meeting the immediate pressing need for sufficient homes.
   b. Collection and distribution of information relating to housing and community planning.
   c. Assisting in the preparation of housing laws, zoning ordinances, statewide regulatory or restrictive housing and building codes, etc.

    d. Study of the means of lowering the cost of housing through better planning in the construction of homes and through their proper location.

    e. Development of a means for using State credits to apply to housing at low rates of interest without loss to the State. To set the standards for the use of such credits and to fix limitations upon the return of money borrowed from the State for housing purposes. To assist in the most practical manner possible in the erection of adequate homes in wholesome environments for workers at a rental cost dependent on the actual cost of land and building. This work to be preparatory to the passage of a Constitutional Amendment suggested as No. 2 of Plan A.

2. The enactment of a Constitutional Amendment permitting extension of State credit on a large scale and at low rates to aid in the construction of moderate-priced homes.

    a. This does not mean that the State itself shall build such homes.

    b. It does not mean that the State is to own or operate houses.

    c. It does not mean that the State is to offer subsidy for the construction of homes.

    d. It does mean that the State shall be enabled to loan money on its credit to limited dividend corporations or to individuals or to organizations, to build houses of such standards as to light and air as the State or community may determine to be desirable, the rentals of such houses to be controlled.

    e. There are many methods by which State credit might be made available. It should be one of the first duties of the Housing Bureau and the local boards to make a thorough study of this matter.

3. Passage of an enabling act permitting cities to acquire and hold, or let, adjoining vacant lands, and if necessary to carry on housing. This legislation should be such as to permit conservation of the increment of land values for the benefit of the community creating it.

The foregoing from Legislative Document No. 78, 1920. Message from the Governor, transmitting the REPORT OF THE RECONSTRUCTION COMMISSION ON THE HOUSING SITUATION.

(Clarence S. Stein, Secretary to the Committee)

---

53 Draft Reprint

[September 1921]

"INTRODUCTION" TO AN APPALACHIAN TRAIL, BY BENTON MACKAYE

The big cities of America seem to have been developed as working places. The homes of workers are congested into the less desirable sections around the factories.

Parks are generally afterthoughts and always inadequate. As the cities expand, they devour the surrounding forests and farms. It is as though man had been created for industry and not industry to serve man's need. The only relief from the noise and strain of the industrial community is the quiet of unmolested nature. The Garden City would preserve something of the outdoors within reach of the urban districts. But this is tame. We need the big sweep of hills or sea as a tonic for our jaded nerves. And so Mr. Benton MacKaye offers us a new theme in regional planning. It is not a plan for more efficient labor, but a plan of escape. He would, as far as practicable, conserve the whole stretch of the Appalachian Mountains for recreation. Recreation in the biggest sense—the re-creation of the spirit that is being crushed by the machinery of the modern industrial city, the spirit of fellowship and cooperation.

The great Appalachian Trail is already started. The Appalachian Mountain Club, the Green Mountain Club, and other similar organizations have for years past been laying the foundation for just such a scheme as is here outlined. They have formed the New England Trail Conference, a federation of twenty-three organizations which have built and are caring for 1072 miles of trail in New Hampshire, Vermont, Massachusetts, and Connecticut. They plan to combine with New York State organizations in a Northeastern Trail Conference. The movement has spread to the South, where the Appalachian Mountain Club has started a chapter at Asheville, North Carolina. The state governments in most of the New England states, as well as New York, are caring for large tracts of forest lands. The nation is preserving portions of the White Mountains and of the southern Appalachians. The possibilities of cooperation among state governments and private individuals [are] apparent in the great success of the New York–New Jersey Interstate Parkway along the Hudson River. Experiments in cooperative camps and farms are being developed by the Hudson Guild at Andover, N[ew] J[ersey], and by the Peoples' Educational Camp Society at Camp Tamiment. In short, all the elements needed for the development of the comprehensive and imaginative project of Mr. MacKaye are already in existence, but to organize the systematic development of the vast recreational plan presented in this article will necessitate the cooperation of many minds and many talents. For the purpose of securing constructive criticism, the Committee on Community Planning of the American Institute of Architects is sending out a limited number of reprints of this article from the October number of the *Journal of the American Institute of Architects.*

To all those to whom community or regional planning means more than the opening up of new roads for the acquisition of wealth, this project of Mr. MacKaye's must appeal. It is a plan for the conservation not of things—machines and land—but of men and their love of freedom and fellowship.

Clarence S. Stein

Chairman of the Committee on Community Planning—AIA

54 To Benton MacKaye

[New York City]   November 16, 1921

Dear MacKaye:

. . . I am glad you are going to see Mr. Allen Chamberlain.[1] Get his ideas on the best manner to start the development of an association to put this thing through.

I have been working very slowly—feeling my way. I have been purposely waiting, as I wanted to give my committee time to send in criticisms before I came out too strongly as representing the Committee on Community Planning being behind the scheme. I wrote to them that, unless I heard from them to the contrary, I would presume that they approve. As yet I have had no answers. Nonetheless, I am continuing to send out copies to various people.

I have had a very interesting letter from W. M. Baker, Assistant State Forester of New Jersey. He tells me of their plans to increase their state forests so as to include the mountain woodland between the Kittatiny Ridge and the Delaware River from High Point, New Jersey, to Delaware Water Gap. This is the country through which we will work with Whitaker, is it not? He says, "While this Department is interested in any projects dealing with the woods and the outdoors, I do not see how we can be of any assistance in this matter, except as I have mentioned, by pushing their own plans. It is of course apparent that any support that can be developed for the proposed Kittatiny State Forest[2] will also be a direct movement for the 30-mile section of the Appalachian Trail."

We should, just as soon as possible, get a large-scale map and start laying out all those portions of the trail that are in existence and those portions that are proposed, either by organizations or state government.[3] Albert Kennedy, the assistant secretary of the National Federation of Settlements, is immensely interested in the project and suggests that it be brought up at the executive committee meeting of their federation. . . .

If you have additional copies of the project with you, you might give them to him to send to the members of the executive committee; otherwise, if you wish, I will send them directly.

As always,

Yours,

C.S.S.

1. Allen Chamberlain, a Boston conservationist and member of the Northeastern Trail Conference, was a friend of MacKaye's. He had provided some information for Stein's introduction to the AIA reprint of MacKaye's Appalachian Trail article for the *Journal of the American Institute of Architects.*

2. The Kittatiny Ridge is part of the chain of New Jersey state forests that extends in a long ridge southeast of the Delaware River, the boundary between New Jersey and Pennsylvania for

about thirty miles. More than half of the New Jersey portion of the Appalachian Trail is located in these forests: Worthington, Stokes, and High Point State Park. The area is twenty miles west of Whitaker's summer place at Mt. Olive, New Jersey.

3. Benton MacKaye did indeed sketch out the location of the Appalachian Trail on U.S. Geological Survey Quadrangles over a period of several months after this correspondence.

---

55   To Benton MacKaye

[New York City]   February 1, 1922

Dear Benton:

Your letter of January 31st has just been received.

Within the last couple of days, I have had a very nice letter from Thomas Adams.[1] [He] says, "I have read through the pamphlet by Mr. MacKaye and think it is a splendid scheme. I am not sufficiently acquainted with the country, however, to be able to make any criticism or suggestions of value. I can only endorse the point of view very ably put by yourself in your introduction. I hope to see you next month in New York."

When he gets here I will have a talk with him about the matter. It is well worth while getting him more deeply interested.

I wrote to Albert N. Turner, chairman of the New England Trail Conference, and have just received a very enthusiastic letter from him. He sent me a map of Connecticut with the state forests and state parks marked thereon. Would this be of any use to you?

I look forward to hearing from you from time to time as your work progresses. I am so deep in other things that I am giving much less time than I would like to the trail,[2] but once you get here I hope to be able to devote more of my time to it.

As soon as you have some maps, I would be very much interested in seeing them.

Cordially yours,

C.S.S.

1. Thomas Adams, the British/American town planner later associated with the Regional Plan of New York, was referring to a reprint of MacKaye's article, "An Appalachian Trail: A Project in Regional Planning," which had appeared in the October 1921 *Journal of the American Institute of Architects,* with a brief introduction by Stein. Adams was returning from England to New York, where he was to direct the preparation of the Regional Plan of New York.

2. Stein was completing plans for the Ethical Culture Society's meetinghouse in White Plains and a residence in Port Washington, New York, editing several articles for the *Journal of the American Institute of Architects*, and making plans for travel to England and The Netherlands with Ernest Gruensfeldt to study European housing policies and projects.

56 To Benton MacKaye

March 20, 1923

Dear Benton:

I know I should have written you sooner, but I have been in a wild rush during the past week. I suppose you have heard that Charlie and Jane [Whitaker] missed the boat. Their ticket said that the boat sailed at 11 or 12 o'clock. They got to the pier at 10:30 and the boat had gone a half hour before. They finally got away on Saturday on the *Baltic*.

Very little is happening in regard to the Appalachian Trail. . . . There was a notice in [Raymond] Torry's column [in the *Evening Post* of New York] last Friday in regard to the meeting of the New York–New Jersey Appalachian Mountain Conference at Bear Mountain on the weekend of April 15th. It said that Benton MacKaye would probably be there. How about it? . . .

. . . The governors of New York and Pennsylvania are saying a good deal about the use of water power. In fact, Pinchot sent a very interesting letter a week or two ago to Smith asking if there could not be some agreements by which Pennsylvania could use a part of the water power of New York. Later it appeared that there was somewhat of a threat behind the letter, for New York City, if its population continues to grow, is going to need new sources of drinking water and the next to be attacked is probably the Pennsylvania source, that is, in connection with the Delaware. All of which points to the need of something much bigger even than a state plan.

We are slowly knocking the Garden City and Regional Planning Association into shape. I hope it is going to be quite big enough to take in your idea. . . .

Cordially yours,
C.S.

57 Memo to RPAA Program Committee

June 12, 1923

FROM   The Program Committee (Mumford, Chase, MacKaye, Stein).
        See Minutes June 7–23
To the Executive Committee, Regional Planning Association of America[1]

Gentlemen:

Your Program Committee, selected to formulate ways and means for carrying into effect the purposes of the Regional Planning Association of America as stated in its constitution, begs to submit the following suggestions:

1. That, as the planning of Garden Cities is an inherent part of regional planning, the development of any Garden City or garden village to be furthered by the Association be based, as far as practicable, upon a comprehensive plan for developing the region which, for industrial, economic, and general living purposes, is tributary to the site of such Garden City or village.

2. That the Executive Committee of the Association continue to cooperate with Professor Patrick Geddes of Edinburgh (during his stay in this country) with the view of getting in touch with the regional planning groups in Great Britain and other countries with whom he is connected and of developing regional planning in America in harmony, as far as possible, with the most advanced thought in such countries.[2]

In connection with advanced thought in such countries, [at] the conference held between Professor Geddes and the members of the Association at the Hudson Guild Farm in Columbia Valley, N.J., on May 19th last, some interesting suggestions were made by the professor as to methods now developing in America which might be applied in some measure in the countries of Europe and elsewhere. The conclusions reached at this conference seem to point to the advisability of focusing attention at present upon carrying out the regional planning project, known as the Appalachian project, which is being promoted by the American Institute of Architects through its Committee on Community Planning.

3. That, in order to illustrate concretely to groups both in this country and abroad what the Association has in mind as a "regional plan" for a type of environment, the Association take measures to initiate a series of regional plans for different environments as constituent plans of the Appalachian project above referred to, and that the Association take up [with] the A.I.A. Committee the possibilities of carrying on this work through cooperation with such Committee or otherwise.

The ultimate tangible object of the Appalachian project is to work out a comprehensive plan for developing and redeveloping the natural, physical, and industrial possibilities of a certain territory (that known as the Appalachian Domain, Exhibit A) for achieving a greater welfare through better community living.[3]

The development in mind is that of a series of services. Certain of these (some of which go usually by the name of "industries") provide for food, clothing, housing, protection, and the preliminary physical requirements for community welfare. These consist of the agricultural, forest, mining, water supply, . . . fire protection, transportation, and other services and their various branches. Then there is the service which provides (on the basis of the preliminaries) the direct opportunity for welfare. This consists of the various forms of recreational service. The form of recreational service being emphasized at this stage of the Appalachian project is that which gives access to the region's natural environment and contact with its natural resources. This access consists of a projected system of walking trails (and camps) to be developed throughout the "Domain." The backbone of this system, divided into a series of links completing circuits from the neighboring cities, is projected from New Hampshire to Georgia (Exhibit B).

Partly to obtain popular appeal but chiefly to emphasize the point that the industrial services are means and not final objectives, the development of the backbone walking trail (the so-called Appalachian Trail) is being promoted as an initial step in the project. A suggested method for handling this development is formulated elsewhere (Chapter VIII of the unpublished manuscript of the book *The New Exploration* by Benton MacKaye).

The method there outlined sets forth the location of trails as a problem in regional planning, the purpose being to interest the public in general, but especially the collegiate and other younger amateurs, in the regional approach to problems of living. As a further means of stimulating this interest, the suggestion has been made of establishing a series of regional surveys for small valley units along the line of [the] Trail as demonstrations. A reconnaissance for such a survey and plan has been made for Columbia Valley, N.J., and a suggested method for handling this line of development (Report on reconnaissance for a regional plan for Columbia Valley, N.J., by Benton MacKaye).

As a means of upbuilding, a technique in regional planning, the suggestion is made in this report that the aid of State experts in various lines, topography, forestry, agriculture, water flow, etc., be solicited and organized. The organization and coordination of this work is something which might well be undertaken by the Regional Planning Association.

The Association might well undertake also (provided arrangements therefore can be effected) the development of the regional planning features of the Appalachian Trail. Plans are now under way for the permanent organization of the administration of this trail; this will probably be effected at a conference to be called at Bear Mountain, N.Y., during next October, through joint invitation of the Chairman of the A.I.A. Committee, of the New England Trail Conference, and of the N.Y.-N.J. Trail Conference. At that meeting it is likely that an "All–Appalachian Trail Conference" will be formed to take over the Trail's administrative features. In connection with this meeting, arrangements might be negotiated for the taking over by the Association of the regional planning features of the whole project.

4. That in case the Regional Planning Association, through negotiations with the A.I.A. Committee, arranges to take over the regional planning features of the Appalachian project, it initiates its work on three lines:

    a. The reconnoitering and surveying of a series of unit valley sections (or small regions) within the Appalachian Domain, in all or some of the several States intersected by the Domain, and the organization where possible of technical regional surveys to follow up such reconnaissances. This should be done, in the case of any particular State, by arranging, through the Governor's office or otherwise, for coordinating several kinds of surveys of the region (topographic, land classification, forest, soil, water flow, etc.), these to be made by the respective State expert. (Equivalent arrangements might be made with the various Departments of the Federal Government in and adjacent to lands, such as National Forests, owned by such Government.)

b. The scouting and organizing where possible, through amateur clubs or groups, of separate links of the Appalachian Trail which would connect points of contact to and from the Trail line by rail or motor road. The result of such organization would be the establishment between the rail points of a section of Trail equipped with camps or equivalent facilities for making the region conveniently and inexpensively accessible for walkers and campers living in the neighboring cities.

c. The making and publishing of a book or monograph, including the results of the surveys conducted under (a) and (b), as a manual of information on illustrations and methods of regional planning as applied in the Appalachian project.

5. That these three lines of work be conducted first within certain key regions and States, as follows: Berkshire County, Massachusetts; the hill country between Bear Mountain, N.Y., and Netcong, N.J.; the anthracite region, Pennsylvania; the Shenandoah Valley, Virginia and West Virginia; the headwaters of the Tennessee River system [and] Tennessee and North Carolina.

These regions are shown in map form, Exhibit C. Within each region at least one valley section is indicated as a convenient area in which to start the reconnaissances referred to under 4(a). One of these units has already been reconnoitered (Columbia Valley, N.J.).

In view of the more advanced development and greater interest in the project existing in the northern portion of [the] Appalachian Domain, the territory within New England, New York, and New Jersey is suggested as that in which to start activities. The work referred to under 4(a) could be started by making reconnaissances of the areas indicated (on Exhibit C) in New Jersey, New York, and Massachusetts. The work referred to under 4(b) could be conducted effectively by scouting the Trail Links leading from the hill country of New Jersey to the White Mountains of New Hampshire (between Netcong, N.J., and Gorham, N.H.). These two pieces of work could be done together in an expedition of about three months over the route names. The work referred to under 4(c) would then be accomplished, for the particular areas and links, by making a monograph on the results of this expedition. These results would have a special value as an aid in demonstrating the objects of the Appalachian project at the forthcoming organization conference at Bear Mountain.

Respectfully submitted, Program Committee
(Mumford, Chase, MacKaye, Stein)

1. The Regional Planning Association of America was an invention of Clarence Stein. A note written on steamship line stationery in 1922, when he returned from a trip taken with Henry Wright to visit Ebenezer Howard and the English Garden City of Welwyn and Raymond Unwin and Hampstead Garden Suburb outside London, outlines his plans for establishing a "city planning atelier." He lists himself, Charles Whitaker, Stuart Chase, Henry Wright, Robert Kohn, Henry Klaber, Frederick Ackerman, Frederick Adams, Alexander Bing, and four others as possible members. The RPAA's influence on American housing and community planning policy is best documented and analyzed by Roy Lubove, Carl Sussman, Daniel Schaffer, and Francesco Dal Co. See Lubove's *Community Planning in the 1920s: The Contribution of the Regional Planning Association of America* (Pittsburgh: Univ. of Pittsburgh Press, 1963) and the complete and concise synthesis (pp. 17–22) in his introductory chapter ("The Roots of American Planning") in *The Urban Community: Housing and Planning in the Progressive Era* (Englewood Cliffs, N.J.: Prentice-Hall, 1967). Sussman's *Planning the Fourth Migration: The Neglected Vision of the Regional Planning Association of America* (Cambridge: MIT Press, 1976) deals more broadly with the group's regional philosophy and planning ideas in a long and perceptive essay that introduces the RPAA members' early published writing in the Regional Planning Number of *Survey Graphics* (1925), as well as *The Report of the New York State Commission of Housing and Regional Planning*.

2. The report is signed by Stein as committee secretary. However, the section on Geddes shows the contribution by Mumford.

3. The language and content of the paragraphs about the Appalachian Trail show very clearly the imprint of Benton MacKaye on the committee's work. They are, in fact, a draft operational plan for organizing a more detailed planning and implementation process to build the trail incrementally.

---

58 Address to Members of the Advisory Council of the Commission of Housing and Regional Planning

December 27, 1923

The Commission of Housing and Regional Planning has called together the members of its Advisory Council for the purpose of reporting on the progress that has been made in the investigation as to the existence of a housing emergency and to consult with them in regard to its future action. Public interest has been so centered on rent legislation that we are all likely to lose sight of the fact that this, no matter how necessary, is merely a temporary expedient.

You remember the story of the little Dutch boy who found a leak in the dike which endangered the existence of his native town. All through the night until assistance came, he held his hand over the hole. That is just what the State has been doing since the Legislature passed the emergency rent laws in 1920 and 1921. The problem that the Commission has been asked to first solve is that of whether the hole in the dike still exists, whether it is necessary for the State to continue this unusual and emergency form of protection. But even if we patch the hole in the dam, the real damage will still exist, the flood will still beat against the wall. The flood is the rising tide of human beings seeking residences within their incomes. Each year . . . masses have been engulfed by it; they have been dragged down into the congested slums. As a result of the emergency, not only these slum homes but those of a large part of the people have been threatened. Patching was necessary, the rent laws were necessary, but we all know that merely their continuation is not going to give us sufficient homes at rentals that the people of New York can afford to pay. After all, that is the problem, how to secure adequate homes to meet the incomes of the people. The problem? It is really a conundrum. How to make inadequate incomes pay for adequate homes? Our next task is to approach as closely as [we can] a solution of this conundrum.

The Commission of Housing and Regional Planning was created by act of the Legislature in May 1923, which defined its powers as follows:

"To study housing needs and conditions in the State and prepare plans adapted to meet such needs and conditions; collect and distribute information relating to housing and community planning, and to study means of lowering rents on dwellings by securing economy in the construction and arrangement of the buildings; assist in the preparation of legislation and regulations in relation to housing, zoning and planning throughout the State; cooperate with local housing boards or similar bodies in cities and localities and with state and federal authorities; and to make a report to the Governor and to the Legislature with respect to matters within its jurisdiction."

The hearings that were held in the City Hall during the week beginning October 15th were so fully reported in the press that I need tell you nothing further in regard to them. Within a period of five days, we heard 145 witnesses including public officials, Municipal Court Justices, civic and social workers, representatives of tenants' organizations, real estate interests, as well as builders and other citizens. Hearings have also been held in those other portions of the State which are affected by the emergency legislation, at Buffalo and Rochester, as well as in the capitol district at Schenectady and Albany. . . .

BLOCK SURVEYS. The Commission has also made a special investigation of rent in relation to living conditions and income in about eight thousand families. These are representative of various income groups living in different parts of Greater New York. In 1920 the Housing Committee of the Reconstruction Commission of the State of New York appointed by Governor Smith made a thorough study of twenty-six characteristic blocks in congested parts of New York City. This time a similar study has been made, with the assistance of neighborhood houses and civic organizations, of eight of the same blocks investigated in 1920. It is therefore possible to make a very accurate comparison of conditions in these blocks in 1920 at the time the Legislature declared an emergency to exist, with those that exist at present. . . . We have investigated not only rentals but the physical condition of the tenements and the effect that the emergency has had on the relation between landlord and tenant. Records have also been secured from a large number of families representing various trades and occupations and living in many different sections of the greater city. There has probably never before been a more thorough investigation of the relation between incomes and rents carried on in this city or elsewhere in the country. The survey of 1920 disclosed many important facts in determining the existence of an emergency at that time. It is hoped that the present survey will prove of equal value.

It is universally recognized that rent legislation will not provide more housing or solve the emergency problem. When the rent laws were enacted, it was admitted that they were but expedients intended to alleviate the situation temporarily and that they were entirely regulatory.

In his message to the Legislature in April 1923, Governor Smith said, "Since my first term as Governor, I have been impressed with the need for the adoption by the State of a definite policy on housing." In his letter which was published at the opening of the hearings in New York City, he said, "The creation of your Commission is the first move on the part of the State toward a permanent solution of the housing problem." Because of the special instructions of the Legislature requiring an immediate report with regard to the existence of an emergency . . . and the necessity for further extension of the present rent laws, the Commission, in the time at its disposal, has made no more than a beginning in the investigation of the broader and more important phases of the housing problem.

However, we feel that our investigation of the emergency has gone far enough for us to prepare for our more important permanent work. The Commission proposes to hold a series of hearings in January and February in regard to the housing problem that has always existed in New York, as anyone who has visited the homes of the poor of this city must know. We have had investigation after investigation since the middle of the last century, but a large portion of the population continue to exist in dark, ill-ventilated, unhealthy tenements, far below the standard fixed by law as a minimum for new construction. As a result of the housing shortage, the standard of living, particularly the standard of housing, of a large portion of the population has been forced downward. Families other than the very poor have been made to live under conditions dangerous not only to health, but to the privacy and general welfare of the family.

We have had many laws in the State of New York that have to do with housing; they have all been restrictive laws. It is time that we did something constructive. Our policy has always been defensive. We have dug into our trenches. Elsewhere in the world they have done the same. But at the same time they have made offensive attacks. No army can win with merely a plan of defense. And that is all that we have in the rent laws or in such restrictive legislation as the Tenement House Law.

The first constructive solution offered the State was that of the Reconstruction Commission. Its program was, first, a State housing commission with local boards. Secondly, State loans at low rates for long terms. Thirdly, if necessary, municipal housing on municipally owned land.

The first step has been taken. We now have a State Commission of Housing and Regional Planning. How shall it carry on its work in developing a practical, constructive program? . . .

The time at our disposal is short. We are therefore going to discuss this question and only this question. We are not going to talk of the existence of an emergency or the continuation of the rent laws; that has been fully discussed at our hearings. . . .

I am going to call on four or five of those present to give us short talks of not more than about ten minutes and then we will open the discussion to all present, limiting the talks to three minutes.

First, I want to ask a fellow member of the Commission, the State Architect, Mr. Sullivan Jones, to outline very briefly the possibilities of a constructive program.

---

59   To Lewis Mumford[1]

May 24, 1924

Dear Lewis:

A most remarkable thing has happened. I went down to the [AIA] Convention [in Washington] ready to fight the whole delegation in defense of our report.[2] There was no fight. They apparently were all strongly behind it. The president spoke of the report in most glowing terms. I think I see Charlie's hand in this but, as far as he understood the report, Mr. Favel [Shurtleff][3] was really enthusiastic about it. I think the same can be said for most of the delegates. Anyhow, a great many of them had very nice things to say about it. I think we should now spread this message as widely as possible. I have just sent a copy to George B. Ford, the distinguished city planner. He asked me the other day whether he could propose me as member of the Institute of City Planners. I told him that I would prefer he did not do so until he had had a chance to read our report.

I am sending you a few additional copies. Why don't you write a little article about it for the *Nation*?

Charlie seemed to be having a grand time selling books.[4] He will be back in a day or so. I hope I am going to see you in town before long.

Cordially yours,
Clarence

1. Mumford and Stein had been introduced by Charles Whitaker in 1920. Mumford had written his first article on American architecture in Philadelphia for the AIA journal in 1921 when Stein was associate editor. He, like Stein, had grown up in New York City. Patrick Geddes, the Scottish social theorist and pioneer of regional planning, was Mumford's acknowledged teacher. They had met in London in 1919, when Mumford was working with Geddes's associate Branford, editor of the *Sociological Review* while Geddes was in India. Mumford considered himself first of all a writer. His first book, *The Story of Utopias,* was published in 1922. Mumford was a very active

member of the group that organized the Regional Planning Association of America in 1923. His working association and friendship with Stein is well documented by their extensive and extended correspondence, which continued until Stein's death in 1975.

2. The AIA Committee on Community Planning had produced a somewhat radical statement on housing policy. It was subsequently published in the *Journal of the American Institute of Architects.*

3. American city planner.

4. Whitaker developed a book publishing program for the AIA which included, for example, an important monograph on the work of Bertram Grosvenor Goodhue. Whitaker marketed these volumes through AIA chapters.

60   Address

Buffalo, N.Y.   June 9, 1924

"ADDRESS OF CLARENCE S. STEIN, CHAIRMAN [OF THE] COMMISSION OF HOUSING AND REGIONAL PLANNING, AT THE FIRST STATE CONFERENCE OF REGIONAL AND CITY PLANNING"

The Commission of Housing and Regional Planning, in its search for fundamental solutions of the housing problem, has come to the conclusion that no permanent solution can be found without attacking the broader problems of city and regional planning. We have found the emergency to be more persistent in direct ratio to the size of the city. I do not say that a housing problem does not exist even in many of the smaller towns of the State. But the scale of the problem rapidly increases, much more rapidly than the size of the center, in our great cities. The cost of homes, the cost of land, the instability of location, the percentage of land covered by building, the congestion of rooms, of houses, and of people all are augmented, until we arrive at the almost unbelievable conditions of the dwelling places of the poor of New York City.

We find a very direct connection between the planning of our cities and these conditions. The concentration of large masses of people in areas too small to comfortably hold them leads to high land values for residential properties, which is one of the causes of the overcrowding of our city blocks. But it is only one of the causes. The planning of our streets and lots without any reference to their purposed use is another cause. As a result we have houses with dark interior rooms, wasteful corridors, and a tendency to build over areas that should be used for courts and gardens. The railroad and dumbbell tenements in New York, the almost as badly lighted flats or two-family houses of other cities of the State, as well as the depressingly monotonous row houses—the mushroom products of our latest housing booms were planned to fit the requirements of lots, rather than to serve the needs of those that dwell in them.

The worst evils of bad housing, the lack of sufficient light and air and of privacy, are probably quite as much the result of the poor arrangement of blocks and lots as of the overconcentration of population in the congested centers. We find narrow courts with resulting lack of decent privacy or sufficient ventilation and light even in the outlying districts of our big cities, where single and two-family houses are built. There may be only 15 or 20 families to the acre instead of 100 to 150 as in the old tenement districts of New York. In spite of the cheapness of the land, the lack of coordination between street and lot layout and the lack of planning and grouping of houses have led to these depressing conditions. . . .

Our homes are arranged, many of them, with the efficiency of a fine piece of mechanism. On the other hand our cities are haphazard growths, colossal accidents, baneful accidents. The main streets are inadequate to handle the flow of men and automobiles. The minor residential streets are wasteful in width of pavement and often in utility layout. Our transit lines are overcrowded. We constantly talk of planning to cure these evils. That is not planning, that is patching. We too seldom speak of planning to prevent such congestion. A well-planned city can control the flow of traffic and transit, just as in a well-planned factory the flow of goods is controlled. Instead of the proper foresight and planning when land values are low, most of our cities wait until it is too late to really prevent congestion. Increased traffic, brought about by widening streets or improving tributary streets, increases property values. This leads to the building of higher structures and thus to increased congestion [and] the need of still wider streets. The evils of this vicious circle can only be prevented in one way, that is, by the comprehensive planning of our cities in advance.

Such planning can be successful only in as far as it is a united effort on the part of a community to organize the physical layout of a city to better serve as a convenient and joyful place for living and working and bringing up children. Such surroundings are not accidental growths. They can only be created through careful and painstaking study of the needs of the community and the best means of attaining these ends. This problem is one of the most important ones that our cities face. The beauty or usefulness of individual buildings serves nothing unless the framework of our cities is such as to produce the kind of community in which men, women, and children can live and work and grow happily. Their lives will always be cramped lives unless the fundamental plan of their community is a sound and sane one. Many of the cities of the State have seen this and have appointed planning commissions for the purpose of studying their future needs and preparing to meet them. . . .

But even the best of our city plans come to an end at the city limits. Evils that experience has taught us to prevent in the planning of our cities are growing up just outside these same cities on land that is almost certain to become part of these cities. The city may have spent much energy and money on zoning, on the development of street and transit plans, on a park system. It may, after many bitter experiences, finally have coordinated its plan, only to find that the plan leads nowhere outside its gates. Its road system may be unrelated to the . . . street layout of surrounding development; its transit lines may be congested by the satellite towns; . . . it may have adequately protected itself with a good water, sanitary, and fire system and building and housing codes against dangers to the health and safety of its citizens. These may all be endangered by the uncontrolled growth just outside of the city limits. This is why we are beginning to talk about regional rather than city planning.

Just as the individual house cannot stand by itself but is dependent for light, ventilation, privacy, sanitation, and safety from fire on the location of surrounding buildings, so in each region the various satellite towns and suburbs are dependent upon the city, and it, in its turn, is dependent on them. No city is master of its own destiny. It is dependent on the flow of food and material from other places, on transportation, on geographic influences. Industry is generally not fed locally. Commerce is dependent on the outside world and the connections with the outside world. The health of communities is interdependent. The disposal of the sewage of one locality may affect the health of other localities. The smoke or odors from the industries that make one town successful may blight the growth of a nearby district, as Bayonne has injured northern Staten Island. The water supply of one city may be rendered useless by the carelessness or neglect of its neighbors. Open country outside the political borders of a city may be the most desirable location for its playgrounds. . . .

It is true that there are certain unquestionable business advantages in the centering of the activities of an industry. But these are many times overweighed by the disadvantages of congestion and increased cost of dispersing the products of industry. The studies that are being made by the Plan of New York and Its Environs are bringing this matter sharply to the attention of all of us. What can we do about it? The curse of New York is the congestion of too many people, too many activities, too much industry on too small a portion of the earth's surface. It is based on miscalculation or, rather, lack of calculation as to the geographic capacity of a limited area to contain and care for concentrated activity. New York is the grotesque caricature of the ultimate aim of all the cities of America that think there is a relation between growth in numbers and growth [of prosperity. Is the need for] more concentration . . . or to really disperse the people of our state, the industry of our state? I don't merely mean disperse them somewhat more widely over the surrounding territory of our big, overgrown cities. I do not mean merely an aggrandized New York Region or Buffalo Region. Each of these parts of the state have important problems that must be carefully studied as individual problems. But their solution is dependent on problems quite outside their borders. They must tie up with the plan of the State, of other states, of the nation, of the continent, and even other continents. . . .

The main framework of New York was planned to meet its natural requirements. We now find that it is growing in [an] uneven, distorted manner. Our great cities are overpopulated. Many ideal localities for industry are underpopulated.

Much fertile farmland is wasted, though the state imports vast quantities of food from the other ends of the continent, that might more economically be grown here. Some of our forests have been butchered; others are permitted to rot. We are only just beginning to think of the development of a statewide park system.

New elements are constantly appearing that should make us reconsider the plan of our state, if we had a plan. One of these is Giant Power, the possibility of controlling the flow of electric energy, of spreading this power so that industry may be more economically dispersed and so that population need not be concentrated, as in the past, in the congested dormitories of our great cities. This and innumerable other inventions of man have not been considered sufficiently in planning the gradual growth of our state. We can plan the state just as efficiently as we can plan a city, but we must consider all the complicated elements that man has brought to bear upon the development of nature. Above all, we must consider the natural resources of the state. Any sane plan must be based on these.

Regional planning is the relating of man to his environment. After all, Buffalo would not exist without the Great Lakes and [the] natural wealth produced [in the region around] these lakes and carried on them. Buffalo and the Buffalo region would lack its present importance without the power from the Falls. New York would not exist without its harbor and without the hinterland of a great fertile state and a great country. Man's ingenuity connected these two centers, but nature gave them their primary importance. In regional planning we must consider, first, nature's resources; second, what man has done with nature's resources and then what man can do to make more efficient use of nature's resources.

---

61 Essay

July 24, 1924

"GARDEN CITIES"[1]

The primary object of the creation of Garden Cities is that of bettering living conditions. The secondary object is that of cutting down the cost of living.

By bettering living conditions is meant: First, bringing men more closely in contact with nature, either as farmers or as gardeners of their own little lots, merely by having fields and streams and woods close to his door so that he may ramble or rest there.

Second: By eliminating the fatigue and waste of time and energy that comes from long trips between home and working place.

Third: Preparing a more beautiful and less complicated setting for living. This can only be done by planning in advance for a community and by the individual making his place a related part of that community.

Fourth: By building up in this better environment better living. The town is but the shell. Unless there be a different spirit, there will not be a different life. It is true that the greater part of the inhabitants of any New Town will be no different than the general run of citizens of the cities from which they come. But with them must be a group, or groups, . . . planning and striving for better ways of living. The cranks are essential to the building up of any new community that is going to amount [to] anything. Let us hope that they may be cranks that can work with others, that can enthuse others and lead them on to new ways of living. Without them, the new community will soon be a dead community.

In preparing for the creation of a new community, we must not forget that communities are made up of men and women and children and ideas, not of bricks and stones. We should start to gather together the little groups that will give soul and vitality to the community at the same time that we make the physical plans for the town and collect the money with which to build it.

The creation of Garden Cities will . . . cut down the cost of living by:

1. Conservation of land values
2. Better planning of houses, roads (widths related to uses, etc.), public utilities, grouping, planning
3. Large-scale construction
4. More orderly, scientific development: opening up streets as needed and building of houses as far as possible as streets are opened up
5. Elimination, as far as possible, of carrying charges on roads, public utilities, etc., not in use. This means also quick development, but against too quick development must be balanced the danger of building up the town so rapidly that there is no time to learn from one's own experience.
6. Economies in construction, including
   a. Large-scale construction
   b. Revision of building law requirements
   c. Cooperative use of certain facilities (plumbing, etc.)
   d. Use of different materials.

Agricultural Belt

One of the essential elements of a Garden City, as originally pointed out by Ebenezer Howard, is the permanent agricultural belt that surrounds it. It is probably this, more than anything else, that differentiates it from the ordinary city. This principle has never been lost sight of by the adherents of the movement.

The soil at Letchworth was not particularly good for farming. Nonetheless, the preservation of the agricultural belt has been held to. Its real and proportional size has been decreased in Welwyn.

The method of development has been changed to cooperative or large scale instead of many small individual farmers. But the agricultural belt is preserved in both cases. The only change in principle seems to be the thought that the open belt is not necessarily permanent in place, that its position may possibly be moved, but there still will be a permanent belt.

What is the object of this agricultural belt? What does it serve? Not one, but a number of things. It limits the growth of the city. It protects the city from possible objectionable outside influences. It supplies food more directly and therefore more economically and fresher.

The elimination of transportation and numerous middlemen is unquestionably a mass or community economy. It is true that it may be more than balanced by less economical or smaller scale methods of production. The point of attack should be toward decreasing these costs. Transportation is altogether too large an element in the cost of running our country. ([Railroads are] the greatest industry outside of farming, and to this must be added building of roads, etc.) The advantage of eating fruits and vegetables the day they have been picked must be apparent to anyone who has lived on a farm.

It keeps the city dweller in touch with the soil. This is the prime object, after all. All of the others are of lesser importance.

For this purpose . . . unused land might in some way serve quite as well—open fields—but, unless these are cultivated or kept up as parks at a vast expense to the community, they are likely to become quite unkempt. These parks may also be necessary, but they are much less important than the productive farm or forest. . . .

General Context

[Welwyn demonstrates] not only that it is possible to build a better town, more attractive and enjoyable to live in, but that in so doing, by an orderly and well-conceived plan and sequence of procedure, these things can be accomplished at a very great saving in cost. (Note, English building [costs are] considered high at this time, very little individual house building being done privately.) This cost saving [is] shown in both . . . building and owning cost at the outset, as well as in the accumulation of future increment values, which are to revert to the community in the case of the Garden City.

We have then a conclusive demonstration not only that a Garden City is economically sound but also that the high cost of home owning in general in the average town or city is caused not so much by high wages or material prices as by the general un-business-like and wasteful method of common practice in land development, scattered and intermittent building, as well as the holding of unused, costly public improvements and the cost [to] the town of serving such communities with all forms of public welfare.

If home owning is to continue, home development must become a direct, straightforward, practical operation without the present cumbersome burdens.

Building Companies

The [technical] advantages of centralized control in building and especially in building facilities are unquestionable. Much of the cost of any operation is set up and overhead. Where a town is building up over a limited and related area, the problem of organization becomes greatly simplified. Railroad sidings concealed but convenient, permanent yards close at hand, just so long as they are needed and not tied by permanent property rights, reduce haulage costs. In both Welwyn and Letchworth, tram lines are left in public roads for considerable periods; same at Hampstead.

All of these and many other advantages are obviously possible for economies as well as increased efficiency. The whole matter hinges upon a social system (i.e., building up an expert and efficient organization which both individually and collectively is capable [of] and willing to operate more [or] less indefinitely on a limited basis, relinquishing all of the profits to the benefit of a community, which may be composed of less fortunate and less deserving units). To constitute in America a Garden City development organization presupposes not . . . a temporary but [a] more or less permanent group of designers, financiers, and managers prompted by motives quite removed from those which usually motivate such businesses.

In starting a Garden City in America, our methods must be somewhat adjusted to the quality and permanency of our staff of managers and technicians. There are examples already of housing developments relatively well done, both in character and efficiency, motivated by eventual capitalistic profit. The problem we must face is whether we can secure the one without the other, over a period of sufficient duration.

A Garden City will not be attained by the mere starting of a better planned, more efficient, and economical community. Duration and continuity of purpose [are required] of the promoters. To secure an intelligent interest on the part of those who are to live in the Garden City is quite as important as to build well. . . .

1. This appears to be a fragment of an extended report that Stein prepared when he and Henry Wright returned from their 1924 trip to visit the English Garden Cities and to meet Ebenezer Howard and Raymond Unwin. The trip was part of the process of planning the organization of the City Housing Corporation and the design of Sunnyside, Long Island, and Radburn, N.J.

62 Essay

[c. September 1924]

"CONDITIONS WHICH HELPED TO PREPARE FOR THE ACTUAL GARDEN
CITIES IN ENGLAND"[1]

A casual study of the English Garden Cities may lead some to say the conditions are
altogether different; the thing might be done in England, but it would be quite
another matter in America. Quite obviously, the English Garden City has not been
produced by magic. It is, moreover, the result of patient work and propaganda on
the part of a relatively few persons. Naturally, these have . . . taken advantage of
such laws and customs as were favorable to their fundamental ideas, but most of
these ideas were new and had to be worked out in the face of unfavorable customs,
laws, and interests, just as they would anywhere else.

The development of certain improved technical methods of planning and building, especially in the realm of town planning economics, had been carried forward
in England previous to organization of the first Garden City both at Bournville,
etc., and especially at Hampstead Garden Suburb. A further development and application of town planning economies has been carried on contemporaneously with
Letchworth and [was] especially developed during the war. The leaders of the Garden Suburb movement were fortunately in charge of the war housing and the later
public housing activities under the ministry of health.

In this manner there have fortunately been built up certain principles of town
planning and methods of house building together with statutory legislation making
these applications not only possible but essential, all of which has been of immense
value in making easier the technical work of especially the second Garden City. But
in all of these the Garden City has been a strong force in promotion of these plans
and laws and cannot be said to have been favored in any special degree by outside
progress. The fact is that by reason of the force and ceaseless activities of the Garden
Suburb and Garden City group, English laws and methods have [been] kept quite
in advance of public methods and prejudices. Whatever advance has been made has
been quite in the face of public prejudice.

English city house building was quite as much botched by building speculators,
quite as set in the method of lot subdivision, street frontage, and other monotonous
and extravagant methods as those in the United States. The small minor street for
residential use, the cul-de-sac, joint drainage, and other improvements and economies were first tested out at Hampstead with quite as much persistence and daring
as would be the case in an American suburb. The Garden City movement is the result of the persistence and hard work of men of ability devoting themselves faithfully to an idea.

1. This appears to have been written after Stein's 24 July 1924 report for the CHC, "Garden Cities."

---

63   Speech at Community Church

January 22, 1925

"SHALL WE SCRAP THE SLUMS?"

No one can deny that the conditions under which our slum dwellers live make it impossible for them to live healthy, sane, normal lives and that [these conditions constitute] a menace to the health and welfare of the community as a whole. The New York slums are among the worst in the world. They are a disgrace to a civilized city. The slums must be scrapped!

For eighty or more years, we have been talking about the horrors of the New York slums and, in all that time, what have we done about them? Practically nothing. We have eliminated a few of the worst dangers to health and safety, and we have passed restrictive legislation, which prevented the repetition of conditions as bad as those in the past. But the poor and the moderately poor still live in the old houses in which they have lived for a century or so. They cannot afford the homes built according to the standards that were written into law twenty-five years ago. More than half of the families living in apartments (and that is a great part of the population of the city) live in buildings below standard in regard to sanitation, light and air, fire safety, and even the possibility of cleanliness which was accepted as a minimum by the community twenty-five years ago.

When we talk of scrapping the slums, we speak of destroying the homes of those who can afford nothing else. If we scrap the slums, can we rehouse those families that are displaced; can we supply additional houses for the newcomers; those who come from elsewhere or who are born and married here? New York adds to its colossal family some 100,000 persons every year. The problem of scrapping the slums is really part of the problem of housing that great mass of the population whose income is inadequate to pay for a home. A comparative study of incomes and rentals, or the cost of housing, shows that a great part of the population are unable to pay for any but the leftover homes. Can we house them, the vast army too poor to pay for new houses? I don't mean house someone else with a better income and leave them out in the cold or to find some other antiquated leftover. There are many people who, in trying to find a solution of the problem, have refused to look it squarely in the eye. They say that the best way to find homes for the poor is to build for those in fair circumstances. Take care of these and they will not compete with the poor for the "better slums." For, they say, there [are] better and worse slums. Some slum houses have a window in every room! A toilet connected with each individual apartment! A more or less safe means of escape for fire! Ceilings that do not leak! A minimum of vermin! If we can take care of the moderately well-to-do, then we can let the poor live in the less distasteful slums.

If we destroy the leftovers, we must face the bigger problem! What shall our policy be in regard to supplying homes for all those whose incomes are too small to pay for them? One answer, of course, is increase their incomes. This problem of the relation of incomes to costs I pass over to the economists or to the hard-fisted revolutionists. But there is another answer: let the State or City pay part of the cost. This is the policy of most of the countries of Europe. They say that the essential thing, as far as the State and the individual are concerned, is that everyone be decently housed, not that everyone have a house in accordance with his income. And it works [in] Holland, England, and elsewhere, where they are producing houses by the hundred thousands, far better than the families that inhabit them could afford, if houses had not been put in the same class as schools and subways, public utilities and public service. But of course, this policy of subsidy is merely a roundabout way of making industry and wealth pay for workers' homes, a roundabout way but apparently an effective one. There is still another way of attempting to solve this problem, that is, through improving our technique through the elimination of waste in planning, in building, in financing, in operating; much already has been done in this direction by Andrew J. Thomas and others. But still more remains to be done.

But let us face the question squarely. Have we now the technical ability to destroy the slums, to replace them with satisfactory homes, and at the same time to properly house the ever-growing number of those too poor to afford new homes? That is problem number one. Can we properly replace the slums? Have we the technical equipment? Can we do it economically or what is called economically? That is, so that the rent paid for the houses will pay the cost of the houses and all the additional costs that go with the production and management of houses.

Another problem that we must answer at the same time because it cannot be separated from the first is can we house every family in New York decently? Have we the technical equipment, architects, builders, labor, material? And can we finance this colossal undertaking? Over half a billion dollars was spent last year for constructing homes in New York City. But little of this, as we all know, went to that two-thirds of the population with incomes of less than two thousand five hundred. Our problem of housing these is colossal. We must face it as a whole. If we cannot do the thing as a whole at once, where had we best begin? That is the question. We must act like the general who plans a campaign. Perhaps he will attack the center where the enemy is most strongly fortified, where the attack is most difficult. But if he is wise he will probably plan to first carry the flanks and thus prepare himself for an easier final victory. The slums must be destroyed. Ultimately, yes. But that is not all. They are but one of the fortifications. The people of New York, all of them, must be decently housed. That is our problem. What is the best attack? What is the practical attack?

In my opinion, the attack on the slums should be made from the flanks, from the outside. We should start by building large quantities of homes elsewhere than in Manhattan because more can be done for less cost.[1]

1. Where land is less expensive.

2. Where it is easier to secure large quantities of land (large-scale operation is essential and only possible in undeveloped sections).

3. Where land can be secured more quickly. This will greatly decrease the carrying charge (taking of land in built-up areas even with right of condemnation is a matter of years). London experience.

4. Where accessory charges, such as those of public utilities, highways, etc., can be cut.

5. Where it is possible, on account of low cost of land, to retain adequate recreational space. The recreation problems must be solved at the same time as housing or else afterward at a greatly augmented price.

6. Where there is more opportunity for experimenting. Here on Manhattan, because type of tenement house has been greatly improved during last few years, we will be tempted to construct houses that in a few years . . . we will consider out of date. What we build here will be built for fifty or a hundred years. . . . We need more experience. We will get little here on expensive land with the restrictions of our old street plan. We can do much more if we work where land is cheap and can be secured in large quantities.

But to be successful in carrying out any program for housing those who can only be housed in leftover homes now:

(a) We must have a large amount of capital at low cost. One way to secure this is through State loans.

(b) Large limited dividend corporations should carry out the work; they must reorganize methods of production.

(c) Cost of streets and public utilities must be cut through better planning and organization.

(d) Cost of transportation of men, materials, and food must be cut by better relation of homes to industry and to sources of supply of food and materials. This means Regional Planning, which must be the foundation on which to build any far-seeing plan for bettering living conditions.

We may not make the direct attack on the slums quite as soon if we follow these tactics, but we will be less certain of failure.

1. This approach to building relocation housing on vacant land at the edge of the city is repeated regularly in reports, articles, and books of RPAA members throughout the decades of the twenties, thirties, and forties. They were a "voice crying in the wilderness." Catherine Bauer reit-

erated and extended the argument behind this opinion in her famous 1953 essay, "Redevelopment: A Misfit in the Fifties," in *The Future of Cities and Urban Redevelopment,* ed. Coleman Woodbury (Chicago: Univ. of Chicago Press, 1953).

---

64 Essay

April 20, 1925

"THE ARCHITECT'S LIMITATIONS"

Most architects look back with a certain regret to their student days when their projects were such as to give freedom to their imagination. The king or president [for] whom we were to plan according to the École program apparently has limitless resources, land without end, and in his happy country there were no building codes, no zoning laws. The sky was the limit!

How different are the realities we face when we start the practice of architecture. After that long wait, when the first jobs come, how our style is cramped by innumerable limitations. There is a narrow deep lot, lost in an endless row of similar narrow deep lots. What a site [for] our glorious dream! A street so narrow that our facade, which was such a lovely pattern on paper, is seen only by those who lie on their backs or so wide that the little house we have planned is quite out of scale to the magnificent boulevard.

And then there is never money enough. "The land cost so much. The mortgage was so expensive," the owner explains, and so we must trim the building. The architect's work is cramped and crippled by a thousand limitations. He accepts them because he has thought they are beyond his control.

The Committee on Community Planning of the AIA has devoted the last couple of years to a study of this problem to find out to what extent the architect can gain a greater control of his own work. It has come to the conclusion that a great part of those limitations are due to faulty city planning and [unnecessarily] excessive regulation. The architect, if he would devote more thought to public affairs, and particularly to community planning, could do much to free himself of these limitations so that his opportunities for service to the community and his opportunity as a creative artist might be more fully realized.

The extent to which the elements that make up the cost of a building are beyond the control of an architect is realized when he considers that, in the normal small house, the architect generally touches but 55% of the cost of a house. The remaining portion covers a multitude of accessory matters, in which public improvement costs, utility connections, carrying charges, and so forth represent the major part. One of the outstanding elements in cost is outside the province of both the architect and the community planner, namely, the rate of money. Yet the New York

Housing and Regional Planning Commission has found in dealing with the problem of rebuilding the obsolete tenements that a 1% drop in the interest rate produces as great a result in the cost reduction as a 15% saving of building costs on the entire structure. . . . This element of money falls outside the field of community planning and is largely beyond the influence of the architect, but this should not be true of the street or plot plan that forms the setting for the architect's work.

The effect of the monotonous gridiron system upon architecture has frequently been noted. The sameness of the plots, the absence of special sites, the sidelong approach to every building great or small, inconspicuous or monumental—all tend to stifle the imagination of the architect. The overcrowding encouraged by our traditional lot plans is nothing but a dead loss.

In all our urban communities, the demand for street frontage has increased the ratio of streets to buildings and has fostered the deep, narrow lot. Insofar as buildings are considered solely as a means for increasing the turnover of capital, this type of layout is admirable. We are gradually learning, however, that the street is a function of the building, and vice versa, so that, if we have wide streets, heavily paved, and carrying a large amount of traffic, we will be driven to erect tall buildings upon them in order to meet the carrying charges; and by the same token, if we erect tall buildings we are driven to further expenditures through widening or duplicating the streets by underground tubes or aerial avenues, and the "economy" of the tall building is to a large degree offset by the vast public expenses that must be incurred in even partially serving it.

The notion that streets can be laid down without respect to use is a fallacy. Wide streets equipped with expensive utilities, prolonged into a suburban area, determine the character of its development: in many cases they make the tenement house of four or more stories all but a necessity, whereas streets planned directly for residence service would make the two-story house possible. We habitually permit the municipal engineer to give a form to the city without determining the functions, whereas the form is meaningless and obstructive except in definite relation to the functions. . . .

When one starts with the community as a whole instead of the individual buyer of land or owner, it is possible to make a great improvement in plot planning. This does not mean that it is necessary to do away with individual ownership; it means only that the size and shape of the individual plot should be determined by the best needs of the whole. Instead of fitting our houses to plots whose size and shape were determined purely on commercial grounds, community planning demands that the commercial arrangements shall be shaped to best serve the character of the whole development.

The next limitation that must be attacked is the customary grouping of houses. The individual detached or semidetached house that is common in our American cities in all their more recent portions gives neither privacy, nor comfort, nor free exposure to air and sunlight; just the contrary. By combining houses in units of six and eight, as was done in the war housing experiments of the U.S. Housing Corporation and the U.S. Shipping Board, a unit that lends itself to more adequate architectural treatment is provided, wasted land is redeemed, and a greater degree of privacy is assured.

It is not only mechanical, city, street, and plot plans that are stifling the architect's imagination and destroying his opportunity for service as weeds destroy the best-planned garden. There are also a multitude of regulations invented by unimaginative reformers and legislators to protect the public from the selfish speculative builder. Thus, the architect is handicapped not only by the bad conditions, but by regulations which are established to combat them. It has almost come to the point where our lawyers and reformers have more to do with the planning of our buildings and communities than our architects. . . .

As long as congestion, high site values, and rapid turnover are the aims of urban buildings, there is little chance of the architect's being able to practice his art with any prospect of stable achievement within our existing centers. Within our growing cities he is hampered by a fine network of established usages, vested interests, high land values, and reckless city plans and city improvements, to say nothing of the procrustean set of regulations designed to reduce the sanitary hazards of bad planning and human hazards of fire.

Does this mean, then, that nothing can be done? On the contrary. . . . Our fresh increments of population may either be added automatically to existing centers, or they may be spotted in new centers. Inertia tends to produce the first development, and our business system, with its eye to turnover and prospective inflation of values, tends to further it. Intelligence and imagination, however, work in the direction of the second development; and farsighted industrialists like Ford, Filene, and Dennison, as well as a large number of industries that put the welfare of their workers on a par with the efficient location of their plant, have here and there begun to favor it.

The architect has nothing to gain from the forces of inertia, the forces that are heaping up and making more intolerable our big cities, for in the long run these forces will dispense with his services. He has everything to gain from the comprehensive and enlightened group action necessary to create the Garden City and to create that new regional framework, based upon the more effective relation of communities and industries to the natural environment, to power, to water, to fresh air and "nature" in which Garden Cities will be possible.

Clarence S. Stein

65   To Lewis Mumford

En route—The California Limited   September 13, 1925

Dear Lewis:

As you see I finally went the other way, west instead of east. The California Institute of Technology [job] finally [came] through, and I am on my way to Pasadena with the drawings.[1]

Your unstamped letter reached me a long time ago. But I have not been able to put my mind on anything but architecture this summer, and so it has remained unanswered.

It has been a great summer, Lewis. No housing, no regional planning, just the drafting board and a pencil. Back to the old drafting days. I am hoping that it is back to stay.

It is queer how changes of this kind come. I suppose I have really known it for some time past, but the realization of it came suddenly. Form and color mean more to me than all the rest—economics, sociology, regional planning. Yes, but I am an architect, or at least I should be. I must slow up on one side or the other and, after this summer's work and fun at design, I have decided that I am not going to slack architecture for some time to come.[2]

This means, of course, that I must give up some other activities. If I could I would resign from the commission at once. But in October and November we must hold housing hearings again. Before January lst we must prepare another report on this subject. In this I hope we will be able to pull together the threads of our other reports. I want to sing my "Swan Song." I know I have tried to sing it before: [now] I will shout it, perhaps, so that at least some will hear. I do feel that I am trying to play "He Who Was Slapped." Only they don't seem to understand the part and instead pat me on the head and say, "Very nice!" There is this housing report and the regional planning report which we will bring out in December. After this I think I should be done.

Of course, if I resign we will give up the advantages of much publicity for what we may have to say. But have we more to say at the present time, more that should be spread in that way? I am beginning to think that Henry was right when he said a short time ago that we should stop and catch up to ourselves. Last year we sketched the outline of a very big canvas. It is all there in rough charcoal line, a bit faulty in drawing perhaps, but essentially right—at least we think so. Now we must fill in the detail and put on the color. But first we each of us must leave the sketch for a while and come back to it with a refreshed and critical mind. Perhaps after all the sketch is not so blamed fine![3]

If we decide that our next step is detailed study, and not popularizing (and I think we will), then I believe the program you outlined, or something very much like it, is the one we should follow. I hope that you will be able to give half your time to it. At least that, if not more, we can finance.

I was going to tell you of architectural impressions along the way, but I am afraid this will be endless. Just this reassuring news I must sent you. All that I see from the car windows looks temporary, millions of wooden boxes, the temporary abode of pioneers. Don't give up hope. It is all to be remade. The waste is terrible. But we seem to have pulled through the war, and we will pull through this, at least America. And then you regional planners will have a grand time.

But I am going to draw pretty pictures and now and then perhaps erect a building, with beauty, a good deal of beauty I hope, and some little sanity.

I will be back in four or five weeks, and then we will talk it all over.

My kindest regards to Geddes if you see him.[4]

As always,

Clarence

1. Stein was associated with several former colleagues of Goodhue's office in the design of a science library addition and a dormitory group for the California Institute of Technology.

2. Stein is here torn, as he is throughout his life, between the personal creative joys of architectural design and his feeling of obligation to apply his skills to the larger issues of reform, especially those he knows the most about: regional planning, community design, and affordable housing policies.

3. The big canvas to which Stein refers is the study he, Henry Wright, and Alexander Bing wrote about a new community in the New York City region and the CHC's first experiment at Sunnyside. This critical note seems to reflect some dissatisfaction with Sunnyside or a realization that their regional planning ideas were impossible to implement with little political support.

4. Geddes met with RPAA members in New York in the summer of 1923. We have no record of another visit to America. So, did Mumford plan to travel to Europe in 1925 where he might meet Geddes?

---

66   To Aline MacMahon[1]

October 13, 1925

Dear Aline:

I will be back on Friday, so perhaps it seems foolish to write. But this letter has been an about-to-be for so long that, now that I have a chance to write, I must do so.

There is so much I want to tell you, but I suppose the tale of the second miracle of Guadalupe will interest you most. Now, you must know that Guadalupe, which is just outside of Mexico City, is the Mecca of Mexico, for there it was that the Madonna appeared to a poor and simple Indian way back in the early days of the Spanish rule, and she told him to go to the bishop and tell him to build a temple to her at that place. But the bishop did not believe and asked for a sign of the Madonna. And she appeared again to the Indian, and she told him to go to the hedge to gather roses in his shawl, . . . and he found beautiful roses where they never had been before. These he carried to the bishop as he was commanded by the Madonna and, when he opened his mantle or whatever it was, there was painted upon it in pigments such as man had never seen the picture of Our Lady as she had appeared to the Indian. Now, if you do not believe, go to Guadalupe. There you will see, framed above the high altar of the great church erected to receive it, the miraculous picture itself! It is hanging in the distance on the back, dim wall, and you cannot get close to it for the crowds of Indian pilgrims that kneel about the steps to the altar, all with candles in their hands, and the smoke and incense add much to the mystery that surrounds the miraculous picture of Guadalupe. But there it is!

A goodly town has grown about this church and the church on the hill where the roses were gathered and the chapel erected about the well near which the Indian last saw the Madonna. The town seems to live mainly on the pilgrims. . . .

I wandered through the market place alone in the crowd, and there I saw a young fellow seated in the roadway, surrounded by . . . various clothes, I believe, but that did not interest me. In his lap was an illustrated magazine. It was opened to a page on which was a full-page portrait. I stopped [and] stared. I mumbled something which he thought meant, "May I look at it?" I picked it up, and surely it was the second miracle of Guadalupe. It was, as you have guessed, the image of my lady, yourself!

And the rest I will tell you when I reach New York.

Clarence

1. Clarence met Aline MacMahon through their mutual interest in the Hudson Guild Theatre, an institution started as part of the Ethical Culture Society's community house in the Chelsea district of Manhattan. Clarence's sisters, Gertrude and Lillie, introduced them to each other in the early 1920s. At that time Clarence was continuing an extended romantic interest in a married woman (editor's conversation with Aline MacMahon Stein in December 1989). In the mid-1920s Aline and Clarence became good friends, and in March 1928 they were married. MacMahon, a talented and well-recognized stage actress in New York, was the daughter of Jennie Simons Mac-Mahon, who had married a Pittsburgh editor. After growing up in Pittsburgh, Aline had been brought to New York City by her mother, who believed tenaciously in her daughter's potential as an actress and who helped her acquire the best training and experience possible for a career on the stage. In the 1930s Aline MacMahon also became a distinguished film actress. Her long stays in Los Angeles for film making meant extended separations from Clarence, which were the reason for the extensive correspondence between them from 1931 until the early 1960s. This correspondence provides a unique and intimate record of the development of their creative lives over a thirty-year period.

67   To Benton MacKaye

January 15, 1926

Dear Benton:

. . . Henry and I are keeping quite as busy as ever. We are already starting to plan for another year's work at Sunnyside. I have been over there all of this morning with him.

Last night I was at a little gathering of the clan, over at Wright's house. Lewis and Sophie were there, as well as the young Unwins. They are about to leave for Boston, where Unwin is going to work with one of the landscape architects for a while. If there is any chance of your getting over to Boston, let me know, and I will send you his address. They are very nice youngsters. . . .

I have just received notice of the New England Trail conference, which I am forwarding to you. Their whole interest seems to be in the little details. I can see no mention at all of the big trail, unless Mr. Turner is going to talk about it.

My best wishes to your brother and to yourself.

Cordially yours,

[Clarence]

P.S. Mr. Unwin's address is: Edwin Unwin, c/o John Nolen, 10 Garden Terrace, Cambridge, Mass.

---

68   To Benton MacKaye

February 1, 1926

Dear Benton:

I think I told you that Henry and I have been making some studies for a new type of farming community for the Russian Reconstruction Farms. Last night we had a meeting with Harold Ware, Jessica Smith, Mr. Stephens, Stuart Chase, etc.

What we have been developing was a purely farming community. Ware brought up the point that we should at the same time develop related industries, such as milling, canning, manufacturing brick and tile, manufacturing wine, and use of by-products. The problem is one not only of finding all-year employment but also (this, of course, is even more important) that of cutting down transportation.

A very thorough study of this whole problem should be made, and it is a regional planning problem, as you see. A study that will be satisfactory, for the time being, anyhow, can be made without going to Russia, as there is sufficient information here, in the opinion of Ware and the others. Will you do the job? It will be possible for us to finance it for about three or four weeks. However, if you are going to do it you should be in New York by Thursday evening, if possible, and not later than Friday. Ware sails on Saturday, and [it] is very important that you have a talk with him before he goes. I hope you will be able to do it.

Cordially yours

[Clarence]

---

69   To Benton MacKaye

March 15, 1926

Dear Ben:

I was delighted to hear from you again and to know that the work for the Russian Reconstruction Farms is progressing so well. I am sending a check for $150 from the Regional Planning Association, which I presume will be welcome. You understand, I suppose, that we can afford to pay for only three weeks or, at the utmost stretch of the treasury, four weeks of your most valuable time. . . .

We have been having exciting times since you left, as you may have read in the newspapers—that is, if you ever do read them. The housing bills have been up before the Legislature in Albany. We had a very fine hearing last week and, I think, may get some constructive legislation.[1]

We are now working to get out the Regional Planning Report. One of the reasons I hope you will be back before long is that I would like you to take a look at it and tell us what you think of it before we send it to the press. George Soule is now attempting to put it into terms that the men in the street will understand. I think it is going to be a very good document before we are through with it. . . .[2]

Cordially yours,

[Clarence]

1. New York State legislation that provided for tax exemption for limited dividend corporations for construction of working-class housing was passed and signed into law in 1926.

2. This is the *Report of the New York State Commission of Housing and Regional Planning,* which Wright and Stein wrote and for which MacKaye did research starting in 1924. It is viewed by many planning historians as a U.S. landmark in state development planning. Its proposals included the germs of the RPAA's concepts of the regional city and the townless highway.

---

70   Draft Memo to Governor Smith[1]

March 26, 1926

In the Hughes Report the State Architect is quoted as saying "co-ordination of state activities relating to the physical development of the state [is required], because what the state itself did in the way of developing its highways, waterways, parks and reforestation will have a profound influence over the relocation and development of industry and consequently upon the drifts of population." In this I heartily agree.

If the proposed plans for a Housing Board and a Housing Bank now before the legislature are approved, practically all of the housing functions should be taken from the present Commission and Bureau and be lodged in the new Housing Board. This would leave the very important function of state planning. The importance of this work is pointed out in the forthcoming report of the Commission of Housing and Regional Planning.

The function of the Division of Regional Planning should be the planning of the physical development of the state. At the present time a series of unrelated plans are being developed in various departments. They cannot be coordinated under any single department head, and surely not under a division head, as is suggested. This is what would be necessary if the Bureau of Regional Planning were placed under the State Architect.

The State Reorganization Commission points out that the functions of the Executive Department will be "somewhat similar to what are termed 'staff duties' in military organization." There is no more staff duty than that of planning a campaign. The function of State planning is in reality the most important work of the Executive. The welfare of the state is more dependent upon it than upon any other word of the Executive. Most of the expenditures of government are connected with proper or improper planning of the physical development of the State.

The Planning Board should serve to coordinate those departments and divisions having to do with the physical development of the state. Therefore, the following should be ex officio members: Superintendent of Public Works, Commissioner of Canals and Waterways, Commissioner of Highways, State Architect, Conservation Commissioner, Commissioner of Agriculture, Chairman of Public Service Commission.

In serving on the Commission, these various heads of departments, divisions, and boards should act in the capacity of a planning board. In this they should be advised by additional commissioners who will have no interest in any specific department. I would suggest that there be at least three other commissioners who should serve without pay. These might be chosen from among the chairmen of the various regional planning boards which will be set up from time to time. At present there is but one such active board, that of the Niagara Frontier, the first annual report of which will be submitted to the Commission of Housing and Regional Planning, and through it the Governor and the Legislature, within a few days.

Respectfully submitted,
Clarence S. Stein

1. This memorandum was the first of four similar recommendations Stein was to make to New York governors for establishing a state planning operation in the executive office.

71   To Benton MacKaye

[New York City]   September 22, 1926

Dear Benton:

. . . I do not know what members of the Russian Reconstruction Farms are in town. Stuart is still away. He seems to be taking one grand, long vacation.

. . . I am awfully sorry I have not been able to get up to see you. This has been a more than usually strenuous summer in spite of the fact that I have quite given up housing work with the exception of Sunnyside. My architectural work has kept me very much on the go. I have been unable to get away for more than a few days at a time, and even this very seldom. Probably I shall go to California early next month. There is more work to be done in connection with the university there.[1] I hope I shall not have to leave before Henry and Mr. Bing return. The Wrights are sailing in a couple of days, and the Bings will be here about the 8th or 9th of next month.

Lewis is doing some work on a pamphlet for the Regional Planning Association, giving the history of past regional studies both here and abroad. We are doing some preliminary groping in connection with the problems of the Garden City. By the way, did I tell you that Lewis and I had found a new name for the Garden City? We propose calling it the "Regional City."[2] I wrote to Ebenezer Howard about this suggestion, and he seems to approve. What do you think?

When will you be here again? I am looking forward to a long talk with you. I hope it will be before I leave for California.

Cordially yours,
Clarence

1. Besides the additions to academic buildings and some new student housing at the California Institute of Technology, Stein was working on this overall plan and several new buildings at the Ethical Culture Society's new school, Fieldston, in the Riverdale area of Manhattan.

2. The reference is to Radburn, which had not been publicly announced, although land acquisition was under way.

72   Memorandum

November 27, 1926

"NEW YORK LABOR PARTY SPECIAL PROBLEMS COMMITTEE FOR A HOUSING PLATFORM PLANK"

The Labor Party hold the following propositions to be true regarding the housing problem of New York State:

The provision of wholesome, attractive and adequate homes for all the people is a public service of primary importance.

Like the services of all other public utilities, adequate housing should always be
   available on terms to permit its universal use.

There is today, however, an increasing shortage of housing for people of moderate means and it is a serious menace to health and happiness.

This menacing shortage, although now for the first time attracting wide public
   attention because of the present acute conditions, is not new.

There has always been an inadequate supply of homes with suitable surroundings for the use of tenants of the wage-earning group.

The reason for this shortage is fundamentally that the margin of profit for investments in wage earners' homes has always been considerably smaller than
   the returns to be secured from investments in expensive apartment houses
   [and] office buildings.

The profit motive has thus failed to supply sufficient incentive to bring into existence the needed housing.

With present prices of credit, material, and labor, investments in homes for
   wage earners show even less prospect of profit than before in comparison
   with the high returns possible from other types of building investment.

It is thus essential, if this vital service is to be adequately rendered, that a comprehensive and fundamental housing program be publicly undertaken and
   immediately started.

Hand in hand with the work on such a program, the people can do much to
   place checks upon rent profiteering, and certain other immediate alleviative
   measures are not only possible but essential.

The Labor Party is convinced, however, that the time has come to attack the
   problem fundamentally with a program which will eventually bring the conduct of the state's housing into harmony with the basic principles of the
   party platform demanding that all public utilities be owned and operated by
   the people.

In accordance with these principles, we insist that housing must be viewed in
   practice and before the law as a public utility in which all considerations are
   subordinated to public needs, to public health, and [to] social happiness.

The foregoing propositions are the result of extensive and disinterested study of
the housing problem. The facts which support our conclusions are at hand. There
are needed today forty thousand medium-priced apartments in New York City
alone. Something over 5,000 were being built on January 1, 1920. The annual rate
of construction in the prewar period was 21,000 apartments; yet last year more
housing accommodations were demolished than were built. A survey of the other
cities of the state shows an equally dangerous shortage.

The present crisis thus only emphasizes a long-standing problem. Before the
war, workers of the unskilled group were housed predominantly in obsolete or

made-over dwellings. It was true then and it is a still true now that this group does not, under a system where profits are taken before a living wage is paid, get a wage sufficient to pay rent to cover the cost of decent housing.

For the skilled workers the provision of housing has been on a speculative basis, which has always been inadequate and now has failed completely to afford housing in sufficient quantity and of a wholesome or artistic quality. The process has been one of building flimsy apartment houses and filling them with tenants at a rent which promised a large return to the owner. The builder would then sell at a considerable profit and leave the new owner to find that his income was cut almost from the start by charges for repairs. As a result, moderately priced apartments tend to deteriorate rapidly into a condition which makes them undesirable, unsafe, and unhealthy.

While we elaborate no program on this point in the present proposals, we realize that the fundamental and ultimate need is to decentralize population through the creation of Garden Cities and thus to eliminate the need of transportation. Meanwhile, transportation should be provided on a non-profit-making basis, which will make possible cheap rapid transit to outlying areas, where garden suburbs can be developed.

Immediate Steps: The following steps can and should be taken at once:

I. Increases in rent should be limited by law as increases in rates are regulated in any other public utility.

II. The amount of the valuation which is used in figuring reasonable rent in judicial reviews of rent increases under present laws should also be taken into consideration in making appraisals and for taxation.

III. The citizens of New York have the right to and should demand the extension of public credits sufficient to meet the existing housing shortage. The method of procedure for using these funds is hereinafter provided.

IV. A federation of the tenant leagues throughout the city, to include all tenants, especially of the wage-earning group, should be formed at once to secure the enforcement of existing laws and to bring pressure to bear to secure public support for the legislation demanded to carry out a fundamental program.

In addition to alleviative measures, however, a new and constructive policy is necessary to bring about a condition of satisfactory housing. The Labor Party proposes the following program.

1. A law should be immediately enacted creating a state housing bureau and local housing boards in all cities over ten thousand population. The function of the state bureau would be to:

a. Administer the granting of state credit for housing projects as hereinafter suggested.

b. Assume control of priority rights in building, giving preference to the building of homes when that is necessary in the interest of public health and safety.

c. Facilitate the organization of non-profit-making corporations of practical building workers as hereinafter described, for purposes of the construction and management of houses and the manufacture of building materials.

d. Educate public opinion on the principles and methods of proper housing.

The function of the local boards would be to:

a. Administer the local application of the state credit.

b. Facilitate the organization of local non-profit-making corporations of practical building workers for building, operating, and manufacturing purposes.

c. Act as sources of information and education regarding housing needs, necessary regulative and restrictive ordinances, etc.

2. A constitutional amendment should be passed permitting the extension of state credit on a large scale at low rates of interest and without regard to the debt limit to aid in the construction of moderately priced homes. This will enable the state to loan money on its credit to organizations and individuals who will build houses of such standards and rentals and under such other conditions as the state bureau and local boards may decide.

3. An enabling act should be passed permitting the state, cities, and towns to acquire, hold, and lease land; to buy, build, remodel, and rent houses; and to engage in the extracting, manufacturing, and fabrication of any materials needed in building houses.

4. Cities should take by eminent domain outlying lands along lines of their probable development and improve them with streets, sewage facilities, etc. Such land should then be rented for actual use on lease with provision that no increment in land values could be taken by the tenant or any association which might build and operate the property.

5. Housing boards should be authorized to facilitate the organization of non-profit-making corporations of practical building workers, and they should be required to give preference to such bodies in the granting of building contracts. . . .

Conclusion

The Labor Party is convinced that the people through state and municipal agencies must take the initiative in financing large-scale housing projects and supplying building materials if we are to be provided with the adequate housing which is indispensable for health and happiness.

The adoption of the above program will mean that, for the first time in the history of the state, there will be at hand a means of supplying the demand for needed houses and of securing homes designed, constructed, and set in an environment calculated to bring the maximum esthetic, physical, and social benefit. In pursuit of that purpose, we submit this housing program with the conviction that it represents an irreducible minimum.

---

73   To Benton MacKaye

May 6, 1927

Dear Ben:

This letter should have been written a week or two ago, but I have been more rushed than ever trying to get things in order so that I may get away. They are by no means in order now, but I sail tonight.

I wanted very much to have a talk with you before I left, as I hope to see Harold Ware and his farms [in Russia]. I have sent him a copy of the report and am taking another copy with me. Of course, you should be along, not only to go over the report with him but also so that you might better see conditions there. But, from what Lewis tells me, it would be a pretty difficult thing to induce you to leave your writing at the present time.[1]

My plans are to go directly to Paris, spend a week or so there, and then go on to Moscow by way of Berlin. I am hoping that Ware may be induced to meet me at Moscow. From there I expect to go down to the Farms, then farther south to the Black Sea, then to Constantinople, and on to Sicily. It sounds like a dream and probably never will be realized, but I am starting with hope.

. . . You must come down to New York for a short time when I return two months from now. . . .

As always,
Clarence

1. Benton is working on the first edition of the *The New Exploration: A Philosophy of Regional Planning* (New York: Harcourt, Brace and Co.), which is to be published in 1928.

---

74   To Benton MacKaye

[New York]   August 3, 1927

Dear Ben:

I was delighted to have your letter of welcome, which was awaiting my return. . . . I am very anxious to see you before long and talk things over, particularly the regional plan of the North Caucasus district. I spent a week with Harold and Jessica and the rest of the crowd.[1] It was very much like being out at Hudson Guild Farm. They live the same type of simple life. They are doing a big job. They have had a very hard time of it, as might have been expected, because they have had to build up a big machine, but I think they are going to make a great success. I devoted a great deal of my week there to going over your report with them.

The general feeling was that, although it was of immense value, we would never get an audience for it in Russia with the people whom we want to reach unless we can put it into terms which they can understand. That is to say, we must find some way of changing American values to Russian values. Besides that, the conclusions we thought must necessarily be carried farther, and we should show how they can be applied to a definite area there in Russia. We have in mind a particularly large plot, the development of which the government is now considering. Besides, I know you have your hands and your mind full with the work that you are now undertaking.

I cannot tell you how happy I was to hear of Harcourt Brace's reaction to your book.[2] . . .

With kindest regards to Hazel,

As always,
Clarence

1. This is a region located in the northernmost foothills of the Caucasus Mountains (about 80 to 100 miles north of the mountain range) between the Sea of Azov and the Caspian Sea. Stein's center of operation was in the town of Arkhangel'skaya about eighty miles north of the city of Kropotkin. Stein sent a postcard to Benton MacKaye on 20 June 1927 from the city of Tiflis, Georgia, on his return trip from the U.S.S.R.

2. Lewis Mumford worked closely with MacKaye on the editing of MacKay's book, and Stein collaborated with Mumford in direct negotiations with MacKaye's publishers.

---

75 To Benton MacKaye

New York City, N.Y.   December 6, 1927

Dear Ben:

On my return from a trip to the West, I found your letter of November 24th on my desk. I was delighted to hear of the progress you are making in regard to regional planning in New England.[1] Of course, whenever the high-sounding name of the Regional Planning Association of America will be of any assistance, please let me know and we will do our best.

We are at last starting actively to campaign for the Regional City. It is astonishing how easily this new name for a Garden City has gone over. I am sending you one clipping in regard to a talk I gave a few weeks ago for the City Housing Corporation advisors. Please send this back when you have read it. . . .

With kindest regards,
Very truly yours,
Clarence S.

1. Benton had prepared several regional plans for Connecticut (the Naugatuck Valley and the Connecticut River Valley) in mid-1927. The RPAA did not want to pursue this opportunity as a group. Benton MacKaye to Clarence S. Stein, 16 November 1927, MacKaye Family Papers.

76 The Radburn Plan

January 13, 1928

"NOTES ON THE NEW TOWN PLANNED FOR THE CITY HOUSING CORPORATION"[1]

This will be . . . the first city that has been planned to meet the problems of the automobile age. In spite of the tremendous progress during the last twenty-five years, particularly in mechanical means of getting from place to place, no really new form of town planning has been evolved to meet the needs of a completely new mode of living. As the number of automobiles has increased, we have widened our streets and laid better pavements. We have placed traffic policemen or flashing lights at the dangerous crossings in the hope of decreasing accidents. The yards in the rear of our suburban homes, which were laid out as quiet places for play and recreation, have been gradually crowded with garages. The typical suburb for a man of limited means, who can afford only a very small frontage on the street, is one mass of roads and buildings. The houses are generally separated from each other only far enough to allow automobiles to pass to the garages in the rear yards. There is practically no place for the children to play in safety. They are forced, like the youngsters in the big city, to make the busy streets their playground. They are in constant danger of accident, if not death, as is plainly shown by statistics in regard to automobile accidents. Even [in the housing areas] that have been laid out during the period of the development of the automobile . . . [it has become] the dominant feature of the life of the town.

The backbone of all our cities and towns has been the highways, the means of getting from place to place. In this New Town the backbone of the community will be the parks. All houses will face on gardens. Every child will be able to walk to school without crossing a single road. Every house will be within a minute's walk of a park as wide as a New York City block. Here the little tots may amuse themselves in the sand. Here the younger children may play in safety. Here the grown children and adults may enjoy themselves with tennis, quoits, or other sports, and here those who want quiet and escape from the mad movement of the automobile may walk for a mile or more in parks out of sight of highways.

How will this be achieved? The houses in this New Town will be arranged in groups of twenty or thirty around courts, which will lead to the main highways. The owner of each house will drive his automobile directly to the garage attached to his house. Although the entrance of the house will be on the side of these court roads, the principal rooms will face on the private garden of each house. The kitchen, on the other hand, will be directly accessible from the road by which general deliveries are made. The living room or the porch on the garden side of the house will have a view of a great park some 200 ft. in width and half a mile or so in length. A short walk through the garden, along a tree-lined footpath, and one will be in the park itself. Here will be about eight acres of land through which no vehicular road will pass. Paths winding around the edge and through the park will lead to tennis courts, small playgrounds for children, space for play of all kinds, bowling alleys, and clumps of trees for picnicking and for spending quiet hours.

In the parkway will be located the school and community rooms for the group of some five or six hundred families that will be housed around these park communities. The school will be accessible not only by the paths leading around the park but also on the exterior of the housing unit by direct automobile roads, so that, although in all probability the children will usually walk to school, they may be taken there directly by automobile in bad weather.

In our old cities it was necessary to have streets at frequent intervals so that the distance by foot or horse from one point to another might be short as possible. This is still true when one walks, and so in the plans of the New Town the paths lead as directly as possible to such important centers as schools and stores. However, a quarter or a half mile more or less in an automobile means only a moment's time, and the sacrifice of this moment means the safety of the whole community.

There will be a series of these small communities of five or six hundred families, each community grouped around its own park and its own small educational and cultural center. These parkways will lead one into the other so that it will be possible to walk a couple of miles through parks without crossing more than two or three highways. Small store centers will be arranged at the junctions of these small communities.

It is very difficult to picture this town of the near future. It differs very much from the normal community built around dusty, busy, noisy highways. Perhaps the easiest way to picture oneself at home in this new community is to think of one's house as facing on one side toward the Bronx Parkway without any auto highways and the other side toward a quiet automobile road easily accessible to the through traffic roads but with none of the noise and danger of the main highway. Homes will have all the peace and quiet which existed in the old New England towns. In these, houses faced on wide parkways with the narrow road running through the center. Even here the roads have now become dangerous ways. The beauty of these tree-lined ways will be preserved in our New Town. The danger will be eliminated.

Clarence S. Stein

1. This draft is the first complete written statement we have from Stein's hand of the intentions of the so-called Radburn Plan. Radburn, developed by Clarence Stein and Henry Wright for the

City Housing Corporation's intended new satellite town in Fairlawn, N.J., strongly influenced American and European urban design concepts for over sixty years. Wolfe Von Eckardt, American urban critic, concluded in the late 1960s that "modern community planning would be unthinkable without Radburn, New Jersey, which was designed in [1927] by Clarence Stein and Henry Wright with Lewis Mumford cheering them on." It was, Von Eckardt continues, "the first community anywhere to put the automobile in its place, to reconcile the demands of livability with mobility."

Radburn provided access to houses by car on cul-de-sac roads penetrating from the superblock perimeter roads. Stein designed a complete pedestrian circulation system for the interiors of the superblocks and thus provided children with access to recreation and schools that was protected from the danger and noise of automobile traffic. His interior foot circulation and park also gave a new focus for outdoor living and affected room arrangements in the houses. For example, he oriented the principle living rooms of the houses toward the green space and away from the streets. In addition, he connected the green spaces within each superblock to adjacent superblocks by underpasses and thus formed a continuous footpath and open-space system for the use of the entire neighborhood.

Convincing evidence for Stein's continuing influence on American and British city planning is provided by the repetition of Radburn-like patterns in residential districts in American and British New Towns, in the planned unit developments of the 1950s, 1960s, and 1970s, in British and American housing design manuals of the 1950s and 1960s (see ULI's *Community Builders Handbook* [Washington, D.C.: Urban Land Institute, 1968), and in the London County Council's 1961 prototype New Town plan for Hook (*The Planning of a New Town*).

By the early 1930s Stein and Wright's innovations had attracted national attention. See, for example, C. S. Stein, "Radburn and Sunnyside," *Architectural Forum* 56 (March 1932): 239–43; "New Towns for a New Age," *New York Times Magazine,* 8 October 1933, 106, no. 6; Lewis Mumford, "The Planned Community," *Architectural Forum* 58 (April 1933): 253–74; Tracy Augur, "Radburn, the Challenge of a New Town," *Michigan Municipal Review* 4 (February–March 1931): 39–41; Alexander Bing, "Community Planning for the Motor Age," *National Association of Real Estate Boards Bulletin,* March 1929; Louis Brownlow, "Radburn, a New Town Planned for the Motor Age," *International Housing and Town Planning Bulletin,* February 1930; Geddes Smith, "A Town for the Motor Age," *Survey Graphic* 12 (May 1925); Henry Wright, "The Autobiography of Another Idea," *Western Architect* 39 (September 1930): 137–41. For recent evaluations of the influence of Radburn on American planning ideas, see Eugenie L. Birch, "Radburn and the American Planning Movement: The Persistence of an Idea," *Journal of the American Planning Association* 46 (October 1980): 424–39, and Daniel Schaffer, *Garden Cities for America: The Radburn Experience* (Philadelphia: Temple Univ. Press, 1982). Stein's publication of a large number of his community designs in the *Town Planning Review* in 1949 and 1950 started the second round of the Radburn Plan's influence on British, Swedish, German, and French urban design.

---

77 To Benton MacKaye

[New York City]   January 20, 1928

Dear Ben:

I am enclosing contracts with Harcourt Brace and Company, Inc., in regard to your book. I have had Lewis go over this contract as expert on contracts with publishers, and he says it looks all right to him. Will you kindly sign on the dotted line and return one copy?

It is Mr. Brace's understanding that Lewis is to edit the mss. To this [I] thought you would have no objection. In fact, I presume you are glad to have him go over it. I took the mss. to him at Sunnyside a couple of days ago. . . .

Henry and I are deep in planning the new development for the City Housing Corporation. Mr. Bing has purchased a very large tract of land in the New York region. Although it is not going to be a regional city, the size of the place—1,000 acres or so—is such that we are going to have a chance to try out many of the things of which we have been dreaming for years.[1] I am not supposed to talk about the details of the plan until next week, when they are to be made public. But I shall be able to write you very soon and tell you the wonderful scheme we have of making recreation instead of highways the backbone of our city plan. We hope to be able to design a city in which practically every child can walk to school through green park or without crossing a single automobile highway.

Do write and tell me what you are doing. How is the idea of a regional plan for New England developing? Tell me also about Hazel and yourself. I hope that she is better.

With kindest regards,\
As always,\
Clarence

1. Planning for the location, finance, and design of the CHC's New Town, later named Radburn, began late in 1927. Early in 1928 Clarence Stein proposed marriage to Aline MacMahon. He had first proposed to her in 1925. (Editor's conversation with Aline MacMahon Stein in her apartment in New York City in August 1987.) They were married on 27 March 1928, and early in April sailed on the *Europa* for a honeymoon in the Cotswolds in England.

---

78   To Benton MacKaye

[New York City]   September 12, 1928

Dear Benton:

. . . Lewis and Sophie were down for two or three days over the weekend. They had dinner with Aline and me Sunday night. Of course, we spoke of you. We want very much to have you come here at the time of the publication of the book. We all feel it is a cause for celebration and would like to give you a little party. When do you think it will really be off the press?

Raymond Unwin is here for a short time. We are seeing a good deal of him as he is consulting with us in the planning of Radburn. A few weeks ago, Aline and I went to Lyme to visit the Hitchcocks and the Unwins. Next Monday we expect to have them all at the house, as well as a few other people connected with the planning of Sunnyside. We wish you could be there.

This weekend we are thinking of going to the Hudson Guild Farm—the first

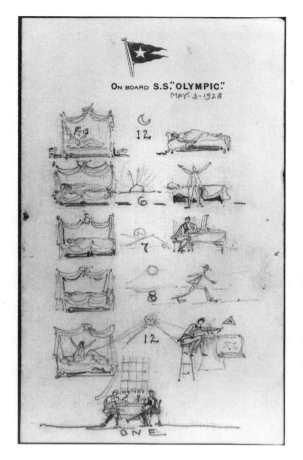

time we have been there since we were married. I know you will want me to remember you to Walter and others there, so I will do so.

Affectionate greetings from us both,

Cordially yours,

Clarence S. S.

---

79   To Benton MacKaye

[New York City]   October 21, 1929

Dear Ben:

. . . I have not had a chance to talk to Lewis about your note of October 10th and your "townless highway." It sounds very good to me. By the way, you may be interested to know that the real estate men are beginning to awaken to the fact that frontage on the through highway has very limited value. People no longer want to live at such places. Most of it is not good for stores. If we could get rid of the gas stations and "hot dog" stands I think it would be a comparatively easy matter to keep most of these highways clear of buildings. At Radburn we have designed a gas station that is not objectionable. In fact, if I were not the architect, I might say it was a very good building to look at. In one of the new Westchester parkways, there are two delightful stone colonial buildings that serve as gas stations. They certainly do not detract from the appearance of the parkway. Radburn gives an example of the difficulty of selling on the main highways. We find the most difficult houses to sell are those on our main streets. People want first of all to buy houses on the park, then those between the park and the main highways. Of course, these main roads are not nearly as busy thoroughfares as those connecting our big cities, which are quite impossible as living places.

I do not know whether we have spoken to you about the suggestion of holding a conference on regional planning [in Williamstown, Mass.] next year. It would form a part of [Williams College's] annual international conference, which in the past

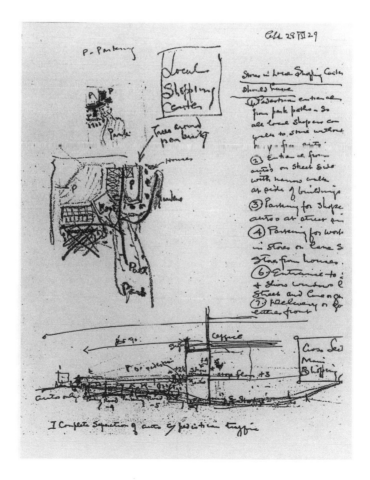

has had to do mainly with political questions. . . . [1] Lewis [Mumford], Henry [Wright], [Frederick] Ackerman, and I think the thing would be well worth while if we are able to do as we did with the *Survey Graphic*, that is, keep the subject of the conference in the right road. We must prevent its becoming so general that it has no direction. Some of those who have been suggested as people who might take part are Stuart Chase, Benton MacKaye, Russell Black, Frederick Ackerman, Thomas Adams, Phillips Bradley, Roger Greeley, Hartman, Reynolds, Robert Bruere, Wright, Mumford.

The success of the meeting will depend to a great extent, of course, upon the presiding officer. We have thought Mr. Unwin would be the best person to take the lead. Henry discussed the matter with him at Rome, and he said that, if we really thought the thing worthwhile, he might consent. What do you think of the idea, and what additional suggestions have you of people who might take part?

Aline sends her best, as does

Yours cordially,
Clarence

1. The RPAA tried to organize a major discussion on regional planning at Williamstown, Mass., early in 1929. Stein proposed that Raymond Unwin chair the roundtable at Williams College and suggested that such well-known American scholars and planners as Thomas Adams, Louis Brownlow, Charles Baird, Stuart Chase, John Nolen, Lewis Mumford, and Rexford Tugwell participate in these discussions. But the conference did not take place. Then in 1931 the RPAA was able to convince Governor Franklin Roosevelt to attend an RPAA conference on regional planning that was held in Williamsburg, Va.

80 To Dr. Wallace McLaren

[New York City]   November 9, 1929

Dear Dr. McLaren:

The Regional Planning Association at a recent meeting of the Executive Committee formulated a tentative program for discussion, which it would be happy to present at the Williamstown Conference. This program would deal with the political, economic, and social aspects of regional planning. Under the first head would come a discussion of geographic regions vs. political frontiers, the problem of planning across existing political boundaries (city, state, and international), the coordination of local and international planning, and the development of regional administration in government and industry. On the economic side, the roundtable discussion would deal with the geographic distribution of population, power, zones of living, and commodities; the question of the balanced region vs. the unbalanced region and of regional planning as opposed to imperialism; and the related problems of a planned economic life. Finally, the discussion would take in regional planning and social life. The existing units of population, their contribution to social and cultural development, and the place of regional planning in creating suitable outlets for the use of leisure . . .

We propose that Mr. Raymond Unwin of London, England, should be the head of the . . . roundtable on account not only of his high standing as a city and regional planner . . . but also because of his active part in international affairs. . . .

Yours very truly,
Clarence S. Stein, Secretary
Regional Planning Association [of America]

23. Interior of the dining hall at Hudson Guild Farm in Netcong, New Jersey. Starting in 1922, Stein designed buildings for the camp of the Hudson Guild Settlement House in Chelsea. A version of the arts-and-crafts style in American architecture was expressed in their stout walls, fireplaces, and rough-sawn timber construction.

24. Interior of Camp Aladdin, in Andover, New Jersey; C. S. Stein, architect (1920–21). The Hudson Guild's first country programs for the children of poor families in the Chelsea district of Manhattan were held at a camp in New Jersey. In his early twenties Stein worked with John Elliott in some summer activities with teenagers from Chelsea. In the 1920s Stein designed some new camp buildings.

25. Interior of the Walter Pollak residence, Morristown, New Jersey. This residence, which incorporated the reconstruction of a barn and the Rose Walter Cottage at the Hudson Guild farm, shared the same craftsman approach to building homes with local materials: fieldstone, rough-sawn timber, and some ashlar masonry.

26. Edwin Wasser House, terrace view (1923). Wasser was active with Clarence Stein around 1904 in the Ethical Culture Society's young men's City Club. The house Stein designed for Wasser was beautifully integrated with its rocky site and had some arts-and-crafts qualities, like other Stein designs of this period.

27. Fieldston School of the Ethical Culture Society. The addition and new entrance to the central courtyard were designed by Stein and Kohn in 1932.

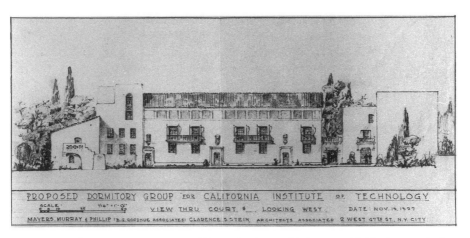

28. Proposed dormitory group at the California Institute of Technology (CIT): elevation looking west, 19 November 1927. When Goodhue died in 1924, some of his California associates continued the work at the CIT campus he had started in 1915. Stein was associated with this group in the dormitory project shown here (not built) and in an addition to the chemistry building, for which Stein seems to have done most of the design.

29. Decoration for supporting piers of the Chemistry Annex being prepared
for installation. Goodhue's use of cast stone ornament was clearly the inspiration for this formal entrance to the CIT chemistry annex and library building
by Stein and several of Goodhue's associates. Stein was very likely the principal designer. There is a clear line of development from the idea of southwest
Indian and Spanish sculptural ornament at the San Diego Exposition, some
of which Stein detailed, to these door-frame columns and later to the entry
ornament of Stein's Kansas City Art Museum.

30. Temple Emanu-El, Fifth Avenue, New York City (1926); Robert Kohn, Charles Butler, and Clarence Stein, associated architects. Preliminary design for the west facade. Concentrated areas of sculptural ornament contrasting with large areas of plain wall were characteristics of the strong art deco aesthetic Stein evolved from his earlier work with Goodhue.

31. Proposed Art Institute, Pasadena, California (1927). This large project, for which Stein developed several designs from 1927 to 1932, was not built.

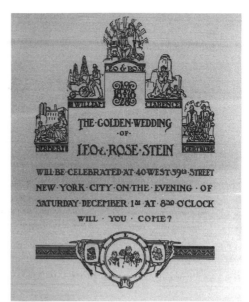

32. The invitation to Leo and Rose's Golden Wedding Anniversary drawn by Clarence S. Stein (December 1928). An outline of the Pasadena Art Institute is drawn above the name "Clarence."

33. The Stein family at Leo and Rose's fiftieth wedding anniversary (1928). Standing, left to right: Herbert, William, Clarence. Seated: Lillie, Rose, Leo, Gertrude.

34. Lewis Mumford (on left) and Benton MacKaye at Hudson Guild Farm, New Jersey (1924). Weekend retreats at the farm were held frequently in the 1920s and early 1930s for discussions and collaborative problem solving by members of the Regional Planning Association of America.

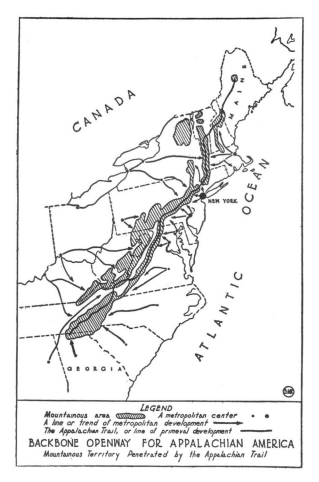

35. Benton MacKaye's plan for the Appalachian Trail. The idea was first published in the *Journal of the American Institute of Architects* in October 1921. A reprint of MacKaye's article with an introduction written by Stein was used in the early efforts to develop the local and regional organizations whose members built the trail.

36. Clarence Stein (on left) at a Russian collective farm in 1927. He made this trip to discuss Benton MacKaye's regional planning studies for agriculture and settlement in the Arkhangel region of the North Caucasus about eighty miles north of Krasnodar in southern Russia.

37. Clarence Stein, about forty-six years old (1928).

38. Henry Wright (c. 1930).

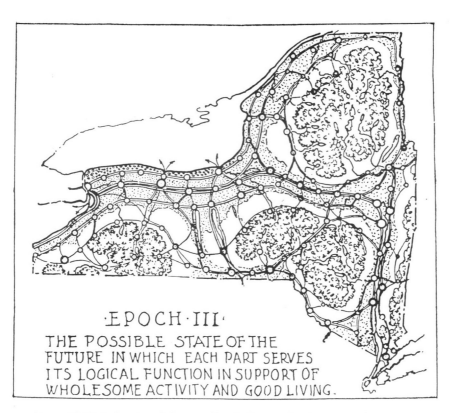

·EPOCH·III·
THE POSSIBLE STATE OF THE
FUTURE IN WHICH EACH PART SERVES
ITS LOGICAL FUNCTION IN SUPPORT OF
WHOLESOME ACTIVITY AND GOOD LIVING.

39. Henry Wright's drawing of the 1926 Epoch III plan for the New York State Region. From the Report of the New York State Commission of Housing and Regional Planning, which Stein chaired.

40. Lewis Mumford (c. 1950).

41. Alexander M. Bing (c. 1928), president of
the Regional Planning Association of America
and organizer of the limited dividend City
Housing Corporation, which developed Sunnyside Gardens, Queens, New York, and Radburn, Bergen County, New Jersey.

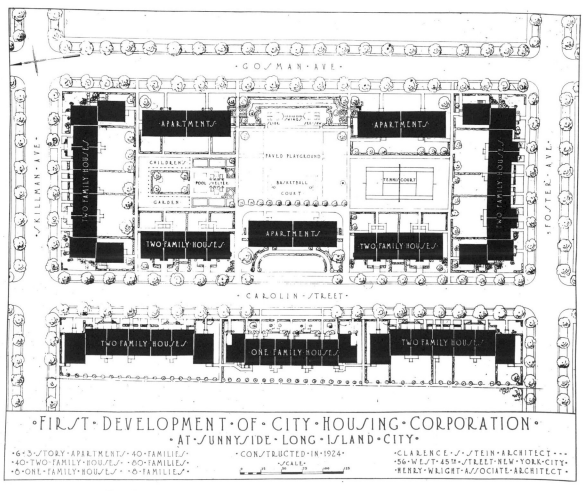

Within the site plan:

- G·O·S·M·A·N · A·V·E·
- ·K·I·L·L·M·A·N · A·V·E·
- ·F·O·S·T·E·R · A·V·E·
- APARTMENTS
- APARTMENTS
- TWO FAMILY HOUSES
- TWO FAMILY HOUSES
- CHILDRENS
- POOL SHELTER
- GARDEN
- PAVED PLAYGROUND
- BASKETBALL COURT
- TENNIS COURT
- SLIDE SWINGS SEE-SAW
- TWO FAMILY HOUSES
- APARTMENTS
- TWO FAMILY HOUSES
- · C·A·R·O·L·I·N · S·T·R·E·E·T·
- TWO FAMILY HOUSES
- ONE FAMILY HOUSES
- TWO FAMILY HOUSES

·FIRST·DEVELOPMENT·OF·CITY·HOUSING·CORPORATION·
·AT·SUNNYSIDE·LONG·ISLAND·CITY·

·6·3·STORY·APARTMENTS· 40·FAMILIES· ·CONSTRUCTED·IN·1924· ·CLARENCE·S·STEIN·ARCHITECT·
·40·TWO·FAMILY·HOUSES· ·80·FAMILIES· ·SCALE· ·56·WEST·45TH·STREET·NEW·YORK·CITY·
·8·ONE·FAMILY·HOUSES· ·8·FAMILIES· 0 25 50 75 100 125 ·HENRY·WRIGHT·ASSOCIATE·ARCHITECT·

42. Site plan of Sunnyside Gardens (1924).

43. Model of the first block of development at Sunnyside Gardens (1924). A separate, shared playground was built at the edge of the community after residents of the first unit complained about the noise of the center-block playground. This demonstrates the experimental attitude of the City Housing Corporation.

44. Central Court at Sunnyside Gardens (1925). The first unit of development featured more investment in landscaping than was found in contemporary housing developments in the same market area.

45. Typical courtyard entry at Sunnyside Gardens (1924).

46. Community Building at Sunnyside Gardens (c. 1928).

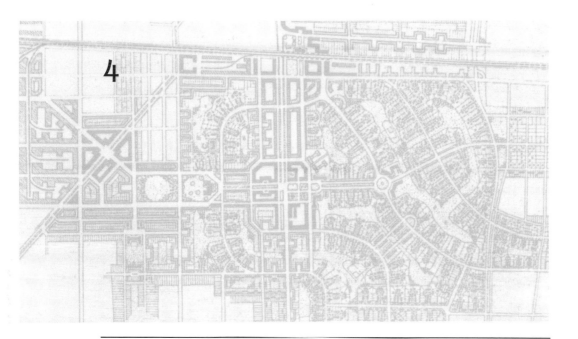

4

Years of Success and Stress
1930-1935

Clarence Stein's letters to Aline, Benton MacKaye, and Lewis Mumford during the early 1930s provide an intimate view of the times and of people involved in Stein's projects, from Chatham Village to Hillside Homes and Phipps Garden Apartments. Sometimes the letters to Aline give a day-to-day account of Clarence's work, meetings, and thoughts and report on his difficulties, disappointments, and triumphs. A small sample of the most interesting letters is included in this section. Stein's perceptive comments on the political and social upheaval of the economic depression of the 1930s provide some of the most interesting passages of these letters. His financial situation was not much changed by the depression because he and Aline both enjoyed comfortable professional incomes backed by their investments, and the depression had little effect on the value of National Casket Company stock, which was a major part of their portfolio.[1] Stein's letters record the complexity of his reactions to the poverty and despair he saw on New York streets. In the last months of 1929 and the first half of 1930, Clarence and Aline traveled extensively in India, and few letters from that period can be found in their papers.

They returned to New York in the spring of 1930 to find that the decline of the national economy had intensified and that Radburn was in deep trouble. Both of

1. A 1942 outline of the Stein's stock and bond holdings located in Aline's professional papers in the New York Public Library includes, for example, shares in American Radiator Corporation, Chase National Bank, General Electric, Rubbermaid Company, and Southern California Edison Company, as well as a large block of National Casket Company stock.

the Steins were sensitive individuals who reacted strongly to the individual and societal pain of the depression. They also had radical political views, which they discussed freely in their letters to each other. Clarence wrote to Aline about many political as well as professional issues, ranging from the plight of Jews in Germany to New York City and national politics, from his arguments with Nathan Straus about building Hillside Homes to FDR's slowly emerging national housing policy.

In 1930, two years after their marriage, Aline MacMahon and Clarence Stein rented an elegant twelfth-floor apartment in a building overlooking Central Park from West Sixty-fourth Street. There they entertained their mutual friends from the theater, including the stage and costume designer Aline Bernstein and playwright Moss Hart, as well as Clarence's friends and colleagues from the world of architecture and planning, including Mumford, Mayer, Kohn, Ackerman, Butler, MacKaye, Bauer, Chase, Wright, and many others. The Steins' dinners were social and intellectual events. Mumford later attributed both the small size of the RPAA and its success as an organization to the size of Clarence's living and dining rooms and the expert quality of the Steins' cooks. From 1930 until 1935 the RPAA met from time to time for dinner and discussion chez Stein, in addition to their more frequent weekday luncheon meetings. Their individual and group productivity in the literature of city and regional planning, as well as in projects embodying their ideals, continued during this period and was without doubt enhanced by the warm hospitality of the Steins' home.[2]

Clarence's letters report on the sad decline of CHC development at Radburn and on Bing's inability to keep the company going. The general collapse of the U.S. housing market between 1929 and 1933 bankrupted the City Housing Corporation. It was forced to end its Radburn experiment and to sell all of its undeveloped land. It had completed less than one full neighborhood. Nonetheless, this work left a legacy that went far beyond serving the community of four hundred families who lived in its realized fragment. Despite the premature cessation of construction at Radburn in the 1930s, the principal ideas of this design strongly influenced the design of hundreds of housing and New Town projects in the United States, especially Columbia (Maryland), Reston (Virginia), and Woodlands (Texas), and in Europe. All of these residential designs made use of the basic Stein-Wright formulation of the Radburn idea, as it came to be known.

During the early 1930s, the policy discussions and research forums of the RPAA were less frequent than they had been during the 1920s, but the group continued to meet and to express its views on New York City, New York State, and national policy issues in housing and regional development. In 1931 Lewis Mumford recruited a new member, Catherine Bauer, who became the executive secretary of the RPAA.

2. Aline Stein, interview with the editor, New York City, 23 December 1989.

Stein's letters report on these activities, the members' mutual criticisms of each other's work, and their collaboration on and integrated presentations of ideas and projects. Benton's work on the Appalachian Trail was well under way, and he turned his attention to conceptualizing and writing in collaboration with Mumford. One of their projects was the "townless highway," Benton's idea for connecting the settlements of the Regional City with limited-access highways but keeping most automobile traffic at the perimeters of the cities.

After the stock market crash of October 1929, Stein believed at first that the scale of national economic collapse would be modest and short-lived. But the national economy steadily declined, with mass unemployment and economic despair by 1931. The economy fell to its lowest level in 1934. The period from 1932 to 1936 seemed unreal to the Steins. In the early 1930s Clarence Stein called the depression an American "earthquake," long before Edmund Wilson so named it in 1958. Clarence was a perplexed and dismayed observer of the effects of the depression. He had some difficulty maintaining his architectural practice but did not close his office. He and Aline were major contributors to a fund in aid of unemployed architectural draftsmen. Sometimes Stein thought that the revolution was at hand—that capitalism could not and perhaps should not survive. His concern for the plight of the unemployed and his political views were very openly expressed in his letters during this period of national despair.

In the difficult years between 1931 and 1935, Stein emerged as a national leader in housing and planning. He wrote about these issues in journals and newspapers and served as a consultant on several seminal housing and town planning projects for nonprofit housing companies in Pittsburgh and New York City. Extensive publication of articles about Radburn soon led to the transfer of its basic concepts to other large-scale, low-cost, and low-rental communities. Early in 1930 the Pittsburgh Buhl Foundation's Charles F. Lewis learned of the CHC's work in affordable housing and retained Stein and Wright to advise the foundation on building low-rent houses for Pittsburgh clerical workers. Their assignment was to prepare preliminary house type and site plans for a forty-five-acre, hilly, wooded site two miles from downtown Pittsburgh. The plans for Chatham Village were a beautiful adaptation of the chief motifs of Radburn to hillside housing sited parallel to the contours. The houses were fronted on the superblock path systems and green areas. Each block was organized around a broad terrace cut into the hillside with parking in basement garages and clustered garage compounds on the downhill side. Chatham Village is a brilliant example of hillside residential area design. A local architectural firm, Ingram and Boyd, designed Chatham Village's simple, elegant row houses, and Pittsburgh landscape architect Ralph E. Griswold developed and detailed the landscape plan. Stein and Wright's overall conceptual plans and site plans were prepared in consultation to the Pittsburgh Buhl Foundation. Clarence's day-to-day correspondence with Aline in Hollywood provides some interesting insights into the new consultant roles of Stein and Wright. In 1931 Stein also designed an addition to his elegant, high-density housing at Phipps Garden Apartments in Queens.

Stein and Wright's extraordinary ten-year collaboration came to a close in the summer of 1933. This split and the reasons for it were the subject of several of Clarence's letters to Aline. Stein and Wright's work together had blended the genius of Wright, an independent thinker whose "conclusions were logical but constantly revised,"[3] with Stein's drive, practicality, and organizational skills. Those ideas developed at Sunnyside Homes and first worked out at Radburn were the model for Stein's personal contributions to residential area design for the next forty years. These concepts became internationally recognized prototypes for many excellent community designs.[4] Sixty years after the completion of its first section, Radburn remains intact. It is enjoyed daily by its residents and is beautifully maintained by its owners. Radburn is regularly visited by urban planners and landscape architects from all over the world. Its name and the names of its principal designers, Stein and Wright, are often placed in the same sentence, so linked are the place and the men.[5]

One of Stein's most remarkable feats of the early 1930s was his "invention" of Hillside Homes, a large housing development on vacant land near the end of the rail transit line at 178th Street and the Boston Post Road in the Bronx. The project, almost entirely his conception, would not have been built without his stubborn persistence in persuading bureaucrats in New York and Washington to build it. Stein designed this notable housing project using an improved T-plan based on the Phipps building type, which provided for great variety and flexibility in laying out multistory apartment buildings and offered cross ventilation for most of the apartment units in a pre–air conditioning age. The project was designed and built from 1932 to 1934 with some design criticism from but without the collaboration of Henry Wright. This relatively high-density apartment complex houses 1,400 middle-income families. The apartment and site design of Hillside Homes is superior to that of many of the more expensive large-scale apartment projects for New York City's middle-class built during the preceding era. Its large blocks and open-connected landscaped courtyards, its low ground coverage, and its extensive ground-floor community rooms were a medium-density variation of the superblock idea employed at Radburn. Hillside Homes was a frustrating but nearly flawless personal achievement for Stein: he selected the site, designed its innovative apartment units, carefully planned the community day care and recreational uses of the build-

3. Clarence S. Stein to Aline MacMahon Stein, 1 July 1933, CSP/CUA.

4. The English town planner Gordon Stephenson, who moved to Australia from England in 1958, transplanted the Radburn idea to influence the design of a number of British New Towns and Australian suburban community plans.

5. Stein, himself, was scrupulously careful to give Henry Wright equal credit for the design of Radburn.

ing's ground floors, prepared the simple but elegant designs for its art deco brick ornament, arranged for its equity financing, and played a major role in the process of
qualifying it in Washington as one of the first housing projects financed by the New
Deal's Public Works Administration (PWA) housing program.[6]

Hillside Homes was in large part the product of Stein's efforts to convince the
landowner, principal investor, and project developer, Nathan Straus, as well as New
York City politicians and financiers, Harold Ickes, and PWA administrators, that a
housing project on vacant land at the growing periphery of the city was a far better
answer to the low-cost housing problem than central city slum clearance and reconstruction. His detailed letters to Aline, who was by the early 1930s in Hollywood
acting in films, tell an inside story of Hillside Homes, along with a blow-by-blow
account of the PWA's first ventures into publicly financed housing. Slum clearance,
Stein believed, would cause displacement of low-income families without providing
relocation housing and would "reward" the owners of the slums. It also would result
in higher land costs and consequently higher population densities. This critical issue in the debate over urban housing policy during the early 1930s was to resurface
in the 1950s and 1960s.

While completing the construction of Hillside Homes in 1933 and 1934, Stein
started working with a group of New York bankers, insurance company executives,
and manufacturers of building materials and plumbing on an idea to stimulate the
national economy by stimulating the U.S. building industry. The strategy called for
the construction of large housing projects for families of moderate income on abandoned airport sites already served by water and sewer lines in Los Angeles and Oakland, California; Milwaukee, Wisconsin; and Valley Stream, Long Island. Stein eval-
uated the sites and prepared a preliminary design for one at Mitchell Field in Valley
Stream. The designs for Valley Stream and its sister projects were influential, in
Stein's view, because they were "an important step toward development of the
Greenbelt Towns." The Valley Stream project was designed to house eighteen thousand people and employed the Radburn idea (superblocks, underpasses, center-
block parks, and separate pedestrian access to schools and shops) at a higher density,
using row houses interspersed with apartments. The proposal extended the Radburn
idea to include a greater variety of housing types, a concept that was realized later
that year in Greenbelt, Maryland. But the corporate investors canceled the "airport"
projects in 1935, when they received unfavorable housing market studies.

Early in 1935 Franklin Roosevelt decided to make major changes in the nation's
emerging housing and community development program. Roosevelt's Resettlement

---

6. See Ann Boyer Cotton, "Clarence Stein and His Commitment to Beauty: Architect First,
Community Planner Second" (master's thesis, Cornell University, 1987), for an account of the dil-
igence, skill, and careful attention to detail in Stein's conception of this project, as well as of its design and execution.

Administration (RA) was assigned to develop a national program of building sub-urban New Towns. Roosevelt appointed Rexford Tugwell, the furthest left of his top advisors, to administer the RA's programs. The staff of Tugwell's Resettlement Administration sought Stein's advice early in their thinking about the design stand-ards and program of the Greenbelt Towns. Stein had taken his Valley Stream plans to the RA offices in Washington, hoping that the RA might want to incorporate the project in their satellite towns, and John Lansill, head of the Suburban Division of the RA, expressed interest in Stein's ideas. Over the next several weeks, Stein met with Lansill about the role he could play in the New Town program.[7] When Tug-well and his staff met for a weekend conference at Buck Hills Falls, Pennsylvania, with representatives of federal agencies that were to play a role in the Suburban Towns program, he invited Stein. At the close of two days of discussions, Tugwell suggested that Stein was to design one of the towns.[8]

But the RA decided that the best approach to speeding up the design and con-struction of the Greenbelt Towns was to locate all of the design staff for all four towns in Washington. Stein wanted to do the work in his New York City office but accepted Lansill's offer to work as a general consultant to the RA for town and housing design review to establish guidelines for efficient housing layouts and to develop standards for community facilities.[9] Clarence commuted almost weekly from New York to Washington during the last four months of 1935 to participate in meetings to review designs for both housing and towns. The Greenbelt Towns ex-periment, one of Roosevelt's most radical efforts to involve the federal government in urban community development, was a part of his multimillion dollar effort to create employment. Stein had a determining influence on the physical form of the Greenbelt Towns, especially Greenbelt, Maryland.[10] His disappointment that he did not have a chance to play a larger and more focused design role in at least one of these New Towns is shared in detail with Aline in his letters to her in California.

In 1935, when Stein completed his consulting work on the Greenbelt Towns for Rexford Tugwell's Resettlement Administration, he had no other architectural or planning commissions in hand. He had hoped to design one of Tugwell's New Towns but did not get the job. He had no way of understanding how effective he had been as a consultant.

In September 1935 Aline took a screen test for a leading role in the film version of *The Good Earth,* Pearl Buck's novel about village life in China. In spite of favora-ble early comments on her screen test, she lost the role to Luise Rainer. Late in 1935, Clarence's consulting and design review work for the RA ended and Aline had no

7. CSS to AMS, 24 and 31 May 1935, CSP/CUA.
8. CSS to AMS, 2 and 3 July 1935, CSP/CUA.
9. CSS to AMS, 16 October 1935, CSP/CUA.
10. CSS to AMS, 24 and 29 October 1935, CSP/CUA.

prospect for a good part in a film she wanted to do. So their long discussions about a trip to the Orient became more serious. In early December 1935, they sailed from New York to the Orient by way of England, Paris, Amsterdam, the Mediterranean, and the Suez Canal. They incorporated long stays in their visits to Indonesia, Siam, China, and Japan.

The Stein's 1935–36 trip to the Orient was a model for much of their later travel together. After reaching Indonesia, they traveled slowly. They stayed for several weeks each in Bali and Bangkok and for a month in Peking, absorbing much more of the sense of those places and their cultures than most travelers do. In Peking they became lifelong friends with Liang Ssu-ch'eng, the Chinese architectural historian, and his wife, Phyllis, with whom they maintained communication long after World War II. The importance of the Orient trip in their lives is shown in the photographs they treasured and the article Clarence wrote about the gardens of Sochow.[11]

11. Clarence Stein, "The Gardens of Sochow," *Pencil Points,* July 1938.

81   To Benton MacKaye

New York City   May 8, 1930

Dear Ben:

. . . Your article in the *New Republic* [about the "townless highway"] stated the case very clearly.[1] I wonder whether you have received a copy of the last number of the *American City,* which reprints a portion of the article. This will give it very wide publicity among just the groups that should be reached.

Did you send Unwin a copy? He is tremendously interested in just that subject in connection with the planning of the London region. . . .

Henry, Lewis, Ackerman, and I were together the other evening and we missed you very much. . . .

Henry has been to Cornell and reports a growing interest in forest preservation and reforestation along the lines we indicated in our regional plan for the State of New York.

Aline and I are getting acclimated but our thoughts are constantly returning to our Indian trip. I hope you will be here soon, and we will be able to tell you about it, if it won't bore you. Aline joins me in sending affectionate greetings.

Cordially yours,
Clarence

1. MacKaye's concept of limited-access regional highways that bypass urban centers, penetrating the built-up areas only as "spur" roads, flew in the face of the desire of commercial developers for direct access at the edges of major highways. His idea, an urban cousin of the parkways then first being built, had a logic based in part on the Radburn plan. Its logic seems to have been too complex for highway builders to consider seriously.

82   To Lewis Mumford

[New York City]   September 16, 1930

Dear Lewis:

Here is the program for the regional planning meeting.[1] As you will see, it is yours with the exception of a few slight alterations. If you think any of these should be changed, please let me know at once, as I expect to send out the programs before the end of the week.

Mr. Kohn sent your article on the townless highway to various people,[2] among others, to John M. Gries, Executive Secretary of the President's Conference on Home Building and Home Ownership. . . .

The following letter from William Stanley Parker was also received by Mr. Kohn:

"Mumford's article is fine. I'm glad he wrote it and hope you can talk more than once with Gries and the President.

"There is only one statement that I fail to understand. He says the 'free-standing house should not be considered sacred,' and adds 'so far from this being an immemorial institution, it happens . . . to be a very direct by-product of the Romantic movement, and in urban communities it is not more than a hundred years old.'"
. . .[3]

I have written a note to Mr. Stern suggesting a program that he might take up with the authorities at Washington. I am now about to write one for Buttenheim to discuss with Gries at Washington in a couple of days.[4] I suppose I shall have to try to make it a little different from Stern's so that they do not all seem to come from the same source.

Cordially,

Clarence S. Stein

1. The RPAA had scheduled a session on regional planning at the Hudson Guild Farm. Its members were also participating in the discussion of President Hoover's national conference on house building and development.

2. Robert Kohn had been an associate of Stein's in architectural practice since 1919. He also was an RPAA member and had served as head of production of housing for war workers in the U.S. Housing Corporation during World War I.

3. Mumford's article argued for higher densities in new development to reduce costs, but at residential densities of twelve dwelling units per acre—the Ebenezer Howard ideal. These densities required attached houses.

4. Harold Buttenheim was editor of the *American City Magazine*.

---

83 To Benton MacKaye

The Regional Planning Association of America, New York City   October 3, 1930

Dear Ben:

Plans for the big weekend are progressing beautifully. Practically everybody has answered yes. . . .

Now as to the program. As I see it at present, it should be something like this. We leave Hoboken at 4:45 Friday and arrive at Lake Hopatcong just after 6:00. Then to the farm and dinner about 7. After that we have our first meeting, say about 8:30. Lewis suggests that I tell them in a few words what we are there for, and then he will outline the past, or rather that which is suggested in the first paragraph of the program. The remainder of the evening and the following morning should, I think, hinge on the idea of a Ten-Year Program. I don't know just why ten years, but anyhow [my talk would be about] how a program of regional planning might be realized. By starting off with the description of the program of a definite region, we can get into all kinds of subjects, of course, and the difficulty is going to be to keep on the track. I should like to have Greeley outline a Ten-Year Program for New England and then have Stuart say a little bit about the Russian plan. . . .

The following morning we might get together from, say, 10 to 12, with Henry leading on the New York [State] plan, and Black following with the plan for the Philadelphia region. Then let's go for a hike in the afternoon and start up again, say, from 4 to 6, taking up the question of the practical plans we should try to realize at once. Some will have developed from the conversation, but the first to consider should be your Townless Highway. For the evening I am arranging for a country dance. Walter Elliott is trying to collect the musicians, and we count on the old farmer, Benton MacKaye, to call the numbers. . . .

How does it all sound to you? I hope you are going to turn up in New York a day or so before the big party so we can rehearse things.[1]

Cordially,

Clarence

1. After this RPAA conference Stein reported to MacKaye that over thirty had attended and discussed "everything from New York State and Philadelphia to Russia and Siberia" and, of course, the townless highway. The key elements of MacKaye's idea were: "1) The Bypass to save the town from the highway and the highway from the town; 2) The Station: to separate commerce from residence within the town and to provide all wayside utilities along the road; . . . 3) The Freeway: to render the motorway as is the railway [free] from frontage development between stations (interchanges); . . . and 4) The Parkway: to clear the foreground of objectionable signs and development."

---

84 To Aline Stein

One West Sixty-fourth Street[1] [New York City]   Sunday, January 4, 1931

Darling:

I am out on the balcony in the noon sunlight, all wrapped up, and it's surprisingly warm—not California warm, of course, but doing very well for N.Y. I miss you even more on Sunday, but I don't know how to express it and I won't try. Your grand letter from Chicago was so full of all the things I can't put in words;[2] I love you says so little.

So let me give you the news. All morning I have been playing with the Springfield Museum—a new scheme.[3] I don't know whether it is better or not. I will have to draw it out this afternoon. Then I will tell you about it. . . .

Yesterday Henry Wright and I planned out the work that must be done to make an exhibition of Radburn drawings at Berlin.[4] Cerone, a city planner of Chicago, called and told us of a plan of Illinois that he is to make for the State Chamber of Commerce, much along the lines of our plan for the State of New York. . . .[5]

Took a bus down Fifth Avenue, but at the library it got so jammed up with all the other buses in New York that I got out and walked. Visited Rosenfield at Macy's to see what hints for museum planning I could get from the display arrangements they are making in the new parts of the building. They are doing more constructive thinking than the museum people, but there is nothing definite to get hold of.

Then to the New School.[6] It is disappointing. The elliptical auditorium was interesting in drawing, but we wondered what would be done to make it acoustically possible, for the dome is the hardest form to treat. In making it a practical place for lectures, all the simplicity of form has been lost. There is nothing left. The library—many of the lighting fixtures and other details are exciting and suggestive—but most of the rooms seem bad in shape and arrangement. I must go back when there is less crowd to see the paintings.

Dinner at the Steins', then to Ethel's to say good-bye.[7] She reports that Jean Dixon says she would give anything to be in the opening at Los Angeles.[8]

I love you,
Clarence

1. Clarence and Aline had moved to the top-floor apartment overlooking Central Park at One West Sixty-fourth Street during the summer of 1930. Stein called it their "sky parlor." In this home they entertained their friends with sustained elegance. Here in Stein's "city planning atelier," the Regional Planning Association of America held many of its meetings. The Steins continued to live here until Clarence's death in 1975. Aline remained in the apartment overlooking the park and the city they both loved until her death in 1993.

2. Aline Stein was en route to Los Angeles as a principal player in the "coast company" of Moss Hart's first successful comedy, *Once in a Lifetime*. She had acted in its Atlantic City and Brighton Beach tryouts during the previous spring. The play was a Broadway hit after extensive rewriting by Moss Hart and co-author/director George Kaufman. Jean Dixon played the female lead in the Broadway opening. In the West Coast company, the quality of Aline's stage acting in this satire of the Hollywood film industry was instrumental in the getting her started on a long and successful Hollywood career. After her successful screen test, Warner Brothers offered her a five-year contract to act in films in Hollywood. This was the Steins' first extended series of separations.

3. Clarence Stein was involved in the Springfield, Mass., competition for the design of a new art museum.

4. For the 1931 Berlin City Planning Exhibit, Lewis Mumford and Catherine Bauer wrote the catalogue copy on Radburn.

5. Clarence Stein and Henry Wright, with the collaboration of other RPAA members, authored the landmark regional plan for New York State published in 1926. This plan was a significant early application of Patrick Geddes's ideas on regional development.

6. The new building at the New School had been designed by Joseph Urban.

7. Ethel Bernstein, sister of Aline Bernstein, a costume designer for Broadway plays.

8. Jean Dixon had played the role on Broadway, and Aline had acted in the first tryouts.

85   To Aline Stein

One West Sixty-fourth Street [New York City]   January 7, 1931

. . . Your telegram about your contract received yesterday sounded fine.[1] I am waiting [for] more detailed news. But I suppose you will find very little time for writing.

Yesterday, in spite of the rain, we started laying bricks at the Phipps apartment,[2] [which] meant that I had to take two trips over there to see samples.

Lunch with Lewis Mumford [in] the late afternoon to help judge the Beaux Arts drawings.[3] These are the problems worked out by the boys at architectural schools all over the country. They, most of them, have gone modern. Although their elevations look "functional" and all that, it is quite apparent that they think of the exterior of their buildings first and then make their plans squirm around to fit it. There were four hundred and fifty competitors. I helped judge from five thirty to half past ten and then gave up and went home to bed. . . .

Love,

Clarence

1. Aline's income at this time was for her stage acting in the West Coast company of *Once in a Lifetime*. She would make more in films. Lewis Mumford reported that she earned up to $52,000 for her six-month film-making stints in Hollywood after January 1932, when she signed the first of many contracts with Warner Brothers.

2. The Phipps Garden Apartments, founded and managed by the Society of Phipps Houses organized by the steel magnate Henry Phipps, were being built on the tennis-court site at Sunnyside Gardens in Queens, which the CHC had sold to the Phipps organization.

3. At this time most North American schools of architecture were members of the U.S. École des Beaux Arts, which wrote programs for architectural problems for all of the members. Several times each year the best designs from each school were submitted in a competition that was usually juried in New York City. This system, which had started early in the century, continued until the post–World War II era, when contemporary or modern architecture became the norm.

86   To Aline Stein

Hotel Schenley, Pittsburgh, Pa.   January 20, 1931

Dear Aline:

Just arrived and bathed, all ready for a day of talk. Henry and I are here to confer with the director of the Buhl Foundation this morning [and] report to the directors this afternoon,[1] then with the Pittsburgh Chapter of the AIA. I'll give them a talk on Radburn and then, God permitting, take the train for New York City. Some program, but the sun is shining in Pittsburgh, so we feel that anything can be done, even find time to see some relatives. . . .

I returned home to hold a meeting with Henry Wright and Herbert Emmerich,[2] whose criticism of our Pittsburgh plans (particularly financial) we wanted. It is the first time I have seen Herbert since you left. He has been having a hard time. His family's fortune has been hit hard, [and] his uncle, who [is] apparently the financial captain of their ship, quit and went abroad. Herbert is apparently trying to salvage the ship. He is cheerful about it.

All my love,
Clarence

1. Clarence Stein and Henry Wright had just been retained by Charles F. Lewis, executive director of the Buhl Foundation, as consultants on their housing program, site planning, and schematic unit design for a housing development for white-collar clerical workers. This project was later named Chatham Village. It was designed in collaboration with Ingram and Boyd, Pittsburgh architects, and is often cited for the excellence of the planning of its hillside site.

2. Emmerich, a civil engineer, played a major role in the design of Radburn and was perhaps the originator of the idea of total separation of automobile and pedestrian traffic. See Clarence S. Stein, *Toward New Towns for America* (New York: Reinhold Press, 1957), 38.

---

87 To Aline Stein

[New York City]   January 25, 1931

My darling:

. . . It is a bleak, cold day, so I am staying in. . . . Over in the park a small group of youngsters are skating. Otherwise, the view is anything but gay. It's all dirty brown.

I was up late this morning and, outside of reading the papers, have devoted myself to calculating minimum rentals for New York apartments on the basis of money borrowed by the municipality. Even the cheaper rate is not enough to meet the problem of the greater part of those who need homes, as the socialists claim.[1] Shall I make a fight for [the] same point of view (which most people will call insane), or shall I just design museums?

Talking of museums, Lee came to the office yesterday afternoon and was almost as enthusiastic as if he had made my Springfield design himself! But what do you say? That is what really counts. . . . Remember it is much better than when I sent it to you.

With all my love,
Clarence

1. Stein probably did not consider himself a socialist at this time, but rather a liberal democrat, labor party member, or independent. His political commitments shifted to the left after 1932, and by 1936 he was voting for Norman Thomas, the Socialist Party's perennial candidate for president.

88 To Aline Stein

Home [New York City]   February 1, 1931

My darling:

Last night I went to bed very early, and so, though it is not much after eight on a Sunday morning, I am sitting in our sunshine, but not on the balcony. It's too cold.

I stopped at the Temple on the way down town to look at some new clerestory windows with Charlie.[1] Not so good.

Much of the day was spent in finishing the drawings for the competition and preparing sketches for Pittsburgh. The museum [design] goes to Springfield Monday. I still am strong for it. Lee [Simonson] and Charlie Butler came in to see it late in the afternoon and enthused. I said that I knew it was all right because you liked it. . . .

Henry will go to Pittsburgh on Monday evening. We are working out some very interesting groupings of houses climbing up hills. It is wonderful how much more freedom one has once one escapes the freestanding house.

At the end of the morning, I went up with R. D. Kohn to locate a new junior school at Fieldston.[2] It looks as though I would be able to go right ahead with the drawings, and I think it will be a [really] modern school, just hanging on the top of a hill. Isn't that grand? . . .

Have they tried you out for the movies yet?[3] Thank goodness, they can't keep you. . . .

Yesterday was a pretty good day, but far, far from perfect. It lacked the one essential—a letter from you. You spoil me, so when there is no word . . . well, I am going to talk to you tonight. Nothing else matters.

My darling,

Clarence

1. Charles Butler, Robert Kohn, and Clarence Stein were the architects of record for Temple Emmanu-El. Stein and Butler were the associates in charge. Much of the decorative work seems to have been designed by Stein.

2. The same associated architects had designed the original Fieldston School building in 1925.

3. Aline was offered a screen test by Warner shortly after the West Coast company of *Once in a Lifetime* opened in Los Angeles.

89 To Aline Stein

[New York City]   February [3], 1931

Dear Aline:

It is a gray and lonely morning.

Yesterday [I was] at the office all morning and at Sunnyside in the afternoon. The apartment is growing up beautifully.[1]

Took dinner at Lillie's. Afterward, Will showed up.[2] He is a changed man. He told us so. A new year's resolution and now I forget just what his new and noble character is, but he still does most of the talking. The party broke up early, half-past eight or so, as both Lillie and Arthur had to go downtown.[3]

Tomorrow evening I am to run a joint meeting of the Architectural League and the New York Chapter of the AIA. Subject: Shall we live in horizontal or vertical cities? I am having quite a time trying to decide how to introduce the subject in such a way as to prevent it running all over the lot. How can I prevent the argument from centering around the question of how tall must a building be to give the best return on land values rather than how high should they be to serve most efficiently for business and to give [the] most satisfactory and happy lives. I have thought I might say that we will not talk of New York but of a new city that each might create as did Peter the Great. In it, land values, lot sizes, and ill-fitting street systems would not exist. Hood and Walker are to lead off for the verticals, Ackerman and Wright for the horizontals. . . .

Which is all the news, excepting that I love you.

Clarence

1. The Phipps Apartments, designed by Stein, were under construction on the site of the former tennis courts at Sunnyside.

2. Stein's brother William had a difficult time making a living. By the early 1930s he seems to have developed a drinking problem.

3. Stein's sister Lillie and her husband, Arthur Mayer, a film theater owner/manager.

90   To Aline Stein

[New York City]   February [5], 1931

My darling:

The meeting last night of the AIA and the Architectural League . . . was a bit flat. They seemed to be talking all around the subject but seldom about it. I am enclosing notes on what I said in opening, more or less. Walker was supposed to speak in favor of the vertical city but got off on a long spiel about the joys of living in his little one-story cottage and then, in a quite disconnected way, tried to show how much more economical and better, too, it would be to put much of Radburn in one building. Wright's talk was not clear, even to me. On the other hand, Hood could not be misunderstood. He definitely believes that tall buildings crowded together make the best places to carry on the business of the world. He talks well, colorfully, and almost persuades you that a "very nice congestion" is . . . desirable. Ackerman did not seem to give much help in putting us on the right track,[1] and so it went on until Lee Simonson got up, and then there was some light, a flame. You can't do anything until you do away with private ownership of land,[2] that kind of thing, you know, but so colorfully expressed. So flamboyantly, Lee striking out all over but holding, carrying his audience.

Back in the rear of the room was Van Allen, and I remembered that unrestrained, rich Hebraic expression of self and ideas [that] so riled so many of the restrained crowd that dined at the Pres . . . back in Paris. Van Allen [is] particularly [good at expressing himself].

Henry Wright came here for the night. He is up.[3] Herbert Emmerich is also coming for breakfast, and then we are going over to Sunnyside.

Darling, I love you,

Clarence

1. Frederick Ackerman was an RPAA member and disciple of Thorstein Veblen. Ackerman lived with his wife in the apartment just beneath Aline and Clarence's at One West Sixty-fourth Street. His commitment to "technocracy" was obsessive. A graduate of the Cornell University College of Architecture, Ackerman was very successful. His work included an excellent overall plan for student housing at Cornell and some of Cornell's most elegant dormitories. His work was frequently published. Ackerman had served as chief designer for the U.S. Housing Corporation in World War I under Robert D. Kohn. During that period he had written extensively on housing in the *Journal of the American Institute of Architects.*

2. This radical thinking was in character. Ackerman, Simonson, and Stein (and probably most of the members of the RPAA and their close friends) were followers of Henry George in his arguments against "unearned value increments" in urban land. Ackerman, who had graduated from Cornell with a degree in architecture in 1905, had been influenced by the teaching of the economist Thorstein Veblen, who taught there briefly during Ackerman's course of study. Ackerman first developed a working relationship with Stein in Washington at the end of World War I, when Ackerman was working in the first federal housing program. Ackerman designed some of the houses and apartments at Sunnyside and Radburn from 1926 to 1932.

3. Apparently, Wright had been ill. While Henry Wright was teaching at Columbia, he frequently stayed overnight in the city (sometimes at the Steins'), returning to his farm in New Jersey on weekends. In a later letter to Aline (in the spring of 1932), Clarence reports that Henry's son and son-in-law had lost their jobs. Henry derived his income from an occasional lecture in addition to his modest Columbia University salary, and so his family all lived off the produce of the farm. Emmerich, an engineer, was closely associated with Stein in the work at Sunnyside, Radburn, and the Phipps Garden Apartments.

---

91   To Aline Stein

New York City   February 14, 1931

Aline dear:

It is one of those damp, murky days we hate so much. All the snow has been washed away in the park, and it's just a mud hole.

Yesterday morning, I took Mr. Lehman of the Phipps Estate over to see the apartment. He is growing enthusiastic but still has the fear that I will put some ornament or pattern on it that might shock the taste of the tasteless. I can't tell you what joy the job is beginning to give me. It *is* good! I wish you could see it.

The day was filled with a variety of jobs. The Pittsburgh housing [Chatham Village] is taking interesting shape. We are just climbing all over the hills with our little houses. We are making some show drawings of Radburn, which means working out, at least in tentative form, many parts of the plans about which we have merely theorized in the past.[1] This is good fun even though not profitable. In fact, nothing is very profitable just now, but what is the difference? We have a reserve and a long future.

After office, about six, Henry and I went to see Charlie Chaplin. They are running it continuously for 50¢ and one dollar. Long lines were waiting in front of both gallery and main entrance. We met the [Charles] Aschers, who were in town to see [the play] *Once in a Lifetime* in the evening. I bet your appearance in California is boosting the New York box receipts.[2] The Charlie Butlers went the other evening and enjoyed. But of Charlie Chaplin,[3] the latter half of whose film we finally saw, of course, he himself is everything you say, but the film is a long time ago, I think. . . .

I love you,

Clarence

1. This was probably the overall plan of Radburn used as an illustration (figure 27) in *Toward New Towns for America* (Univ. Press of Liverpool, 1951), 50.

2. During the West Coast run, Aline had an opportunity to see some of Clarence's 1920s architectural work for Goodhue: the California Building, the arts building at the San Diego World's Fair, the Marine Corps base, and the Naval Air Station at San Diego.

3. This film, *City Lights,* Chaplin's fifth film as the "little fellow," was a silent film masterpiece, though made during the first years of the use of sound in films. It was eloquent, moving, and funny.

---

92 To Aline Stein

New York City   February 21, 1931

Aline darling:

At the office my time has been devoted mainly, for some time past, to the general plan of Radburn. The preparation of drawings for the Berlin Exhibition has been the immediate incentive, but the main objective was to have a completed plan of Radburn. And that we have at last. I don't doubt that it will change and grow. But at least it is a unified, thought-out plan, and I think a damned good one.

But that was only one step. The difficult thing was to get [Alexander M. Bing], to whom anything that looks beyond the next move is theoretical, to accept it. And that we did yesterday. He accepted it for exhibition purposes, but he will get so accustomed to seeing it around that it will be *his* plan of Radburn. A little more work on certain details of the big plan and we can retire at anytime, if necessary, feeling that we have said our word, set the mold, and that others can carry on. . . .[1]

All my love,
Clarence

1. Stein believed at this stage of the depression that much more of Radburn would be built. A few years later, the balance of the land assembled for the project was sold off. Today the residential layout of the area surrounding Radburn is conventional post–World War II subdivision.

---

93   To Catherine Bauer

New York City   February 25, 1931

Dear Miss Bauer:

Both Mr. Wright and I were very much interested in your excellent article on Frankfort housing. It seems to me a very clear, concise statement. There are just one or two points that I questioned. The main one is your statement in regard to Satellite Cities on page 4. I do not feel quite as positive about the impossibility of ultimately being able to carry on developments of this kind around certain of our cities, Philadelphia, for instance.

You speak on page 8 of "Mr. Stein's plan of Radburn." It should be Stein and Wright.

Mr. Wright has just left on a short lecture tour. When he returns I hope that it will be possible for you to lunch with us so that we may have an opportunity of discussing the Frankfort scheme and other things that you saw abroad.

I am returning your manuscript herewith.

Cordially yours,
Clarence S. Stein

---

94   To Aline Stein

[New York City]   February 28, 1931

My darling:

The sunshine in our window is so warm that if you were here you could imagine yourself in California, and would not that be perfect for me?

Last night I heard Frank Lloyd Wright speak, but first I dined with the Butlers. It was nice. I feel more and more at home there, in spite of the stuffy surroundings. And a good dinner, beautifully served with appropriate drinks, does help the flow of spiritual (as the French might put it) conversation. Lee could not go with us to the lecture. She has pretty nearly lost her voice.

Although Wright has given two or three other talks in New York this week, the auditorium of the New School was crowded to the doors, with an audience that paid to get in! That speaks well for architecture. Henry Churchill acted as chairman and did it graciously.[1] Wright, a stocky, handsome chap with a great head and much white hair, read his talk. They say he talked extemporaneously the night before when he fought with [Raymond] Hood about the Chicago Fair. I wish I had heard that. His reading was poor, and I don't know just what he was shooting at. I seem to have heard it before. . . .

Then I went to the reception that the Churchills were giving for Wright, way up in the sky, at 1 University Place. It is a two-story apartment with terraces at both levels from which you got breathtaking views of the moonlit skyline. Inside [is] but partially furnished, with bookcases climbing up sides of walls; lights, long lines of them, set in ceiling; and angular things—very well designed, but so unlived-in. It looks as though the angles never would come off: fine for receptions or to illustrate magazines. But home, no. [The Lewis] Mumfords, [Douglas] Haskells,[2] and others of interest [were] there, and the bubbling Lee [Simonson], who considers you one of the world's great letter writers.

Just room to say I love you.

[Clarence]

1. Henry Churchill was an architect and community planner, who was later associated with Henry Wright, Albert Mayer, and Alan Kamstra in the design of Greendale, the New Jersey Greenbelt Town not built in FDR's Resettlement Administration program. Churchill was the author of *The City Is the People* (New York: Reynal and Hitchcock, 1945).

2. Douglas Haskell was soon to become editor of *Architectural Forum*.

---

95   To Aline Stein

New York City   March 1, 1931

My darling:

After a week of beautiful sunshine, today, when I was to sit out on our balcony, it had to be raining. The view across the park is misty and mysterious.

Last night it sparkled and then grew a little hazy, but the air was balmy and we were able to go out on the balcony from time to time. There was quite a crowd of us: Hilda Swarthe, the Ernsts, the Moskowitzes and son Joseph Israels for dinner— then afterward Lee Simonson. It was one of these parties that just rolled along with a lot of talking; the sad end of the *World,*[1] what its editors will do, the theater, the censor, Frank Lloyd Wright, the theater ticket racket, with "Mom" and Henry M.[2]

competing to give the latest inside dope until Lee came and swept them all off their feet. Lee was talkative, and after he had talked of the whiskey which I received as sole fee for [architectural] services to the Midtown Hospital, he held the floor against all competitors. Mrs. M. had warned me when I invited her in the morning that they were going to a concert. They were still here at twelve-thirty.

Thomas Adams came in to see the plan of Radburn yesterday noon and liked it.[3] I told him that if his report on housing was as reported, I did not agree with it and thought it did not face the problem. He said there were sentences that insinuated things that could not be safely expressed. His thinking grows muddied.

Al Bing is again putting his mind on Radburn. We had a long talk a few days ago. He is more and more bewildered. We fuss too much. Architecturally, we may be all right, but it isn't good architecture people buy. They want joy. We have got to do things differently. I feel that the end is probably in sight, and now I do not care. The plan of Radburn is made at last. The mold is there. I want to write a report, a guide for the future, and then it will not matter if I get out or not so much. I feel free at last.

Your letter that suggested that the play may not run forever was the best news I have had for a long time.

If you were only here . . . but tonight I will hear your voice, my beloved.

Clarence

1. The *New York World,* an old and respected newspaper, had closed that week.

2. Henry Moskowitz was Belle's husband and also became her biographer.

3. Adams, the English town planner, headed the preparation of the *Regional Plan for New York and Environs.* He disagreed with all of the ideas of the RPAA, and they frequently did not agree with his.

---

96   To Benton MacKaye

[New York]   March 5, 1931

Dear Ben:

. . . Aline has been away since the first of January. They suddenly asked her to go out to Los Angeles to play in *Once in a Lifetime* and, although she had only twelve hours' notice, she was so delighted to have an opportunity to start acting again that she went. The play is a big success, and there is no telling how long it will run. Aline promises me that she will try to get back by the 15th of April. In the meantime, naturally I am very lonely. Why don't you come down to New York for a week or so and stop with me? . . . [Y]ou could do your writing just as well up at the apartment. We will be able to get the whole crowd together, as Stuart is back from Mexico.

Among many other things that Lewis and I want to talk over with you are the plans for the Virginia conference. It is definitely fixed for the week of July 6th.

Brownlow is to act as chairman, and we are trying to get Governor Roosevelt to start the thing off. You probably saw the program that he has sent to the Legislature of the State of New York in regard to a land survey and gradual taking over of the unused farmland for forestry purposes. The proposal is a big step in the direction of carrying out our plan for the State of New York. The *New Republic* had an editorial comment on this and pointed out the possibilities of national planning in case Roosevelt should happen to be elected president. . . .

I am much interested to hear more of your Washington work. I was delighted to see the start of your New England history in *New England*, as well as the reprint of "Super By-Pass for Boston."

Do try to come down and keep me company for a little while.[1]

As always,
Clarence

1. Clarence obviously missed Aline very much and needed the company of old friends. MacKaye's proposal was for a half-circle bypass with a five- to ten-mile-wide park strip between the one-way "motorways" and included a public foot trail in this wide park. It was published in the *Boston Globe* in February 1931.

97 To Aline Stein

New York City   March 6, 1931

Aline dear:

Last night I went downstairs to dine. Quite informal. Frederick Lee [Ackerman] wore his house slippers, but the stage is not set for formality. There is such dignity and finish, too [much] perfectness. As we sat among the furniture after dinner, Ackerman said, "Well, I passed Bolshevism a couple of years ago." I thought, "The stage director has slipped. This is the set for the scene depicting the lush, beautiful, overripe civilization."

I returned to the bare and empty rooms above. Well, I guess you are right. Some of the furniture can stand re-covering and, well, an extra chair or so, perhaps. But I like my garret, and after April 15th, there will be nothing that need be added to it.

Yesterday morning was difficult. Alone with Al Bing for hours. His spirit has fallen low. He has been hit hard by the financial crash, but that does not seem to worry him so much any more, . . . he has so much company. He still has enough left to hold on to his many homes and possessions, but it's City Housing that worries him. Can it weather the storm? He is no longer able to keep it afloat with his hundreds of thousands, and he can think of nothing but mistakes of the past, of which he takes the blame for having accepted poor advice. I've visited the housing development of our principal competitors and saw how much vulgarity they were able to sell for less than our prices, and Al said, "I know when I am licked." And I, who know only when not to say anything, remained silent.

I don't know just how it will all end—what form of retreat Al will attempt (if retreat is possible). I know my own feeling has changed. I will help if I can. In spite of his muddle-mindedness, Al has given himself to a big work in the biggest way he knows how. I will remain true to him, as long as he remains true to his ideals, but I will not join the retreat.[1]

On the way back we were able to forget Radburn troubles for a while and talked of more personal things: of how little the Ethical Society means to either of us; of how Florence [Bing], with no children left to worry about and her interest in charities and other things left in the past, knows not where to turn for life; of Robert [Kohn], his qualities and weaknesses—and the barrier that had grown up between Al [Bing] and me somewhat weakened. . . .

I send you all my love,

Clarence

1. Stein, apparently soon after this letter was written, dissolved his business arrangements with Bing and the City Housing Corporation because he did not want to participate in the sale of its assets, which were mainly its land at Radburn.

---

98   To Aline Stein

New York City   March 19, 1931

Aline darling:

Today's letter, which should have been written this morning, has had to wait until evening. This has been a busy day and I overslept, or rather I got up just in time for eight-thirty breakfast. We both will have to start to revive our habits if we are going to get back to breakfast together, but that is over a month from now.

So you are not coming home until the 25th. I dare not say anything. Perhaps I may be tempted to take another job, and then I would not be able to go abroad.[1] This busy day has been spent with Mr. Lewis, who represents the Pittsburgh crowd. It looks as though the Buhl Foundation may want Henry and me to go ahead with the job instead of having it done by a local architect.[2] It is an interesting job and the office is more than broke, but I want to go away with you, so I have my problems also.

Yesterday, Henry and I had luncheon with Miss Bauer, who has been in Germany studying the new architecture. She is a keen young person whom I met at Lewis Mumford's. She studied to be an architect but has taken to writing.[3] Her descriptions made me long to see the New World the Germans have created since the war. Shall we go my love, in spite of everything?

Clarence

1. Clarence was planning to attend the 1931 meetings of the International Federation for Housing and Town Planning (IFHTP) in Berlin and Stockholm, where the latest Radburn plans would be on exhibition. Aline had proposed that they revisit the Cotswolds (where they had spent part of their wedding trip), London, Paris, and Vienna before and after the Berlin meetings, but Clarence, worried about the expense of preparing the exhibit drawings of Radburn and "getting more and more behind financially," suggested that they should "somewhat limit [their] extravagance."

2. This did not happen. The Pittsburgh architectural firm of Ingram and Boyd were the principal architects, with Stein and Wright serving as consulting architects and site planners.

3. Catherine Bauer was actually a graduate of Vassar, but she spent her junior year at Cornell University studying architecture.

---

99   Memo to FDR for RPAA

[New York City]   March 23, 1931

"MEMORANDUM TO GOVERNOR FRANKLIN D. ROOSEVELT SUGGESTING A REGIONAL PLANNING BOARD IN THE EXECUTIVE DEPARTMENT"[1]

In your message of January 26th to the Legislature, formulating a definite land policy for the whole State, in regard to farming and forestry, you showed how "such a survey and land policy will help us to attain the highest maximum efficiency in planning farm to market roads, rural electrification and telephones, and scientific allocation of school facilities." You also pointed out how closely tied up with this survey is the question of local land assessment.

Should not this program be broadened to take in [industries other] than farming and forestry? The same wasteful, unguided tendency that you have pointed out in the development of land exists also in the location of industry and living quarters. The tendencies of an era in which concentration of the industrial population was made necessary by the limitations of steam power have been continued far into a period in which a much wider distribution of population throughout the state is not only practical but desirable.

The present is an ideal time for State planning for the purposes of assisting industry as well as farming. Since the War, the need of a complete change in the economic and social pattern of the State has existed as never before in its history. The development of long-distance transmission of electric power and of motor transportation are but two of the factors that have been potential possibilities of completely remolding the State.

The industrial depression has led all thoughtful men to consider whether the wasteful, unplanned development of industry can be continued. The extent to which industrial costs are related to the location of industry and homes is only vaguely understood. But those who have studied this problem deeply are more and more convinced of the difficulty of solving the housing and recreational problems of workers in the old congested centers. They feel convinced that there is, in the development of plans for new communities, much better opportunity of economically working out the social problems that have developed in this new age of the motor and increased leisure.

Cities such as New York have already passed the limits of efficiency. They are becoming increasingly less desirable places for industry and, particularly, for living. The impetus of the past will continue the growth of New York and other great cities for some time to come. But, ultimately, the disadvantages, the multiplying costs, and the difficulties of carrying on work and of sane or healthful existence will reach the breaking point. In some industries, the advantages of the larger cities have already been counterbalanced by their waste. As cities grow, more industries will be so affected. There are many signs that we are approaching the end of concentration as typified by New York and entering a period of decentralization.

In fact, decentralization of population and industry is already beginning to take place. New methods of roadway transportation less confined to the valley grades [and] new methods of power generation and power distribution offer new possibilities to revive old towns and build new ones in long-forgotten and dormant areas. Desirable changes of this kind can be encouraged and accelerated if the State so directs its energies and plans its public facilities.

The need of a master plan to which, at least, the activities of the State shall conform is obvious. The location of roads, power houses, and schools, as well as parks, hospitals, prisons, and all other buildings constructed for the State should be planned to conform to the future location of population. It is, therefore, of utmost importance that the State be consistently studying the trend of growth both of industry and agriculture.

In the same way, the plans of county and local government expenditures should be controlled by the desirable development of the future. This again applies not only to roads, water supply, sewage disposal, but to all types of governmental structure.

It is true that there is a point at which effective control of the development of the State by governmental agencies ends and private initiative steps in. But there is no question that progressive leaders in industry and business welcome the information that can be collected and put at their disposal by the State. The State cannot dictate the policy of industry, but the coordination of State and industrial development will give us a sane and better-organized social and economic structure than the present planless development.

In 1926, the Commission of Housing and Regional Planning made a study of the relationship of the resources of the State to its economic history. The Commission, in its report, said,

"This is no academic study. Its purpose is the practical one of preparing for the future. This report is not a plan. It is a collection and analysis of some small part of the final data that will serve as a basis of future planning. In this study, the Commission has attempted to ascertain and measure the forces which have shaped the present state and to evaluate the new forces which are now altering the present mold. Its purpose is to find a basis for a plan for the future development of the State. A plan of the State is not a thing to be willed into being by any one man or Commission or power. It is the result of many forces—physical, economic, and social. Although it must rest on the unchanging physical conformation of the State, it is subject to constant revision as a result of changing habits and economic relations of men and of their ability, through better understanding or invention, to harness nature to their need.

"In carrying forward its studies, the Commission has been more and more impressed with the need of a permanent agency for planning the physical development of the State. At the present time, several State Departments are engaged in the preparation of unrelated plans. Coordination may best be accomplished by a Planning Board in the Executive Department.

"The Commission recommends the establishment of such a Board with the personnel composed of the heads of the several State Departments charged with the expenditure of funds appropriated for permanent public improvements and representatives of planning boards created under Chapters 267 and 539 of the Laws of 1926."

Such a Board should have as its chairman some citizen of the State who is not identified with any individual department, but who has a broad understanding of all the social and economic problems of the State.

The value of setting up a Board of this type is made more apparent, it seems to me, by your plans for a land survey. The coordination of these plans with the location of highways, schools, etc., for which you point out the need, would be an important work of such a Board. They should, at the same time, start a master plan for the State—a plan which would be a living, growing, and not a static affair.

If the portion of the General Municipal Law relating to the creation of Regional or County Planning Boards is strengthened, as is proposed by Senate Bill 1185, Int. 1075, these Boards will be given a more important role in the planning of the various regions of the State. This bill has been amended so that, although the Planning Boards are to make a comprehensive master plan for the entire area of their county or region, this plan will not deal with State projects. A State Planning Board would serve not only to coordinate the work of the Regional Planning Boards, but would harmonize them with the plans of the State.

Such a Board should be in the Executive Department. It has to do not only with public works, parks, and conservation, but with the whole policy of the State in regard to planning. If such a Board existed, it not only would serve to coordinate the various agencies, both governmental and private that are gradually remaking the plan of the State, but it would also help the Governor and the Legislature in formulating the budget so that the expenditures of the State would be of the greater permanent value.

Clarence S. Stein

1. This was the second of five proposals Clarence Stein made to New York governors to establish regional planning at the state level as a cabinet department. Stein's approach to Roosevelt on state regional planning policy was a logical continuation of the work on regional planning which he and other members of the RPAA had done for Governor Al Smith in the mid-1920s.

---

100   To Aline Stein

[En route to New York]   March 24, 1931

I am on the way back from Albany. I had lunch and a long talk with the governor, and I think he is a great guy, or a good actor, or both.[1]

We lunched in the Executive Chamber in the Capital. The governor's bowl of soup and cup of coffee was served on his desk; my lunch on the table next to it. We had towels as tablecloths and napkins, and the food from the restaurant in the basement would just about have passed muster at Child's. Roosevelt takes his noon meal at his desk because he doesn't want to leave headquarters while the legislature is battling upstairs and because it is such a task to move his crippled leg. You don't notice that he is an invalid, he is so full of life, unless you look under the desk at the brace on his leg.

He did most of the talking. His land policy (see the enclosed clipping) was only a first step. He wanted to find a way of reviving small industries in the farming sections so that the farmers would find something to do during the long winter months of unemployment. Those industries could be carried on in the old, deserted factory buildings to be found all over the state—left there since the days when steam power replaced water power and drew workers into the big cities. These industries should be run cooperatively. They would be experimental at first and might have to be assisted by some foundation.

His state land policy was applicable to the country as a whole. As we decreased farming in New York State, we would become more dependent on better production in the West and South. He spoke of Russia and how she was calling for large-scale imagination in national industrial planning. State planning—yes. Everyone was talking about the planning of the smaller elements: town planning, city planning, county planning. We must work from the bigger unit down—state planning. He had had it in mind right along. But in a governor, the political sense was of the utmost importance. He must not tell the whole tale at once, the public mind could not grasp it. First, the land policy, the small industry for the farmer's spare time, and then state planning. They must have an advisory State Planning Board in the Executive Department.

Now and then I got in a few sentences. How much did I suggest the subjects that led him to a point of view? I always seemed to be following along. He was speaking of the things I had come up to suggest before I had time to outline them, or did he grasp it from the suggestion of a word? He shook his head yes, yes, as he read my memorandum. "Some people would call it communism, I suppose. But the heads of our big industries would understand."[2]

I wonder—if his next visitor were a stand-patter, an individualist, government-mind-its-own-damned-business, what Roosevelt would he meet? But I have no right to say that. The only one I know is one of us. He and Stuart Chase and Lewis Mumford belong to the same gang.

The talk was interrupted from time to time by the secretaries hurrying in with telegrams, messages, or long reports of what the Senate was doing. If I did not know what [a] joke the legislature upstairs is, I would have felt myself in the center of things. Anyhow, it would make good theater, Aline Stein. He probably will go to Virginia, though he could not promise. Anyhow, it was worth the day's trip. . . .

[Clarence]

1. This letter is less optimistic about FDR's agreement with the RPAA's stated planning proposals for New York than are Stein's subsequent letters to Aline about the same subject. It shows a keen politician's insights into Roosevelt's chameleon-like political persona. Many Roosevelt scholars have noted FDR's ability to persuade all of his advisors of complete empathy and agreement with all arguments, no matter how disparate. This quality of FDR's interaction with his advisors may have been one of his most effective political tactics. He anticipated their ideas and seemed totally with them as they tried to persuade him to their course of action.

2. Roosevelt was a strong supporter of government planning. After he was elected to the presidency in 1932, he established national planning and asked his uncle, Frederick Delano, to lead the formulation of his urban and regional policy. FDR's National Resources Planning Board was the strongest national planning unit that ever operated in the United States. One of the instruments of its policies was financial support for state planning organizations. Stein's effort to insert specific urban policy issues into Governor Roosevelt's agenda was not very successful. Later, Roosevelt incorporated in modified form some RPAA ideas for regional development into New Deal programs including the TVA, the Greenbelt Towns program of Rexford Tugwell's Resettlement Administration, the housing policies of Harold Ickes's Public Works Administration, and the proposed Housing Act of 1936. After his first term, however, FDR's national planning and urban development policies took a turn to the right.

101 To Benton MacKaye

[New York City]   March 25, 1931

Dear Benton:

Yesterday I went to Albany to ask Governor Roosevelt to take part in the Virginia conference. He seemed immensely interested, and I believe he will come if he possibly can.

I spoke about an hour with the governor, and I find that he has a very broad point of view in regard to state planning. In fact, he is already thinking in terms of national planning. You have seen his program for a land survey for the whole state, have you not? The next step he has in mind is that of setting up small industries in the farm areas. In short, it would be a return to the days of water power. He feels that something must be done to make use of those long winter months in which the farmers' time is unoccupied. He sees very clearly that a careful study will have to be made of the types of industries that can be carried on, on a small scale. I suggested that Ford had been doing this, but the governor says that, although Ford has written much about it, he has not carried out the theory. The governor would like to see these small industries possibly carried on in the actual factory buildings that were used in the time of water power and run on a cooperative basis. I think if we can find any examples of where this sort of thing has been tried, the governor would be glad to hear of them and they may be of help.

Of course, he has no idea of setting this up all over the state. He sees clearly that we must eliminate farming except in the most fertile areas of the state.

The third step he sees is state planning. As he says, everyone has been talking about the smaller elements, town planning, city planning, county planning. It is about time that we started at the top and worked down.

I gave the governor a memorandum, copy of which I am enclosing. It seems to me that there is a very good chance that he will set up some sort of Advisory State Planning Board before his term is over. . . .

I will probably see Brownlow tomorrow, and we will be able to work out plans for the Virginia Conference more definitely. I think it is going to be a great meeting.

As always,
Cordially yours,
Clarence

---

102 To Aline Stein

220 West 98th Street, New York City   March 30, 1931

Aline dear:

I must admit it, I have had an unhappy night. First you were coming home on the 15th of April, then the 28th, and now it depends on how much the movies offer. . . .[1] But I will say nothing until I receive your letter.

I was just looking forward, twenty-five years from now. I have just written my 999,999th letter to Los Angeles, and [I] hobble out to the balcony to look up at New York. And there on the thousandth floor of the Metro Goldwin Mayer building is Metro Goldwin Mayer himself, announcing that after twenty-five years, Aline MacMahon, in person, is returning to her old home town. Therefore, the president of the United States has decreed this Husband's Day, and the whole city blazes forth: Welcome, Aline! And there you land in your own plane on top of the last of the Eighth Avenue trolleys. I still know you; you look just like your pictures. Murphy is holding back the hordes of 65th Street with one hand and saluting you with the other, just as though you had left but yesterday. And you wave me a kiss. Oh, but I have a surprise for you! I let down my long white beard, so that you can climb up to me. You falter a minute. After all, you are an actress first. You turn to your director. He gives the signal. The cameras click. You climb to me!

I will wait for you. I love you so.

Clarence

1. Warner Brothers had given Aline a screen test early in March and then negotiated a multi-film contract.

---

103 To Aline Stein

Home   Sunday, April 12, 1931

Aline dear:

Out on our balcony, the sky all blue. The air is so clear that the buildings stand out, hard, naked, masonry. New York needs its mists to give it majesty. It's the mystery of its massing, not the endless repetition of detail, that gets you: mists or black night.

Friday night I was up on top of No. One Wall Street. There are observation balconies, all enclosed in glass. Reminds you at once of a ship, a ship moored high up above the world. The black masses hedging you around are fantastic—pyramids, rectangular forms of all sizes and [proportions,] seem to lift themselves up to you. Long lines of street lights parade toward you from all directions. Dramatic grandeur.

These balconies are outside the big hall at the very top of the fantastic structure that Voorhees, Gmelin, and Walker have just finished for the Irving Trust Company. The New York Chapter of AIA held its annual dinner there, and before and afterward we had [the] opportunity to examine this outstanding example of conspicuous work. After visiting the richly mosaicked vestibules and the colossal director's room with its golden ceiling, we finally reached the giantesque hall at the top of the building where the bankers rest after wrecking or making the fortunes of a nation. All of the architects were bowled over.

No one really put this over on a client. It was Walker's joke: he had the chap that designed the "Beggar of Baghdad" set build the Arabian Nights room just as a joke on the profession.[1] The walls wiggled all over the place, and so did [the] plan and outline of fireplaces, doors, everything. What's more, the walls were covered with an elaborately designed fabric (very expensive, I assure you) that also wiggles. The walls go up and up, oh, so high. They don't end, but somehow hang. Way up, there is a ceiling all covered with mother of pearl. Believe it or not, it's covered with mother of pearl. I am trying to find a simile to describe the place—a luxuriously fat and painted lady dancing the hoochy-koochy and dressed, overdressed, in nothing but five-and-ten-cent jewelry. Tip-top vulgarity.

What a setting for the final act of the red revolution: The Trial of Bankers. And then they will walk a plank out into dizzy nothingness above New York.

Now tell me about the movies.

I love you,
Clarence

1. Ralph Walker's designs for Irving Trust may be an architectural precursor of the type of design prank at which Philip Johnson became so proficient beginning in the mid-1960s. The best known are Johnson's "Tootsie Roll" forms for the science buildings at Yale and "giant Sheraton grandfather clock" form for the AT&T corporate headquarters building on Madison Avenue.

---

104   To Aline Stein

[New York City]   April 15, 1931

Aline, my darling:

I can't write today, dear.

Now there is only you—otherwise, the world would be empty.[1] She loved you so. You were so much to her. I am sure you made up for all I could never give of myself. *Regretons nous jamais.* Sometimes it is so hard.

Clarence

1. Clarence's mother had died very unexpectedly the day before.

---

105   To Aline Stein

May 3, 1931

My darling:

What do you suppose I have been doing all this beautiful morning? I have been seated here in the living room reorganizing and rewriting a talk I am to give tomorrow evening on the history of Jewish architecture. I have found it a fascinating subject and quite different than I had thought. The form of building that we have in the Temple Emanu-El, which is so much like a theater, with auditorium and stage, is of very modern derivation. The ancient form of the orthodox synagogue has persisted for 2,500 years or more. It is found in the old examples that are being excavated in Galilee, and the identical form of plan exists in the Portuguese Synagogue on Central Park West, in which I will speak. It is very lovely. . . .

Between the reading desk and the ark is a large open space for processional and ceremonies. Real pageantry, real beauty is possible in such a setting.

Research work has been done by Miss Bauer. Did I write to you about her? I met her at Lewis Mumford's some months ago. A youngster who studied architecture but took to writing, instead. She went to Germany last year and studied the modern housing, particularly in Frankfort. She sent an article on the subject (quite socialistic in character) into a competition run by the magazine *Fortune,* which asked for something under the title of "Art in Industry." The big department store in Pittsburgh financed the competition expecting to get a nice story about how the [knickknacks] they sell are made. Instead, [Norman] Bel Geddes, who was on the jury, insisted on giving them Miss Bauer's story. She was here for dinner last night and has an intelligent young mind. You will like her.

Day before yesterday the Empire State Building opened. I climbed, or rather was lifted, to the so-called 102nd floor up in the so-called mooring mast . . . .

In the evening, Lee and Lillie for dinner. Then to the Brooklyn Museum to see a very fine show of modern furniture, fabrics, photographs, etc. Lee is president of the association that put it on. . . .

All my love

Clarence

---

106   To Benton MacKaye

[The *Europa*]   May 15, 1931

Dear Ben:

Less than a week after Aline returned from Hollywood, we sailed for Europe. We wanted to be together for a while and get away from things. Besides, we wanted to see the new world that is being created in Germany.

I am sorry I have not had a chance to keep you posted in regard to the Virginia meeting the week of July 6th. I asked Lewis to do so just before I left, and I suppose you have heard from him. It promises to be a bully good talkfest. I am enclosing the present tentative program. Most of the speakers have promised to play their part, and there will be [a] chance for some good differences of opinion: Goodrich and Henry Wright, Mackenzie, and Lewis [Mumford]. At first we thought of having only the Southerners speak on the cultural aspects, [so] they could argue as to whether the South should stand pat or attempt to meet the cultural problems of the machine age. But we felt that, although the main time of the morning should be devoted to this, some other region should be brought in (New England, for instance) and, of course, you are the one to handle that. I [will] talk it over with Lewis if he has not already written to you. I think the expenses of the speakers are paid, if that makes any difference.

. . . On your way to or from, we hope you will stop at 1 W. 64th St.

Aline sends affectionate greetings,

As does

Clarence S

[P.S.] I have just read an inspiring little book, *The Russian Primer: Tale of the Five Year Plan,* written for Russian children. It makes you and I feel as though we were the children. Our regional plans are all hedged in by private ownership and selfish private interests. So we dip and turn 'til there is nothing but a shadow or a hope left. They can plan. They *have* planned. So big and sane that the rest of the world looks foolish.

Perhaps they will not succeed. Perhaps the Russian people have weaknesses of character—inability to organize or to become technicians. I don't know. But that does not prove that their kind of planning is not the only way out for civilization. I think it is.

CS

107   To Lewis Mumford

July 17, 1931

Dear Lewis:

. . . I did not stay for Saturday morning, but I hear from Ascher that there was a fairly good crowd. Brownlow read Stuart's paper.[1] It is too bad he was not there to round off the week's discussion.

The two days you missed were very valuable. I have the papers and will either keep them here for you or send them to you, whichever you wish. Thursday was particularly good. Fletcher and Barr both gave well-rounded talks. Barr's was a beautiful piece of literature. Benton certainly looked and spoke like a Yankee after the two Southerners. He was good, but a little bit too long. He stuck to the subject of culture most of the time but, of course, insisted on getting in the townless highway, which he connected up by saying it was the means of preventing the metropolitan civilization from flowing through the Shirley Centers.[2] The room was crowded; in fact, every seat was taken, and there were a good many standees. Brownlow kept the discussion well in hand. I am sorry you weren't there to take part.

Mackenzie made the Friday meeting worthwhile. I must say I haven't the slightest idea just what Odum was talking about. Mackenzie had a greater collection of figures than even Goodrich has ever played with,[3] and one could get a little meaning out of them. The statistics had to do mainly with the flow of population and showed that the actual trend still is toward the big metropolitan centers and that they are absorbing the population of the country even quicker than I had thought. He has an interesting, clear, snappy type of mind. It didn't appeal to Fletcher at all. I walked over to the Commons with Fletcher after the meeting with the idea of lunching together but, when I told him that I had an engagement with Mackenzie, he said, "That statistics fellow! I don't want to meet him."

Friday afternoon, with the Blacks and Augurs, I drove down to Williamsburg. We got there too late to do very much sight-seeing until the following morning. It is a remarkable affair. They are going to have a modern museum of the Pennsylvania museum type, but on a gigantic scale. Along the main street, at the present time, there is a quaint mixture of old and new. Some of the typical twentieth-century boxes have not yet been destroyed. We spent the night in a large, shapeless, wooden building with the latest of modern plumbing and all that. We were told that this, along with everything else [that] did not speak of Colonial or Early Republican days, would be destroyed in a short time. It is all going to be fine if they can only induce the population to wear the costumes of the period.[4]

On Saturday afternoon we drove up to Washington. In all, we must have passed through 250 to 300 miles of Virginia in the two days.[5] After seeing the mean little farms, I can't, for the life of me, see how they are ever going to make Virginia an agricultural state, no matter how many of them "take their stand." It is true that I have not seen the Shenandoah Valley, but that is certainly not sufficient to support the whole state. My strongest impression of the week is that I was in a country more foreign than England. Their problems of the future seem even more difficult of solution than those of England. Virginia may have had a past, but I can't see that there is a great deal of it left except here and there in spots. England, at least, has a chance to carry on an old culture and civilization and can find some way of paying for it. Virginia, and I presume most of the South, has got to build anew. . . .

Let me know when you expect to be in New York again so that I can be sure to see you.

With kindest regards to you and Sophie.

Cordially yours,
Clarence

1. See Stuart Chase's papers in the Library of Congress. Some copies of the papers read at the Virginia Conference are preserved in the Clarence Stein Papers in the Cornell University Archives. They were never published. The collection includes papers by Lewis Mumford, Louis Brownlow, Franklin Roosevelt, Benton MacKaye, Barr, Fletcher, Mackenzie, Floyd Odum, and others. They are of very mixed quality. FDR's paper consisted mostly of anecdotes and truisms.

2. Shirley Center was Benton MacKaye's home village, and Stein used it as a metaphor for all small communities that needed protection from the ill effects of metropolitan civilization.

3. Goodrich was a Harvard professor whose professional work and research on planning and housing was an early effort to bring social sciences to bear on the subjects.

4. As we know, of course, Colonial Williamsburg did arrange for costumed people to staff some of the restored buildings in this museum/town.

5. Aline and Clarence motored in Pop Stein's Lincoln from the Virginia conference back to New York.

108   To Benton MacKaye

New York City   August 18, 1931

Dear Ben:

The Wisconsin State Planning job certainly does look interesting. There is no question that they are stepping off in the right direction, and you are just the man to help them. Is there anything I can do to arouse further interest on their part? If a letter from the secretary of the Regional Planning Association or former chairman or anything you want will do any good, let me know.

The same day that I received your letter, I had one from Lewis containing a copy of the Wisconsin Act and also a very interesting memorandum by John M. Gaus on "Land Use Policies." Lewis says that Gaus is La Follette's principal advisor. He certainly has a very clear understanding of the whole problem. I think it would be a good thing if Lewis wrote to Gaus that you are available for work of the kind they need done. I will suggest this to Lewis when I write to him today. . . .

I now have here at the office all of the Virginia Conference material (i.e., the talks as originally printed and notes of the stenographers [for] the speeches). There is a possibility that the whole may be put into a book of some kind. I had thought that possibly Lewis might be induced to edit such a book. Brownlow suggests Odum. What do you think of him?[1]

There is very little news here in New York. We have had an awful stretch of heat. Aline is acting for three weeks. She has been taking the same part in *Once in a Lifetime* that she did in California. I wish you were here to see her. She sends her best greetings, as does

Yours,
Clarence

1. Lewis Mumford agreed that Odum should edit the proceedings, but the conference proceedings were not published. Inspired by the conference, Catherine Bauer started an article on regional planning for the *New Republic*.

109   To Benton MacKaye

[New York City]   November 5, 1931

Dear Ben:

We have been wondering where you were last. Glad to hear that you are finally coming back to New York. . . .

Lewis and I have been considering the advisability of having a meeting of the Regional Planning Association. . . . One of the many things that we want to consider at this meeting is the drawing up of a memorandum to Governor Roosevelt in regard to new towns. He has appointed a Commission on Rural Housing. In doing so he expressed himself even more definitely than at Virginia in favor of decentralization and the forming of a new [towns] committee. Although he expresses the thing very much as old Ebenezer Howard would, Lewis and I doubt whether he understands just what it all implies. We think it would be worthwhile to write a memorandum which would set forth in as simple terms as possible just how to go about the forming of new communities and connect the whole thing with a regional plan for the state.

As always

Clarence

---

110   To Aline Stein

[New York City]   Friday, January 8, 1932

Aline darling:

I had a letter from Will today in which he told of the grand time he had at Palos Verdes. He certainly is appreciative. Have you seen any more of him? . . .[1]

Someday, if you have the time, go and see California Institute of Tech. again. Take a look at the Chemistry Annex, for which I am responsible. I was trying a decorative stunt on the north elevation. I don't know whether I altogether succeeded, but Lawrie's sculpture is interesting in detail.[2] Also, take a look at the library.

I am anxious to hear of the other movie part they are offering you, and how long it will take you?[3]

I haven't spoken about the Regional Planning meeting night before last. For dinner, at six-thirty, Ackerman, Aronovici,[4] Black,[5] [Henry] Wright, and Emmerich.[6] We had such a desire for . . . seniors talking before the others came at eight-thirty that I, for one, had lost much of my pep for the discussion of state planning and settlement of new communities. Others must have felt the same, for though we had the able assistance of R.D.K., Bright, Mumford, Greely of Boston (whose boy was here the last time and who had come over for the meeting),[7] and Miss Bauer, we did not settle these simple matters before the punch was served.

Russell Black stayed here for the night and left early the next morning.

I am dining with the Ackermans tonight, so you see, I am quite the gadfly.

And your adoring, etc., etc.,

Clarence

1. Clarence does not look forward to visits by his brother William.

2. The sculptor Lee O. Lawrie had worked with Augustus Saint Gaudins, taught at Yale and Harvard, and done much decorative sculpture for Goodhue's buildings at West Point. The sculpture Stein had retained him to do for the Cal Tech Chemistry Annex was inspired by Mayan or Aztec designs.

3. Aline's second film for Warner Brothers was *The Mouthpiece.* She did not like the script but, when the picture was released, she was pleased with the footage.

4. Carol Aronovici was an important addition to the RPAA membership. He was active in U.S. housing and planning policy in the 1930s and 1940s and authored several books on housing and community planning, including *Housing the Masses* (New York: John Wiley and Sons, 1939).

5. Russell Van Nest Black, planner and environmentalist, was a pioneer in state and metropolitan planning.

6. Herbert Emmerich was a civil engineer who had joined the Architects Associated firm. He participated in the site planning of all the major Stein and Wright projects and later was to become an important player in FDR's pre–World War II and "defense housing" policy.

7. Roland Greely was a landscape architect who taught city planning at Harvard.

---

111 To Aline Stein

[New York City]   January 14, 1932

Aline darling:

Meeting Diego Rivera was a memorable experience. He is a radiant personality. He is big and round, a face like the sun, and all smiles and kindness, a round body, but not fat, and trousers like round stove pipes—a great big boy, but a boy, all right. He knows what life means to him, and he seems to love the world and the path he has definitely chosen.

Lee had invited a dozen of us to meet him—all men. Even Caroline wasn't there. There was Littel, the two Biermans, Frank, Morice Ernst, and the like. The language spoken was French, as no one but Rivera seems to know Spanish, and he spoke a very passable French, better than most of us.[1] The talk was general until Lee passed the punch. Then he asked Rivera to speak, which he did quite simply and informally. I am tempted to tell you all, I found it so attractive, but it will keep until you come back. I got away about twelve-thirty. Oh, yes, one thing we talked about will interest you—Eisenstein's film of Mexico. Rivera has seen it and says it's wonderful. Shows the life of Mexico from south to north. Starts with the rich, beautiful, aboriginal life and leads on to the Americanized, Mexican-influenced civilization.[2]

Stayed home and wrote, most of the morning. . . . This noon to a luncheon to hear an old Scots-American builder's idea of a New Town. A group of real idealists talking of Utopia . . . all so crazy, and so much saner than reality.

Love to you.

All my love,
Clarence

1. Rivera studied art in Paris from 1911 to 1920. The Mexican mural painter worked on several projects in the United States in the early 1930s. His mural at the Detroit Institute of Fine Arts was denounced as irreligious, and his Rockefeller Center piece, "Man at the Crossroads," which included a portrait of Lenin, was eventually demolished. Later "Man at the Crossroads" was rec-

reated by Rivera in the Palace of Fine Arts in Mexico City. His murals at the New School in New York City have now been preserved and will remain in place.

2. Sergei Eisenstein's *Que Viva Mexico* (1931) was made in collaboration with Upton Sinclair. The film was to be apolitical, and the world rights were to be the property of Mary Sinclair. After eleven months of filming, Upton Sinclair interrupted the shooting on financial, political, and moral grounds and he sequestered the film. Eisenstein returned to Russia demoralized. He was received coldly and did not begin another film for four years. Some of the material he shot in Mexico was used in *Thunder over Mexico* (1933) and in two short films, *Death Day* and *Eisenstein in Mexico* (1934). Upton Sinclair later claimed that he ended his association with the Russian filmmaker because of pressure from his wife, Mary Sinclair, and her rich parents.

---

112   To Aline Stein

[New York City]   March 22, 1932[1]

Darling:

It was so good to hear your voice, even if it was such hard luck stories you had to tell. . . .

Al B[ing] phoned me today. Sorry he [cannot] be at the meeting Wednesday evening, at which Lewis is to discuss the *Plan of New York and Environs*. He hopes we will not combat too hard.[2] Thinks he might have to resign from the RPAA board. . . . He is also on the board of the [Regional Plan of New York], that is trying to put the plan over. (He admits he does not altogether approve of it.) Sez I, "Why not resign from their board?" "Oh no, those connections are too important to the City Housing Co." "The hell," sez I to myself.

But you want the real news.

This morning This evening

And both yours,
Clarence

1. Aline seemed to have made a quick (one-month) trip to New York City. We have no letters from Clarence to her or from her to Clarence from February 13 to March 22, 1932.

2. Mumford's article on the subject, published in the *New Republic* a few months later, was a scathing criticism of the plan, which generated a strong response from Thomas Adams.

---

113   To Aline Stein

[New York City] Thursday, March 24, 1932

Aline darling:

And now you are in California. Well, the sun shines here also, only it is having one hard time trying to get from behind those misty clouds.

Your letter from the late *20th Century* was so beautiful.[1] If I were only the Clarence you seem to see. And when you say it so wonderfully, I wonder and I step upon the clouds. And you, I never seem to be able to tell you why I love you so utterly.

Did you get the telegram I sent to Pasadena? If so, you know that Lewis Mumford knocked out Thomas Adams in the first round, to the delight of the Regional Planners.[2] Around the ring were Ackerman, Wright, Geddes Smith, Bruere, Gove, Aronovici, the Blacks (both of them), and Miss Bauer. Oh yes, and Bruce Bliven of the *New Republic,* for which Lewis is going to write the article on the Plan of New York and Environs. It is going to be strong stuff. Afterward, we had one of those famous Stein suppers for Lewis, the Blacks, Miss Bauer, and Henry Wright. . . . Henry slept here.

This housing meeting for the 13th of April is becoming a nuisance. Committee at my office yesterday. Endless detail. These women get all lost in the details: what kind of paper to use for the invitations, the dinner and the camp, stools for the meeting afterward, and how many will come, and how will we get money? I don't know whether they remember what it is going to be about or why.

I love you,

Clarence

1. He meant her letter from the *Twentieth Century Limited.* The train was running behind schedule.

2. The previous evening Stein had talked to the Greenwich House Housing Association on the role of government in housing. He thought it "could not be more incompetent . . . than the Lending Institutions." He reported to Aline that Edith Elmer Wood had been at the meeting "to help put the audience to sleep."

---

114   To Aline Stein

[New York City]   Thursday, March 24, 1932

Dearest:

Back to New York after a few hours in Albany—hearing by Governor Roosevelt on a Housing Bill. I was lined up with the Housing Board against the City, which made it somewhat complicated as I explained that I believed in the City going into housing but not this way. I went up to Albany with all the good citizens and came back with Ed Doyle,[1] who represents the interests, real estate and others. I must say that Doyle is the more amusing company, but I can't stand three hours of his constant chatter. So I have retired to the bar car.

The governor always gives [me] the impression of a sincere student of governmental problems.[2] He seems keen and alert and gave his decision in a decided manner. If I didn't know too much about him, he could have my vote. . . .

This morning, before I left the office at 11:00, I was busy for an hour proving [my case] to various people who I want to speak at that housing meeting of the

13th. [The] program is about full, but I am getting good and tired of it. How I wish there was some architecture to do!

I think I will go to Pittsburgh Sunday night with Henry Wright,[3] who is on his way west.

> I send you
> All my love,
> Clarence

1. Edward Doyle, New York City political figure.

2. Roosevelt was, as usual, well briefed, but Clarence Stein had returned to his skepticism about the political will of the Dutchess County patrician to carry out a radical national housing policy.

3. Both were consulting with the Buhl Foundation on the design of Chatham Village.

---

115   To Aline Stein

[New York City]   March 29, 1932

Aline dear:

Manhattan Transfer! Home again, home again. No, home is in California now. Home is you.

I arrived in Pittsburgh an hour and a half or so late. We got into a bad snowstorm during the night. Henry Wright had taken an earlier train and was waiting. So, with Mr. Lewis, the architect Boyd, and the landscape man,[1] we went up to Chatham Village, which is what they now call the Burke development. It sits up on a hilltop overlooking a park. The group of brick houses are simple in design but charming, partially because of the careful way in which they have been related to the site and to each other and partially because of the infinite care with which every simple detail has been studied. The construction is very good. In fact, I think it is the best moderately priced housing development in America. Of course, it does not go quite as far as Radburn in meeting the problems of the motor age, but most of the Radburn ideas have been followed in Chatham Village.[2] And the people want something of that kind, . . . proved by the fact that the houses were 100% rented some three months before they were finished, with a long waiting list.

They are not ready yet to have us start with the second development, but they will be in a month or so. There is one job anyhow. . . .

> [Clarence]

1. Griswold was a Pittsburgh landscape architect who worked on the site planning for Chatham Village.

2. This excellent hillside housing for "clerical workers" was designed by the Pittsburgh architectural firm Ingram and Boyd, with Clarence Stein and Henry Wright as consultants and site planners. The project probably owes its conceptual excellence (large open spaces with nuclear in-

ternal parks) and its brilliant hillside site planning to the consulting services of Stein and Henry Wright and the work of Griswold as its landscape architect. It is still regarded as an excellent example of residential site planning.

---

116   To Aline Stein

[New York City]   Sunday, April 3, 1932

My beloved:

I was up early. I must get that article for the *Nation* written today.[1] Why is writing such a task for me? It seems so easy when I promise to do an article on a subject that I know. It is so hard to compress one's thoughts into words. And then I can get a little afraid of it. That's bad. Things seem so long in getting done. But I suppose worthwhile things are like that. Only I wish I had [the] talent of writing with ease.

It is a gray day. The park is surprisingly empty—not an automobile in sight for a few minutes. . . . There was a group of men on bicycles with bright sweaters, and for some reason it took me back many years to the Bois de Boulogne. I don't know why.

The office is an empty place on Saturday—none of the men there, but all the more chance for me to work. Lunch with Catherine Bauer, Lewis Mumford, and Stonorov, a young Russian who is practicing architecture here.[2] Lewis has been asked to write a series of articles for *Fortune* on housing and city planning in Europe. I think they are giving him a fairly good sum of money (from the point of view of a writer, not a movie actress).[3] He will probably have Miss Bauer collect certain of the information in Germany and Rosenfield in Russia. There may be money enough to make it possible for Sophie to go.[4] I think I dropped the hint that led to all this at Minna Cortina's the other evening.[5]

Darling, I am so lonely for you. If I were not all tied up in preparing for this meeting on the 13th, I would just jump into a train and go out to you. I can only send you all my love.

Clarence

P.S. Why don't you go to San Diego? If you do, see [Reginald] Johnson.

1. "Housing and Common Sense," *Nation,* 11 May 1932. Reprinted in *Readers Digest,* October 1932.

2. Oscar Stonorov later practiced architecture in Philadelphia from the early 1930s into the 1960s. He also worked with Catherine Bauer on housing policy in the mid-1930s.

3. Lewis Mumford also received a Guggenheim Foundation grant to support his research trip to Europe. Bauer worked with him for much of the trip during the summer of 1932.

4. Sophie Mumford seems to have joined Lewis in London near the end of the trip.

5. Archibald MacLeish, a *Fortune* editor, had discussed housing with Clarence at Minna Cortina's home.

117   To Aline Stein

Tuesday, April 5, 1932[1]

Aline dear:

Here is news, headline stuff, *I Have Fired Emma.* Of course, I haven't the slightest idea she will remain fired. But the mere fact that the deed was done, the words spoken, after all these years is news. I told her I was going out to California and that business was bad, so I would have to let her go, that she could have two weeks to look for another place. I don't know whether she expected it, but she said nothing but "Yes, Mister Stein." Perhaps she was stunned. More likely, she has guessed what the maid told on her this morning. Same old tale of cruelty, but when she told me, among other things, that Emma did not give her food enough I decided that I could not stand for any more. Perhaps I should have talked it over frankly with Emma. Perhaps I will have to do so ultimately. But I decided the fewer words the better. And now let us await results.

I don't know why I told you this first, excepting that it is the last thing that happened. The real event was seeing the preview of *The Mouthpiece* at Arthur's place.[2] You are wonderful, darling, but the photographer certainly did not bring out your beauty, but he could not destroy your acting. I didn't see the end. I had to leave after you had revived him from his drunk. Your work is fine, as far as I could see, beyond criticism. But lordy you must get something other than those hard-boiled parts. One more perhaps, then something like yourself.

All my love,
Clarence

1. As he often did during these years, Clarence wrote two separate letters to Aline on 5 April, probably early in the morning and again in the evening. Only one of the two letters written on the fifth is included here.

2. This film, directed by Elliott Nugent, drew excellent reviews: "First rate all the way."

118   To Aline Stein

[New York City]   April 9, 1932

. . . To the Cloud Club, which is upon the sixty-something floor of the Chrysler Building to lunch with R. M. Wollett, who is the head of the American Radiator Co. and the Standard Sanitary Co. and what not. He was late, so I waited in a fake English room that did not quite fit into the office building, with [a] theatrical fireplace and the usual imitation antique furniture. The Cloud Club is apparently the lunch place of the big little men that made America what it is today. You know, the well-brushed kind. . . . Mr. Wollett, when he turned up, explained to me that the bottom of the stock market had dropped out and that was why every one looked so worried. Alfred Stern had not turned up,[1] so Mr. Wollett and I lunched. He is a genial old soul, seventy or so. We talked large-scale housing. Then Alfred came and told him that the only way to start it going was for the manufacturer of the building materials to help. Wollett seemed impressed. Anyhow, I am taking him and Stern out to Phipps [Garden Apartments] on Monday. . . .

Evening. Dinner for three in front of the window [with] Lewis Mumford [and] Catherine Bauer. It has been decided that she is to [go] abroad to collect material for the series of articles that Lewis is to do on housing. We discussed what they should look for and much else. What a joy to be with such people. Makes thoughts go up, up. Is that how your Chinaman would put it? And they (little big business men) called their club [the Cloud Club]. Cloud Ku-Ku land is what it is.

What a meal we had. I mean in our Cloud land. I almost unfired the tragic Emma. How will I do without her?

Breakfast time. So farewell my beloved.

Clarence

---

1. Stern was active in the Chicago housing and slum clearance movement and later served as a member of the Chicago Housing Authority.

---

119   To Aline Stein

[New York City]   Wednesday, April [13], 1932

Aline darling:

These were sad days—leaden skies, rain, rain, rain, drowning rain. But I guess it is mainly that I received such reproachful letters from my beloved.[1] How thoughtless of me not to have telegraphed you. Just as soon as I heard from you, I started to see if I could not arrange things. I just took for granted that I would go if I possibly could and thought you would understand. And when a cold voice came over the telephone on Sunday, I just didn't understand. Isn't it strange how you can be so inconsiderate without even knowing it.

Yesterday I was at [it] in that strenuous way. You know, wearing myself out so that I will feel my vacation is well earned. At nine met at the Grand Central Station: Mr. Wollett, Alfred Stern, and [Ernest] Gruensfeldt. . . . Pop's machine was waiting, and we went over to Sunnyside and the Phipps. Wollett was enthusiastic. I showed him the drawing we made Saturday of a great development of apartments of the Phipps style [Hillside Homes] forming a community of some six to eight thousand people with all the safety features of Radburn. Then I took him out to the property near Jackson Heights. Did I say that Ernest was the salesman? Back to New York and the Radiator Company Building until after one, looking at the experimental work they are doing in new construction and discussing the possibility of financing my scheme.[2] Perhaps! My problem [is] to arouse their interest sufficiently before I go [so] that it will still be there when I return from the coast. My danger [is] not to get them so excited about it that I can't get away. The real truth I suppose is that nothing will really happen.

Back to the office to be deluged by telephone calls—the big meeting Wednesday and everything.

. . . at City Club in evening. Ackerman speaking high-minded philosophy from another world. Walked home with him and Henry Wright. . . .

Clarence

1. Clarence had planned to travel to California early in April. He delayed the trip so he could visit Sunnyside Gardens with Wollett and encourage him to invest in large-scale housing, beginning with Hillside Homes. He seems to have been slow in letting Aline know about the change. She was very unhappy about it. He did leave for the coast on 14 April and returned on 3 May 1932.

2. This work was the basis of the site selection and design of Hillside Homes (as the project was finally named). Wollett did participate in its financing. The design had considerable influence on quality large-scale housing design in the United States. Stein's work on community facilities (including Hillside Home's community rooms and day care facilities, which he designed for the ground floor) had a broader and more pervasive influence. The Bronx high-density apartment project was designed entirely by Stein, but it was not yet financed.

---

120   To Catherine Bauer[1]

[Los Angeles, California]   April 26, 1932

Dear Miss Bauer:

. . . I am glad Lewis finds that he can do his share of the *Fortune* article, but I hope Henry Wright will get some of *Fortune's* surplus. As for yourself, I don't know whether you should be congratulated or not. Perhaps you can still get something out of a flying visit. I know after my last trip, I can't. But enjoy it, for I warn you, I am going to have lots of work waiting for your return.

If you get a chance, check up on community equipment, stores, etc., to see whether they really have a [new] approach over there. The essential things about the [survey of Queens, Long Island] at this moment are highways and [utilities], their physical and legal status, transportation, and possibly character of surrounding properties.

I would send MacKaye's article to *Harper's*. We can try the others afterward, if necessary.

By all means, have cards with RPAA title.

If you have books of mine or material that I may want to refer to, please leave them with Miss Thomas.

I hope Miss Thomas has paid you all we owe you. She will if you remind her and, if you really have to have fifty dollars allowance, perhaps she can be induced to make out a check for it.

Now as to the climate. It's cold and damp.

But this little house of Aline's just turns its back on all the world and looks out over one of the most peaceful and lovely views in the world.[2]

Of [Henry] Wright's book and his work, some other time.

Aline sends greetings. Bon voyage and all that.

Cordially,

Clarence Stein

1. Catherine Bauer was working part-time for Clarence on community facilities at Hillside Homes, on a housing site in Queens, New York, and on an article he was writing for *Architectural Forum* (May 1932) about his procedures for planning community housing. She was planning a trip to Europe to do research for her book, *Modern Housing* (New York: Houghton Mifflin, 1934). She also wrote (with Mumford) articles commissioned by *Fortune* magazine. Bauer and Mumford traveled together in Europe in the summer of 1932, beginning a two-year love affair. Bauer, a creative thinker and effective writer on housing policy, was a major figure in the shaping of U.S. housing policy in the 1930s, 1940s, and 1950s. After her work with Stein and Mumford, she worked with Oscar Stonorov, Henry Churchill, and others in the Housing Study Guild in Philadelphia and became an effective Washington lobbyist for the national housing legislation that was passed in 1937.

2. Aline had rented a house in the Brentwood section of Los Angeles.

---

121   To Aline Stein

[New York City]   Thursday, May 16, 1932

My darling:

This has been a full day. This morning with [Andrew] Eken the builder, his assistant, and Frank [Vitolo] to the Navy Yard section of Brooklyn and then to the further ends of the Bronx, 178th or something (it seemed 2,000th Street after endless time in the subways) to examine apartment houses built under the state law.

Finally arrived at my office at two-thirty to hear that a Mr. Rosoff's office had been trying to get in touch with me in regard to doing some housing.[1] His secretary had tried to make an engagement a couple of days ago. Frank explained that Rosoff was the fellow who built the subways and bought immense gravel pits, everything he needed, even a railroad, to carry out his work.

I went over to Rosoff's office. Left my body guard, Frank, out in the vestibule. Rosoff, a big, burly, Russian Jew, [is] all energy. "When I want a thing, I go after it. I want things done yesterday."

He loves to use his trucks, his machines, his men to build houses. Sometimes he finds a way of borrowing money from the government. . . . He [referred to Wollett] (you remember, of the American Radiator Co.). Wollett says, "You must have Stein as architect," or something of that kind. And so we talked in snatches of building in Manhattan, in Queens—twenty million dollars worth of houses—between Sam Rosoff's telephone calls with the various parties. "Yes, buy the old car barn." "How much?" To his secretary, "How much?" "Seven dollars a square foot," says the secretary. Rosoff over the phone, "Not one cent over five dollars." To someone else, "Sure, I will see him about the Pasadena water works." "We bid on 'em." "Yes, I went down to Washington, and I told the president." "Say, I told the mayor I would run the subway myself for five cents." And behind this volcano, on the wall hung a large photograph of a Russian-Jewish peasant, a calm, dominating Jewish mother. Rosoff's mother, apparently.

Frank came in and we talked big figures, but it was difficult to take it seriously. It was musical comedy stuff. Oh, for the pen of Moss Hart! And then Rosoff, himself, must produce it in the movies. He is the kind that has made the talkies what they are today.

He telephoned to Wollett and made an engagement, and over we all went to the Radiator Building: Frank, the secretary, Rosoff, and I. More big talk about millions and millions and millions.

Dreams are strange, but they are more real than conferences with the great of this topsy-turvy world.

I breakfast tomorrow with Rosoff at the Savoy Plaza at eight and then [go] to see the Phipps and properties on Long Island. Perhaps it's real and we may not be able to go to New Mexico. Anyhow, it's amusing while it lasts. Someday something will be real. Anyhow, let's hope we have our trip. You and I, we are real, anyhow.

My love,
Clarence

---

1. Sam Rosoff was a very successful building contractor and a New York subway builder of the 1920s and 1930s.

---

122   To Aline Stein

[New York City]   May 18, 1932

Aline darling:

After a dinner alone, dressed in pajamas last night, I suddenly got the idea that I must see [George Bernard] Shaw's play before it closed.[1] Fool. So, I rushed into clothes and to the Guild Theatre. A dull show, so unbelievably dull. And the actors were more bored than the audience. They just said their long lines while the rest of the actors' thoughts were far away, or they had their own jokes and spoofed the audience. A disgraceful performance, but no worse than the scenery.

Lunch with Stern of Chicago and the builder Eken, mainly to talk of the bill in Washington to spend untold millions on housing. It is almost unbelievable, but it may pass.

Went to Jamaica, in connection with this famous Sunnyside case. Luckily, I arrived too late to be called on the stand. But I stayed and was much amused to hear the results on humans of all these restrictions we had so often theorized about. How they resent anything that is not the commonplace.

Drove back to town with Lewis [Mumford], Isaacs, and Al [Bing]. Al asked me up to the house, sat out on the roof, and tried to keep off the subject of depression, but with difficulty. Even Al thinks the economic system may be busting. Then looked at art books. Florence arrived and dinner. Al had to go out to his art class—he is really studying painting in a class—and I stayed to gossip with Florence. . . .

Otherwise, there is nothing to say but that you're all the world and my darling.

Clarence

1. *Man and Superman.*

---

123   To Aline Stein

[New York City]   Sunday, May 29, 1932

Dear Aline:

Yesterday I stayed home. I was going to write. But what I did was to put books and things in order so as to facilitate writing. Order consisted in moving them from one shelf to another or at least getting some of the old papers or pamphlets in the scrap basket. That is a relief, when they are in their final resting place and you don't have to come on them ever again and think, "Well, in which box shall I file these?" Most of the technical or philosophical papers of just a few years ago began to seem so dated. I guess that was what was really troubling me. I had intended to get back to my book, but I was really dodging it, for way down at bottom I think I am feeling, well, what kind of world are your new communities to be built in? Will it be anything like the civilization we are going to know by the time the book is written? Are we going to have mortgages and all that nonsense? What materials will we build with? Are communities to become more fixed, or will we live on wings? Here in the East, where there is that feeling that our economic-social system may be on the skids, it becomes harder and harder to talk of a definite future. But I will try.[1]

In the evening to Lillie's. Her flower pictures continue to be more and more amazing.

Until tonight, when I will again hear your voice, good-bye my love.

Clarence . . .

1. The day before this somewhat sad soliloquy, perhaps a precursor of his later serious depressive illness, Clarence had traveled to Long Island City to visit the Phipps Apartments. He wrote: "The garden is lovely, beyond any of the kind I know. . . . It certainly gives one a thrill to have a partial responsibility for an accomplishment of that kind. . . . Like seeing oneself in a movie, I guess." Then he had visited the property where he hoped to design his "next big development" in Long Island.

---

124   To Aline Stein

[New York City]   May 30, 1932

My darling:

Eight o'clock on Decoration Day or some holiday. I never can tell one from the other. Isn't it queer that I should be spending my time developing new ways of organizing communities when I do everything I can to escape all these community get-togethers. It's a beautiful blue-sky day and cool. So let them enjoy their parades and speeches and everything. I am going to stay home and write.

Yesterday was cool, too, welcome after these hot days, but gray. In Pop's machine I went out to see Radburn and visit Mrs. Cautley.[1] It is pathetic what they are doing to Radburn. They are trying to get on the bandwagon and be as loud and vulgar as any cheap speculator. Thank goodness, they haven't much money to spend, and the trees in time will hide much of it. I am glad that Henry and I are in no way connected with the job.[2]

On the way back, [I] stopped at Radburn again. The Morrisons were out. I called on the Walkers. He is taking Brownlow's place. . . .[3]

Clarence

1. The landscape architect for Sunnyside, Radburn, and Hillside Homes was Marjorie Cautley, who studied landscape architecture at Cornell University and graduated in the class of 1919.

2. During the brief time since Clarence's break with the CHC, its directors seem to have decided to develop some of their land in a conventional pattern, perhaps in an effort to gain sufficient cash flow to save the rest of their assets.

3. Louis Brownlow, a Chicago lawyer and housing reformer, served as a resident manager during the first years of Radburn's development. Major John O. Walker, Radburn's manager at the time of this letter, later became a close associate of Clarence Stein's in connection with his work on the Greenbelt Towns in 1935.

---

125   To Aline Stein

[New York City]   Wednesday eve., June 1, 1932

Aline dear:

Your letter of Saturday was so much more cheerful that I have been happy today.[1] But your enthusiasm about my letters (though, of course, it delights me) at the same time [surprises] me. Your letters are so much better written. They are so much you, all the warmth and richness and kindliness and everything of you. Well, let's not quarrel about it. Your letters are you and mine are me, and so there you are and where are you? . . .

A good deal of my time [the] last few days has been devoted to the problems of the unemployed draftsmen. With a mighty effort we have collected what seems quite a sum of money. We have 30 thousand dollars left to spend. Now, if we put our two thousand unemployed draftsmen to work at the large salary of fifteen dollars, we could keep them going for just one week. Isn't it absurd? There isn't any question in my mind that by next winter the government will be handing out doles (or whatever Mr. Hoover prefers to call it) for a large part of the population, and we will have governmental control of the distribution of a great deal of the food supply and possibly even of housing. You movie folks don't seem to even know there is a depression. But just you wait until Warner's stock completely goes under and then where will you be? In *Once in a Lifetime,* says Aline, whom I love.

Clarence

1. Aline was discouraged about the direction of her work and her performance in the film *One Way Passage* and was concerned that Warner Brothers would not release her to Universal Studios to act in their production of *Once in a Lifetime.*

---

126   To Aline Stein

[New York City]   Saturday, June 4, 1932

Aline dear:

Your grand, long letter of Tuesday arrived yesterday. It was so full of news and you.
. . .

At the office I tried to keep a two-ring circus going, dictating my radio talk and working with the boys on plans for the only not-yet-dead job, the [Hillside] housing one. It is a good deal a matter of dollars and cents. The Phipps rents for an average of about $16.85 a room. Can we design an attractive, livable apartment with great gardens to rent for $10 or $11? It is true [that] building costs are cheaper. Nonetheless, we have a lot of simplification to do, or we have to find quite new methods of building. We go through one of these after another, and each time comes on a catch—unions, laws, safety, costs. It is not as easy as it sounds when you read the articles in the architectural magazines.

The radio talk is going to deal with the Wagner Bill, which proposes to lend national money for housing. I really think there is a chance of its passing.[1] Then the danger will be that the money will be wasted on the wrong kind of building or get lost in the banks.

Your picture is all over the front of the theater where they are giving *Week End*

Marriage. They have your name fourth. Were you not to have third billing? My picture also is appearing in *Fortune* as one of *the* five city planners.[2] I knew it was me because of the name under it. I wonder where they picked up the photo. I don't think much of it.

But while we are boasting I might say that my article is really going to appear in the *[New York] Times* magazine section.[3]

I love you,
Clarence

1. It did five years later! Senator Wagner's 1932 Housing Bill was much amended and finally passed and signed into law in 1937. Clarence's radio talk on housing legislation was given on 7 June 1932.

2. *Fortune Magazine,* June 1932.

3. The *New York Times Magazine* did not publish this article until October 1933.

---

127   To Catherine Bauer

[New York City]   June 7, 1932

Dear Miss Bauer:

I was delighted to receive your interesting letter from Frankfurt. I have never seen the Fuggerei, nor have I been to Ulm. I certainly will try to get to both places next time. It is astounding that so few Americans have stopped to see Oberbaurat Feuchtinger. Ulm's experience is going to be of more value to us, I should think, than almost anything that has happened in Germany. I do not think that it will be long before our big cities will be recapturing land that has already been pretty well ruined by subdivision. In fact, [the RPAA is] working at a model State Housing Law . . . (I hate the word "model," but what else shall we call it?) and hopes to make one of its essential features the taking of land not only for housing, but for replanning.[1]

The present activity in regard to a State Housing Law grows out of the possibility of our having the use of national money for housing very soon, probably even before you get back to this country to tell us how it might best be used. A group of the Democratic senators, led by Wagner, are proposing large loans to the states for self-liquidating projects and to limited dividend companies for housing and slum clearance. The president's proposals are very similar, though he does not specifically mention housing. The money will be loaned through the Reconstruction Finance Corporation [RFC].[2] We are working very hard to induce the powers that be to set up adequate technical boards to pass on the merits of projects. If we can get a central board, we will then try to have similar regional boards set up. These should, as soon as possible, be replaced by State Housing Boards. I wish we could call them Housing and Regional Planning Boards. Anyhow, we will try to arrange, in the outline for housing laws, so that such boards will have, as one of their functions, the study and guidance of the location [and] distribution of population and industry.[3]

Architecture is still quite dead. We are working hard at schemes for large housing developments in an attempt to see whether the Phipps type of thing cannot be simplified so as to be rented for $10 or $11 [/room/month] instead of $16 or $17. It is just as well that you didn't spend your last week making that study of the Queens property, as we probably will work first in some area closer in.

One of these days we must set up a simpler outline of procedure in gathering facts for proposed projects. Ours is so complicated that I fear but few people will use it. Just as soon as they send me a bound copy of the three reprints, I will forward one to you. It will be interesting to find out whether they have worked out anything of the kind in Germany.

Research for the book is going along very slowly. Just at present, a few of the unemployed draftsmen, under the guidance of Mr. Rosenfield, are studying the school problem and its relation to neighborhoods.[4] I am not at all satisfied with the conclusions at which we arrived after our Radburn study. I am enclosing a rough outline, which I have just set up for Mr. Rosenfield's guidance. You might be interested to see whether there has been any definite attempt in Europe to relate the size of neighborhoods to the school system or to any other unit. I have the impression that quite a number of housing developments in Holland were built around a single school. Is this a fact? I have also outlined, very roughly, a study for playgrounds, a copy of which is enclosed.

Aline is still very busy. She has given up specializing as a secretary and has been a head nurse, adventuress disguised as a countess,[5] and is about to play her old part in *Once in a Lifetime.*

Do write and tell me more of what you are seeing and doing.

With kindest regards,
Cordially yours,
Clarence S. Stein

1. This was, surely, one of the first U.S. proposals to establish direct municipal intervention in the urban development process through public ownership of land. It was the precursor of the public policies later called *urban redevelopment* and *urban renewal.*

2. The RFC loans to housing were eventually awarded to only six projects carried out under various state programs for limited dividend housing, one of which was Hillside Homes. With the small limited dividend subsidy, rents were too high for families with the lowest incomes.

3. This was an early proposal for state "guidance" of industrial location.

4. Stein and Bauer did some of the earliest qualitative and quantitative research in the United States on standards for community facilities in relation to population. Their work included outdoor and indoor recreation spaces, nursery schools, and shopping facilities. It was published in reports used in the planning of Hillside Home's social and shopping facilities and in *Architectural Forum* in 1933.

5. In the film *One Way Passage,* Aline plays an adventuress and con artist, working with Kay Francis and William Powell.

128   To Aline Stein

Ossining, New York[1]   June 19, 1932

Aline darling:

I passed over the halfway line yesterday night, and I am just the same youngster.[2]

Yesterday morning I went down to the office, in spite of the fact that it is supposed to be closed on Saturday. I wanted to start designing another dream housing development. When one of them becomes a reality, I won't believe it.

I opened the mail. There was a very nice letter from Miriam Price to remind me that I was fifty. Isn't it funny how people have found out. And after I had opened all the envelopes marked in such a way that I knew where they came from, I cut one with a return address which I did not know. An advertisement, I supposed. And inside was a check for five thousand dollars from the Phipps Estate, with a note saying that they made their extra payment because they thought I had done such a good job. How was that for a birthday present, a hundred dollars for each year. If I had only been a hundred years old, they might have made it ten thousand. Perhaps I will give them a chance one of these days. . . .

The main thing is to get housing started in a big way. Did I tell you I had a scheme?[3] Let the building industry start things itself. Form limited dividend corporations under the state law, and what money it can't get from lending institutions put in the form of materials and work. It may go in spite of sounding a bit wild. Tomorrow we have a meeting to talk it over.

And so it goes.

My love,
Clarence

1. Clarence was spending the weekend at the summer place that belonged to Theodore and Aline Bernstein.

2. On the previous day, Clarence's letter to Aline had anticipated a different reaction to his fiftieth birthday: "I go over the crest. It is strange how it distresses me. It's only numbers. Fifty!"

3. The Bronx large-scale housing project (Hillside Homes) on a site selected by Stein and designed by him and his associates turned out to be a major contribution to the development of ideas about good quality large-scale housing. It was the prototype for many such projects from 1932 to the early 1960s. Most were successful. Those that "went sour," such as the Pruitt Igo project of the St. Louis Public Housing Authority, gave the term *housing project* an undeserved bad name. The developments that failed did so mainly because of very complex social and management reasons. Efforts by postmodernist critics and social scientists to blame the failures on their designs are not conclusive. Professor Roger Montgomery's research on the myth of Pruitt Igo has raised serious doubt about the validity of these causal arguments. Phipps Garden Apartments, for example, is well maintained and well managed, and it has experienced few of the problems of other large-scale rental housing projects.

129   To Benton MacKaye

New York City   June 21, 1932

Dear Ben:

I was delighted to hear from you.

Your letter to [Arno B.] Cramner, [director] of the National Parks Service, seemed very good, but I wonder whether we are going to make any headway in preventing the whole trail being turned into an automobile drive unless you arouse all of the Appalachian Trail Associations. Complaints from one or two are not going to make very much effect, but I think, if all of the various groups and associations along the line of the trail would work together, there might be a chance of preserving the top of ranges purely as trails.[1] . . .

I would be delighted if you would come down to New York for a week if you feel that it would be worthwhile getting in touch with the various magazines again. In fact, it would be great if you would come if only to make a visit and enjoy the quiet of the big city. We promise not to turn on the radio! . . .

As always,
Clarence

1. MacKaye started his struggle with the National Park Service over the construction of the Skyline Drive late in 1933. He objected to the destruction of the wilderness aspects of the Shenandoah and other Appalachian parks by the proposed ridge-line parkway. He proposed a valley parkway or a flank road that would free wilderness areas of automobile and radio noise and development. Cramner thought that ridge-line parkways would help conserve wilderness areas.

130   To Lewis Mumford

[New York City]   June 21, 1932

Dear Lewis:

Bruce Bliven sent me the proof of Adams's answer to your two articles. I would forward it to you, but he says he has already sent you a copy. I can see no value in our answering it. It would simply lead to endless arguments, and there is not the slightest question that out of the pudding he can pull proof of any statement that he wishes to make. In his lengthy, detailed answer, he, of course, misses the main point and, I presume, purposely so.[1] Although there is nothing to be gained by continuing the articles in the *New Republic*, I think it is worthwhile to have criticisms appear elsewhere. Aronovici is writing one now.[2]

Congress has, as yet, taken no action in regard to housing, although it is possible that something will happen within the next couple days. The portion of the Wagner Bill allowing loans for that purpose was dropped by the committee, but

Senator Wagner promises to move that it be reinstated. We are all working very hard to see that, if government money is to be spent, its use will be directed by a technical project board rather than by the banks. Robert Kohn points out that, if this were done, it would be possible to base the order in which work should be taken upon need rather than financial return. Even if the work lasts for only a short time, it might set a precedent which might be of value in the future.

I am constantly working at a study of apartments in the hope of producing plans as good as, if not better than, the Phipps, at much less cost. Eken, of Starrett Bros. & Eken, is helping in securing estimates.[3] We had hoped in the beginning to be able to do a great many new things in construction, but we find, as we compare prices, that we are gradually coming back to the old methods. I still have confidence that there is going to be a great change in methods of construction and use of materials in apartments, but it is very difficult to take the first step. The building material people are experimenting, but none of them, American Radiator and others, have anything ready that one can use in a large development with assurance. It is very discouraging, but we will have to keep pegging away and bring in one new process at a time.

Henry [Wright] is still spending most of his time at the farm. He has not yet found out how he is going to finance his European trip. Nothing seems to be forthcoming from any of the foundations. I do hope that some means will be found to send him over, as he seems to have his heart set on it, and I think it is of great importance just at this stage of his study. . . .

Robert Kohn was asking me the other day just what has been written about Geddes here in America after his death. I find that Aronovici wrote a short article for the *Survey,* and, although I did not see it, Bruce tells me that they had an editorial. You did write an article about him a year or so ago in the *New Republic,* did you not?[4] I wonder if it wouldn't be an awfully good thing if you would write about him again. Just what Geddes stood for does not seem to be recognized except among a very few here in America. . . .

What you say about German housing interests me very much. I saw some illustrations of it last year at the Berlin Exhibit, but it was very difficult to get very much of an impression from the group pictures. . . .

Cordially yours,
Clarence

1. Mumford's article in the *New Republic* attacked both the basic ideas of the Russell Sage Foundation-funded Regional Plan of New York and Its Environs and its compromises with the real estate–formulated form of urban growth, which meets the financial requirements of the market but disregards the social and environmental needs of the larger community for affordable housing and natural open space.

2. Aronovici had also been awarded a fellowship to travel to Europe to study housing and planning. In an earlier letter, Clarence had lamented the fact that Henry Wright, who also wanted

so much to research European housing, had not received such support. By midsummer 1932, Wright, Aronovici, Mumford, and Bauer were all on the trail of money to support their research on European housing.

3. The design of the second stage of the Phipps apartments provided Stein an opportunity to improve on the T-shaped building to improve internal circulation and provide as much cross ventilation as he could. The changes were to continue that year with the development of the first unit plans for the Bronx, N.Y., project later named Hillside Homes.

4. Mumford was, as much as any American scholar, "the discoverer" of Patrick Geddes. He visited him in Edinburgh in 1922 and wrote extensively on his contributions to regional planning.

---

131   To Aline Stein

[New York City]   June 29, 1932

Aline dear:

. . . The work at the office is interesting, although it hasn't come to a head as yet. Every few days we have a new site. And we arrange our houses in new patterns, like playing blocks. Build up the side of the hills. What nice views they have out the windows, one house above the other. The buildings run north and south as far as possible so the sun will get in every room. Garages here to protect the houses from the noisy street. Playground, stores, everything. Now let's try another!

Last night, Robert Kohn, Carl Stern, and George Gove were here. We worked at the outline of a model state housing law.[1] They will want it in various states if the Wagner Bill passes, permitting the use of national money by state housing boards.

. . . We started at six and worked until near ten, with a good dinner in the middle. Henry Wright [was] also here, though he isn't so much interested in state housing laws. . . .

Love to you, darling.

Clarence

1. New York's first local housing authority–enabling legislation had been enacted in 1930. It provided for local tax exemption, the use of eminent domain in acquiring housing sites, and resale of this land to limited dividend corporations. Stein and his associates were adapting and updating this law as a model for other states.

---

132   To Aline Stein

[New York City]   Friday, June 30, 1932

Aline dear:

Just a few minutes before I rush to catch the 11:30 evening train for Lake Champlain. Henry Wright and I have been up in the Bronx inspecting the property that we are now studying. It is a wonderful plot, a hill, so that the buildings will gradually build up. I can see possibilities of a beautiful site.[1] But it is an awful distance up there. It would be hard to believe that anyone would go up there if there were not already so many houses, large and small. It was beginning to grow dark when we arrived, and we finally had [to] find our way around by electric lights. . . .

Love,
Clarence

1. This was to become the site of Hillside Homes, Stein's excellent high-density apartment project.

---

133 To Catherine Bauer[1]

[New York City]   June 30, 1932

Dear Miss Bauer:

. . . There is really no news here. We are still working along at dream housing developments. Nobody has money to go ahead. I, anyhow, am learning a great deal in regard to the fundamental requirements of community development within the city. We have made studies for quite a number of large plots both in the Bronx and the borough of Queens. It is astounding how many places there are with twenty acres or more in farmland and still close to existing schools. As I see it at present, the fundamental question, in deciding whether a development is large enough to form a community, is that of the recreation space.[2] This, of course, applies within cities, such as New York, where you can pretty well depend on the municipality's taking care of school requirements. From what I have observed of late, it seems to me that the play facilities, in connection with these schools, [are] inadequate. One should, of course, try to organize a community in such a way as to make it possible to get at the playgrounds without crossing dangerous roads. This means that the area of the development must be large enough so that you can afford an adequate playground and at the same time be able to distribute the cost without putting too much additional expense on each apartment.

The only reason I am writing to you about this . . . is that I thought you may want to see how they handled this problem in Germany and Holland. If they are willing to set the play space in the middle of the interior court, it is simple enough. Our difficulty is that we have found the noise of the larger children [to be] troublesome and, therefore, at Sunnyside we were forced to separate the playground from the houses entirely.

The question as to whether there will be money for housing in the near future is, to a great extent, dependent on whether the Wagner Bill is passed. I wrote you of this the last time. Since then the bill has been amended so that monies will only go to those limited dividend housing corporations which are completely regulated by state or municipal laws. This means, of course, that if the Wagner Bill is passed there will be a tendency, on the part of a good many states, to immediately pass housing legislation. I have been working with Robert Kohn, Carl Stern, and George Gove on an outline of suggestions for laws in other states. A real educational campaign is going to be needed to prevent states from either [aping] too closely the New York law or doing something that will set housing progress back, instead of forward.

[Henry] Wright tells me that *Fortune* has suddenly decided to slow up on American housing. I don't suppose, however, that this will affect their interest in the material that you and Lewis are gathering.[3]

Mr. Rosenfield left a couple of days ago. I hope that he will have an opportunity to see you on his way to Russia. The American Russian Institute has given him letters to various authorities, suggesting that they send over an exhibit illustrating city planning and housing.

Aline is hard at work on *Once in a Lifetime.* She will have a couple of weeks off when it is over, and I hope that we can meet at one end of the continent or somewhere halfway between.

With best regards to the Behrendts and any of my other friends you see.

Cordially yours,
Clarence S. Stein

1. Bauer was in Berlin.

2. This seems to be a variation on or an extrapolation from Clarence Perry's neighborhood unit concept for planning urban residential areas. In this concept the elementary school serves as the nucleus of a neighborhood; its pupil population is used as a basis for calculations of the number of families to be housed in the neighborhood and thus the appropriate population size. The theory generally works well but does not account for the aging of the population in a given neighborhood and the consequent variation of a school-age population.

3. *Fortune* published Mumford's articles on European housing: "England's Two Million Houses" (November 1932) and "Machines for Living" (February 1933). These articles emphasized the importance of functionalism in German housing and the use of public credit in British housing programs.

---

134 To Benton MacKaye

New York City   July 11, 1932

Dear Ben:

I was glad to hear from you again but was sorry that you are not coming down to see me now. Perhaps it will be better later. Lewis writes that he will be back the second week in August. Come then and we will all be able to get together. Judging from Lewis's letter, he and Catherine Bauer are going to have a good many interesting things to tell us. . . .

I don't know that I am quite as strong for Roosevelt as I was last year. He is a fine fellow and an excellent talker, as you were able to judge at Virginia, but I have not very much faith in his ability to make up his mind or to keep it made up. I am afraid he would make a pretty weak president, but who shall we vote for—if at all? . . .

Yesterday I was out to the Hudson Guild. It must be the first time [in] about two years.[1] The place looks wonderful and Walter Elliott and Miss Whitson are the same as always, doing most of the work and giving everybody a good time. My father and Margaret, Herbert's daughter, were all along. Afterward we went over to Henry Wright's place. Most of the family, including the grandchildren, were there, as well as Harris Whitaker and his new wife. As though this were not enough, Henry is starting [an architectural and housing design] school with dormitory and drafting room in the building connected with the old mill. There are four men out there now. We had a fine time of it.

Cordially,
Clarence

1. Robert Kohn allocated some of the grant from the Rockefeller Foundation he was managing to Wright's New Jersey School.

---

135 To Lewis Mumford

[New York City]   July 11, 1932

Dear Lewis:

I was immensely interested in your letter of the 29th of June. I did not get a chance to get a very definite impression of the Beacontree Estate. It is too bad that the London County Council should have fallen down on this, its biggest experiment. I was very much disappointed in the latest of their apartments which I saw. They seem far behind our better plans in regard to economical use of space.[1]

I am having a perfectly wonderful time, at present, studying possibilities of various large tracts in the Bronx [Hillside Homes] and Queens.[2] It is wonderful what one can do if the plot is large enough and it is possible to change the location of streets, or, altogether, eliminate a good many of them. Of course, we do not know yet just how the city will take our proposals for closing streets. What I want to do is to get them to take a space equal to the streets closed and put it altogether in a single park, which will be placed across the road from the existing school. It is astounding, as soon as one gets into really good, large-scale planning, how many, many laws or regulations one has to break or have changed. So, even if we are able to get money to finance any one of these large operations, which is still very questionable, we are going to have our hands full inducing the city to permit us to do something good.[3]

In regard to financing, the only hope seems to be the passage of the proper legislation at Washington. The two Houses did pass [the Garner-Wagner] bill, which
included loans on housing, as you probably have read, and I presume that before
the day is over President [Hoover] will have vetoed the bill. [There are] Congress
[ional] proposals to pass the bill again, changed in such a way as to contain housing
or not; . . . [this] is questionable. Even if the bill is passed, our difficulties will not
be all over. I do not believe that the national government will lend more than 60%
to 65%, and this, of course, will merely take the place of the loan that one would
expect to get from the [usual] loaning institutions. The Metropolitan [Life] Insurance Company and all the rest of them are lending nothing at present, so we still
. . . have to get equity money. We are hoping that we can get the building industry
to come in to a certain extent. But all that remains to be seen.

In the meanwhile, the boys in the office and I are learning a great deal about
large-scale planning that may be of use someday. I am looking forward to long talks
with you and Catherine Bauer to find out just how certain [of the] problems, that
are giving me the most trouble, have been met abroad. I am thinking, particularly,
of the problem of securing adequate and properly placed play areas.

I was out at Henry Wright's place yesterday. He is getting his school started, at
last. With the help of some of the boys, he has been remodeling the building attached to the mill so as to form a drafting room, dormitory, and kitchen. Four boys
are starting in work. Henry certainly has his hands full. Most of the children are at
home, as well as the grandchildren. . . .

I may go out to California again this weekend, unless a real job turns up. Aline
cannot come east at this time as she has only a very short time between pictures.
She is in the midst of *Once in a Lifetime.* She has one more picture scheduled, and
then I hope in September she will be coming back to New York.

Do remember me to the Unwins. Tell them that I have intended to write them
but haven't known just how to go about congratulating a knight. Is Sophie with
you? If so, my best to her as well as to Miss Bauer.

As always,
Clarence

1. Stein was referring to the Beacontree Estate of the London County Council. Mumford had
just traveled in England and was in Paris.

2. In a letter to Aline written the same day, Clarence reported on a conversation with Eken of
Starrett Brothers, the builder of his Bronx project. "Ekan has talked things over with the man
who owns the land [they] want to use." The owner was Nathan Straus, who later organized the
limited dividend company that developed Hillside Homes.

3. The plans to close the streets were not accepted, thus making impossible the superblock
with a central pedestrian spine of open space that Stein had planned for the Hillside community.

136   To Aline Stein

[New York City]   Tuesday, July 12, 1932

Aline darling:

Things are coming along. The owner of the land on which we want to build our houses says o.k. He will come in on terms that are very easy and will help put through the project with whatever influence he has. It seems that he has quite some. I learned this morning that he is [New York] Senator Straus.[1] Tomorrow morning Eken and I go to show our scheme to Mr. Wollett. A few more drawings and then, perhaps, I will be free to go to you. . . . More prospects: Voorhees and Walker hope to get a job as housing consultants. In which case, they want me to consult the consultants. We had lunch together. Something is coming soon.

We have completed the outline of a model state housing law, and Robert Kohn has succeeded in getting a donation of $5,000 to use in educating those who should have housing laws inflicted upon them. [The] Henrys, Klaber, and Wright are to be sent out to preach the law. Perhaps Aronovici, also.

To Fieldston School this morning to decide on colors.[2] The end is in sight.

Love to you, my beloved,
Clarence

1. Nathan Straus, the owner of the large parcel on which Hillside Homes was built, later became a senior policy maker on housing in the Roosevelt administration. He was appointed by FDR in 1937 to administer the new Federal Housing Agency established by the Housing Act of 1937. Straus's book on American housing policy, *One Third of a Nation* (New York: Macmillan, 1939), provides a good summary of his understanding of, analysis of, and ideas about housing policy.
2. Clarence Stein and Robert Kohn had completed their design for the Fieldston High School of the Ethical Culture Society in Riverdale.

137   To Aline MacMahon

[New York City]   July 13, 1932

Aline darling:

Another step today toward the success of the project and toward freedom to leave for California and you. Eken and I called on Mr. Wollett, and Eken told him about the project. I have never seen such a salesman! The finest housing development that has ever been done (well, perhaps it would be) and assured financial success, etc., etc. Hamilton, Mr. Wollett's assistant and president of something very important in the world of plumbing and heating, came in with a very big cigar, and they all began to get excited. Not only would it pay [for] and use thousands of bathtubs and

W.C.'s, but says Mr. Eken, "Think of the social good." Says Mr. Wollett, "That is the way I look at it, and that is just what Mr. Hamilton had been thinking of." Who says that big business has no heart?

Tomorrow we try out the Housing Board or, rather, its chairman. We need the board's backing to get the exemption and a chance at a governmental loan. The chairman, Mr. James, will not be so easy. He is a banker, and bankers don't like good, cheap housing in the Bronx, where it will compete with older and poorer buildings that the banks have mortgaged. We will see. If we do succeed, then I will just finish our show drawings and leave Eken to straighten out the finances and fix things with [the] Tenement House Department while you and I spend a week on the beach. . . .

Clarence

---

138   To Aline Stein

[New York City]   Saturday, August 20, 1932

Aline, my darling:

I am just back from Amenia, where I have been visiting the Mumfords. A day of talks with Lewis all about his travels, our mutual friends, and housing, housing, housing in Europe and here.

They live in an old house of many rooms, colonial-like on the outside but for a blue, blue main door.[1] Inside, the furniture is simple and meager. There is much disorder, excepting in Lewis's study, where I slept on a very comfortable bed. The interior has been much rearranged by the Mumfords and will be very attractive, if it is ever finished. Guess it is job enough to just keep a house going if you have no servants.

Sophie was hospitable enough, but I am never quite sure. Geddes is still a beautiful youngster. He is full of life, so full he gets a little on the nerves of his mother. Be warned before it is too late! And this boy just came through another serious illness. Luckily, they did not cable his parents, who were just about to sail home. The woman who nursed him and her pale little daughter were guests, as well as the head of the Sunnyside School, a very blond Scandinavian or, perhaps, German.

[Benton MacKaye] comes next week after visiting the Mumfords. And so it goes. Much more to tell, but it will keep until tomorrow.

All my love,
Clarence

1. This house was on the old farm property in Dutchess County, N.Y., which Mumford had acquired in 1926 for a family summer retreat from New York City. In 1932, when they moved from their home at Sunnyside, Long Island, they renovated the Amenia house for year-round use.

139   To Aline Stein

[New York City]   Friday, August 26, 1932

Aline darling:

Well. Life began with a bang in the Hollywood Theatre, and MacMahon stole the headlines, anyhow, in the *Times*.[1] I didn't see the opening and haven't yet had time to see the other papers. Among our friends who were going were the Moskowitzes. Saw them at Arthur's Tuesday night. They looked forward to seeing you in all three showings of which I wrote you. Belle and I had much to gossip about concerning housing. She (I mean, Al Smith) is to be editor-in-chief of *Outlook* magazine.[2] So we will have another means of telling the people what's what. . . .

I didn't write yesterday because I was out at Henry Wright's. . . . Henry's students are doing a grand job. [They are] studying ways of building group houses [on hillside sites by] working with drawings and models. Great enthusiasm in the nothingness. At six we all went in swimming: Henry, the four boys, as well as Albert [Mayer] and Kamstra of my office, who had come out for the day. After dinner we had a long talk on theoretical phases of housing and town planning in the future. They kept me hoping mentally. There is something thrilling about these young minds that is altogether lacking in the dead brains of the practitioners who have "arrived." Arrived where? . . .[3]

Clarence

1. The film *Once in a Lifetime* opened in New York on August 25, 1932.

2. The importance of Belle Moskowitz's contributions to Al Smith's communications of all kinds has been noted by many biographers.

3. Henry's "school," which operated in the summers of 1932 and 1933, was partially funded by the Rockefeller Foundation. Its students included some who later exercised major influences on American housing and planning, including Robert Mitchell, the founder of the University of Pennsylvania Planning School, and Chloethiel Woodward Smith, a Washington, D.C., architect and planner whose designs included housing projects in the Southwest Washington Urban Renewal Area and housing in the New Town of Reston, Virginia.

140   To Aline Stein

[New York City]   August 30, 1932

Darling mine:

I suppose you wonder why I don't tell you about the progress of our [Hillside Homes] housing development? It's because every day it looks as though there would be something definite to tell tomorrow and that tomorrow never comes. There are so many things outside of making it a better and better plan, which I think we are doing. Above all, we must get the Reconstruction Finance Corporation's approval at

Washington if we are to have the needed finances. And we can't get that until we have the o.k. of the State Housing Board. They keep on putting us off. Truth is they are scared of the opposition of the Bronx real estate men if we put up our good houses to rent for less than their rotten ones. So the board says it wants housing on the lower East Side to replace the slums. Of course they do! The slums don't pay the landlords any longer, and building there may save their financial life. But the trouble is that [that] land is held at such a high price that they can't build there cheaply enough. The Housing Board should know this, but they do not want to face the facts. The members of the board are sentimentalists or bankers. They don't know how to see simple facts and see the straight. But ultimately they will be forced to let housing outside of Manhattan go ahead or do nothing. And then, I think we will be first. After that, there are whole bundles of other difficulties: closing streets, a new type of construction, and so on. It is a long, long fight, but we are going to win. So now you know.

And how's your job? It's my opinion that it's about time you quit it, if you want to know. I am getting homesick, and home, as I have told you, isn't a place—it's where my love is.

Clarence

---

141   To Aline Stein

[New York City]   Saturday, September 2, 1932

My darling:

There were two long days without any letter from you. And then last evening the long sweet one of last Tuesday, so full of you, but lacking the one piece of information I want. When, when are you coming home? It is getting so long, this waiting.

Yes, we will have a grand shopping spree, particularly if I get the housing job. . . . Someday, if we can forget the boys who are sleeping over in the park and waiting for a nickel to get coffee at Columbus Circle, and the 2,500 unemployed draftsmen, and the actors' lunch place that is having a hard time. Life is complicated. . . .

Yesterday was unbelievably hot, and I had to spend the whole day running around town. Housing Board in the morning. They say they will approve our scheme next week and take it to Washington. But this is endless, and there are so many chances for political slips. Then to discuss things with Eken and Mrs. Moskowitz, who is doing our publicity. The office. And then another conference. Talk, talk, talk, with Straus and Eken. . . .[1]

I love you,
Clarence

1. Straus, the owner of the land on which the Hillside Homes project was to be built, had become an active partner in the enterprise. The builder, Eken, was a significant force. His Starrett Brothers Construction Company, which built many of the RFC- and PWA-financed housing projects in the mid-1930s, was well financed by New York bankers.

142 To Benton MacKaye

New York City   October 6, 1932

Dear Ben:

Just a few lines in haste.

Of course, there is nothing to be done with Roosevelt now. However, I agree that we should prepare a plan for him. I will discuss this with Lewis when I see him and then write you what we think the best way of going about it.

It is grand to have Aline here again. She is staying until Nov. 12th or thereabouts. I hope we are going to see you before then. . . .

As always,
Clarence

143 To Benton MacKaye

New York City   November 12, 1932

Dear Ben:

Well, Roosevelt is elected, and I wonder what it is going to mean as far as regional planning goes. Of course, I haven't the slightest doubt that he will say very nice things about it, but what will he do in a practical way? I think it would be a good idea for us to write out a program and see whether we can influence him.[1] The attitude toward national highways should be a very definite part of such a program. Let's think it over and try to get together some time in December. . . .

Aline left yesterday. She was awfully sorry that she didn't see you while here in the East. I am hoping to be able to go out there for a week at Christmas time, and she will be back in a few months.

I talk to Lewis over the telephone now and then but seldom see him. He is keeping busy, and I have been very much on the go. If you have not entirely given up the habit of reading the newspapers, you may have read that the Reconstruction Finance Corporation has decided to lend money to the big housing development on which I have been working. . . . If we do go ahead, it will be an immense step in housing.

When am I going to see you?

Yours,
Clarence

1. Late in September, Benton had written to Clarence about the probability that "FDR would 'get there' and if so . . . how [could] he run the country unless the RPAA tells him about it?" MacKaye was pessimistic about FDR listening to them. "However," he wrote, "let not our own small chances go completely by default" to argue for "communities, townless highways, parks, and forests." On 4 November 1932 he wrote to Clarence that he expected "to remain conservative and vote for Norman Thomas."

144   To Aline Stein

Pittsburgh, Pa.[1]   Tuesday, November 14, 1932

Aline beloved:

I will write you another note today, as I will be back in New York and the struggle tomorrow and there may be no time.

This afternoon we went to see the Buhl houses. There is a thrill in having played a part in building such a community. It is beautiful.[2]

They certainly need beauty in this God-forsaken town. We were taken on a bus trip to see the engineering feats with which they have been trying to make this impossible hilly site into a great, functioning city. We went through six-million-dollar tunnels into barren valleys with a few forlorn wooden shacks, over extravagant bridges into the smoke of ugly factories and dilapidated slums. The engineering waste of bridges, highways, tunnels is worse than those subways you have heard so much about.[3] And to think that my friend Fred Bigger has been devoting the best years of his life to making this mess and labeling it *city planning!* Why don't people know when to quit?

This noon I had to preside. I didn't prepare so it was all right.

This evening [Louis] Brownlow and [Thomas] Adams on community life fifty years from now. You are right, the latter is a stuffed shirt. There is something sound about Louis Brownlow. Anyhow, he says it so well he makes you believe.

And now, it is time to catch a train, so good-bye, my darling.

Clarence

1. Clarence was attending the annual meeting of the American Institute of Planners.

2. Chatham Village has, if anything, increased in quality after sixty-five years. It provides such an excellent living environment that it shows clear signs of gentrification. In the mid-1980s efforts were made to convert it from a cooperative to an "equity cooperative" ownership. Many Pittsburgh architects and planners live there, and the parking areas have some Mercedes Benz and BMW automobiles in them.

3. Clarence "Subway" Stein was a lifelong hater of New York's subways. Mumford expressed well their shared opinion of this modern form of transportation, calling them "people sewers."

---

145   To Aline Stein

Pittsburgh, Pa.   Tuesday, November 15, 1932

Darling:

A second clear day in Pittsburgh. Who will say that even a depression hasn't advantages? The factories are closed; there is no black smoke.

This is a talky conference. Yesterday morning Henry Wright and R.D.K. and Ackerman were the program. The latter mystified his audience with technocracy. Robert [Kohn] and Henry [Wright] roused that Doughboy, [Edward] Bassett,[1] father of your schoolmate, who said a good word for the abominable wooden houses of Queens. (I think he is retained by companies that hold the mortgages.) Henry came back at him in good form in the evening, when he showed pictures of the rotten stuff along with such good housing as the Phipps and Buhl. The boys do have fun!

[As] the office did not do the talking in the afternoon, we went out for a walk— Henry [Wright], [Russell Van Nest], Black, and I—to see a housing/city planning exhibit at the Carnegie Institute. Going to and from it, we passed through vast galleries lined with sugary paintings, the leftovers from the annual international exhibits.

Just had a letter from Frank Vitolo. He says that Straus is all excited and seems to be ready to fight.[2] I can't wait to get back.

Henry Klaber, Ascher, and Brownlow . . . say the Chicago papers had your picture taking breakfast, and [you] saying your family affairs were none of their business, or something. . . .[3]

And all my love,
Clarence

1. Bassett, an attorney/city planner, was an expert on zoning law.

2. Local and national difficulties with the approval of the Hillside Homes project had convinced Stein that the project might die an early death.

3. Aline, now becoming a celebrity, had been interviewed by the press in Chicago before boarding *The Chief* for Los Angeles.

---

146   To Benton MacKaye

New York City   November 16, 1932

Dear Ben:

Just a line to acknowledge receipt of your letter. I spent Sunday afternoon over at Sunnyside with Lewis. We both think that the Regional Planning Association [the RPAA] should definitely draw up a program for Franklin D., even if he never has time to look at it. So, send along your suggestions. Try to put the idea that you had in the "Open Door" about housing, highways, and wilderness areas into a few paragraphs.

We are having a grand old fight in regard to the building of the housing development on which I have been working so long. All the property interests in New York are against us, but we haven't given up hope!

As always,

Clarence

---

147   To Aline Stein

[New York City]   Friday, November 18, 1932

Darling:

Three letters from the train have come, but not a word since you arrived. I want so much to hear about how you found everything, and what you are doing, and, of course, what you are to play.

Today is the hearing before the Board of Estimates in regard to the [tax] exemption of housing. Yesterday morning it looked gloomy for us. Seemed as though everyone would appear on the other side. I got to work on a talk or newspaper release for Straus, whom I thought would represent us. About one, Eken phoned from Washington that he and Straus would have to stay there and continue the argument with the RFC. I suspect Straus just didn't want to be here. His position on the battlefield is apparently not at the front. But, perhaps, after all, it is better that we do not appear ourselves. After all, the hearing is not supposed to be about the Hillside Housing, but about the tax exemption as a whole. But someone must appear, and our [presentation] . . . must be organized.

I got to work at the telephone. I found that the civic clubs were o.k., not shouting for Hillside, but for postponement of the hearings, which will serve. Then I called up Eken's office and discovered that they had at last got the labor unions in line. It seems someone had been telling them lies, that we were importing all our materials and what not. Now they are all het-up and ready to insist on work going ahead. A lawyer of Straus's, to whom he had phoned, came to the office, and he started calling up everyone in the Bronx and telling them to come to the hearing with their organizations. I don't know whether they are to invite their organizations or not. Anyhow, there will be a crowd, and they call it Architecture.

Here is all my love,
Clarence

---

148   To Aline Stein

[New York City]   Wednesday, November 22, 1932

Aline dear:

Last night I went to a dinner at the New School. Fool affairs these serious dinners. Subject: housing. Victims: Robert [Kohn], Henry [Wright], and Albert Mayer [the builder], to say nothing of the seventy or so listeners. But what can you say to a room full of human sponges? Anyhow, it all seemed too technical to me, and then to cheer things up they asked Edith Elmer Wood to say a few words, and she got started and forgot how to stop.[1] Thank God, I said nothing to bore them. Nothing to the crowd. I don't know about my neighbors. There was a bejeweled aunt of Ernest's across from me and a young matron who I couldn't see through the paint next to me. It looked bad. Then came an elderly man to sit at my left. He was introduced as [the banker, Frank] Vanderlip,[2] and I asked myself what can I talk about to a banker? And would you believe it, we had much in common. Goodhue did his sister's house, which I know well; he knows California Tech. He owns the beautiful Portuguese Bend and wants us to call on him next time we pass, and he is bugs on technocracy. Attends their meetings, has copies made of their graphs, knows Ackerman, and thinks it would be o.k. if they weren't going to do funny things with money. Bankers can be human, too. . . .

Love to you, my beloved,
Clarence

1. See Eugenie Birch, "Woman Made America," in Donald A. Krueckeberg, *The American Planner* (New York: Methuen, 1983). This is an excellent review of Wood's contributions. RPAA member Edith Elmer Wood's interest in housing reform as a young women led her to focus on housing economics in housing policy in her graduate studies of political economy. Wood opposed Lawrence Villier's approach to tenement house design reform and minimum standards. Her 1919 book, *The Housing of the Unskilled Wage Earner* (New York: Macmillan), is considered the first scientific discussion of the problem. Her extraordinary knowledge of housing statistics

and strong and detailed views on public policy were published in several important books and may have made her speeches more complex than most.

2. Frank A. Vanderlip, a New York banker, was unhappy about Hoover's inaction in response to the economic depression. He was a member of a group of liberal Republican businessmen who voted for Roosevelt and formed the "Committee for the Nation," which proposed planned price inflation to rebuild purchasing power. He was involved in discussions about financing several housing ideas in which Clarence had an interest.

---

149 To Aline Stein

[New York City]   Saturday, November 26, 1932

Beloved:

It is but a few hours since I wrote you at the Lafayette, but I have re-read your letters just now, so I must scribble a few lines before going to the office. Your letters are grand. So warm, so you! And it's fine to know that the Foxes appreciate you and that you are having such a grand time.[1] There does not seem to be anything to answer.

At the office yesterday we went on improving our plans. They are just about set now. The little model is a wonder. I must get a photograph of it for you. And now Straus has the idea of having another model made at the same scale showing a typical part of the Bronx, housing an equal number of people. It is going to be done and, if the comparison does not lead to the ultimate destruction of and replacement of the rotten stuff, I am a poor guesser. It will not be the worst of it that we will show, not old, large tenement houses, but those that have been built since 1900. Even these are unbelievably bad.

I had suggested to Straus that he induce the [New York] Times to ask Lewis Mumford to write an article on the meaning of our development. At first, they said yes, but afterward phoned that this was a controversial matter and an economic rather than an architectural one, so they would get someone else. When I heard this, I told Straus that we did not differ between the architectural and economic. He answered that he had discovered that I approached architectural problems differently from other architects and that, if he had known me sooner, it might have been a good thing for him, as well as for me, which is probably what the Honorable Al Smith calls "baloney."

Nonetheless, I love you.

Clarence

1. Fox Studios had bought part of Aline's time from Warner Brothers so she could act in *Heros for Sale* with Loretta Young, Richard Barthelmess, Grant Mitchell, and Ward Bond.

150   To Aline Stein

[New York City]   Saturday, December [3], 1932

Aline darling:

Two grand letters from you and [a] very beautiful one from Belle [Moskowitz]. Made me feel like excusing her for having a son named Joe.[1] By the way, Eken has faced her, and it is arranged that we are to have her personal time. We will see. Trouble is, she tries to do too many things. Running the governor is job enough for one lady. Did you see his plan for reorganizing the city government? He certainly knows how to face problems of government and think them through. Not that his answer to our problems is very original, but it is an answer. And he even is willing to admit that we must pay for the subways. If he only would go one step forward and—you know the favorite speech of Clarence "Subway" Stein.

The models [of Hillside] are wonderful. The one showing existing conditions is unbelievable. I have to look at the airplane views of the Bronx to believe that we have not [exaggerated it]. But there are miles of this brutal congestion. I feel like a crusader. I am going to destroy it. But first, we will exhibit the two models in the window of the Empire State Building. I will send you photographs of them. . . .

With much, all my love,
Clarence

1. Belle Moscowitz had left her son in charge of the publicity campaign for Hillside Homes. Clarence Stein was not pleased with the job he did.

151   To Catherine Bauer

[Los Angeles, California]   January 11, 1933

Dear Miss Bauer:

I have just re-read your two letters. There seems nothing to answer. It sounds as though the exhibition work [is] moving as quickly as possible.[1] But we have only a month, so we will have to soon get after those who have shown no sign of action. It may be worthwhile collecting information from other sources (magazine write-ups, for instance) and sending them to those responsible for projects for checking if they are too lazy to collect the data we have asked for. Probably you have done this.

I am not quite certain how I will route my home trip. I have just had a telegram from Dallas, Texas, asking me to stop there. The chances are, however, I will go by way of Chicago. I will do so unless I telegraph the office within the next few days. You might write me c/o Alfred Stern at Chicago for any information you want there.

The outline of advice to a future president looks good, but apparently, after we have told him why he should be good, we will have to make up our [mind about] just what he is to do if he wants the RPAA Sunday school medal. I hope Lewis's draft arrives before I leave.[2]

In spite of temptation to spend all the time in loafing here in the land of springtime, I am devoting some four hours or so a day to what approximates work. As a result, three and almost four chapters of the book are in rough draft form. I am afraid to re-read them for fear I will throw them in the fire. I will have a third of the book in form to judge what it is going to be like before I get back. I am discovering innumerable fields for research.[3]

Aline sends her fond regards.

Cordially,

Clarence S. Stein . . .

1. Bauer continued to work for Stein and the RPAA part-time until late 1934. She became secretary of the organization and did extensive research for Stein in preparing exhibitions of his projects and articles on community planning and housing projects.
2. The RPAA was preparing its housing and planning policy recommendation for FDR, who was to take office as president of the United States on 5 March 1933.
3. Clarence Stein continued to work on this manuscript on housing until mid-1934. A copy of the work in its last state is in the CSS papers at Cornell.

---

152   To Aline Stein

[New York City]   January 20, 1933

Aline beloved:

Benton [MacKaye] just arrived and has had breakfast with me, and we have talked of you, and of Shirley Center, and of technocracy. Ben was one of the original workers of the Technical Alliance with Scott and Stuart Chase, you know.[1] We have just started, Ben and I. We will go over it all again as we walk down.

Benton didn't know whether to come on account of the expense. But Lewis Mumford and I decided that now was the time for him to look around for a publisher and for us to give him what help we could with his book. So I sent him $25 (told him funds were low so I didn't send more).

The Steins at this end of the continent are economizing, or trying to. Miss Morris and I have cut down the office budget as far as we could. Boat [to Europe] is out for the present. Albert [Mayer] and [Alan] Kamstra cut to twenty dollars [per week] with no promise after a month. At home Mia has agreed to try to cut household expenses to twenty dollars a week (though she is still feeding me with the fat of the land), and we will probably only have the laundry woman every second week. Mia [is] doing some of it. I have almost forgotten what the interior of a taxi looks like, and I eat only three good meals a day.

And then I get orders to go and buy out Creighton and Stan and Andrews, no less.[2] Well, I will go and see what they have, but the buying will probably wait until you come back. Anyhow, Tugwell of Columbia, economic adviser of Roosevelt, says, "Don't inflate." He at least is considering the plight of the poor movie actress.

Lunch with Al Bing yesterday. We are such close friends again now that we are not working together. Florence is enjoying a nervous breakdown at one of Al's hotels.

Lewis spent a good part of the afternoon here at the house reading all that I have written of my book. He thinks that it certainly should be published [and] likes the style of the first chapter, which is more or less the way I want to write it. Says I did a lot of work, and generally he made me feel happy.[3]

My darling,
Clarence

1. The Technical Alliance was a small, relatively short-lived organization through which Thorstein Veblen, who was its "Chief Engineer," proposed to further his criticism of the political economy outlined in his book *The Engineers and the Price Systems* (New York: Viking Press, 1921) and his wavering ideas of a revolution organized by technocrats. Frederick Ackerman, Stuart Chase, Benton MacKaye, and Charles Whitaker were also members. There was a considerable overlap of members of the alliance with the RPAA, although their objectives were quite different. See Max Lerner's introduction to *The Portable Veblen* (New York: Viking Press, 1948), 16–18.

2. These are New York retailers for fine silverware. Aline seems to have decided that sterling silver tableware would be a safe investment in this phase of the depression.

3. Mumford was also preparing copy for the Architectural League's 1933 housing exhibit catalog.

---

153   To Aline Stein

[New York City]   February 3, 1933

My darling:

Your letters are a joy. We had a grand dinner party. Lewis Mumford, Stuart Chase,[1] Benton, and I. Frederick Lee [Ackerman] came up for a little while before dinner and talked technocracy. He is still [so] full of it that it is difficult to keep him on any other subject. During dinner there was much reminiscing about Scott and the early days of the Technical Alliance. Later we discussed our message to the president-elect. Stuart had just received news of Roosevelt's proposal to remake the Tennessee River Valley region, which appears in this morning's paper. So our suggestions for regional planning sounded merely like an echo of his ideas. Guess we will have to be a little more radical, anyhow in words, to keep ahead of the president.[2]

Stuart [Chase] will be in Pasadena about the 16th and will get in touch with you. He and Marion look forward to seeing you.

All my love,
Clarence

1. Stuart Chase, a long-time member of the RPAA, taught economics at Columbia University, where he was an associate of Rexford Tugwell, perhaps the most radical of Roosevelt's close White House advisors. He was the author of *A New Deal* (New York: Macmillan, 1932), which outlined many of the public works, national planning, and social and economic program ideas that became part of FDR's policies during his first term.

2. For a summary of the ideas sent to FDR by the RPAA, see document 160, their letter to him of 1 March 1933.

154   To Aline Stein

[New York City]   February 4, 1933

Beloved:

Last evening dinner for six, the [Russell Van Nest] Blacks, Catherine Bauer, Gertrude,[1] Benton, and me. Gertrude got the stage and held it most of dinnertime. Her tales were interesting, but perhaps the others had interesting things to tell. Who will ever know? But their time comes later. Nature sees to that. While Gert's eyes close for a few minutes, we discuss the welfare of cities, states, and the nation, and particularly the day letter the Regional Planning Association sent to Roosevelt today telling him that he was a good boy.[2]

The Blacks were in town because of a meeting of the City Planning Institute. Ackerman and I attended in the morning—a small group of men growing old. As I looked at some of them, they seemed to turn into skeletons with a parchment skin sticking on—old men talking like babies. Again and again I whispered to Ackerman, "Let's get out; I can't stand any more of this drivel." But he was fascinated. He had to stay and hear the ancient mariners. I left at noon. . . .

Clarence

1. Gertrude was Clarence Stein's sister.
2. A day letter is a form of telegram, delivered the day after it is sent.

155   To Aline Stein

[New York City]   February 5, 1933

Aline darling:

. . . Robert [Kohn] came back yesterday from two days [in] Washington, appearing before congressional committees. Monday he meets with Robert Moses's committee, of which he is a member, to decide which of the many proposals that have been made to the RFC they should try to induce Washington to finance at once.[1] I was curious to see whether Robert would fight for the Hillside housing or whether he would refuse to back it for "ethical" reasons. My fear is that the Moses committee is going to sidetrack Hillside, telling us that they are first going to back those things against which there is no public objection, that they will put over French's lower East Side proposal,[2] to which the bankers seem to have no objection. They say housing has been taken care of.

Robert [Kohn], when I discussed it with him yesterday, seemed to be weakening on the French proposal. He will not oppose it in spite of the fact that it is contrary to all the arguments he has raised. He says at least it would get something going. As to Hillside, he is searching for arguments that will rationalize his desire not to back it. He does not want people to say that he is using a public position to help a job of his associate,[3] but he tried to argue with me that it was too far away, that it should replace existing buildings, that it should be in Brooklyn. All that kind of thing, that he can answer as well as I. I don't know how he will ultimately stand, but I feel pretty badly about it.

Fact is, I feel more discouraged about the job than I ever did. I guess that I will accept the fact that it is not going ahead, that the Realtors and the bankers have been too much for us. Perhaps then, old friend, contrary luck will come to my help.

Anyhow, it's a good world. There is still you, whom I love.

Clarence

1. Robert Moses, who later became chairman of the New York City Housing and Slum Clearances Committee in addition to his role in highway park and power decisions, was chairman of the committee that decided which New York City projects would be submitted to the RFC for funding.

2. F. F. French developed several high-density housing plans for "slum clearance" on the lower East Side of Manhattan in New York in the 1930s. Werner Hegemann, the German urban design authority who edited *The American Vitruvius: An Architect's Handbook of Civic Art* with Elbert Peets in 1922, was very critical of French's plans because of the high density and high ground coverage of the proposal. Stein, Wright, and other RPAA members argued that the owners of slum tenements, who had exploited their tenants, should not be further rewarded by being paid high prices for their property in slum clearance schemes. The correct strategy, they believed, was to build affordable housing on vacant land at the edge of the city for low-income families and to move industries and their jobs in industry to the periphery (perhaps to New Towns but, if this was not possible, to large vacant tracts). Thus, they reasoned, the "antisocial" dollar value would be squeezed out of the slum properties. The RPAA opposition to slum clearance without proper rehousing was an early statement of this position in an argument that continued into the 1960s.

3. FDR had decided to appoint Robert Kohn to head the housing division of the PWA under Harold Ickes. Kohn was later criticized in the press because he had approved Hillside Homes, a project designed by his associate Clarence Stein. So his fears were well grounded.

---

156   To Aline Stein

[New York City]   February 7, 1933

Beloved mine:

New York is as exciting as in the days when the great war was starting. I can't wait until the next newspaper comes out but, as a whole, people seem relieved rather than frightened. At last something is happening. "The weather has been heavy and threatening so long, let her rain and get [it] over with." Everybody wants to show you how little money they have. Lunched at the big table at the City Club and was joshed for having come to eat on credit. I wish I could see and read the Russian papers: "America's banks all closed—The End of Capitalism!" What a great laugh must roar from end to end of Soviet land. But I am afraid they are wrong. We are not done worrying about where we invested our hard-earned paycheck. We have got to let the bankers and the Wall Street boys and the Los Angeles Realtors crank things up once more.

Anyhow, last night on the floor below here, Ackerman tried to tell us about life under technocracy,[1] where there will be no jobs for the above-mentioned gentlemen and where each will have what he needs of plenty. And where a movie queen or a damned good architect will receive no more than anyone else who does his own job as well as he can. Which will be enough? All he can carry? What shall we take? A whole lot of old silver coffee pots? And we can use that precious National Stock to start the fire, so why worry?

My love,

Clarence . . .

1. About a week later, Clarence reported that Oscar Armenger, the socialist editor, had had a discussion with Ackerman, in which Armenger had compared his "formulas to Marx's doctrine" and had "admitted that socialism didn't seem to fit the problems of this age or this land." Oscar Armenger edited several socialist publications, including the *Oklahoma Leader,* later published nationally as the *American Guardian.*

---

157   To Aline Stein

[New York, N.Y.]   February 9, 1933

Aline dear:

Yesterday my faith in the building of Hillside reached its lowest point. The morning papers announced that the Moses committee was going to ask the RFC for money for French's lower East Side housing and take no action for the time being in regard to the Bronx. James of the Housing Board had made a very bad case. Robert [Kohn] told me that his hands were tied, as an engineer on the board had made a point of not voting on a proposition on which one of his associates was working.

Guess the best thing to do is to forget it, if I can.

Lunch with Lewis M. and Catherine B., then to a meeting of the Unemployment Committee.[1] (They are endless.) I presented your check, which I have been carrying around in my pocket. It was received with vast enthusiasm.

Home to work. Robert [Kohn] phoned to ask if I would come up to [Westchester County to] talk with him. As Ben was to be out, I accepted with pleasure.

All is peace and joy, and the Hudson looks beautiful out of the window and perhaps, just perhaps, we may sometime have a house in the country. Who knows, in this world of uncertainty? Only this is sure:

I love you,
Clarence

1. The architects' committee formed in New York to aid unemployed architectural draftsmen.

---

158   To Aline Stein

[New York City]   February 16, 1933

Darling:

At last the housing exhibition is hung.[1] It is a telling show. It will do much to get over, in picture form and through contrast, just what we have been talking about. Something big is likely to happen soon. You turned housing prophet at just about the right time to walk off with the honors. People here are talking of a Housing Authority—the government, state or municipal, going in and replacing large areas. In Cleveland the same idea is taking form. It is the big way to get men working, working usefully. Even if the government at Washington has to lose on its investment, it is better than a dole. They are beginning to see that, some of them, but, of course, Mr. Real Estate, if he realizes what this means, will again say, "Nothing doing!" They are trying to pretend now that slum clearance will not compete as Hillside does, but I can't see how they can put that idea over, not if I get a chance to design the new housing community anyhow. It is all very exciting. I am enjoying it, even though I have not yet taken off my mourning for Hillside.

Our housing exhibit is just a side show of the architectural exhibition, which is at its old [New York Architectural League] home on 57th Street. Joe Urban has built a complete new interior in the three big rooms as a setting. [It's] beautifully done.

There is unity and yet he has focused attention on individual objects by planning corners and niches to trap the visitors' interest. Just my idea of what a museum should do. There is little architecture this year. The smallest of the rooms shows all that was worth showing and some that wasn't. The big hall is given to sculpture and murals, [and] the other to what looks as though it would be an excellent exhibit of theatrical arts—models and masks and all. . . .

Enclosed is Henry [Wright]'s sad note [about his European housing research trip]. Albert Mayer is back,[2] and I will see him tomorrow and hear more of Henry.

My love,

Clarence

1. The Housing Exhibition of 1933 was hung separately from Phillip Johnson's seminal 1933 exhibition of works of modern architecture at the Museum of Modern Art, which generated the cannon's appellation "International Style."

2. This was Albert Mayer the civil engineer and architect, who had been working in Clarence's office for several years. He was just back from a European trip to study housing. The other Albert Mayer was a builder and friend, whose wife was an actress. The architect Albert Mayer seems to have had the means to study European housing on his own.

---

159   To Aline Stein

New York City   March 1, 1933

Darling:

I am up early. The world as seen across [Central] Park is sunny and cheerful. I think I hear the chirp, chirp, chirp of birds through the drone of the automobiles. The window is part open. The air is clear and soft. . . .

Fred Ackerman called yesterday morning, and we walked down to the office. He said he could not see anything in the proposed Tennessee development. It would be another Mississippi Bubble. It was foolish to attempt to do anything until we could do the whole thing, now that nothing can be done under the price system. Fundamentally, Ackerman is right, but I said we should take every possible opportunity of practicing ways of creating a better environment. It is true that Sunnyside and Radburn could not be complete successes under the limits imposed by the present economic setup, but they were worthwhile. No, says Ackerman. There is nothing about the planning of either of these places that any number of us did not know. Give the technician freedom to use his ability. That's all that is needed.

I am finding a growing difference among those to whom I am close mentally: Frederick Lee [Ackerman], Lewis [Mumford], Robert [Kohn]. All of them are after the same objective—a saner world, but off on different roads.

Another letter from Henry Wright yesterday. Less cheerless. They're off to Stuttgart. I hope they see the sun.

Love, my love,
Clarence

---

160 To Franklin D. Roosevelt

[New York City]   March 1, 1933

Dear Mr. Roosevelt:

The Regional Planning Association of America has publicly endorsed your plan for the development of the Tennessee Valley.[1] We believe that it offers the opportunity of using the present emergency to build a better world in which to live when the emergency is over. When our permanent industrial unemployment is translated into the more valid form of leisure, it is only by creating a richer environment that the new leisure will be anything but a curse. It is because your broad-visioned program offers the opportunity to develop just such [an] environment that we wish to point out certain features that we believe should be employed in the realization of the plan.

I. Location and design of new communities in connection with industrial decentralization with the object of building a usable environment. All of our experience of the past indicates that this cannot be attained by speculative land development, individual house building, and chaotic town and village growth. It can only be secured by planning and building complete [and] integrated communities, both small and large. Such towns can be set in the midst of parks and play fields that will offer ample space close to all homes for gardening and outdoor life and will provide the possibility of varying the routine of industry and business with crafts and arts and productive outdoor activities. Radburn, New Jersey, indicates the possibility of relating the plan of a New Town to the actual requirements of living, with a lowering of costs and an increase of human facilities. Your Tennessee program offers the opportunity of broadly developing this [kind of] environment in terms of the house itself, the neighborhood unit, the balanced industrial and agricultural unit, the community, and the region. It should serve as an example for the redevelopment of much of our country.

II. Reform of the transport system by "townless highways." The highway system connecting these individual communities, designed for living, working, and trading, should be regarded essentially as a means of getting from one place to another and not as an excuse for a noxious extension of the towns. Therefore, the roads should be equipped at convenient intervals with stations for entrance, exit, gas, food, and comfort, but with the stretches for fast, safe driving between stations absolutely inaccessible to man or motor car.

III. Conservation of wilderness environment. Your conservation policy in New York State has indicated how, in connection with reforestation, the primeval wilderness can be restored. Now, a wilderness must be difficult to arrive at if it is to retain its untamed character. This kind of natural, wild country is actually being jeopardized in the National Parks, whose special purpose is wilderness preservation, by the building of ill-considered [skyline] motorways. We do not believe that it is the common interest that all public land should be equally accessible. Therefore, we advocate that, side by side with timber growth and stream control in the mountain sections of the Tennessee region, the wilderness character, as such, should be maintained as one of the forest resources.

Your program has fired our imagination and enthusiasm. The Regional Planning Association of America believes it offers the possibility in the present emergency of securing a stable future rather than salvaging the speculative past.

Very truly yours,

[Clarence S. Stein]

1. This proposal, transmitted to FDR by Stein, was a product of the collaborative efforts of Stein, MacKaye, Mumford, Bauer, and other RPAA members. Stein's hand was clear in the first proposal, and MacKaye's in the second and third elements of the recommendation, in which he continues his defense of wilderness preservation and his opposition to the Shenandoah and Smokey Mountain Skyline Drives as destroyers of true wilderness.

---

161   To Aline Stein

March 5, 1933   New York City

Aline darling:

I have just read and re-read the president's inaugural address, a nice collection of short sentences that seem full of meaning and yet, when you try to get at it, most of it, it is not really sharp and pointed.[1] The direction in which he is aiming is apparent, but whether he is going to shoot at the bull's eye or just vaguely in the direction of the target is not plain. True, our "money changers" are bad boys, but will Roosevelt act to take the control of credit out of the hand of the bankers for all time? He is right. Men must be put to work by direct recruiting by the government, as in time of war, but will he have the backbone to use that army to build homes and cities, even if it decreases the "values" of existing property? Excuse me . . . I seem to have forgotten that this is a letter to my darling, and not an editorial. . . .

I suddenly got the idea yesterday morning that I had better draw something out of the bank so as to have ready cash. I have been so deep in my work at the office that I had not heard the gossip that a moratorium would be declared. Ethel [Bernstein] told me of it Friday night. Saturday morning Fine said that Governor Lehman was not going to close the banks. When I asked Miss Morris to go around to the bank and get some money, she said that all the other papers [had] announced the bank holiday.[2] Luckily, I have forty or fifty dollars in my pocket, and business will probably be mainly on credit here. These sure are exciting times. No need of traveling to see revolutions and such like.

Tonight I hear your voice again. There is so much to say.

My darling, I love you,
Clarence

1. FDR's rather short speech compared the national distress to the perils of the nation's pioneers, which had been overcome because the pioneers lacked fear and had faith in their future. He blamed the "money changers" for the crisis and called for unity of spirit and cooperation.

2. New York Governor Lehman issued a proclamation declaring a bank holiday on 5 March 1933 at 4:20 A.M. Illinois and other states followed quickly. So by the time FDR was inaugurated, U.S. banks were closed.

---

162   To Aline Stein

New York City   March 6, 1933

Aline dear:

Yesterday was a good day. I stayed home. There was a lovely sun, so I spent much of the morning out on the balcony all blanketed and comfortable, too comfortable, in fact, to do much work. So I read through the first two chapters to see where I was, to start writing, and I found them so interesting that I did no writing before lunch at half past one. Lunch was good, all but your empty place. Perhaps they will close down the studio, and in a week or so it will not be empty! Afterward, I did not get far with the book. I got thinking about and sketching the new housing development for Cleveland. Real problems are so much more important than theories, or is it merely that they are more fun because they are easier for me.

Then I walked down to 42nd and stopped a while to see a Russian picture just showing off their aeroplanes flying over the Red Square and the crowds so proud of them, and all their big guns, and army, and everybody dancing for joy. And then the American newsreel. Roosevelt making his inaugural address the day after all the banks closed. We haven't been willing to recognize Russia [because] she was economically unsound. I wonder if she will be willing to recognize us now.

Of course, all conversation here drifts around to the banks and did you draw any money out? Will they issue script? What will the president do? [I] dined last night at Lee and Caroline [Simondson's]. There were the Louis Untermeyers, and the Lewis Mumfords, and a daughter of Morgantane, and one or two others. Says Lee, "You don't suppose the bankers will let Washington take any of their power away from them." I suggested that the timely thing for the Theatre Guild to do would be for them to put on a play like George O'Neil's, in which the last act could be us comfortably discussing Lee's question and the first would be set in a salon in Paris just a few days before Louis XVI was thrown in prison with a group of nobles gaily telling each other what the king will do to punish the insolent common herd. Of course, this is a different kind of revolution. It is more like an earthquake: something we can't control. Perhaps it isn't going to bust open this time.[1]

Who is philosophizing now? Who but your darling? And I don't know anything, excepting this, that you should not buy real estate—not in California!

And I love you.

Clarence

1. In 1958 Edmund Wilson titled a collection of his essays about the follies of the 1920s and the period of economic depression and change in the 1930s *The American Earthquake: A Documentary of the Twenties and Thirties* (Garden City, N.Y.: Doubleday and Co., 1958). These essays provide a view of the period that complements Stein's attitudes about society and politics at a time when "the whole structure of American society seemed actually going to pieces."

A little place — but we call it home —
A.M.S & C.S.S.

163   To Aline Stein

[New York City]   March 8, 1933

My dear:

It is like London. The air is so thick and soupy that the buildings at the other side of the park just aren't there. Last night it rained. How it rained! Benton and I had to take taxis to and from Pop's apartment, and I would have you know that taking a taxi these days is an event. . . .

It is exciting at the office, creating, or reasoning into being, this little town to place in the midst of Cleveland. So many things to consider—gardens, and who shall take care of the stairs, what kind of heating, and shall we induce the city to pay for the playground? How to group the houses to take advantage of every breeze on sultry days, and where to hang the wash? Where to hang the wash—that is giving me more trouble than anything else. In the office, at home, as I walk along the street, I am trying to hang out the laundry. It is all over the place.[1] Meanwhile, Frank [Vitolo] adds up long lines of figures and says, "At $8 a room we are in the red." Always in the red, and nowhere to hang the laundry. That's architecture. Downstairs, they are in a different business, a sort of Bergdorf Goodman architecture. Robert [Kohn] and Charlie [Butler] designing monuments with lots of sculpture for Estelle [Kohn] to carve.[2] Robert has ideas, and his designs have force, but— I won't say the rest. . . .

The fog is still thicker—59th Street is gone, and most of the park is lost.

I love you,
Clarence

1. Before the days of electric and gas clothes dryers, "the wash" in high-density, upper-middle-class residential areas was done in commercial laundries or hung out to dry in the rear yards of lower-middle-class and lower class tenement houses. In the first of the new working-class "garden apartments" of the 1930s, which Stein was trying to invent, the laundry was hung in basement rooms, on special racks in bathrooms and kitchens, and in "drying yards."

2. Clarence Stein's architectural firm was entering a competition for the design of a major memorial in Cleveland, Ohio.

---

164   To Aline Stein

[New York City]   March 13, 1933

[After dinner] Lillie [Stein] and Henry [Wright] had to go to concerts, and later Arthur [Mayer] disappeared. The rest eyed our watches from time to time so that we would not fail to turn on the radio at ten to hear the president. The machine [the radio] worked! Roosevelt is certainly clear, and I guess it is all reassuring, but where do we go from here? The banks will reopen, and before long the "money changers" will again be ruling and making or breaking us. I guess [D. H.] Morris [one of FDR's conservative advisors] is right; we are going to have inflation and another spree. I am afraid Ackerman will have to wait until the next time. But let's wait for another act before we decide. . . .

[Balance of letter is missing]

165   To Aline Stein

[New York City]   March 18, 1933

My beloved one:

I have been home all morning working at my book.[1] I have come to the biggest and hardest part of it. I am attempting to explain the relation of the planning of communities and the remaking of our cities to the big picture of reshaping America as a whole. In the other room is Ben, surrounded by maps on which he is trying to chart a scheme of development of our national forests in accordance with the proposal of the president. New communities, reforestation, a plan of the United States! Dreams, yes, but some of the dreams or some part of them may be realized, tomorrow or the next day.

And along comes you and says, "Let's go to Japan."[2] I would love to [see] Japan or anywhere you and I can be together and away from things that separate us. I feel so lonely apart from you. Our letters help bind us, but now and then I feel in your letters that we are apart. Being one with you matters more than anything else. And Japan would be a lovely setting. Japan in spring, but I fear it is not to be. Whether housing is coming in July, as you say, or before is anybody's guess. I should be here, awaiting. . . . Which conclusion is open to momentary change, and we may be sailing to Japan in a month, though I doubt it. I think we will have to find our oneness here this time.

Robert [Kohn] has been down in Washington conferring with the powers, Miss Perkins, Senator Wagner,[3] etc. We will know better what is likely to happen when he returns. . . .

And I love you,
Clarence

1. There was no work at the office. Clarence had speculated in the previous day's letter about letting Catherine Bauer go, even though he felt that "this is the sensible time to work on the book." And he hadn't "the heart" to fire Albert Mayer and Alan Kamstra, but he had cut their salaries again from $20 per week.

2. Plans for travel to Japan or China were a major topic of the Steins' correspondence during the early 1930s. They did travel to China and Indonesia in 1936.

3. Francis Perkins was FDR's secretary of labor, and Robert F. Wagner was a N.Y. senator from 1927 to 1949. Wagner was very much the legislative architect of housing policy during that period.

166   To Aline Stein

[New York City]   March 24, 1933

Beloved:

Last night I dined at the Steins'. . . . I left early and went to Catherine Bauer's. Charles Ascher there, and so [there was] no end of housing talk. Did I tell you that C.B. was going to write a book on European housing using the material that she collected last summer?[1] Lewis [Mumford] induced the Rockefeller Foundation to give her a thousand dollars to help pay expenses, and after much search she found a publisher who was willing to get out the book if she took no royalties on the first thousand. So you see how popular housing books are. I am just as well satisfied to have her work a little less for me during the present financial stringency. . . .

Love, my love,
Clarence

1. Catherine Bauer's first book was *Modern Housing* (Boston: Houghton Mifflin Co., 1934).

167   To Aline Stein

(Our Fifth Anniversary) [New York, March 26, 1933]

. . . If we could only get perspective. We are in the midst of one of the world's great revolutions. Tomorrow there may be no jobs for anyone, no movies, no salaries, and National Casket stock may be only good to start a fire with.

Ackerman came up in the morning and spent a couple of hours fitting the world's troubles into mathematical formulae. . . .

168   To Catherine Bauer

[New York City]   April 10, 1933

Dear Miss Bauer:

I have gone over all the material from Fritz Gutheim,[1] which I am returning herewith. I think you should write to him, sending him a copy of our letter to the president (which is enclosed) and telling him that we have made this as short as possible, but our purpose was to emphasize the fact that the purpose of the development of the Tennessee Valley should not be merely industrial.[2] As far as we are concerned, the working out of better human relations is of much greater importance. This can only be done, as you have indicated in your letter of April 8th, by complete land control.[3]

You might tell him, if you want, that Benton MacKaye is in Washington and can be reached in care of F. M. Kirby, 1322 New York Avenue. MacKaye probably understands the situation as well as anyone else. I do not, however, want to have MacKaye and his knowledge used as a means of helping Nolen or someone else to get a job making another survey. (This, of course, you will not tell Fritz in just these words.) A survey should be made, but what is of greatest importance is the point of view.

If you want to discuss this with me further, I will be at home until 6:30 this evening.

Cordially yours,

Clarence S. Stein

1. Frederick Gutheim was serving as a staff member of the Brookings Institute and later served on the staff of the American Institute of Architects in their Washington office. He was instrumental in inserting into the TVA Act sections 22 and 23, which gave the TVA the rather vague regional planning authority it exercised with so much political caution.

2. A copy of the RPAA's letter to FDR is in the Bauer Papers at the University of California at Berkeley and in Benton MacKaye's papers at Dartmouth College.

3. The RPAA believed that project development in the region should make extensive use of public initiatives based on public land ownership.

---

169   To Benton MacKaye

[New York City]   May 6th, 1933

Dear Ben:

Lewis and I thought that it was about time that we had a meeting of the Regional Planning Association. I would prefer to have the discussion hung around the possibilities of developing the Tennessee as a region and as a sample of what should be done in the rest of the country. Of course, if we do have that as the subject we will need you here. Possibly you will have Washington and the rest of the U.S. organized sufficiently by the date of the meeting so that you can run up here and lead the meeting. Otherwise, we should have a complete report from you on the state of the nation.

I hope that things are going to be cleared up sufficiently so that you will be able to give [Raphael] Zon a definite answer in time to make sure of the job he offered [you], in case something better does not come along. But, of course, it would be much better if you could be connected with the Tennessee affair.[1] That, I think, is much more important than writing. You will get time to do all the writing that is needed, I am sure, even if you are doing an active job, and now is the chance for you to lead them in the right direction, not only by word, but by action.

Your letters are tremendously interesting. Do continue to keep us posted on doings at Washington and particularly your doings. When you get your plan of Tennessee far enough developed, if it isn't too much trouble, I would like immensely to get a Photostat copy or a blueprint with any description that you may have written. . . .[2]

Best wishes from both of us,

Yours,

Clarence

1. Stein, Whitaker, and Chase were working together to secure a post for Benton in the new TVA program, but they were having great difficulty getting information because of the chaos of the early days of the New Deal. Benton had been offered a job by an old friend in the Interior Department, Raphael Zon of the U.S. Forest Service, working with the American Indian program in New Mexico, but he really wanted to work with Arthur E. Morgan in the Tenneessee Valley Authority.

2. Benton MacKaye had started a "plan for planning" in the Tennessee Valley, which included several sketch plans for a 600-square-mile area. Copies are in the MacKaye Family Papers at Dartmouth.

---

170   To Benton MacKaye

[New York City]   May 26th, 1933

Dear Benton:

I have just had a letter from Charlie Whitaker in which he says that [Arthur] Morgan, who has been made head of the Tennessee Valley experiment, knows him very well and that he would be very glad to say a good word for you or give you an introduction. . . .

Robert Kohn has been back and forth between here and Washington a number of times. I am sure he would look you up when he is there, but he is always rushed. It looks as though something could really be doing in regard to housing. But one of the great difficulties, of course, is going to be that so few people there have the slightest idea what it is all about.

As a result of the discussion at the meeting of the Regional Planning Association the other night, Lewis and I have been working on a very simple memorandum. It is still in rough shape, or rather Robert Kohn has offered a great many criticisms and suggestions that we want to put into the final draft. Just as soon as it is in a little better shape, I will send you a copy.

The meeting of the Regional Planning Association was a fairly lively affair. It was attended by Messrs. Black, Bright, Kohn, Mumford, Wright, Gilchrist, Emmerich, Albert Mayer, and Mrs. Wood and Miss Bauer. There was plenty of difference of opinion, but finally we worked out a pretty definite and straightforward program. . . .

Best wishes from Aline and

Clarence

171   To Benton MacKaye

[New York City]   June 3, 1933

Dear Ben:

Your statement in regard to the Tennessee Valley is a masterly job. I haven't yet been able to work out just what is going to be the best way to get it to Mr. [Arthur] Morgan. I feel that, if it were handed to him without preliminary preparation, it would merely get into the files. To me, its meaning is very clear because I know so much of the background of your thought that has been boiled down in this thing. To give it to someone else, no matter how intelligent, would need a certain amount of preparation. I have thought of the possibility of our just writing to [Arthur] Morgan, sending him copies of the letters we have already sent to the president and possibly your *Survey* article. I don't know whether that is the best thing or not. Perhaps he should have word from one or two people as to just who we are. Let me think a little bit more about it, and send me your ideas. . . .

To come down to procedure or personnel, we certainly would have a tough time, if it were our job, to find the people who could properly carry out this work. There are very few landscape architects, in my opinion, who are good for anything excepting laying out pretty gardens. As for chief planner, who would you suggest for that job?

Under maps on page 6, Lewis suggested that the words "a possible goal of," appearing before the word "resettlement," be eliminated, leaving just the word "resettlement."

I hope you get the Indian job. I think there is much more likelihood of something being done there than in connection with the Tennessee Valley affair. At the present time, doing something real, no matter how small, is, after all, better than just dreaming big plans.

We had a grand time at Lake Champlain. Aline sends affectionate greetings.

As always,
Clarence

172   To Aline Stein

[New York City]   June 11, 1933

Darling:

Early morning. The sun is shining brightly on [Central] Park, but the breeze is cool. We live again!

Yesterday all day at the office. The Radburn apartment group [plan] should be in Washington by Tuesday.[1] Herbert Emmerich came over to help prepare papers, and he lunched with the rest of us, including Pop (a bit worn by the weather), Charlie [Butler], who has taken a new lease on life since we got this job (knock wood), and Henry Wright. The latter came back from Washington with Robert this morning. He saw Benton. In fact, he set up his way to the West. There [Benton is] to be a big chief.[2] It seems Ben was bowled over by the fact that he at last had a job. I guess, really, he would have liked to escape it. And he had to have a hundred and fifty dollars or something of that kind to get west. So Robert and Henry lent him all they had. . . .

Your philosophical letter from this side of the Chicago Fair arrived and also [the] enclosed telegram, which you may be able to translate. All I care is that it is from my beloved.

Who I love,
Clarence

1. Al Bing and the directors of the City Housing Corporation had decided to go ahead with a long-planned apartment project at Radburn and to seek RFC financing. Frederick Ackerman designed it.

2. MacKaye had taken a position at Gallup, N.M., with the Department of the Interior's Forest Service and the Bureau of Indian Affairs on the Indian reservations of New Mexico and Arizona.

---

173   To Aline Stein

[New York City]   June 16, 1933

Dearest mine:

Early morning—back from Washington. It seems such a long time that I have been away. But I did not leave here until 10:30 yesterday morning and did not get to Washington until 3:30. It was half past two there. So there was afternoon enough to do much running around with Robert [Kohn]. He certainly is on the move. All problems no one else can solve, they send on to him. "What's that got to do with me?" he says, but he enjoys it. The new public works government doesn't exist yet, as the president hasn't signed the bill, but they are all as busy as beavers. They are, most of them, officers. Generals and majors, and the chap who runs errands is a lieutenant (ha, ha, or something). It is like playing school.[1]

All my jobs were there yesterday. I brought down the drawings of Radburn. [Andrew] Eken came down about Hillside, and I met the head of the Cleveland project. That is the only one that troubles me. They do not know where they are going, and just as soon as they get the promise of money they will have to go fast: six weeks to start building.

In the evening with Robert to a dinner meeting to discuss the advisability of the government developing small farms as part of its housing program. Present: brain trusters, secretary of agriculture and his followers, engineers and other in Public Works, etc. Our host was a Mr. Harriman, president of the U.S. Chamber of Commerce, or some such impossible organization. And he started things off by saying, "Of course, we all agree that we must have decentralization. Our big cities must be broken up." The world does move, says your

Subway Stein,

who loves you

1. In 1933, the work of Stein and others on specific housing projects in New York and several other cities was out ahead of and possibly therefore "hung-up" by FDR's policy makers and administrators. Stein had started the work locally and applied for a loan from the Reconstrcution Finance Corporation during the Hoover presidency. Even though the fabled "first hundred days" of FDR's New Deal presidency were over by late June 1933, there was residual uncertainty and confusion about New Deal housing policy and its implementation. Administration of these programs was precariously balanced between the liberal Republican Secretary of the Interior, Harold Ickes, a new group emerging from the young people working under "Brain Truster" Henry Wallace, including Rexford Tugwell, and a White House group, including Utah banker Marriner Eccles, who were drafting the private sector-oriented Housing Act of 1934. Stein and his Hillside Homes projects were caught in the crossfire between these contending groups, while FDR, as was his style, waited for the dust to settle.

---

174   To Aline Stein

[New York City]   June 18, 1933

Aline dear:

This housing with governmental assistance is like a dream where you struggle up a great stairway, only to find that the stair has reversed, and what seemed the top is really the bottom of a much longer flight. When I was in Washington, it looked as though it was all set. I saw all those who were to be in charge of housing. They were all ready to go into action as soon as the president signed the Recovery Bill, and it looked as though one of my projects would be first in line for action. The president signed the bill and left on a three-week vacation, but he did not appoint the group that R. D. [Kohn] and the others had so carefully organized during the past weeks. In fact, as far as they can find out, he forgot all about them. So there they are, there I am, all in a heap at the bottom of the stairs. Perhaps Mr. Roosevelt may stop sailing long enough to push a lever and throw the bottom of the stairs up to the top. Dictators are fine, when they are on your side. . . .

Mrs. Paul Baerwald told Gertrude that Jennie seems to be getting along with the present German government and is continuing her work. . . .[1]

Until tonight, goodbye, my love.

Clarence

1. Jennie Baerwald, a friend of Clarence's younger sister, Lillie, had taken on the task of assisting the immigration of Jewish intellectuals persecuted by the Nazis. Stein's letters to Aline reported regularly on Jennie's work from 1933 to 1935. Mr. Paul Baerwald, Jennie's father or father-in-law (we are not sure which) was very active before and during World War II in the efforts of New York Jews to assist in this life-saving immigration.

---

175   To Aline Stein

[New York City]   June 20, 1933

Darling:

I slept late and there is much to be done at the office, so this will be a short note.

I have just gone through the newspaper carefully to see what is happening in Washington in regard to Public Works. But I can't make head or tail of it. Have Robert's plans all been smashed? Are the politicians instead of the engineers and architects going to determine policy and give out jobs? What a chance for either an orgy of graft or a big step forward in public policy and real planning.[1] We will see. Robert was called down to Washington again Sunday. No word from him yet. Meanwhile, I am trying to get things ready in Jersey to put through the Radburn apartments if Washington approves them. [I went] with Frank and the lawyer of the City Housing to see the secretary of the Public Service Commission, which is in charge of such housing. More politics.

The birthday flowers were lovely, both here and at the office. I wish I knew what they were all called. . . .

Catherine Bauer dined here. Then to see Fred Astaire. He is the show. He dances all over. There is a seriousness about his movement, like the Spanish. And gaiety. A studied art.

My love, I must go.

Clarence

1. On June 17 FDR had signed the Bank, Rail, and Industry Bills and the National Recovery Act. In New York City, $25 million in federal aid had been requested for construction, and another $50 million was being readied. By June 19, the *New York Times* had reported that 1,619,000 jobs had been created during the preceding two months. On June 24, $900 million was allocated to New York's road system, including funds for the Triborough Bridge.

---

176   To Benton MacKaye

[New York City]   June 22, 1933

Dear Ben:

Every day since I had news of your departure for the West, I have intended to write to you. . . . It was fine that Henry Wright and Robert Kohn could be there when the great news came. . . .[1]

Gutheim stopped at the office yesterday for a few minutes to talk about you and about Tennessee. He brought your plans with him. Apparently, Gutheim has had no contact with the authorities of the Tennessee project. However, he has seen a man who was appointed to be in charge of planning and housing. Perhaps he has written you about him. He is a southern landscape architect and, from what Gutheim tells me, not at all the man to head up regional planning.[2] In fact, I don't think he knows what it means. Gutheim was very much worried, but Brownlow, whom he saw, told him that this chap would probably not do much more than a single town.[3] That's bad enough, of course, unless he really is more of a man than Gutheim seems to think he is.

I have tried to find out what the best approach to [Arthur E.] Morgan is.[4] I think it is very much better if he knows about us before I go to him than if I just send him a letter, as we did to the president. The fact is, I would like to go with Robert Kohn and have been hoping that the appointments would be made in the Public Works Administration. If Robert Kohn got the important position there, he could, as a fellow office holder, call up Morgan and make an appointment. However, nothing has developed in regard to the appointments in Public Works. The president signed the bill and went away on a sailing trip, leaving everything up in the air. There are good things to be said about dictators but, if they are going to run a job like the U.S. and keep everything in their own hands, they will have to work more than 24 hours a day and every day. . . .

I was in Washington a week ago. It was a hurried trip in regard to housing. I tried to get in touch with Fritz Gutheim but could not reach him. In the evening I attended a meeting called to discuss the subject of Subsistence Gardening Housing. It appears that somebody dropped into the Recovery Bill a little paragraph which put aside some $5,000,000 or $25,000,000 (I never can remember just what the figures are in that bill) for Subsistence Gardens. Nobody seems to know just how they are to be organized. So they got together the highlights of the Agricultural Department, including its head [Henry Wallace], and those who are to take charge of Public Works, along with some of the famed members of the Brain Trust. Robinson, president of the U.S. Chamber of Commerce, of all people, called the meeting. He started off by saying of course there is one thing we are all agreed on—that is, that we are going to have decentralization and our big cities will be broken up. Nobody was willing to say "No" to this, but I cannot see that anybody knew just what to do with the Subsistence Gardens, particularly the agricultural people, who are trying to puzzle out just what to do with our so-called oversupply of food!

Anyhow, I was glad to be at the meeting because I had a chance to have a short talk with Tugwell. I told him that I was anxious to get in touch with the Tennessee Authority, and he said that it was a one-man affair and that I would have to get to see Morgan.[5] Then someone who was with us said that Tugwell's great problem at the present time was to know what advice to give in regard to spending the money that had been appropriated for highways. I said there was no problem there—put it all into townless highways. He seemed to know what I meant but didn't see just how it could be done because of legislative restrictions. I told him of our effort to do away with those difficulties at the last session of Congress. He promised to get me in touch with the man in charge of highways the next time I came down.

I hope to go up to see Lewis at his retreat this weekend. He is hard at it, trying to get his book finished. Henry is off at Cleveland at present in an attempt to get the housing situation there straightened out.

I am glad that they have landed you at or near Gallup, N.M. Aline and I on our way to and from California always pass through that station. So we will look forward to seeing you and your tribe there next time our train stops. Aline is back in California. Were she here, she would join me in sending her very best.

Yours,

[Clarence]

1. MacKaye had accepted a position with the Bureau of Indian Affairs at Gallup, N.M., working on Zuni and Navajo lands in Arizona and New Mexico. Robert Kohn and Henry Wright had seen MacKaye off when he left by train for the West.

2. The landscape architect Earl Draper, who had worked for many years with John Nolen in the Southeast, was indeed placed in charge of land planning for the TVA.

3. That was what happened. The single town was Norris, Tenn., designed by Tracy Augur along Radburn Plan lines and built for workers constructing the Norris Dam.

4. Arthur E. Morgan, the champion of the small community and an innovative hydraulic engineer who was then president of Antioch College, had been appointed chairman of the three-person TVA board of directors. Morgan was eventually eclipsed by Lillienthal, who was not at all sympathetic to the regional planning ideas of the RPAA.

5. Mumford was working on *Technics and Civilization,* which was published in 1934 (New York: Harcourt Brace).

---

177 To Aline Stein

Amenia, New York   The Mumfords' place[1]   Late Sunday afternoon, June 25, 1933

Dear Aline:

. . . I was greeted at the Amenia Station by the Mumfords and two guests   embryo regionalists [Frederick] Gutheim and [Oscar] Stonorov, cultured young gentlemen.[2] The latter is a Russian architect, polished by a roaming education through most of Europe. Gutheim is young but determined to put the world to right at once.

Sophie seemed overjoyed to see me [and] greeted me with a kiss!

We went swimming in a lovely private lake and did no end of talking 'til I turned in at nine.

Home again, and just telephoned to you, beloved one.

The Mumfords' place is simple, one of these old houses that grew. Upstairs, all steps up and down and much half finished. Sophie does most of the cooking, and good enough, too. Lewis is writing with tireless energy, up and at it before 6 or 6:30 this morning, as usual, and hard at his typewriter until long after noon, I'm told. Today he quit at 10 to go walking with us. At noon, when we were were rid of the other guests, Lewis and I could spend a long afternoon taking the world apart and putting it together again.

All my love,

Clarence . . .

1. Mumford's summer home was a farmhouse at Amenia, N.Y., in Dutchess County, eighty miles north of Manhattan.

2. Stonorov was now practicing architecture in Philadelphia.

---

178   To Aline Stein

New York City   July 1, 1933

Beloved one:

The heat mists hang over the park, so I can see the mass but not the detail of the buildings across the way. By afternoon I will be in the country, but I doubt if it will be any cooler up there. It will be good to be with the Bernsteins.

Lee [Simonson] has left, and Mia is gradually getting the apartment into shape again. Lee looks upon the place as one great ash tray and, although Mia spotted the place thick with little silver trays, there were never enough. It was for such as Caroline that heaven was invented.

Henry [Wright] and I had a talk yesterday as to our future relations. I am glad it was his suggestion. It has been growing more and more apparent to me that the relation of partners in any of these jobs is difficult. I have got to have the right of final and definite decision in conferring with such people as Eken. In fact, in any housing problem where there are so many possible solutions and so many factors to be considered, a time comes when someone must decide on the road to take and then stick to it unless reasons of the greatest weight for change come along. Henry, as you know, is not one to cooperate on final decisions or to take the responsibility of action. On the other hand, he is an inspiring (if sometimes annoying) critic. Hereafter he is to be consultant on my work, as on that of other architects.[1] That will be better, don't you think? I will see that he is well paid on my work. And I suggested that I should [help] him in making agreements with other architects as to what they are to pay him. He agreed that that would be of great help.

The first section of Henry's book is coming out in the magazine *Architecture* this month. He is in seventh heaven. . . .

I love you, my one,

Clarence

1. Disagreements about Hillside Homes and several other New York City housing projects led to a separation of these longtime associates. Wright wanted the recognition of equal partnership. Stein had always been and continued to be chary of such fixed relationships. Wright was a consultant architect and site planner on the Cleveland, Ohio, slum clearance and public housing projects that became Lakeview Terrace and Cedar Apartments.

---

179   To Aline Stein

[New York City]   July 10, 1933

My darling:

Robert is well satisfied with the world and himself.[1] He has insisted that he did not want to be director of housing, but he would have been heartbroken if he hadn't been appointed. And he is the only man that can do the job, if it can be done at all. He wanted to tell me all about it. Of his meeting with the cabinet, and how they asked him what policy he would pursue, and how radical he was, giving them something much like the proposals of the Regional Planning Association [of America] (which was in the *Octagon* I sent you),[2] and how they accepted it. And how Sawyer, the acting administrator, had neglected to tell him of his appointment for two weeks after it had been approved by the Cabinet. And all that he hoped to do. We talked. He talked, all morning. Meanwhile, we took a long walk through the woods to the Gerard Swopes. . . .

Clarence

1. Robert Kohn had been formally appointed chief of the Housing Division of the PWA by FDR.
2. The 1933 volume of *Octagon,* the journal of the AIA.

---

180   To Benton MacKaye[1]

New York City   July 11, 1933

Dear Ben:

. . . Robert Kohn has been appointed as head of the Housing Division of Public Works. He has a great opportunity and, as you can well imagine, is probably going to have a big fight to put through his program. He is going to follow, as far as possible, the program of the Regional Planning Association. . . .

Kohn is likely to surround himself with other members of the Regional Planning Association either as full-time workers or as consultants. Klaber, Mrs. [Edith Elmer] Wood, [Russell] Black, Henry [Wright], possibly Ackerman, may all be called into the game. I am going to stay on the outside and try to get some of the houses built. I understand that Bob Bruere is already at the Capitol working under Johnson. We will have to get you back there before long and move the headquarters of the RPAA.

Nothing definite has been done in regard to the Tennessee Valley. I really think we have been wise to wait, as we will have a much better approach now to Morgan through Kohn, as they will probably have to work together.[2] I have asked Kohn to try to arrange for a meeting with [Arthur] Morgan and possibly the other members of the Tennessee Valley Authority. . . .

Write soon and tell us more of your adventures.

My very best to you.

Clarence

1. This letter was addressed to MacKaye in Arizona.
2. Through their various friends in Washington, RPAA members were, by October 1933, instrumental in generating an offer to Benton of a position as Regional Planner in Earl Draper's division of the TVA staff.

---

181 To Aline Stein

[New York City]   July 13, 1933

Beloved one:

It is clear and cool, cool enough. (Yesterday morning it was almost cold and I wanted a fire, but, of course, there was no wood. Mia hates that fireplace.) This morning it is a fine and pretty world, and I feel like crowing along with our rooster in the park.

So I guess I am well again. That's what I get for persisting yesterday working, even when I grew tired. Oh, I know it was foolish, but there was so much to be done. All these wonderful dream jobs: Radburn apartments to be revised, slum clearance in the nineties on the East River to be discussed with Eken and then new drawings made. He (Eken) is just back from Washington and sure Hillside will soon be approved. Finally, a pilgrimage to Wall Street in taxi to all the winged bankers, who seem to be really serious about making housing spring up simultaneously in all corners of the U.S. and at once.[1] There is so much information that must be collected if we are to do it wisely. What can workers afford? What are building costs? What kind of houses do they prefer in each place? Etc., etc. Today's job is to start getting that information from Pittsburgh, Milwaukee, the New York region, and Los Angeles. I don't think I can trust any of the real estate men, even

Harold, and I am not sure enough of the architects. They might blabber. Here is a really good job for you and you waste your time in the movies!

Last evening there were four of us for dinner—Lewis [Mumford], Henry Wright, and Frederick Lee [Ackerman]. Such a stimulating group. We dined in front of the living room window. Our blue room doesn't have a chance these times. It just has to be satisfied to be beautiful. . . .

My love, my love,
Clarence

1. Clarence was referring to an idea for building housing developed by a group of New York financiers, including his new friend, Frank A. Vanderlip, a New York banker and FDR advisor. They planned to build large-scale housing projects on obsolete airfields near large cities. In the summer of 1933, Frank Vitolo of Stein's office made an extended flying trip to evaluate these sites.

---

182   To Aline Stein

[New York City]   July 16, 1933

My darling:

Robert [Kohn] was in town during the morning. He has no organization as yet, as those higher up insist that salaries be cut to the bone and RDK refuses to offer starvation wages to the trained technicians he wants. So far he has only Henry [Wright], who is working on a per diem basis. Robert saw the governor, who nervously paced the floor. [I] guess he doesn't know what to do, as the city is trying to pass him all its troubles.

In the afternoon Charlie, Frank, and I went out by the railroad to see the aeroplane field on Long Island. I don't know just what to say about the site we looked at. It is true that there are plenty of houses around, new ones, with people living in them, but I don't know why. Yes, the Rockaways are nearby, but why should anyone want to go to far Rockaway? Well, anyhow, it is a great big piece of land all in one ownership, and I guess I will see what I can do to turn its bleak flatness into a place of green beauty. They cut down all the trees and now we will have to put them back. Today is rainy, so there is something to do—thousands of little houses lost in trees.[1]

I love you,
Clarence

1. Floyd Bennett Field on Long Island was one of the old airport sites being considered for large housing developments by a consortium of New York bankers and manufacturers of building materials. Stein's plan for Valley Stream (the new development) was a high-density version of the Radburn Plan. The housing projects designed for abandoned airfields were canceled in 1934 because of negative market reports.

183 To Aline Stein

[New York City]   July 18, 1933

Aline darling:

Yesterday was a fine day. There were three letters from you. Two short ones written in the early hours came in the morning and then a big, fat one all about taking the picture out on location.[1] What good time we make of our work (they call it work), you and I.

How I wish I could spend the three weeks with you, but my weeks now are like months. Perhaps everything I am doing now is just futile. I mean, as far as the projects turning into jobs, but I feel that it is giving me a command, almost a mastery of my metier.[2] I am getting the feel of the orchestra director, of knowing just what note to draw from each instrument and how to fit and weave together the various sounds. Not all yet. There are parts of the orchestra that still seem to be in the darkness, that I have not yet reached. I must get to them, understand their instrument, make them join in. You understand, it is just what you have been going through in acting, but you have been finding, and coming to know, you can command all the instruments within you. And when we have the whole orchestra, ready, in our hands, keen to go, you and I will not care very much, will we? We will throw down our batons and go to Japan.

Perhaps, but I guess I will be tempted to realize just one or two of my dreams. I felt so yesterday at Radburn. Radburn came so close to being. The fundamental ideas are there, but compromise, compromise, compromise.

Herbert Emmerich and I were showing the place to the young city planner [Earl] Draper, who is to be in charge of planning in the government's great Tennessee project. From what I could gather, they are attacking the problem from the right angle: a great social experiment, the world in which man will have a new selection of industry and leisure. May they have the strength to carry through and not lose their track when the hyenas of private interest and real estate start to attack them.

My love, I love you,

Clarence

1. Aline was working on the film *The World Changes* with Paul Muni and Mary Astor.

2. Stein was working on his plan for Valley Stream and the designs for a half dozen other abandoned airport sites being considered for large housing developments in New York, Milwaukee, Pittsburgh, San Francisco, Los Angeles, and elsewhere. Valley Stream, Long Island, was to house four thousand families. It made extensive use of the ideas first employed at Radburn. Stein felt he was operating at his best as a designer in this work.

184   To Aline Stein

[New York City]   July 21, 1933

Aline dear:

. . . The day was another day of strenuous designing of new villages. Catherine Bauer has reported that Milwaukee looks promising. So we are preparing to house some 10,000 Milwaukeans.

The newspapers reported yesterday that RDK's assistants had been appointed. Looks like the roll call of the Regional Planning Association: Henry Klaber is chief technician, and among the consultants are Russell Black, Henry Wright, Fred Ackerman, and [Edith] Wood. . . . Paul Bruere is connected with a nearby office. It looks as though we would have to move our headquarters to the Capitol.

Love to . . . you,
My darling,
Clarence

185   To Aline Stein

Washington   August 4, 1933

Darling:

Yesterday was a day of great adventure. I flew.[1] I know you said don't, but dear, we can't stand still. It's absurd. There is no more danger than from auto. Not as much as there is from careless drivers around Los Angeles. But it's foolish to argue. I knew that you really would not mind, and it's going to make it so much easier for us to be together when we *both* want to. I can spend weekends with you.

What a thrill it is. And the loveliness of the patterns of country underneath. Long Island Sound, Manhattan with Central Park just below, the Hudson, Jersey, bunched houses and patchwork patterns of varied colored farm land, rich farms and giant smoke stacks of industry in Pennsylvania, and then the mountains. I thought they would be bumpy, but they weren't. Not much.

I was with Cowden in the famous *Kingbird,* in which Frank flew across the country. We went to Pittsburgh just to show Buhl to a couple of men [Keith Morgan and Joseph E. Davies] who are interested in the big housing scheme.[2] The latter [are] very close to the president. They were immediately impressed and thrilled by the idea of doing that kind of thing all over the country. Davies particularly is enthusiastic about the conception of all that I have been talking about and now am putting in the shape of drawings. He is going to try to get the president [to] do it. Perhaps it is going to be realized. I wonder, I wonder . . .

We had a long session here, at Davies's spacious Washington house, last night with Robert and Frank, who brought . . . a great colored drawing of one of the developments down from New York.

> More tomorrow,
> Clarence

Evening.

Back in New York. I only fly, hereafter! Please don't object, my love.

1. His first flight.

2. He was referring to Chatham Village. The *Kingbird* airplane was owned by Joseph E. Davies, a New York City banker and later FDR's ambassador to Belgium. Keith Morgan was a Wisconsin insurance executive and millionaire, later appointed a U.S. ambassador to the U.S.S.R. by FDR. Morgan, a conservative Democrat, was indeed close to FDR.

---

186   To Aline Stein

[New York City]   August 9, 1933

Darling:

I had a letter from Henry Wright yesterday in which he says, "I have, after a very long struggle, come to the conclusion that it would be wiser for me to withdraw from the association of the past 10 years." Friendly enough the rest of the note. This has been coming on for some time, as you know. Henry has been becoming more and more of a teacher and a theorist, with fewer and fewer moments to spare in criticism of my work.[1] I have come less and less to turn to him for it. I have come to enjoy being on my own, completely, even in those problems of town planning that I formerly left mainly to his guidance.

The final break came last Saturday. Henry has the idea that the only way to get anything good done at once in New York housing is to get together a group of important architects to work as a single body. His theory is that [the] city would not dare refuse to be guided by them. It would be awed into doing so, or RDK would refuse to lend money unless they did. I said that the Chicago Fair and Radio City had taught me all I wanted about architecture born from the group mind. I was out. Then Henry said, "Will you let us have all the studies you have made as a starting point for the group's work?" It is my humble opinion that the studies I have been making come much closer to a solution of the New York problem than anything else that has been done, and in this, I believe, Henry agrees. I said *no.*

I owe much to Henry, so much I can never repay him. That flame of his has helped light me on my way. It would have been a somewhat different way without it.

But just now I prefer to follow the path alone, even if I must lose my way from time to time.

Marion got back to the farm. She had left Henry's auto somewhere in Hoboken. She did not seem to know just where. Poor kid.

My love, my love,
Clarence

1. Wright had started lecturing at the Columbia School of Architecture in 1932 and by mid-1933 was also working intensely on his book, *Rehousing Urban America*. Lewis Mumford considered the breakup of the Stein/Wright team to be one of the great tragedies in the history of urban development planning.

---

187 To Benton MacKaye

New York City[1] October 16, 1933

Dear Ben:

I was both astonished and delighted to see your handwriting. You certainly are coming on. It is quite apparent that you have the very best of care—not only medical, but spiritual.[2] It certainly is fine having such a good doctor as Alexander and such a good friend as Harvey Broome. I imagine the only thing you need now is patience. Don't rush things too much. You seem to have so many friends around that time should not hang heavy on your hands. It surely would be better if you took a thorough rest before starting in to work again.

In regard to the hopes of work, I can't say anything as yet, as I have not heard further from the Tennessee Valley Authority. I presume they are as slow as all government offices. . . .

As to my own jobs, I don't know from day to day whether I have any. Last week we were working along at a great old rate; we had about fifteen men over the drafting boards. Then, suddenly, word comes that there was another tangle in the red tape in Washington. So, Friday everything had to be stopped. It was terribly hard to tell those boys, who have been out of jobs for a year or more, that they would have to quit again, even though in all probability it was only temporarily.

I don't know whether the government is really going to get anywhere with its housing program. Those in charge are so honest and so afraid that someone will take advantage of them that they are doing nothing, or practically nothing. The latest thought is that the government, instead of giving money to others to spend, will go directly into housing. That's fine. The only trouble is that it will take time, and it means that there will be no work done this winter. It seems to me that what they should do is to go ahead and get the building industry started, even if they have to take chances on there being some waste. Meanwhile, they might be developing a policy of direct governmental action. I am afraid the whole program of public works is going to amount to nothing, or next to nothing, unless they get started and started in a big way within the next month or so. . . .

We all send our best wishes,

As always,

Clarence

1. Clarence had gone to California on 14 August 1933 and returned to New York City on 3 September 1933.

2. Soon after his arrival in Knoxville in September 1933, hoping to work on the TVA regional planning staff, MacKaye experienced a life-threatening episode of digestive tract pain. He underwent an operation to remove his Meckel's diverticulum. The cost of his medical treatment and support during his recovery was paid by Clarence Stein. MacKaye was not able to start his TVA work until April 1934. See Daniel Schaffer, "Benton MacKaye: The TVA Years," *Planning Perspectives* 5 (1990): 5–21. MacKaye resigned in the fall of 1936, disenchanted by FDR's focus on economic development rather than on the RPAA's vision of regional planning for the social and physical environment.

---

188   To Lewis Mumford

[New York City]   December 4, 1933

Dear Lewis:

The following from a note just received from Aline may interest you:

"I've read Lewis Mumford's very succinct article in *Common Sense*. Thanks for sending it. It's the first tangible program for the New Life I've come across. Pleased to see housing is the cornerstone of the world to come—as, of course, it must be—but it looks more certain in print."

Ben is slowly improving.

My best to you and Sophie.

Clarence

---

189   To Aline Stein

[New York City]   December 10, 1933

Beloved:

. . . Yesterday morning, Robert [Kohn] was at the office, but there is no talking to Robert. He seems to be going so many places, he is going nowhere.[1] He appears to be working at so many problems that he cannot reach a well-thought-out or steady program in regard to any of them. He seems to constantly wobble. I fear that it is because he has never developed a sufficient housing philosophy or understanding of technique for himself. He has accepted thoughts from Henry, from me, [and] from others. A case in point: The committee RDK has called into existence to work out plans for a New York Housing Authority is split on the question as to whether the City Authority should come under [the] controller of the State Housing Board or not. Robert is representing the government that is to put in the money, [and] Kantoff and others think [he] should decide the matter. But he seems to take both sides, as did Roosevelt when he was governor.

[Robert] and Estelle are coming here for lunch, and I will try to keep away from housing. He is so worn out, so harried. He needs change of thought so badly. Estelle stayed around the office most of yesterday, while Robert held meeting after meeting. At last she got him to go up to the country in the afternoon. She's going down to Washington with him now for a long visit.

Frank and I lunched at Henri's yesterday. A changed place, half crowded, and most everyone ordering drinks: cocktails, wine, liqueurs. It is like suddenly waking from a long bad dream. . . .[2]

Goodbye 'til tonight.

My love,
Clarence

1. Clarence did not yet know if his Hillside Homes project would be approved. The complex approval process involved the New York City government, New York State, and the new housing division of the PWA, which Kohn headed.

2. The atmosphere of Clarence's favorite luncheon restaurant had completely changed with the end of Prohibition.

---

190 To Aline Stein

December 14, 1933   New York City

Darling:

. . . I had lunch with Charlie Whitaker at a little French restaurant where you can eat enough for a week for 50 cents. Not bad. Even the wine is good. Charlie told me more about his book, the economics of architecture, or rather architecture and world economics. He is going to show how the expenditures for buildings impoverished Egypt, Constantinople, and France of Louis XIV, etc., all of which proves? I don't know.[1] . . . Anyhow from Charlie it sounded like a really hopeful note. So I took another glass of wine, a number of them, and so probably I didn't get it all straight. . . .

Goodbye my love,
Clarence

1. Whitaker's book, *The Story of Architecture: From Ramassus to Rockefeller* (New York: Halcyon House, 1934), is a very negative history of architecture and architects—Whitaker's tragic tale of

the megalomaniac rulers' use of the skills of craftsman builders to glorify themselves. There had been, he noted, "a few smaller scale efforts to build examples of communities in which people might live with decency and comfort."

---

191 To Aline Stein

[New York City] January 30, 1934

My darling:

Yesterday was a busy day! A whole bunch of days rolled into one.

The office just filled with men, and things rolling along, so much I must go over carefully, for now the final decisions must be made. A pile of letters and pamphlets on my desk—most of them can wait. And the telephone bell jingling. The excitement of being back![1]

We had a meeting at the Empire State Building for hours. Eken and Straus and all. Straus says it will take a number of weeks to transfer the property to the Hillside Corporation. The lawyer says the government will not pay out anything until land is transferred. I said they would have to either give me a contract or else pay my draftsmen. So it is somewhat of a mess. That, I presume, will be cleared up today or tomorrow. If not, the office will just close down. Have you ever heard such a tale? And they call themselves businessmen.[2]

Alfred Stern came in late in the afternoon to tell me that the only way the housing situation at Washington could be cleared up was for R. D. K[ohn] to get out. It seems that Ickes and he hate [each] other like poison. I listened and said nothing.

Shreve came up to the house for dinner.[3] He is running the slum clearance studies, you know, and what a lot of gossip. They are getting deeper and deeper in the fog, like our trip out of San Diego. Shreve says Robert has got to hold on until he has a clear issue on which to resign. There seems to be a general agreement that RDK has got to go, but his friends don't want him to be made the scapegoat. Poor Robert. I wish I could do something for him.

Your lovely letters keep me cheered up. Hillside could go, everything here, as long as there was you, it would still be the best of worlds.

My love,
Clarence

1. The lack of correspondence between Aline and Clarence from mid-December 1933 until late January 1934 suggests that Clarence spent that time in California. In later letters to Aline early in February, he refers to a "vacation, and such a vacation!"

2. Eken agreed the next day to meet Stein's payroll until Straus's corporation started receiving funds from the PWA-approved RFC loan for the Hillside Homes project.

3. New York architect Harold Shreve was a principal of Shreve, Lamb and Harmon, architects of the Empire State Building, among many others.

192   To Benton MacKaye

[New York City]   February 1, 1934

Dear Ben:

I finally did break away from California, and since Sunday I have been in New York. I was about to say, here at home, but I am not quite sure just which end of the continent home is at present. . . . It now looks as though the Hillside job is definitely going ahead, and the office is as busy as it was in the good old days. . . .

I am awfully glad to hear that you are feeling so much better and that you are making real progress in your regional planning pamphlet. Now is the time to get out something of that kind. I don't know whether you noticed the other day that Governor Lehman made a speech in which he promised to appoint a State Housing Board. I find they were talking of passing legislation in California for the same purpose. There is a strong movement on at present to appoint all sorts of planning boards. . . . Now is the time for you to talk up.

I hope, however, you are going to finish with that soon because I am sure your friend Richards needs you down in the Tennessee Valley. I wouldn't put off going to him too long, if I were you. All these governmental offices are constantly changing their policies and point of view so, if I were you, I would take the job as soon as you can put your hands on it. . . .

My best to you,
As always,
Clarence

193   To Aline Stein

[New York City]   February 2, 1934

Aline dear:

The Stein family had dinner with Jennie Baerwald at Henri's. We were there in full force: Pop, Gert, Lillie, Margaret, and even Mike.

Jennie is a wonder. So vital, so direct. She is over here to try to get her citizenship papers. If she is an American, she feels that they will not be able to interfere with her work. As it is, a number of times it has looked as though [the Germans] would put her away in one of their camps. At first it appears they objected that the great percentage of the people she helped were Jewish, and then afterward they [encouraged] her to make it altogether Jewish. The tales she tells seem unbelievable. There is no way for the professional men and women to turn. They can't leave Germany. Anyhow, they can't take their money out. Their jobs are gone and, if they were in government jobs, they can't even have their pensions. Jennie's organization is the only hope for a great many of them. She, of course, is spending much of her time here collecting money. She says her great difficulty is that all the Jews think only of sending their money to help the German Jews to Palestine, and a great part of them can't go there. . . .[1]

All my love,

Clarence

1. The Steins supported Jennie Baerwald's work to aid the Jews in Europe throughout the 1930s and during World War II. Baerwald's work in Germany was discussed in another letter to Aline on 12 February 1934: "J. has her passport and American papers straightened out and is returning to Germany on Thursday. She is like a soldier who has been on leave, returning to the front. She sees no immediate hope for the Jews. She believes that if there is a war there is likely to be a pogrom. She is not worrying about the future. Her job is in Germany and she wants to get back." Later, in a November 1935 letter to Aline that is mainly about their travel plans, Clarence reported that "Emile Baerwald [Jennie's husband?] called on me the other evening for a short time. . . . He [said] that he and Jen are going to stick to their job, as they expect worse trouble to come." This comment, apparently about the Baerwalds' work to rescue Jews from Nazi persecution, is the last reference in the Stein Papers to Jennie's work in prewar Germany.

---

194 To Aline Stein

[New York City]   February 4, 1934

Aline dear:

After I wrote you Friday evening, I went down to the Union League Club (me at the Union League again!) to a dinner meeting with a group of architects and Langdon Post.[1] He is the Tenement House Commissioner and will probably run things in the new [New York City] Housing Authority. A very nice young chap, but a politician who wants his name on the front page. He is using Housing for all that it is worth, promising everybody everything, even though he never can deliver the goods. His intentions are perhaps all right, but he doesn't know, and so many are telling him things.

New York is just full of "housing experts," now that it is going to be good business. This bunch had much to tell him, too, seeing that they were responsible for more and taller skyscrapers than any other group. They ought to know all about little four-story apartments. But there were one or two there with a little sense, particularly Albert Mayer,[2] who had evolved a scheme the rest of the crowd had agreed to back to clear three blocks on Manhattan (probably lower East Side) but not attempting to rebuild there. Make it into a park, then do a large slum clearance and rehousing job in the bad areas in Brooklyn, where land is cheaper, and a still larger one outside in Queens, where there are no buildings. That, as you see, lays the emphasis on the attack from the outside but starts to get rid of the rotten stuff inside. Most of the architects don't altogether understand the significance of the attack.

276

But it looks like work and they want jobs. Formerly they hunted for them one by one, but now they are so hungry they hunt in packs. As to their victims, Post acted like a gentleman and smiled and spoke sweet words but, when he thinks it over, he will see that there is more front page in building on the lower East Side. . . .

My love, tonight we talk.

Clarence . . .

1. Langdon Post was the second chairman of the New York Housing Authority (1934–37), the author of *The Challenge of Housing* (New York: Farrar and Reinhardt, 1938), and the arch enemy of Harold Ickes's centralized administration of the PWA housing program.

2. Stein's former associate, Albert Mayer, was now practicing architecture on his own in New York and was championing the RPAA's strategy of increasing the stock of moderate-rent housing by building on vacant land before clearing slums in the city.

---

195   To Aline Stein

New York City   February 5, 1934

Dearest Mine:

A gray and white morning. Gray skies and a white ground and air that is filled with "go."

And I sure am going these days. Having a job, and having had a vacation, and such a vacation! There is no stopping me, so I say, now that I feel confident that Hillside is going to be realized.

Frederick Lee came up and we decided that R. D. K[ohn] ought to take his stand (probably his final stand) before the week is over. I think his position is hopeless. If he can only get out without their dropping the whole load of criticism of his division on his head.

I discussed with [Ackerman] what I should say if I [see] the mayor (I had already pretty well decided), and [Ackerman] read me his latest writing, which I understood!

In the afternoon, met Straus and his wife at the office, where they enthused about the model. Straus says the matter of the land is all straightened out, excepting that they will have to advertise in the newspapers for two weeks before they can actually transfer it. . . .

My love, have patience,

Clarence

196   To Aline Stein

[New York City]   Tuesday, February 6, 1934

Aline darling:

. . . Yesterday, another busy day at the office. All the boys working with such energy with the joy of having something to do. And me, all over the place. Ward was right. There are other incentives than profit.

Eken came in, so appreciative (sentimentally appreciative) of how I had been willing to give in last week about simplifying the exteriors of the building. [It] is one grand joke. Hunter, Eken's hard-boiled partner, had been picking [on us] just on principle. [He says] that architects are wasteful, that there were too many bands [of brick] on the exterior. [They] couldn't get the bricklayers to lay up a thousand a day. He didn't get anywhere. So last week he phoned [that]he wanted to bring Eken up and we would fight it out. OK, says I. In the couple of hours before they came, I made some new studies concentrating the bands and I added a decorative frieze, which I didn't have on the old drawings. The new design was different, but just as good as the old. I didn't show the new one to them, but led them on to criticize the old one, so as to force me to do just what I had drawn in the new arrangement. So, after a few explosions, we were all happy.

By evening time I was good and tired. Dinner in bed. So comfortable. Read an article in *Fortune,* by MacLeish, on the Housing Division at Washington.[1] He shows how events have driven what was to have been a lending institution in a capitalistic society into a purely socialistic brand of government. He makes Robert his principal character and pretends that he has guided the ship, but in accordance with winds of which he knew not. I could not help thinking as I read: "He should have known," and wondering, "Does he ever know where he is blowing?" And I would do anything for Robert. . . .

Here is all my love, my love,

Clarence

1. Archibald MacLeish's article "State Housing" appeared in the February 1934 issue of *Fortune.* It was a tongue-in-cheek story about Ickes's housing policies "accidentally falling into socialism." But MacLeish praised the professionalism of Kohn and his assistants: "If any personnel could make a socialistic division of government successful [they] should certainly succeed." It was a strange performance from an influential author who in other situations urged government intervention in the housing market as a component of FDR's New Deal.

197   To Aline Stein

February 15, 1934   New York City

Aline dear:

Yesterday and Thursday [were] filled tight with architecture, mainly [the] consideration of whether to do Hillside in white brick instead of red. The builders claim that an immense saving can be made if we change. I went early in the morning to take a good look at the Cornell Medical Center, [which is] just simple masses of white with delicate detail in lines rather than relief. Of course, we will have a poorer material, but something could be close with it, and so we made studies in white [with] green foliage through the day. But still, I am afraid of it, children writing on it, dirty finger prints all over it. Isn't architecture a complicated game?

Lewis Mumford and Albert Mayer came in during the morning. They have been writing a series of articles, with Henry Wright, on the present housing situation for the *New Republic*.[1] Don't miss them. The first by Mayer appeared last week. They wanted me to go over the final article with them. It's fine.

The Housing Authority is appointed, very socially minded, but quite ignorant of the practice of housing. I say that in spite of the fact that one of the members, [Louis H.] Pink,[2] has been on the State Housing Board and should know something. But somehow these very good people (social worker types) let their wish for a better world and their hatred of the slums blind them to the practical problems they must meet. They concentrate so closely on the little black spots and their desire to eradicate them that they can't see any large pattern.[3] The chairman of the board, Post, who is also Tenement House Commissioner, is a nice gentleman with political ambitions. He wants to use housing to put him on the front page. . . .

My love, I love you,

Clarence

1. "New Homes for a New Deal," *New Republic* 78 (10 February and 2 March 1934): 7–9, 41–44, 69–72, 91–94. In this three-part article, Mumford, Mayer, and Henry Wright (whom Stein does not mention) were highly critical of the New York City housing program, which had been based on Hoover's PWA/RFC loan program. In two years it had produced little new housing; it was, in the RPAA's opinion, misdirected at slum clearance without the provision of new relocation housing for the displaced slum dwellers that they could afford. They noted that it was based on a weak federal-city debt structure and rewarded a handful of slum owners at the expense of the rest of the city. Catherine Bauer's article, "Slums Aren't Necessary," also based on the RPAA's discussion of housing policy, was published at the same time in *American Mercury* 31 (March 1934): 296–305.

2. Pink, an advisor to Governor Alfred E. Smith in the 1920s, wrote *The New Day in Housing* (New York: John Day, 1928).

3. Later this same day Clarence Stein ate lunch at the City Club. After hearing his companions complain about the lack of bankers on the Housing Authority Board, he decided that social workers were all right.

198   To Aline Stein

[New York City]   Washington's Birthday, 1934

Aline, my darling:

If you were only here. The snow is so lovely in the gray dawn. I want you to be looking out the window with me. Just sit up in bed and look, and then you can yawn and turn over, if you want.

I am so busy that there is nothing to write about. Just drawings, drawings, drawings, windows, thousands of windows, all to make patterns on the exteriors of walls, but every one placed just where the women inside the room will want it. Windows, windows, regiments of windows, and steps, and never one on which to slip or trip, and closets in which you can put your hand on every suit. Five thousand closets. Hooks and hinges and incinerators and slop sinks and recreation rooms and door knobs and nurseries and the size of brick joints. That's architecture.[1]

By three yesterday I reached the point where I could not look another window or brick joint in the face, so I wandered home and to bed. Now, after fifteen hours of repose, I am fresh as a daisy. Bring on your windows! . . .

Clarence

1. Stein seems to be in a manic phase of his mental life, enjoying every moment, with boundless energy, creativity, and high expectations.

199   To Aline Stein

February 23, 1934   New York City

Dearest:

. . . Henry Wright came up to dine with me last night. Poor Henry, so brave but so bewildered in this hard-boiled world, and yet, in flashes, so clear minded. I guess he has been having a pretty tough time of it. Cleveland hasn't as yet paid him a cent for all the work he did.[1] It must be the little he gets from the English job that keeps him going. Henry does get a punch from having his little group of students around him, and he bravely refuses to waste any more time working for the government with its present setup. His book is finished, but the publishers say they can't afford to bring it out unless they get some financial aid.[2] The book looks complicated, but it's what the men in the profession need, and, above all, Henry needs to have it brought out. So I guess it is going to be up to me to see that it is published. . . .

I love you,
Clarence

1. Wright and Stein had served as architectural and site planning consultants to Walter McCormack, chief architect for Cleveland's first slum clearance project.

2. Wright's book *Rehousing Urban America,* a classic in the field, was published by Columbia University Press in 1935 after Stein and others provided some subventions.

---

200   To Aline Stein

[New York City]   February 24, 1934

Darling:

. . . Yesterday Aline Bernstein and I had lunch together at Henri's. We had so much to tell each other. Aline, so troubled that she does not get the right plays to do, and all the other difficulties of being an artist working for a business (you know!). And writing is so hard. (I told her she had not discovered that. And what has she to complain of on that score? Her book is selling and she is at work on another). Life in a hotel. Well, it isn't just life in your own home. But in spite of her complaints, we decided that there were worse fates than that of Aline Bernstein. She is a grand one.

Robert [Kohn] and Estelle were in town. I had a very frank talk with Estelle: told her, from all I heard, I thought Robert would be much better off if he resigned and that they were going to drop all the failures on his head one of these days.[1] She said she thought there was hope and he had to fight it through. With Robert, it is difficult to have a talk. He is in such a hurry, jumping from one thing to another. But when I spoke of the apparent hopelessness of it all, he said there was a possibility of getting housing out of Ickes's department.[2] RDK saw the Rockefeller Foundation people, and there is a chance that they will put up 50 thousand or so to train architects, managers, etc., to do housing work. This is an idea that Robert has had for over a year. I promised to outline the work for an advanced school of this kind, with the assistance of Lewis, Henry, etc., so that RDK can present it to them next weekend.[3]

There is much, much more to write, but what matters? All that is of importance is . . .

I love you,
Clarence

1. Robert Kohn resigned his federal housing post four months later in June 1934 under a cloud of Ickes's vituperation. Clarence wrote a few days later that Robert's only hope was to "escape from Ickes's department. Victory? There can be no victory for Robert in this war. He merely troops on. He had no plan of campaign. He never has had time to really consider the objects of the war. . . . He is battling in a fog with his face bravely turned toward a distant light called 'Right' or 'Ethical' or something, . . . in spite of which I would do anything for him."

2. The hope was new legislation that had been introduced by Senator Wagner to establish a separate national housing administration, but it was not passed into law for three years.

3. Wright had established a school for unemployed architects at the Hudson Guild farm in New Jersey but had higher aspirations in teaching city planning.

201 To Aline Stein

[New York City]   March 1, 1934   This month you come home!

Darling:

Sometime in the middle of the day yesterday Mia came down to the office to have her weekly argument with Miss Morris on the high cost of living. She brought with her two letters from you. . . . My, my, so you have decided that Franklin D. is no radical![1] And it would have been better to let it all go to hell. That's what I think up in my mind, and then somewhere else inside (perhaps it's in my belly) I reason, "The worm won't turn in America, no matter what it suffers. There is no chance of revolution among the middle class, and they are all middle class, on their way up, if not actually, at least in intent." I have been reading more of Beard's *Rise of American Civilization.* The whole framework of the Constitution is capitalism, but you are more interested in what happened to CSS yesterday?

All morning, meeting with Eken's blustering partner, Hunter, on details. If you had heard my heated arguments, you would have known well that it was more important than the fate of capitalism.

The lawyer phoned that my Hillside contract was now in the form I wanted it, but there was no telling yet just when it would be signed. The lawyers still are setting up obstacles of words, and the opposition to Hillside has by no means disappeared. In fact, yesterday afternoon a photographer from the *Journal* came around to take a picture of our office door. I guess they want to show that RDK and I are partners.

I phoned Ackerman at Washington, and he agreed that he would accept the position of advisor [to] the New York Housing Authority. I hope there will be no slip there. Talked to Ethel [Bernstein] over the telephone. We will probably go to see Gertrude Stein's madness tonight. . . .[2]

And I love you,
Clarence

1. Less than a year after his inauguration, the Steins, along with many other liberal reformers, had become disillusioned with the slowness and conservative nature of FDR's moves to reshape social and economic policy.

2. Gertrude Stein's opera, "Four Saints in Three Acts," had just opened in New York City. Her prose was set to the music of Virgil Thompson, and the show was considered an avant garde theatrical performance.

202   To Aline Stein

[New York City]   March 3, 1934

Darling:

Last night the New York Chapter of the AIA hung a red ribbon round Robert Kohn's neck, and at the end of it was the gold medal, and Robert was very happy. Something like being knighted. (Sir Robert! The funny part would be Estelle as Lady Kohn, not half as quaint, say you, as Lady Stein! Thank God for democracy!)

Before dinner, a number of us met at Charlie Butler's, so as to fortify ourselves with drink for the very mediocre food of the Architectural League.

Robert's talk was one of hope after defeat. He admits the little that has been done, but he looks forward to great things. In speaking of the medal as an approval of his architecture, he handed some bouquets to Charlie and me in his best Robertian manner.

Yesterday noon I met [Eliel] Saarinen, the Finnish architect, at luncheon. He is working here and at a school near Detroit.[1] He knows what it is all about. I must get to know him. . . .

Here is love, and love, all my love,
Clarence

1. The Cranbrook Academy for Boys at Bloomfield Hills, Mich.

203   To Aline Stein

[New York City]   March 14, 1934

Aline dear:

It is three. The Whitakers and the Behrendts,[1] who were here for dinner with Jennie Mac,[2] have just left for the Philharmonic. This morning it was 10 before I got up. I spent most of the morning with Ackerman, gossiping and philosophizing. His appointment as New York [Housing Authority] adviser has been announced. In a week he will finish his Washington job and start up here. I am anxious to see what he will do with reality. RDK will miss him at Washington. He is the only really analytic mind there has been down there; [the only] one that could see the thing as a whole. Poor Robert! They have had him on the go this week. I guess the newspaper men have been after him because of our former relations. He sent up word to take his name off the office door and off our letterheads.

Evening. I have just phoned. In a week you will be on your way. Nothing else matters: Hillside, Warners, to 'ell with 'em! I saw Joe Price. He seems fine in spite of what they say. Bob Moses was there.[3] I haven't seen him for years. He is a human, likable chap anyhow, when he is not playing Mussolini. He had much to tell us about the mayor. If this administration doesn't go on the rocks, I am a bad guesser.

But what does it matter? You are coming home.[4]

And I love you,
Clarence

1. Walter Curt Behrendt was a German architectural historian whom Charles Whitaker, Mumford, and Stein helped to extract from the danger faced by Jews in Hitler's Germany. They found him a teaching post at Dartmouth College. Clarence and Aline helped pay his salary for the first year by gifts to Dartmouth. Behrendt's Dartmouth lectures formed the nucleus of his book *Modern Building*, published by Harcourt Brace and Company in 1937. His survey of the origins and development of the "new style" from the "moral revolution" of Ruskin and Morris through the European and British pioneers of art nouveau, Van de Velde, Peter Beherenns Loos, and Berlage connects their ideas to the German *werkbund* and the American contributions of Sullivan and Frank Lloyd Wright, as well as showing Wright's influence on European architecture. It is a neglected classic.

2. Jennie Mac was the stage name of Aline's mother.

3. Robert Moses supervised a number of U.S. National Relief Agency projects for New York City, which was a major recipient of FDR's public works largess, even though Roosevelt and Moses were arch enemies.

4. Aline seems to have returned to New York City in mid-March 1934 and stayed for three months, until mid-June.

---

204   To Aline Stein

[New York City]   March 14, 1934

Beloved:

I don't know if there is any chance of this reaching you before you leave, but I will take chances.

Left early to attend the memorial ceremony for Belle Moskowitz at the Women's City Club.[1] Miss [Francis] Perkins spoke with feeling but a little oratorically.[2] And then Al Smith told, for the first time publicly, just how great was his personal debt to Belle. He said she could have had any position in his power to give her, but that she had preferred to remain in the background. He admitted that she had written or helped him write many of his state documents and articles. He said, "As everyone knows, my English ain't so good, particularly when I get excited." Then he told of her family life.

Yesterday everything went wrong in a big way. My contract [was] all muddled. Permission that was promised us by the Building Department [was] withheld, apparently for political reasons. It is all topsy turvy. But there is always a sun shining somewhere behind the thickest clouds, so cheer up, Clarence, Aline is coming home. What matters the rest?

I love you,
Clarence

1. Belle Moskowitz was a welfare worker, reformer, and political leader in New York City during the first three decades of the twentieth century. In 1913 she chaired the "Women's Division of Al Smith's Campaign" for governor and became his trusted advisor on social and economic problems. She was his publicity director in all five of his major political campaigns.

2. Francis Perkins, secretary of labor in FDR's cabinet.

---

205   To Aline Stein

June 13, 1934   New York City

Beloved:

Last night I took dinner at the old homestead along with the rest of the Stein brothers. What strangers they are. So far away. Afterward with Pop, Margaret, and Herb to the Plaza to see [W. C.] Fields. He is the funniest man in the world in *You're Telling Me*. Will showed up there later with his lady friend, but we were not introduced.

This morning Ackerman came up for breakfast, and we walked down. He seems to think the Housing Authority is getting somewhere, anyhow, far enough to let him go off for a few days' rest to Nantucket this weekend.

The brick situation looks more hopeful, but news from Washington is bad. I think they are about ready to drop the whole load of troubles on Robert's head and throw him out. Why, why did he wait? The government is trying to play some more nasty tricks on me, but these are so unimportant compared with what they are doing to Robert.

Henry Wright and Albert Mayer [were] here for dinner. Henry to spend the night. I am so glad. I feared being alone.[1]

I am so lonely for you my dear, my beloved.

Clarence

1. Aline's absence from New York during her acting assignments in Hollywood may have been a major factor in Clarence Stein's increasing bouts with depression.

---

206   To Aline Stein

[New York City]   June 16, 1934

My darling:

The news from Washington is bad. Herbert Emmerich phoned me last night saying that Henry Klaber and all of Robert's other principal assistants had been fired but that Robert's resignation had not yet been accepted. Herbert had telephoned Brownlow at Chicago, and they were agreed that Robert should go right down to Washington to be ready to answer any publicity and to lay the matter before Senator Wagner and, if possible, the president. They wanted me to talk to Robert. I called him up and told him what Herbert had said. Robert said he was not physically able to go to Washington. I offered to go up to see him, but he said he thought it best that I should not and that he would not go to the office for some time.

Along with my feeling for Robert and Henry (isn't it awful!), I must say I am thinking somewhat about Hillside. We are in for trouble in plenty (that crowd down there [is] not interested in the facts, just in making trouble), but we have been there before, so don't you worry. . . .

My love, my love, don't worry about me. I always do have you, and you, me.[1] That's all that matters.

Clarence

1. Aline's letters at this time reveal that she was very concerned about Clarence's deep sadness over their separation.

---

207   To Aline Stein

[New York City]   June 18, 1934

Darling:

Estelle [Kohn] came to the office this morning. She says that Robert is in pretty bad condition—can't sleep. Things weren't improved by a savage letter from Ickes. But he is receiving many letters from those who have faith in him.

Next one to get it will be CSS, I suppose.[1] They will connect Robert and myself and try to catch some neglect on the job. In spite of all we have done, they will probably be able to find something that can appear to be neglect. So I have been trying to check through the contracts to see all the many complicated requirements and have been trying, above all, to make sure that all our bookkeeping is OK. There can be no question of our drawings and specifications. Of course, it is nonsense. No one knows it better than I, but it has me worried.

Your letters help so much at these times when little things take on big proportions through the night. It is grand to know that there is you and you are, well, *you*. What more could you be, my darling, my strength.

Clarence

1. Clarence expected Secretary of the Interior Ickes to instruct the PWA/RFC to drop the Hillside project.

---

208   To Aline Stein

[New York City]   June 20, 1934

My darling:

I am again myself, sitting on the top of the world, and to hell with it! And yesterday and the days before it was atop of me, a great load, just pressing down. Isn't it strange how we come bobbing up again, and why?[1] Perhaps because the sun shone today and the weather was of the loveliest. More likely because I heard your dear voice last night.

Anyhow, there is little in the facts to justify my renewed joy in life. The Housing Board has not yet given its final decision [in] regard to the brick, and we can't find a red brick that is within our means that has any character. The board will probably throw us down, though how they can do it after reading the technical report, I don't know. Eken and I talked at great length this afternoon, trying to decide what to do then. If we go to Washington and complain, [New York City Housing Authority Director] James will use every technical excuse he can get in the future, and he can find plenty to hold up the job and kill it, if possible. On the other hand, if we take his decision, we are wasting 75 thousand (Eken says more) and getting a poorer material. But this is a bad time to go to Washington. They are looking for trouble, and the storm of last week has not yet calmed.

This is what they call architecture!

My love,
Clarence

1. Clarence had come out of the deep depression that had followed Aline's departure for the West Coast. His mood was upward bound to a manic phase.

---

209   To Aline Stein

Hay-Adams House, Washington, D.C.   June 27, 1934

Aline dear:

I am writing this on the train bound for New York. Frank and I came down late yesterday as a result of a telegram from [PWA's] new director of housing. When I received it I thought they were preparing to make trouble for Hillside, but quite the contrary. They wanted to find out about the job. They had cleaned house so completely that there was hardly anyone left that knew anything about the drawings or anything else about the jobs. In fact, they asked us to bring all our copies of the official drawings and specifications (a colossal bundle), as they might not be able to find theirs. We spent all morning schooling them. Frank's still at it. I am glad we went, as we now have direct personal contact with all the authorities, until they have another house cleaning.

It is hot in Washington, another reason I am glad I am not part of the government.

The only one I know who is really getting a great kick out of working for the U.S. is Herbert Emmerich (the rest got kicked). From all I hear he is making a great success in a very important Executive office. He takes it quite calmly. We had a long talk. He fears that it is going to be difficult for Henry Klaber to get another government job, though he thinks the best recommendation in the world should be that Ickes fired him.[1]

The sky outside is almost black, and against it is an almost perfect rainbow. The white brick was definitely washed out yesterday. Now we will see if we can get a good-looking red [brick] Hillside.

My love,
Clarence

1. The Housing Act of 1934 would pass Congress on 30 July 1934. Henry Klaber would go to work for the agency in 1936.

---

210 To Aline Stein

New York City   July 7, 1934

Darling:

Heat haze hangs over the buildings across the park. There just can't be so many hot days in succession.

I wish I could completely close the office today, but Albert [Mayer] and [Allan] Kamstra must finish the competition drawings before evening. The rest of the crew can enjoy the heat of the suburbs.

The competition drawings are a long and tedious job, and I don't believe anything will come of it. Ickes's department and the Housing Authority are beginning to quarrel like two little boys: "It's my Housing!" "No, 'tain't, it's mine." "Mine!" "No, mine!!!" I wonder why I have wasted my time, but the problem was interesting, and we have done the best job yet, even if the jury doesn't find it out.

Robert came to town again. All week he has been working at his letter to Ickes, answering the latter's accusations. He has had much legal advice: Stanley Isaacs and Carl Stom and I don't know whose else. Too damned much. He showed me the letter. It hasn't any fire, like a bunch of firecrackers that don't explode. It is so polite.

In the evening, Alfred Stern came up to dine with me. . . . He is chairman of the Illinois Housing Board, you know, but he thinks the whole situation is so hopeless at present, with Ickes in command, that he is just going away. He sails on the *Paris* today. He hopes things will get bad enough so that there will be a change. That's about as constructive as he is.

He had asked Vladeck to come around after dinner.[1] Vladeck is a member of the New York Housing Authority, a Socialist, editor of the Jewish Socialist paper in fact. He was in the Russian revolution of 1905, thrown in prison there when he was sixteen, and has seen much of labor and municipal politics here. His interest is centered in housing now, but, like the rest of us, he doesn't know where to go from here. He agreed with me that we must start at the bottom, [to] work with those who need the houses rather than [with] the government. In short, create a demand by labor groups, a demand that government will have to listen to.

All my love to you darling,

Clarence

1. B. Charney Vladeck, the editor of the *Forward* and a member of the Socialist Party, was elected the leader of the majority coalition of the New York City Council in 1937. Vladeck Homes, a 240-unit city-subsidized New York City Public Housing project at Corlears Hook on the lower East Side, was named in his memory in 1941.

---

211   To Catherine Bauer

[New York City]   July 12, 1934

Dear Miss Bauer:

At last, the famous Store article has been reprinted![1] Charles Ascher is seeing that it is broadly distributed among city managers and city planners and such like. He has sent me a limited number of copies. How many do you want?

When will you be in town again? I was awfully sorry to miss you last time and hope we can arrange to have a long talk when you come here again.[2]

Cordially yours,

Clarence S. Stein

1. This article, "Store Buildings and Neighborhood Shopping Centers," written jointly by Stein and Bauer, was originally published in the *Architectural Record* 75 (February 1934).
2. Bauer was in Philadelphia working with the Housing Guild and with architects Oscar Stonorov and Henry Churchill in an effort to develop labor union support for housing legislation.

---

212   To Aline Stein

[New York City]   July 14, 1934

My darling:

That is great news about the possibility of your doing *The Good Earth*.[1] Here's hoping.

I have been reading *A Chinese Testament* and will send it to you soon. I find it very interesting and yet hollow. One sees these yellow figures move around like marionettes, but they seem just stuffed with rags, as are the purposes that guide a people with a long, fixed past. So inevitable, even when they are in revolution, that they do not waste time on philosophizing, on the inner motives that guide action?[2]

At the office our attention is centered on Wichita.[3] We really have to do all our drawings and specifications over, and it must be done quickly or Friend Ickes will take the money away. The little rump of the building we are able to do may not be bad looking, if it is well executed. It will consist of the main entrance and approaching stairs and terraces, more approach than building, I fear, but it may induce them to build more. Inside will be fine exhibition rooms on the upper floor and an auditorium (though we can't afford the seats) and toilets downstairs. At least, Herr museum architect Stein may have a museum to his credit!

I love you,
Clarence

1. The film version of Pearl Buck's novel.

2. In a letter the next day, Clarence expressed sympathy with the Chinese boy rebel who was the main character in the book and wrote, "How I wish the boys in our universities were in revolt. I wanted to be a boy again, but am I too old or only too well fed."

3. Construction of the Wichita art museum, which Clarence Stein had designed, was about to begin. A small amount of PWA funding had been approved. Only the small central part of Stein's Wichita art museum was built in 1934. Additions of the 1960s completely enclosed this part but left much of the original exterior decorative elements of Stein's design as interior decoration.

213   To Aline Stein

New York City   August 21, 1934

Beloved:

It was a very successful party last night. It lasted until long past eleven. Much talk in small groups on the balcony or in the living room while sherry was served. Dinner at eight. There were sixteen of us: [Raymond] Unwin, Ernest Kahn of Frankfort, Miss Samuel (a round and talkative English woman), Ernest Bohn of Cleveland,[1] R. D. K[ohn], Shreve, Gove, A. M. Bing, Lescaze, Catherine Bauer, Margaret, Aronovici, Albert Mayer, Charles Ascher, Henry Wright, and CSS—some party?[2]

Mia's dinner came close to following the menu we sent her. Only she seemed quite undecided as to the temperature. We were to have a cold meal if it was hot, and vice versa. We started with cold soup, then hot fish, then cold vegetable plate. But it was good.

Afterward, much talk, which I fear bewildered our foreign friends as much as it informed them in regard to our point of view of housing.

Robert stayed here. It is about time I awakened him.

Hillside is alive at last. Steel and brick growing up all over the place. I am back just in time. I spent all afternoon there.

It is breakfast time.

Until tomorrow, good-bye.

My love,
Clarence

1. Bohn was establishing his reputation as a major player in American housing from his political base in Cleveland, Ohio, where he founded the Regional Association of Cleveland and the Cleveland Metropolitan Housing Authority in the mid-1930s.

2. This was Unwin's fourth visit to the United States. The visit was sponsored by the Ernest Bohn National Association of Housing Officials (NAHO), with Charles Ascher as executive director. The Rockefeller Foundation sponsored the commission, which included Unwin, Ernest Kahn (a German housing economist), and Alice Samuel (an advisor to the housing ministry in Great Britain). The guests were an interesting mixture of American and British housing officials and American housing experts and architects who were to advise NAHO in developing U.S. national housing legislation. During their tour of the United States, they visited Radburn, Hillside, and the TVA. They spent an hour with FDR discussing housing policy.

---

214   To Aline Stein

[New York City]   August 23, 1934

Aline dear:

. . .

I have spent almost all day at Hillside. My legs are good and tired. I walked around the long walls and up the hill, following the work of one bricklayer after another, changing a pattern here, rejecting a brick there. It is growing, growing, growing. What a feeling of power, of existing one has, of creating.[1]

And outside the wire fence that surrounds the job are a hundred or two hundred men, pressing against the gate, bricklayers waiting to be taken on, waiting from early morning to long after the five o'clock whistle. Poor fellows, they haven't had a job, most of them, for two years. And why should someone else be taken on instead of them? There are endless complaints of favoritism. One of them told me that no Jews were being taken on, and the Italians all get after Frank. We try to keep out of it, but it is heartbreaking. When you think of them going home to the wife at evening. . . .

Last night we saw the *Thin Man,* and my faith in movies has returned. If they would only give my darling a chance.

My love,
Clarence

1. Stein's satisfaction with this accomplishment was enormous. The following day he continued to enthuse: "In spite of all the care with which drawings are made, it all has to be gone over again at the job, with real bricks instead of lines. In fact, I have in some small manner changed almost every pattern on the buildings to fit the size of the brick. It is great fun, building—really building. Escape from all the theory of housing for a while." And later: "It's laying bricks, the joy of it, to see the conception unfold, rise, grow, by the hand of men—long rows of them, men not machines, and to mold the details of that growth—to be part of it and have it part of you. The petty troubles of Hillside are forgotten. Now it is pure joy!"

215   To Aline Stein

[New York City]   November 21, 1934

Beloved:

This will have to be a rather hasty note. I should be on my way up to Hillside, but I slept a little beyond my time, as the result of getting to bed around one.

Yesterday evening was judgment of the Beaux Arts program which I wrote.[1] Subject was a group of apartment houses, something of the nature of Hillside. Some good stuff. The boys turned out serious and sincere attempts to find solutions [to] a problem that they consider vital. I don't know whether it is because it is vital to our civilization (or whatever you call it) or vital to their making a living. The jury, mainly the older men of the profession (to think that I am becoming one of the older men!), seemed quite as keenly interested. We started at five-thirty and were not done with our final decision until midnight. And were my legs tired!

The rest of the day was devoted mainly to meetings with the representative of Ickes to try to get some action on unsettled Hillside matters and with Mandel, who is [in] charge of stores for Straus.[2] How I despise these nasty speculators!

I must go. Frank [Vitolo] is waiting at the end of the subway.[3]

My love, I love you,
Clarence

1. Stein and Henry Wright both taught at the Columbia University School of Architecture in the early 1930s. One of the mysteries of Stein's relationships at Columbia is the lack of any evidence of contact between him and Werner Hegeman, the German urban theorist who fled from Berlin during Hitler's rise to power in 1933, and who also taught there.

2. The previous day Clarence had reported to Aline that he had seen the *New York Times* Building News Sign announce Straus's resignation from the New York State directorship of Roosevelt's NRA. The sign then, to Stein's astonishment, continued that Straus "will devote all his time to the Hillside project." Three days earlier Clarence had complained to Aline: "That D. F. of a Straus! He and Eken getting together in my absence and settling things!"

3. At the Hillside Homes site.

216   To Aline Stein

[New York City]   December 9, 1934

Beloved:

. . . Henry Klaber was in town yesterday, officially. He is in charge of the large-scale housing of Moffit's department [in the Federal Housing Administration].[1] He came here with other officials to pass on the property that Charlie [Ascher] wants to develop up in the Bronx. . . .

And Mr. Ickes is still dawdling. The Housing Authority seems to be walking around in circles, and the architects who thought they had won a job as well as a competition are softly cursing and, all in all, it looks like an inactive winter. "China!" sez you.

Tomorrow I am going over to see whether I can induce the Phipps Estate to build an addition to the building at Sunnyside.[2]

No time to throw down a job. Yet I did my damnedest Friday to give up the [Hillside] store job, but I didn't succeed. Straus came up to the office. I told him I did not care to work with Mandel, if he had anything to say as to the design or construction of the buildings. He insisted on my not getting out. I agreed to stay if my dealings were directly with Straus and not through Mandel, and if I am in charge of design and the character and quality of construction, and if we have a reliable builder, Eken, if possible. He agreed. Now to see if he holds to it. If he had promised Mandel something else, I may still be on my way out. Does this detail bore you?

My love,

Clarence

1. In addition to its provision for mortgage insurance loans to repair and build new single family homes, one of the sections of the Federal Housing Administration (FHA) provided for federal mortgage insurance for multifamily housing projects. After a lag of two to three years, this provision added substantial momentum to the growth of apartment building in the United States.

2. The addition to the Phipps Garden Apartments was started in 1935.

---

217 To Aline Stein

[New York City]   December 11, 1934

Aline dear:

Yesterday, I tried to get a job. The Phipps Houses seemed to me the most likely victim. So I went to see Mr. Lehman, who runs the estate. He is a hard man to get hold of. He spends most of his time at a telephone telling the members of the Phipps family how to invest or spend their money. When, after an hour and a quarter wait (you see I was very determined), I did get to him, he explained to me that there were now about thirty-five members of the family (three generations) and that this was his busy season because they all were in New York, just before Christmas. I think Lehman decides everything for them, even down to how many diapers they can afford for the new baby. So, you see, he did not have much time to consider whether it was advisable to put up an addition on the property they have at the side of the building I designed. "How much will it cost?" he asked. "About

$400,000." So he called in a telephone. "How much have we in the bank and investments of the Phipps Houses?" The answer was "about $400,000." So that looked all right. Anyhow, Mr. Lehman wasn't opposed. I had better see Mr. Burg or some of the other trustees.

I saw Al Bing in the afternoon. [He said:] "How can you tell what will happen? Everything is so uncertain. Perhaps the government will do a lot of building, and how can we compete with that. We better wait." I guess architecture is going to continue to be mostly a waiting game.

Thank God for Hillside.

In the evening I went to a meeting at which the mayor, and Bob Moses, and the borough presidents explained the need of sixty million dollars worth of roads, cutting across the city, as though there wasn't enough crazy rushing and moving around in this mad house world. . . .

And I love you,
Clarence

---

218   To Aline Stein

[New York City]   December 15, 1934

My darling:

Yesterday I received such good news. Last evening Lydia Behrendt phoned to tell me that the university was so pleased with Curt [Behrendt] that they had decided to apply for the money that the Rockefeller Foundation had offered to contribute, an amount equal to that collected.[1] So Curt will receive $600 more each semester, and he feels wealthy! More, the university is going to publish his lectures. Tomorrow is his fiftieth birthday. They will have something to celebrate. Isn't that grand? You see there are good little gods as well as cruel ones. . . .

Yesterday morning to Hillside with Charlie Butler, Albert Mayer, Henry Churchill, etc., all seeming enthusiastic. The weather was good. The bricklayers were once more busy. We have everything up to the roof excepting the six-story buildings.

I wish I could send you some of our lovely clear weather, but, instead, here is all my love.

Clarence

1. Walter Curt Behrendt, the German architectural historian, wrote extensively on European housing and city planning in German periodicals and for the *Journal of the AIA* when Charles Whitaker was editor.

219   To Catherine Bauer

[New York City]   [December] 1934

Dear Catherine Bauer:

Books really do get published! The sight of your [*Modern Housing*] gives me hope.
Perhaps, someday, mine will also be a reality. But I doubt it. It seems so impossible.
. . . But that isn't what I was going to say. I wanted to thank you for the book, and
tell you it looks fine. I think it is well set up. . . . It reads easy and [it] is clear that
the facts are there and a real understanding of those facts. [It] is fine that one who
knows [them] can express them so clearly.

Kindest regards.

Cordially,

Clarence S. Stein

220   To Aline Stein

New York City   January 12, 1935

Beloved one:

. . . Yesterday morning I had breakfast with Ben [MacKaye] at the Parker House
(where they grow the famous rolls). It has the charm of long ago. Benton and I had
a grand old talk. He is so delighted with his job. He is thinking about the TVA. No
one is hurrying or pushing. I only hope it lasts. . . .

My talk at MIT was all right, I think.[1] [There were] about forty students. I seem
to have got the idea over (only one of the boys dozed), and even though it did not
roll over and build up as well as it will one of these days, a good part of the class
stayed for twenty minutes after. I had lunch with Emerson, the dean, and Young,
who is in charge of the city planning. They are trying something quite new in this
country: city planning as a part of architecture rather than landscape architecture or
engineering.[2] That is the way I practice it, of course. Emerson had discussed the
plans for the school with R. D. K[ohn], Ackerman, and me before he started, and
so they wanted to know what I thought of their work. I had to go back to the
school to look over drawings.

By the time I got to the Art Museum, it was almost closing time. I could not stay
overnight at Boston as I have too much to do here, so I will have to go up again for
the museums. That will be when you come. . . .

I love you . . . perhaps that will help too!

Clarence

1. Stein was lecturing in the new graduate program in City Planning at MIT. In the 1930s he
lectured at the new schools of city and regional planning, including Columbia and Cornell in
1936.

2. This was the beginning of MIT's formal two-year graduate program in city planning. Its first graduates in 1937 were Carl Feiss, Jack Howard, and Thomas W. Mackesey. Feiss taught at Columbia University and later was the first director of the Housing and Home Finance Agency, which administered the urban renewal programs initiated by the U.S. Housing Act of 1949. How-ard was planning director in Cleveland, Ohio, in the 1940s when the landmark general plan of Cleveland was developed, and Mackesey established the graduate program in Regional Planning at Cornell from 1937 to 1962. In 1951 he became dean of the College of Architecture at Cornell.

---

221   To Aline Stein

[New York City]   January 24, 1935

Beloved:

It did stop snowing after all. 1888 still holds the record, but I bet it was no more beautiful than today. I wish you were here to see our front yard.

Yesterday, another check from Hillside. They really do pay! $11,400, or some-thing like that. So I sent Pop a check for what I owed him and ordered some more Treasury Notes for you. Mia has made out another record of the coming and going of our accounts, which I enclose.

. . . I had tea this afternoon with [the] Spingarns, the ones that gave Lewis his house at Amenia.[1] Her English sister, Lady Something-or-other, was over and wanted to talk of the London Housing she is philanthropizing. It was a good talk, and I got in a few words of instruction to the old story, but there are only three weeks more.[2]

My love,
Clarence

1. Spingarn was an important influence on Mumford as a critic. He also introduced Mumford to the region of Amenia, N.Y., where the Mumfords' summer and later full-time home, apparent-ly given to them by the Spingarns, was located. In *Sketches from Life,* Mumford states that he "ac-quired" the old farmhouse in Amenia with two acres of land in 1929. Lewis and Sophie Mumford spent summers there (eighty miles north of Manhattan) after 1929 and, in 1936, moved per-manently to Amenia from their house at Sunnyside in Queens.

2. Stein was quite familiar with the history of philanthropic contributions of individuals and family foundations for the construction of housing for families with low and moderate incomes. So his reaction to "Lady Something-or-other's" account of her philanthropic work in housing naturally was that he could add to her knowledge. He probably was bored and would much rather talk to Aline, and so he comments on her pending return to New York.

---

222   To Aline Stein

[New York City]   January 30, 1935

Aline dear:

Things move so slowly. I have had drawings for Phipps [apartments addition] ready for over a week, but I can't get hold of Lehman, who is the one who must approve of them before we can put the matter up to the board of directors. Nothing seems to be happening in regard to the Municipal Housing. [I'm] lucky Hillside is still there to worry about. But I want a new one, something to dig into.

I had lunch with Stacey May today way up near the top of the Rockefeller pile. It looks as though the Foundation may go into housing in a big way: Education, research, and that kind of [thing]. Mr. Rockefeller has been stung so badly in his experiment with Thomas that it is going to be quite a job to draw him into building for awhile.[1] But I think there is much they might . . . bring out—the real facts in regard to our cities and housing: the actual cost factors, all about subways and community buildings, and those old things, in the books your husband never wrote.

Well, anyhow, Stacey and I had a very nice talk and an excellent lunch. . . . They treat those highbrows pretty well once they enter the golden doorway. It's pretty soft for the professors. It must be like heaven up there in the sky, after the struggle most of the learned ones have.

As you see, there is not much new.

"Come home, come home, wherever you are." That's all I can think.

I love you,
Clarence

1. Andrew Thomas was the architect for much of New York City's early philanthropic housing for families of low income, including the 1928 John D. Rockefeller, Jr.–financed Thomas Garden Apartments in the Bronx and the Paul Lawrence Dunbar Apartments in Harlem, built in the same year as a cooperative for black families.

223   To Aline Stein

[New York City]   February 2, 1935

Beloved:

. . . Of course, I want to go to Yucatan and Mazatlan. But I don't think it can be two weeks from now. Firstly, it will be difficult to drop certain work at present.

1. Models: I must criticize them from time to time, and I must be here to see that Lawrie pushes them along.[1] I think the Wichita people would be justified in feeling I was neglecting my job if I did not see it through now.

2. The method of coloring the ornament is not yet determined. We are still experimenting. We may reach a conclusion next week. Then I may be forced to go out to argue the matter with the board. I can't quit for any length of time until it is determined.

3. I must keep after Phipps. The office holds another job. Though progress is slow in getting Lehman and their board to act on the plans, I must keep after them.

4. There is Hillside. Marjorie Cautley is working at landscape plans. I must criticize these and then get the government's approval. Besides, we are just beginning to put up partitions.

I want to be here to see all of the various types of apartments in actuality so that I can be sure no change is necessary before they are duplicated again and again.

Possibly, I would like to stay put for a little while. I have been looking forward to you being here with me, and our enjoying New York together, and my settling down to my writing desk, if I can't find reason to settle down to my drafting board. . . .

Leave home, come home. I want you here, beloved. . . .

My love,
Clarence

1. Lee O. Lawrie's models were for the sculptural ornament that was a major feature of Stein's Wichita Art Museum design.

---

224 To Aline Stein

[New York City]   February 17, 1935

Darling:

I am delighted that you were happy about *The Good Earth* [screen test], no matter what they may think.[1] Your letter about the tests arrived today. It sounds very exciting. The Chinese food must have been of great help, and the real water buffalo! . . .

Last night, when you spoke of my saying I was going to get out of the housing authority work, I did not know just what you meant. I remembered afterward I said I didn't want to be connected with the first job.[2] It is like a dish that has been on the fire too long: [that's] cooked to death, and too many cooks. Today we met with Commissioner Post and he told us how the work was to be divided (if any). It is all very complicated. I will tell you about it when you get back. But, in short, Washington has decided we are to be divided into teams, and the principals on the first job are to be the executive team. So I am out of that. I am to be one of the five to run the second. They think there will be three jobs. Post and LeComme (who seems a good guy) are with me, and I think we can play together and can make the rest of the crew play ball, if they don't do it of their own free will. So, something worthwhile may come of it.

This morning [I was] at Hillside. It is moving rapidly now.

It is hard writing letters now. You are so nearly here.[3]

I love you.

Clarence

1. Aline had tested for the lead role in *The Good Earth* and very much wanted it.

2. At this time the first large New York City project was to consist of slum clearance and rebuilding on a site on the lower East Side of Manhattan. It was to be designed by a "team" of architects.

3. Aline seems to have made a trip east in mid-February 1935.

---

225   To Aline Stein

March 11, 1935   New York City

Beloved:

. . . Yesterday, I stayed home most of the day. I am trying to outline a series of studies that might be made by the Rockefeller people in regard to cities and housing. Naturally, I want them to prove the facts I have been indicating, but I have got to put it in a way that will not show too plainly just where they will land when they come to the end of their laborious search. What I want are the actual facts and figures uncovered, analyzed, and published in such a way that they will be brought home to the public. Perhaps they can and will do it. (I am not sure.) Then, the whole thing will not be too much of an indictment of business.

Ben left at about nine. Albert Mayer came up for a long talk and took lunch with me. Albert is a good one. He is doing a fine job trying to get New York out of its housing mess. His great trouble is, I think, that he is forever getting lost inside himself. He is trying to find Albert Mayer.

I went out to see a few exhibits on 57th Street. I was not impressed. Even Noguchi, who has a one-man show, did not say much, though he was trying to show sculpture as an expression of the community spirit. Most of it looked ugly or crazy to me. But there was one architectural [piece], . . . a man [and] a play mountain for a park that was delightful in form. Not sculpture, just man and beautiful flowering, lines, steps, and ranges.

No use talking more about the temptations of Yucatan. We will have much to say about that one tonight.

I love you here, or in Yucatan, or anywhere.

Clarence

226 To Aline Stein

[New York City]   May 21, 1935

Beloved:

Yesterday I wasted the greater part of the afternoon up at Hillside. The real estate editor had been invited up, and for some unexplainable reason they had to be fed and thanked before [they saw the project]. So we sat around a second-rate Italian joint until two-thirty. Eken was expansive and told his neighbors all about how he had done the job. Yes, yes, there was an architect. He apparently came in somewhat late in the picture. I smiled. I can see the story grow as time passes. Andrew becomes the sole designer of Hillside (of course, presuming that it is a success).

Zoe showed the place to the editor, ultimately, and they seemed duly impressed.

Straus was there, of course, and had to tell me how bad he thought all the planting [was]. He apparently thought he was getting a private estate with the choicest of trees. He is a D. F., but I must keep him away from Mrs. Cautley as much as possible until a few people tell him what beautiful planting he has.

Yesterday morning I received the last letter written on the train. Today I expect to hear from Brentwood.

[rest of letter missing]

227 To Aline Stein

[New York City]   May 24, 1935

Aline dear:

Yesterday morning we presented the Valley Stream scheme, drawings and figures, to the Tugwell branch of the government.[1] Fine! Just the kind of thing they want, and all that. There is something the matter. Things don't go that easy excepting in dreams. And the arrangements for financing were such as one meets only in Wonderland. No interest! Amortization of building costs but not land. In short, the government pays for the land and forgets it. The cost of labor and materials is paid back over a period of years. But the sacred god of capitalism, interest, they will have nothing to do with it. This is relief. It replaces the dole, not a limited dividend housing operation. And, of course, there is where we will find one of the great difficulties when it comes to counting costs. Relief labor is paid, but it does much less.

Another interesting problem is that of how to give so much of the work to the unemployed in the neighborhood, rather than putting too much of the cost into materials made elsewhere. It seems to be one of those crazy conclusions that the topsy-turvy conditions have led them to. They are trying to solve a national problem, but in each locality I am trying to see its narrow, local angle. We begin to consider how we might make our own windows and cinder blocks, etc., no matter whether we could get them in from existing factories elsewhere in the country at a slightly lower cost or not. We can, of course, for the simpler manufacturing processes in the big hangars. It is all very exacting. They all want to do nothing but whole towns, all at one time.[2] And what arrangements would I suggest as payment for architectural services. Of course, it is a dream, but don't awaken me too readily.

Anyhow, in reality or in the dream, they [the financial bankers of Valley Stream and other similar projects in other cities] told me that Eckes, president of the New York Life, had promised to lend 80% of the cost if Colean would approve the loan.[3] Colean is Henry Klaber's boss, and their department [Federal Housing Administration] can [insure] loans of this kind. So I took them over to see Colean, and he thought it looked OK, as they are ready to put in the rest of the cost, part in land which they own free and clear and part in capital.

He could not definitely approve it until he had evidence that there would be an easy market for renting the housing and until he saw designs and a cost statement. But it is most promising. So Hanson is starting back to gather statistics in regard to the need, and I will soon be on the way out, if we can make satisfactory arrangements. I guess we can, as they seemed set on having me as architect.

Now don't awaken me, anyhow not until I get to California. I want to wake up on the sleeping porch and hear the hummingbird and Brother's bark and look over and see you wake up, so surprised.

I love you,
Clarence

1. Stein was to present the Valley Stream plan to PWA officers but ended up presenting it to the new staff of the Resettlement Administration, which FDR had established the previous month. Rexford Tugwell, one of FDR's domestic policy advisors, had been appointed to direct the Resettlement Administration.

2. This was the first indication (in his correspondence) that Stein was seeking work as part of the Resettlement Administration plan to build New Towns.

3. Clarence seems to be discussing two conversations about the Valley Stream plans: one with Tugwell's group and another with the FHA about financing the "airport projects" and another project with institutional investors to be insured by the FHA. Miles Colean, a housing economist, was a major figure in U.S. housing policy for the next two decades.

228　To Aline Stein

[New York City]　May 26, 1935

My darling:

I am back from a long trip [or] so it seems. One sees so many people at Washington that one knows, it is the way Paris used to be in summer. No, they are the more interesting ones in Washington. Breakfast at the Hay-Adams, downstairs, of course.

What a lot of architects: Voorhees (who is chief architect of Princeton for a month)—I had wanted to discuss the museum [with him]; Sullivan Jones, who was on the Housing Commission with me; and . . . George Gove, who was secretary of the commission at Washington with a lot of the other housing experts to criticize Catherine Bauer's report.[1] George [was] looking glum and hopeless about it all, and there is the Chicago crowd, Mr. Rockefeller's boys, all a-smiling. They have their jobs, houses or no houses: [Coleman] Woodbury and the rest of them. Charles Ascher over at the corner table with what looks like a good-looking girl, unless the distance deceives me.[2] And, well, what's the difference?[3]

Quite a different world over at the Willard, where the museum convention is gathered. I spent yesterday morning with McCabe, the superintendent of the Chicago Museum, discussing their experiments with glass [block] walls. They are doing much of the experimenting that will be needed if my Princeton museum is to be a success. So it may be just as well if they pioneer my ideas.

Lunch with Catherine Bauer and Armenger at the Occidental. Good food and good talk.

Then Catherine and I went to the Freer [Gallery] and reveled in the screens. Afterward the director of the museum showed me a new method he had developed for storing pictures.

And now to work: To arrange my notes from Washington, to try to plan how I would do the job if any of the dreams come true.

I love you,
Clarence

1. Bauer was working with the Housing Study Guild (Wright, Churchill, Stuart, and others) on ideas for housing policy and was lobbying for national housing legislation.

2. Charles Ascher, who worked as a legal advisor to the CHC, drafting the covenants for open space at Sunnyside and Radburn, was very active in planning and housing circles during the New Deal era.

3. Stein seems to be feeling a bit left out of the interesting things happening in Washington.

---

229   To Aline Stein

[New York City]   May 28, 1935

My darling:

Yesterday was one of those never-ending days, jumping from one job to another: Valley Stream, Palos Verdes, Lochita, Phipps, Hillside. It started early in the morning at my desk, then a long talk here with Frank. It is so much calmer here. Then the office, with a thousand crosscurrents. Lunch with Harris and architects in regard to Valley Stream. Then to Hillside. Renting going fine, but trouble again about street closing. We are to have another meeting this morning, and I believe the villains are all set to kill my pet idea.[1] It was quarter of seven before I was finished going over garden plans with Mrs. Cautley. Dead tired, I wondered whether I really wanted to start off on another big proposition [with] all [its] nagging details. I must get away and see it in perspective.

California, here I come! At least, I hope the Palos Verdes crowd will agree to my terms.[2] Soon, soon, soon, let's hope.

And if you have nothing else to do, you can go out to Palos Verdes with me and tell me where to put the houses and what they are to look like and everything.

My love, my love,
Clarence

1. Several of the 1932 site plans for Hillside Homes indicated a continuous east-west automobile-free pedestrian circulation path in the center of the blocks between the Boston Post Road and Hicks Avenue. By September 1933 it was clear that legal closing of all or most of the north-south mapped streets was going to be a lengthy and perhaps unsuccessful process. In Stein's later plans no buildings were located on those mapped but unbuilt streets, with the hope that someday the city would approve the legal vacation or closing of these rights of way.

2. The "Palos Verdes crowd" were the developers of and investors in an apartment project in Los Angeles that Clarence hoped to design.

230   To Aline Stein

[New York City]   May 28, 1935

Beloved:

. . . We had it out hot and heavy with the enemies of closed streets [at Hillside Homes], and we certainly licked 'em, but the battle was not final. Straus seemed so happy to see someone get the better of Eken and Hunter! I almost forgot how much I dislike him.

Well, I suppose I should say something about the late lamented NRA.[1] But, what should I say? . . .

All my love,
Clarence

1. The National Recovery Act had been declared unconstitutional by the Supreme Court.

231   To Aline Stein

[New York City]   May 31, 1935

Beloved:

Yesterday Frank and I went to Washington just for an hour and a half's interview with one person, but what an important interview.[1] [It was] about the terms on which I would design a complete town if (of course, there are a lot of ifs), and I still look upon it as nothing but a dream. But we talked seriously of architectural fees that would amount in a year to almost half a million! They want a single architect with concentrated control and responsibility. That is the only way they can get efficient "spend and speed." Spending the money on employment in a year is the essence of the program.

The trouble is that [John R.] McCarl, the controller who controls expenditures, says there must be a competition on the basis of price for architects (which would cut me out) or a group of architects.[2] I am opposed to this, and so are those in charge of the program for building these towns. So now we must wait. I don't know just what to wish. I hate the idea of a big office, even for one year, and yet, and yet, we will leave it to the gods and McCarl.

Washington or, rather, the governmental offices were mostly closed, so Frank [Vitolo] and I spent what time we had in seeing some of the sights: Goodhue's Science Building, Cret's Pan American, etc.

There is much more to write, but I must go to work.

My love,
Clarence

1. Stein met with the staff of the Resettlement Administration, which was launching the program in which the Greenbelt Towns were built (1935–37).

2. Stein, an active member of the American Institute of Architects, opposed the selection of architects on the basis of the lowest fee for services.

---

232 To Aline Stein

[New York City]   June 3, 1935

My darling:

Yesterday I did not write. I was so disappointed about the prospect of my not going out to see you, and there was still an uncertainty. There still is, but the odds are against my going just now.

Saturday I was at the office all day. All the boys and Miss Morris came in also to help me get ready to go. Word did not come until the afternoon that the results of Hanson's survey of the need, or rather demand, for the kind of housing we were proposing [at Valley Stream, Long Island, and other abandoned airports in other cities were] not very promising. He thought he needed more time.[1]

It was a blow. I had been going full steam, and here was a rock on the tracks. Well, well, you and I must get used to taking these things as you said last night. I began searching around for my mother's rosy spectacles. With the Valley Stream affair so imminent, or so possible anyhow, I should be here. I had more preparatory work to do on Valley Stream.[2] We have only been separated two and a half weeks. It would be better to go later, etc., etc.

These big beautiful prospects are exciting, even if nothing ultimately comes of them. I don't know when I have been so full of energy and "go" from six thirty in the morning on through the day. It's grand.[3]

It is good of you to take this disappointment as you did. You're a darling, my darling.

And I love you so,
Clarence

1. Stein had been planning to go to California to see the site of the Palos Verdes housing project. The project was postponed and eventually scrubbed.

2. The old-airport housing projects of the National Housing Corporation did not materialize either, providing the second of a series of "no starts." This was to leave Stein without any major design commissions by the end of 1935.

3. This may be a good example of one of Clarence Stein's manic phases, which often led to a sharp drop into depression during the days following.

233 To Aline Stein

[New York City] June 4, 1935

Beloved mine:

For weeks I have been flying through air and grabbing at stars, going way up! Just sweeping along. All the old pains forgotten, I was never tired.

It couldn't go on forever, of course. The postponement of the California trip was like a bad air pocket. Down, down, down. Yesterday afternoon, all of a sudden, I was all tired. So I went home, and at five thirty I was in bed. A good dinner, a good sleep. Now I am up early and ready once more to fly off into space, to fight the dragons, or anything.

But let's come down to earth for a moment and talk finances. I will pay your taxes this time. Foolish for you to keep on getting rid of your bonds. And I think the account book says I owe you something.

Ackerman's coming up to breakfast at eight. There is an hour and a quarter in which to work before then. There is plenty of work, so my love, good bye until to-morrow.

Clarence

234 To Aline Stein

[New York City] June 5, 1935

My darling:

There is so much to do here. I wonder now how I really would have gotten away. The Phipps addition took most of my time yesterday. Something unforeseen happened, and we will be digging a hole for the foundation in a week or so.

Yesterday morning, Ackerman had breakfast here. He is pretty hopeless about the [New York City] Housing Authority getting anywhere. I can see the forewarnings of just what is likely to happen in the near future. Newspapers yesterday said that the four billion must go mainly to labor; too much goes to materials and land in housing, they say.[1] The money must be spent before July 1936, they say (I guess that is so that it will assure the reelection of FDR), so there isn't time [to] clear . . . the Valley Stream project, you ask? Probably it will. . . . There is a chance that [Valley Stream] might get by. The land costs would be low, and we could set up factories in the old [airport] hangars. But I don't really believe it will happen. Nonetheless, I am going to get ready. . . .

My darling,
Clarence

1. This large federal appropriation intended to generate employment was at first managed by Harry Hopkins. Most of it went to his new Works Progress Administration (WPA), and some went to the PWA for housing. Tugwell was allocated a small portion for the Resettlement Administration, including a smaller amount for New Towns than he had originally hoped.

---

235 To Aline Stein

New York City   June 14, 1935

Aline dear:

It was hot yesterday, sweltering hot.

Not much to report. Just work. Enjoying myself rearranging the plans for the Phipps East River job, then to see Lehman. It looks good, but I don't know if I will do it.[1] If I do, it should take a month or so to get out the drawings, and I guess I would have to stay right here. If it doesn't go ahead, I should be free to go west before long.

The Washington situation looks more and more hopeless. I can't see how they are going to be able to do housing. They are setting up one obstacle after another; practically all the money must go to labor, none for materials. The money must be spent in a year, but all suggestions must be passed on by so many authorities at Washington that much of the time will be wasted before anything can be done, etc., etc. In short, they are busy at Washington building high walls that will keep them out of the promised land and me out of the job of building a Garden City. But the time will come.

. . . The book, that sounds good. We will publish the book. But which one![2] My love, my love, my love.

Clarence

1. The Phipps East River Apartments job would be scratched in a few weeks.
2. Aline was trying to encourage Clarence to work on his book on housing and planning or his book on museums, both of which were stalled.

---

236 To Aline Stein

New York City   June 17, 1935

Darling:

It is queer. When you told me last night that other architects were going to do the Pasadena Museum, I felt as though I had just lost something, something precious to me, when I have known for a number of years that I would not do that building but never believed [it]. Didn't Johnston tell me the other day?[1] But, all of a sudden, I seemed to realize last night that it was done. My dream was ended. I suppose that, when a man is being tried, no matter how badly the case may go, there is always the hope: the jury, the judge. And the verdict "guilty" always comes [as] a surprise. I don't know why I talk on about this. I know it is merely an incident. There are many dreams, many sketches before there are buildings, and the world can be thankful for that. And, after all, that design for the [Pasadena] Art Institute is no longer [for] me.[2] [But] I do like it. I would be tempted to build it if I had the chance, and I know more about what a museum should be. So, you see, I have not lost Rosie's spectacles.

The morning I spent in writing. I am catching up to myself.

It was a lonely day. I miss you so.

My beloved,
Clarence

1. A chance meeting with Reginald Johnson in Washington the previous day had revealed that Myron Hunt was doing sketches for the Pasadena Art Museum. This was the third potential design commission to slip away from Stein in 1935. The East River Houses for Phipps and Valley Stream and its parallel projects will be the fourth and fifth. Finally, the opportunity to design one of the RA's Greenbelt Towns will be lost a few months later in this long series of disappointments.

2. Stein's design proposals for the Pasadena Art Institute drew from the Spanish colonial work he had done for Goodhue in San Diego and on his own for the California Institute of Technology in the late 1920s. His papers include a perspective of his proposal.

---

237 To Aline Stein

New York City   June 19, 1935

Aline, my darling:

I just heard your voice, and so this is a very happy birthday. I never thought while we talked that it was still night at your end of the wire. Four o'clock, and dark. You are a darling to call me. It made me glad to have a birthday.[1]

I am getting a bit fearful of this annual record of the passing years. I want to hide my head in the sand until this day is passed and forget these numbers they give the years. Well, I will have Pop here tonight to remind me that, to the Steins, they make no difference.

Even then, I can't altogether believe. I have this fear of aging. I don't mean the aging of the body. You're right, I should let this masseur chap help take care of that. But it is the fear of aging inside. The flowers you sent are so gay: long stalks of blue and purple. I wish I knew what they were all called.

Yesterday was made more gay by a visit to City Hall to see his Honor the Mayor. It is difficult to take government seriously when one sees it close up. It is there for Moss [Hart] to photograph for us as an annual revue. I went to see La Guardia in company with one of the younger Swopes, who is in Tugwell's division at Washington, in charge of subsistence homes and New Towns. Tugwell seems to have surrounded himself with a group of the sons of wealthy dads, who know about as little about the subject with which they are dealing as he does.[2] The mayor had heard of the possibility of their doing some housing and thought there might be a chance of getting some of it for New York. I was taken along as someone who might know something about housing and the possibilities of any suggestion of location the mayor might make.

Our guide was Mrs. Rosenberg, who is the New York head of the late, defunct NRA. She knew you from the days of Aunt Sophie,[3] she told me. She is another Belle Moskowitz, as far as knowing her way around politically. [She is] the friend of all the statesmen, large and small, around the city hall, from mayor and borough presidents down to secretaries and the policeman on guard at the mayor's door. They are all good friends of hers. She is Belle Moskowitz, all but that spark of genius that made Al Smith what he was and is no more.

We waited hours before we saw the mayor, but it was all good serious comedy there in the outer office, and then the roly-poly mayor with this vest hanging over the back of his chair. I will tell you about the talk some other time. It was long, but it didn't get anywhere.

My love, how I wish you were here. Not only your dear voice . . . you, you, you.

I love you,

Clarence

1. This was his 53rd birthday.

2. Stein's disdain for these latecomers to the causes of better housing and communities for the working class and poor was not even thinly veiled in his letters to Aline.

3. Aunt Sophia was Sophie Loeb, Aline's demanding critic and mentor, the older, "successful" sister of Jennie Mac.

---

238   To Aline Stein

New York City   June 20, 1935

Beloved:

. . . I found that birthday presents still thrilled me, but not as much as a telephone call, a telegram, and two letters, all in one day from you.

There were some presents. Ely's book came yesterday.[1] I had ordered it some time ago. It looks good: well illustrated, good press work, and it is short. . . .

And, at last, Noguchi decided to let us have your bust.[2] We tried it at various places, and it finally climbed to the top of the mantle in the dining room. The marble, says Noguchi, is a great sculptor. He feels the shape of skin stretched on bone, but it doesn't say you. The shape of the head, yes, but not what Jim has in his sketch, the dear you. Noguchi's lady is so serious, so head up in arms. You are almost there, but not there. He probably lost you between the clay and the marble. Something around the mouth and the eyes.[3] He says he will find it when you get back. But what he wanted now was the fifty dollars that was still coming to him. He is off to Mexico, with a stop at L.A. on the way. Perhaps I am all wrong. I shouldn't try to judge the bust until I have lived with it. . . .

I love you,
Clarence

1. Ely Kahn's book of photographs of his architectural work.

2. Five days later, Clarence wrote to Aline, "I'm falling in love with the bust on our dining room mantle. First thing in the morning when I get up, I greet it."

3. The Noguchi head of Aline MacMahon Stein is now displayed in the Performing Arts Branch of the New York Public Library at Lincoln Center, which also houses some of Aline's papers related to her stage and film career. When Aline complained to Noguchi that the portrait sculpture did not look like her, he is said to have responded: "It will."

---

239   To Aline Stein

Wichita, Kansas   June 27, 1935

Darling:

There isn't much to say after our talk of last night. It was good to hear your voice.

I am out at the job. There it is [the Wichita Museum], a little affair, but solid and fresh and gay.[1] It is good and so full of promise, not only for this building when it is all there, but for others to come. Architecture with color and with gaiety and dignity, color that can be handled freely.[2] The trouble with most of our architectural color is that it has to [be] made at distant shops permanently in terra cotta and such like, without the opportunity of judging it in the light and surroundings in which it will be seen. Here, Charlie and I decide things right on the scaffold. You must see it. I think you will like the interiors, also—what there is of them. They are simple, but they are varied. And I think [they] will make good settings for whatever art they put in them.

It is fairly hot here. The favorite costume of the natives is shirtsleeves. . . .

I probably will leave here tomorrow night. I will not telegraph Sunday, as I expect to be out at Tugwell's conference somewhere in the country.[3]

All my love,
Clarence

1. The Wichita group was able to finance only the central part of the art museum that Stein had designed for them.

2. Stein's early study of color in ornament at the École des Beaux Arts was reinforced by the decorative work he did on Goodhue's San Diego buildings and on St. Bartholomew's, as well as on several of his own New York City buildings.

3. The meetings, which he will describe later in a letter to Aline (document 242), were to be held at the resort Inn of Buck Hills Falls in east-central Pennsylvania.

240 Speech at Dedication of Hillside Housing

[Bronx, New York]   June 29, 1935

Last year, while Hillside was being built, the children of Public School No. 78, which adjoins Hillside, carefully followed the building operations. Their notes and sketches, which were made into a book by Mrs. Robson, their principal, showed how it was built from foundation to roof. Most of the students described some process of construction, but one little girl illustrated Hillside as it was before we started building. She wrote: "This is the hillside. We played in the grass. We sat on the rocks. We picked wildflowers. It is all gone."

Yes, for a time the grass and trees were gone, and there was only mortar and steel and brick and scaffold and apparent disorder. But now we are bringing nature back, grass and flowers and trees. The trees are still small, but they will grow, and there will be places to sit in the shade while the youngsters play or wade in the pools. It will not be long before the vines have grown and the bushes and trees and the lawns have softened the outline of the buildings.

It is that that will make Hillside different from the rest of New York. It will be a quiet, peaceful park surrounded by houses. Hillside will be a place of safety and re-pose, a place of sunlight. From every room one will look out on broad vistas of gar-dens and restful lawns or gay play spaces.

The rest of New York was beautiful, as was this hill. But when the builders de-stroyed nature elsewhere, they never let it return. The homes of New York's millions look out upon bare walls and open onto noisy, dangerous, treeless streets. What ar-tificial beauty they might have had for a time was wiped out by the degradation of neighboring buildings. Blight has destroyed the social as well as the economic value of a large part of New York.

Hillside will never be blighted. It was planned, was built, and will be operated as a complete, integrated neighborhood. It will control its own environment. It will be managed by a company that knows that its success depends on the preservation of its unique features.

Above all, the people who will live here will preserve and develop the gardens and recreation spaces that offer an opportunity for a finer and more abundant com-munity life.

241 To Aline Stein

[En route to Buck Hills Falls, Pennsylvania]   June 30, 1935

Beloved:

This is written on a train of the Delaware and Lackawanna Railroad. I am on my way out [to] the conference of the Tugwell group, which is to be at Buck Hill Farm up in the hills of Pennsylvania, beyond Delaware Water Gap.

Yesterday's affair up at Hillside was, on the whole, a fool affair, as all such things are likely to be. Mainly [there were] a lot of prominent nonentities, who had nothing to do with the long battle that made Hillside possible, making themselves as prominent as possible while Frank Vitolo and Jack Bower, who did the building, stood in the background. Don't take this as a complaint as far as I am concerned. There were very nice things said about the architect by the governor and most of the others. [This] was good because that was what Pop had come to hear, and he seemed satisfied. He sat with the rest of us on the speakers' platform, and I think it was a great day for him.

And finally there was Mayor [LaGuardia]. He came late, in fact after the show was all over. Straus and I took him all around and he was immensely interested—intelligently so. He was constantly asking me to compare what they were planning for slum clearance with what he saw. And I, at last, got an opportunity to drive home the need of really getting the streets closed. So we have arranged that I am to go down to his office sometime this week, and he will get hold of the lawyers that are setting up obstacles. So it was worthwhile going back to New York after all.

Good-bye until tomorrow, my beloved.

Clarence

242 To Aline Stein

July 2, 1935

Darling:

This is a queer place. [It is] a tremendous hotel set in the green hills [with] immense corridors, and porches, and "sitting around places," with chairs, regiments of chairs. The Macy's of country hotels. It's Quaker: no drinks, and smoking [is] considered a nuisance. I remember, when I was working over at the factory, we made a casket for a rich Quaker. It's hard to be as simple as possible (yes, regardless of cost), made of pine, but the very, very finest pine. That's this place.

The conference has been going on interminably. There are about fifty or sixty experts in education, health, recreation, housing, community organization, home economics, and everything. They are heads of all the associations and of various departments of the government. They are shooting at this idea of how to build, manage, and create a new community, from every possible angle. It's hard to make any sense of it all: an orchestra of diversified prima donnas, all of them accustomed to having the whole show. Now and then a clear note comes over. But there are interesting people, and so the between times are worthwhile.

Most in charge still have hope that they may be able to go ahead with Valley Stream or something of the kind. They say they may know next week. They always expect to know next week.

And now for another talk fest.

My love,
Clarence

---

243 To Aline Stein

July 4, 1935

Beloved:

After all, it was only a dream. Last week I really thought we might, we would be on our way across the Pacific in a fortnight or so, but now it looks as though China [will] have to wait.

Here is the the way it is, as far as I am concerned.

Toward the end of our meetings at Buck Hills Falls, it was suggested that a small committee be appointed to summarize the meanderings of these three days of discussion. When Tugwell looked over the list, he said, "I don't know whether Stein can serve. He is to design one of our towns." Of course, they may never do any, but it does look as though, after all the talk, they probably will be given a chance to start something. And it seems that I have a very good chance if they do.[1] It certainly would seem folly to be at the other side of the Pacific if that chance came. Anyhow, we should wait a little. Don't you think so, darling?

And then yesterday, O'Conner (who is the chief of our little army of slum-clearing architects) called up to say that Pop had just told him we would probably get the budget of the slum replacement job . . . at Red Hook.[2] . . . It was not sure, but were we ready to start making studies? So that puts it right up to me. Shall I go ahead with them? It is tempting if I am really given complete charge of planning. But I am afraid there will be endless talking and squabbling and compromising. The sensible thing is to get out, but, well, anyhow, I will talk it over with O'Conner and Pop tomorrow.

And so, for a while, our dreams must continue to dream. And we must content ourselves with these meager realities.

All my love,
Clarence

1. It is clear that, at this point in the planning process for the Greenbelt Towns, Tugwell expected Stein to play a very different role in the program than the one to which he was finally assigned.

2. This Brooklyn, N.Y., project was one of the largest in the city at that time. Its architects were many. Stein was a member of Red Hook Project Associated Architects for the early planning period. Alfred E. Poor was chief architect. This group was in turn associated with other single firms, including W. F. Dominick, W. I. Hohauser, E. O. Litchfield, W. T. McCarthy, J. Moskowitz, and Z. J. Robin. The project, finally built in 1937, did not much please Stein, who seemed to have played an advisory role in the design decision making.

---

244   To Aline Stein

At the Bernsteins   July 7, 1935

Aline dear:

All the family here, of course, send love and talk of you constantly. They are all well. Aline is blooming. She is taking much exercise, and writing.

There always seems much to write of my paltry adventures and problems. But your problem, your everlasting problem, seems so much more pressing. If I could only help. It is such an everlasting affair that there is none but a partial and temporary answer, no solution because it is always there in a new form.

The trouble is that your art is not the art of an individual. It is a cooperative undertaking: author, rewrite, director (to say nothing of supervisor, the distant chap in the main office, and the guy that always knows what the public wants), the cameraman, and the actors. Not just one actor even. Now, of course, one may become actor-director, but there is generally something unsatisfactory about that. They are different fields. It is like trying to talk and arrange a photograph of a group of which one is part. One can make oneself so indispensable that one can condition all the other elements that make the production. But unless one is to write and direct, as well as act, the expression of one's individual idea will be blurred in the production.

In short, as I see it, in any cooperative art, such as making a play or a picture or building a city, there are very definite limits in each single work to the individual's progress in expression. Neither you nor I want to lend ourselves to undertakings that do not carry us a step forward in the direction we want to go. But I do not believe that we can hope to make such [an] undertaking the complete and perfect realization of what we see at the moment as the ultimate. I always have to look for examples in my own work.

Wichita is a valuable experiment in color and texture of concrete. It is mediocre, but not bad as art museum planning. My choices, when the work went ahead, were to give it up entirely or take the opportunity of doing as fine a job as possible in the expression of the building, with the idea of stepping forward in the internal management in the next job and the other parts of this museum. In Phipps, I was able to put in a few private gardens. They were stepping-stones toward the best feature of Hillside, the many private terraces. Hillside is the best yet in apartment communities, but it's just full of imperfections, partial attainments.

Now I guess I am getting too involved. Do you get what I am trying to indicate? I think that you have to accept definite limitations in every job but that you must always know the direction in which you are going and take some step in that direction. A really fine job in acting, if it is not just repetitive, may be worthwhile even if the play itself is anything but perfect. There are certain limitations of surroundings in which one cannot progress but, if one waits endlessly for the perfect environment, one may never grow for lack of opportunity.

Don't get the idea that this is meant as any criticism of your policy of aiming at the stars and refusing to compromise by taking an easy way in some other direction. I am just wondering if the way to the stars is a single and a straight road.[1]

The truth is I think you are perfect. But what is the use of preaching, even if it is Sunday? You are always right, and I love you.

Clarence

1. Stein's remarkable sensitivity to the similarities in the complexities of his and Aline's careers was no doubt one of the solid rocks on which their marriage was founded.

---

245 To Aline Stein

[New York City]   July 21, 1935

Beloved:

Selma Weiss phoned this morning that Aline is better.[1] She recognized Theo.[2] The doctors seem surprised at her resistance but fear her lungs have been affected. She was unconscious for two days, from Thursday noon until yesterday. Fate seems to be fighting for her, or is it against her?

Saturday morning I spent at Hillside with the other eight architects of the Red Hook project. I had brought blueprints of the studies Albert and I had made, but before showing them we visited the various courts of Hillside so that we would all see the scale of things the same. Then we got together over the plans spread on a table in the community room. There was much criticism. The plans, which were in a sense diagrams of ideas, were intended to arouse suggestions and to crystallize a common point of view, if that is possible. There was only one type of comment that made me hot. It was, "The Housing Authority (or the PWA) will not stand for that, or don't want that." I said our job was to find out what we thought was the best solution and fight for it unless the authorities could show us what was the matter with it. Our meeting was not over until after two; then we adjourned to a nearby Italian restaurant.

Since then I have been wondering: is there any chance of our evolving anything worthwhile? Will we be forced to a compromise plan? Can nine architects really produce anything but a hybrid? If the answer is no, the quicker I get out, the better. What have I to gain: Money? Not worthwhile that way, and there probably will not be any anyhow. Reputation? Of one of a group that produced a neo-grandiose, commonplace work for the office? It will not be done in the office. On the other hand, I may, if I fight hard enough and constantly enough, take another step forward in developing a complete community, a larger community than Hillside. I can't quite make up my mind.

Mixed up with it all is the desire to get away with you to the strange places.

It is you I love.

Clarence

1. On 20 July 1935 Clarence had written to Aline that "Aline [Bernstein] has done it at last. She took an overdose of her sleeping medicine." According to one of Thomas Wolfe's biographers, Andrew Turnbull, *Thomas Wolfe* (New York: Charles Scribner's Sons, 1967), 356, Aline Bernstein, who had begun an affair with Wolfe in 1926, attempted suicide in despair over the deterioration of their relationship in March 1931. At the end of his 1935 novel, *Of Time and the River* (New York: Sun Dial Press, 1944), 907–12, Wolfe described their meeting in 1926. Suzanne T. Stutman, editor of *My Other Loneliness: Letters of Thomas Wolfe and Aline Berstein* (Chapel Hill: Univ. of North Carolina Press, 1983), concluded that Aline did not attempt suicide in March 1931. She believes that Aline's letter of April 1931 to Wolfe disproves this belief of "some scholars." In this letter Aline describes "the problem with her blood circulation" in some detail and suggests it as the cause of her collapse in mid-March 1931.

Turnbull describes a tense scene between Aline and Tom Wolfe in the Scribner's office of Wolfe's editor, Max Perkins, in mid-July 1935. The date seems to have been 11 or 12 July. Aline expressed her concern to Perkins over the recent publication of Wolfe's account of their affair. "At one point [on July 11 or 12] Wolfe and Perkins (Wolfe's editor) left the room to discuss something privately. On their return they were horrified to see Aline putting a vial of pills in her mouth. Wolfe knocked it out of her hand and a doctor [later that day] ascertained that none had been taken."

The attempted suicide that Clarence Stein described in his letter to Aline of 20 July 1935 seems to have occurred on 19 July, a few days after the incident in the Scribner's office. This suicide attempt was not mentioned by Turnbull, who did note that Wolfe left for a trip to the West on 27 July, two weeks after the Scribner's meeting, and that when he returned in September Aline Bernstein helped him furnish his new apartment. Did Turnbull not know of Aline's suicide attempt on 19 July, which seems to have been a more serious effort than the attempt on 11 July that he reported?

2. Theo was Theodore Bernstein, Aline's husband, a Wall Street banker. Ethel, Aline Bernstein's sister, was a very close friend of Clarence and Aline Stein. Edla was Theodore and Aline Bernstein's daughter. Teddy was their son.

---

246   To Aline Stein

New York City   September 22, 1935[1]

Aline dear:

It is such a lonely house and so sad, in spite of the fact that Mia has covered the floor with all our gay carpets.

Last night, after I wrote you, Catherine Bauer came up for a while. She looks quite prosperous. She is acting as consultant for various departments [in Washington]. [She] says she can earn a living with ten days a month, but she considers $50 a month a living.

Catherine tells me that Tugwell's department got some money after all, but I guess they are not going to do Valley Stream. Perhaps they will call on me to do something. Who knows? . . .

The *Times* spoke kindly of Moss's show this morning.

And I love you very much.

Clarence

1. Clarence's plans to spend a month or two in California late in the summer of 1935 seemed to have materialized. There is no correspondence between 29 July and 22 September. Aline returned to New York about 1 August and stayed there until 21 September.

---

247 To Aline Stein

[New York City]   September 24, 1935

Beloved:

I went to Phipps [Apartments at Sunnyside] this morning. Such a bully job it is—so well built. We should be doing a great many more, says I to Frank, and, of course, Frank says OK.

I telephoned to Washington and told Tugwell's crowd that I did not want to butt in, but we should do one of their towns. We have the organization already to jump in, and we know how. I don't think there is a chance they will let the work get out of Washington,[1] but, anyhow, I think I will go down there Friday and talk to them.

For lunch, Robert, Frank, and I went to an Italian joint and ate everything from pasta to spumoni with a good bottle of Chianti. After an hour . . . Robert had to leave; Frank and I stayed on over our coffee just as though we were abroad. Frank said, "It's a shame Mrs. Stein not being here when you have a little time." Frank knows everything.

Hunter telegraphed from Washington that the bids for Hillside's gardens had been approved. Thank God!

My love, I love you,
Clarence

1. Clarence was right. Despite Rexford Tugwell's earlier statement (at the conference at Buck Hills Falls) about Stein designing one of the RA's Greenbelt Towns, Stein's role was to be that of general consultant. They called on him to develop the design criteria for the Greenbelt Towns they had decided to build. Stein also served as a general consultant to the RA, especially in design review. In these roles, new to him, he had very considerable influence on the towns' design, espe-

cially that of Greenbelt, Maryland. See K. C. Parsons, "Clarence Stein and the Greenbelt Towns," *Journal of the American Planning Association* 58 (April 1990): 161–83.

The RA's leaders decided to do all of the design and contract drawings in Washington. By October 1935 Albert Mayer, Henry Wright, and others were working in Washington full time designing these towns. Several dozen planners, architects, landscape architects, and engineers worked in the spacious rooms of the RA's leased offices in the former Walsh MacLean mansion on Massachusetts Avenue at Twentieth Street. They were under the direct supervision of the former planning director of Pittsburgh, Fred Bigger.

---

248   To Aline Stein

[New York City]   September 27, 1935

Aline dear:

. . . I am writing to you again today for fear I will be too rushed in the morning. I take the early plane to Washington. I am going down to see if I can get them to give me one of the jobs that Tugwell's department is going to try to push through before December 15th. I feel certain it would be the sensible thing for them to do. We have the organization and we know how, if anyone does. I will do everything within reason to show them why. I feel it is up to me to do so, and yet I don't think I have a chance if they have a lot of reasons why the work should be done in Washington. . . .

Beyond that, there are some of them that don't like my architecture. I got that from Henry Wright, who was down there yesterday.[1] I was glad he told me. Made me feel a little sore at first that anyone should not like Hillside. But why should everyone like it? They may not take you for *Good Earth,* but you're the best actress to do it, nevertheless. I don't need anyone to tell me that Hillside is a pretty good job, but really I would like to hear frank criticism. I can't learn anything from those who say, "It's grand." I would like to hear what people think is the matter with it— they might even be right! And I would know what not to do the next time.

I may stay in Washington for a day or so and see what is happening, or what they think is happening.

All my love,
Clarence

1. Wright and Catherine Bauer advised Warren Vinton, who was organizing the work of the Greenbelt Towns division of the RA under Tugwell, that Stein "was pretty good on site planning, but best used as consultant." (Note card in Warren Vinton's Papers, Cornell University Archives.) Catherine Bauer's part in Warren Vinton's decision to offer Stein a consultant role in the Greenbelt Town program was important. She was having an affair with Vinton when she advised him that Stein would be "best used [by the RA] as a consultant." Stein's friends and associates, including Wright and Bauer, surely had a significant influence on Vinton's decision not to place the design of one of the Greenbelt Towns in Stein's hands, but Stein's resistance to moving to Washington to work on a design was an equally important factor in his loss of this opportunity.

249 To Aline Stein

[Washington, D.C.]   September 28, 1935

Beloved:

I flew here yesterday morning. [I] left New York at 8:30 and got here at 9:30. The difference between daylight savings and standard time gave me an extra hour.

I didn't succeed in showing the Tugwell crowd that they would do much better to give me one of their towns to take back with me to New York. They are all set on building a departmentalized organization here to turn out the three or four towns.[1] City planning, site planning, architecture, engineering, building, community organization—each as a separate compartment, but all working together—that's their idea. My claim is that they all must be one, or rather not only all under one head but also an organization that is accustomed to work together as a single unit. It takes a long time to develop a group that can take the problem of layout [of] a town and make it work. We have the nucleus of such a group in the office, with the cooperation of the engineers that have worked with us at Radburn and Hillside.

Well, what's the difference? They didn't see it. Perhaps I am a poor salesman when I seem to be selling myself. It embarrasses me to seem only to be trying to get something for myself when I am trying to get the thing done in the best way. (I guess the motives are really mixed, after all.) If I were just a go-getter, I could probably put up a better argument, but I don't want to. Perhaps they really are tied up by governmental regulations so they can't let the jobs go out, as they say. Anyhow, I didn't get what I wanted.

What they have asked me [to] do is to set up the community requirements for their towns.[2] It is a problem that I want to get to the bottom of. What can a poor community afford in community facilities, how to plan them and make them pay their way, and all that. [This is] just what I was trying to get at in my last unwritten book. I didn't promise to do any more than outline the attack on the problem for them, but I guess I will do the job. It is really the essence—the heart of the whole problem of building new communities.

Perhaps they are just trying to sidetrack me, but why should I care.

I must get going. It's nine, and there is much to be done in Washington today.

All my love,
Clarence

1. The RA was rapidly gathering a large staff of architects, engineers, landscape architects, and city planners to work in teams (one to a town) to finish the design in time for construction to begin before the end of the calendar year. Stein may have influenced the RA's decision to organize an interdisciplinary team for each town's design. The original plan to build eight or nine towns had been reduced to three or four because of local opposition in several locations and the reduc-

tion in Federal Works funds allocated to the RA's program. Ickes had secured allocation of the lion's share of this special appropriation for his housing and public works projects.

2. This was to be Stein's consulting assignment for the RA Greenbelt Towns program.

---

250 To Aline Stein

[Washington, D.C.]   September 29, 1935

Aline dear:

Washington again. [I] left New York at 7:30 yesterday morning and was here at quarter of ten. I spent most of the day over at the Resettlement Administration. [Tugwell is] laying out research work for various statisticians and the like. Catherine Bauer is supposed to be assisting me, but she has tied herself up with [so] many other jobs that she isn't of much use to me. I am trying to set up a budget of the expenditures of running a town inhabited only by workers of low income to see what equipment they can afford to have, what it costs for education, recreation, sanitation, care of health, and all. It is an interesting job, but why I should be doing this instead of designing one of their towns—it's absurd.[1]

Fred Bigger was in town yesterday. I hadn't seen him for years. We had dinner together at the Occidental and then walked around the parks. There was much to talk of. Even when you have lost contact with old friends, there is so much in past recollection and bringing things up to date that still bind you or at least make an evening agreeable for conversation.

And now to work.

All my love,
Clarence

1. Clarence Stein was still having difficulty accepting the role Vinton had chosen for him in the Greenbelt Towns program. This disappointment, along with the loss of the California housing work, Valley Stream, and the Pasadena and Princeton museum design jobs, meant that he was without new major projects at the beginning of October 1935.

---

251 To Warren Vinton[1]

[New York City]   September 30, 1935

Dear Mr. Vinton:

I spent all day yesterday trying to set down a method by which we might attack the problem of the community setup for the four towns the Suburban Resettlement Division is preparing to build, without constantly bumping up against question marks. From our conversation of Saturday afternoon, it was apparent that we will get nowhere unless we at least tentatively clear up some of the indeterminate points.

Therefore, don't you think we must take certain things for granted for the time being so that we may make a tentative setup of some kind? Accordingly, I suggest, for purposes of determining what equipment will be needed and what our financial setup will be, that we presume the following:

1. That family incomes of the inhabitants average $1,250 a year.
2. The families will average four persons.
3. That, in considering the capacity of the inhabitants to pay for what they are receiving, for the time being, we will consider only the cost of the original plant (i.e., dwellings, public services and utilities, educational and recreational facilities, stores, etc.).
4. The equipment and buildings to be supplied under original investment shall be adequate to meet the requirements of good housing and good community living.
5. These facilities will be adequate to compete with the neighborhoods from which the population has been drawn. (I mean not only that they shall be better from the point of view of experts, but they shall be so much more attractive to the people who are to be served that they will be induced to move to the new settlement.)
6. That all costs of operation and maintenance will be covered by rent, either of residential or commercial property.
7. That the entire community plant will be held in single ownership. This includes not only the properties to be rented and those facilities that are normally run by the government, such as educational and recreational facilities, but also certain utilities, such as gas, electricity, and water, that are sometimes supplied by private companies. I am not here proposing that all these shall be supplied by the community, but merely that, for purposes of first test, we set up our figures so as to cover these costs. We must then follow with studies to see in what cases it would be cheaper to give franchises for some or all of these utilities to commercial companies.
8. The planning and construction of the town, its building, and equipment be such as to minimize cost of maintenance and operation.

Although it seems important that we follow through as quickly as possible along all lines to find out just what equipment will be needed and what can be afforded, your Planner seemed to be particularly anxious to get an immediate answer to your store problem. I suggest, therefore, that you set some competent person to work on that at once. You will note in the report that Catherine Bauer and I made, "Store Buildings and Neighborhood Shopping Centers," we used the United States Census of Distribution, 1929, as the basis for working up figures in regard to Radburn. We found out what was spent at stores of similar size and economic capacity in the

New York region. Your towns are going to have smaller purchasing power. I, therefore, suggest that we take ten of the poorest towns in each of the regions in which it is proposed to put a development. They should be communities of 5,000 population or thereabouts and should be independent as possible of the main center. What we want to get at is the list of average annual per capita sales in different types of stores.

I hope that on Wednesday or Thursday we will be able to take up the matter of educational facilities and come to a tentative conclusion. To do so we must know in the case of each town:

1. Whether State supervision must be accepted.
2. What State financial aid will be given.
3. How will the acceptance of State supervision and State aid affect the standards of school building and curriculum.

Can you have someone started on getting this information together before my return to Washington? I expect to be in Washington Wednesday morning. However, if for any reason Catherine Bauer and you cannot work with me or if there is any other reason why you think I should postpone my visit, I would appreciate it if you would let me know at once. If anything comes up here to prevent my going to Washington on Wednesday, I will telegraph you.

Cordially yours,

Clarence S. Stein

1. This is Stein's first written report to the RA on his assignment to assist them in establishing standards and criteria for community facilities and town design.

---

252   To Aline Stein

New York City   October 2, 1935

Darling:

I have just re-read your letter of Sunday. Life seems good, even if we can't have just the parts we want or design the towns we want.

You ask, do you want to meet with a group of serious pinks? Why not? I have always thought I was going to be a red, if I ever had time to decide what shade really matched my own point of view. But first I had to find out just what that point of view was. It keeps on moving, excepting during the long periods of active work when it goes to sleep. If one joins a movement or a party, one has got to stop moving, I mean as an individual, or else become a leader, which takes so much time. And yet I am always sure that tomorrow or the day after I will join a revolution. I suppose on my eighty-fifth birthday I may be ready. So perhaps you better go and

find out if I am going to [be] making a mistake, or whether you are coming along.
. . .

My Washington trip has been postponed until tomorrow.

I love you,
Clarence

---

253   To Aline Stein

[New York City]   October 10, 1935

Beloved mine:

It is growing warmer and the leaves are turning. [It is] a wonderful day to take that trip to New England or here. If you were only here. But if you were, I suppose we would discuss it all morning and then walk across the park, and in the afternoon . . . But what's the use? I am just going to stick to my desk until noon and then work with Major Walker all afternoon. (He is coming here for lunch.) We will set up a government for these diagrammatic towns which we have been inventing all week.

I have been working hard, but what fun. There are so many angles at which to attack the problem. The good life: economy of play, construction, management, government, school, shopping centers, recreation, houses, gardens, street cleaning, health center, etc., etc., etc. Each a separate, complicated problem that must be simplified and then made part of a simple plan of [a] town and a good plan of living. It is like making a great stained-glass window [where] all the different pieces of colored glass must be made and cut, pieced together as small elements, and then made into a single related design—simple, unified. . . .

And now to work, my love.
Clarence

---

254   To Aline Stein

[New York City]   October 12, 1935

Beloved:

Nothing definite was decided as to just what my relation to the [Resettlement Administration's] Suburban Town group should be. [John] Lansill told me he was reorganizing and needs a few days more to get things decided. Meanwhile, I have plenty . . . [to study] for the economic basis on which the towns must be built. . . . Spent most of the day organizing the research that is to be followed up by the boys that were formerly here in the Housing Study Guild and Catherine Bauer and various young statisticians. Statistics is Washington's speciality, with long lists of figures that generally lead nowhere. My job was to try to keep them tied . . . to reality and [to] gather the essentials first, so that we will know something about what it is going to cost to run our towns before we have them built and it is too late to modify the design to meet the income of those who are to live in them.

I flew home in the dark with the beautiful, star-spotted pattern of cities below me. Washington was fascinating—the dome of the Capitol flooded with light and the web of lighted ribbons leading to it.

At home were your letters and your telegram. I must go to Washington every week.[1] It is such joy to come home to your letters. So glad you are enjoying the picture and that they like you so. How can they help it?

I love you,
Clarence

1. Clarence found some relief from his trips to Washington on the weekends in New York. In mid-October, he attended the opening of Moss Hart's musical, *Of Thee I Sing.* After the show, Hart commented to Clarence that "he was going out to get drunk." "Think of that," Clarence commented, "of having to wait until Monday to know your fate."

---

255   To Aline Stein

[Washington, D.C.]   October 16, 1935

Aline darling:

The Tugwellians were delighted with the preliminary job I have done. They see that this type of economic-social study must be the basis of their physical planning if it is to be successful. I had a long talk with [John] Lansill, the head of this Suburban Towns division. He wants me to continue as consultant and map out what should be the makeup of the four towns that are to be built. I said no, that I did not intend to be sidetracked as an economist. I had [of necessity] based my planning on the type of economic-social studies that I had started for them, but . . . I was not going to be labeled as a researcher or social-economist. There is the same danger as of your becoming an actor of serious parts, or something of that kind. Lansill said what he wanted was to have me act as one of his chief advisers, along with Fred Bigger and Henry Wright. We came to no conclusions, but if he agrees today that I am not only to work up the program of community equipment and government, but am to have a definite say as to the physical form that the towns and their buildings will take to carry out the social economic plans I will develop, I will take the job temporarily.[1]

It would have the advantage over being in charge of the planning of a single town, which was the job I thought I wanted, that I would not have to stay at Washington all the time. I could come down here for a couple of days a week, and I probably can do a better job sticking to the big essentials and not getting lost in the details. We will see. . . .

My love,
Clarence

1. It is astonishing that Lansill's and Tugwell's other chief advisors did not devise a more direct role for Stein in the design of the Greenbelt Towns. Mumford later discussed the "all but total neglect" of Stein by the Roosevelt administration in their housing and planning programs. In his RA work, Stein, it seems, had no idea of the influence of Henry Wright and Catherine Bauer in Lansill's decision to employ him as a consultant.

256   To Aline Stein

[New York City]   October 21, 1935

Aline darling:

Yesterday I went out to see the site of one of the future Garden Cities—beautiful, rolling farmland in Jersey near industrial towns.[1] A great opportunity if it can be realized. This may be the next step: Sunnyside, Radburn, and . . . we will see.

Albert Mayer and [Ralph] Eberlin and a young architect were along. We drove back and forth across the great expanse of land they are thinking of taking and then by Radburn [on the way] home. We covered some hundred and fifty miles during the day. It was a beautiful day and, although most of the country was not as rich in brilliant foliage as Westchester, there were many spots of glory.

I spent some time at Radburn with Major Walker checking over government costs, then to walk around the parks. Radburn is mellowing. Nature and time are making the buildings one with their setting and place. We will do better in the future. . . .

I hope the trip is coming off.[2] I am collecting dope [information] for it anyhow. . . .

My love,
Clarence

1. This was the site of Greenbrook, N.J., which was to be the fourth of Tugwell's Greenbelt Towns. It was being designed by the team of Henry Wright and Alan Kamstra (town planners) and Albert Mayer and Henry Churchill (architects). Kamstra and Mayer were both soon to be on leave from Stein's office while they worked in Washington.

The day after the trip to Greenbrook and Radburn, Stein wrote to Aline, expressing depression: "These are sad days—sad and lonely. You seem so far away." The Greenbelt Towns project at Greenbrook, N.J., was shut down by the RA in early 1936 after several unfavorable local court decisions in a suit brought against the RA by landowners near the proposed site in New Jersey.

2. In late October Clarence and Aline Stein were already planning a trip abroad for mid-December, when Clarence planned to finish his consulting work for the RA.

257   To Aline Stein

[Washington, D.C.]   October 24, 1935

Beloved:

Yesterday was a busy day here. I had little time [during the day] for my study of the economic-social setup and so I had to stay overnight instead of returning to New York yesterday evening, as I had planned.

Henry [Wright] and Catherine Bauer and I were called in to criticize the plans of houses that were being made for the first of the Garden Cities.[1] So we sat around a table all morning and afternoon with the group of architects that made the plans, as well as the architects that are to do the other projects. Fred Bigger presided. He is becoming a sort of general manager with the reorganization of the office here. Catherine was there to give a consumer's rather than technical reaction. And so the heavy work of criticism fell to Henry and me. The plans were unpardonably wasteful. They had nothing to do with low-cost housing. They were the result of the architect's desire to have every American live like a king or better, a suburban bank president. We dealt with generalities most of the morning, principles of planning, but we finally had to rip into the plans.

It was a hard thing to do. I so hate this authoritative know-better-than-thou attitude toward a fellow professional. But what else was there to do? Time is short. They must start building. The possibility of building Garden Cities means too much to me [to] let the whole thing be set back because these first ones are so extravagant that they become laughing stock of all practical builders.

I am going to keep the ship from sinking if I possibly can—if only for the memory of old Ebenezer Howard.[2]

And now I must get back to work.

My love, my love,

Clarence

1. These probably were the designs for houses to be built at Greenbelt, Md.

2. Stein's commitment to building New Towns in the United States was total. It mattered a lot to him that he was not designing one of the RA's Greenbelt Towns, but he gave generously of his conceptual talents with a sense of mission. It is clear that he would have much preferred to be participating in the design of one of the towns. It is also clear that, when Lansill, Vinton, and other RA officials had decided by mid-September 1935 that all of the towns would be designed in Washington by teams of architects, engineers, and town planners, Stein was not asked to join (let alone lead) one of these teams. As to what his decision would have been had he been asked to move to Washington to work at the RA offices, we can only speculate. His personal commitment to the idea of building new settlements as a major component of urban policy was so strong that it seems very likely that he would have been willing to give up the comforts of his life in New York City for a few months to participate in this opportunity. It also seems likely that he was not asked to do so.

258 To Aline Stein

[Washington, D.C.]   October 29, 1935

Beloved:

It was a busy day yesterday. It was just mainly plans trying to help the designers here simplify their house plans and to relate their cost, at least remotely, to what the people who are going to live in them can pay. They seem to have the idea that, because the original cost will probably be wiped out and forgotten, they need not worry about it. But the more elaborate house is going to be more expensive to maintain and operate. Besides, if this that they are doing is going to be of any use as a demonstration in any but a technocratic society, they must try to save in the cost just so as to find out how it can be done again.

Trouble is, no one seems to know just who is going to live in the houses in this first development between Washington and Baltimore [at Greenbelt, Maryland]. I am trying to drive them to a decision with my economic studies.

Had lunch with Fred Bigger. He is trying to get some order out of the [RA's] chaotic architectural office. Fred's methods are somewhat Machiavellian, though always, of course, for the good. He has been handling committees of bloated millionaires in Pittsburgh and making them back plans for the good of the city which they always thought were for their good. He has been a diplomat for so long; he walks around a mile even though he will tell you a straight line is the shortest way there. But I like Fred. Perhaps that is just a habit.

Time for me to get back to work.

I love you,
Clarence

259 To Aline Stein

New York City   November 3, 1935

Darling mine:

Sunday morning—dreary, cloudy, heavy weather. What I need is a good day in bed. And I am going to have it in spite of the fact that I had planned to work on my studies for . . . Rexford [Tugwell's Resettlement Administration] to pull them together and get them in order once more before going down there tomorrow morning.[1]

I wonder how much use they will be to them. They must move quickly; they must build.[2] I am not sure that the instrument I am trying to put together can be formed hastily so that it can be used by anyone excepting he who makes it. In this kind of planning, there is so much that depends on individual judgment that comes from a mixture of long experience and I know not what. I should be doing a job, not telling others how to do a part of it. I am not fooling myself about that. Perhaps I am lucky I am not doing it. Probably it is all going to be done so hastily that there will be no worthwhile chance. Perhaps I am lucky that I am having this opportunity to round out my study of the fundamentals.

But, of this I am sure, I am no longer feeling badly that I was not given the job of doing a town. That will come one of these days. I know I can—that's what counts. I have a growing confidence in my own ability to find a way, to find the right foundation, to create a better human environment. I feel more ready to do my job when it comes than I ever have before. Somehow or other that makes me very content.

I wish you could feel that way about O-Lan and Faith.[3] What if your chance comes today or tomorrow? What if the Thalbergs or the Warners recognize your talent now or later? I know, and you must know, that you are one of the ones, one of the very few, and your job is to go on broadening and deepening that talent until the opportunity comes. And if it doesn't altogether come, somehow it seems to me it doesn't altogether matter. Just to have prepared for it, to have prepared oneself seems somehow as important or more important than to have done.[4] Or is this just Sunday morning?

What matters after all is I love you,

Clarence

1. Stein's letters transmitting his last studies for the RA Greenbelt Town program to John Lansill were dated 19 and 23 November 1935.

2. The RA was working to a congressional timetable that required the New Town's construction to start before the end of the year.

3. Aline was still trying to land the lead role in *The Good Earth*.

4. Aline's and Clarence's disappointments at these crucial points in their professional careers are uncannily similar. After Aline did not get the role she wanted and Clarence did not get the job of designing one of the RA's New Towns, they both felt rejected and believed that they were functioning below their potentials.

---

260   To Aline Stein

[Washington, D.C.]   November 5, 1935

Beloved one:

. . . Yesterday was a day of plans. I criticized the houses and town layout of the Garden City [at Greenbelt, Maryland] they are to build near Washington. There is something terrifying, and tempting too, in being accepted as an authority. Here are a group of architects who have been working at this project for months and yet they are ready to let me change things around.[1] Is it respect for my opinion or merely fear that I represent those in control? I try so hard not to impose an idea but rather to change their point of view through their working out the thing with me. Sort of schoolboy, isn't it?

Anyhow the odds are slightly against the client today.

I love you,
Clarence

1. The team designing Greenbelt, Md., included Douglas Ellington and R. J. Wadsworth, architects, and Hale Walker, town planner. Judging from the extensive use of Radburn-like ideas in the plan for this town, it is clear that Stein had a very substantial influence on the overall form of the design and the specific details of the town's layout.

---

261 To John Lansill

[New York City]   November 19, 1935

MEMORANDUM TO	Mr. John S. Lansill[1]
FROM	Clarence S. Stein
SUBJECT	Studies of the relative improvement costs of various schemes of house grouping.

The purpose of these studies is to measure the comparative efficiency of various methods of grouping houses as affecting street, yard, and park improvement costs. The same type of house has been used throughout. We have compared houses facing on main roads and on lanes with and without vehicular roads, similar lanes of different lengths; houses in groups of different lengths with and without garages attached, as well as freestanding houses; houses with long and with narrow side toward the road.

The attached table showing cost per family indicates that improvement costs may vary as much as approximately 54% in Schemes 4 and 11. This would make a difference of approximately $457,000 for a development of 1,000 houses. These figures naturally do not take into consideration the possible differences of contour and soil conditions. They are based on approximate costs in [the] New York region at the present time under normal building conditions. They indicate, however, the relative—if not actual—difference in costs. Bearing this in mind, a few of the conclusions that may be drawn from these studies are:

1. The cost of improvements per house is greatest when houses are built facing on main roads. (Houses on main traffic ways are also probably the least desirable for good living.) Schemes 10 and 11 show similar arrangement of houses, the one on a lane and the other on a main road. The estimates of these two indicate that, conditions of soil and contour being equal, the latter will cost about 38% more than the former.

2. Improvement costs of houses on lanes are increasingly cheaper per house as the length of lane increases. (See comparison of Schemes 2 and 3.) It is apparent that a superblock of 1,000 ft. in width offers economic advantages over a block of half this width unless there are site conditions that overbalance the saving from decreased length of main highway and main lines of utilities per house.

3. The cheapest arrangement, as affecting improvement costs, is that of row houses on lanes without vehicular roads in the lanes but with garages grouped at entrance to lanes. (See Schemes 1 and 4.) This arrangement has great advantages from the point of view of good living. It offers increased safety and quiet on the service side of the houses and, at the same time, it permits complete privacy on the garden side. On the other hand, some planners may prefer to sacrifice these advantages for the convenience of direct access to each house by automobile, . . . greater ease in the delivery of bulky goods and fuel, and easier fire protection.

The lanes without roads show a cost advantage of about 18% over those with roads (see Schemes 1 and 2). However, the length of lanes without vehicular roads must be limited to facilitate delivery of heavy and bulky goods and of fuel. The proportionate difference of cost is greatly decreased when lanes with roads are increased to the greater length that their arrangement makes practical and acceptable. (See Scheme 3.) But the economic advantage of the lane without roads will be increased on hilly sites where road construction is difficult and expensive.

This study has been made with the assistance of Ralph Eberlin and of Albert Mayer.

1. This is an example of the series of memoranda Stein sent to Lansill in late November 1935. A number of these memoranda were later included in Stein's book, *Toward New Towns for America*. Their approach to the problem and the ideas developed in them have had a continuing influence on the economics of design of residential areas in the United States.

---

262   To Aline Stein

The Hay-Adams House, Washington, D.C.   November 20, [1935]

Aline darling:

The end of another busy day—mainly in a drafting room with a hundred or so draftsmen.[1] The plan takes shape. A plan of a community is an ever-changing affair. For a while it seems to all take form and hang together, and then some element is out of place, and the pattern is lost, and one must go back and piece it together again. I imagine composing music is like that. It is a complicated pattern I am weaving, made up of simple motives. It gets you, but it is wonderful when it finally clicks.[2]

Breakfast with Benton, . . . Stoddard, and Filene of Boston. Benton should not have been out. He has a bad cold. He returned to bed afterward. When my work was done, I called him. What a bedraggled old house. All its outer ugliness has no effect on the beauty of Benton's inner self. I gave him your love.

I am waiting now for Sam Ratensky to take me to dinner. I must get ready.

All my love,
Clarence

P.S. I have postponed the painting at 1,000 Years so that we would not have to keep the heat on all week.[3] I will get at [it] this spring.

1. Several large RA drafting rooms were located in the former ballroom and kitchen of the Walsh MacLean mansion in Washington, D.C. The building is, at this writing, the Indonesian Embassy.

2. C. S. Stein seemed to be working on the plans for Greenbelt, Md. The "simple motives" are the sweeping curve of the main roads of the town, the alternating parking bays and pedestrian paths leading between the rows of "town houses" to the central green spine, and the central green park and pedestrian route. In short, he worked to combine all of the elements of the Radburn residential layout on the site of the Greenbelt, Md., New Town.

3. The Steins seemed to have purchased a small farm in Yorkville, Westchester County, which was to be their summer and weekend retreat.

263 To Aline Stein

[New York City]   November 24, 1935

Aline dear:

I don't suppose you will get this, but still it may reach you before you leave.

I don't know whether I am going east or west half the time. I am even tempted by the last scheme which I sent you, which means not getting back until late in April.

What do you think of the itinerary of November 16? If we are not going to sail on the 29th of November, can we wait [until] the following week? You will note that the Dutch boat is the *Olden,* which they say is the best of the Dutch boats to the Indies and that it sails from Genoa. I understand there is a special train from Holland to the boat. I am ready, but if you can get the part in *Good Earth* I will visit China on the set instead.

Friday evening, foolishly [I went] to the old homestead to celebrate Albert's birthday. Saturday [I was] in bed again—no serious complaint, but just a suspicion of a cold. Quite enough, however, to call up and call it off. And am I happy! It is gray and rainy and cold. What a miserable time they are having, and I am up and alone and all full of energy. But [I] will take it easy today, and tomorrow I will be fine again, and the weekend will be over.

Yesterday afternoon the office moved up here—Albert [Mayer] with drawings and Miss Morris with all the papers that had been cluttering up the desk for a long time. We threw most of them away and then had tea. It is good to be home.

Soon you will be here [and] then it will really be home. And we will put our home on a boat and sail to . . . what matters, as long as you are there.[1]

You, who I love,
Clarence

1. Aline did not get the part she wanted as Olan in *The Good Earth.* The Steins left New York for Europe in early December 1935, sailing to England and then to Amsterdam and then traveling by train to Genoa, where they boarded a Dutch ocean liner for Egypt, the Suez Canal, Indonesia, Siam, and China, returning to San Francisco in April 1936.

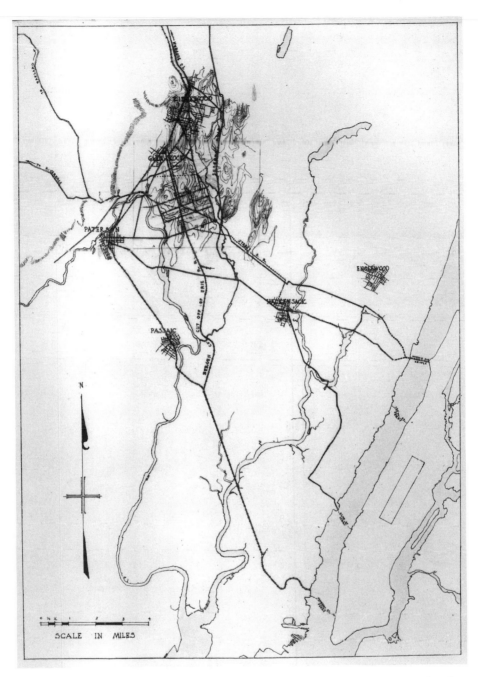

47. CHC map showing the region around Radburn. Almost two square miles were purchased in the gridded area south of Glenrock. Note the inclusion of commuter connections to Manhattan. The developers were not able to implement their early plan to develop industrial land with rail connections three-quarters of a mile south of the first neighborhood.

48. Presentation of the Radburn New Town proposals to a Bergen County planning commissioner, standing at left (c. 1931). Clarence Stein is seated at right. Others in the photograph are not identified, but the man seated next to Stein may be Alexander Bing. The person pointing at the map probably is Herbert Emmerich, Stein's civil engineer, a collaborator in planning Sunnyside and Radburn. As late as 1932 the CHC planned to complete the town.

49. Drawing of a bird's-eye view of the Radburn idea (c. 1928). The footpath to the school passes under the collector road at the lower right. Garden-side paths lead to the linear park along the bottom of the drawing. Alternating with the footpaths are wide automobile lanes that lead from the collector street to cul-de-sacs, around which houses are clustered.

50. Radburn: A plan of the first development areas, with shading indicating houses and apartments completed in 1929. Footpaths and future building locations had been planned in detail for the development of northern, eastern, and southern sections of the town site owned by the CHC.

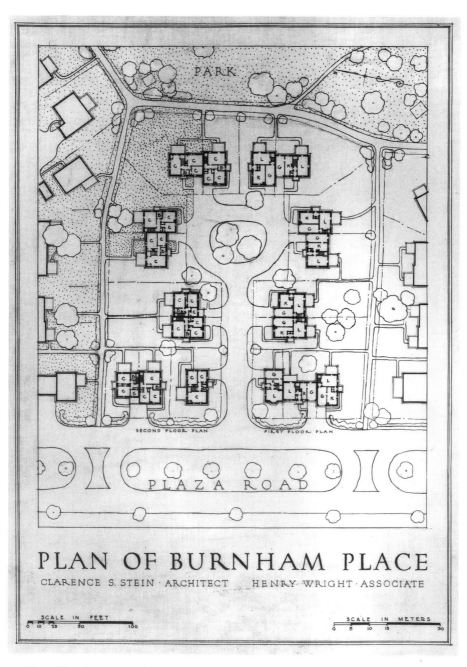

PARK

SECOND FLOOR PLAN   FIRST FLOOR PLAN

PLAZA ROAD

PLAN OF BURNHAM PLACE

CLARENCE S. STEIN · ARCHITECT   HENRY WRIGHT · ASSOCIATE

SCALE IN FEET
0 10 25   50   100

SCALE IN METERS
0 5 10 15   30

51. Plan of Burnham Place, showing house plans with principal living areas located on the "park side" and garages and kitchens to the "automobile side."

52. Pedestrian bridge across Fairlawn Avenue at Radburn (1938) was demolished in the 1950s.

53. Pedestrian underpass at Radburn (early 1930s).

54. Radburn center-block park owned and maintained by the Radburn Association for the use of all of the residents (1930).

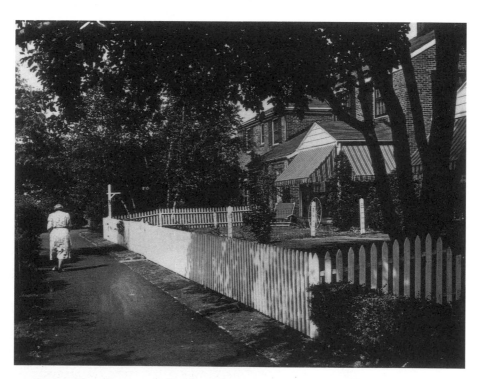

55. Garden-side walkway at Radburn. Socializing seems to occur over these fences, as well as around the cul-de-sacs on the service sides, yet homeowners still have good-sized private gardens.

56. View of cul-de-sac at Burnham Place (c. 1948). Since this photograph was made, increasing automobile ownership and the difficulty of getting large cars in the 1930-width garages have caused some cluttering of the lanes with parked cars.

57. Apartments at Radburn; Andrew Thomas, architect.

58. Swimming pool at Radburn (1949).

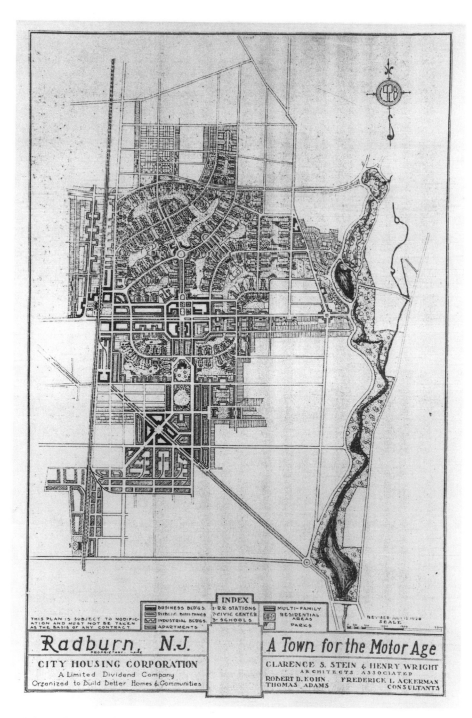

INDEX

	BUSINESS BLDGS.	1- R.R. STATIONS		MULTI-FAMILY
	PUBLIC BUILDINGS	2-CIVIC CENTER		RESIDENTIAL AREAS
	INDUSTRIAL BLDGS.	3- SCHOOLS		
	APARTMENTS			PARKS

REVISED JULY 11 1928
SCALE

Radburn, N.J.
CITY HOUSING CORPORATION
A Limited Dividend Company
Organized to Build Better Homes & Communities

A Town for the Motor Age
CLARENCE S. STEIN & HENRY WRIGHT
ARCHITECTS ASSOCIATED
ROBERT D. KOHN   FREDERICK L. ACKERMAN
THOMAS ADAMS   CONSULTANTS

59. Town plan of Radburn, New Jersey, prepared by Stein and Wright in 1928 as the basis for development by the CHC. These plans called for a larger town and civic center and higher densities
than the 1932 plan, which called for more commercial development near the railroad station.
Street patterns were also modified in the later plan.

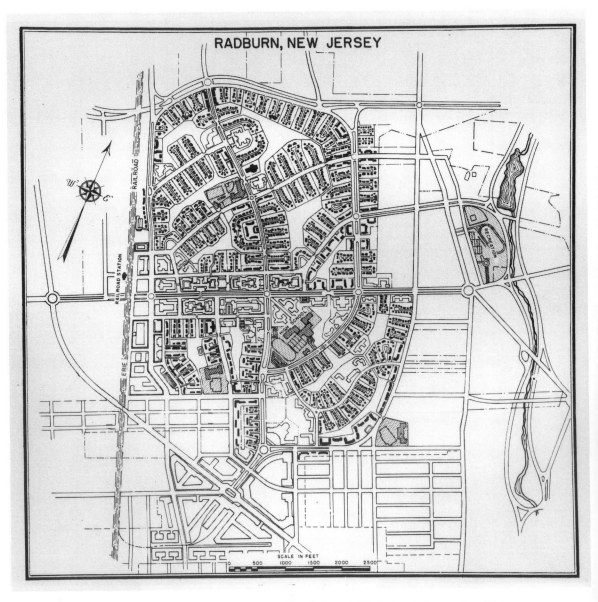

60. Town plan of Radburn, New Jersey, prepared by Stein and Wright for the International Federation for Housing and Town Planning Exhibition in Berlin in 1932. Soon after the plan was completed, the City Housing Corporation started selling land to meet other obligations as the housing market collapsed during the depression years of the 1930s.

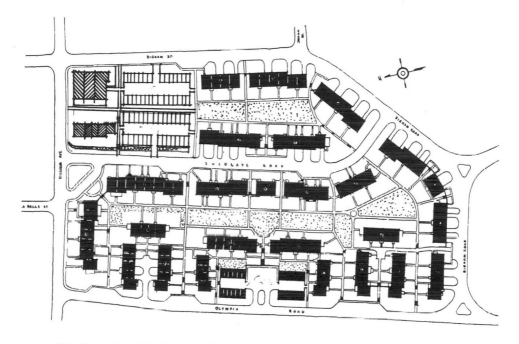

61. Site plan study of the first unit of Chatham Village in Pittsburgh, Pennsylvania (1932), built by the Buhl Foundation: Clarence Stein and Henry Wright, consulting architects; Ingham and Boyd, architects; R. Griswold and T. Kohankie, landscape architects.

62. Preliminary design perspective of Chatham Village in Pittsburgh, Pennsylvania (1932). This proposal seems to have preceded the final plan, which made more effective use of the hillside to screen parking and enclosed the northern end of the lower courtyard.

63. Garden-side walkway, Chatham Village (c. 1935).

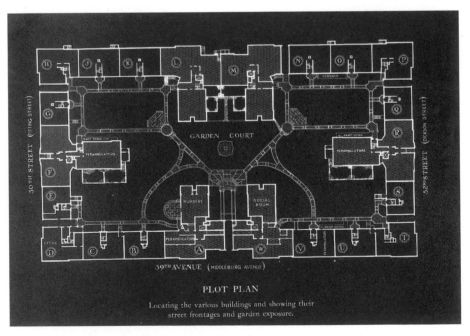

64. Phipps Garden Apartments; Clarence S. Stein, architect; Henry Wright, associate architect (1931). This was the first building of a planned two-stage development.

65. The inner courtyard of the Phipps Garden Apartments (c. 1935).

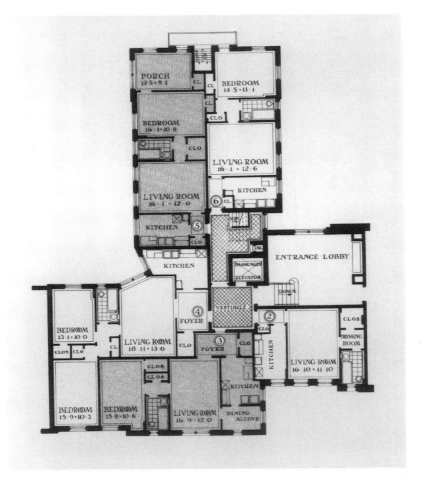

66. Floor plans of efficiency, one-bedroom, and two-bedroom apartments at Phipps Garden Apartments (1930).

67. Suggested treatment of the porch of an apartment from a 1931 promotional brochure for Phipps Garden Apartments.

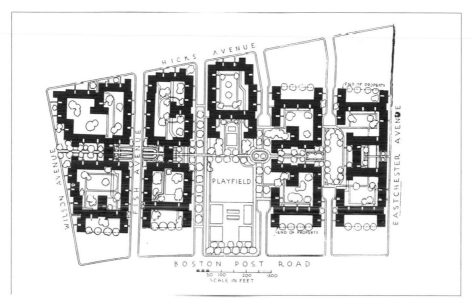

68. Site plan of Hillside Homes in the Bronx, New York (September 1933). Stein's original intent was to close most or all of the north/south avenues to form a superblock. This early design includes an underpass for the main east/west pedestrian way under Fish Avenue. The New York City Engineering Department would not approve the street closings.

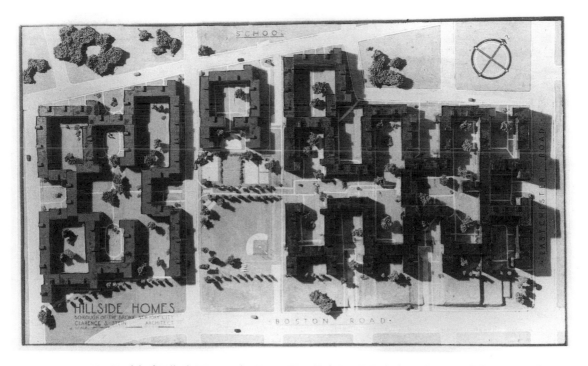

69. Model of Hillside Homes, the Bronx, New York (1933). Stein hoped to extend the courtyard garden quality of Phipps Garden Apartments to his project designed for lower-income families. Lower rents were achieved by higher residential densities, smaller rooms, and large-scale construction. The development was approved for PWA low-interest loans in 1934.

347

70. Entrance to units at Hillside Homes from the courtyard. Stein's use of brick art deco decorative elements at Hillside was more restrained than his design of Phipps Garden Apartments. Some of the apartments on the lower floors of the downhill side were designed for families with children and elderly persons. The above-grade rooms on the uphill side provided space for day care nurseries and other community uses.

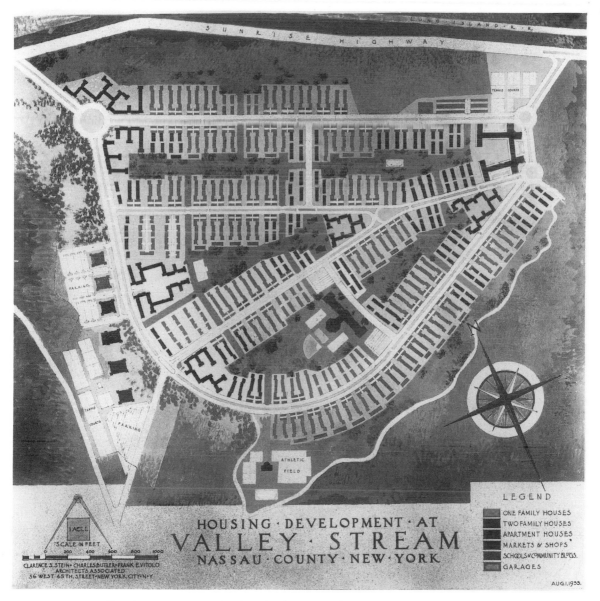

71. Site plan of a proposed housing development at Valley Stream, Nassau County, New York (August 1933), which was not built. Radburn's principles of residential layout were applied in this higher-density development proposed by the National Housing Corporation for the site of Floyd Bennett Field.

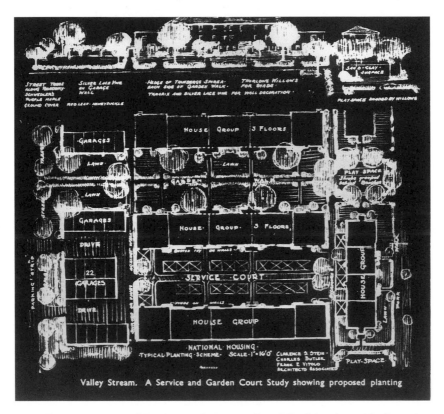

Valley Stream. A Service and Garden Court Study showing proposed planting

72. Valley Stream Proposal (1935): Detail of a typical module of the plan, with alternating formal gardens and service yards. Parking is provided at the ends of row-house groups.

73. Stein leading a tour of Radburn for members of the International Housing Commission (summer 1934). The Rockefeller Foundation financed the Housing Commission, which was organized by Ernest Bohn and Charles Ascher of the National Association of Housing Officials (NAHO). The International Housing Commission visited fourteen U.S. cities and prepared a report proposing a large U.S. program of public housing. They also met with FDR on housing policy. Its members included Ernest Kahn (a German economist), Henry Wright, Ernest Bohn, Raymond Unwin, and Alice Samuel (British housing manager; at right in the photograph)

74. A pause in the commission's tour of Radburn. Left to right: Herbert Emmerich, Clarence Stein, Henry Wright, unidentified person, Alice Samuel, and other unidentified persons.

75. Clarence Stein and Benton MacKaye at MacKaye's home, Grove House, in Shirley Center, Massachusetts (c. 1934).

76. Preliminary study of the Art Institute in Wichita, Kansas (1934). This is the only one of Stein's four museum designs that was executed. Only the center part was built. Some of the building's walls and decorative elements are preserved in the core of the expanded museum. His proposed designs for museums in Pasadena (California) and Springfield (Massachusetts) and at Princeton University were not built.

77. Clarence Stein seated on the entry stair of the Wichita Art Institute (1935). The sculptural and mosaic decoration was by Charles Lawrie, who had worked with Stein on several Goodhue buildings. Stein considered himself an expert on museum design. He wrote several articles and a long unpublished manuscript on the subject.

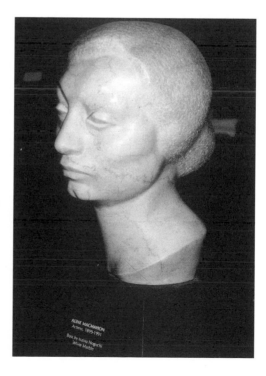

78. Portrait head of Aline MacMahon Stein in marble by Isamu Noguchi (1935). The portrait was commissioned by Stein in 1934, but when it arrived he wrote to Aline that "Noguchi's lady is so serious." A few days later he decided that he liked it and wrote, "First thing in the morning when I get up, I greet it." The head was given to the Performing Arts Division of the New York Public Library with Aline's professional papers and is on display in the reading room.

79. Drafting room of the Resettlement Administration's headquarters in the former McLean Mansion on Massachusetts Avenue, Washington, D.C., November 1935. Clarence Stein is standing in the aisle at left.

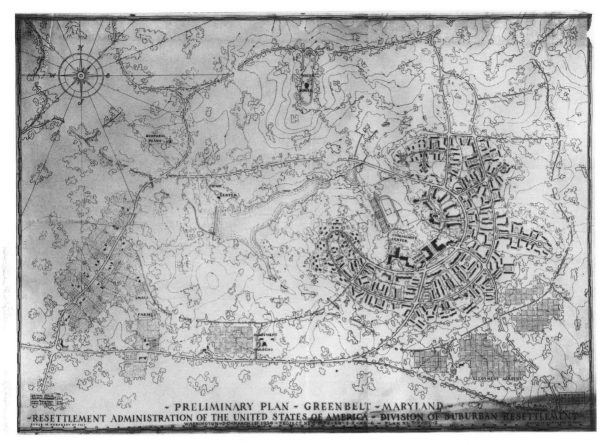

80. Preliminary plan of Greenbelt, Maryland, by the Resettlement Administration of the United States of America (March 1936). Stein had considerable influence on the design of this, the best known of FDR's three Greenbelt Towns.

81. President Roosevelt with Rexford Tugwell, the director of the Resettlement Administration (seated behind him), visiting the partially completed new town of Greenbelt, Maryland (c. 1936).

82. Theater in the Greenbelt shopping area, with apartments on the hill in the background (1939).

83. Pedestrian underpass at Greenbelt (c. 1940).

Photograph of bearer

84. Clarence and Aline MacMahon Stein's passport photos (1935). Clarence had no interesting projects in his office, and Aline had not been selected for a leading role she wanted, so they took a long-planned trip to Asia.

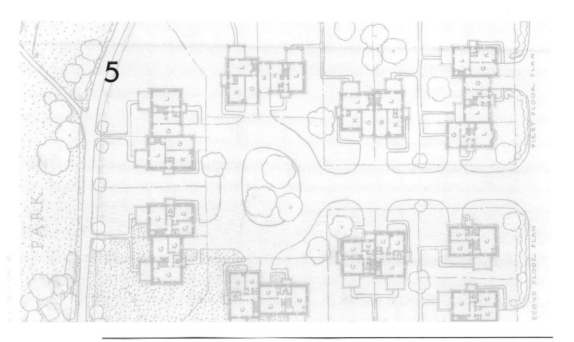

Time of Troubles
1936-1939

The late 1930s were troubled years for Clarence Stein. But 1936 began joyfully, during the Steins' much-anticipated trip around the world, which included long stays in Bali, Indonesia, and Peking, China. While on board ship, Clarence worked on his books on museum and housing but finished neither.[1] When the Steins returned to New York in the early summer of 1936, there was very little work in his office. Their journey had refreshed them, but Clarence's basic problem, not having any architectural or planning work, was not solved by their absence. The only jobs were a preliminary design for a movie theater renovation for his brother-in-law Arthur Mayer (not built) and a house in New Jersey for his sister Gertrude. These were not the kinds of projects to which he aspired. The theater proved infeasible, and his design for Gertrude's house, which was built, was disappointing.[2] In mid-1936 Aline departed for Hollywood, where she started another film, *When You're in Love,* with Grace Moore and Cary Grant. The daily correspondence between Aline and Clarence resumed, and it includes a detailed account of Clarence's struggles, including his loneliness.

1. He was still trying to finish both of these manuscripts. Copies are in his papers. He did not complete either one but did start another book in 1948–49 by writing a series of articles for the *Town Planning Review,* which were put together in a book published in 1951 as *Toward New Towns for America* (Liverpool: Univ. Press, 1951).

2. CSS to AMS, 15 October and 6 November 1936, CSP/CUA.

Later in 1936, Stein was appointed to the Design Review Board for the forth-coming 1939 New York World's Fair. He secured an assignment from Nelson Rock-efeller to help program the building space needs and write the design program for the Museum of Modern Art. He also continued discussions with his friend, Aline Bernstein (the stage set and costume designer), about her idea for a costume mu-seum. These jobs filled in the time, but they did not lead to architectural work. Then there were the books he was trying to write. He continued to struggle with the manuscripts of a book on museum design, which he had started on shipboard, and another book on housing. Completion of these manuscripts seemed to him an impossible task.[3] Stein's general mood was despair. His friend Henry Wright died in early June 1936. Aline Stein was in Hollywood most of that summer and fall, and the small architectural projects in his office did not satisfy Clarence's desire to prac-tice community architecture and work for housing reform.

In December 1936, Clarence visited Aline in California and then, at the end of the year, she spent a few weeks in New York. After she returned to Los Angeles to work at the Warner Studios early in 1937, Clarence's mental health collapsed. He experienced what was then termed a *nervous breakdown* and was hospitalized. This was the last stage of a serious bout of depression that had been getting worse throughout the last half of 1936. Evidence of his downturn was expressed in the in-creasingly confused and unhappy letters he wrote to Aline during this period. His hospital stay lasted for two and a half months. By mid-March 1937 he had recovered sufficiently to move to the Silver Hill Sanitarium in Connecticut. From there he re-turned to New York City late in April 1937. These four or five months of deep de-pression were the first of a series of disabling episodes of mental illness Stein expe-rienced over the next decade. Some of the letters to Aline and his close friends Lewis Mumford and Benton MacKaye from Silver Hill, written while he was recov-ering, are included in the following section.[4]

3. The C. S. Stein Papers at Cornell include detailed outlines and substantial manuscripts for at least eight books that were never published. Two are books about New York City, which were begun in 1922 and 1924. There are three outlines and partial manuscripts for books from the early 1930s: *New Communities, Community Housing,* and *Rebuilding America*. Parts of Stein's 1935 book on museum designs have also survived, as have several outlines and manuscripts for books on *Housing and Communities* (1939) and *Building New Communities* (1943–44). The last efforts formed a basis for articles in the *Town Planning Review* that were written in 1948 and 1949 and published in 1951 in Stein's only completed book, *Toward New Towns in America*.

4. Many of Clarence Stein's letters to Aline written from the hospital and Silver Hill Sani-tarium are in Stein's papers in the Cornell Archives. Some of these letters go into more detail about his experience with depression and his treatments than do those included here. A clearer understanding of the nature of his illness, its causes, and its relationship to his creativity would re-quire a thorough study of these letters and of his medical records by someone with extensive knowledge of manic-depressive illness, clinical experience, and access to Stein's records. The re-cent works of Dr. Kay Jamison, *An Unquiet Mind* (New York: Knopf, 1995) and *Touched with Fire*

Clarence's strongly contrasting moods of energy and depression were noted by Aline and several of his close associates and friends, particularly after the middle of the 1930s. Aline sometimes commented to Benton MacKaye about Clarence's "nerves," and his own letters show marked periods of deep discouragement during which he would stay home in bed "working." During the onset of these periods of depression, his handwriting changed from a relatively clear script to an almost baroque handwriting characterized by curling letter formations in which the tail of the *y* extends downward, sometimes an inch below a line of script. His depressed periods usually followed periods of intense work activity, elation, energy, and enjoyment of the urban visual scene, the landscape, his friends, and life in general.

These mood swings suggest an almost classic manic-depressive illness very similar to those of other creative, imaginative individuals. His mood swings from elated enthusiasm to downcast despair seem to have had short, medium, and long periodicity. Sometimes they varied from day to day or week to week, but usually they were suffered over longer periods of months or years. His manic and depressive tendencies usually lay tightly together just beneath the surface of his everyday calm. Stein in his most energetic and creative periods was always optimistic and enthusiastic, but he was a sharp critic of the urban scene, as well as an articulate prophet of the grand possibilities of achieving major gains in the means for shaping urban growth. He was a creative contributor of ideas for improved urban life. In his first well-documented period of depression late in 1936 and early in 1937, his withdrawal and inactivity were almost total. During the contrasting, very productive period of the 1920s and early 1930s, his work on Sunnyside, the *Survey Graphic* articles, the New York State Regional Planning study, Radburn, Hillside Homes in the Bronx, Phipps Garden Apartments in Queens, Chatham Village in Pittsburgh, and Greenbelt, Maryland, was completed during a long and energetic "up" period. Then, during the period following these most productive years, from late 1936 to 1947, he was pessimistic about his work and the world and not very productive. During this period he experienced several extended and severe episodes of debilitating depressive mental illness in 1936–37, 1940, 1941–42, and 1945–46.

Stein was only 55 years old in 1937, when he experienced his first well-documented bout with depression. By mid-1937 he had returned to writing, including articles on the Housing Act of 1937 for *Architectural Forum*, to his Planning and Design Review Committee assignment for the New York World's Fair, and to complet-

---

(New York: Macmillan, 1993), provide an admirable model for those who aspire to understand the gifts and pains of productive and creative people whose lives are deeply affected by manic-depressive illness. For Clarence Stein, electric shock therapy and the psychiatric counseling of Dr. Zahbriskie seem to have helped. These treatments are used today as they were in the 1930s and 1940s. However, lithium and other medications, which are widely prescribed now to treat manic depression, were not in use during Clarence's "time of troubles."

ing his work with Nelson Rockefeller on the design program for the new building of the Museum of Modern Art. He struggled to continue to practice community architecture, but the political context was not supportive. The social objectives of architecture he considered vital to excellence were often overshadowed by strong economic and time constraints. Getting back to work after his first long period of mental depression was not easy.

Little work was available for community architects. The slow evolution of national housing policy from the era of the PWA housing project loan to the direct subsidies of the Housing Act of 1937 required the establishment of local housing authorities. Early in 1938, Stein secured several jobs designing large-scale housing projects for local housing authorities and private land developers in the Los Angeles area. He worked on these West Coast projects in association with his colleagues from Goodhue's former California office. This gave Clarence an opportunity to spend more time with Aline, who was back at work on films for Warner Brothers. In Los Angeles he also met Walter Arensburg, who on several occasions involved him in plans to build a museum for his great collection of modern art. These activities are well documented in his letters of this period.

The California work included two projects of the newly organized local housing authorities of the City of Los Angeles and Los Angeles County: (1) Harbor Hills at Long Beach with Cecil Shelling and (2) Carmelitos with Reginald D. Johnson. In a third Los Angeles project, called A Thousand Gardens, Stein again was associated with Reginald Johnson of the architectural firm of Johnson, Wilson, Merrill, and Alexander. This community housing design developed later into an FHA-insured rental project named Baldwin Hills Village.

Baldwin Hills Village is one of Clarence Stein's most significant architectural design associations. The design for this project continued to evolve the Radburn concept into a market-rate, row-house-density, residential project. It had an exceptionally fine conceptual plan, a brilliant site plan, handsome, well-planned houses, and excellent landscaping. Stein served as consulting architect to Johnson, Wilson, Merrill and Alexander. Robert Alexander, a sometime associate of Richard Neutra, was the chief designer. A proposed extension of Baldwin Hills Village in the mid-1940s would have occupied the balance of the large Baldwin family estate in Los Angeles to provide triple the number of housing units, an elementary school, and a neighborhood shopping center. But the developers could not secure funding for the expansion after World War II. The residential district around Baldwin Hills Village was, like the area around Radburn, built as a conventional postwar FHA-style subdivision of freestanding single-family homes.

Making the film *The City* was another less-conventional project of Stein's in the late 1930s, which greatly satisfied his drive toward "community" architecture. He had seen Pere Lorenz's documentary film *The River* in February 1938, and it had given him the idea for a "picture" about the city. After discussing it with his brother-in-law Arthur Mayer, who understood film production costs, and with John Keppel of the Rockefeller Foundation, who was "very much interested," Stein wrote: "I'm crazy to do that film, but I don't think I will try it unless I can do a good job."[5] By midyear he reported to Mumford that Pere Lorenz had agreed to write the script and the shooting script and to make the film. Stein, who became the executive producer, involved his RPAA friends, including Lewis Mumford, in the project. The result, a much-admired documentary, *The City*, has a deep-voiced narration written and spoken by Mumford, an alternately gloomy and spritely musical score by Aaron Copland, and many negatively critical images filmed in New York City's and Pittsburgh's smoke and slums contrasted with positive historic and new community images filmed in Benton MacKaye's rustic, quiet home village of Shirley Center (Massachusetts), Radburn (New Jersey), and Greenbelt (Maryland). Stein was the conceptualizer, organizer, and driving force in the production of this brilliant documentary film—a clear and compelling statement of the problems of the city and of community planning ideas of Clarence Stein and the RPAA.

In the summer of 1938, while Clarence Stein wrote to Aline about his work on three projects for Los Angeles housing and on *The City*, he also designed and built a birthday present for her. It was a simple but elegant, small, redwood structure on the hill above the farmhouse they had purchased in 1935 at Yorkville in Westchester County. This minimalist structure, inspired by the Japanese tea house, was unlike anything Stein designed before or after. It was inspired by Asian residential architecture in its proportions and simple use of wood, but it was also Californian in its openness. Its location was the site they had considered for a larger house to replace the small farmhouse that they called "A Thousand Years" after a story in *Tales of the Genji*. This was their weekend and summer retreat from the hubbub and heat of New York City summers. The smaller redwood house, sited above the old farmhouse, provided good exposure to cool breezes and a sweeping view of the surrounding hilly landscape. The simple rustic retreat was used by the Steins for entertainment, for writing, and for sleeping on hot summer nights at "A Thousand Years."

At the end of the 1930s, there is increased correspondence with the founding members of the RPAA who had scattered from New York: Catherine Bauer had gone to Washington in 1933, where she had become director of research for FDR's newly established U.S. Housing Authority, and Lewis Mumford now lived year-round in Amenia, New York. Aline, of course, continued to travel regularly to Los Angeles for her film work, and Clarence was spending more and more time there with her. His letters to her and others continued to provide a rich account of his professional and personal life.

5. CSS to AMS, 9 February 1938, CSP/CUA.

264 To Lewis Mumford

[New York City]   June 20, 1936[1]

Dear Lewis:

I have very sad news. Henry Wright died last night.

We heard last Sunday evening that he was in the hospital at Newton and that the family had given up hope. It was the first I had heard of his being seriously ill. Aline and I went out to Newton at once. Eleanor and all of the children were there. There seemed to be nothing to be done. It was a case of hardening of the arteries that was affecting the other organs.

It is well that it should happen just now when Henry was feeling that he was on solid ground and that he could devote himself to passing on to the younger men that flame of his.[2]

Clarence

1. In the Stein collection at Cornell, there are no letters to Aline or others from Clarence Stein during January to June 1936. The Steins may have returned to New York from their trip to the Orient as late as May or early June 1936. Stein's holographic letter to Mumford is characterized by the long vertical tails of the letter *y*, which appeared in his script when he was in periods of depression and were not present when he was feeling good.

2. Henry Wright had only recently completed his first year of teaching full-time at Columbia in the new program in city and regional planning.

265 To Aline Stein

[New York City]   October 9, 1936

Aline darling:

My two days in Washington were so full that I found no time to write to you yesterday. I will have to . . . condense my description of what I did and who I saw.

Wednesday morning I went out to see the New Town [of Greenbelt, Maryland] that is being built by Resettlement between Washington and Baltimore. Quite a delegation went along to show it to me. Jack Lansill, who is the head of the whole undertaking, Fred Bigger, who keeps the organization going, Walker, the city planner, and so on. It is a grand site, lots of woods, a hilly contour with a plateau on top for the village, and they have the beginnings of a Garden City! If old Ebenezer were only here to see it. It is a good job that they are doing as a whole.[1]

The afternoon I spent in the drafting room looking over some of Fred Bigger's records.

. . . Fred Bigger and I had a long lunch together. He told me the whole inside story of his job and all the prima donnas that he, as stage director, has had to keep in some semblance of harmony. Fred just needed to get it out of him, and I am a good listener.

[In] the afternoon [I went] to see Coleman of the Museum Association and Walker, formerly of Radburn, then [took] the six o'clock plane back to New York.

At eight thirty I was having my dinner in bed and reading your last letters.

Grand news about the Hertzes and [that] you are enjoying your work. If I only had a job, too.[2]

My love, my love,

Clarence

1. This is strong evidence of Clarence Stein's generosity. He easily could have been justifiably bitter about being left out of any direct role in the design of these New Towns. Instead he praises the accomplishment.

2. Aline was working on the film *When You're in Love*, with Grace Moore, Cary Grant, and Thomas Mitchell. Opera star Moore hires Cary Grant as her husband. The film was a mild success. None of Clarence's efforts to secure an architectural or planning job had materialized. He was still designing a new house for his sister Gertrude.

---

266   To Aline Stein

[New York City]   October 11, 1936

Dear beloved:

Talking to you has cleared away some of the gloom. I feel happy again, and I have been way, way down.[1] This damned book! Why must I inflict it on myself and the world! Writing is a form of self-torture. And after a day of it . . . I have been at it since seven thirty this morning. I am sure I will never be able to write anything that makes sense. Then I pick up the bit I wrote about Henry [Wright] tonight and I say: "It will come."[2] But when? There is that, and no jobs, and just general blues. Guess that has something to do with you. It is probably all just love lorn for my Darling.

And so you don't like your job. I am so sorry. But a job's a job. You know that when you haven't any.

Today has been an all-alone day—home in pajamas.[3] Three meals without company. I tried to get Thaz for dinner, but she was still out in Pennsylvania Dutch Country. I should have liked to have been out in the country with the [Russell Van Nest] Blacks. The colors must be wonderful, and the day was perfect. But I called it off. I just felt I must write.

Tomorrow is a holiday, so I will make another try.

Your voice was like sunshine.

I love you,

Clarence

1. This seems to be the onset of another bout of depression. Clarence Stein's decline in mood continues until his mental collapse early in 1937.

2. The books on housing and museums are both stalled.

3. The comment and the behavior would both be ascribed by some doctors to a person on the verge of a serious episode of depression.

---

267   To Aline Stein

[Boston, Mass.]   October 30, 1936

Aline dear:

I am at the house of the Emerson's,[1] where I have spent the night. . . . The Emersons are delightful and belong so much in this house. They have made me feel so much at home. The Unwins are here also.[2]

Yesterday at Emerson's office at [MIT], we spent [the] morning and afternoon discussing the education of city planners. About twelve of us, of those you know: [Russell Van Nest] Black and [Eliel] Saarinen (who had come all the way from Detroit), and [John] Nolen, Charles Ascher (also representing someone of the many Rockefeller interests and all that), and there were Harvard professors, and so on. About twelve. I found it much worthwhile. I found my own thoughts clearing. Talking things over is one of the best ways of thinking, anyhow, for me. . . .

The Emersons say they are so sorry you are not here. How I wish you were. You would have liked them so, and then we could have had a day in the museum and—

I love you,

Clarence

1. Professor Emerson was developing a graduate program in city and regional planning at MIT.

2. Sir Raymond Unwin had come to America to take over Henry Wright's post in Columbia University's new graduate program in city planning. Carl Feiss was serving as his assistant.

---

268   To Aline Stein

November 3, 1936   New York City

Aline, my darling:

. . . And now I must decide who I am going to vote for. Not [Norman] Thomas, not Roosevelt. I had decided that the Communist offered the best means of protest. And then I read in this morning's *Times* the last speech of [Gus] Hall. So wishy-washy. "Democracy is in danger. Our duty is to fight Fascism (the Republicans) now. Save the Constitution. Afterwards we will form a Labor-Farmer party."

In short, he suggests voting for Roosevelt. Now I guess I will have to vote for Norman Thomas.

But it all seems to make so little difference. It is only you that matters. What if I go and write in my candidate, Aline who I love.

Clarence

P.S. As to autos—seeing you don't know what you are going to do with it, I favor the cheapest operable car. If I had a vote, it would be for Mr. Ford.[1]

1. Aline was buying a car in California.

---

269   To Aline Stein

[New York City]   November 8, 1936

Dearest:

It is half an hour before telephone time. I suppose I will repeat most everything I write now when I speak to you. But here goes: what little there is.

I have been struggling with that damned book most of the day. It had me desperate this morning. There was a hard wall right near the beginning and no getting by it. But this afternoon I had an idea. I just let it go and walked around it. I wrote other parts. Some day I will go back and try again.

Pop came for dinner, which was at two-fifteen. It was good! Hilda is surely coming along. And always trying new things.

Afterward I gave Pop the second part of the [museum] book, which is beginning to take shape in the second draft. I was afraid he would be bored. But not at all. He grew enthusiastic about the idea of small museums. Just what he had always wanted. (I have recollections of him many years ago asleep in front of Leonardo's picture of the Salon Cane. We always looked for him there.)

I am seeking what I can do about a ticket for Jennie Mac on the *Franconia*. She says she wants minimum fare. But I guess she should have something better. Yes?

Have you any pictures of your little house? Send me some if you have.

10 minutes and I talk to you who I love.

Clarence

---

270   To Aline Stein

[New York City]   November 19, 1936

Aline dear:

Yesterday morning Mike Mayer met me for breakfast.[1] We had a long talk. Mike has definitely decided that our economic system can't work. He is on his way. He is a grand boy.

After, I spoke at [Columbia] before a crowd of some thirty architects and city planning students. I told them how Hillside came into being. I am afraid I tried to tell too much, so that they didn't get much (or perhaps I am just generally pessimistic about everything I do these days). After my talk of an hour, I continued on the same subject answering questions of the small group of city planners (some twelve), so that was better. We got somewhere. We went on for another hour and a half.

. . . [In] your letter from B Bar H Ranch, it all sounds grand. . . .[2]

My love to you, darling. How I wish we were together. I need you so.

I love you so,
Clarence

1. Mike Mayer was Clarence's nephew. A few days later, on 23 November 1936, Stein reported to his wife that "tonight Catherine Bauer dined with Lewis and me. She is just back from the Scandinavian lands and brimming over with what she saw. What a vital person, a real one."

2. Aline Stein was on location, working on the film *When You're in Love*.

---

271   To Aline Stein

[New York City]   November 28, 1936

Aline beloved:

It is midnight, but I must write now, as I neglected my letter this morning. We have had such a lovely evening. Lewis, Sylvia, Gert, Fred Bigger, and I went to see *Iolanthe*. That delightful nonsense blows away all one's foolish troubles. They don't exist, they evaporate. Green as the Lord Chancellor was ridiculously superb. Lydia enjoyed it so. We all did, but to the Behrendts it was new.

Before, we had a very good dinner chez nous. Pop was also with us.

Fred is spending a couple of nights here. We have just had a long talk while looking out on the moonlit scene. And Fred says, "What do you think are the prospects of building more private capital [residential projects] like Radburn and Chatham Village?" And I found myself saying, "I find it difficult to advise people to do so on an investment basis, because how can we tell what will happen in thirty years? There certainly will probably be no interest in investment without interest." I thought, Is this why there are no dreams? Is it the uncertainty of things, of the future? I have been wondering, since you wrote me, what has happened to those dreams of mine. No, it isn't that, but something has happened. I must find out. We must have our dreams again.

Now I just have you, my love.

I love you,
Clarence

---

272   To Aline Stein

[New York City]   November 28, 1936

Aline, my darling:

Fred Bigger slept here last night and is here again tonight. . . . In the evening Fred and I dined with him [my father] and Lydia [and Curt Beherendt]. Fred told us the whole long history of the Resettlement division and his work there. He seems to have the feeling that, in spite of its fine objectives and the fact that it has really started to build Garden Cities, it has lacked clear policy. He wonders if his year there was worthwhile, if he should see it through. He just had to talk it out with someone, and Curt and I were the ones. It was an interesting talk, though a bit long. Perhaps it helped Fred to tell it. Listening is what friends are for, I guess. . . .

My love,
Clarence

---

273   To Aline Stein

December 31, 1936

Aline dear:

Yesterday was a busy day. I worked on the house [and] then a meeting of the Fair. Things are moving. The design of the central building, which is being made by [Wallace] Harrison, promises to be original and interesting. Perhaps some good stuff will be developed by the Fair after all.[1]

Later in the afternoon [I went] to a meeting with Aline Bernstein and Irene Lewison about the Costume Museum. It seems that Aline had a meeting with the Fashion Group day before yesterday. They were very enthusiastic about the museum and are considering the possibility of collecting the money for the building! At least, so says Aline.

In the evening to a musical at the Steins. First, dinner there with Florence and her two boys, the Behrendts, and, of course, Pop and Gert. Hans, it appears, is a very conservative young man and a strong believer in Germany, and he does not seem to be sure that the Jews were not, to a great extent, responsible for what happened to them. They made themselves too prominent [he said], and so there was a very heated argument between Curt and Hans.

The Behrendts have just left. It has been good to have them here, and I am so sorry to have them leave. Gertrude is returning with them to Hanover [New Hampshire] to spend the weekend. She needs to get away. It's too bad she can't make it a real vacation. . . .

I miss you so, my darling. Last year we were starting out for Europe at this time. A lot has happened since.

I love you, I love you,

Clarence

1. The 1939 New York World's Fair was a great, popular success with its Trylon and Perisphere theme building. The film produced by Stein and directed by Pere Lorenz was shown daily but did not draw the big crowds who visited the "Futurama," General Motors' giant model of the "city of tomorrow," replete with freeways and skyscrapers. No Radburn there.

---

274   To Benton MacKaye

New York City   February 21, 1937

Dear Ben:

I have put off from day to day answering your call to another conference at Shirley. There is nothing Aline and I would prefer to being with you and out in the country. But just at present I am under doctor's orders, and he says stay here for the time being. Trouble is nerves. As a result I have been staying away from work for some time. Luckily, Aline has been here, and we have had a grand time just being together. I have been gradually getting back to things during the last week or so.

I want very much to see what you have been writing and talk about no ends of things. . . . And so does Aline. We will try to make use of the timetable you sent before long. If not, you must come here.

I see Lewis now and then. He still comes down to town almost every week. He has decided to drop the *New Yorker* and follow your example of retiring to the country and digging in[to] his next opus.

Our very best to you.

Clarence

275   To Benton MacKaye

1 W. 64th   New York City   March 7, 1937

Dear Ben:

Your good letter of a week or more ago has remained unanswered because of our uncertainty as to whether we could leave New York just now. We would love to be with you, to talk to you, and walk with you, to enjoy the peace of Shirley and of your philosophy, or common sense, or whatever it is. And we would like to sit at either side of you and look at the scrapbook of your old Knoxville gang. But it can't be just now. The doctor wants me to start doing a little work at the office, gradually break into it. So here I must stay for the time being. Aline is here taking good care of me.

Perhaps before long we will be able to get away to see you.

The next best thing to seeing you is hearing from you. So do write again when you have time.

As always,
Clarence

276   To Aline Stein

[Silver Hill]¹   April 11, 1937

Beloved:

You are gone only a half hour, and I am so homesick for you, but it was a good day, and next Sunday there will be another. And before long . . .

Here is the article on *The Good Earth* that came out in the *Evening Post,* as well as the one in the Sunday. Not so good, the first one, is it? By the way, have you seen *The Good Earth,* or are you saving that for me? There is so much we are going to do.

I love you, I love you,
Clarence

1. In the CSS papers there are no letters to Aline from 31 December 1936 until March 1937. Clarence seems to have become seriously depressed during early January 1937. He was hospitalized for several months, during which time he received electric shock therapy. By late February 1937 he had recovered sufficiently to leave the hospital for a sanitarium at Silver Hill, Conn., where he stayed, except for occasional short weekends, until mid-May 1937.

277   To Aline Stein

[Silver Hill]   April 20, 1937

Aline, my darling:

Such days! And you are not here. A year ago it was Japan; no, we were on the way back, were we not?

Yesterday I rode bicycle for an hour and butchered some more good wood and tried pastels. (No success. It is a special trick. I must get it.) Late in the afternoon, Dr. Dubois and I took a long walk, and I slept, you bet I slept. . . .

All my love,
Clarence

278   To Lewis Mumford

[Silver Hill]   April 27, 1937

Dear Lewis:

It was good to get your letter.

I have been here almost six weeks now, and either the doctors or the springtime is working its magic upon me. I am looking out on a bright and hopeful world again. I want to be back in New York and doing again, but I know it is going to be hard to leave the country. I have never really seen a spring in the country here in America. I am enchanted by its beauty—the glow of color, a sort of haze of color that seems to surround the trees before they burst into blossom. But why should I try to tell an old country man?

I am glad you are back at the book. I am looking forward to seeing it. By all means, take your trip. Take all you can of life as you go along, Lewis. That seems to be one of the few things I have lacked.

I have read Curt Behrendt's book with such pleasure.[1] He has told his tale so well, so clearly and so concisely. And, above all, he has something to tell. I do hope the publishers are going to give the book good publicity. It should have a large sale and give him an opportunity to do a lot of lecturing, if he is interested.

What do you hear from Benton? How is he? And how are you and Sophia? My very best to you. I hope I am going to see you soon.

Clarence

1. *Modern Building* was published by Harcourt Brace in 1937. It is an excellent history of the evolution of the Modern Movement in architecture from Ruskin and Morris through Art Nouveau in Vienna, Sullivan and Wright in the United States, to Taut and Mendlesson in Germany.

279   To Benton MacKaye

Silver Hill   May 18, 1937

Dear Ben:

For the last two months, I have been up here, taking a rest and trying to find my old self (which explains my not writing to you). I am going back to the big city next week, a healthier and, I think, a wiser man. I have discovered springtime in the New England countryside. Ben, do you know, I have never spent a spring in the country in America. It has been a great experience. Such a wealth of beauty, from the time branches glow with color through their season of budding. But there is no need of telling you. I have taken to painting again in the mad attempt to perpetuate some of the beauty. At least, I see it clearer as a result.

And you, Ben, what have you been doing and planning? And how is the "opus"? Have you been up at the Center all this time? We must get together soon. Are you coming our way? If not, Aline and I must try to get up to Shirley.

Have you seen Curt's book? It is a fine job. Clear, sincere, intelligent. . . .

If Aline were here she would send love, as does

Clarence

P.S. By the way, Ben, if finances are low, I hope you will let me know.

280   To Catherine Bauer[1]

[New York City]   July 1, 1937

Dear Catherine:

Thanks very much for the suggestions for Mr. Eberlin. They will be a great deal of help to him.

Also, thanks for the Wagner-Steagall Bill. As soon as the revised bill comes out of committee, will you kindly send me a copy?[2]

Cordially yours,

Clarence S. Stein

1. Bauer had set up an office in the Hay-Adams Hotel in Washington to lobby for the legislation that became the Taft-Ellender Wagner Housing Bill, the Housing Act of 1937.

2. There are so few letters from this period that it seems useful to include this one to show that Clarence Stein was once again engaged in the world of affairs after his long illness. In November 1937, *American Architect and Architecture* published the extended comments of Coleman Woodbury, Clarence Stein, Langdon Post, and Albert Mayer on the "Wagner-Steagall Housing Act of 1937." Stein's comments were very detailed and essentially positive. Later in November Stein wrote a long essay, "Housing: The Next Chapter," which was to be sent out as a news release by the AIA. A copy is in the Stein Papers at Cornell.

281   To Lewis Mumford

[New York City][1]   August 24, 1937

Dear Lewis:

I was going to write to you yesterday, but in the rush of things I didn't find time. At last, I am getting busy again, architecturally. I don't know whether I am happy about it or not, as I would like to have more time for my book.

Your letter came this morning. I quite agree with you that it was altogether too hot for a conference over the weekend.

In regard to the manuscript,[2] I have read all of the first part a second time. It looks much better to me now than it did at first. In fact, I think it is a fine job. As I went along I wrote notes on the margin: I wanted to read and explain these to you. I don't know whether you will understand them, but I am sending them to you nonetheless. The rest of the manuscript will be forwarded within a few days.

The first of my notes, as you will see, offer additional examples of your point of view, rather than criticism or correction. Most of them, probably, will be of no use at all, since you are in the process of cutting down.

There is one general criticism that I do want to offer. I do not think you bring out plainly enough the connection between our present form of metropolitanism and capitalism, nor do you explicitly enough show that the present form of city growth can be changed but to a small degree as long as capitalism exists. Ackerman, I think, showed the limitations of technology under what he calls "debt economy" very clearly in his articles which were published by [the] New York City Housing Authority. They may be of some help to you, so I am sending a copy of the publication [to] which I refer.

. . . All these arguments you have considered, I know, but nonetheless I thought you might want to read these statements, which are the clearest ones that have come from him.

I found it very helpful just at this time to read and reread your material. It is going to be a great deal of help to me in connection with the course that I will probably give at the Federation Technical School. You probably know that this is a school sponsored by the Federation of Architects, Engineers, Chemists, and Technicians. My first idea was to try to develop with a group of more advanced boys a plan for [a] city under a noncapitalistic society. After having a couple of talks with the instructors of the school and some of the probable students, I decided that they were not ready for this as yet. They want to see the relation of what they are studying to their present work. What I am going to try to give them is something that will show them how to think through these problems. My idea of just how the subject should be handled for this purpose is growing and changing from day to day. Its present form is somewhat indicated by the outline which I am enclosing. What do you think of it?

I'd like to get Benton down [to New York] in connection with [Lecture] Number VI, Development of a Regional City in the Connecticut Valley. He might spend the whole evening discussing the Connecticut Valley with the idea of getting the boys to think through with him the best location for a new regional city.

I haven't heard from Benton for a few weeks, but a couple of weeks ago Gertrude and a friend of hers were in Massachusetts [and] they went over to see him and spent the night at his place. They found him in very good condition.

My best to you and Sophie.

As always,
Clarence

1. Only a few of Stein's letters from this period have survived. This letter and the one written to Mumford in November 1937 were typed on the stationery of Stein's office at the Architects Associated, 56 West Forty-fifth Street, New York, N.Y.

2. Mumford had sent him the draft manuscript of *The Culture of Cities,* which was published in 1938.

---

282   To Benton MacKaye

[New York City]   September 23, 1937

Dear Ben:

I don't know when we are ever going to be able to eat all that candy, but we are doing our best! Thanks very much.

Sorry you were not with us last night at the opening of the Henry Wright Library. It was a simple affair, but the expressions in regard to Henry were heartfelt. I presided, Albert Mayer said something about the library, and then Robert Kohn and Sir Raymond Unwin spoke of Henry.

It is in the library that we are going to carry on our famous course. The first of the lectures will be next Monday. I will write to tell you how it comes off. . . .

Our best to you.

Yours,
Clarence

---

283   To Lewis Mumford

[New York City]   November 16, 1937

Dear Lewis:

It will be wonderful for the "Henry Wright Library" [at Columbia] if you lend them your City Planning library. You are quite right in not giving it to them until you are certain whether you will have to refer to it again. I found during these past weeks, when I had to prepare my lectures in the very limited time I could find outside of my work, that there was no chance to go to the library to do reference work; I had to make out as well as I could with what I had at home and at the office.

The further I go with my lectures the more strongly I feel the need of a clear expression of the Regional City idea. We must reawaken the Regional Planning Association [of America].

In that connection, I have just received a notice from the International Federation for Housing and Town Planning saying that our organization is entitled to the appointment of one member of the council. Frederick Ackerman has been our representative, but as he has attended no meetings I am going to ask whether he wants to continue. If not, I will be glad to accept the nomination if our honored secretary wants to voice it.

You sent me some plans of Wythenshawe.[1] What shall I do with them?

I haven't yet given up hope of finding a picture of Sunnyside. I will try again. The trouble is that all our photographs were taken when the planting was young. I haven't so far located any good pictures taken since that time.

As always,
Clarence

1. The Manchester Council's large satellite settlement at Wythenshawe was planned by Barry Parker, Raymond Unwin's early associate. In the late 1920s and early 1930s, Mumford thought it was a bold updating of the Garden City concept to meet the needs of the motor age. Unwin's biographer, Mervyn Miller, believes it "the most striking example of the municipalization of the Garden City." *Raymond Unwin, Garden Cities, and Town Planning* (Leicester, England: Leicester Univ. Press, 1992).

284   To Catherine Bauer

[New York City]   December 8, 1937

Dear Catherine:

. . . I noted in last night's paper that the atmosphere up on the Hill seems to be cleared and that the Hillside matter will not prevent the confirmation of Mr. Straus.[1] So, apparently, there is no use attempting now to tell you the tale of the 100-ft. frontage on Boston Road [at Hillside Homes] as I remember it. It is a long story, and I don't know whether all of it would be of help to you. However, if you still want it, let me know by letter or wire, and I will write out everything that I can remember.[2]

The housing situation here is certainly a mess. What they need even more than a good chairman of the board is a well-paid director—somebody who would have both the power and ability to build houses. We need someone with drive and a knowledge of the fundamentals of housing and community building and operation, as well as the ability to get along with the prima donnas. I think Herbert Emmerich could do it, but I don't suppose he would.

Thanks for suggesting me for the position on the City Planning Commission. However, I hope that I am not embarrassed by being offered it. I am afraid it is not for me. The New York City Planning Commission, I presume, will have to see that the tax structure does not go to pieces. As you know, the kind of city planning that I would favor in New York would deflate a great part of the property values on which the income of the city is at present based. It would be good for the city of ten years from now, but I am afraid it might be pretty hard medicine to take at the present time.[3]

When you get tired of running the government,[4] I hope you will come up to New York so that we can have a chance to talk to you.

Cordially yours,

Clarence

1. Nathan Straus had been appointed by FDR to be administrator of the newly established U.S. Housing Authority.

2. Clarence was referring to Straus's behavior regarding the development of commercial buildings along the Boston Post Road at the edge of Hillside Homes. Stein would have preferred a planted buffer strip that was part of the housing development, but Straus wanted to realize some profit from commercial development of this narrow strip of land.

3. Conventional city planning was clearly not Clarence's cup of tea. It would have been very frustrating for him to serve in the planning commission post for which Catherine Bauer had suggested him.

4. Bauer was now serving as director of research in the U.S. Housing Authority, the new housing agency set up under the Housing Act of 1937, for which she had done much to secure passage in Congress.

---

285   To Aline Stein

February 9, 1938

Aline dear:

Last night Ben and I dined with the Arthur Mayers. . . . Arthur and I discussed *The City*, my plan [for a] picture.[1] RDK [Robert Kohn] had told me in the morning that Keppel told him that they were very much interested, but the cost was too much.[2] *The River* has cost much less. Both Arthur and I had been getting information in regard to *The River's* production costs during the day and had found that they were probably all wrong. Much of it is hidden in bookkeeping. I am crazy to do that film, but I don't think I will try it unless I can do a good job.

Otherwise, no news. I can't wait to hear from you and all about everyone and a job?

Love to you, my beloved,

Clarence

1. This was Clarence Stein's first mention of his concept for the film that was to become *The City*.

2. Keppel was an officer of the Rockefeller Foundation.

---

286 To Aline Stein

[New York City]   February 18, 1938

Beloved:

Your voice sounded so good, and you seemed cheerful. You were just in time to catch me before I left the office to present the report on the Museum of Modern Art to Nelson Rockefeller.[1]

He is quite a boy—seems keen and with a very good sense of the practical aspects of planning and building. What is most important in connection with the mess they have got into [is that] he is quite willing to take responsibility. Barr and Maybury said, "We better submit Mr. Stein's report to the other members of the building committee." Nelson Rockefeller answered, "What's the use? It will just excite them. Let's decide what must be done, and do it." So there is some hope. But we have by no means found a solution; all my . . . report does is to clarify the problem. Rockefeller seemed much impressed.

From there to a meeting of the directors of the Museum of Modern Art. Irene has a way of going on and on and on. Everything must be discussed and rediscussed. . . .

Tonight I talk on housing [at the Architects' Federation School].

Sunday, we will throw a party. You better come home. You are missing it all.

And I miss you. But have your fill of California while you are there. . . .

My love,
Clarence

1. Clarence continued his role as a member of the New York 1939 World's Fair design review board throughout 1938 and seems to have had a contract to assist in the programming and preliminary design analysis for the new building for the Museum of Modern Art.

---

287 To Aline Stein

[New York City] February 1938   Washington's Birthday

Aline, my darling:

. . . Yesterday noon lunched with [Andrew] Eken.[1] I took him to the Canton Village, and how he enjoyed the food: soup, lobster, vegetables, and all. Funny conversation. I wanted to find out about one thing. He appeared to want to tell me about it. But he claimed he had promised not to discuss "a certain subject." This was quite apparently the 100 million or so that the Metropolitan Life is reported to be about to invest (not lend) in large-scale housing. (The legislature at Albany has just passed a law permitting what Eken's firm has been doing building for the Metropolitan. . . .) Says he, "There is a certain person with whom I have been discussing this important job. I want you to be the architect, Clarence, but if I push you too much, he will oppose you. I just keep on mentioning Hillside. I have got to work him around to the point where he asks for you. I have at least got rid of someone else" (presumably [Harold] Shreve). All of which would have sounded OK if I had any faith in the speaker. . . .[2]

Last night Ben took my place as lecturer. Good talk.

Now to write my spiel for next week at Boston Technology [MIT].

Good-bye for a day, my love,

Clarence

1. Andrew J. Eken was the building contractor who had built Hillside Homes in 1934–35.

2. The Metropolitan Life Housing program was finally started in 1939 with the building of Stuyvesant Town. Needless to say, Stein did not get the job.

---

288   To Aline Stein

[New York City]   February 22, 1938

Beloved:

Yesterday was like another Saturday—home all morning, Frank's for lunch and the afternoon.

I worked at my lecture for Boston Tech [MIT] in the morning on "the architect's approach to city planning." It is all getting so much clearer and simpler. It is beginning to form itself into short, decided sentences, many of them figures of speech. The soft edges on involved sentences are falling away. Perhaps it is getting too simple. I am projecting myself mentally into the future, to the time when we will be free, or at least freer of the bonds of Frederick Lee's "Price System."[1] I know it must and will go. Why give it all [the] attention . . . Ackerman does?

I read back over some of my writing of the last decade. It sounded like formative stuff. Not quite jelled. I was glad my other books were stillborn. And then I wondered, am I ready now?

Lunch at the Vitolos'; no, it was dinner. Heaping plate of noodles. Steak and all, including vino again. One of Frank's Tammany friends was there—perpetual office holder. Amusing tales of how we really are governed. But best of all was the story of how he got out of public office for a while and ran a club. It was made up of Jews of all degrees of orthodoxy and reformation. None of them would trust the other, so they hired this Catholic Italian. "I studied all about their religion and habits and holidays. Someone would say, 'Let's throw a party on such and such a day,' and I would say, 'Gentlemen, gentlemen, we can't do that on Yom Kippur!'"

Just—I love you,
Clarence

1. Frederick Lee Ackerman, who studied architecture at Cornell at the end of the nineteenth century, may have been a student of Thorstein Veblen, who taught there in the early 1890s. Ackerman had read Veblen's books and worked with him on the Technical Alliance. He was an active proponent of technocracy.

---

289   To Lewis Mumford

New York City   March 24, 1938

Dear Lewis:

The Culture of Cities arrived over the weekend. It is a fine-looking job. I have only had a chance to make a start with the reading. I am tempted to stroll leisurely through the illustrations and the descriptions each time I pick up the book.

In Boston [on] Tuesday, Aline and I breakfasted with Ben, who looks fine. Then I condensed my 16 lectures on the "City of the Future" into one two-and-a-half-hour talk. I have been trying to rest up some.

Wishing you the same,
Clarence

---

290   To Benton MacKaye

New York City   May 6, 1938

Dear Benton:

Lewis and I are seated here together so you can count this letter as being from the two of us. Lewis and Sophie are in town for a few days to see the sights.

But it is not of that that I wanted to write to you. It is about the picture . . . *The City*, of which we have already told you our hopes. Well, it is going ahead. The Rockefeller Foundation has given the money. Lewis has been working at the story. As it stands at present, it begins in a Colonial Village, which you may guess is Shirley. The first thing we want to do is to take some pictures up there before spring is over. We are wondering when you expect to go back because Shirley without Benton MacKaye won't amount to very much.

I was delighted to see in the letter that you wrote to Aline that you think if the administration goes off on a spending spree you are pretty sure of a job. Of course, we in New York think that the government down there in Washington is mad enough to do anything. We certainly hope they will have sense enough to take you on in the Forestry Department one way or the other.[1]

Our best from Lewis and myself.

As always,
Clarence

1. In July 1938 Clarence wrote to congratulate Ben on his new job in Washington.

---

291   To Lewis Mumford

[New York City]   June 15, 1938

Dear Lewis:

Just a few words to report on the progress of the film [*The City*]. Lorentz has agreed to write the script.[1] He is first to prepare a short outline, which we are to check and criticize. Then, in cooperation with [Richard] Steiner and Van Dyke, he is to write the shooting script. I think that you have stated the story clearly enough to him so that he will not get off the track. Anyhow, I think we have to take a little risk because he certainly is our best bet. He has unquestionable ability, and his name is going to help. I only wish I could nail him down to his job. Every time that I think I have got him at work, I discover that he has run down to Washington to do something else.

While we are waiting for him to finish his writing, Van Dyke and Steiner are going to do some scouting. One of them will go down to Pittsburgh, and the other to Greenbelt. Then they both will visit Radburn and other places around here.

I presume that you are having a wonderful time and it is going to be difficult to get you back to America.[2] We were only in Honolulu for a day. We spent the greater part of it at the Academy of Arts. We did have time at noon to go to the Halekalani Hotel, where we had a swim and a delightful luncheon out in the open. We will never forget it.

I have just had a cable from Schenck, director of the [National] Academy of [the] Arts, saying that they are going to have our Chinese friend Liang give a course of twelve lectures. I hope you will have an opportunity to stop in to see Schenck. If you do, tell him how pleased I am. Also, if you hear of anyone who has a good little house that the Liang family (consisting of father, mother, and two small children) might use while they are there, which will probably be in November, without any great expense, do let me know about it. I am sure Liang Ssu-ch'eng and his wife are going to be a great success in Honolulu, both socially and otherwise.

My best to you.

Cordially yours,
Clarence

P.S. Just had a postal from Lin Yutang in Paris. He says, "Reading Lewis Mumford's book. I was delighted to find your name there and hear about your close association with him in the most important problem confronting man in the modern age. . . . I am going to get L.M.'s *Technics and Civilization*."

1. Stein had made considerable progress with his idea: he had secured funding from the Rockefeller Foundation, had worked with Mumford to lay out the film's basic idea, and had involved the writer and director of several excellent documentaries, Pere Lorenz.

2. Mumford was doing consulting work on the city plan for Honolulu.

292   To Johnson et al.

[New York City]   June 27, 1938

From: Clarence S. Stein

To: Reginald D. Johnson and Wilson, Merrill and Alexander, Architects Associated

In regard to the job that you are hoping to do with the local [Housing] Authority, I am very much interested. I agree with you that it would be foolish to try to discuss compensation until we know more definitely just what the project is to be and the extent to which my services will be needed. I don't know how we are going to be able to arrive at that without my going out to California. It would seem to me that the thing for you and your associates to do, as soon as the project takes definite shape, is to arrange for me to come out. If I am able to get away at that time, I would be glad to arrange to come on the terms that we made in our agreement of April 5th, 1938, in regard to Thousand Gardens. . . .

293   To Aline Stein

[Los Angeles][1]   August 24, 1938

Aline, my darling:

Jennie Mac and I met here at two and had a delicious lunch out on the terrace. What beauty—the distant circle of hills part hidden by brownish mist, the water of Naples Bay, and such luxurious trees and flowers around us. Do you remember it all? The foliage has grown much richer since we were last there together. And do you recollect the patios?

Jennie Mac brought your letter of Thursday along. What a weary, dreary letter. Shake out of it! You can't have the whole world made to your order. I think they have been pretty nice giving you a six-week guarantee instead of four. Why not give them two days of work for nothing? [Making] movies isn't business unless you make it so. The whole trouble is Sophie Treadwell. If she doesn't want your criticism, talk to her about the weather. But what is the matter with me anyhow? By this time you have forgotten your mood of Thursday and are probably having a grand time with the picture.

I have been working out at Long Beach all morning.² That project is really taking shape. There is every chance of its being a really good job, the sort of thing I have been trying to get started these last six years. Only thing that can stop it is Harry Cheney's pigheadedness. He is technical adviser of the [Los Angeles] County Housing Authority. But there is nothing technical about Henry. All sentiment and a lot of city planning and housing hang over from the past. All of the architects working on these projects have got his number and disagree with his point of view. But I guess it is going to be up to me to fight it out with him, if I can't get him into believing that we are carrying out his ideas in a slightly different way. But enough of that.

Let me fill my lungs with this good air, and take another look at all this beauty, and tell you how I love you, and wish this was our terrace at "A Thousand Years."

Jennie Mac, of course, sends love.

Clarence

1. Stein had accepted a role as consulting architect on several public housing projects in Los Angeles. Aline was on location away from Los Angeles.

2. One of the housing projects was being designed for the Housing Authority of Long Beach, California.

---

294   To Aline Stein

September 21, 1938   Pasadena [California]

Aline darling:

. . . Last night [I had] dinner [with] two of the "big" architects of L.A., Dave Allen's son and Donald Parkinson's, with wives, of course. Much talk, nothing said. Of the family, in addition to Reg [Johnson] and Mrs., there was only the tall daughter, handsomer than ever. By the way, she is at the office now acting as secretary.

Yesterday I worked on a couple of the jobs.¹ I will try to explain to you what they all are one of these days, unless they all disappear before then.

At noon we had a luncheon of all the principals concerned with A Thousand Gardens.² [There was] young Baldwin of the famous Baldwin Estate, on which we are to build, the head of the *L.A. Times* (an elderly guy who just eats an apple for lunch, while we put away a fat meal at Reg's club), [and] his nephew and advisers. The old man is part owner of the land along with the Baldwins. The architects and builder [were all there]. I had to give a little talk, which went all right, as it wasn't prepared.

In the afternoon I visited the head of the [Los Angeles County] housing authority, who wants very much that I act as advisor of both county developments. It seems, when my name was mentioned, Straus spoke well of me. Strange things happen!

Jennie Mac telephones [from Beverly Hills] that there is a letter from you awaiting me.[3] I can't wait to read it.

All my love,
Clarence

1. These were the two jobs for the Long Beach and Los Angeles County Housing Authorities.

2. This private rental project would develop into one of Stein's most important consulting opportunities, later named Baldwin Hills Village.

3. Aline's mother had purchased a home in Beverly Hills and was now living in Los Angeles. Clarence stayed there during most of his 19 September to 4 October working trip to California. The schedules for his meetings on the three L.A. housing projects on which he was consulting and his trip to San Francisco to meet William Wurster are detailed in a three-page "Diary" in the Stein Papers. Stein's "endless trips" back and forth across the city were noted in one letter to Aline: "Oh what an ugly—endlessly ugly—place the realtors have made of Los Angeles."

---

295 To Aline Stein

September 22, 1938   Jennie Mac—Los Angeles

Aline, my darling:

Yesterday was another strenuous day, but it had the best of endings. When I got back here, there were letters from you, two for me and one for Jennie Mac.[1] The very detailed description of the trip on Saturday from Gert's to our side of the river was just the thing I needed. The fact that you liked the color of the garage door is really much more important to me than that the British have sold out [to Hitler]. It is even more important than what the Housing Authority of the County of L.A. may do about housing.

I met with them yesterday morning. They don't know what it is all about. Luckily, they think I do. They stop their endless discussions about unessentials or unattainables to listen to the expert from distant parts. One has to be the man from Mars . . . to have authority. If I could only make them believe in New York that I really came from California.

I am not going to try here to explain the various jobs and the different housing authorities for which I am working. I will try to make a diagram or something when I have time. . . . Yesterday I appeared before the County Housing Authority first with Johnson's group, that is to do the Palos Verdes development, and then with architects that are planning a community in Long Beach. I also had a little meeting with the [Los Angeles City Housing] Authority before the architects appeared and, in fact, with the commissioners when the other architects appeared. The elderly chairman . . . wanted to know what part of Germany we came from and tried to tell me the history of his family and the part of the country from which they came, while Reg Johnson was trying to explain the Palo Verdes project, and the lady member of the commission was sentimentalizing about sweet little houses, and the hard-boiled builder on the Authority was booming about being practical, and everyone else was butting in.

Then came lunch with Gallo, the chairman of the City Housing Authority. Another group of architects, with Reginald as chairman, were getting acquainted with him, for the City Authority may have millions to spend on housing. Gallo is the head of one of the biggest wine-making concerns. He dresses in broad-patterned shirts and suits and is deeply interested in his housing job.

In the afternoon I worked on 'Thousand Gardens.' And now I must be on my way to Long Beach.

All my love,
Clarence

1. Aline was back in New York acting on Broadway. Clarence and Aline Stein have traded places.

2. This was a private residential development proposed for the Baldwin Estate, south of central Los Angeles.

---

296   To Aline Stein

[Los Angeles, California]   September 27, 1938

Darling:

. . . Last night I told Walter Arensburg all about museums.[1] After his wines had made me particularly fluent, I told him that the first principle was that a museum wall should never be crowded. There must be space around each object. And all the time I looked at the surrounding walls covered like wallpaper with his fantastic art. He has been made a member of the board of the museum out here, and perhaps he may someday house his own collection. Anything can happen.

In the morning there was another meeting of the County Housing Authority, and they approved the preliminary sketches of both projects. We have them eating out of our hands.

Lunch with Reg Johnson, Luillio (the head of the City Housing Authority), and Manchester Boyd, editor of the *Daily News*. Travel is broadening.

And I love you,
Clarence

1. This was the beginning of a long friendship. Stein became an advisor to Arensburg during the years when he was seeking an appropriate site and design for the museum he hoped to build for his important collection of modern art.

297   To Melville Dozier[1]

[New York City]   October 31, 1938

Dear Mr. Dozier:

As you see from the enclosed memoranda, I spent two days at Washington last week conferring with various people at the United States Housing Authority in regard to the two projects of the Housing Authority of the County of Los Angeles.

In general, the conferences were very satisfactory. [Nathan] Straus seemed very much interested in what you are doing and very anxious that you go ahead just as soon as the drawings go through the regular routine at Washington. I found the attitude of those with whom I conferred very broad-minded. They did not want, any more than necessary, to tell us what to do. They simply wanted to give us whatever suggestions they could and emphasized the need of economy, particularly economy of maintenance. . . .

Cordially yours,

[Clarence S. Stein]

1. Dozier was the executive director of the Housing Authority of the County of Los Angeles.

298   To Cecil Schilling

[New York City]   October 31, 1938

Dear Mr. Schilling:

As you will see from the enclosed, I spent a couple of days in Washington last week discussing your plans, as well as the other development, with the United States Housing Authority. Mr. Straus seems very much interested in what is being done and is very anxious that we get things going as soon as possible.

If you have any questions in regard to my memorandum of conferences, please let me know. I don't know just what the final criticisms will be, but I thought it would be helpful to have these notes so that we may start making further studies.

On the basis of the criticisms and of the studies I have been making of your plans, I have a number of suggestions to make. The easiest way to make these will be in the form of sketches. I have one of my men working on these at present. Just as soon as they are finished, I will send them to you. I think you should then make comparative estimates of various types.

In general, the criticisms of grouping and of roads seemed to me to be very sound. I only hope that somebody suggests eliminating all or most of the freestanding houses. They look very wasteful to me compared with simple rows. . . .

Cordially yours,

Clarence S. Stein

299   To Cecil Schilling

[New York City]   March 24, 1939

Dear Mr. Schilling:

Since my return I have not had time to study the revised plan of the Carmelitos Housing Project in detail. However, I am surprised at the complete change in the site plan. It is apparent, however, that the purpose is to cut down costs. Because I have not received the cost figures, I cannot judge just how far the changes were necessary to bring the costs given in the Job Program within the amount that Washington was willing to allow. Since we started work I have been in complete sympathy with you in regard to the need for economy. I have no doubt [that], as I study the revised plans carefully, I will discover detailed changes that served to greatly decrease site costs.

It seems to me that, in making the changes, many of the most important features of the town plan that would have served for good living have been sacrificed. These features are (1) safety against hazards of auto accidents, (2) location of community facilities, including recreation building and playgrounds, (3) spaciousness. Just a word as to each of these.

(1) Safety against hazards of auto accidents

In the original plan there was a complete separation of auto and pedestrian way. This plan was arranged so that it was possible to walk from any house to playgrounds, community building, or one's neighbor's house without crossing a vehicular road. The new plan, in my opinion, sets up numerous hazards. . . .

(2) Location of community building

In the original plan, the community building was placed on the park leading to the school playground. It had spacious surroundings and adequate space adjoining it for the recreation of youngsters and for gatherings of the whole community. It had adequate parking space. It was so placed as to take advantage of the site in arrangement of [the] basement and to show up to the best possible advantage from the park inside the development, as well as from the outside approach along Orange Avenue.

The new plan replaces this location with cramped surroundings, inadequate setting, and without sufficient adjoining space for playgrounds or community gatherings. The parking area here seems quite insufficient for public gatherings in California and is located at a particularly dangerous spot. . . .

(3) Spaciousness

In the original plan open spaces were so organized as to open into each other in such a way as to give broad outlooks. In the new plan green spaces have been broken up into small areas. I sympathize with the attempt to cut down the areas of public upkeep, but it seems to me that, in doing so and particularly through the distribution of these open areas, the attractive quality of the original plan has been sacrificed. Moreover, there is inadequate space for recreation, organized or otherwise. . . .

Had I had the opportunity to give these criticisms while the plans were being studied, they would have been of greater value.[1] Nevertheless, I hope it is not too late to make some use of them.

Cordially,
Clarence S. Stein

1. It appears that Stein's housing design concepts had not been fully accepted in these projects: The U.S. Public Housing Authority tendency to cut costs (due partly to criticism from the real estate industry) had already made it difficult, if not impossible, to include the safety features and amenities that had characterized Stein's housing designs of the late 1920s and early 1930s.

300   To Cecil Schilling

[New York City]   April 3, 1939

Dear Mr. Schilling:
I have your letter of March 24th.

I appreciate the trying period through which you and your associates have been going and the unexpected amount of work you have had to do, yet I cannot allow your inference to stand that I suggested I had influence in Washington which would make it possible to put your plans through without trouble. I refuse to consider having my fee reduced on the basis of failure to render service neither called for in my contract nor promised at any time, nor one that honestly could have been offered to you by anyone.

In the interest of professional amity, may I suggest that you withdraw entirely both your letter and its inferences? I shall then be willing (and only then) to consider a request for modification of the contract payments, provided the request is based on the known facts regarding your greater work caused by the unpredictable requirements of the Washington departmental critics: the consequent increased cost and lesser profit to your group.

I am returning your letter herewith. I shall look forward to receiving from you another, and quite different one.[1]

Sincerely yours,
[Clarence S. Stein]

1. Shilling's letter was rewritten. He had suggested a reduction in Stein's fee based on the extensive changes required by the U.S. Housing Authority, which Schilling's office had not expected.

301   To Benton MacKaye

[New York City]   July 26, 1939

Dear Benton:

. . . Now, whenever possible, we go out to the country Thursday evening and do not return until Monday for dinner. Things at the office have been particularly slow. I have been trying to do some writing on what may be either an introduction to a book containing the illustrations of *The City* with Lewis's narration or else the first part of my [museum] book. It has been going rather slowly. . . .

We are very anxious to have you come up. Your suggestion of coming to 1,000 Years on Sunday is fine. Make it soon and, if possible, make it for more than one day. We now have a room down in the old farm where I think you would find living comfortable, even though there are none of the modern conveniences. . . .

. . . You ask about the Unwins. I just had a letter from Sir Raymond. They are leaving for the United States on August 18th and will be in Connecticut for a while. I wrote to him yesterday about the possibility of having a get-together out at Radburn some time in the autumn. . . .

I want very much to talk to you about another museum. Both Lewis and I have been discussing with the director, Charles Adams, the possibilities of the development of a really good State Museum in Albany. There is [a] chance to develop a museum there on the basis of the Housing and Regional Planning Commission's report on a Plan for the State. There are lots of other things to talk to you about, also.

Our best to you,
As always,
[Clarence]

302   To Reginald Johnson

[New York City]   November 3, 1939

Dear Reg:

I was delighted to hear from you and to learn that things are at last moving. All of this housing seems to be a game in which the authorities set up one obstacle after another to try out the architect's patience. You, Lew, and the others have certainly shown plenty of patience.

I am anxiously waiting for the plans of Harbor Hills, which you say are being sent. I am curious to see to what extent the USHA has insisted on changing things. I can't quite understand from your letter whether they really have done away with our chevron plot plan.[1] I hope not. You say you hit the ceiling when it was suggested. I don't blame you.

I am particularly anxious to see Thousand Gardens under way. I believe, as I have for some time past, that this should be the finest housing development in the country. The plot plan that Lew sent me unquestionably showed great improvement over the last ones. However, it was at such small scale that it was very difficult to study any of the detail. I hope you will keep me posted as things go along.

Alexander's experience here should be of a great deal of help.[2] I met him from time to time, and he impressed me as a very able person. . . .

Cordially yours,
Clarence

1. Much of this pattern survived in the final site plan for Harbor Hills.
2. Robert Alexander, an architect in Los Angeles and a sometime associate of Richard Neutra, was a key member of the design team for A Thousand Gardens (Baldwin Hills Village).

---

303   To Benton MacKaye

[New York City]   November 30, 1939

Dear Ben:

I was up at Columbia a couple of days ago and saw Carl Feiss.[1] Both he and one of the students with whom I had a chance to talk seemed very enthusiastic about the plans for the Connecticut River survey. Carl told me of the suggestion that I go along. I can't promise, but I will do so if I can.

I hope that, on your way through New York, you are going to stop in to see us. Above all, I hope you will get up to 1,000 Years. The old farmhouse is now almost completely civilized, with heat, hot water, and all the other newfangled things. There is even a radio, but we will promise to turn that off if you come.

Our best to you
As always,
Clarence

1. Feiss, who had graduated in 1937 from MIT's new graduate program in city and regional planning, took a position as Sir Raymond Unwin's assistant. After Unwin died in 1940, Feiss assumed his teaching duties.

85. Clarence Stein on the SS *Dempo* on the Indian Ocean, working on the manuscript of a book on museum design (1936). The Steins' trip to Asia took them east to England, France, the Suez Canal, India, Indonesia, Thailand, China, and Japan.

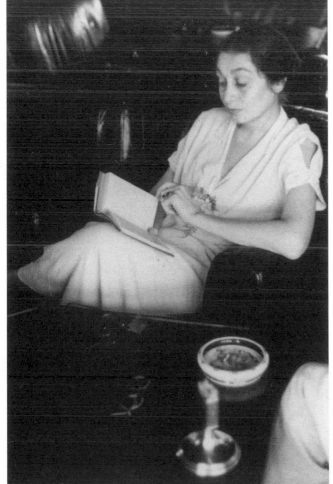

86. Aline Stein reading on their trip to the Far East (1935–36). One of their favorite books was *Tales of the Genji*. After they returned to New York in April 1936, they named the small farmhouse they had purchased as a summer retreat A Thousand Years after a passage in the book.

87. Stein with his walking stick outside their temporary home in Peking (1936). The Steins' travel style was to stay in one place for an extended time (one or two months) to see and understand it.

88. Clarence Stein on the Great Wall of China (1936).

89. Clarence Stein in China with Phyllis Liang and Dr. Liang Ssu-ch'eng at the Summer Palace in Peking (1936). Liang was the first Chinese historian to carry out systematic field work, measurement, and research on ancient buildings of China. Liang visited the Steins in 1946 while working with an international committee of architects on buildings for the United Nations in New York.

90. Aline's 1938 birthday present from Clarence was Hill House, a redwood retreat up the hill from A Thousand Years, near Yorktown in Westchester, New York.

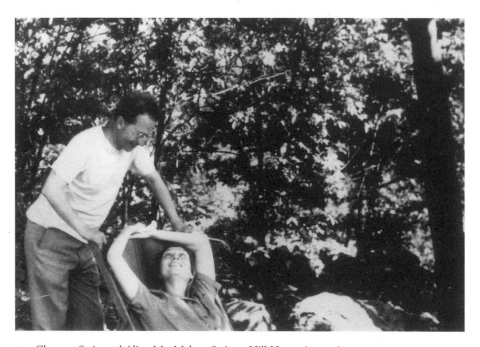

91. Clarence Stein and Aline MacMahon Stein at Hill House (c. 1937).

92. Clarence and Pop Stein at the house Clarence built for his sister Gertrude (c. 1937).

93. Autos and gardens at Baldwin Hills Village. In this section, where parking areas are near entries to the service areas of the houses, low brick walls and landscaping provide a kitchen garden for each house.

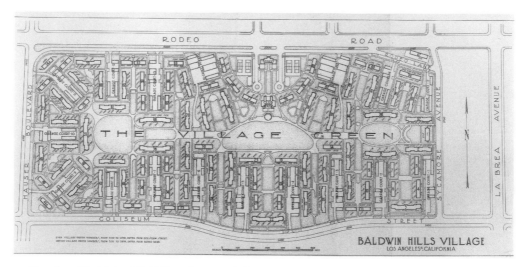

94. Site plan of Baldwin Hills Village (1940), which was first called "A Thousand Gardens" when Stein began consulting work on the design for development of a large tract of land in southern Los Angeles in 1938 with Reginald Johnson, Wilson, Merrill, and Robert Alexander. The 80-acre/620-dwelling unit project was built in 1941 after long delays in FHA review. "Here," Clarence Stein wrote, "the Radburn idea was given its most complete and most characteristic expression."

95. Clarence Stein in a relaxed moment at Aline Bernstein Fraenkel's summer home in Armonk, New York. Bernstein had worked with Aline MacMahon at the Hudson Guild Theatre in the 1920s. Their long friendship included many summer weekends at the Fraenkels' large country home.

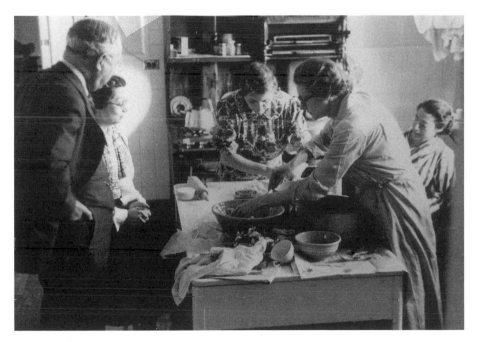

96. In the kitchen while visiting the Fraenkels in Armonk, New York (1939). From left: Mark Holstein, Aline MacMahon Stein, Aline Bernstein, Ethel Fraenkel, Edla Cusick (Aline Bernstein's daughter).

6

The War and Postwar Planning
1940-1949

During the early 1940s, Stein continued to develop his strength as a consultant to architects engaged in large-scale housing design. He also was a consultant on "defense housing" policy and design and designed several defense housing communities, including a prototype project near Washington, D.C., and three in and near Pittsburgh. There simply was little conventional architectural work coming his way. His work on state and federal policy for housing and community development also occupied more time. And, of course, he kept up his extensive correspondence and wrote a few articles on housing and regional planning. For example, he advised the New York governor's office on specific legislative changes needed to adapt the state's laws on limited dividend housing companies to the realities of federal housing subsidy programs for the lowest income families under the Housing Act of 1937.

He went back intermittently to his interminable book writing, now with a new outline for "the city book," which he discussed with Mumford and Harcourt Brace. Its working title was *People, Place and Price—The New Technique in City Building*. Various drafts of the outline and of chapters of the unpublished work are preserved in the collection of Stein's papers at Cornell University. None of this writing has been included in this volume of his unpublished work. He was seldom satisfied that he had "got it right," and that frustrated him. He knew that there would be a great deal of "community building" after "The Emergency," a euphemism for the United States' serious buildup for participation in the war in Europe.

When FDR's pre–World War II "defense" buildup started in 1940, Clarence was recruited to assist his old friend and associate Ralph Eberlin, who had been appointed administrator of the Federal Public Housing Administration (FPHA). The FPHA was assigned the task of building new housing in dozens of communities where increases in defense spending were causing major increases in employment and subsequent housing shortages. Stein's first assignment was in Washington, where he negotiated and wrote guidelines and physical standards for defense housing projects. He advised on standardizing the planning procedures, the types of housing layout, and the densities for defense housing built by the federal government from 1940 to 1944. Later in this program he reviewed for FPHA many of the projects that were built. At Stein's urging the agency rejected efforts of the more conservative policy advisors to build conventional single-family subdivisions that could be sold easily to individual homeowners after the "emergency." His recommendations for higher-density, more efficient dwelling designs and site layouts were first tested in Stein's 1940 design for a demonstration project at Indian Head just south of Washington, D.C. These assignments and the rigors of his prewar travels between New York and Washington are described in regular letters to Aline.

After his work on policy making and prototype design in Washington, he was given commissions to design three projects in the suburbs of Pittsburgh, a center of much-increased prewar industrial activity. Two of his projects were built in Shaler and Stowe Townships, suburbs of Pittsburgh, for the Allegheny County Housing Authority. Both were characterized by excellent site planning, and they were designed and built at breakneck speed. Stein, always an intense, hard-driving individual, worked arduously on these emergency defense housing projects in New York and Pittsburgh. This required air travel weekly among New York, Pittsburgh, and Washington. Stein usually spent his weekends at "A Thousand Years," but this extensive travel and the heavy workload, which he reports in happy letters to Aline, took their toll mentally and physically. By early 1942 Stein was back in the hospital with a bout of depression. It took him over a year to recover. He was treated at Silver Hill in Connecticut and at a ranch in Arizona. By the following year, 1943, he had recovered sufficiently to do consulting work with the FPHA, evaluating the war housing program.

Aline and Clarence Stein were together much more during World War II than they had been during the 1930s. She was acting on Broadway in Thornton Wilder's *Skin of Our Teeth* in 1942 and Maxwell Anderson's *The Eve of St. Mark* during the summer of 1943, and Clarence traveled with her to California that autumn to stay the winter while she played a major role in the film version of Pearl Buck's *Dragon Seed*.

Throughout 1944 and early 1945, Stein began to develop a plan for an organization to provide consulting design services to public and private large-scale urban development organizations after the war. Some of the correspondence that deals with these efforts is included in this section. He also began writing articles about postwar community planning.[1] Sadly, Clarence's plans for a consulting practice after the war did not materialize. From May 1945 through the end of the year, he suffered yet another nervous breakdown, his third since 1937 and one from which he did not recover until early 1946. He was sixty-four years old; however, after these episodes of bad health and disappointments with his career, the best days were yet to come. Some of his major contributions to urban development policy and design were still before him.

In the late 1940s Clarence built a new life as a consultant, critic, policy advisor, and author. Gradually, after the war ended, he revived discussions with his old friends Lewis Mumford and Benton MacKaye. He began to work with new friends like Frederic J. Osborn, a central figure in the formulation of British policy on New Towns, and Gordon Stephenson, editor of the British planning journal, *Town Planning Review*. His circle of correspondents grew and became more international. In 1947 he became engaged in saving FDR's Greenbelt Towns from obliteration as models for the types of communities he believed should be the units of new regional systems of cities. He lobbied for modifications of federal legislation, with the goal of providing a basis for Regional Cities, in which New Towns would be a major element for the restructuring of metropolitan areas. In these efforts he worked with Catherine Bauer and his Republican friend of the mid-1930s, Ernest Bohn of the Cleveland Metropolitan Housing Authority. He also reinvigorated the RPAA, adding new members and setting a new agenda. Perhaps his most important initiative during these years was that he began to write more effectively, with support from Gordon Stephenson, editor of the *Town Planning Review*, and Lewis Mumford.

In 1948 he abandoned his "city book." He had written himself into a corner. Now, with the encouragement and support of Mumford and Gordon Stephenson, he started anew and quickly wrote several long, clear, persuasive, and well-illustrated articles about the designs of Sunnyside, Radburn, Hillside Homes, Chatham Village, the Greenbelt Towns, and Baldwin Hills Village. These articles led directly to more widespread knowledge, understanding, and subsequent adoption of many of Stein's ideas in projects in England, Sweden, and America. The publications also helped to launch Stein on a new career as a consultant and writer. They gave him a new platform from which he wrote, lectured, consulted, and designed for the next twenty years. As always, he spread his ideas generously, with convincing arguments about the need to design for the larger-scale urban environmental needs of metropolitan regions.

In the late 1940s, Clarence and Aline Stein traveled widely in Europe and America, much more extensively and much more often than they had since the early 1930s. Clarence consulted on and studied urban projects in England, Sweden, Den-

1. See, for example, "City Patterns: Past and Future," *New Pencil Points* 23, no. 6 (1942): 52–56.

mark, France, Finland, and Italy. Aline acted in films and on stage in England, Denmark, and Germany. On his visits to England to work with Gordon Stephenson on articles for the *Town Planning Review* in 1949 and 1950, Clarence also worked with Stephenson and others on the first designs for the pedestrian-favoring town center of the British New Town of Stevenage, which incorporated many community functions (town hall, library, community college, theater, etc.), along with the commercial center and some light industrial land uses. By the end of the decade of the 1940s, Stein was well on his way to developing a second career as an international urban statesman.

304   To Aline Stein

A Thousand Years[1]   January 12, 1940

Beloved:

And thus the moon sunk behind the redwood house early this morning. And now, as I write, the sun is just rising above the rocks behind me, and you are not here. There has been a rousing fire in the fireplace in our room as I dressed. It seems so wasted without you—you in the bed with half-awake eyes.

It was one of those superbly beautiful days—very cold, dry, part cloudy.

[balance of letter is not in the Stein Papers][2]

1. A Thousand Years is the name that Clarence and Aline Stein had given to their suburban New York retreat in Westchester County, which they had purchased in 1935. There, Clarence had designed and had built a hilltop cottage of redwood above the principal residence, an old farmhouse.

2. On 1 March 1940, Stein, acting as president of Modern City Films, Inc., signed a contract with the Museum of Modern Art Film Library for educational distribution of *The City*, which the corporation had produced.

305   To Aline Stein

[A Thousand Years, Yorktown Heights, N.Y.]   May, 1940

Aline dear:

It has been a peaceful day. Hilda and I came up on the ten o'clock train.[1] The Hudson was beautiful, particularly toward the end of the trip. All gray clouds, palisades,

[and] distant hills, with just a streak of white where the sun struck the ice on the river.

. . . I walked again for a short time up to the redwood house, after lunch. It is glorious at this season, and the little house is in the best spot, I thought: even better than the site we chose for the house that was never built—a broader view of distant hills and the contrast of the cottage in the valley below. I sat before the living room fire and then started the bedroom fire and read in bed.

How I wanted you to be there. I would have bored you by reading bits from the book. I had started on the train this morning and have been reading most of the day, between walks and dozes. It is Harold Laski's *Where Do We Go from Here?* It tells more clearly than anything I have read or heard what this crazy war is about.

The background against which he writes is his belief that democracy and capitalism are contradictions. The middle class, which came into power with the French Revolution, needed the masses to give them the economic power and to protect that power through the State. But the welfare of the people—of democracy, in fact—was always a restraint on the fundamental purpose of capitalism, unrestrained profits. The governments of France and England could not prepare for war nor carry on a wholehearted fight because they loved capitalism more than democracy. In fact, they feared the growth of labor's power and demands more than they did Hitler and Mussolini. Laski believes that we are witnessing the breakdown of the old social order.

When then? I find it difficult to wait until I get to his last chapter, "What Are We to Do Next?" Perhaps he has hit the right answer. But it seems to him that we must search for the answer, some answer at least. Without it, all we do is meaningless. No, perhaps acting may go on in any framework, just good technique and the joy of acting, and designing buildings for clients, making them sound and good looking and to meet the requirements set up by the client. . . . But when it comes to the task that I have set myself, that is another matter—to help build the background for the future. But what future? What social order? What culture? Without some idea of the frame into which the picture I am to paint is to fit, there is no meaning in my work or my words.

And so for the moment I hang upon the words of Laski. Let's hope he does not let me down.

All my love,
Clarence

1. During this period when Aline was in Los Angeles, Clarence and the Stein's maid would frequently travel to Yorktown Heights to A Thousand Years on Saturday mornings and return to New York City on Monday.

306 To Benton MacKaye

New York City   July 26, 1940

Dear Ben:

I have just received a copy of "Defense Time Conservation" in its final form. . . .

I am sorry that I have not been able to give more time to much further development of my part of this idea. I have been pretty well tied up on other work and particularly on the scheme for the redevelopment of the lower East Side. The mayor and other city officials are very much interested, and there is really hope that something may happen. . . .

I have been trying to develop at greater length the short memorandum that I had when I was in Washington. All I have succeeded in doing so far is a rather technical memorandum to help [Miles] Colean. This deals mainly with the comparative cost of developing and operating a community built on farmland and one that is a rebuilding of an old section of an existing city. . . .

Because of the lower East Side work and the other housing job at the office, I am not at all sure just when I can get down to Washington. I would like to make it sometime next week, but I have grave doubts as to how it can be done. . . .

> Best from Aline and
> Clarence

307 To Benton MacKaye

[New York City]   October 21, 1940

To Ben:

Still in bed at 1 West 64th Street, but not a permanent fixture there any longer. On Saturday we went up to 1,000 Years. In spite of the cold there was much of autumn's blaze on the hilltops. I sat all morning in an easy chair, in the bright sun, absorbing heat and color.

Early this morning we drove in and I went directly to the office. Half a day was all I could stand, and now I am here, . . . enjoying the other side of the park. Not entirely a bad world.

Jennie Mac is still here. She and Aline would send their best if they knew I was writing. Mine goes without saying.

> Clarence

308 · To Benton MacKaye

[New York City]   November 1, 1940

Dear Ben:

I have postponed writing to you because I thought that I might be able to get to Washington before the end of this week, but I am finding that it is very slow work getting back to complete strength. I am trying not to overdo, and I think within a week or so I will be myself again. Next week they are going to take X-rays of me, and they think they will find out just what's the matter.[1]

I'm glad that you voted for the right man. We will have our chance next Tuesday.

This Sunday evening I am going to have a confab with Albert Mayer, Henry Churchill, and Oscar Stonorov up at my apartment. We are going to discuss the question of how the services of the technicians in planning can be made use of in the Defense Program. . . .

Next Wednesday noon Lewis and a few of the rest of us are coming together to plan a few meetings to discuss the subject that you and I have been talking about for some time (i.e., the Defense Program), that will lead to something worthwhile when defense is no longer needed. . . .

As always,
Clarence

1. Stein is in the first phase of recovery from another bout with depression, which had started in the late summer of 1940 and seems to have been associated with lung problems.

---

309   Aline Stein

[New York City]   January 18, 1941

Aline darling:

. . . So much has happened during the last week that my news is way behind. I told you of my first day at Washington, how Hardie [Phillips] and I visited the Navy & Army. I spent the evening at Greenbelt with the Fulmers. . . .

The next day I went in search of housing work. First I visited Clark Foreman, the housing assistant of the big brass, [and] John Carmody,[1] who Congress said should spend the money for industrial housing. You remember that I told you the last time that Foreman froze when I made suggestions to him. This time he asked me if I would act as their housing consultant. I said I was eventually after a job for the office but that I was delighted to help in any way I could. Ten minutes later I had been transferred from the U.S. Housing Authority.

I told Foreman that I had been looking at the site plans at [the] Public Buildings Administration (the architecture factory) with Kline Fulmer and that I thought the principal difficulty with their work, in addition to the fact that they needed site planners, was the fact that they had no program. For instance, they are laying out their development on the basis of the [property] being sold as individual lots. This means more expensive utility layout and less attractive places for living.

Mr. Carmody is in favor of planning as a community, but the head of Public Building, Reynolds, just takes for granted that the proper way of disposing of houses is to sell them to the little guys. I suggested that Carmody was the client or representative of the client, Uncle Sam, and that it was his business to provide the architect [with] . . . a program: a clear statement on a few sheets of paper [that] would save lots of time and talk. "Funny that nobody thought of that," said Foreman.

So, I was asked to write the program, which I did that afternoon, aided by Keene Fulmer and Catherine Bauer, who was still in Washington. Next morning I presented it to Foreman and it was . . . at once approved by Carmody. It is likely to be anything but popular with Public Buildings, and I guess they will not love me when they learn I was the author. . . .

But over at Carmody's office they know. So the next morning, Foreman asked me to make studies for the site plan of a development near Washington on which Reynolds's office had started. . .[2]

Love to Jennie Mac and Ethel and all the rest to you.

Clarence

1. FDR had succeeded in increasing arms production for shipment to England under Lend-Lease laws. This, in turn, required the production of housing for defense industry workers and contractors engaged in expanding military installations. Carmody was in charge of the work.

2. This was the prototype Indian Head defense housing site south of Washington, D.C., on the east side of the Potomac.

---

310   To Aline Stein

The Hay-Adams House   Washington, D.C.   Tuesday, February 4, 1941

Beloved:

Two days in Washington, busy days. Yesterday everything seemed to go wrong. Today it is all fine and dandy. I am still working at the Indian Head Development. We are about ready to lay out the roads on the ground. It is a good site plan, but the thing may look like the devil. It is going to consist of 650 knock-down houses that are individually anything but beautiful. We will see.

Spare time I spend trying to locate a job for the office. Long waits in outer offices, and what a job it is to get to some of them. In the Navy building you must be registered and wear a big badge that they give you and have a card signed to permit you to carry out a briefcase. They are having just as much fun as though there was a war. All the secretaries are most courteous, but that does not get you anywhere. At last, one of the housing agencies offered me hope this afternoon. I said make it California if you can, which, of course, they will not.

Ackerman is here. We dine together. Everyone comes to Washington. Last night dinner with Ben. He is done with his cold. . . .

Love to Jennie Mac and to you, my darling.

Clarence

---

311   To Aline Stein

Thousand Years   February 8, 1941

Aline dear:

I returned from Washington yesterday evening with a certain feeling of content. I had won out. The plan I had been working on for the Indian Head Development was accepted in place of that proposed by the Public Buildings Administration [PBA]. This should mean the acceptance of the idea of community planning in place of the old type of subdivision, not only for Indian Head, but as a dominating policy for the future. [I] say "should mean" because I know that the fight is by no means done. The old real estate methods do not expire as a result of a single blow.[1] But we have the old-timers on the run.

It is too complicated a tale to tell you it all here. Most of it will have to wait until I can tell you by word of mouth. But here it is briefly.

I told you that my first job with the Federal Works Agency was to suggest a basic policy, one section of which was that all projects be planned for future disposal as a whole, rather than as individual home properties. Carmody signed and sent it to Public Buildings Administration. They did not like it, and, in fact, seemed to pay no attention to the directions.

Meanwhile I had been making the plan of Indian Head, which was an extreme illustration of community planning. [It is] much the same idea as Radburn, but adjusts to the beautiful site above the Potomac River. The Public Building site planners made a plan for the same place. It was a banal real estate subdivision, endless rows of similar lots. We had about as great a contrast as possible.

Foreman (Carmody's Housing representative) and I put the two plans before the big boss. He called the chief architects and site planner of PBA over and made it clear to them that, as far as he was concerned, the old real estate [ideas] . . . [for] handling these problems were in the way. Selling to the poor was not good policy, and community planning was desirable.

It was arranged that I was to meet with the advisory committee of PBA the following day to consider the two proposed plans. Much to our surprise the big boss, Carmody himself, turned up. (He had to come from the other end of Washington.) In picturesque language he made it clear that he wanted a change of policy and more action. He stayed for almost an hour. When we left, they considered only one of the two plans and, with slight changes, they accepted my plan. Whether they will butcher it in drawing it up is to be seen. I will go back later next week and try to prevent it.

This meeting was interesting in bringing out the personalities of the members of the advisory committee. Matt, who is chief land planner of the Federal Housing Administration, was clear and concise and completely dominated by the idea of lot sale. He and I were two extremes, without compromise. But Fred Bigger, another member of the Advisory Board of planners, was all for adjusting the plan so that it might be either this or that, "We can't be sure."

Compromise, compromise, compromise. Fred always tells me that we are of the same point of view. Yes, but I am afraid Fred has too long been making surveys and writing reports, judicious reports, that weighed all the pros and cons so carefully that there never was a clear idea left when it had gradually been whittled down by his honest judgment. . . .

Love to Jennie Mac.

[Clarence]

1. The idea that publicly built housing of any type should be designed to sell as individual buildings or dwelling units was persistent. In the 1950s and 1960s, the Public Housing Administration design guidelines required that site plans for its projects show possible property lines for each building so that it would be clear how the project could be sold off to purchasers of single apartment buildings or individual row houses.

---

312 To Aline Stein

[New York City]   Saturday, February 15, 1941

Dear Aline:

. . . It is impossible to write everything when so much is happening. I have been in Washington again for two days, most of the time plugging away at the one job, and yet I don't seem to be able to give you a clear idea of what I am doing or where I am getting. I don't know that I am altogether clear myself, but I feel sure that the direction is right, and I have made some strides.

They seem to be trying to carry out my plan of Indian Head as fully as they can. They want me to spend as much time as possible directing the work. Indian Head is important. It is close to Washington and so is likely to be the show example of Defense Housing. . . .

I am getting no end of letters of congratulations about that medal.[1] Queer those things should matter. All that really counts is work and you.

My love,
Clarence

409

P.S. This morning it was cloudy. And now the sun is bright, and I am not at Thousand Years.

Lewis Mumford is coming here for dinner and to stay. He has been at Simonson's, but they have no maid. So chez Stein gets him.

1. In 1941 the New York Chapter of the American Institute of Architects had awarded its gold medal to Stein for his work on housing design.

---

313 To Aline Stein

[New York City] February 22, 1941

Aline dear:

It is Saturday morning. I look out upon a gray park and gray clouds. [There's a] promise of snow perhaps, and so we are off to the mountains but not to be snowed in. That must wait for you.

There may be many things to do at the office, but they must wait. Thousand Years calls me.

I got back late yesterday evening from Washington. It was a busy day. I attended an all-day session of a committee of housing folk to write a revised national program.[1] Events have moved so quickly that much revision is needed. It was a well-chosen group, some twenty-five or thirty. A good many of them [have] very clear minds and a great deal of experience. We did not get very far beyond [the] outline. But that was enough to bring out some fundamentals. I advocated the importance of housing as part of the rebuilding of our cities and the whole physical framework of America. And now I must try to put my ideas into clear writing this weekend.

Between sessions of the housing meeting, I had to return to the drafting room to keep the Indian Head project going. It seemed in pretty good shape before I left.

I had breakfast with Herbert Emmerich, who is now running the government. Good stuff, Herbert. But he did have to show me what the newspapers had to say about him.

There is much more to write, but I must be on my way to the train.

More from the country, and tomorrow we speak.

All my love,
Clarence

1. After 1940 Stein increasingly became involved in discussions of housing policy in the executive branch of the U.S. government. This letter reports on his work with a large committee advising FDR on defense housing policy and postwar reconstruction.

314   To Aline Stein

[New York City]   Friday, March 14, 1941

Aline dear:

Last night I returned from Washington. That trip is becoming a bore. The night train down and then four hours in an uncomfortable Pullman seat coming back. I will travel by air—as soon as spring comes. Weather is too uncertain in winter, fogs or clouds over LaGuardia.[1] Besides, I don't think I will have to go so much in the future. The layout of Indian Head is pretty well done.[2] I have helped write out the rules of the game, and now I have designed one community as an example. Now they should give me some of the work to do here in the New York office, where I can put a job through as it should be done and where perhaps we can make enough to support a simple living in three or more home-sweet-homes. . . .

There is also a good prospect of my getting something from the Public Buildings Administration, just as soon as Congress votes another hundred and fifty million for housing.

But, of course, nothing is certain. So don't talk about it to anyone. Let us have our disappointments all by ourselves. . . .

My love,
Clarence

1. The airport serving New York City had already been named for the mayor.

2. The Indian Head project had a Radburn-like site plan, with grouped parking courts. It was a very influential prototype for much defense, war, and public housing during and after World War II. For a more complete account of Indian Head and Stein's later defense housing projects, see Kermit C. Parsons, "Clarence Stein's Middle Years: The Transition from Greenbelt Consultant to Urban Policy Statesman," compiled by Laurence Gerckens, in *Proceedings of the Fifth Biennial Conference on American Planning History* (Columbus, Ohio: Society for American City and Regional Planning History, 1994), 88–105.

315   To Aline Stein

[New York City]   Monday, March 17, 1941

Dearest:

Gertrude, Lydia, Arthur, and Lillie are going to be here for dinner. Arthur will be able to tell me what he thinks of your scenario, which he has had over the weekend.

. . . You write of reading "great letters." I spent much of Saturday reading minor ones (my own of years back to 1935). I took some metal file boxes up to the country to put them in [order]. While arranging them, I read them. How things repeat. Tugwell promising me a town to do—all those hopes and then that dark period, when I suffered so.[1] But there was little sign of it in the letters. I kept it pretty well hidden, only there was that house of Gertrude's—always wrong.[2] I don't think it will happen again. I must steel myself to hear that I am not getting any of the housing jobs, not even Honolulu.[3] That will be hard. Hardie and I lunched together. We are so well prepared to do that job, and wouldn't it be grand to go there?

I phoned Caroline [Simonson] this morning. She was up to see Lee Simonson, took a long walk with him, and dined at Silver Hill. He is much better.[4] They think he will be on the mend this week after they open a theater on which he was consultant. This is his Gertrude's house.

I know there are a lot of other things I wanted to tell you, but I can't remember them now.

My love,
Clarence

1. Clarence's disappointment about his 1936 Greenbelt Town assignment as general consultant and design review team member rather than as designer of one of the towns clearly was, according to this recollection, one of the causes (along with losing several other important jobs) of his 1936–37 "nervous breakdown." He had served as a consultant and as a "loyal soldier" in the RA's Greenbelt Town design process, where he had had a very substantial influence on the design of the Greenbelt New Towns, especially Greenbelt, Md.

2. Stein designed his sister's house in New Jersey when he and Aline returned from their 1936 trip to the Orient. It was not up to the quality of the single houses he had designed earlier in his career.

3. Stein and Hardie Phillips, one of the Goodhue "alumni" who was registered in Hawaii, had discussed several defense projects in Washington a week earlier.

4. Simonson seemed to have been having mental health problems. He was staying at the same recovery sanitarium in which Clarence had stayed when he was recovering in 1937.

---

316   To Aline Stein

The Hay-Adams House, [Washington, D.C.]   March 20, 1941

Aline darling:

Yesterday I had decided not to [go] to Washington, in spite of the fact that I was supposed to attend a meeting here to write a housing program. But I woke up at quarter of six and the weather was so beautiful that I phoned the airline. They had a seat on the 7:50. At nine thirty I was here.

In the plane coming down with me was Mrs. Rosenman, who has ambitions to be another Belle Moskowitz, but specializing in housing. I offered to take her to the meeting in a taxi. She said she had to drop her bag first. "What hotel?" I asked. "The White House," [she said]. Her husband the judge was Roosevelt's right-hand man when he was governor,[1] so they just stop at the White House. This is the kind of democracy worth fighting for.

It wasn't really necessary for me to come down. Everybody, or enough of them, anyhow, are slipping gradually to the left in Housing, and I will be pushed off the edge soon. There was nothing of importance to fight for. So, although the meetings are continuing tomorrow, I am taking the eight o'clock plane back tonight.

The planes are wonderful. [They are] so much more restful than a train. . . .

All my love,
Clarence

1. Judge Samuel I. Rosenman put together FDR's "brain trust" in 1933. He wrote an eyewitness account of FDR's New York governorship, *Working with Roosevelt* (New York: Harper, 1952). See esp. chapter 2, "The Genesis of the New Deal." Rexford Tugwell notes in his volume, *The Democratic Roosevelt* (Garden City, N.Y.: Doubleday, 1957), 149–50, that "Judge Rosenman . . . was more intimately concerned in formulating [FDR's New Deal] ideas than any other individual."

---

317   To Aline Stein

A Thousand Years, [Yorktown, N.Y.]   Saturday evening, March 22, 1941

Darling:

. . . The Ackermans are coming this noon and Kenneth Reid and wife. He is editor of *Pencil Points*.[1] I want to see if there isn't some way to make the younger architect to understand the scope of the problem that is before us in the years after the war, the physical rebuilding America, countryside and cities alike. I was astounded at the extent to which the committee with which I met in Washington last week accepted this rebuilding as the basis of the housing program. Just as soon as there is a general recognition of the scope of the problem, the approach of housing authorities and architects will have to change. It will no longer be a matter merely of housing for the poor or patching the old cities here or there. We will have to shoot the works and get down to fundamentals. What a big job there is ahead, to clear the issues first and then to actually do the work. How badly the architectural profession is prepared.

(Says I), who hasn't yet got a job, but I am still hoping for the CIO one.[2] If I only knew it wasn't coming right away, I would take a plane out at the end of next week to see you setting the clock back. . . .[3]

More later,

Love,
Clarence

1. *Pencil Points* was an architectural journal of the 1940s and 1950s. Clarence wrote "City Patterns, Past and Future" after this conference. It appeared in the June 1942 issue of *New Pencil Points* 23, no. 6 (1942): 52–56.

2. The labor union Congress of Industrial Organization (CIO) was considering postwar housing policy and projects. Its officers contacted Stein about a consulting assignment.

3. Aline was working on the film *Journey for Margaret,* a World War II drama about children left homeless by bombing attacks.

---

318   To Aline Stein

[New York City]   April 24, 1941

Aline dear:

I went to Pittsburgh to get a job. It seems pretty certain that I will get a job there, but somehow I am not very happy about it.

There is a great need of more workers' houses throughout the whole Pittsburgh section. There are to be some 5,000 units in the city and county, just as soon as Congress passes the additional appropriation for $150 million for houses. Meanwhile, the housing authorities of the city and county are preparing themselves to carry on the work with the utmost speed just as soon as the order comes. The directors of both authorities,[1] Dr. Hoved and Mr. Palmer, were very cordial and seemed to be delighted to have me as one of the architects.

The trouble is that all the larger developments have already been promised to local architects, which is natural. So they offered me a small project outside of the city. . . . I asked for two jobs. They both will have to be done at the same time and in a period of four or five weeks. It will be, to a large extent, personal work, so I am taking on plenty.[2]

Dr. Hoved had objected to any local architect having more than one job, but they agreed they would try to arrange so that I got two. It is like being offered two parts in a play. Quite a compliment, but two minor parts. I guess I will have to take them if the offer comes. I must work (sounds like my wife talking) and if I refuse those little affairs, even if there is nothing constructive about them, the bigger ones will cease coming. . . .

I think that one of the reasons I am anything but happy about the prospect of this job is the fact that, if I do it, I cannot see how I can go out to Los Angeles to give the week of talks. But I have had no message from [the] University of Southern California.

Your letter about your jobs just arrived.[3] When do they start?

All my love,

Clarence

1. The Pittsburgh City and Allegheny County Housing Authorities.

2. The project designs were excellent, but the pace of this work and other defense housing work during 1941 may have been more than Stein could manage. Early in the fall of 1942, Clarence would experience another nervous breakdown, a bout of depression more serious than the one he had suffered early in 1937.

3. Aline had taken a part in the film *Out of the Fog.*

319   To Aline Stein

[New York City]   April 29, 1941

Aline dear:

I saw a wonderful exhibit this afternoon, the architectural work of the TVA. What characterful stuff—big and at the same time beautiful, overwhelmingly beautiful. The power and grandeur of great objectives expressed with simplicity and straight-forwardness. What luck that a new, fresh movement was able to get an architect like Roland Wank with a fresh and modern point of view. I met John Carmody of the Federal Works Agency at the show, and he asked me how they happened to find Wank. And I took the opportunity to suggest that Wank should be brought to Washington some day and [be given] a [a role in the] Public Buildings Administration. Roland at lunch had told me that he hoped that might happen some time. He [Wank] would make a wonderful chief architect of that division, which [under Carmody] is in charge of the design and construction of public buildings.

Wank and I had a fine talk. His angle on the future rebuilding of America and mine fit together. They were not able to come to dinner, as the TVA crowd were going to the theater. Both Wanks asked about you and sent regards.

The . . . exhibit opened with talks by Boon, the mayor, and Lillienthal [chairman of TVA]. [There is] also a new movie about TVA—a very talky, teachy movie, but interesting.

I am just about to leave for Pittsburgh—two days there. I hope I return with assurance of a job or two.

Clarence

320   To Aline Stein

The Pittsburgher, Pennsylvania Railroad   May 13, 1941

Beloved:

Nearing Pittsburgh—clear skies beyond the smoke and soot, brown waters. rows of houses perched on crags.

And me, to quote, is about to bring home the bacon. So we hope. We will know before the day is over.

And then work, steady work until July 2nd, which is the date on which the design of the two developments must be finished. After that, unless another job comes, I may be tempted to go west if the Casa is not crowded. Who knows? Who knows what will have happened to our world in the next six weeks?

But now I feel fit to do anything.

Last night, after dinner in our "sky parlor," Gert, Ben, and I went to the Hudson

Guild to see a special performance of the Cellar Players. As I told John Elliott,[1] it thrilled me more to see Will Gowrie again than it would to see Booth. Gowrie is my past, and he is still good at sixty.

Clarence

1. John Elliott was Clarence Stein's old friend and teacher, who had now taken over the work of Felix Adler in the Society for Ethical Culture in addition to his work at the Hudson Guild settlement house in Chelsea.

---

321   To Aline Stein

[New York City]   May 20, 1941

Beloved:

I expect to fly [to Pittsburgh] at seven tonight, spend the night with the [Isidore Simons],[1] and then, if possible, return tomorrow night. I can't stay away from here long. Ten men working on the job now, and I have to keep pouring out ideas and decisions to keep them going.

[Clarence]

1. Isidore Simons was Jennie Simons Mac's brother, who built the FHA-financed garden apartment complex Morewood Gardens in Pittsburgh.

---

322   To Aline Stein

Morewood Gardens, Pittsburgh   May 22, 1941

Beloved:

I am seated at a window looking out on small brick houses surrounded by great trees.[1] In the cloudy distance: church steeples, no sight of belching smokestacks. It is difficult to believe that this is Pittsburgh. There, the church bells ring. It is like an English collegiate town.

And do you know where one of my housing developments is? In Stowe township. When I go out there, I always think of the Cotswold and you, and me. How lovely it was. Stowe here is different. It has a beauty, but not a tender beauty. It is high up above the Ohio River, and below is the fierce, ugly beauty of industrial Pittsburgh.

I am enjoying these jobs. Everyone here is doing their best to help. Generally, Housing Authorities want to show authority, little toads blowing themselves up and looking wise, but these folks are giving me everything I ask for, pretty nearly. They believe in me and so naturally I have got to give them everything I have.

Yesterday [Ralph] Eberlin and I spent a busy day gathering information and visiting the sites. . . . Then Eberlin and I went to visit Mr. [Ralph] Griswald, who is to do our landscape work. [Eberlin] returned to New York, but I stayed over to get approval on drawings I brought from New York.

In the dark beside me, you look straight at me from [Steichen's] beautiful photo of 1933, my darling.

Virginia and Is send love to you and Jennie Mac, and so do I.

Clarence

1. Stein's defense housing projects in Shaler and Stowe Townships outside Pittsburgh were, as were most of their kind early in the war, of simple but permanent construction. Both are distinguished by their excellent site planning.

323   To Aline Stein

[New York City]   May 22, 1941

Dearest:

I am home again, after a rocky air trip, but there were letters from you—two, such dear letters. You are so happy. We might as well live as fully as we can, and meanwhile I want to do my job, think it through, the physical world we will make, if the Nazi heel doesn't stamp us out.

And meanwhile design, build, that is the best of all, and they pay me for it! At last this afternoon I got a contract. Over ten thousand dollars and most of the expenses paid. I can't send any to you now because it is only a promise and I have to finance an expensive office, but it will come. So cheer up, even more, and we will get some of the bank debts cleared up and pay the back taxes, and live happily ever after, even if it may be very short.

So it is kind of mixed sentiments, you see. . . .

Give my love to Jennie Mac and my best to Johanna, and keep the best love for Aline.

Clarence

324   To Aline Stein

[en route to Yorktown, N.Y.]   May 23, 1941

Aline dear:

I have just left a noon meeting with AIA [members] Carl Stern, Ralph Walker, and Harold Buttenheim. . . .

I am trying to write this on my way to Harmon, bouncing along, with the beautiful Hudson outside the [train] window and me very tired after a strenuous week at Washington. So it will be short.

My headquarters now are transferred to New York. I am going to try to put the requirements of community facilities into diagram form in the office. I will go to Washington [as general consultant to the Federal Works Agency on defense housing] perhaps a day each week, or someone will come from Washington.

Just at present the whole thing seems so big and complicated that I wonder how I will pull through in time to be of use, but I know a good, restful day at the farm will make everything look different.

I have been working on the per diem basis, which really does not leave much in the treasury when expenses are paid. I have been trying to have this changed to a contract basis, which was finally agreed to on Thursday. Expenses of office and self (when traveling) will be paid, and there will be a fee. Just how much was not settled, but the important thing was to get an agreement that my drafting was to be covered and that I could make headquarters in New York.

. . . So delighted about *Journey for Margaret.*[1] Tell me about it tomorrow. Your letters are wonderful.

Love,
Clarence

1. Aline's film, with Robert Young, Laraine Day, Fay Bainter, Nigel Bruce, and Margaret O'Brien, was a successful World War II drama.

325　To Aline Stein

[New York City]　May 28, 1941

Aline darling:

I was so tired last night [that] I went to bed long before the president spoke. But I got up to hear him—great talk. But I missed something, a positive purpose. It is a war of defense we are to fight, we must fight, so that we who are Jews will not be destroyed. But, on the positive side, the president is not so clear. Democracy and world trade are mixed motives. When he talks of "freedom of the seas," he is thinking of capitalism, not democratic freedom. I wish we had a more positive picture of a better world we were going to fight for, but fight we must if only so that we may have the chance in the future of doing something with our little pieces of the world.

The Pittsburgh projects are moving along. I think I am going to develop something that is just another step forward, but I can't be sure yet.

The rest of this paper is on the way.[1] I could not resist sending you a sample.

All my love,
Clarence

1. Clarence had had new stationery printed with a sketch he had made of Casa, Aline's Los Angeles home, at the top.

326   To Aline Stein

[New York City]   June 12, 1941

Beloved:

Yesterday, all day, in Washington. The morning I spent at the office of [the] Federal Works Agency, showing Klein Fulmer and others my Pittsburgh jobs. . . .

I attended the weekly meeting of review of progress of the housing work under way. John Carmody, all energy, driving the 200 million dollar program ahead top speed at a desk way at the end of a great paneled office. In front of them the chiefs of districts and agencies, the lawyers, and what not behind large diagrams showing just where each job stands. Carmody [is] bellowing "Why? Why can't you get the land there? What is holding up the survey here? Why not move the tenants in there?" Have got the sense of something happening for defense.

In the afternoon [I] drove out to Indian Head to check progress. It is going through the messy period where nothing has jelled. Such ugly knockdown houses. Trees are the only thing that will save them.

Back to town just in time to attend a reception at the White House for a housing organization whose meetings I was supposed to be at. The White House is a lovely place for meeting folks. I mean, the gardens are such a gracious place—great lawns and lovely old trees. Mrs. Roosevelt smiled at each of us as she shook hands. What a bore it must be. There was a long tablecloth from which lemonade and cookies were dispensed. And all the housers were there and partook. . . .

All my love,
Clarence

327   To Aline Stein

[New York City]   June 26, 1941

Darling:

It seems foolish to write. I will be with you so soon. That is, unless another job gets in the way, and it certainly would have to be very big and bulky. My thoughts are in California, and I hope that next week will find the rest of me there. We have been at the two ends of the world too long.

Meanwhile, it is grind, grind, grind. Time is short; time is flying. Decisions must be made immediately. The work of the various technicians must be coordinated. The form of and plan of the house and the site work, the sewers, the water lines, the gas lines and the electric poles, the roads and paths and steps—every step just where it belongs and a place for the garbage can. And then the landscape work—each shrub and tree in its place, and each engineer must know what the other is doing so

12322-23ᴿᴰ HELENA DRIVE · BRENTWᴼᴼD HEIGHTS · LOS ANGELES · CAL·

June 25. 1941

that the electric poles and the trees don't get in each other's way. They must know at once, so they waste no time, and we all finish on the dot.[1]

It is great fun. We are doing some new things. I am learning. One of these days I will really be ready to do that city. If I were only younger . . .

My love,
Clarence

1. Clarence was working to a July 1 deadline for both Pittsburgh projects (in Stowe and Shaler Townships). When he had submitted the drawings, he would go by train to California and stay until late in July.

---

328   To Benton MacKaye

[New York City]   August 1, 1941

Dear Ben:

Since my return I have been hard at it again to get out another of these Defense projects. They are really the stuff—just the kind of thing I attempted to describe in my *Common Sense* article. I am very anxious to show you the model that we have just made of this last project.[1]

I have not yet found time to get to Washington, but I propose to go there either the end of next week or the beginning of the following week.

Next Wednesday I am going to Lewis [Mumford's] to spend the day with him. In the evening we are going to talk at the Housatonic Valley Conference. The subject is The City: Past, Present, and Future. The other speaker is Earle S. Draper.[2] Lewis [will] start off with an historical introduction, then I am going to make a very quick sketch of what I consider the elements of the future city. I think Draper will probably agree as to the general elements but will argue that we should rebuild old cities. I will talk in favor of starting off with the building of New Towns. We may get into somewhat of an argument; anyhow, we will try to keep the good citizens of the Valley awake for a couple of hours.

I am very anxious to see both you and Lewis. I feel that the time is ripe for a good deal of active public instruction on the subject of the building of cities. Just what the best way to go about it is, I do not know. But the way there is an excellent article in the last number of *Common Sense* called "Build Garden Cities Near Aircraft Plants" by a young architectural draftsman, Alan Nathan, who works in Detroit. He takes the same point of view that I did in my article but has a great deal of interesting factual material.

Do write and tell me what you are doing and whether anything has developed for the future.

As always,

[Clarence]

1. The third and, Stein believed, best of his projects was southeast of Pittsburgh at Clairton in Allegheny County. It included more community facilities than did his other Pittsburgh defense housing projects. It was not built.

2. Draper was a planner for the TVA.

---

329   To Aline Stein

[Amenia, N.Y.]   August 8, 1941

Aline darling:

Wednesday morning I went by train to Amenia. By noon I was there. It is pleasant, quiet country, but none of the excitement of the wild west.

Lewis and I had a long leisurely talk through the afternoon. So much of the world to put aright. He looks wonderful. Getting away on a trip to San Francisco and the Northwest was good for him. Sophie also looks all right—aging a little. [She is] the good wife with an interest in local affairs. She has accepted the role of the wife of the noted writer, Lewis Mumford. He is about to disappear into the making of his third great volume.

In the evening we drove over to Connecticut and performed. Why they got three of us to talk to some seventy people (and they are to pay us each a hundred dollars) is hard to explain, but we enjoyed it, and they don't have to suffer often, those sleek, well-fed highbrows of the Berkshires and the Housotanic. . . .

We are finishing the drawings of the Pittsburgh job, even though it will not be built at once.

Love,

Clarence

330 To Aline Stein

[New York City]   August 17, 1941

Me on a Sunday morning—at the top of the world, on high in our redwood summer palace.

I have been reading *The Coming Struggle for Power,* and I had just reached "the capitalistic system is dying and cannot be revised" when Hilda appeared with a great basket of breakfast, which she spread on the table beside me. . . . Outside I could see Ted working for us, and below is the sound of Johnson's hammer and his son's sawing as they build shelves in which to preserve our apples for us. And I lean back and say, "This is a beautiful, comfortable world in which to wait for the end of capitalism. How long?"

Certainly not before I see you next Wednesday.

My love,
Clarence

331 To Melville Dozier[1]

[New York City]   October 23, 1941

Dear Mr. Dozier:

I was so sorry not to see you while I was in California this last trip. As your office has probably told you, I tried a number of times but had bad luck in calling and telephoning when you were away.

I visited both Carmelitos and Harbor Hills.[2] I was delighted with the appearance of both of them. Harbor Hills in detail is, I think, one of the best projects in the country. Carmelitos is very attractive. However, I still think that the scheme we originally developed would have had more charm. . . .

May I ask you for just one additional favor? I noted in your office some months ago, when I called on you, some airplane photographs of the model of Carmelitos as we originally laid it out. If you have extra prints of any of these, I would appreciate having them.

You will be interested to know that the architectural magazine *Pencil Points* is publishing a rather lengthy article on Harbor Hills in its next number.

The next time I am in Los Angeles, I hope I have better luck and that we may have an opportunity to visit Harbor Hills and Carmelitos together.

With kindest regards,
[Clarence S. Stein]

1. Dozier was executive director of the Housing Authority of the County of Los Angeles.
2. These are the Los Angeles public housing projects designed by Clarence Stein in 1938, working in association with local architects. An article on the "Harbour Hills" public housing community appears in *Pencil Points* 22, no. 11 (1941): 667–83.

332   To Benton MacKaye

[New York City]   [Jan. 16, 1942]

Dear Ben:

Above is pictured my first venture out of doors. Yesterday I was guided from bench to bench by the boss.[1] It was sunny, almost springlike, and we covered two blocks going and coming! You know the feeling. . . .

The Truman Committee certain[ly] lambasted them. Stone . . . had the dope.[2]
We mailed (or expressed) you a book to the house yesterday.

Our best,

Aline and Clarence

1. The sketch at the top of this letter shows Clarence with Aline walking along Central Park West in front of their apartment building. Stein was recovering from his second or third nervous breakdown, caused by overwork in his consulting on and design of defense housing in Washington and Pittsburgh. This work had required months of triangular commuting by rail and air among New York, Washington, and Pittsburgh.

2. Senator Truman had chaired a Senate investigation of the costs of defense spending. His committee's sessions were based in part on the information developed in Is Stone's investigative reporting. His reports revealed overcharges by various defense contractors.

---

333   To Benton MacKaye

1 W. 64, NYC   March 17, 1942

Dear Ben:

I had hoped to get to Washington before you left to say good-bye. But I am afraid there is going to be nothing doing. So we will have to do our talking by letter.

Robert Kohn has written a letter of introduction for you to Dr. Sidney Schwab of St. Louis. He doesn't remember his address but says you should have no trouble finding him, as he is a well-known doctor.

Days here are a bit dreary, cloudy, and rainy. But the feel of spring is in the air. Nonetheless, we spent the weekend in the city. I [was] in Pittsburgh Thursday and Friday, climbing muddy hills to see my housing (not so bad). Got back Saturday morning, a little tired. It was raining pitchforks. Good day to spend in bed. So we stayed here. Sunday more loafing and a little writing. In the afternoon we walked across the park and down the avenue, filled with folks practicing for Easter. The rain had ceased and the sun appeared now and then. And so to the Hitchcocks', where we called on Lady Unwin. She has hurt her back, but they are taking good care of her and it is much better.

Aline is busy with her big job. The theater wing has appointed an excellent committee [to provide entertainment for war industry workers] representing the various elements connected with the theater. Aline is secretary, and I guess boss. Anyhow she is enjoying it.[1]

No work for me as yet. Housing apparently hasn't settled down to work yet. Meanwhile, I am gathering strength for the spring drive.

Aline and I send our best to you. May St. Louis be a place of new adventures and new discoveries. And so, the New Deal briefcase moves on.

Clarence

1. During the early years of World War II in Europe, Aline was active in organizing entertainment, including theatrical performances for U.S. defense industry workers. After the beginning of direct U.S. involvement in the fighting, she helped organize New York City performers for the United Service Organizations (USO) entertainment for military groups.

---

334 To Aline Stein

[New York City]   April 18, 1942

Aline darling:

. . . It sounds fine on location at Lake Arrowhead. When do you go?

. . . The Paul Kerns were there. They are so much younger than I expected. And he was not at all explosive, as one would judge from the newspapers. They have the sixth-floor apartment here, to which we are supposed to retreat if the enemy attacks us. Quite a nice party we will have there: the Ackermans and the musical lady on our floor (she is [Jerome] Kern's aunt), Henry Arensburg, and so on. Later came others, including a Negro writer, Wright.[1] We talked far into the night on the lack of clarity of war objectives. How difficult it must be for the young soldiers. How the attitude in America toward the Negro (in army, navy, the housing development at Detroit) is harmful to hope of solidity with colored races in India and elsewhere in the orient.

Thursday evening I went to a dinner of the Architectural League and enjoyed it! Not the food, of course, but the spirit of the talk. Hugh Ferris has made a trip to [the] Tennessee Valley. Great and useful architecture has been created as of late. He went on a scholarship and has brought back a series of exciting drawings. At last Ferris has found subjects where he does not have to exaggerate the scale. He spoke well. And Albert Kahn, who designs the miles of great factories in Detroit, told us how his army of draftsmen is producing at top speed. He is a shrewd one but a good, straightforward architect, also.

The star of the evening was Roland Wank. Many of his mighty and beautiful jobs were illustrated on the wall. He spoke well, quietly and naturally. Against the background of that great work [for the] TVA, he showed how the architect's functions and opportunities were broadened when he was serving the people and not an individual. It was a thrilling talk.

Yesterday noon I lunched with him. He sends his best.

All my love,
Clarence

1. Richard Wright, author of *Native Son* and other works depicting the struggle of blacks against racism in the south and Chicago in the 1930s.

335   To Aline Stein

[New York City]   April 21, 1942

Darling:

Here I am home again, home again, after a day in Washington.[1] It is spring there, blossoms everywhere. Such masses of white and pink dogwood and deep purple blossoms. . . . In spite of nature's joyfulness, the Washington folk seem tense and jittery. [I] guess they feel a bit uncertain about their jobs. My impression comes mainly from housing folks, who have gone through a couple of official earthquakes and don't know yet just where they are landing.

Herbert Emmerich, who is up on top, shuffling the cards, has plenty of troubles. I had a long talk with him, five hours or so, at his house late Sunday afternoon and evening. He is tired, but I think he is going to like his job; at least he will do it if it can be done. As Herbert says, at present it is much like swimming in mucilage. . . .

. . . We spoke of the work that is to be done around Washington, and I told Herbert that I hoped they would not lose the opportunity of building at least one satellite community with a department building serving as industry.[2]

Herbert gave me the name of the man that he had just appointed as head of the Washington area. Klein introduced me to him the following day, and I told him I would like to do a job, and so it goes.

Herbert may want me to head up a study of the community needs of the new developments, perhaps. . . .

Love,
Clarence

1. Stein had recovered sufficiently from his illness to resume consulting duties on housing policy with the Federal Works Administration (FWA)/Federal Public Housing Administration (FPHA) on the national program of housing for war workers.
2. This was a recurring idea of Stein's, which he would have an opportunity to develop after World War II, when Truman and his advisors on national security made a serious effort to disburse federal government workers to satellite employment centers as protection against atomic attack from the U.S.S.R.

336   To Aline Stein

Washington, [D.C.][1]   Wednesday, April 29, 1942

Aline darling:

It is almost eleven, time for bed, and am I tired. . . .

For two days I have been busy getting a bird's eye view of my job and trying to escape the temptation of getting into—or too deep—in any of the details of the problem.[2] My headquarters is in the office of one of the people that you met, Howard White, who is in charge of management of community facilities for housing. Everyone in the office remembers you. The secretary was so thrilled to have Aline MacMahon['s husband] call on her. I have become a special favorite as a result. Miss Reeder is attending all of our meetings. She wants to be remembered also.

Today we were in constant sessions from nine to almost five. We discussed recreational facilities with Britter of the Recreational Association in the morning. The requirements are completely changing in these war communities as a result of (1) the three shifts and therefore need of quiet around the houses, (2) higher incomes, (3) threat of air raids, (4) need of keeping up morale, (5) migratory workers with no roots in the community, (6) the mothers possibly becoming workers. This means, among other things, that there must be care for the preschool children away from the houses, nursery schools or something.[3]

In the afternoon we took up stores. Tomorrow morning we will meet with the doctors and discuss health problems. Then there are schools and restaurants, [which need] fire protection and everything, and somewhere there [have] got to be halls in which plays can be given!

I was going back to New York tomorrow afternoon to attend a housing meeting at which Herbert Emmerich is going to speak, but I guess I will have to stay on another day. Then back to New York and the farm to let some of this soak in, then probably here again Monday. . . .

All my love,

Clarence . . .

1. This letter was written on stationary with the letterhead of the Federal Housing Administration, which meant that it came from the office of Eugene Henry Klaber, Clarence's longtime friend, who was now working for the FHA. Clarence stayed at his home in Washington during his weekly stints of work on war housing policies for community facilities.

2. The character of Clarence Stein's handwriting was changing from that of letters written earlier in 1942. The long horizontal strokes and long vertical downstrokes on his *y*'s in this and following letters were similar to changes in his handwriting before his sessions of mental depression in 1936.

3. The quality of day care in war worker communities was quite good. For extended analysis of day-care policies, see Dolores Hayden, *Redesigning the American Dream: The Future of Housing, Work, and Family* (New York: W. W. Norton, 1984).

---

337   To Aline Stein

The Hay-Adams House, Washington, D.C.   Wednesday, May 6, 1942

Aline darling:

This week we are concentrating on the dormitories. There are no end of community problems. The disappearance of the auto is going to mean isolation for these units. They must, therefore, be grouped around community centers that will contain not only recreation rooms—medical care—at least preventative and isolation rooms, but also eating places.

We devoted this afternoon to restaurants with a group of experts who had had varied experience in feeding large groups of people. . . . One of the most interesting was a Mr. Weber, who had been invited over to Russia to advise them on their problems of mass feeding. They really planned, those Russians. They had limited quantities of everything. They could not waste it. They learned—how to do more with less by planning and by discipline. I wonder if we can learn after our years of wasted plenty. Their cafeterias were wonderfully well organized; food was determined on a scientific basis—health and economy and as much enjoyment as possible. In the beginning all feeding for new centers, such as the city they built around the Denieper Dam, was in the social centers, each of which took care of about 500 people. The children had separate dining halls from their parents. There is probably a good deal we are going to learn from the Russians during this war, but we are not going to tell Congress about it.

The . . . housing representative developer was present and suggested that the cafeterias be made cooperative under the unions at such places as Detroit. He said that was the best way to prevent the men complaining.

I opened the meeting by calling attention to the difference in the point of view we must make in planning these communities from our normal outlook. The essential objective must be to win the war. Efficient workers, in [the] sense of productive capacity, means scientific, wholesome eating in pleasant surroundings. The basis of operation must be good diet, not profit. The three shifts brought up complications of operations, as did [the] lack of transportation.

This feeding problem is only one of the many things we are trying to get settled quickly enough to get community facilities for the dormitories that are being planned, built, or are already lived in.

I love you my darling,

Clarence

---

338   To Benton MacKaye[1]

[New York City]   May 25, 1942

Dear Ben:

For weeks I have been intending to write to you, but I have been so much on the go, running back and forth between here and Washington, that there never seems to be time enough to tell you all about it. I have decided not to attempt to do so, but just to get off a letter that will tell you that I am still here.

Most of my time has been spent at Washington. I have been returning to New York for weekends and have been able to spend Sundays up at the farm. The only trouble I find is that the seasons have been rushing each other a little bit too quickly: I miss a great many of the changes between weekends. The apple blossoms were there one Sunday, and a rainstorm did away with them. The next weekend the dogwood trees were in bloom, and now they are gone, and the trees have taken on an almost summer foliage.

Washington is more and more of a madhouse. Nobody seems to know where they are going. The situation is made more complicated every day because of the growing scarcity of various materials.

There are a few good things to report about the place, however. One of them is that Herbert Emmerich, whom you remember, is now head of the Federal Public Housing Authority. He knows something about what it's all about as a result of having worked with all of us at Radburn when he was manager of the City Housing Corporation.

I can't remember now just how much I have told you about my job. Here's just a brief outline. Emmerich asked me to help determine just what is needed in community facilities for the different types of workers' villages. As you know, the last administration left out everything, or practically everything, but shelter. And even now there isn't anything more than a feeble beginning at supplying that. Detroit alone will need 100 to 120 thousand new workers' shelters after every house there is filled. Rubber and gas is giving out: there isn't enough material to go around to build the houses. To conserve building materials, there is a strong tendency to build dormitories for workers—both men and women, with the idea that the number to be housed will be immensely decreased if the families are left behind.

The question of community facilities to be supplied must be determined on a quite different basis than that of peacetime. The conservation of the working power and the enthusiasm of the worker are essential factors to production, and luckily we have in Emmerich someone who is aware of it before it is too late. Against the need of adequate living quarters and facilities for recreation, for good eating, for care of health, and all that must be balanced the critical need of conserving most kinds of building material.

Some of the unusual conditions that we have had to consider in determining what we would recommend are (1) long hours; (2) three shifts (necessitating quiet around homes and dormitories and bringing up the question of day care of children in the case of family units); (3) workers isolated from their families (means greater need of community facilities and health care and meals they would normally get at home); (4) limitation of transportation (which makes isolated communities of a good many of the communities which, in the old days of the auto, would have been near the movies and all that); (5) the essential importance of contented, healthy workers; (6) the growing number of women workers; (7) production plants in isolated or overpopulated areas.

It has been an exciting and fascinating job. How well I am going to find answers that can be realized in this mad rush is to be seen. I shall probably be working on it here in New York from now on, for the most part.

More when I get more time. Do keep on writing to me, even if I don't do my part.[2]

I phoned Aline yesterday; she is fine.

My best to you.

[Clarence]

1. MacKaye was in St. Louis on government business.

2. Community planning associated with war housing was a challenge to which Clarence seemed to have given his full energy. Again, as in the case of his consultation on the Greenbelt Towns program, he believed that he would prefer to be doing community planning rather than assessing policy options. And again he was assessing policy thoroughly and learning much from the process.

---

339   To Aline Stein

[A Thousand Years]   Sunday, June 7, 1942

Aline dear:

I am writing this lying on the bed up in the sky house. The Carl Sterns and the Ralph Walkers were here. A delightfully successful party. The Sterns walked with me around the circle and were properly enthusiastic. We had a fine dinner and much good talk and missed you very much.

I feel so much better after this and last night's party at the Bernsteins—got away from the mental grinding chase. It was such a relief to talk to you about it. I hated to pass any of my troubles on to you, but it seems so foolish to keep anything hidden. I feel now as though I were going to get things in hand. I will try to go at a slower pace. Don't worry about me. I know what I should do, just as though you were here to tell me, and I will do my best as far as the job permits. I know I must go at it slower if I am to be of real value. . . .[1]

It would be unbelievably wonderful if you were coming home for a while. But don't let it interfere with the job. My love to Jennie Mac.

Beloved mine,

Clarence

1. Clarence seemed very much aware of the symptoms of his breakdown, but he was denying them and was trying to overcome the downward slide he was experiencing.

340   To Aline Stein

[Silver Hill, New Canaan, Conn.][1]   Monday evening, July 6, 1942

My darling:

I have been reading Lin Yutang's translation which you brought me, and my thoughts have gone back to those lovely days in Peking and Sochow and to you, my beloved—you, you, you. How I love you.

There has been so much that we have had in the past, and there is so much that we will have together in the future. But there are just a few days that we will try to cut out of the picture.

We have had a heavy storm this evening, and how the air is clear and fresh.

And things are clearer here, too. Next Sunday we will be in another world, our old world.[2]

I love you so. That is everything.

Clarence

1. On 19 June 1942, Clarence Stein was sixty years old. The stress of his continual travel between New York City and Washington while working on FPHA community facility policy and programs, the loneliness of being separated from Aline, and the technical and political difficulties of his tasks in Washington overcame Clarence's determination to continue in the job. Sometime between a letter of 10 June to Aline and 6 July (the date of the first letter in the Stein Papers from Silver Hill in 1942), Clarence experienced another mental collapse. After hospitalization (probably in New York City), he moved to the sanitarium at Silver Hill in New Canaan, Conn., for a long recuperation that was extended until the end of 1942.

2. In July 1942, Clarence was already spending some days away from Silver Hill visiting Aline at A Thousand Years and their New York apartment.

---

341   To Aline Stein

[Silver Hill]   Saturday, August 29, 1942

Aline dear:

Yesterday was bright and clear and cool. This morning is cloudy after a rainy night.

Everything is moving along. I saw Dr. DuBois yesterday morning. He laid out a program of taking things easier and slower. I have a young nurse, Mrs. Runyon.

Yesterday morning we went through the regular morning program of breakfast, newspaper, study, walk, but at a more leisurely pace than before. Then I wrote to you. This afternoon—rest and shop. We had tea at the Terhunes', a biggish house of stone and a good deal of colonial. The spacious English house is American.

After dinner [I] played Liverpool rummy, a more complicated gin rummy, [and then had] a good night's sleep.

The crowd here is much as it was. A few have gone, and there are a number of new faces.

I was so happy to receive your letter of yesterday. I am so glad that you are so enthusiastic about the play.[1]

Sunday will be difficult without you, but I will be looking forward to the next week.

All my love,
Clarence

1. Aline was back on Broadway acting in Thornton Wilder's play, *The Skin of Our Teeth*.

---

342   To Aline Stein

Silver Hill, New Canaan, Conn.   October 27, 1942

Aline dear:

It is beautiful[ly] clear. The air is cool, almost cold and dry. The trees are, to a large extent, bare, but here and there are masses of brilliant leaves—a day of days. I wish you were here.

We have just returned from a brisk walk around the "big loop"—some three and a half miles or more. I feel top of the world, not quite top, but on the way. This afternoon I expect to put on my warm clothes and go out and paint.

Early this morning I had a long talk with DuBois. He is convinced that this grew out of the Washington experience: that I was not physically 100% when I started; that the traveling was a physical strain; that I took on too much of a job or rather went at it too vigorously and that it got a hold of me psychologically. Sounds simple. He does not believe there are hidden causes, such as we discussed. He tells me he is convinced of a cure and that he sees me well on the way.[1] The cure, he says, can be permanent.

I think it is up to CSS with some of Aline's sense.

It was so good to have the two days with you, darling. Home, home, home, our lovely home and you, that is the center of the universe.

I called on the Bernsteins for a short time after you left. It seems that they had spent the weekend in town, and Ethel (who is looking much better) could have come up for a later supper.

It was all fine, and next week—the farm. Meanwhile, take care of yourself, beloved.

All my love,
Clarence

P.S. I heard Wilkie over the radio on my return. Sounded good, but I want to read parts of it.

1. Early in the month (on 1 October), Dr. DuBois had told Clarence Stein that he was on an upward swing.

---

343 To Benton MacKaye

[New York]   November 23, 1942

Dear Ben:

Am in town just for a couple of days. Have been enjoying the view from our sky parlor. Last night the full moon was out, and this morning the sun rose in a brilliant mass of clouds. I wish you could have been here.

Aline's play is making a great success. No telling how long it will go on running. We are very anxious that you see it, and, of course, we want very much to have you come East before long. Was terribly disappointed that you couldn't arrange to meet me at the farm Thanksgiving time.

Cannot tell you how much I appreciate your continuing your one-sided correspondence. Both Aline and I were so delighted with your message to the ATC [Appalachian Trail Club]. It is queer that a play by Thornton Wilder that opened last week, *The Skin of Our Teeth,* attempts to approach problems that we are facing in very much the same way. Although it was a fantastic play, it looks as though the public [is] really interested.

I will be writing you more in detail soon. Affectionate greetings from Aline.

As always,

Clarence

I am going back to Silver Hill this evening but hope to be here in New York before long.

---

344 To Benton MacKaye

Silver Hill, New Canaan, Connecticut   Dec. 6, 1942

Dear Ben:

Your postal of Friday arrived today. I am glad you are off on your field trip and will have a chance to find out what the middle-west farmer really thinks about it all.

I find myself growing more and more skeptical about the possibility of our winning a peace that is worth all the sacrifice that is being made. I, of course, recognize the need of a war of defense. But as to any clarity [of] purpose: of a better, saner world, of preventing the possibility of future mad wars, I think there is much less sign than there was the last time. Michael Straight makes that clear in the *New Republic* of November 30th. Do you remember how we were thrilled by [President] Wilson's talks and messages? We had an awful letdown afterward, it is true. But this time there seems to be so little constructive[ness] for which Mike and the rest of the boys are giving their best years, and maybe all.

Aline's play shows that the fight must be made. By the way, the play is a great success, but it looks as though it [will] go on and on for a long time.

Meanwhile, we olders should be planning some way of making a stand against "the business as usual" gang. They sure are going to take us for a ride way up. I can see the foundations being laid, housing and city . . . building already. The banks and insurance companies are coming out for large-scale building and management. All the good ideal, but the government to buy the land and then practically give it to them, with the Realtors running that show and the State Department prepared to write a peace treaty and probably putting the Demons in power. Seems to me it is about time you and I and a few others should begin to raise hell. I will be wanting to help in something constructive soon. How about talking it over, over a big "se-gar," and straightening things out a bit?

Weather here has been wonderful—cold and clear. It was so good that I did not make my regular weekend trip to New York.

If Aline were here she would send her best,

As does
Clarence

---

345   To Aline Stein

Silver Hill, New Canaan, Conn.   December 10, 1942

Aline beloved:

The first snow is very beautiful. From my corner room I get broad views of it. The loveliest part are the golden weeping willows against the white-outlined firs—fond recollections of One Thousand Years.

I have been painting as never before—real freedom and control of color and movement. [It is] far the best thing I have done, even though it is only a pile of vegetables.

The snow is freezing a little, so that one must walk with care. But we still do the loop. In fact, life goes on with the regularity of the clock, come snow, come rain, come sunshine, and it has been mainly sunshine.

I have been about to write you for days, but I have thought I would be with you. I probably will be before this reaches you. I am so happy that you are on the go all the time, but I hope you don't overdo it.

I had this nice note from Jennie Mac, also a box of wonderful figs, etc.

Take care of yourself, my darling. I love you.

Clarence

346   To Aline Stein

Double U Ranch, Tucson, Arizona[1]   January 17, 1943

Aline dear:

I have just talked to Jennie Mac. I had hoped to get her before you did so that she could pass on my message to you. But you had talked to her just before.

We have been here two days now, and I have postponed writing because we have been trying to take things easy. And yet there is so much to see and so many things that we want to do. Arthur has probably told you of Lillie's letter and telegram, so you know something of the place and our adventures.

The ranch is in a flat valley surrounded by brown, craggy hills. I say brown but, of course, they change with the varying effects of clouds and sun. These last two days we have had more than our share of overhung skies. It's very beautiful, but a little chilly and not so good for sunbaths. We had one the first day, which was perfectly clear, and there are prospects of the sun coming out again this afternoon. But sun or shade, the air is wonderfully invigorating.

The surroundings and the ranch are very reminiscent of the places we visited outside of Palm Springs. There is a central building with lounges (and dining—of which I will tell you more some other time.) We had a steak that could almost compete with the Pacific Dining Car, if any steak can.

Lillie and I have a cottage with good-sized rooms with windows on three sides. Each of us has a bathroom. All is the simple Mexican. All [is] very spic and span. Around are cacti of various kinds and trees of various kinds, of which I will be sending you sketches once I get my hand in again. The birds—but they can wait. . . .

[Clarence]

1. By mid-January 1943 Clarence was sufficiently "himself" (as he sometimes put it) to leave Silver Hill. His doctors decided that he would recover completely and more rapidly by moving away from the excitement and cold winters of New York City to the peace and warm climate of Arizona. His sister Lillie accompanied him west. His nurse, Miss Robertson, went with him for the first few weeks. In addition to his other problems, Clarence now had contracted a case of shingles.

347   To Aline Stein

Double U Ranch, Tucson, Arizona   [March] 3, 1943

Aline dear:

Your letter written on the balcony a couple of days ago was so full of spring and joy that I feel sure that you are all right again.

As to myself—I just took a walk with Ella Robertson with the idea of telling her that I thought that I would be able to get along without her within a couple of weeks. She got ahead of me and suggested that she leave by the middle of the month. The skin trouble is gradually getting under control. One by one, the sore spots are passing away and new skin is forming. It has been slow work and takes no end of time painting them and all that. The bandages are long gone from my hands, and those on the legs we only put on when I go riding. We have come to the conclusion that the dry air, even more than the sunshine, is curing them. I can put on the salve and even the bandages now that the areas are restricted.

Miss Robertson has done a swell job in taking care of me. She has lots of common sense and tact, and she knows her stuff. She has personality. In fact, she has been one of the most popular persons here since we came. We were certainly lucky in getting her.

As far as the news now, there is no question that [my nerves] are immensely better, as Lillie must have told you. The trouble is not all over, but it is on the way out. It takes time, as we know only too well, but not much more. Anyhow, there is nothing Miss R. can do about that. It is up to CSS and time, with some help from the calm of this desert.

I will be home by the beginning of April or perhaps in time for our wedding anniversary. I have thought of going out to the coast, but Jennie Mac is coming East, and I will want to get home as soon as I get through here. I will make a beeline for New York, ready for work, if any. . . .

I am glad that Gerard Swope finds everything looking shipshape at the farm. That's fine. It was good of him. . . .

We have had our first rain since Lillie left. There had been a week of threatening clouds, [and] last evening and through the night we really had it—good thing. There has been too much dust. This morning there [are] alternating blue skies and dramatic clouds over the mountains. Miss Robertson and I took a good walk up high enough to get a good view of its grandeur.

She telegraphed Doctor Terhune, asking his approval of her departure on the 15th, as we both think it is all right. His answer came this morning. OK. So, that's that.

This rain should have cleared the air by the time that Henry [Klaber] arrives Saturday morning. I will see that he gets a good rest when he first gets here.

Write me about your play. How is it coming? Have you got good actors to take the place of the boys who have gone? Is it as popular as ever?

Hope you keep feeling fine.

Love,
Clarence

348   To Benton MacKaye

Double U Ranch, Tucson, Arizona   March 6, 1943

Dear Ben:

. . . This dude ranch, with all the comforts of home and the convenience of what we call civilization, is close to the wilderness, or near wilderness. Sometimes we ride over the mountains and into Bear Canyon. There is nothing there that is made by man excepting the narrow trail, and that is mainly the work of the horses, I guess. It crosses back and forth across the rapid stream that flows between the precipitous hills at either side of the canyon. Beautiful they are, warm brown rock above, strange, weird cactus below, tall monsters and little ball-like affairs that stick into you unless you look out. The trail leads up the mountainside, and sure-footed ponies take us to high points, from which we get broad views through the canyon to the desert valley and beyond to the distant hills. . . .

The peacefulness of the spacious valley, along with the clear, dry air and the warm sun, seem to be doing the job for me. I am getting as brown as an Indian. The skin trouble is gradually disappearing, and the old devil nerves is turning tail and slinking back into the desert like the coyote. Soon I will be ready to go back and find some way of doing my share in the big job of the present or in preparation for the future. . . .

Aline is leading an active life with her play (and the project for giving workers in the war industries a chance to be entertained) and no end of other things. I am sending you something she wrote about the young director of *The Eve of St. Marks.* . . .

More of my activities, or nonactivities, in a future letter.

Henry sends regards.[1]

My best to you,
Clarence

1. After Clarence's sister Lillie had left, his friend and former École des Beaux Arts roommate Henry Klaber had come to the ranch to "keep [Clarence] company and get a good rest."

349   To Aline Stein

[Double U Ranch], Tucson, Arizona   March 25, 1943

Aline dear:

The early morning is so beautiful from here on my porch. It is warm and clear. The sky is all blue and the mountains even lovelier than usual, if that is possible.

Henry [Klaber] and I are going to town [Tucson] to get our hair cut so that we will look somewhat civilized when we get home.[1]

My thoughts are all turned homeward. Yesterday afternoon I began to get my things together for packing. In the morning I finished the last picture I will make of the mountains. This time it is good, the best I have done. It is for you and our wedding anniversary. It will arrive a few days late, but what matter? We will celebrate when I get back.

I have been thinking yesterday, as I walked over the hills, of the good life we have had, you and I. You have made it, darling. Last year has been hard, but there are many to come and you are right—we have everything with which to make life good.

I can't wait to get back home and to you.

My love,
Clarence

1. Gertrude, Clarence's sister, helped pay the expense of Henry Klaber's vacation at the Double U Ranch as a companion for Clarence during the last weeks of his recovery.

---

350   To Lewis Mumford

New York City   April 4, 1943

Dear Lewis:

I got back from Arizona a few days ago and found your letter waiting for me. I was very happy to hear from you, although the news of the Mumford family was anything but joyful. We are . . . very sorry that Sophie has had such a bad time of it and that your students have disappeared. Although I would like to have you back here, I hope the army is going to take you on to teach the boys something about the future. It is going to be . . . very cold in the house at Amenia.

I returned to find Aline laid up with grippe, which has kept her away from the stage for a week, the first time she has had to let the play go on without her. But she expects to be back tomorrow. *The Eve of St. Marks* is a great success, still filling the house. It is a great play, and Aline does a wonderful job. It looks as though it [will] go on for some time. I hope it will still be here when you and Sophie return.

As to myself, I am well again; at least, I think I am completely my old self, excepting that I am taking things a little slowly—only a few hours a day at the office. There is no work. But I really don't care, for the present. I just want to be sure that I am back. And I want to think a while about the future.

I am at the problem of New York again. These last two days I have been outlining the after-war program, that is, what might be the program if anyone can be awakened to the fact that we actually face the Decline of the Great City—and particularly, this city. It was at a distance when we prophesied some twenty years ago, but it is here now. New York is not a war center and, when peace comes, it will find it hard work to regain its old place. New harbors, new industrial plants, new techniques are going to make it tough sailing for the old town, unless it is ready for drastic change. At least, so it looks to me, as I find myself out of the fog in which I was for so many months. I want to study some of the key industries of old New York and the trends of commerce and transportation, as far as we can see them. But more of this some other time.

Arizona was a great experience. I was there two and a half months on a dude ranch near Tucson. . . . The sun, clear dry air, the rest. Something out there seems to have done the job of curing me pretty thoroughly. So here I am, back in good old New York, which I love so much, in spite of all the faults I find. . . .

From Ben, I hear constantly. He seems to be enjoying his job.

Write me soon. I promise not to be so long in answering the next time.

Aline joins me in sending affectionate greetings to Sophie and you.

Clarence

---

351   To Benton MacKaye

1 W. 64 St., NYC   April 8, 1943

Dear Ben:

I am home again. It is wonderful after those months of absence. And I am my old self again, which is even more wonderful. The fog is gone. The mind clicks. It is too good to believe. So good that I am taking it back slowly and carefully, that fine, pretty world of ours. I fear I may lose it again unless I am careful.

Here it is, the view from our sky parlor, with the first glow of green just touching the trees. The sun rising over the buildings, so far north that I can just see it from my bed. And those superb afterglows of the evening—another beauty to compare with that of Arizona, and our very own. And then there is the apartment, all the lovely, familiar things. Here is New York; how I love it, in spite of all I may write or say of its mad disorder. And here are so many of my friends, who welcome me . . . so cordially. Only you I miss. But you have been with me constantly, as a result of our one-sided correspondence. I can't tell you how much your letters have meant to me this last year. And here, above all, is Aline.

Aline, poor dear—it has been her turn to be the sick one. For the last couple of weeks, she has had a bad attack of the grippe, which has kept her in bed most of the time. She even had to let the show go on without her for a week. She is back again since Monday but still has to take good care of herself.

As to my occupation, I have none. But, nonetheless, I find that there is much to do. There is no work at the office. That does not bother me now. I want to have time to get my feet on the ground, to get a perspective of things, and to prepare for the future. There is a vast accumulation of papers, books, drawings that I want to get rid of so that I can travel more lightly. So far, in the three hours or so a day that

I spend at the office, I have only succeeded in cleaning off the part of my big desk which is piled with things that have gathered since I left.

At home I am beginning another explorative survey of the future of New York. It looks as though the future that we foresaw some twenty years ago is now about to take shape. New York is losing ground. The city is not a war center, and, unless there are radical changes, the time is approaching when it will not be *the* peace center. The war has developed new forms of factories that will not fit into the compact cities or areas. [We have] improved other ports; [the country] will turn us toward the West far more than toward Europe, I believe. [We are] developing the airplane and its routes so that commerce may flow. . . . And so I am sitting down here again and trying to find where are we going? Where will New York best fit in the New world? And a whole lot of other things. I will not bother you about it, until it is more clearly outlined in my mind. I just wanted to tell you that, even without a job, there is much to be done in this fine, pretty world.

Aline joins me in affectionate greetings.

Clarence

---

352 To Lewis Mumford

1229 Ozetta Terrace, Los Angeles 46, California   October 6, 1943

Dear Lewis:

I have been here almost two months. I have intended to write you again and again, but there has been much to do.

I have been visiting no end of housing developments and studying the mad things that the government has been forced to do, often as a result of postponing action too long.[1] I have been particularly interested in the community facilities that have been set up. It's true that a good many of them are inadequate. Nonetheless, a good many important steps have been made in advance. They are now attacking the problem of the care of infants whose mothers are working. Some of the nurseries are very attractive places. They have also set up dispensaries in a great many of the larger developments. Some of these centers are so good that it's too bad that practically everything is now being built on the temporary basis. But all of this I'll tell you when I get back.

Just at present I am more interested in working out a scheme for an effective planning agency for the state of New York. Governor Dewey has expressed an interest in the matter, and [Harold] Buttenheim has asked me to work up a report to be submitted to the governor. To prepare me for the task, he asked quite a number of the planning agencies of various states to send me their reports. There are some forty-two of these state planning boards, or whatever they call them, and they have all been busy getting out voluminous documents—a good many of them the kind of thing that Benton calls the Chinese "laundry list."[2] I finally put them aside and tried to look at the problem that we face in New York State. It's really not very much different than it was some eighteen years ago, when our famous [1926] report was written. The problem is no different, but the need of a solution is even greater than it was then. Since that time, they've had a couple of planning agencies. They've been so one-sided and so powerless that they really have gotten nowhere.

As I think of it, I find that the old words "state planning" are now very unsatisfactory. Words certainly do get worn out by use. The Regional Plan of New York [and] Environs pretty well battered the title Regional Planning, and the state planning boards have given so many meanings to state planning that it says very little now.

It seems to me what we really need is a state redevelopment agency and one with power and ability to really do things. I don't think that a board composed of a good many [of the best] people gets anywhere. Look at housing in New York. Neither the State Housing Board nor the New York City Housing Authority ever had a new idea that was worth anything. The only good, live housing agency that we've had was under Winefield, who acted as a single state commissioner. It seems to me that, if we're going to get real results in state redevelopment, we need a single commissioner, and he will have to have standing and power. Unquestionably, it's going to require an all-around person. He'll have to know the state and enough about regional planning to know where he's going. Besides, he'll have to combine Bob Moses's ability at getting things done with Benton's understanding of what should be done.[3]

I have jotted down a few notes on an outline for my report, which I am enclosing. If you have time let me know what you think of them. . . .

Aline has finally started work on *Dragon's Seed*. They built a whole Chinese village out in Calabasa, with terraces to represent rice fields climbing up the hills behind. She starts at seven in the morning and doesn't get home until about seven in the evening. As Calabasa is about as hot a place as there is in this neighborhood, and this is the hot season for Los Angeles, it's not all fun.

I expect to get back to New York in about a month. I look forward to seeing you then.

Affectionate greetings to you and Sophie from Aline and

Yours,
Clarence

1. The FPHA had retained Stein to review progress on selected war housing developments.

2. The federal government, through FDR's Natural Resources Planning Board (NRPB), had funded the staff operations of a large number of state planning agencies during the 1930s. This work continued well into the early 1940s. Stein's seemingly low opinion of their work may have been caused by his very definite ideas of the need for strong state intervention in the urban and regional development process—a view not shared by most state planning agencies or, more importantly, by many state governments.

3. New York State came close to the ideal type of Clarence's proposal when Governor Nelson Rockefeller appointed Edward Logue to head the New York Urban Development Corporation in 1968.

---

353   To Benton MacKaye

Los Angeles, California   October 7, 1943

Dear Ben:

Just so that I keep [you] posted as to some of the things that I am doing, I am sending you a rough draft of a report I have been working on. Governor Dewey says he is interested in decentralization and state planning, so Harold Buttenheim has asked me to get together some ideas on the subject. I found after looking through the reports on the work of some forty or so State Planning Boards that I don't think very much of "planning" anymore. It's a kind of worn-out word, don't you think? It has meant too many things to mean anything. *Redevelopment* seems a good deal better to me. "Re" suggests that we are going to do things over, "development" gives the idea of change and continued movement, adjustment, and revision. Let me know what you think about this and what suggestions you have to make.

By the way, in my reading I have come on a couple of very complimentary criticisms of the state planning report that we prepared for Governor Smith. Both of them give you due credit for the help that you gave in creating that famous document. One of these pamphlets I think you'll be interested in. It is called "State Conservation of Resources" and is by Clifford J. Hynning, published by the National Resources Committee.

As always,

Clarence

---

354   Essay [A note to himself]

[c. November 1943]

"THE NATURE OF COMMUNITIES"[1]

[For community, we must have] common activities in which all members of the community can or do take part, in which all have an interest, [and] which bring them all together. Often this is a common antagonism—need of union for defense may be the first cause of union.

The people of Marin City organized for the purpose of meeting with the Housing Authority in regard to such problems as furnishing. Their association since has made itself responsible for various community activities. It is self-governing through an executive committee representing the artificially divided districts. [The executive committee members] keep in touch with the community through a weekly paper, which is self-supporting due to advertisements.

There is always danger of an individual or a small group getting in a controlling position through assertiveness, leadership, . . . control of community association, or editing the local newspaper (as in Banning Homes).

Often [communities] are more interested in an outside threat than in the practical good of the community. The forming of the association in Knickerbocker Village, New York, was an example of this. . . . The management gave cause for the forming of an organization of opposition rather than cooperation by its bad handling of the opening of the building to more tenants than could be taken care of by elevators and other facilities.

At Hillside and Sunnyside, tenants' associations were ultimately a thorn in the flank of management. I wonder if they really need have been?

Sunnyside trouble, I think, was quite separate from its community organization program. It arose out of the financial breakdown and the depression. The Sunnyside folks were fighting against the unfair attitude of the real owners of their homes: the holders of the first mortgage. The City Housing Corporation was squeezed between the resentment of the little so-called homeowners and the power of the big financiers, who refused to recognize the actual change in the value of the dollar and were determined to get the last drop of blood, no matter what it cost society. The City Housing Company took the legal side and not the common sense or humanitarian (moral) side. So they lost the backing of the citizens of Sunnyside.

The Sunnyside folks had no stronger case than [did] the hundreds of thousands of little "homeowners" throughout Queens. But they were a community that had had experience in working together through its association, which was started and developed by the company that the citizens finally fought.

Hillside trouble seems to have been in trying to limit the discussion of its association to matters that did not criticize management. Discuss this with George Gove and Miss Blackham.

The Metropolitan Insurance Company apparently decided that safety lay in having no community. So at Parkchester they neither planned for nor built community facilities (no meeting or recreation rooms, no schools, no churches, only a limited number of playgrounds). They formed no community association. (Check on this. What has happened? See Lowe and Gove.)

Radburn offered leadership in organization of various activities. (See "Radburn: A Plan for Living.") It tried not to impose the management's ideas. It acted through the Radburn Association, which was a semigovernmental agency—with power of taxation up to one-half the taxes of the borough. How has this worked through the period of stress? See the manager, Goldberg—also Eberlain. Also, discuss the beginnings with Major Walker and Charles Ascher.

At Radburn, the strength of association in activities is apparent in the theatrical groups. Walter has held onto his house in Radburn as long as he could so as to remain in the theater. Afterward he still continued to visit Radburn so as to design and make their scenery.

The Morrisons were bound to the group that lived near them through common interest in the activities of their children. They helped each other in the difficult period when new children were coming. I wonder how large a group they felt themselves a part of, whether it was the whole neighborhood. Ask them. Does this kind of neighborliness differ from the ———,[2] with its objectionable loss of privacy and individuality?

Upper D-2 Camp Humphrey, Virginia, is an example of how common needs fostered by close and continuous association led the smaller men to act as though they were a tribe apart. When their members temporarily secured the power of appointment of officials, they distributed the desirable jobs in upper D-2.

The nature of a neighborhood community is strikingly illustrated by Bali. The common interests and activities dominate the lives of all. The community festivals require drama, orchestra, dance, costumes, and the background of the temple grounds. These are woven together to form the life of the communities. To [these activities] the people give most of their time. Their individual work is secondary to their bigger occupation: community ceremonial, recreation, or play. For it, all their arts of dance, music, painting, fabrics and clothing, all type of decoration, including that of musical instruments, are welded together with the art of living—of living together.

Even in Bali there can be too much community for some. These individuals can escape within themselves by painting a sign upon their forehead, as a result of which they theoretically disappear by common consent.

If it is true that a thoroughly democratic community develops out of common interests in which all the members can take an active part or have an effective influence, then . . . a community must be limited to those that have a common activity or interest close enough to them geographically and close enough to them practically or spiritually so that they can either take part in the activity or in its management. This should give a guide to the geographical or numerical size of a neighborhood community.

Common interests or activities might be:

1. Occupational, lending to business or industrial associations, labor organizations, Lions, or such.
2. Religious.
3. Recreational: theater; games: active or quiet; parties, picnics, etc.
4. Cultural: music, art, oratory, etc.
5. Education: schools, classes, workshops.

The first and second are interests of limited parts of the neighborhood. Their community may be in association with other parts of the neighborhood or other neighborhoods entirely. But they are likely to be bound together as a group within the neighborhood. In the medieval days the church was common to all and dominated functions. The theater and other recreational activities took place on the church ground or even in the church. Even the commercial fair was there, just as it still is in China. It all was a matter of ceremony that brought the community together. It gave them a feeling of common interest and union when the community was small enough.

The school is the dominating common interest of the American community. Every family with a child has a special interest in the school. Every taxpayer has a different form of interest: most of his taxes are spent on education.

The citizen of a small town takes an active part in governing and guiding the local school. (Does he?) Talk it over with educational people at Washington. Ask Lewis Mumford about Amenia. When the schools in the country are amalgamated, they become more distant and are likely to be governed by boards appointed by [outsiders].

In a city, particularly a large city like New York, the local school policy and activity is decided by a central Board of Education. A single program serves for all neighborhoods. The neighborhood has little or nothing to say. As a result we have Parent-Teacher Associations. (To what extent do these unite the parents and the neighborhood? Have they any influence with the Board of Education? Could the neighborhood parents effectively guide the school? Educationally or in neighborhood activities?) [Ask Mark McClosky.]

Have school activities been a common interest that has served to bind neighborhoods together? Can they be made to? How about Greenbelt's experience, where the numerous other community activities outside of the education of the children took place at the same building? [Ask Klein Fulmer and someone experienced in Parent-Teacher Association affairs. . . . See my Greenbelt Report.][3]

The elementary school has been accepted as the ideal focus center of a neighborhood. It is close enough to all neighbors within a built-up neighborhood—one-half mile walking radius. Check this for six families to the acre and 10 families.

How has it worked? Where? Radburn [not well], Greenbelt [very well]?

The other community activities should be centered with the school to form a real neighborhood focus. [But appropriate facilities within the school need to be provided for adult use.—L.P.B.]

How American communities have become encumbered with duplicating activities. Social activities of churches, YMCA (American missionaries to American heathens), political clubs, clubs of various social groups.

Movie, auditorium, theater (in Greenbelt); [there is] neither movie nor auditorium with adequate stage for theatrical production. The movie, being commercial, not serving for local activities and the hall in the school having a flat floor.

What happens to community activities when no foresight is shown in planning or building facilities? Parkchester. See Frank Lowe.

1. From time to time Clarence Stein uses the process of writing out his current thinking on a subject as part of his thinking process. There was no apparent recipient for this note, but it revealed much about his ideas in 1943 on the problems of community in America. The note was also a research agenda.

2. Blank space in original text.

3. The copy of this document in the Cornell archives includes a number of notations by L.P.B. (Louise Blackman). These handwritten comments are set off by brackets in this letter. Similar notes from L.P.B. are included in documents titled "Government and Management in New Communities" and "How Large Is a Neighborhood?"

---

355 To Mrs. William Wurster[1]

[New York City]   November 11, 1943

Dear Catherine:

I was delighted to hear from you and to know that all is well with you and Bill.

I am glad to have your spiel on the London Plan. I hope I may keep it for a while. I would prefer not to look at it until I have had an opportunity to formulate my own point of view. As yet, I have not received a copy of the report. Somehow or other it has got lost at the British Information Bureau. They have promised to lend me their copy tomorrow. I will send your article back just as soon as I have outlined my article and have had a chance to read yours.[2] I have also received one from Professor Gauss. By the way, I was tremendously interested in his article that was prepared for the Harvard Planning School. I am amused in looking at the list of those that the *Architectural Review* has chosen to criticize the plan. They seem to have left out all the regular planning boys.

I just got back the day before yesterday. I have had a perfectly wonderful three months, mainly out on the coast. It was like going to school again. I have been making a study of the housing work and particularly community facilities from San Francisco down to Santiago and then stopped off on the way back to see what was being done for Willow Run. Kline Fulmer came over from Cleveland, and we spent three days together, two of them at Cleveland, where I went over their various site plans and saw some of Ernie Bohn's work. I am not going to talk to you about it here, but I do hope you will be able to come down here for a weekend so I can see you and Bill. I will open up the farmhouse in the country, and we can have a good walk and talk.

Aline is busy doing Pearl Buck's *Dragon Seed*. It looks as though there will be about three months more of it, so if I can I am going to get back to the coast, where

I find I can write and even do a little thinking instead of constantly dangling at the end of a telephone. My best to you and Bill.

Cordially,

[Clarence S. Stein]

1. Catherine Bauer was now married to William Wurster, who had been appointed dean of MIT's School of Architecture. They lived in Cambridge, Mass.

2. Clarence Stein's article "Technique and the London Plan" was completed in March 1944 and appeared in *Architectural Review* 96, no. 578 (1944): 79–80, as part of a series of comments on the 1943 *County of London Plan* by Abercrombie and Foreshaw. The other authors in this series included RPAA member Catherine Bauer, as well as John M. Gaus, Frederick P. Clark, and Jacob Crane. The Abercrombie Plan, as it became known, was the first of two famous and influential postwar plans for the metropolis. The 1944 *Greater London Plan* was the other. From this time onward, Stein and Mumford developed an intense interest in British planning for the London Region and played a part in its evolution.

---

356   Proposal

[New York City]   December 13, 1943

"PROPOSAL FOR A DIVISION OF PLANNED DEVELOPMENT IN THE
EXECUTIVE SEPARTMENT [OF THE] STATE OF NEW YORK"

Prepared for Governor Thomas E. Dewey by a Special Committee of the Citizens' Housing Council; Clarence S. Stein, Chairman

The purpose of this proposal is to give conscious direction and planned form to the physical development of the State. This in the past has taken place in a disorderly way as a result of the uncoordinated activities of the legislature, various state departments, local authorities, functional groups, corporations, and individuals.

Need

The need is urgent.

1. Other states and other cities will compete with the Empire State and the metropolis of New York for supremacy immediately after the war. Many of them have been strengthened and modernized during the war far more than New York City and State.

2. Postwar building and public works will form and harden the mold of [the] future. All the State's activities should harmonize and form part of a plan for the future, rather than as additions to an obsolete past.

3. Disorderly decentralization must be replaced by purposeful decentralization with coordination in the movement of industry and workers.

4. A more wholesome relation between rural and urban sections of the State must be developed, with less unproductive movement of goods and people.

In fact, the two should be made one with the closest possible contact between city and country.

Form of the Planned Development Agency

A Single Commissioner. A staff position in the Executive Department along with the Budget Bureau, acting as advisor and eye and ear of the governor.

1. Analyzing tendencies and needs as basis for governor's development plans.
2. Harmonizing the planned development activities of state departments and local and regional planning agencies with each other and with the desires and needs of the people and of various functional groups.
3. Preparing capital budget for coming year and tentatively for five to ten years in cooperation with the budget director.
4. Assisting the legislature or legislative committee on request in matters relating to planning and development of State. [There should be] a small, compact, but skilled staff with an adequate budget. Experts in various departments should cooperate with and assist [the] development commissioner so as to prevent duplication of effort.

A State Coordinating Board. Consisting of the heads of all departments dealing with development of physical or human resources and facilities of the State (perhaps the governor's cabinet plus certain legislative leaders).

1. Shall meet six times a year and at call of governor.
2. All department heads shall attend or be represented by assistants with power to vote; however, in regard to special problems only those heads of departments and legislative committee dealing with these subjects need attend.
3. The plans of all departments and agencies shall be made available to the Planned Development Agency at an early stage of their conception and development.
4. The coordinating of activities of state departments affecting State redevelopment will require great tact as well as force. The commissioner of the Planned Development Agency, as agent of the governor, ultimately must have the power to hold up projects until conflicts can be resolved, or the governor must keep in close touch with him so that conflicts may be settled by executive decision. Otherwise, unrelated activities of various government agencies will continue to dissipate the wealth and energy of the State.

A Local Governmental Coordinating Board.

1. Shall coordinate the development activities of local and regional planning agencies with various state departments through discussion and explanation of policies and activities.

2. Shall meet four times a year and at the call of the development commissioner.

A Public Advisory Board.

1. Composed of representatives to be appointed by the governor from various functional groups, such as agriculture, industry, transportation, retail and wholesale business, labor, engineering, architecture, etc.
2. Purpose is to harmonize the activities of governmental agencies on various levels with desires and needs of the people of the State, industry, agriculture, and commerce.
3. To meet from time to time on call of commissioner.

---

357   To Catherine Bauer Wurster

[New York City]   January 10, 1944

Dear Catherine:

That is a splendid article about cities in flux.

The more I look around, the more I feel that after the war we are going to have a repetition of the crazy, purposeless growth of the twenties. Even where there are pretenses of broad postwar planning, the habits of the past and the force of those who have property interests promise to be too strong for any common sense reasoning. For example, I was up at Syracuse University and had time to quickly glance at the work that was being done on the much advertised plan for the future of the city and the region.[1] As far as I can see, when they are through getting a consensus of the opinion of all interests, they are just going to have another zoning plan and another compromise highway plan. *Fortune* will not know the difference.

All we can do about it is to state the case for common sense as clearly as possible. That you have done in your article for the *American Scholar.*

By the way, I had completely forgotten how much studying we were doing on the subject of community facilities way back in 1932. Looking through the files yesterday, I came on some old cards that you and I made out. There were notes of our talks with Major Walker and Albert Kennedy, etc. It does not look to me as though we have learned [very much] since then.

How is Bill? Give him my very best. The railroads permitting, I will be bound for California in about a week. I hope to see you and Bill out there before I return. I don't know whether Lewis let you know that he already has departed. His address in 694 Alvarado Road, Stanford University, California.

Cordially,

Clarence

1. This large effort was funded in part by *Fortune* magazine.

358   To Frank Palmer

[New York City]   February 5, 1944

Dear Frank:

I have given a great deal of thought to our talk of last Sunday, during the week. The only reason I have not written sooner is that I have wanted to prepare an outline of the type of organization that should be formed.[1] Putting it down has led to many currents of thought that I am trying to clear up in my mind.

But here are a few things that I think are plain: First, things are getting under way for the postwar period. We should start looking around and letting folks know what we have to offer—as you suggested. Secondly, the field that we must cover to do a comprehensive job of creating new towns and neighborhoods is a big one. But, unless we define the type of work we intend to do in the beginning, we will find ourselves drifting into all sorts of related fields. Here is how I see it:

The Nature of the Work We Desire (and to which we will limit ourselves).

A. Creation of new towns or neighborhoods from the ground up.
B. Redevelopment of existing cities or neighborhoods, but only on the basis of being clean-cut jobs without crippling compromises.
C. Serious work that is to be carried out thoroughly and which can be financed.

We Do Not Want to Participate in:

A. Patching jobs.
B. Compromise undertakings.
C. Speculative operations.
D. Small developments—less than a comprehensive neighborhood or town.
E. "Planning" jobs—consisting merely of surveys, statistics, pretty reports, and such dream stuff destined for files, not realization.

To do a thorough, comprehensive job in the large field, we will need a variety of talent. And there is the great difficulty. I fear big organizations. They master you. Ultimately, the chiefs find that their main job is chasing jobs. They are forced to accept work they do not like, to compromise their ideas. In short, to sell out, and for what?

I have seen overhead kill so many good intentions and make servants of brilliant technicians who might have been valuable leaders. That is the problem I see big as . . . any other: how to hold a group of tip-top specialists ready to put a job at call and not be swamped by overhead between jobs?

That's what has got me thinking as I start outlining a prospectus of what we will offer in services. It can be done, but how? What are your ideas?

Meanwhile I will go on with my outline of purposes, services, personnel, and all that to be sent to you later for criticism.

Kindest regards,

Cordially,

Clarence S. Stein

1. Stein had decided that he needed to mobilize like-minded professionals in a consulting group to offer community planning services in the post–World War II era. Palmer was the executive director of the Allegheny County Housing Authority; Stein had worked with him on three defense housing developments in 1941. By August 1944, after discussion with several other former associates, Stein will have developed a full prospectus of Clarence Stein and Associates, to which he will have appended a list of the twelve major housing developments in which he had been principal or major consultant from 1924 onward.

---

359   To Benton MacKaye

Los Angeles, Calif.   March 8, 1944

Dear Ben:

It must be a couple of weeks since I wrote you. I got involved in writing an article. It was [a] subject on which I apparently knew too much, and therefore [I] couldn't get it boiled down to make sense. You know how that is. It was about the County of London Plan. A great job, as far as the rebuilding of a metropolis goes, but it still leaves a colossus that is bound ultimately to die of its own bigness. The easiest way to tell you about it is to send you a copy. You might return it, unless you think there is any good reason for keeping it. I won't mind, in fact, I will be delighted to have your characteristic underlining.

Now that this job is done, I can get back to the bigger one: the tremendous number of notes that have to be put into some order. My, what a lot of time it all takes. . . .

Aline has been done with her picture for some weeks now. She has been enjoying a well-earned rest, and I am enjoying having her at home. Perhaps it hasn't all been rest for her. She has been doing a lot of cooking—and such good cooking it seems a shame to waste her talent on acting! . . .

Affectionate greetings from Aline, Jennie Mac, and

Clarence

360   To Ralph Eberlin

[New York City]   March 11, 1944

Dear Ralph:

I was delighted to get a letter from India. I have been wondering where you were.

. . . I was immensely interested in what you had to say about your impressions of India. . . . My activities, as far as jobs go, have been not very great. The truth is I have made very little effort to get any government housing work. It is all cut and dried now. All the drawings for buildings are canned and sent out from Washington. In most cases the architect merely crosses out certain things in the drawings. The main thing an architect has to do is site planning, and you know how well most architects are prepared for that job. . . .

. . . In California some of these community centers including schools, public auditoriums, nurseries, and all the rest have been worked out with a great deal of unity and interest. Here is something that will really be of permanent value after the war, even if some of them are destroyed. This part of the work is being frozen in the Washington office. Everything is standardized. It is only by chance that the buildings that are now being done meet either conditions of site or special requirements. . . .

That is the very question I have wanted to study. Really, I have been very glad to be free of regular office routine in order to do some investigating and to think things through in regard to requirements of a community. Here is the way I see it. We are going to or, at least, we should build a lot of new communities after the war. It won't matter whether they are new sites or whether they consist of rebuilding of neighborhoods. . . .

Now, I would like to say just a word about the future. I don't know whether you want to think or talk about after the war now, but you will remember I spoke to you about the possibilities of forming an organization for the purpose of creating new communities. I have been doing a lot of thinking about this since. Here is just the briefest outline of what I have in mind.

The idea is to get together a small but experienced group that can do a complete job in the creation of new towns and neighborhoods or the rebuilding of existing cities or neighborhoods. No attempt would be made to do any patching or compromise jobs, nor would the organization go into speculative undertakings or "planning" jobs consisting of surveys, statistics, pretty pictures, and all the rest of it that is generally filed away.

The organization should be able to do a comprehensive job from exploratory services through the execution of the job, including city planning, architecture, site, . . . structural and civil engineering, landscaping, and supervision of construction. It is my idea that the organization will not do all of the detail work in connection with the execution as much as possible. It seems to me it should be done by local professional men and builders under the supervision or guidance of the members of the organization.

However, I have forgotten one point. I think that a function that is essential in the creation of such communities is the setting up of government and management. This is the sort of job in which John Walker or somebody of his kind is needed. Such an organization should consist of a very limited number of key men. They must know their own business and know how to work together. As I see it at present, they should look upon the work of their organization as their principal job. However, it probably will be more sensible if everybody continues to do his professional work at times when the organization does not keep him occupied.

This whole thing is still in a very preliminary state in my mind. I have spoken to hardly anyone about it. . . .

One way or another, I will be writing to you again very soon about the things that may interest you to hear. Mrs. Stein joins me in sending you kindest greetings.

Cordially,
Clarence S. Stein

---

361 To F. L. Palmer

[Los Angeles, California]   March 27, 1944

Dear Frank:

I have again postponed replying to your letter until I had sufficient leisure to answer it in full. I ought to know by experience that that time never comes.

In the first place I want to tell you that I am delighted at your attitude in regard to our discussion. . . . You wrote that "the real point to my questions comes on the issue of whether the group will always await the principal who awards the commission as against creating that principal when necessary." In my mind there is no question that we should seek the type of work that we want to do. My experience has been that the best way to get new and better things started is to initiate them. Let me give you a couple of examples of what I mean.

Hillside, at the beginning, consisted of nothing except my idea that a community of apartment houses should be built so that it would be an example of how urban areas in such cities as New York should be rebuilt. There was no land. There was no client. There was nothing but an idea. Radburn was well under way, and I was anxious to see whether the Radburn idea of a community developed around common interests, large, open green spaces, and safety of number could be built into a community consisting entirely of apartment houses. The quality of living in the Phipps apartments seemed a desirable standard, but to make it successful for large groups it was necessary to produce this at a lower rental. Further, I felt that a community large enough to form a neighborhood with central community facilities and playgrounds adjoining a school was essential if it was to serve as an example for future urban redevelopment.

Many studies of plan and size were made before land or client was sought. The first one to become interested in the idea was Clarence Woolett, head of the Standard Sanitary Corporation. He brought in Ecker, the builder. Straus joined us only after we discovered he had one of the two large pieces of land that seemed to fit our program.[1]

Here's another example of creating the client. A few weeks ago I felt that the next thing to do in New York housing was to develop a large run-down area for the use of the middle class as well as poor. . . . As an example of how New York should be rebuilt, we needed at least one complete community with adequate recreation, shopping centers, [and] apartments of different types and heights planned for safety and peaceful living, close to working places and yet with convenient means of getting to open country—all this at a cost within the means of those to be served.

It seemed to me that it was desirable, if possible, to create this kind of environment not merely for a single economic group but for different economic levels who would live as closely in the same neighborhood as possible. To carry this out it was apparent that a large enough tract of moderate-cost land was needed. This required government cooperation but not necessarily direct action, along with adequate sources of investment finance at low rates of interest.

After searching around the lower East Side for the best available property, I took the matter up with Louie Pink, who was then head of the State Insurance Department and who, as a former member of the State Housing Board and City Housing Authority, was deeply interested in the proposal. He called together a joint meeting of the heads of the large insurance companies of New York and city officials. The mayor was very much interested. He induced Robert Moses to take the leadership. The savings banks were drawn in to cooperate with the life insurance companies. The FHA gave its tentative approval to plans. Finally, a coordinated scheme of large investment for white-collared workmen, financed jointly by the insurance companies and banks, was developed in relation to two public housing developments. One of these was to be financed by the state [and] the other by [the] federal government. They all were to be related to a large municipal play area, to existing schools, and to complete revision of [the] street plan.

This scheme did not go through because one old duffer on the Finance Board of the New York Life was opposed.[2] But the idea and its development greatly influenced the attitude of financial institutions in the city toward redevelopment of New York.

I have described these two experiences so as to show you how much I think progress requires leadership and initiative. I do not think we will get very far in working up new things if we wait around for clients to initiate new neighborhoods.

I am particularly interested in bringing labor units into this field, just as you are. It probably will be necessary to assist them first in understanding just what should be done if they want to live in good communities and how best to carry it out. If we want ultimately to develop communities that will be made up of more than one economic group, we will probably have to do a good deal of organizing, ourselves.
. . .

I shall write to you again before long and hope that I may hear from you.

Cordially,

Clarence S. Stein

1. This is the most detailed, simple, and complete description in the Stein Papers of the evolution of the idea of Hillside Homes. The project's birth and some of these events were also described in Stein's correspondence with Aline during the early 1930s (also in the Stein Papers).

2. There is no file of this proposed project in the Stein Papers, but there is a large file and much correspondence about another possible life insurance company project at Fresh Meadows, Long Island. The golf course site was later developed by the company to the plans of others after World War II.

---

362   To Roland Wank

[New York City]   June 28, 1944

Dear Roland:

Ever since we talked here, I have been intending to write to you. Our conversation set me thinking all during the long weekend that followed.

In regard to the Metropolitan Life Insurance Company's first housing experiment, I went to see George Gove, who is now in charge of housing for that company. He tells me that, during the last twenty-one years, with the exception of the three first years of the depression, the Metropolitan has cleared a good six percent profit after all expenses were paid. At the same time they have cut their equity down a million and a half dollars or more. This is pretty good business.

He also called my attention to the fact that the Annual Report of the City and Suburban Homes Company had just been published. This company, which was started as a semi-philanthropic affair almost half a century ago, has some ten million dollars invested in real estate. Last year their net income after paying income taxes and everything else was almost eight per cent. In their 3,821 apartments there are only two vacancies.

The limited-dividend projects that have been erected under the New York State Housing Law seem to me an outstanding example of successful investment in good housing. Rents are lower than in anything that is at all comparable. However, it is very difficult to get people to accept these as examples of what can be done with government capital. They say that they are not in the competitive market because they receive tax exemption on a large part of their value. I therefore asked the Acting Housing Commissioner if he would have his office take Hillside and one or two other developments and find out just what rental would have to be paid without the exemption to put their earnings to the equivalent of what they are at present. Hillside [renters] with the exemption now pay a rental of approximately $11 a room per month; without the exemption they would [pay] $12.90. Boulevard Gardens would have to pay a rental of $13.25. The only large-scale groups that seem comparable at all with these are those built [with loans insured by the] Federal Housing Administration. . . .

[Balance of letter missing from the Stein Papers]

---

363   To John Walker

[New York City]   November 9, 1944

Dear John:

When I left you in Washington, I promised to repeat in writing my somewhat hasty description of the organization which I am forming and of which I hope you will be a member. Here it is. It has taken me some time to get to it on account of other jobs that had to be done. I am going to try to set it down in as compact a form as possible. You know so much of the subject that I do not think it will be necessary to fill in all the details, and I know that you will ask me for anything to clarify where necessary.

The Purpose of This Organization is to give comprehensive technical service in creating new towns and neighborhoods, from preliminary studies to completely constructed communities, equipped and organized with government and management as well as buildings.

Services Are Offered to industries desiring to move to new localities; seeking to improve living conditions of workers; to build a new community replacing temporary "war housing" near modern wartime plants; labor organizations, such as Auto Workers Union, proposing to create better communities; large-scale investment corporations, such as insurance companies or banks, planning redevelopment in existing cities or the creation of new communities; governmental authorities and agencies in connection with regional studies, such as those for the Columbia River or for the Central Valley in California; states desiring to foster industrial decentralization by assisting in building towns; municipal housing authorities desiring advice in forming future programs or criticism of past work; federal agencies in connection with colonies for ex-soldiers, old folks, etc.

Services Will Include explorative surveys for relocation of industries; determining the location, nature, and form as well as the management and governmental organization of new towns and new or redeveloped neighborhoods; estimating approximate costs of constructing and operating. Preparation of preliminary plans of towns, site, groupings, and buildings; programs and budget for construction and operation; recommendation for government and for management, and operation of housing, public, and commercial properties. Execution or supervision of planning and engineering of all types; construction, site work and landscaping; organization of government and housing management.

The Organization Consists of experienced specialists in planning and design; regional, city, town, site, landscaping, housing, and community buildings; engineering: civil, site, structural, and mechanical; government and housing management; building construction.

Form of Organization. As far as possible the organization's functions will be advisory. It will carry out detailed work only to the extent that it is necessary to do a comprehensive and complete job. Just as far as is possible for the execution of the work, local architects, engineers, and builders should be employed, but the organization should make the preliminary, exploratory surveys. They should assist in the determining program, and they must see that it is carried out by giving adequate supervision and continued advice.

The Chief Functions Should Be

Design, Policy—from house up to region.

Survey and Programming—industrial, geotechnical, labor, government, etc.

Engineering—including site, civil, and utility work.

Construction—consisting not of the actual building but merely estimating, coordination, and, when necessary, supervision.

Government or management of town and housing.

I am hoping that ultimately Ralph Eberlin will do our engineering and possibly construction, with specialists under him in utilities and other branches.

You unquestionably are the man to take charge of the fifth branch. I know from my experience with you at Radburn and in connection with the reports that we worked out in connection with Greenbelt, [Maryland,] no one else can do it with more competency and authority and with better spirit of cooperation. I feel very strongly that the work of the organization would be incomplete unless we covered the field of government and management along with that of physical planning and building. The two must go hand in hand from the period of conception to that of completion. . . .

The job is one of important possibilities, as you see.[1] The kind of guidance that we should be able to offer is going to be badly needed in this important period of redevelopment. I feel that there should be plenty of it to be done and that our problem is going to be to definitely limit ourselves to complete, integrated communities or parts of them: no land subdivisions, no speculative enterprises, or no big plans intended for future reference that will be shelved away.

Do let me know what questions there are in your mind in connection with the scheme.

With kindest regards,

Yours cordially,

Clarence S. Stein

1. Stein's plans for this orgaization made up principally of his former associates in housing and community building were never implemented. Stein's personal health problems and other interests of his intended collaborators mitigated against success.

---

364   To Lewis Wilson

[New York City]   December 28, 1944

Dear Lew:

You couldn't have given me a better Christmas present than that telephone call. I had been wondering just what had happened, and it was sure good to talk things over.

The Baldwin Hills publication of *Pencil Points* has created a lot of discussion here in the East.[1] It's really the outstanding example in the country, anyhow, as far as organization and grouping of buildings around [a] superblock goes. It would be an easy matter to make it far more valuable as an example if its size were doubled. You will remember we talked about this when I was in Los Angeles.

What should be done is to build on the land toward the hill what would be, in general scheme, a duplicate of what has already been done. Experience in operation would probably suggest certain variations but, on the whole, the scheme is good. That would give a community large enough really to support adequate community facilities. These include, among other things, playgrounds and a community director with assistant.

Also, it would probably make it possible to have the proposed school moved to a location in the center of the development—that is to say, on Colosseum Street. Possibly this street could be dead-ended so as to make a connection between the two superblocks.

One of the buildings in the existing block might be moved so as to open up the connection between the two central greens.

None of this is new, but I am just repeating it because you have been so busy at other things that you might want to be reminded.

How could we go about realizing this? The financing should not be difficult. We might even try to get the New York Life interested. It was my impression that the Baldwin people would not be opposed. What's needed is somebody to get things going.[2]

Mind you, I am not asking you to do so if you still have the same feeling as you did when we talked things over in my apartment when you were last here. If you do not want to get into things now, what do you think is the best thing to do? Should I suggest it to the Baldwin people?

As both you and I recognize, the really difficult thing is our feeling toward Reg [Johnson].[3] Of course, what I would like to see is the job done by you, if you are ready to get back into harness; otherwise, possibly by your brother and [Robert] Alexander, with me acting as consultant. I probably would go out, in that case, to Los Angeles and spend a good part of my time at it.

Give me your idea on this, but don't let it change any plans that you are making for yourself.

How are you and Sonny? Aline and I are going down to Florida on the 12th of January. I am giving a talk at Miami University. Our best for the New Year!

As always,

Clarence S. Stein

1. Catherine Bauer, "Baldwin Hills Village," *Pencil Points* 25, no. 9 (1944): 44–60.

2. Unfortunately for Clarence, as well as for the development of residential planning with a focus on community and for the future residents of the Baldwin Hills development, this extension of the original 1939 project did not materialize. An ironic development of the decades from the 1950s through the 1970s was the completion of conventional single-family development in areas adjacent to the original project and the conversion of the original townhouse development to an adults-only community.

3. Johnson had been a frequent associate in projects with Lewis Wilson, Robert Alexander, and Clarence Stein.

---

365   To Elliott V. Bell[1]

[New York City]   January 2, 1945

Dear Mr. Bell:

I want to thank you for giving me so much time over the telephone at this busy season. I was glad to have a preliminary talk with you regarding the proposal for a Commissioner of Planned Development in the Executive Department.

The two big difficulties that you brought out have troubled me a great deal. I agree with you that it is impossible to find a man with all the knowledge and ability required to lay out and coordinate the work for dynamic development of the State. But this same difficulty exists in more important fields. The fact that nobody is of the caliber to handle all the various tasks that come to the president of the United States is no reason why we should do away with that office.

The redevelopment task that faces the State after the war is so great and is of such importance for the future that it seems to me that New York must find a man who can assist the governor in doing this work.

Now, as to your second point: we recognize the administrative difficulty of anyone attempting to coordinate the planning activities of the various heads of departments. We have tried to meet this by proposing that the commissioner have a staff position in the Executive Department. The Agency would then be similar to the Budget Bureau. The commissioner would act as adviser and "eye and ear" of the governor. He would not be a competing head of department but merely an agent of the governor. This probably would facilitate his dealings as coordinator with the various planning departments.

I recognize that there still would be difficulties and that, even though the head of the Division of Planned Development would speak only with the authority of the governor, he still must be a man of great tact and political understanding. That, of course, is making it even more difficult to find the man.

May I have a chance to talk to you about this at greater length some day when you are in New York? If you prefer I would be very glad to come up to Albany to see you. I am certain that Harold Buttenheim and George Hallett would also be very glad to be with us.

Meanwhile, I am sending you a copy of the memorandum proposing a Division of Planned Development that was prepared by a Special Committee of the Citizens Housing Council at the request of the governor. I also am enclosing a report on the Development of the State that was prepared for Governor Al Smith, which I think will interest you.

With kindest regards,
Cordially yours,
Clarence S. Stein

1. Elliott Bell was Superintendent of Banks for New York State.

---

366   To Lewis Mumford

[New York City]   March 13, 1945

Dear Lewis:

I cannot tell you how distressed I am about Curt [Behrendt]. There seems no question about the fact that he should not be attempting to carry on his teaching. I can very well understand how he hates to give in, but I do hope someone (Lydia or you) will make him see the need of preserving his strength.[1]

Is there anything we can do about the matter of the doctor? I, of course, cannot judge whether having a specialist come up there again will be of any value. Apparently your judgment is that he needs the care of somebody like Dr. Wechsler. Would it be worthwhile trying to have Curt moved to New York? Naturally, I will do anything that I can to help. . . .

It is good word we have had from Ben. He is on his way to the new life.

Affectionate greetings to you all.
Clarence S. Stein

1. Within two months of Clarence's expression of concern for Curt Behrendt, he was himself back in the hospital. The June 1945 episode of mental breakdown seems to have been more severe than the 1937 and 1942 episodes. He spent almost a month at the New York Neurological Hospital at 158th Street for electric shock treatments for depression. In a letter to Aline late in July, he referred to not remembering what had happened during this period. On July 24, Dr. Terhune wrote to Aline from Silver Hill Sanatorium: "I brought Clarence out here today following successful electric shock treatment. He was still a little confused and [his] memory [is] hazy. Mood is excellent." Clarence wrote to Aline at this time, mentioning a briefcase of her letters that he had but did not remember reading previously. On July 29 he wrote to Aline, "It probably will be a long time before I know just where I have been. . . . It is still very mysterious."

By July 30 his confidence and fierce determination had returned. He wrote from Silver Hill to Aline in California: "I am not done, that is sure. My work may be consultative, that we will see, but I have some important things ahead of me. I can't see life otherwise. . . . I feel the fog rising."

By early August he had gained weight and was reflective about the future: "There are so many complications in our way of living that [will] have to be straightened out, even if we should decide to make the West our center of action. . . . I might get rid of the load of past materials, . . . all those files at the office and our homes that apparently drove me here. . . . Someone else must clear the files and do the business."

It was apparently at this time or shortly afterward that the main files of Stein's architectural practice (from 1919 to 1945) were destroyed. Files that had been kept at West Sixty-fourth Street in New York, at A Thousand Years in Yorktown, and in Los Angeles seem to have been kept for the most part. They are in the C. S. Stein Collection at Cornell University.

During his recovery Stein reflected on his old slogans (CSS to AMS, 5 August 1945): "A Thousand Years," "Nous regrettons jamais," "Time is our servant," and "As I am I mean to be," and vowed, "I must learn how to use my experience to create new communities, as well as our means of living, without getting lost in the machinery."

---

367 To Lewis Mumford

Silver Hill, New Canaan, Conn.   August 8, 1945

Dear Lewis:

Your letter arrived here yesterday. Nothing could have given me greater joy. How I long to see you and talk to you of the world that must be created.

I have been cut off from it so long—a month in the hospital (a thing to be forgotten)—and now here regaining my strength. I don't suppose you could come up here. But, before long, perhaps Thursday or Friday of next week or early the following, I may be able to go to New York for a day. Could you possibly meet me? I need your guidance.

Sony, Ben [MacKaye], and the Kizers were in Washington when I went to my apartment two weeks ago.[1] I am glad to hear of your book. . . .

My warm greeting to Sophie, Allison, and you. Aline is producing a play of Pearl Buck's at Palo Alto. It is about an American girl that marries an Indian and the mother (Aline) who becomes part of the Indian life.

Clarence

1. Ben Kizer was a Seattle lawyer who was active in regional planning in the Northwest. Stein and Kizer became close friends during several trips Stein made to the Northwest in the 1940s. By August 11, Clarence had returned permanently from Silver Hill to the apartment in New York City, where he had lunch with Carl Feiss, Ralph Walker, and several other old friends at the "Sky Parlor" on West Sixty-fourth Street. He and Aline continued to discuss, by letter, the choice of New York or California as their "center," and Clarence looked forward to the "glowing autumn" at A Thousand Years. Aline was to return to New York City on August 19 to act in a new play on Broadway.

---

368   To Lewis Mumford

[New York City]   December 10, 1945

Dear Lewis:

I was delighted on returning from the country last night to find your letter. I had postponed writing you for so long, in spite of the fact that I have so much to talk about, possibly because I still have some distance to go before I can get really active.

Arthur Mayer returned from his trip to India, China, and Japan for the Red Cross. I spent all day yesterday in the country with him, listening to his adventures and the interviews he had with everybody from MacArthur down to the wild young radicals of India. He called on Ben Kizer and had a long talk with him. I already had heard that they hit it off remarkably well, as was to be expected. He tells me that Ben is being run ragged. He has a tough job and insufficient assistance.

I am so glad to hear that you are getting the *Culture of Cities* in form with new illustrations for distribution in so many lands. I will try to get hold of Abercrombie's *Plan of Greater London.*

You will be interested to know that, out of a clear sky, I received a letter from C. B. Purdom relative to my article in *Theatre Arts.* He says, "Your reference to regional cities interested me. A new form of city has to be developed, if civilization is to be what it should be. Regional cities, in the sense of cities that are definitely parts of regions, are necessary; but cities that are split up into separate parts so that the whole disappears do not represent an idea that appeals to me or that seems to me to be sound. That is one of the faults I have found with the Country of London Plan, the criticism of which by Lewis Mumford is one of the best bits of town planning criticism ever written." . . .

Affectionate greetings to you, in which Aline would join me if she were here.

Clarence

369   To Lewis Mumford[1]

1229 Aezeta Terrace, L.A. 46   February 14, 1946

Dear Lewis:

Your postal in regard to [Sir Frederic] Osborn just reached me.[2] I wish I had had your advice earlier, before I wrote to Buttenheim that I would contribute toward bringing him over [to the United States] if someone else would arrange lectures and other contributions. I doubt if they will, so I guess it is safe, particularly as you doubt if he would come now.

I am sorry that you seem so discouraged about the world we hoped to help build . . . twenty-five years ago. I still hope to find a way to create our new cities—which [seems] absurd, after a few hours' drive today through the new slums and the endless dull miles of shop-lined avenues to the ugly harbor. Practically every open buildable piece of land [is] planted with the seeds of ugly waste.

Lewis, I wish I could talk it all over with you again. Anyhow, we would like to see you while you are out here. Isn't there any chance of your coming down here on your way back?

Do tell me what your plans are.

Clarence

1. Mumford was in California teaching at Stanford.
2. The RPAA was to bring Osborn to the United States to speak on British postwar plans, especially New Town proposals, with the objective of trying to influence U.S. policy.

370   To Lewis Mumford

1229 Aezeta Terrace, L.A. 46   April 15, 1946

Dear Lewis:

It was good to hear from you. I hope you will have an opportunity to get a good rest before you leave for England. I presume they will keep you on the go once you get there. I got some idea of your program from Osborn's letter and from our last talk. Hope you will have a chance to write one more about it.

I was particularly interested in the subject of your R.I.B.A. [Royal Institute of British Architects] lecture. The confusion in regard to the housing of the United Nations certainly needs clarification. I attended a meeting of the Shag Club before I left New York, at which Dick Childs spoke at length about his adventures with the international committee in search for a site—for what?[1] Seemed to me that what they needed was a program. Childs's interest was in large part to see that principles of community ownership of underlying land [were followed], which he and the rest of us tried to induce the steel trust to use a quarter of a century ago. . . . But, as a large part of those who will visit the world capital [United Nations office] may come there only for meetings and will not require permanent homes, it seems to me that this was not the place to try out principles that would have worked well at Gary. I got an idea that the committee had no time to think about what would happen in the world capital or meeting place. I wondered how much real imagination had gone into the requirements that had been set up for them in London. It showed much understanding of transportation here and now. We use the auto so much more here. . . . I left New York's LaGuardia at 4:15 P.M. on the Constellation and arrive[d] here just after midnight. So why locate so close to New York on the most expensive suburban land in the world? Dick Childs quoted your letters a number of times but not enough to give me a clear idea of your conception. I wish there was some way I could take a look at what you had written.

Clarification of program, understanding of purpose, of what is to be done, and how it is to affect folks is what we need before the architects start messing things up. Or should the architects' essential job be that of helping to develop the program? I have been wondering a good deal about that since I got here. . . .

And that is how American cities grow. Architects? Planners? They may call them in to try to redevelop, but not now. Even our limited experience in building communities during the war is being put aside, probably to be discussed when we have more time.

I have been studying what is being done to see whether there is any chance of doing anything constructive, that is, when I am feeling completely fit again. What chance is there of successfully building and operating rental communities based on the experience of Baldwin Hills? Something of that kind is needed, I believe, not only for the GI, but also for the future of Los Angeles. Can it be successful? I don't know. Anyhow, I am seeing how cities grow without purpose. . . .

But it just all goes to show how much the kind of guidance you are giving in connection with U.N. is needed in all these growths. So much more to say, but some other time. Our very best to you and Sophie.

Clarence

---

1. The search for a site for the United Nations lasted over a year. Stein was concerned that the site search seemed not to be based on a program for the UN's building needs. The Rockefellers' offer of the site at Turtle Bay on New York City's east side finally won out.

371　To Lewis Mumford

1229 Aezeta Terrace, L.A. 46　July 14, 1946

Dear Lewis:

I was delighted to get your postal from England, which was a long time in getting here. I know you will have no time for letters, but I hope that I will hear from you when you return. Better still, I look forward to seeing you when I return to the East in September so that I can hear what actually happened in a country that at least plans for peace.

Things have bogged down here completely. I just have received the latest reliable report from New York prepared for Citizens' Housing Council by Carl Stern's committee. It is gloomy. The promises of Robert Moses, Housing Dictator, last December called for 43,300 [new private sector] housing units and 127,000 permanent units [to replace the temporary housing units built during the war] plus public and private. So far, the only production by public agencies is 11,700 [dwelling] units, all temporary. . . .

Worst of all, [there is] no big plan or prospect of it nearby. This has to do not only with distribution of material and control of prices. It means plans in the arrangement of dwellings and all· the building of new cities and rebuilding of old ones as modern regions. We must not lose this opportunity.

So I hope you will return with good news that plans are going to be realized and improved. I hope that some of Osborn's Garden Cities will be realized. I saw some illustrations in *Sphere* of the first town that is proposed to make into a Garden City. I don't like it. Guess the people up at Shirley Center might feel the same. How about Ben? Would he lead the movement at the town meeting for the preservation of the past? . . .

[Balance of letter not in the Stein Papers]

---

372   To Lewis Mumford

1229 Aezeta Terrace, L.A. 46   September 5, 1946

Dear Lewis:

. . . I probably will be home again by the 15th. I hope you will be coming down about that time so that we can both see Ben.

I read in the *Architectural Record* of August that FPHA [Federal Public Housing Authority] has started to sell the units they took over from the Farm Security Administration. This includes the three Greenbelt Towns. I have been trying to find out why this is happening. Has to do with requirements of Lanham Act that they [be] disposed of, I am told. It is a shame if this is permitted to take place. The Greenbelt Towns were the most important step in the direction of Garden Cities that has been made in America, in spite of their lack of industry. Otherwise, all the elements were there. As experiments in economic as well as social and physical planning, they are important, and that value will in great part be lost if the towns get in the wrong hands or are sold off in lots.[1]

You remember I laid out the budget for operation of the town. Since then I have followed their development (particularly Greenbelt) and checked actual costs of various government functions against original estimates. This should be continued. We are going to need all their experience badly, when the attempt to build up the old cities from within breaks down. And it should be of help as means of comparison for our British friends, if it can be put in order and kept up.

Aline sends greetings to you both.

As does
Clarence

1. Clarence spent a considerable amount of personal time over the next several years in efforts to save the Greenbelt Towns, especially Greenbelt, Md.

---

373   To Lewis Mumford

New York City   June 8, 1947

Dear Lewis:

It was good to hear from you. I am very much disappointed that Osborn is not coming. The Brave Housers seem to be in retreat or seeking hiding. They need news from Britain to hearten them, if they still have heart and hope.

Just when we get reports of the Labor government's proposal to wipe out land increment, Washington is planning the liquidation of the Greenbelt Towns. At least, at last, I have word from [Oliver] Winston that they have plans and reports in regard to [the] future of Greendale. Monday I will see them in Washington. I hope they do not sell out.

I wish I understood better just what is proposed in Britain. Perhaps you can suggest references, or possibly you may be able to lend me a few of the best things that explain the present British thought and action.

We are planning to go to California at the end of the month.[1] Benton will be here Wednesday for a week. Then, if I can, I will go up to Cambridge for a day or two. Vernon de Mars, who is there now teaching at Tech., is going to dine with us tonight. This morning we went out to Sunnyside. I was surprised how well it was preserved. The Phipps are in superb condition. A really fine job in building is an economy, and a well-kept garden makes good living possible, even in a New York apartment.

I saw James Dahir: not so young, but intent on doing another scrapbook. I have not finished reading his first booklet.[2] But it does seem too bad that vital problems must be discussed by those who know the facts from what they found on library shelves rather than in actual experience.

Do try to get here before the end of the month. Affectionate greetings to you all from Aline.

Clarence

466

1. Aline's new film, *The Search,* about a mother's search for her son missing in World War II, was to be made in Los Angeles and Germany. It would be a critical success.

2. Stein was referring to Dahir's book on the use of the neighborhood unit in city planning practice.

---

374   To Aline Stein

A Thousand Years   July 8, 1947

Aline dear:

Ruth drove us out here after dining with me last evening. . . .

I ate breakfast and lunch by the side of a glowing fire. Another is prepared for tonight with the [Robert] Kohns coming.

I have been reading F. L. Osborn's experience of building and operating old Ebenezer's two Garden Cities—Letchworth and Welwyn.

It occurred to me that there was a similar analysis of our attempts for Radburn and the three Greenbelt Towns. Why were they such partial successes? With all our good intentions and hard work, why haven't these towns been all they should have been, all that Howard visualized? Don't take this as a regret. I know only too well the importance of these towns, and I recognize that the bridge between the past and the future can't be planned and built without many trials. To move on, we need not only experience but [also] understanding of our past work. So I spent the day outlining a study of what was intended and what accomplished at [Radburn] and the Greenbelts.[1] Such an analysis will be of value to F. J. Osborn when he comes here to us. . . .[2]

[Clarence]

1. This was the beginning of the two years of study of his own community designs that (late in 1949) produced the articles about Stein's work, from Sunnyside to Baldwin Hills. They were published in the *Town Planning Review* in 1949 and 1950.

2. Reading Osborn's book, *Greenbelt Cities: The British Contribution* (London: Faber and Faber, 1946), also seems to have stimulated Stein to begin rebuilding the RPAA, which was initially intended to act through regional New Towns committees to stimulate action to build new towns. See minutes of the Regional Planning Association of America, 22 April 1948, CSP/CUA.

---

375   To Liang Ssu-ch'eng[1]

[New York City]   February 12, 1948

Dear Ssu-ch'eng:

The letters from you and Phyllis gave us great joy. We have read them over again and again. Your sister has read them. By the way, I don't know whether I told you that she has been here a number of times since your departure. The last time was a particularly enjoyable occasion. She brought the children to see the famous Macy Parade on Thanksgiving Day from my balcony. There were some fifteen to twenty other children, and they all seemed to have a grand time.

. . . Wally [Wallace] Harrison [architect for many Rockefeller projects and at this time coordinating the design for the U.N. Headquarters] is such a busy person and jumps around the map at such a rate that he is very difficult to get hold of. I finally had a good talk with him by telephone a month or so ago. He told me that he was very anxious to get the Rockefeller Foundation interested. . . .

. . . The work on the United Nations buildings is moving along. I visited Soilleuse at the headquarters of the drafting force, which I presume you know was moved to the building that was erected by the New York Housing Authority on the site. A large force of draftsmen were busy making a new set of working drawings of the revised design. The purpose is to secure estimates now that the buildings have been cut to the bone. Those in authority were afraid that, if they asked the United States Government to finance the $65,000,000 loan, they might afterward discover that prices had gone up to such an extent that the work would cost more, and there would be no way to secure the additional money needed.

The design has been very much simplified, and as a result it has been improved in a good many ways. The library seems to have been omitted. I think they have the idea that they can use for that purpose the building in which they are now doing their drafting. There is talk also of postponing the construction of the tall building to the north. . . .

I have seen very few others of the U.N. planners. Nowicki is still working. I saw him at a meeting last evening and expect to have a good talk with him next week. He sends kindest regards to you. Ralph Walker is just back from a European trip. . . . A couple of months ago he was down in South America. Oscar Niemeyer was invited to give some lectures at Yale. For some unearthly reason the State Department refused him admission to the country, claiming that he was a Communist. . . .

I have been in the best of health and very active. I am still hard at work on my book. Getting together material on a subject of the kind I am trying to cover is certainly a big job. I would find it easier to build a few more little towns than to tell about the ones I have already completed.

I am also starting an association for the purpose of backing the idea of New Towns for America. We talked of this matter for years past, but nothing much except Radburn and the Greenbelt Towns have come of it. I think now that the time has arrived to really remake America on a big scale. . . .

In spite of all of the disagreeable things I have to say about the big metropolitan cities, I have to admit that Aline and I have found New York both exciting and enjoyable this past winter. There is a certain pleasure in being in the center of things, particularly if you can see it all from the height of our "sky parlor," with the green of the park as a foreground. Even the series of heavy snowfalls has not troubled us too much. It has made the park supremely beautiful.

To return to the question of your institute,[2] I will let you know just as soon as I can get further information from Wally [Harrison]. . . .

Aline joins me in affectionate greetings to Phyllis and to you.

Cordially,

Clarence S. Stein

1. Liang was a Chinese architectural historian whom the Steins had met in Peking during their 1935 stay in China. Liang served for a brief period on the international committee of architects who designed the United Nations Headquarters in New York City in 1947. Clarence Stein served as a consultant to the group and developed close friendships with three of the committee members: Liang of China, Nowicki of Poland, and Markelius of Sweden.

2. After many years of difficulty for the institute's field research, including Japanese occupation of much of China during World War II and temporary loss of many drawings and photographs, Liang's work was edited by Wilma Fairbank and published in 1984 by MIT Press as *A Pictorial History of Chinese Architecture*.

---

376 Essay

[New York City]   March 18, 1948

"NEW TOWNS FOR AMERICA"

The replacement of our obsolete, decaying cities is America's most urgent need. The breakdown of our urban centers is apparent in the flight of families in search of spacious, healthful homes in safe, natural surroundings. The outmoded incongruity of the centralized metropolis of the nineteenth century is further emphasized by the outward flow of industry to open areas beyond city borders. The migration of people and factories has so far been, in the main, a disorderly rout, lacking coordinated plan or development. It has left the old atrophied cities encumbered with debt, with artificially pyramided land values and taxes, crowded with outdated structures and with street patterns antagonistic to modern living and working. In most of the newer suburbs beyond the old cities' borders, the extravagant process of build, stagnate, and decay starts all over.

We cannot afford to continue repeating the same mistakes. We know how to build cities that will fit the needs of spacious, safe, healthful living, efficient work, and satisfying recreation. We know how to relate these communities to each other so as to bring living, working, marketing, and recreation closer to each other and to nature. Thus, we can eliminate the colossal waste of unproductive travel and conserve time, energy, and money for better living and more efficient work. We can bring our lives, our cities, and our countryside into harmony with our desires and with twentieth-century technical progress. To do so we must replace the obsolete patterns of the past. The mere patching of outmoded urban structures is futile. These cities built for another age are fundamentally antagonistic to our needs. Reliance on palliatives is throwing money into a bottomless pit. A new approach to city building is urgent. This cannot be developed within the restricting limits of the old city framework. A fresh start is essential. New towns must be built throughout America.

When these New Towns have been created in such a way that workers may live a good and economic life close to working places and to open country, there will be fewer obstacles to rebuilding the old cities as desirable communities. The modern pattern of streets, open places, and neighborhoods will have been thoroughly demonstrated. Sufficient population will have been drawn to the New Towns to adequately decrease congestion in the central areas. Then the old cities will be reborn—in a form appropriate to the needs and opportunities of the twentieth century.

To create New Towns and then to remake the old cities is a gigantic task. But our choice is not whether we shall rebuild or not. America is always being rebuilt. The question is [whether we shall] fit our new structures into the old mold and thus assure [their] early strangulation or . . . create complete, balanced communities that fit today's needs and will therefore live and grow.

A new policy of urban development cannot be postponed. Immediate action is required. We are on the threshold of the greatest period of construction this country has ever known. Nothing can stop it—the need for factories, homes and community structures, or highways and utilities is too great. They will surely be constructed on a vast scale, if good times continue. Now is the time for decision. The new physical form of America's communities will in large part determine the economic destiny of cities and countryside and, above all, the happiness and the good life of generations to come.

---

377 Memorandum

[New York City]   April 9, 1948

TO Catherine Bauer [Wurster], F. L. Ackerman, Frederick Bigger, Stuart Chase, W. Roger Greeley, Eugene Henry Klaber, Robert D. Kohn, Benton MacKaye, Clarence S. Stein

The Regional Planning Association of America has been dormant for some ten years. Meanwhile, the program that was advocated has become both more urgent and more probable of realization. As a result a new association is being formed to advocate New Towns.[1]

It seems apparent that the RPAA now should determine its future policy.

Shall it be revitalized?

Shall it terminate its work and its existence?

Shall it combine with the new organization?

To answer these questions, to discuss the past and consider the future, and also to decide what should be done with the small sum in our treasury, there will be a meeting of the RPAA on Wednesday, April 21st, at 1 West 64 Street, Apartment 12 A, at 8 P.M. If some other hour would be more convenient to you, please let me know.

Clarence S. Stein, President

1. This call for the first RPAA meeting since 1936 showed Stein's ambivalence about reviving the RPAA in a New Town advocacy role. Catherine Bauer responded negatively to Stein's suggestions. She thought that the revitalized organization should concentrate on regional planning, with a subgroup organized for the New Towns effort.

---

378   To Catherine Bauer [Wurster]

[New York City]   April 27, 1948

MEMORANDUM—Subject: Regional Planning Association of America

Your letter was superb: clear and logic[al].

I agreed after reading it. But have waited to discuss the matter with others.[1]

I could not get all of them together, so met Chase and Kohn separately. Stuart Chase agrees we should go on. Robert K. was more interested in the New Towns movement at the moment and had some helpful suggestions, but he was not opposed to continuation of [the discussion of] RPAA [at our] meeting [on] Thursday, April 22nd.

Ackerman, Bauer, Klaber, Mumford were all much impressed by your letter. We decided to go on with RPAA. Details later, but this is important: We must gather a younger group. (Lewis said, "Catherine Bauer is the only younger member that we took in." So you see where you stand.) The amalgamation with New Towns [was] not as unanimously received. I asked that I be allowed to study it. I want to talk it over with you. Are you coming here for N.P.H.C. [National Planning and Housing Conference]? If so, let's make an engagement in advance.

Benton MacKaye writes, "I vote with Catherine." Fred Bigger wrote a typical[ly] judicial note. He is on both or either side, as I understand it! I may be in Boston May 27, 28, and 29. Will you be there or at Cornell?[2]

1. A copy of her 13 April 1948 letter to Stein is in her papers in the Bancroft Library at the University of California, Berkeley. She discounts reviving the RPAA and using it to promote New Towns rather than setting up a special new organization for that purpose alone.

2. Bauer had been invited to give the Messenger Lectures at Cornell University. This was perhaps the most distinguished visiting lectureship in the university and carried the understanding that the lectures were to be published in a book.

---

379   To Lewis Mumford

[New York City]   May 30, 1948

Dear Lewis:

I saw Ben in Boston. He looks and feels fine. Catherine is also OK, and so is Bill.

With them and with Roger Greeley, I discussed Regional Planning Association of America and New Towns. What the relation of the two should be has had me stopped ever since the last meeting of RPAA. Now I think my mind is clear enough so that I can start going again. Here for your criticism is a setup:

RPAA for development of policy and programs in relation to broad planned development, including natural resources, population flow, industrial locations, and, therefore, New Towns and means of circulation, also regional authorities and governmental administration. New Towns Committees to go out and do things. Get needed legislation (after consultation with RPAA), see that workable administration is set up, study specific district problems of industrial and population flow, interest and educate industrialists, merchants, and the public in their area, find sites, organize corporations for creation of town, build it, and get it going.

It takes two different kinds of groups for RPAA and N.T. The first should be the same as the old RPAA, with new blood mixed with the old. All going [toward] the same place or at least in the same direction, though they follow different paths and use varied means of transportation. The size of the group doesn't matter; it's its mental quality and integrity. I think the main difference between then and now is that our goal is nearer. Nineteen-twenties was spring. We planted the seed. Now is summer and, perhaps, soon will be autumn and the crops will be ripe. Who knows? Anyhow, we must see that it does not rot.

The New Towns Committees require on their boards manufacturers and merchants, senators, administrators, and such like: go-doers. Let's hope they will will turn to RPAA for guidance.

RPAA should be national.

New Towns Committees should be formed as separate organizations in regions that seem ripe for action. New England, New York State, the Northwest (or Columbia River Basin)—their problems are different: the approach will not be the same. They might be tied together through a central board with representatives of the regional New Town Committees, or the RPAA might be the central stem. Anyhow, I hope their letterheads will read something like this:

NEW TOWNS COMMITTEE of NEW ENGLAND
Affiliated with the Regional Planning Association of America

What do you think of all this? Also, give me your opinions of these suggestions for new members coming from many sources. Also, give me more names. But remember, it's not numbers we need.

I am going to Greendale for the 10th anniversary next Thursday. Hope to see you when I return.

As always,
Clarence

---

380   To Aline Stein

Flagship Fleet—In Flight with American Airlines from Washington back home
June 23, 1948   6–7-1/2 P.M.

Dear Aline:

An interesting two days around Washington—from one office to another trying to find who was responsible for the order to sell out the Greenbelt Towns to the highest bidder. I didn't want to go directly to the head of the public housing, Jack Egan, fearing I would get a definite answer—"our policy is determined"—which would make it difficult to go higher. I suspected that he was following the advice of a little-minded lawyer who did not want to take chances. But the three fellows who were supposed to be in the know, as to housing politics, thought orders were coming from higher up —Foley, who is head of the top administration. Only thing to do is to get the White House to send word to Foley to change. Better see Kaiserling to get introduction to see the right one at the Executive House.

Next day, today, Paul [Oppermann] and I went over to see Vinton. Warren didn't have time, but I insisted, as he is close to the head of public housing and always has been supposed to be strong for the Green Belts. There, we at last got on the right trail. They are scared. They have the foolish notion that they might appease the enemies of public housing in Congress by throwing the Green Town overboard. And there *is* a lawyer that advises caution no matter what happens to the town folks.

Only thing to do is to go up to the legal top—Foley's lawyer and principal advisor. So we saw [John] Fitzpatrick this afternoon. He is all for the disposal of the Greenbelt Towns in such a way that their character will not be changed, 100% with us. Policy would have to be approved by his office. He hadn't heard of any decision to sell to the highest bidder without any restrictions. I told him I believed the order was being given. Paul will now follow up to see that Fitzpatrick asks Public Housing what they are doing. Such is my life in politics.

[Balance of letter is missing]

381   To Lewis Mumford

Palo Alto, California   August 13, 1948

TO   Lewis Mumford
FROM   Clarence Stein
SUBJECT   RPAA and all

. . . We are delighted with life in Stanford. Aline was great fun in *The Rivals*. The year 1775, when it was first presented, made me wonder if General Howe and the other leisurely leaders of the British did not have their minds on the easy life rather than that of the Rebels.

As to the RPAA, I think our dinner or get-together might be on the 10th. What do you think? I think it should be purely a RPAA affair, with perhaps a few guests. It might celebrate 50th anniversary of Ebenezer's book, RPAA 25th, and rebirth. I hope we will have new members before then.

Will you please draft a memo to go to prospective members telling them what we stand for, our history, the problems before us? Could you let me have it soon?

I have had a couple of good talks with [Jack] Kent. His department at U.C. [Berkeley] he hopes will be mainly research. He wants to start with metropolitan area problems. I have tried to show him that the frame is too restricting. He will make the same misjudgments as the R.P. of N.Y.& E. [Regional Plan of New York and Environs]. . . .

[Balance of letter missing]

382   To Lewis Mumford

Lake McDonald Hotel, Glacier National Park   September 1, 1948

Dear Lewis:

It is early morning and I am trying to keep warm in front of a great log fire. Luckily, I brought along a winter suit and woolen shirt. Days get warmer but not really hot.

We stopped off here after a rather energetic week of exploration in the Columbia River Valley. It has given us time needed to light and to begin to organize the varied impressions of the new land they are making. We saw both big dams and passed through some of the million dry acres that are to be made to bloom within the next few years.[1] Through Kaiser's aluminum plant, we traveled miles by jeep. It is too vast for the pedestrian. And I talked with a good number of those who have taken leading parts in the building of this great empire, finally with Ben Kizer. . . .

I hope I will have a chance to see you before long and talk over impressions of the Columbia Basin. It certainly seems time that the RPAA's great opportunity is in helping in the development of these new lands. Here is opportunity for pioneer experience.

Talking of the RPAA, I have been going over the ballots for new members. I do not find one from you, though most of the old-timers have responded. Was yours mislaid? It would help a good deal if you would write a short memo of invitation to new members describing our past and the future possibilities of usefulness. I need it when I return next week. I would like to get our new members joined up, so that we can have a reorganization meeting early in October. What do you think of combining such a meeting with the celebration of Howard's book and our twenty-five years? I would like to see it a leisurely get-together lasting all, or anyhow half, a day. Let's talk things over and get oriented. I should think that the Sunday before the meeting of ASPO [American Society of Planning Officials] would be the best. . . . Let me know what you think of this.

To you both,
affectionate greetings,
Clarence

1. Grand Coolee and Bonneville Dams were part of FDR's Columbia River Basin development.

---

383 To Aline Stein

In Flight AA American Airlines [en route to New York City]   October 20, 1948

Aline dear:

Now that I am floating godlike above the clouds, it is all clear.

1. Make your speech. Speak out for the right of minorities to be heard and of the duty of those who believe to speak out.[1] Even if you should not mention Wallace, you will serve your cause—and your conscience.

2. Refuse to resign from your job. Force them to fire you and to state (better, to write) why. I question that the congressional requirement—"nonpolitical"—prevents individuals from taking part in our democratic process.[2]

3. Get Osmond's opinion of this. If he agrees that there is no legislative restriction of the kind they suggest, fight it out as a member of ANTA.

And I love you,
Clarence

1. Aline Stein was active in the politics of ANTA [American National Theater Association], the actors' union.
2. This episode was connected with a speech Aline made in support of a political candidate. It was Aline's brush with the McCarthyism of the late 1940s and early 1950s. She and those close to

her suspected that her name was on the Hollywood blacklist. It is true that she experienced difficulty in getting work in the 1950s, but it is not clear whether the testimony of her associates in the film industry had resulted in the placement of her name on the film studios' infamous blacklist.

---

384   To Aline Stein

The Little House, L.A.   November 4, 1948

Aline dear:

Two days after election, and I haven't got over the shock—pleasant shock! We still live in a democracy. The people still rule and, when they get sore and make up their minds, the best political sales organization with all the money of Wall Street behind it might just as well shut up shop.

I don't think that the president carried in a democratic Congress with him. It was just the other way. The people were disgusted [with] the actions of the last Congress, so they put 'em out. Mr. Truman was wise or well advised—he campaigned against the reactionary Congress and, with a Democratic Congress, he went in. That's my diagnosis. I can't be more wrong than the political prophets.

Perhaps the new Congress will get rid of the Un-American Committee. And those that spoke for Wallace and freedom of speech may become respectable citizens again.

It was a fine talk you gave—much better than the first draft, though that was delightful. Keep them both. I will send the last one back to you. . . .

By the end of the week I should know if I have a job. If no, I will perhaps go up to San Francisco (it would be a shame to waste my round-trip plane ticket!) for a day or so. [I'll] see a few more folks here, and then home. Otherwise I *hope* Thanksgiving.

It has really been a pleasant experience. It is good to work out a problem and be convinced you know *the* answer. And if I lose, I am still much better off than Dewey.

Jennie [Mac] is fine. Tonight we dine with the Simons and the rest of the family. I will try to be silent when the election is discussed.

All my love, darling,
Clarence

385   Draft Letter

[New York City]   November 17, 1948

[DRAFT LETTER ON THE RELATIONSHIP OF NEW TOWN DEVELOPMENT TO
PROPOSED NATIONAL HOUSING LEGISLATION]

. . . Urban redevelopment should be postponed; . . . most, if not all, new construction must be on open land; . . . fringe development must be stopped. In this, I emphatically agree with you.

New Towns for industry as well as good living should be the primary objective or a realistic Federal Housing Law. By New Towns, I, of course, mean communities of a limited size, favorably located and sanely planned, built, and operated. Naturally, I include the planned enlargement of existing small towns.

We have long needed a constructive national program for New Towns. That need appears more urgent and more immediate now, on the basis of national security. Industries are being asked to decentralize. But a sensible policy of industry requires at the same time relocation of workers and essential services: in short, a broad program for creating New Towns and of locating them properly to serve industry and the nation. Such a program can only be carried out through the cooperation of government. This probably will have to be the federal government—anyhow, in the beginning.

Therefore new legislation should be framed to assist in the development of New Towns, properly located, at least in regard to the following:

Land should be secured by the government. It should be taken by right of eminent domain, if necessary. Adequate land should be taken in the beginning for the future growth of towns and their surrounding green belt. One of the principal difficulties of starting New Towns in America has been that of purchasing adequate land at a reasonable price. But an even greater difficulty has been that of holding the land while it was being gradually built upon. Therefore, government (probably national, but possibly county, state, or, in the future, regional) should hold the land until it can be developed).

Utilities and Highways: Financial assistance should be given liberally for them in the beginning. This should be in the form of land on easy and long terms. Possibly, where immediate movement of industry seems essential, the best kind of subsidy would be in connection with the purchase of land for the future and the installation of utilities and highways.

Subsidized Housing should be as easily obtained for desirable New Towns as for existing cities. In fact, the new law should completely separate the Siamese twins slum clearance and subsidy. Let them each stand on their own feet.

Self-liquidating Housing should for the time being be predominantly in New

Towns. Therefore, FHA insurance should be given preferably to large-scale planned communities for industry and good living.

Location of New Towns should be according to broad national and regional plans. Therefore, an agency is required for purpose of study and action in this field. This means the amalgamation of Public Works and Housing—and probably much more.

Cordially,

Clarence S. Stein

P.S. This is my personal opinion. The Regional Planning Council of America has taken no stand on new housing legislation, but I hope we do so early in December.

---

386   Draft Proposal for National Legislation

December 29, 1948

MEMORANDUM: LEGISLATION REQUIRED FOR URBAN DEVELOPMENT AS WELL AS REDEVELOPMENT[1]

The need of federal aid in the redevelopment of blighted areas of our cities as approved by the Senate [but not the House] last spring has been widely accepted in our large cities. But such redevelopment is temporarily impractical, for in most cases it requires the demolition of many homes. At the present time no habitable dwelling should be destroyed. Therefore, although legislation is required so that redevelopment may go ahead in the future, such activity should be postponed. The urgent problem today is not redevelopment, but new development in outlying areas. Most new construction for the time being must be on open land. Such developments, if they are to be economically or humanly sound enough to pay their way, must be planned, built, and operated as well-balanced communities, consisting not only of homes and community facilities, but also of industry. They must be planned to arrest the present trend of chaotic, unrelated fringe development of industry, as well as dwellings.

At the present time the primary emphasis should be on the development of economically and socially balanced communities, either through the establishment of New Towns or the enlargement of existing small urban centers. We have long needed a constructive national program for such New Towns. That need appears more urgent and more immediate now, on the basis of national defense. The National Security Resources Board is urging industrial decentralization. To be successful, such decentralization requires relocation of workers and essential services, in short, a broad program for developing New Towns and of locating them properly to serve industry and the nation.

478

Such a program can only be carried out through the cooperation of government. The federal government must take the lead—anyhow, in the beginning. . . .

State as well as federal legislation is essential to make possible building [of] the badly needed new communities. The states should permit setting up of local or regional governmental agencies to supervise such activities; the states also should give such agencies power of taking land by eminent domain. However, the federal government should take the lead by giving the development of new communities on open land equal opportunities for loans and other financial assistance, with redevelopment or slum clearance.

Clarence S. Stein

1. This draft letter is an outgrowth of the RPAA members' discussion of the Housing Act of 1948, which was not passed. In the revised Housing Act of 1949, some limited provisions were made for use of federal loans for vacant land development by local government redevelopment organizations, but they were little used in practice. Though Truman, Stein reported, said he would favor new communities being assisted by the federal government the same as redevelopment, major national housing and community development legislation was not passed until the 1949 legislative session. By this time it included no specific federal grant assistance for the state or regional New Towns programs RPAA had proposed.

---

387   To Catherine Bauer [Wurster][1]

[New York City]   January 3, 1949

Dear Catherine:

Thursday last I spent a very full day at Washington in regard to the disposal of the Greenbelt Towns and urban development as well as redevelopment. I saw Leon Keyserling and Jebby Davidson [and] also Senators Sparkman of Alabama and Flanders of Vermont.

Everyone seemed jittery. Leon and Davidson apparently had their minds on the president's State of the Union and economic messages. Keyserling told me that he would get in touch with me when he came to New York. Davidson, as a result of your letter, had apparently been looking into the matter of the disposal of the Greenbelt Towns. He was under the impression that there was no longer any danger. For the time being, I think he is right. I talked the matter over earlier in the day with Joe Orendorf in Foley's office. He, I know, was very sympathetic with our point of view. I was particularly interested to find out whether Foley wold hold up sale of Greenhills as well as Greendale so that legislation for negotiated sale might be considered by the 81st Congress. It is Greenhills, as you know, that Jack Egan wants to put on the block as early in January as possible. I now understand that Jack Egan's office has been directed to send any proposed prospectus to the Housing and Finance Committee before they take any action. This should give time for the passage of the needed legislation, if the backers of the Greendale veterans group act quickly enough.

I note that, in the *Milwaukee Journal* of the 27th of last month, Foley warns that such government-owned properties must be advertised for sale to the "Highest Responsible Bidder." In the *Sentinel* of the following day, however, it is said that Foley would not advertise Greendale for sale until Congress has been given a chance to enact legislation permitting negotiated sale.

The Alabama senator's reaction to New Towns was interesting. At first, he didn't seem to grasp what I was after. Finally, he said, "Yes sah, we're going to build them out in the cotton fields." Senator Flanders was too engrossed in a committee report that he apparently wanted to get out before the 80th Congress faded away to concentrate his mind on anything else. However, he had a nice young chap who discussed things with me at length. The senator apparently prefers to have his food predigested. I left two short memoranda with the senators, copies of which I am enclosing.

I finally had a very nice talk with Gen. Fleming. He seems very sympathetic to the whole idea of New Towns. I think in time we can get some real help from him.

Lee Johnson was a good deal of help to me, both in making engagements and telling me about folks. His health seems to be OK again.

My general impression of Washington and particularly of the Hill is that the new New Deal may be very short. The sooner you can get action on housing the better.

I am glad you're going to do the article for the Sunday *Times* in regard to New York planning. I think your idea in regard to it is very sensible. It is much better to offer a constructive program than to attack anybody. If I can be of any help, just call on me.

This morning Albert Mayer telephoned me. He wanted to tell me how important he thought it would be to have you here on the 18th, when [John] Gaus is going to lead our discussion about Planning and Government: Federal and Regional. Isn't there some way that you can arrange to come?

We've come on a queer one in trying to get the RDCA incorporated in the state of New York. They say our name is too much like that of the Regional Planning Association of New York and Environs. That sounds like a good joke. We were in existence, as you know, long before they took the first part of our name. They must have known of our existence because ours was one of the few organizations that attacked the work of the boys that were working at the Sage Foundation. Nonetheless, it looks as though the New York association, which might say that they have no objection, will block our way. I haven't had a chance to talk this over with people, but I am wondering what you would think of our changing our name to the American Regional Planning Conference, if it becomes necessary.

Thanks for your help in paving the way to Leon's and Davidson's offices. In the long run I think they will be a great deal of help. The fact is, I hope it will be possible to induce Keyserling to join the RDCA, or whatever it may be called.

My best to Bill and you.

Clarence

1. Bauer was teaching in the City Planning Department at MIT.

---

388 Essay

[New York City]   [February 1949]

"THE REGIONAL CITY: PROBLEMS CONNECTED WITH THE USE OF OPEN
GREEN AREAS FOR AGRICULTURE, FORESTRY, ETC."

"The Regional City consists of a group of communities, which, in aggregate, should be large enough to support economically the essential equipment of a modern American city. Each community, in addition to its residential function, may serve one or more specialized functions required for the group—industrial and commercial, cultural and educational, finance and government, entertainment and recreation. Community character is permanently established by a surrounding protective area of natural green. The open spaces between communities are kept permanently open for their related uses as farmland, recreation area, or natural woodland. Because the unit of scale of the Regional City is the free, safe use of the automobile and the airplane, the residents of any community within the city are as near in time to the other communities and to the open spaces between them as the residents in the outlying areas of the sprawling metropolis are to the center."[1]

Attached diagrams show the various elements making up the regional city. The basic unit is the neighborhood, centered around elementary school, shopping center, and community meeting place. This is very well illustrated by Greenbelt, with its population of 7,500. This could form a community by itself, but in general I am counting on there being towns consisting of groups of neighborhoods. The size of these towns would vary, but they will be limited so that everybody living in the town could be in close touch with the areas that surround it.

All of the units that are shown on the "Diagram of a Regional City" will vary in size. For example, the neighborhood, which is given as one square mile to serve a population of some 7,000 or so, may be a little smaller or larger. The regional city as a whole, as here shown, is for a population of approximately one million people. It might be half that population. The area covered, which I have given as 1,000 square miles for this million population, more or less, would actually depend mainly on the requirements for open areas, which separate the towns. That is why the question in regard to its practical use for agriculture, forestry, and so on is so important. The urban built-up areas, as shown on the diagram, would actually only come to about 160 sq.m., and this is based on these towns being very open developments. There would therefore be, as shown in the diagram, more than 800 sq.m. left as open area. These open areas, in addition to serving as places for recreation, should be used as far as practical for agricultural and forestry purposes.

1. This is probably a quotation from an earlier RPAA document that seems to be missing from the Stein Papers.

---

389   To Catherine Bauer Wurster

[New York City]   March 11, 1949

Dear Catherine:

It was good to hear from you. In regard to RDCA your advice will be of a great deal of help when we work out a final statement in regard to our purposes and organization. Final? That's just what we don't want it to be. We must make this organization flexible enough that its methods and even its purposes can grow and change. But now that we have the blessing of the secretary of state of New York and a name, it is time that we get organized. I don't know whether this will result in a constitution or not. Perhaps that is too formal, but at least we must have something that we call bylaws. The secretary of state, for some reason or other, is curious to see these. Then we will send out bills for dues. After that is done we will know who really are the members.

It looks as though, and I hope it is, a fact we are going to remain a small organization. In regard to additional members for the organization, I wonder whether we can't find some way in which the local groups as they develop will suggest new members. That's what Kent did in San Francisco. Do you think it would be a good thing for you and Bill [Wurster] and [John] Gaus to start a group in Cambridge?[1] If so, [could] you suggest additional members for the Boston area?

You asked about progress in regard to the Greenbelt Towns. There was a hearing on S-351, Senator McCarthy's bill, the last time I was in Washington, the week of February 21. The American Legion Community Development Corporation of Greendale was well represented, and there were representatives also of the central organization of the Legion. However, the two other towns were not represented. Walter Kroenig was in town, and after the hearing I suggested that we do what we could to get Greenhills and Greenbelt lined up. He telephoned to Larry Tucker in Cincinnati, and as a result the Greenhills Legion telegraphed the same night to the Ohio senators and congressmen, as well as Egan and Foley, in favor of the bill. Since then, the veterans in Greenhills have been organized in very much the same way as those at Greendale, and they will probably give good support.

Things don't look as well at Greenbelt. I went out there before leaving Washington and talked the matter over with Mr. MacDonald, who is now town manager. He agreed that similar organizations should be formed and assured me that the matter would be brought up before the veterans. I've telephoned him a couple of times since, and I don't believe he got very far with them.

The trouble is Col. Westbrook, whom you probably know, started some time ago to organize some kind of cooperative association in Greenbelt. He got a lot of people to sign up because it only cost $5 to do so. This probably is tying them to the organization, even though they don't know just what they are going to get out of it. From what I have heard of Col. Westbrook and the developments for which he has been representative in the past, they won't get very much. MacDonald has phoned me he was bringing the matter before the town council. I'll try to get out to Greenbelt when I am in Washington next week and try to see how I can help get the matter straightened out.

Of course, I'll try to see Lee Johnson. His advice is always of great value. I know he feels as I do that the Greendale veterans made a great mistake in letting the matter be brought up by Senator McCarthy. But that is done, and now we've got to see what can be done with the House committee.

With kindest regards,
Cordially,
Clarence S. Stein

1. Bill Wurster and Catherine Bauer lived in Cambridge, where Wurster was dean of the School of Architecture and Planning at MIT.

---

390   To Ernest Bohn[1]

[New York City]   March 17, 1949

Dear Ernie:

I note that Catherine Bauer sent you a copy of the letter that she wrote me on March 15 in regard to the disposal of the Greenbelt Towns. Here are a few notes that may bring you up to date in the matters.

I am enclosing a very short memorandum that I wrote on January 15 in regard to the disposal. Attached to it is the excellent summary of the action that the members of the Legion at Greendale propose to take. A bill to authorize the Public Housing commissioner to sell the three towns without competitive bidding has been submitted by Senator McCarthy of Wisconsin. This is S-351. A hearing was held by the subcommittee in regard to this bill on February 22. This was attended by representatives of the American Legion Community Development Corporation of Greendale and also of the national office of the American Legion in Washington and by

Jack Egan. I believe Foley also attended. I am told that the committee seemed to be favorable. However, the absence of representatives of the other two communities was noted, and I think they are going to have another meeting with the expectation of representation from Greenhills and Greenbelt. . . .

The main reason for my writing to you about this is that I hope, as Catherine does, that you may be able to suggest the way in which we can put Charlie Taft straight in regard to this matter. When I first got interested in seeing that the Greenbelt Towns were not sold down the river, I thought that the Taft brothers would be on our side. I don't know just what has led Charlie Taft to go over to the enemy, that is, if he definitely has. Anyhow, you, Ernie (who know everybody), must know how to get this matter before Charlie Taft. Can you talk with him, or do you know who will?

If you want further information, let me know.

With kindest regards,
Cordially,
Clarence S. Stein

1. Bohn, the director of the Cleveland Metropolitan Housing Authority and chairman of the Regional Association of Cleveland, had a long association with Stein and Bauer in developing national housing policy. He was a liberal Republican, but Stein thought he might be able to talk to Taft even though the senator was a conservative on most issues.

---

391   To William Wurster

[New York City]   April 13, 1949

Dear Bill:

I was glad to have a copy of your letter to John Nolen. I do not agree with you that the National Capital Housing Authority is the right body to take over Greenbelt.[1] I do not know much about this organization personally, but I am told by a very able observer who lives in Washington that the Capital Authority has shown much less interest in community facilities and community organization than most other housing authorities. The importance of the Greenbelt Towns is the fact that they are experiments in community planning, development, and operation. They should be put in the hands of people who are interested in further developing them as communities and not merely what are called "housing projects."

There is another reason why I am not interested in putting up a fight to have public agencies, and particularly federal public agencies, run these towns in the future. That is the fact that I believe Congress is determined not to dispose of the towns to other than federal agencies.

What I had hoped the National Capital Park and Planning Commission would suggest is that adequate greenbelt areas be retained and taken over either by your commission or by the state. This is of the utmost importance. The great danger, in my opinion, in connection with all three of the towns, is that their character may be lost if the greenbelts are not nailed down before the rest of the land is sold.

Greenbelt, Maryland, is partially protected because of the lands that were transferred to the National Agricultural Research Center. This is to the east. The northern land is also owned by the Research Center. On the west sufficient land should be retained for a greenbelt between the town and the proposed Washington-Baltimore Superhighway. To the south there should be a park or recreation area serving as a protective belt.

Both the House and the Senate bills neglected to offer means of protecting the character of the towns from the possibilities of future sale for speculative purpose of these lands, utilities, and buildings that remain under governmental care. I therefore proposed to Senator Paul M. Douglas the following addition to Senate-351: "However, streets, roads, public buildings, federally owned utilities, playgrounds, swimming pools, and parks, including adequate open land completely surrounding each project, shall be transferred to the appropriate nonfederal governmental agency without monetary considerations."

I believe that he will use this or something similar. You will note that I did not refer to greenbelts so much, but called them "open land completely surrounding each project." This the senator agreed would probably be more acceptable to certain of the senators.

I expect to have a none-too-easy time in getting this into the final law. The House bill, which has already been referred out by committee, does not include any clause of this nature. (Note that last week a number of other changes were made in House Bill 3440, before it was completed.) My other difficulty in regard to the change that I have proposed and that I consider essential is that the American Legion is not with me in this proposal. At the present Maxwell Elliott, representing the Legion, and I have been preparing the revision of the Senate bill at the request of Senator Douglas. We have agreed on a number of things that are desirable. Among these is permission for limited dividend corporations as well as cooperatives or mutuals to purchase towns. However, Elliott tells me that the Legion does not favor transferring the things that I have listed to other governmental agencies directly. They want to have them sold first and then let the purchaser turn them over to the town, county, or school board. This, I am sure, is too risky, [putting] too much power in the hands of the cooperative or limited dividend corporation instead of the people or proper governmental agency.

Please let Catherine see this. I am going to need the help of both of you when the fight really starts. . . .

Aline and I will probably be in Los Angeles from the middle of June on. If this matter is at all clear by that time, I'll be able to discuss it with Walter Arensburg.

My best to you both.

Cordially,

Clarence S. Stein

1. Wurster was a member of the Washington, D.C., Fine Arts Commission and so knew John Nolen, Jr., the executive director of the Washington National Capital Park and Planning Commission.

---

392   To Gordon Stephenson

[New York City]   April 18, 1949

Dear Gordon:

I hope you will excuse my having taken so long to answer your letter asking me to write an article for the *Town Planning Review.*[1] I can't think of any magazine that I would prefer to write for. My trouble has been that I have already promised Cedric Firth to write a lengthy article about the Greenbelt Towns. You have had a letter from him about it. It's turning out to be much more of a task than had expected— it always is! Besides, I have had to give a good deal of time to legislative problems. There is a bill up before Congress at the present time to dispose of the Greenbelt Towns. I am spending quite a lot of time in Washington so as to prevent their selling them without a guarantee of the preservation of the good quality of the towns.

I have not wanted to say no to you, and therefore I have just postponed writing from day to day until I could think of some way of working out a really thoughtful appraisal of the work of which you speak. I'll try to do it if I can, but before I can positively say yes I must have a little information from you so I can know whether I can fit it into the rest of my program. When would you want the article, and how long would it be?

I have been thinking about the matter over the weekend in the country. The title might be "Motor Age Planning" or "Evolution of the Town of the Motor Age in America." It would deal with:

1. Sunnyside as prelude to Radburn and as showing the impossibility of motor-age planning with the gridiron street restrictions.
2. Radburn, with the beginnings of the development of superblock and neighborhood, but limited by lack of industry and greenbelt.
3. The Greenbelt Towns, showing the advantage of the greenbelt and further emphasizing the need of industry.
4. Hillside Homes as an example of apartment house neighborhoods.
5. Baldwin Hills Village, showing the evolution of the service street.

There might also be a mention of Chatham Village, Pittsburgh.

486

Is this about what you mean? I think we'd have no difficulty in finding very good illustrations of all the developments.

Both Mrs. Stein and I enjoyed very much having you and your wife visit us [in New York].[2] We both send out best wishes to you both.

With kindest regards,

Cordially,

Clarence S. Stein

1. Stein had already started to write about his earlier work. This effort was soon turned into a series of articles in the *Town Planning Review*. This series was so well received that its editor, Stephenson, arranged to have the articles published by Liverpool University Press as the book, *Toward New Towns for America*.

2. This was the beginning of a long and productive friendship.

---

393 To Gordon Stephenson

[New York City]   April 27, 1949

Dear Gordon:

I was glad to get your prompt answer to my letter regarding the article for the *Town Planning Review*.

Just a few questions: You suggest July or October issues, and say that you would like to get the material as soon as possible. Exactly what date would you like to have it for the July number? I hope that you can run off a few hundred reprints for me. As to length, I can't say as yet. I want to make it as short as possible because I presume your architects may be like ours, who have time for plans but very little for reading. However, there is so much that I would like to say about the various developments.

I am drafting the part about Radburn now. When I have it roughed in, I will try to eliminate everything that will not be of value to those who are planning towns now. Perhaps I'll send you parts to get your judgment and criticism as I go along.

Don't weep about the disposal of the Greenbelt Towns. We have known for a long while that they had to be sold. What I am fighting for now is to prevent their getting in the speculative market. The special legislation that is proposed would limit their sales to cooperatives or limited dividend corporations. I am trying to get a clause into the law that will preserve the character of the towns in their future growth and, above all, prevent housing being built on the greenbelts. Before my article is completed, a decision will probably have been reached.

Aline and I may be in Denmark and Sweden this summer. In that case we'll try to end our trip in England. I'm very anxious to get better acquainted with those who are doing the planning work for the [British] New Towns. Particularly we want to see you and Flora again.

There is much that we have to talk about. Among other things I want to hear more about the plans for your new department and for the new buildings.

With kindest regards from both of us to both of you,

Cordially,
Clarence S. Stein

---

394   To Gordon Stephenson

[New York City]   May 13, 1949

Dear Gordon:

I'm having one time of it trying to condense the material that I have into an acceptable article for the *Town Planning Review.* So I thought I'd review matters with you before I go too far.

Here, to begin with, is the maximum number of words that I am counting on for each development. Sunnyside: 1,000, Hillside: 1,000, Radburn: 2,000, Greenbelt Towns: 2,000, Chatham Village: 750, Baldwin Hills: 1,000. This doesn't leave much, if anything, for conclusions.

In regard to each of these, I am proposing to [cover] the following subjects more or less in this order: (1) background: economic, political, and housing legislation; (2) purpose; (3) promotion; (4) site; (5) plan: unit, group, site, community; (6) construction; (7) research; (8) life in community; (9) results.

For your criticism I am enclosing a first draft of the section on Hillside Homes. Although I have cut it a great deal I can see that it must be pared further. Possibly some material can come under the illustrations. I'd appreciate it very much if you will let me know just as quickly as possible which of the subjects in my outline and in this draft will be of greater interest to your readers. In other words, I want to know what you think I can expand and which decrease or eliminate. It is pretty difficult for me to get proper perspective of the importance of the various jobs. All my architectural children are too dear to me.

I am enclosing one of the two excellent articles that appeared in regard to Hillside Homes. This is merely so that I can get your reactions in regard to illustrations. In the first place let me ask you whether you can reproduce from illustrations such as the two on page 2, one of the general plan and the other the cross section. I am going to find it very difficult to get original drawings or photographs of a good many of the plans and diagrams. . . .

Aline and I are both preparing for our trip. My time is growing short, so I hope that you will answer my main questions either by return air mail or cable.

Cordially,
Clarence S. Stein

395   To Lewis Mumford

[New York City]   June 1, 1949

Dear Lewis:

I was delighted to hear from you. I knew that you were deep in your book so had not expected to have any word from you earlier. I know now from my own present experience just how much concentration is needed when when one gets to the point where writing has to be produced.

I am spending most of my time at present on the article for *Town Planning Review* concerning the permanent results of my past. Gordon Stephenson seemed to like the one section that I sent him and has told me that it's all right if I spread myself a little bit more than I thought was possible. He says that he'll be glad to devote a whole number of the magazine.[1] I'm getting a lot of illustrations, and it may be all right. I wish there were an opportunity to go over some of it with you to see what you think, but that probably will not be possible.

In regard to the outline of the book, I think we'd better wait until this autumn. By that time you probably will be freer and be sailing along easily with your book. I will have returned from my trip. The additional notes which you have sent me are going to be a great deal of help in our visit to England. In regard to our dwelling, we are in luck. We are going to have the whole floor of Raymond Unwin's old house.[2] Isn't that wonderful?

Aline is flying to Denmark either today or tomorrow.[3] I'll be following her on the 13th.

Benton is fine. He has actually finished (I hope) all four parts, and I feel convinced it is a book. I wish he would forget his friends at the *Survey Graphic*. Anyhow, he agrees with me that the thing to do is try to find a publisher. Matthew Nowicki, who was with us over the weekend, read a good part of it, and he was tremendously interested and enthusiastic. He suggests that it be published by the North Carolina Press—whatever it's called—and Ben is giving him a copy to take with him. I think it would be a fine thing if you would write to them and tell them what you think of Ben and his ideas.

Our very best to you both.

Cordially,
Clarence S. Stein

1. In the end, two issues of *Town Planning Review* were devoted largely to Stein's long article (vol. 20, nos. 3 and 4 [October 1949 and January 1950]).

2. The Steins did stay in this old house of Raymond Unwin's in Hampstead Garden suburb.

3. Aline was acting in Denmark in *Hamlet*.

396   To Lewis Mumford

Helsingor, Denmark   June 23, 1949

Dear Lewis:

Do you think you can find time to run through the article I have been preparing for Gordon Stephenson? Your criticism would be very helpful at the present. All of the manuscript is in rather finished draft form, with the exception of a section on Greenbelt Towns, which will be #VII. The whole thing will be illustrated very fully with preliminary schemes, final plans, and photographs—excellent ones from all of the jobs excepting Sunnyside. Neither it nor Radburn seemed to have been photo[graphed] for some 20 years. I had Radburn [photographed] a day or so before I left.

Gordon and I will get together at Wyldes about the 15th of June. If we could have an expression of opinion from you at that time, it would be of immense assistance.

I have tried to follow roughly the same sequence of topics with each job, starting with the economic background. The first page will be a graph which will show, I think, to a certain extent, how "time and place and the so-called economic cycle mold the ultimate reality of our dreams." I have tried, where I knew the facts, to show how each development served as a place to live in and how it affected people's life. Perhaps I have laid too much emphasis on this in some cases—Radburn, for instance. I hope to have a compact "Conclusions," as in Chatham Village, after each development.

Gordon has asked me to end with a glance into the future. I might show what we or, at least, what I have been trying to accomplish toward building New Towns. What do you think?

And what change of emphasis should there be, or what do you think I have neglected? Can you think of other phases of these problems that would be of help to our English professional friends?

This has been a delightful experience here at Helsingor. Our balcony almost overhangs the waters that separate us from the Swedish shore. In [a] few hours that shore will be ablaze with fires to celebrate, during the few hours of the sun's absence, the longest day. The nights are astounding. The foreglow of the sun colors the sky long before midnight. The water is a deep, dark blue, and the crescent moon and sun compete for mastery of the heavens.

Beyond the picturesque village is the castle in which Hamlet lived, and there each night Aline plays his mother. It is a brilliant production, a thing of gay color and movement—much the flow and unity of a ballet. The natives come with their Danish script and were surprised that the lines have been rearranged. It is their Hamlet (he was one of their boys). They are experts, having seen the play by the best actors of many lands. Experts are conservatives. And this is far from a conservative production, but is a great one. Aline is enjoying it immensely and, of course, doing a fine job.

Ever best to Sophie and to you.

Clarence

. . .

---

397   To Lewis Wilson[1]

North End London N.W.3, Wyldes   [July 6], 1949

Dear Lew,

After our travels through Denmark, Sweden, and Germany, we have settled down in London. We expect to stay here for a month or so, so at last there is time and leisure to write to you.

I've just said we are in London, but you wouldn't guess it if you looked out of the windows. We are almost surrounded by open country and the woods and fields that form part of Hampstead Heath. We had the good fortune to rent a very old house—some five hundred years, they say. It is spacious and lovely and, what means much to me, it was the home of my dear friend Raymond Unwin. We have the feeling of living here instead of being tourists.

I am spending a great deal of time with various planners and others who are at work on the New Towns. I find they are very much interested in what we have done in America, particularly . . . Radburn [and] Greenbelt and, when they hear about it, Baldwin Hills Village. I believe that what we did in the Village in regard to the organization of service roads, etc., can be a lot of help to them. That is why I am anxious to make the article that I am writing for the *Town Planning Review* in regard to Baldwin [Hills] and the other places just as thorough and explicit as possible. . . .

[Clarence]

1. Lewis Wilson, Reginald Johnson, Robert Alexander, and [Edwin] Merrill were associated architects for Baldwin Hills Village, Calif., for which Stein was consultant.

---

398   To Benton MacKaye

[London]   August 2, 1949

These are happy days, Ben.

I am writing this in the room where Raymond Unwin studied and designed and wrote in the early morning. After I prepared that first cup of black coffee, I read his book. Then later in the day I rambled around Hampstead Garden Suburb, for which Wyldes forms a part. It is Unwin's greatest work in site planning and is discussed at length in his book. He was a great master in site planning in placing buildings in relation to each other and to the lay of the land. No one that I know surpassed him. Henry Wright came closest to him. He had a wonderful sense of topography and how it could be used to make a development more habitable. But he had too little sense of the beautiful. Raymond Unwin created beauty out of a combination of form and place. His work was in harmony with the material form of place but molded to serve man beautifully.

Last week Gordon Stephenson was here for four days. . . . We had a busy time, checking proofs and locating illustrations. The article has gradually expanded to the point where it will fill much of two numbers of the magazine. And Gordon proposes to make a book of it.

There is much more to write about. I will do so soon. Aline sends love.

Clarence

---

399   To Lewis Mumford

North End London N.W.3, Wyldes   August 6, 1949

Dear Lewis,

I was delighted to receive your letter of July 5th. It has been a great deal of help. The reason it has remained unacknowledged for so long is the fact that I have been somewhat overwhelmed by the job of getting the manuscript into final shape for publication. . . .

I was delighted that you like the manner in which the material was presented. I have given a good deal of thought to your main . . . criticism that equal attention was given to all of the developments. I think the comparative proportions will be changed as a result of the illustrations. Just before leaving New York, I had a wonderful set of photographs made of Radburn. They show the wonderful growth and beauty—all the trees now dominate the whole picture—but also the varied and happy life that goes on there. I think the quality of these illustrations will do much to lay particular emphasis on Radburn. This is important because of the extent to which the planners in England, as well as Sweden, are depending upon the Radburn idea for inspiration. Sunnyside is less well pictured. So far as I can find out, neither have any worthwhile photographs less than twenty years or so old. From Baldwin Hills I was able to secure some photographs, made recently.

There is only one point on which I do not agree with you in regard to the matter of importance of the various developments. Hillside can and should be of greater influence than it has been. Apartment houses rather than a row of freestanding houses are being used to such an extent in developments, not only in America but in the Scandinavian countries, that I think our experience in trying to create a neighborhood community of apartment buildings is worth restating at some length. . . .

This trip has been a delightful adventure. I cannot attempt to tell you about it all now. There has really been too much of interest. Most of it will have to wait until we all get together again. Then I will tell you why I am so enthusiastic about the manner in which the Swedes are developing great new communities—not just planning on paper but actually determining the location of buildings in their mass and in building them that way. I also can tell you a little of the sad way in which the German cities, or at least Munich, are losing the opportunity of rebuilding their cities as modern, functioning communities. At present, I am devoting much of my time to the New Towns here. I started with the Ministry of Town and Country Planning, trying to find out from their administrators and planners their procedure for building these New Towns and how it is working; then I am going to study the plans themselves with deSoisson and the others in charge of specific developments. It is all very exciting!

I also wish you were here to walk around Hampstead Garden Suburb with me. In the early morning I re-read Unwin's book; then when I can find time I stroll across the heath to the center of the suburb and take in its beauty and study the wonderful way the buildings have been related to each other. Unwin was certainly one of our great site planners. Henry Wright had a similar ability [to] locate . . . buildings in relation to the natural form of the land, but Henry lacked the adequate sense of beauty. Revisiting the Garden Suburb has made it clear to me that Unwin was not as great a city planner as he was a site planner, but of that more when I see you. . . .

Affectionate greetings to Sophie and to you from Aline and

Clarence

P.S. I forgot to say that your detailed criticisms of *Toward New Towns for America* have all been followed.

---

400   To Catherine Bauer Wurster

[New York City]   December 21, 1949

Dear Catherine:

When we last talked about the research in regard to community facilities, I told you I would send you some preliminary research I had started in regard to health. I had been so driven by my editor, Gordon Stephenson—who objects to my getting more than a month behind the deadline—that I have had no time for anything else. But now that that is about done, I found a copy of what I called "Tentative Outline of a Comprehensive System of Public Health Care in New Communities." This, I think, will serve to show how, in general, I think the problem of recreation, etc., etc., should be handled. At least, it will serve as a basis for your criticism.

I don't know just why I am taking the credit for this study, as you will see that most of the work was done by Dr. Margaret W. Barnard, New York Director of District Health Administration, and her assistants. I think they did a splendid job. It was my idea to get the opinions of certain regional leaders in this field in other parts of the country. This would be followed by a more architectural study. In this one should show the relation of health building and other elements in community centers. Also there should be, expressed either by diagrams or by words, some idea of the latest requirements for structure, that is, hospital, health center, etc.

It seems to me that it is on somewhat this basis that a study of this subject of community facilities should be made. Any research that is limited to smaller units, such as housing developments, [is] likely to be too restricted. The housing development, as far as community facilities go, must always be considered as a portion of something bigger—neighborhood, town, or a region. After a talk with Eddie Weinfeld yesterday, I am not as hopeful as I was of getting this job done as part of the research by Foley's crowd.[1]

Here is best wishes for Christmas and the New Year from Aline and myself to you and Bill. We do hope that when you come this way we will see something of you. Let us know in advance so that we can be sure to be free.

As ever,

Clarence S. Stein

1. The Housing and Home Finance Agency did finally develop, in connection with the American Public Health Association, a monograph on the full range of community facilities, a subject on which Clarence and Catherine had started working during the planning of Hillside Homes in 1932. The work done by others was published in 1950 as *Planning the Neighborhood.*

97. The small former farmhouse at A Thousand Years (January 1941).

98. Catherine Bauer Wurster, Bill Wurster, and Sadie, their daughter, at their home in Berkeley Hills (1940).

99. At the Steins' home, A Thousand Years. From left: Clarence Stein, Robert Kohn, and Charles Butler (c. 1940).

100. Stowe Township Defense Housing was renamed Ohio View Acres. Two such projects designed by Stein at the edges of Pittsburgh were built at breakneck speed during FDR's mobilization for World War II. The buildings were substantially renovated by the Allegheny County Housing Authority from 1978 to 1993.

101. The Steins' New York City apartment was at the top right, facing on Central Park—apartment 12A, 1 West Sixty-fourth Street (c. 1948).

102. Clarence and his sister, Lillie Stein Mayer, at the Double U Ranch in Tucson (1943). Stein was recovering from a nervous breakdown caused by the time pressure of his defense housing work and the long hours of travel between New York City, Washington, D.C., and Pittsburgh.

103. Proposal for a development called Fresh Meadow Park (drawn in 1944). In the last years of the war, Metropolitan Life Insurance commissioned Stein to do preliminary design for a large residential community on Long Island. His wartime health problems contributed to his loss of this commission. The Fresh Meadows project that was built was designed by his good friend, Ralph Walker.

104. At the Steins' weekend home A Thousand Years (1946). From left: Benton MacKaye, Jennie MacMahon, and Clarence Stein. The companionship of Benton and of Aline's mother, Jennie MacMahon, played a major role in Clarence's recovery from the mental illness that plagued him during the war years.

499

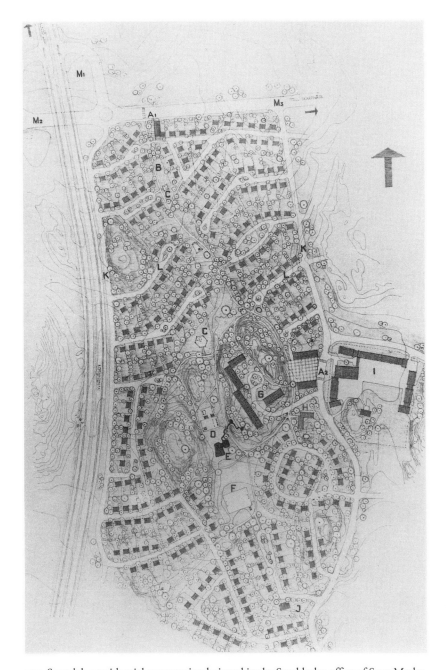

105. Scondal, a residential community designed in the Stockholm office of Sven Markelius, was much influenced by Radburn, which Markelius and his colleagues had probably visited during his trips to New York as a member of the international team of architects working on the United Nations Headquarters. Scondal, built in 1947 with only minor modifications of this plan, was an experiment in using the Radburn idea, which led to similar layouts for the higher density and better-known Stockholm satellite New Towns of Vällingby and Farsta.

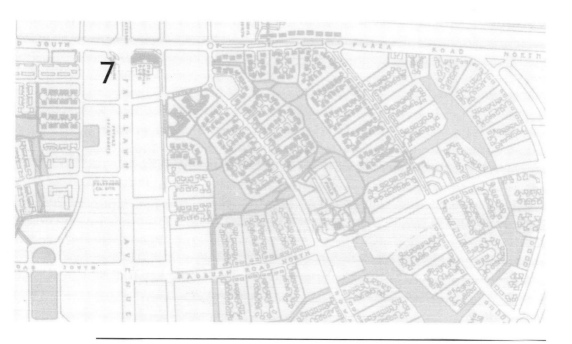

Fulfillment and Recognition
1950-1959

High energy, joie de vivre, and intense focus characterized Clarence Stein's days in the 1950s, especially during the early years of the decade. This was quite a contrast to his demeanor and daily program during the last years of World War II. The change had started in 1948, when he, Lewis Mumford, and Catherine Bauer had re vived the RPAA to launch an effort to develop a New Towns program in the United States and "save" the Greenbelt Towns. Then Stein wrote an important series of articles for the *Town Planning Review*. Through the influence of Gordon Stephenson and even more through Stein's publications in the *Town Planning Review*, Clarence Stein exerted a significant influence on British New Towns built during the 1950s and 1960s. Stevenage's later residential areas and the residential neighborhoods of many other New Towns built in England and Scotland after 1953 adopted the pattern that had now become known as the *Radburn Plan*, alternating footpaths and automobile access between rows of houses with substantial open space in the cores of the superblocks around which these subareas were organized.[1]

Clarence and Aline spent more time together in the 1950s, in New York, in Los Angeles, and on trips abroad, than they had in the 1930s and 1940s. During their long visits to England in the 1950s and 1960s, Clarence renewed his friendship with Raymond Unwin, whom he had first met in 1922. The Steins stayed at Unwin's

---

1. K. C. Parsons, "British and American Community Design: Clarence Stein's Manhattan Transfers—1924–1974," *Planning Perspectives* 7, no. 2 (1992): 181–209.

home, "Wyldes," south of Hampstead Garden suburb. In London, Clarence attended professional meetings, where he met William Holford, Frederic Osborn, and many other leading British town planners. One might say that he became a very familiar figure in British town planning circles because of his writing, lectures, and consulting activity. He admired and envied the British New Towns program. British town planners, particularly the younger ones, admired and used the ideas about New Town design that Stein had pioneered in America. These ideas were perhaps even more influential in Sweden, through their publication and through Stein's direct interaction with Swedish planners and community architects, especially Sven Markelius.

The circle of Stein's European professional friends and associates grew considerably in the 1950s and so, of course, did his correspondence with them. In addition to Stephenson, Clarence Stein corresponded with many English architects and planners, including William Holford, F. J. Osborn, and Charles Coote. In Sweden and especially in Stockholm, where the Steins made several extended visits and acquired many new friends, he corresponded with Sven Markelius, Yngve Larsson, and Göran Seidenbladh, planners of the Stockholm metropolitan region and its radial satellite New Towns, including Vällingby and Farsta. In Denmark, Clarence established a close relationship with Steen Eiler Rasmussen and his colleagues. Clarence Stein understood, appreciated, and influenced the work of these leaders of post–World War II European New Town planning. We have a very substantial record of his written interaction with them in his correspondence of this decade.

The Steins' travels also often took them west to California during the 1950s. Aline worked in films and with the Art and Drama Department of Stanford University as a visiting artist. Aline's film roles occupied longer periods of time for each film than had her early work with Warner Brothers, and Aline's mother, Jennie Mac, who had achieved recognition as an an actress in her sixties, moved to Beverly Hills, where she purchased a modest cottage. This provided a base for Aline's work in Hollywood and a home for Clarence during his extended visits to be with Aline and to work on a series of projects and studies of plans for community and open space in California.

A Stanford faculty committee was set up to study the possible use of land adjacent to the campus that belonged to the university. The chairman of this committee had seen Radburn, and he wanted Stanford to sponsor development of similar quality. Unfortunately for Clarence, and some would say for Stanford and Palo Alto, the decisions on the use of Stanford land that was located in the path of San Francisco Bay area urbanization were made by the trustees and leaders of the university without Stein's advice. In the early 1950s, Stanford decided, to Stein's dismay, not to follow his idealistic community planning concepts. Pressure for the development of commerce and industrial research was great, and so Stanford's decision makers treated the land development planning process as a series of very profitable, very attractive, and very useful real estate projects generating needed income. They possibly failed to realize the full community planning potential of Stanford's ownership of so much land surrounding its campus. The San Francisco office of Skidmore, Owings, and Merrill prepared the urban district plan for the university, which incorporated a number of separately planned real estate investment projects.

Clarence Stein was somewhat more successful in his professional role in shaping President Truman's emerging metropolitan dispersion, a policy of the federal government employment centers in the Washington, D.C., region. His involvement in high-level discussions about dispersion of federal employment in the Washington, D.C., metropolitan region was short lived. But perhaps his ideas about using New Towns as a framework for population dispersal in the region influenced the form of the dispersion that has actually taken place. Nevertheless, his proposals provide a window on Clarence's thinking in the 1950s about the relationships between planning for metropolitan regions and New Towns. This process is revealed by Stein's correspondence with Tracy Augur (the urban planner for the federal Public Buildings Administration), with Carl Feiss (the head of community planning for the Housing and Home Finance Agency, the predecessor of HUD), and with his colleagues Lewis Mumford, Albert Mayer, Catherine Bauer, and others, who revived and enlarged the Regional Planning Association of America and renamed it the Regional Development Council of America (RDCA).

The impetus for the 1950–51 discussion of federal employment dispersion policy was Russia's acquisition of atomic bomb technology. This unexpected development prompted President Truman's defense policy makers to consider the possibility that a single, well-placed Russian bomb could destroy almost all of the nation's leaders and program administrators. If federal employment centers were to be dispersed, Stein reasoned, so should their housing, residential services, and related employment centers. As Stein reflected in his letters of the time, he searched for sites for New Towns for these federal workers in the Maryland/Virginia countryside north and west of Washington. For a time, the federal reaction to fear of the bomb became the major reason in Washington and elsewhere in the country for direct federal intervention to restructure population distribution. However, Congress did not approve funds for a dozen dispersed 5,000- to 10,000-employee federal office centers. Nor did Congress seriously consider the plans Stein prepared for the General Services Administration (GSA) for an arc of New Towns to house their employees. Later, during the Eisenhower administration, the government did build many "atomic bomb-proof" deep shelters in an arc twenty miles north, west, and southwest of the District of Columbia. What is remarkable is the fact that these shelters in the foothills of the Appalachian Mountains, much war-related federal employment, and New Towns built in the late 1950s, the 1960s, and the 1970s seem to follow the Augur-Stein dispersion plans. Correspondence and some records of RDCA discussions about this federal policy initiative are included in the Stein Papers of this decade.

We also find in his papers examples of Clarence Stein's 1950s conceptual thinking, leadership, and organizational ability in his correspondence with Albert Mayer and Julian Whittlesey about the new cities of Chandigarh, a new provincial capital in Punjab, India, and Kitimat in British Columbia. Stein served in a consulting role on the first plans for Chandigarh, for which Albert Mayer, his longtime associate, had the planning contract, with Matthew Nowicki as architect.[2] A number of Stein's reports to Mayer are in the Stein Papers at Cornell. A few are included here. Later in the planning for Chandigarh, Le Corbusier was retained as its architect planner. By that time Mayer and Matthew Nowicki, with considerable consulting backup from Stein, had established a basic superblock, pedestrian-preferring structure for Chandigarh's plan, which Le Corbusier later modified.

In Kitimat, British Columbia, Stein played a larger, more direct, and more influential role in the conception and development of a community plan. In mid-1951 Stein signed a contract with ALCAN to direct overall community planning for the new town, and he served as coordinator and director of planning for Kitimat during the critical first year and a half of its conceptualization. He chose, brought together, and coordinated the work of a team of specialists assembled to develop ideas for Kitimat "far broader and more all-inclusive than a physical plan, . . . a complete plan for living." Clarence Stein's friend, Lewis Mumford, who seemed at times to misunderstand and undervalue Clarence's abilities and influence, noted that "Stein got [the job] because he was the one person [among the many planners who tried to get the job] who showed [ALCAN] that he had any grasp of the political and administrative realities of founding a New Town. . . . Once more at the top of his powers, [he is] almost the same man I knew in 1925, though he is now almost 70. That kind of opportunity is better than a magical injection of hormones to promote rejuvenescence!"[3]

The Kitimat job was more than a youth-restoring experience for Clarence Stein. It was, perhaps more than any other project or writing of the 1950s, very satisfying work for the new urban statesman, as Osborn dubbed Stein. Directing his group of specialists and working with Albert Mayer and Julian Whittlesey in his sky parlor above Central Park strengthened Stein's confidence in the efficacy of his ideas. With the assistance of Roger Willcox and strong support from Julian Whittlesey, Clarence Stein was able to continue as Kitimat's director of planning until early 1953, despite a mercifully brief return of his old problems with mental health. He also

2. Albert Mayer, "The New Capital of Punjab," *Journal of the AIA* 14, no 4 (1950): 166–75.
3. Lewis Mumford to Frederic J. Osborn, 8 December 1951, in *Letters of Lewis Mumford and Frederic J. Osborn,* ed. Michael Hughes (New York: Praeger, 1972), 200–202.

started to write again, more clearly and vigorously, about the successes and problems of New Towns in Britain and Sweden, about the Regional City idea, and about the sustained livability of his earlier residential designs. A Regional City book began to take form again, but it was never completed.

The fulfillment of Stein's goals to continue his work in regional planning and community architecture was accompanied by recognition from his peers. In 1956 the American Institute of Architects awarded Stein its highest honor, the Gold Medal, for his distinguished work as a community architect. The American Institute of Planners, at its 1958 meeting, gave him a Distinguished Service Award. Their citation stated: "No other man in our time has had a more effective influence in furthering regional and city planning worthy of a human enlightened community. With a generosity of spirit that sets a high example to his peers and successors, his talents as both organizer and designer of new communities evoke . . . admiration and gratitude."

Throughout the 1950s Stein's circle of correspondents grew, and many new correspondents appear in letters selected for inclusion here from the large number preserved. The number of his correspondents and the range of his interests are staggering. In 1957 he was sixty-five years old, but he had almost ten years of productive life before him.

There is much of interest in Stein's writing during the last decades of his life. Toward the end of the very productive decade of the 1950s, his thoughts returned increasingly to the past and to the joys of everyday life. He and Aline traveled together more; they took long trips to England, France, Italy, Iran, and Israel, and Clarence commented at length in letters to his hosts and friends on city and regional planning in these countries. He drew deep pleasure from each day when he was "at the top," which was most of the time. Sir Frederic Osborn, writing of Stein's aesthetic sensibilities to his friend Lewis Mumford, noted, "In [Stein] again, as in New York ten years [previously] at sunset, the ecstasy that essentially urban architectural effects give him [was] quite as acute, [he thought], as that of the aesthetes who edit the magazines."[4] Stein's intellect was functioning, too, in concert with his sensibilities. In another letter Osborn wrote, "Clarence seems to have taken another dose of monkey glands, or something; at any rate, I have had a stream of inquiries from him about New Towns' experience and policy which necessitated copious replies."[5]

4. Frederic J. Osborn to Lewis Mumford, 25 October 1958, in Hughes, *Letters of Lewis Mumford,* 283–84.

5. Frederic J. Osborn to Lewis Mumford, 21 November 1960, in Hughes, *Letters of Lewis Mumford,* 297–98.

CLARENCE S. STEIN, 1 WEST 64TH ST., NEW YORK 23 · EN. 2-8065

401   To Yngve Larsson

[New York City]   January 4, 1950

Dear Yngve:

I was delighted today to get your letter and new year's greeting. I will ask someone to translate your article about Sven Markelius just as soon as possible.

Although I have not written to you for some time, my thoughts have been with you often. There are so many pleasant recollections of the altogether-too-short time that I spent at Stockholm, the cordiality of Mrs. Larsson and you, the great help that you gave me in getting acquainted with the city and so many of its activities, and your friendly assistance—along with that of Sven Markelius, Blum, Nils Ahrbom, Eskil Sundahl, and all the others.

The only reason that I have not written to you earlier is the fact that, ever since my return to America, I have been trying to make up for my long vacation and also to finish the series of articles that I was writing for the *Town Planning Review* of Liverpool. I hope that you have received the copy of the series that includes the description of Radburn that I asked them to send you. The lovely photographs were taken as a result of the visit with you and Mrs. Larsson. After that visit I wrote the few paragraphs "Radburn Revisited," and I was surprised to find that I really had no pictures that represented the present beauties of Radburn. All the photographs that existed seemed to have been taken in the early days, some twenty years ago. Therefore, on the last couple of days that I was in America, I succeeded in having these pictures made by a very intelligent young woman photographer [Gretchen Van Tassel].

After I left you in Stockholm, I spent a short time in Germany, where Mrs. Stein was acting for our soldiers. We then flew to London, where we spent two months in the former home of Sir Raymond Unwin. It is delightfully situated on the edge of Hampstead Heath and had been remodeled from the [500-year]-old dairy called Wyldes. . . . My time there was equally divided between writing the articles for the *[Town] Planning Review* and getting acquainted with the New Towns that are being built in England. I visited the administrators and particularly the technicians in the main office in London and then went out to see the towns themselves and the group of architects, engineers, and others who are building them. Perhaps I exaggerate when I say they were building them. Financial conditions in England have been so difficult that progress has been very slow.

I have not had a chance since I returned to study my notes and plans that I brought back from England. I presume that I will find that the English planners are really making a great contribution. But as I look over the summer, it seems to me that the strongest impression of progressive movement in planning was that which I got in the short time that I was in Sweden. It may have been that your hospitality and the thoughtful guidance of all the others bewitched me, but I think not. I think that a tremendously valuable contribution is being made, not only in the orderly manner in which the remainder of Stockholm is being planned and built as a single process, but also in the design of the neighborhoods as units related both to the requirements of living and the form of the land. My first impression of the unusual approach of the Stockholm planners I received when I arrived by air and saw the new houses, partly hidden among the old trees that were left standing. This relating of every building and every group of buildings to the site conditions impressed me even more strongly as I studied the developments on the ground with you and others.

I have been wondering if there was not some way in which it would be possible to give the general public here in New York some idea of this procedure and the results. I discussed the matter only the other day with Mr. Philip C. Johnson, who is in charge of the architectural department of the Museum of Modern Art. He was very enthusiastic. He suggested a comprehensive exhibition at the museum. I think that would be of great value at the present time, as the last Congress passed the housing bill, which means that there will be a large appropriation for more housing, to be spent here in New York, among other places.

Here is just a brief idea of what I think should be expressed by such an exhibit:

1. The planned developments of neighborhoods as a whole and as part of an integrated city pattern.
2. The relating of buildings to the actual form of the site in such a way as to preserve, as far as possible, trees, streams of water, rocks, and in general the form of the land.

3. The design of buildings of varied heights and uses as a coordinated design.

4. Procedure of planned development from the original concept in Markelius's office through the study in massing and in relation to ground, use of models, to the construction by Sven Wallender's cooperative organization or other means.

There is much to be said on the subject. As the audience is to be mainly the general public, it will, of course, have to be expressed in very simple terms. It [would] probably be best if the material were available to take a single development and show it through the project periods and on to the time when it is completed and the living place of many families. Possibly Reimersholme might be good to take as a key example. Markelius, of course, I presume, would be the best person to judge. My suggestion is not that the exhibition need be restricted to showing a single settlement, but that it would be easier for the general public to understand if we made a single place the central feature.

What do you think of this suggestion? Do you think that it would be possible for Stockholm or Sweden to bring together material for such a display? Mr. Johnson tells me that, although the museum would be very happy to meet the expenses of putting on the show, they have not the funds at present to pay toward the collecting of material or its transportation as far as New York.

I know that such an exhibition would be of great value to us in New York. I also think that it would increase America's understanding [of] and respect for the Swedish people and the outstanding work that they are doing in planned development.

If you are interested in this suggestion and think it is practical, I hope that you and Markelius will take my outline in regard to the exhibition as purely tentative. Do let me know as soon as you have had an opportunity to consider this proposal.[1]

My best wishes to you and Mrs. Larsson. With kindest regards,

Cordially,

Clarence S. Stein

P.S. *The Ten Lectures on Swedish Architecture* is of great interest.[2] A short time ago Alva Myrdal was here. Although she had written one of the articles, strangely enough she had not yet seen it.

I have sent you Louis Sullivan's *Autobiography of an Idea*. It is not only the tale of one of our greatest architects, but also I think one of the loveliest descriptions of the life of a child.

1. Stein's proposal did not lead to an exhibit of Sweden's urban design achievements at the Museum of Modern Art (MOMA). A book by Kidder Smith, *Sweden Builds* (New York: Bonnier, 1950), provides an excellent overview of the Stockholm satellite towns. Stein's article "Stockholm Builds a New Town" in *Planning 1952: Proceedings of the Annual National Planning Conference*

Held in Boston, Massachusetts, 5–9 October 1952 (Chicago: American Society of Planning Officials), 56–83, describes the Swedish planning and design process.

2. *Ten Lectures on Swedish Architecture,* ed. Thomas Jacobson, Thomas Plaenge, and Sven Sillows, trans. William Cameron (Stockholm: National Association of Swedish Architects, 1949). The book includes a long chapter, "Town Planning in Stockholm," by Sven Markelius and Göran Sidenbladh. The most recent complete discussions of Stockholm's satellite New Town building experience are found in David Pass, *Vällingby to Farsta: From Idea to Reality, the Community Development Process in Stockholm* (Cambridge: MIT Press, 1973), and David Popenoe, *The Suburban Environment: Sweden and the United States* (Chicago: Univ. of Chicago Press, 1977).

---

402   To Albert Mayer and Julian Whittlesey[1]

[New York City]   February 8, 1950

TO	Mayer and Whittlesey
FROM	C. S. Stein
SUBJECT	Chandigarh
RE	Separation of Roads and Paths Should Be as Complete as Possible

1. Such separation has been successful over a period of many years at Radburn, Greenbelt, Baldwin Hills Village, and elsewhere. Compared with the old method of road and path combined as [a] single street, it is safer, more peaceful, [and] more beautiful.

2. It is criticized as more difficult to police and therefore dangerous for women and children. That is contrary to the experience in America during the last 20 years. An inhabitant of Radburn for over 18 years says that she has never heard of an assault or robbery in the park. But she was relieved once of her pocketbook near the store building. There is more danger of this kind on the streets than on the park walks, she says.

Baldwin Hills Village paths in the park are used for walking, says a tenant since the beginning, rather than those along the outside road. They are safer. When his young daughter goes to the movies at the end of Baldwin Hills Village by herself, her parents insist that she go by park path, because outside the young men might annoy her. There is only an old man as watchman in the park, but that is found sufficient.

At Greenbelt, in spite of my close contacts with the town for ten years, I have never heard of complaints of danger there, nor was any [such] report made [in] later lengthy studies of how the plan had worked . . . by Kate Edelman and in a different form by Louise Blackham.

The police force is small and has many other jobs, but none of the past town managers I have known has complained of, or even mentioned, dangers in the parks. The present city manager, Charles McDonald, has just told me that he is not aware of any.

3. *The Additional Cost of Lighting* is another objection given [by] those favoring the customary relation of road and walk. Mr. McDonald considers this cost unimportantly small. It can be minimized by careful planning and design. But even if it could not, the advantages of separation are so great that they would be worth paying for.

4. *The People of India* are different, it is said. So were the Americans before 1928. The street pattern and relation of road and walk seemed fixed. But at Radburn the new arrangement of separate walk and road made sense to the people who moved there. And so it has been accepted at Chatham Village, Greenbelt, and Baldwin Hills Village.

5. *The Manner of Detailed Planning* will differ in India. There will be larger crowds walking (and thus additional safety), for one thing. But the basic need of safety and natural beauty exists in all contemporary civic design.

1. Albert Mayer and Julian Whittlesey were under contract to design Chandigarh, a provincial capital city in India, and they retained Stein as a limited consultant. Stein recommended that Matthew Nowicki become a member of the Mayer and Whittlesey staff in India. Their preliminary plans were sometimes reviewed in the Steins' sky parlor when the principals returned to New York. Replacement of Mayer and Whittlesey by Le Corbusier, Maxwell Fry, and Jane Drew in 1952 did not undo the general concepts of the Chandigarh plan that Mayer and Whittlesey had developed with Stein's criticisms.

403   To Matthew Nowicki

One West 64th Street, New York 23, N.Y.   March 21, 1950

Dear Matthew:

We had a long and interesting meeting in regard to the two proposed plans of the capital of East Punjab. Your suggestion had been drawn up to compare with the earlier suggestion, which had been further developed. I am sorry you could not be present.

This very partial note [is] in regard to plans I thought might interest you.

When are you coming again? . . .

Our very best wishes to all four of the Nowickis,

Cordially,
Clarence S. Stein

404   To Benton MacKaye

[New York City]   September 8, 1950

Dear Ben:

Your [draft] letter of September is received. I agree, in view of the complemental purposes of our organizations (Regional Development Council of America and the

Wilderness Society), that a joint offer of our aid to the Washington Regional Planning Council would be appropriate. This, as you say, would be aimed not to "refine the plan" which the Washington Council itself has in charge, but to "win acceptance for it" through our respective memberships, in case, of course, we believe the plan to be in line with our objectives.

Our objectives are really one—regional habitability, the attainment of a region's proper balance between the urban, the rural, and the primeval environments. The RDCA enters this problem through the urban door, and the WS through the primeval. The RDCA is concerned immediately with the building, or rebuilding, of communities and, hence, the maintenance of a healthy urban influence in the country, not forgetting its equally vital antidote, the primeval influence. The WS is concerned immediately with the maintenance of a healthy primeval environment, not forgetting its complemental urban environment.

Such is our relation, couched in abstract terms. The Washington dispersal project might afford us an opportunity to do a useful job in concrete terms.[1] In no sense should we suggest any possible duplication of the work of the local body (the Washington Council), but I can see a possible supplementation of their efforts by getting their conceptions before the country at large, with such reactions in the country's Congress as might be.

If, for instance, their conception is that of the "Regional City," it would fit precisely our own visualization, which we might help pass on to the public. There are two visualizations of urban expansion: (1) a continent and (2) an archipelago; a solid metropolitan mass and an open regional fabric. Ours is the latter, a city of cities, the parts kept distinct and individual by substantial open belts and spaces, the urban and the wilderness influences side by side. American urban expansion, unfortunately, has taken usually the metropolitan form (wherein wartime danger is now added to its accepted aberrant qualities). "Greater Washington" has got started toward this dangerous form (1), but a vigorous patriotic demand might yet steer it toward form (2).

I should be glad to consider with you further this absorbing and timely subject, with a view especially of approaching the Washington group.

Yours sincerely,

Clarence S. Stein

1. Stein, always an optimist in such matters, had no idea of the strength of the opposition that would develop to a federal role in the development of New Towns during the Truman and Eisenhower administrations. His work with Tracy Augur on the dispersal of federal workers in the Washington region in the early 1950s included consideration of New Towns as an element of the dispersal. The legislation authorizing this dispersal did not pass in the Congress. The atomic bomb shelter aspect of the plan was implemented during the Truman and Eisenhower presidencies. For an examination of the Washington dispersal plans of 1950–51, see K. C. Parsons, "Shaping the Regional City, 1950–1990: The Plans of Tracy Augur and Clarence Stein for Dispers-

ing Federal Workers from Washington, D.C.," in *Proceedings of the Third National Conference on American Planning History* (Cincinnati: Society for American City and Regional Planning History, 1989), 649–89.

---

405   Memorandum to RDCA Members

[New York City]   October 5, 1950

Next Meetings
Friday, October 20th, 4:30 P.M. C.S.S.'s apartment, 1 W. 64th Street, N.Y.C. Lewis Mumford will lead discussion on Regional Redistribution of Federal Government Functions. This meeting will be the first of a year-long series devoted to restudying the objectives of regional planning. See discussion below. . . .

Summary of Decisions by Executive Committee Meeting, September 27th, in N.Y.C.:

Present: E. Carlson, L. Mumford, A. Mayer, H. Pomeroy, C. S. Stein, R. Willcox.

Schedule of Meetings, 1950–1951: Last year we held 12 meetings in this area. Most were well attended and worthwhile. However, several members have asked for a regular monthly meeting date and a continuous program of discussion. It was agreed to hold regular meetings as announced above and additional special meetings when unusual circumstances warrant.

Program for Regular Meetings: Those present agreed with Lewis Mumford's opinion that no useful self-education is possible unless it has a definite objective. During the 1920s the old Regional Planning Association of America members had the desire to promote Garden Cities and a new way of organizing regions. Today, if we wish to successfully continue the work of the RPAA, we should recognize the need for establishing and working for definite objectives.

After further discussion it was agreed that the theme of our regular meetings for 1950–51 should be a reexamination of the assumptions on which we work in the general field of regional planning; development of Garden Cities, creation of desirable regional patterns of development, regional redevelopment. Each meeting should be a continuation and extension of the main theme as it has been developed during the previous sessions. It was agreed that Lewis Mumford should lead off the series by examining the position of the federal government with regard to present and potential requirements for governmental decentralization.

It was further agreed that, when deliberations of the Council reach definite form with respect to some current issue, such as the Washington, D.C., situation,[1] that the Council members would be advised as to suggested action to take.

New Members: It was agreed that both the Council as a whole and the loosely formed and potential regional groups of Council members would benefit by an increase in membership of the Council. Members are hereby encouraged to recommend people for membership, especially those interested in the problems of regional development because of its special impact on their own professions—be they doctors, lawyers, sociologists, engineers, union officials, executives, architects, city planners, economists, population experts, bankers, or other!

1. Stein was at this time serving as a consultant to Tracy Augur, who, as regional planner for the General Services Administration, had played a leading role in the development of proposals for President Truman's National Security Resources Board to disperse federal workers in the Washington, D.C., region. These proposals included Stein's recommendation for an arc of New Towns northwest of the capital city to house workers in federal "Employment Centers" sixteen to twenty miles from the White House. In January 1951 Stein wrote to Vernon DeMars about this project: "At the present time I am kept pretty much on the go, particularly in connection with the Washington Dispersal problem. I am one of Tracy Augur's consultants in regard to this problem. Just what will happen I do not know, and of course I cannot tell you in any detail what we are considering. But it is, as you can imagine, a very exciting affair." In April 1951 Congress rejected Truman's plan for dispersing workers.

---

406   Memorandum to Lee Johnson

[New York City]   October 13, 1950

SUBJECT: THIS HOUSING EMERGENCY AND THE NEXT

War or defense housing should be built as permanent housing and as part of permanent communities. The greater part of it will be used for a long time. We have never caught up with one housing emergency before the next one has us on the run. Therefore, for long peacetime use and because contented workers are [a] primary essential in war:

(1) Standards of size, etc., of public housing should not be lowered. Standards of minimum FHA should be raised.

(2) Community equipment, including plentiful open spaces, are essential parts of all housing development. If all equipment cannot be built at once, space should be left for it.

(3) Dispersal is a basic requirement of both peace and war.

(a) If war comes or the threat of atom bomb is realized by the public, there will be a flight from the big centers.

(b) Industry, particularly big industry that requires spreading, one-story buildings, is on the way out. They are going out to stay. This is not a war or defense measure; it is just business sense. Locations that are good for war are best for peace—most of them, anyhow.

(c) Workers must be conveniently related to these industrial sites. If they are they will be in the best location both for defense purposes and for future peaceful living.

The communities of houses should therefore be designed, grouped, and built for the future:

1. as community neighborhoods interrelated for shopping, education, and recreation;
2. surrounded by countryside, farms, and forest;
3. well served by means of transportation.

All emphasis should now be put on the building of such open-land communities or the building up of small communities close to carefully selected industrial sites for defense and peace.

Redevelopment should for the time being take a back seat. It can wait.

This change of emphasis requires revision of laws: federal, state, and local. For instance, we need state legislation for regional or county housing authorities, planning boards, and perhaps even town building corporations. There must be centers and offices for planned distribution of industry and community development, both federal and state.

Clarence S. Stein

---

407 To Tracy Augur

[New York City]   November 8, 1950

Dear Tracy:

Dispersal it shall be hereafter. We are delighted that you can come here on November 17 to tell us all about it.

I note that you say that the project is still classified. That's another word that will have to be explained to us! But I can assure you that Roger Willcox will not send out the minutes of the meeting until you have had a chance to go over them and cross out anything that should not appear.

I have heard from Fritz Gutheim and Carl Feiss that they also will be here. I presume that you will have an opportunity before you come here to discuss the manner in which you prefer to divide the subject.

I am hoping to be in Washington next Monday. If so, it would be fine if we could all get together.

Now as to another subject—that is, Civic Films. We have, as you know, a very small board of directors, and as a result of Fred Ackerman's death there are only four of us left—Robert Kohn, Harold Buttenheim, Lawrence Orton, and myself.

The City, I needn't say, has been a great success, and there is still a demand for it. We feel that the time has come for us to decide on doing other work in this field, and we therefore want to slightly enlarge our membership. We think that you could be of a great deal of help to us. I am therefore asking you to be a member of the board. Of course, I haven't forgotten that you were a member some time ago, as president of the Planning Institute, but I hope that you will again join our ranks. So that you and Carl Feiss, whom we are also inviting, may become better acquainted with what we are doing, we are calling a meeting for the same day as the RDCA meeting (that is, on Friday, November 17). The meeting will be at 12:15 at the Town Hall Club, 123 West 43rd Street. Ask for Harold Buttenheim.

The meeting of the RDCA will be at four-thirty promptly, at my apartment, 12-A, at One West 64th Street.

Cordially,
Clarence S. Stein

---

408 To Aaron Copland

[New York City]   November 21, 1950

Dear Mr. Copland:

This is to confirm our conversation of this morning in regard to the picture *The City.* You said that you would be good enough to give all rights that you might retain in regard to the motion picture *The City* to Civic Films, Inc. As I explained to you, Civic Films, Inc., is a nonprofit organization. We receive a small amount for the rental of the picture, but all this money is put aside for use for educational purposes. In the future we hope that we will be able to collect enough to produce another film of the same general type as *The City.* The directors of Civic Films, Inc., are architects, planners, and others interested in developing better types of cities in America. In the distribution of the film, we have been represented by the Museum of Modern Art.

Thanks very much for your cooperation. I don't want to miss this opportunity of telling you how much we feel indebted to you for the music of *The City.*

Yours cordially,
Clarence S. Stein

P.S. Will you kindly sign the enclosed formal release and return it to me in the enclosed envelope?

---

409 To Catherine Bauer Wurster

[New York City]   November 30, 1950

Dear Catherine:

Lewis and Sophie will be here for dinner with you on Sunday, December 10. Albert will come later. Benton MacKaye will also be here. We are looking forward to the party.

We have been trying to arrange an Executive Committee meeting of the RDCA during your stay here. The best time seems to be Tuesday, December 12, starting with lunch at one and going on through the afternoon. There is much to discuss, but the main subject is that which grows out of the memorandum "Creative Decentralization for Defense and for Living," that Albert prepared, a copy of which was sent to you and Bill. This was discussed at our meeting this Tuesday. It was decided that the RDCA, with the approval of the organization as a whole—including members outside of New York—should:

1) Send a letter to the president on this general subject
2) Follow it up as far as it can with a campaign to drive home some sort of sane policy in regard to decentralization.

Lewis volunteered to re-edit Albert's memo. That will be ready early enough before this meeting so that it can be sent to the members of the Executive Committee.

The purpose of this is to induce you to keep Tuesday lunchtime and afternoon open. Let me know whether this is OK just as soon as you can, please.

I don't know whether you have heard that we are really making an active effort here in New York to set up something similar to the big housing cooperatives in Sweden. This is to take in only the New York region to start with. There is a good board of directors, and it looks as though there would be some action. The office force consists mainly of a young man of the name of S. F. Boden, who I think is going places. I would like very much if I could arrange to have you meet him while you are in New York. We have just been discussing over the telephone the need of formulating (1) some type of statement of what we mean by "cooperative"—this in light of the fact that face cooperatives are spreading everywhere—and (2) what type of housing and community we are interested in fostering. Boden would like to get some general impressions from you.

I can see that you are going to have a nice, leisurely time here in New York! Greetings.

As ever,

Clarence S. Stein

---

410   To Carl Feiss

[New York City]   December 1, 1950

Dear Carl:

I have again read the preliminary statement of the *Slum Clearance and Urban Redevelopment Program* dated October 30, 1950, on the subject of *The General Community Plan—A Preliminary Statement.*

It is a very clear summary of the elements of the general plan. All of this is needed to determine whether a redevelopment program is going to fit into the general framework of the city under consideration. But it is not in itself sufficient to judge whether a proposed change is really worthwhile. The important thing about the program of redevelopment is to relate it to a city—as it is being remade for the future. If you and those who are working with you are to judge this, they must know more of the objectives of the city under consideration—that is, of its planners, its administrators, of its people—than is generally apparent in those items that you have listed under "Plans for Physical Development" or "The Existing Administrative and Regulatory Measures." It seems to me that there should be something even more than can be expressed in what you have called "Programs of Development and Redevelopment."

A statement of the broad purpose of the program of development is required. What kind of city is to be developed and why? It is quite apparent in all of our cities that we have reached a point where radical changes are needed in the form of the basic framework. The requirements of living of the present, of technical abilities and all that, have made that necessary, as we all know. What is more, certain very apparent trends of decentralization of industry and workers suggest radical changes. The expression of this, it seems to me, is not necessarily adequately defined by the basic parts or elements that you have outlined under the three main headings. With these should go a statement of purpose and program.

On the basis of such a program, one should be able to judge how an individual redevelopment scheme will help to carry out a broad idea and purpose of redeveloping the city as a whole. Take, for instance, a central slum area. It is certainly not enough to merely replace this with better housing. What type of buildings or open spaces are to go into a redeveloped central area will depend on the extent to which various elements of the city are tending to decentralize or should be decentralized.

I don't know just what form such a statement of purpose should take. I am sure that you can formulate such a thing much better than I can, but I do think that it should be part of the requirements. Otherwise the statement looks OK to me.

Cordially,

Clarence S. Stein

---

411   To Lewis Mumford[1]

[New York City]   December 4, 1950

TO   Lewis Mumford

FROM   C. S. Stein

SUBJECT Notes on Proposed RDCA Memo

---

1. A period of vast expansion of industrial plant in the USA is beginning. No matter whether war comes or not, this will continue for many years.

2. Rapid development or expansion of required production is dependent on hav-

ing adequate supply of the right kind of workers where and when needed and of keeping them.

3. Supplying housing communities is an integral part of war preparation. The production of homes for workers must proceed or keep pace with the growth of industrial operation. If it lags behind, production will be crippled, no matter how efficiently factories are planned or equipped.

4. If houses are inadequate in size, equipment, or surroundings or if community equipment and facilities for shopping, gathering, and entertainment are missing, the turnover of workers will be high, with resulting loss of productivity. If workers are forced to live at too great distance from working places, they will waste time and energy and good disposition in travel: work will suffer and turnover increase.

5. We need no further experience to learn this. We know it to be true from our experience before and during our two last wars. (Shall we summarize these experiences? For the First World War, 1918–1919, see *Housing for Defense* (20th Century Fund, 1940). For Second World War, see reports of Congressional (Truman) Committee.)

6. Conclusions that are inevitable from these past and parallel experiences are:

A. Adequate housing and community facilities where and when needed are an essential and integral part of industrial preparedness.

B. The supply of transportation and communication is part and parcel of the solution of all industrial plant and labor supply problems.

C. Planning and construction of housing communities and highways require as much (sometimes more) time than factories.

D. The integrated location, planning, and development of

Industry
Housing
Community facilities
Communication

in an emergency such as the present becomes a primary federal government responsibility. No matter by what means these are to be financed or built, an agency of the government must decide on the what, where, and when of these interdependent elements in industrial expansion and relocation.

Lack of integration and paralleling of development of housing communities and highways (transportation) with industrial plant expansion crippled or slowed production both in 1918–20 and in the early forties. (The United States Housing Corporation opened its first community on January 1, 1919, about two months after the Armistice. See further HOUSING FOR DEFENSE.)

7. The present preparedness emergency problem is intensified as compared with the past by the inescapable need of dispersal. Dependence on existing housing and community equipment will be minimized compared to the two other preparedness

periods because of the need of moving both factories (and offices), as well as living places, out of range of attack of large bomb targets.

Because of the menace of bombs, not only must industrial plants be separated from concentrations of population, but there must be no concentration of factories of a single type of production.

8. There are two basic elements in the needed coordination of industry—community housing and transportation—that require active leadership of the federal government.

I. The Distribution and Location of industry and related housing and
    transportation.
    The Regional and broad planning aspects of the problem.
    What? How much? Where?
    This is parallel to the function of the Central Defense Staff in the Pentagon,
    but applied to physical development. This may be the job of the National
    Security Resources Board. If so, they are not doing it. Nor do they seem to
    know how to go about it—nor have they up to the present had the guts to do it.
II. Planning of the Physical Plant for production.
    This includes:
    A. Housing—that is to say, complete communities for living.
    B. Highways and means of transportation.
    C. Factories and office buildings.

The location and scale of these and their integration can be—in fact, must be—determined by the federal government. Whether private industrial builders or state or local government carry out the work rather than the federal government, the financing as well as the determining of the policy—including that of the form and manner of decentralization and dispersal—must come from the federal government. It must select location and determine plans, whether or not it builds.

The first and immediate move must be the concentration in one federal agency of all physical planning and building activities. These include all three divisions of what were the Public Works Administration: i.e., Public Roads, Public Buildings, and Community Facilities; also all agencies now under the HHFA [Housing and Home Finance Agency], as well as any other agency having to do with the building of communities and their integration with industrial plants. This might be called Housing and Works Administration or by some more inclusive title.

---

1. This was the draft of the RDCA's document on dispersion and defense, which Stein had suggested be sent to President Truman.

412   To Gordon Stephenson

[New York City]   December 4, 1950

Dear Gordon:

Your letter of November 28 contains much good news. In regard to Stevenage I am particularly delighted that both Nersome and Henry Morris accepted the new location of the County College and its relation to the town as a whole.[1] This seems to me of the utmost importance. I am naturally delighted that there is to be a fully equipped town theater. I hope that much study will be put into this to make it a truly contemporary theater. I feel that you and Holliday will win out against those fool engineers. How often I have gone through that same fight, to prevent their putting roads where they will do more harm than good—in fact, where they destroy all meaning of modern planning. We must not budge an inch on the essential principles of the thing. The details require infinite study, of course, but I feel certain that basically we have a sound plan.

Again, I must thank you for the splendid way in which you are following through on the book. I am sure that the paper cover is going to come out fine. With all that Lewis has written about me, I can't see that you need any more in regard to me. Nevertheless, I am sending you some biographical notes, even though I don't think there is any reason for making use of them on the cover.

In your postscript you speak of my articles on Paris and Venice. I did not give them to you as editor but as friend. I don't think they are ready for the *Town Planning Review*. They require a good deal more study and possibly even another visit to the two cities. I do, however, very much want your criticisms and comments. Points of view that I may have found new may be quite the same as impressions of other planners. To me, much of it was fresh discovery. Do give me a thorough criticism, as I am about to go ahead with research and writing.

Cordially,

Clarence S. Stein

1. Stein continues to follow up on the controversial "Pedestrian Center" scheme for Stevenage New Town, for which he had served as a consultant early in 1950.

413   To Benjamin H. Kizer

[New York City]   January 22, 1951

Dear Ben:

There is just one reason why I have not written to you often in the past months. Every time I started I found that there was so much that I wanted to tell you and talk over with you that I just didn't have time to do it. The more I postponed, the

more there was to say. Therefore, I am going to write you a short note now and then try to follow with other letters in the near future. . . .

I am so happy that you are writing the article for Gordon Stephenson about the Columbia Basin. He presents material very well. The number of subscribers to the magazine is not great, but most of them are people who would be very much interested in what you have to say. I wish there were some way in which we could have your article reprinted for broader circulation.

My book, which is made up of the articles that appeared in the *Town Planning Review,* with an additional article in regard to hopes and plans for the future of New Towns, is being printed now. I have been saying for a long time that it will be here in a month, but the printers in Liverpool are slow workers. You will be interested in a long, fine introduction by Lewis Mumford, which deals with the history of community development from our angle.

I have been spending much of my time of late at Washington. I have been acting as consultant in connection with the proposed location of new office buildings twenty miles away from the center of the capital. You have possibly read among the various papers that RDCA has been sending you that I presented a memo on this subject at the hearings held by the Senate committee. That was before I had started acting as consultant to the General Services Administration. There is a challenging opportunity in this, but whether the government will be able to visualize the problem as a whole and act is yet to be seen.

We spent about three and a half months this summer in Europe. It was a great experience. We visited few places and had been to all of them before. We settled down in Paris, Florence, and London long enough in each place to feel at home. We actually did have our own home in each place, an apartment or a house. There was time and opportunity to get reacquainted with these cities and to see them in a sense with new eyes, based on experiences since the time when I was a student and spent lengthy periods at least in Paris and Florence. . . .

Among other things good about the trip was that we escaped to a great extent the feeling of inevitability of doom that seemed present in America. We have not come to completely understand it, even after the months we have been back here.

China is very much in our minds, the China and the Chinese that we knew for a short time while we were there. That is why we sent you the *Peking Diary.*[1] By the way, Gerard Swope has promised to invite Aline and me to his house when the author, Derk Bodde, visits him in the near future.

Aline just finished another book about China, and I have started it. We both think it is even more interesting than the diary, for it is based on a longer experience and is the work of a very keen observer. It is *Two Kinds of Time* by Graham Peck. If you are interested I will be glad to send it to you.

Now I must stop. Aline joins me in warm greetings to you and Mabel.

Cordially,

Clarence S. Stein

1. Derk Bodde, *Peking Diary: A Year of Revolution* (New York: Schuman, 1950).

---

414   To Louis Justement

[New York City]   February 18, 1951

Dear Louis:

Thanks for sending me the clippings. I had already received news from Washington that the National Capital Park and Planning Commission was gaining ground. I judge from these clippings that there is, however, some chance that they will take over. If so, something strenuous should certainly be done about reorganizing the commission. They need a good strong chairman who knows something about the problem and who can stay on the job. It should be someone living in the District, I presume, and, above all, the technical staff certainly needs strengthening—and that's putting the thing gently.

It is too bad Tracy did not have the opportunity to show more initiative and leadership. But I guess it is a pretty hard thing to do in a government office where your chief is at a distance and interested in many other things.

I telephoned to Tracy the other day that I expected to go to California for a month on Monday, February 26, and that, therefore, if he wants me in Washington he should let me know. He said that his office was preparing a preliminary or tentative report to go to Jess Larsson. I wrote to him again today telling him to let me know if he wanted me to come to Washington at the end of this week.

It was good fun working with you and Fred. It is too bad we didn't get any further.[1]

Cordially,

Clarence S. Stein

1. Stein already was developing a sense that his proposals to Augur and those of other GSA consultants, including those of Louis Justiment, for an arc of New Towns around Washington did not have much support from the GSA, let alone the president or Congress.

---

415   To Frederic J. Osborn

[New York City]   February 28, 1951

Dear FJO:

You asked me about the policy statement in regard to dispersal as prepared by the RDCA. This, in its final form, has not been distributed as yet, but I expect to send it out very soon. The reason we have been holding it back is because we intend to take it up with some of the higher officials of the government before, rather than after, we make a public statement. I will send it to you just as soon as it is ready for publication. We have given it a great deal of study, and the writing in the main is that of Lewis Mumford.

I do not know just what our follow-up will be in regard to this matter, but it is very certain that we are going to keep at it in some way or other. Albert Mayer has already written a number of articles on the subject that have been published: one in last month's *Survey,* another in the *Journal of the American Institute of Architects,* and a third which has just come out as an editorial in the *Journal of the Planners' Institute.*[1]

Yesterday I sent you copies of my testimony before Senate committees: one, on December 18, 1950, on "Current Proposals for Decentralization of Federal Office Buildings" and the other, on February 19, 1951, on S-349, The Defense Housing and Community Facilities and Services Act of 1951, insofar as it has to do with the policy of dispersal.

There is no question that there is a real interest in Washington in regard to this subject of dispersal. The day after I appeared, the *Washington Post* had a summary of my testimony on the first page.

Aline and I are leaving in a few days for California. We expect to spend a month there, mainly in Los Angeles. However, in all probability we will go up to San Francisco to visit our various friends. Do let me know from time to time how things are developing, and I will try to keep you posted in regard to progress here in America.

Kindest regards to you and Mrs. Osborn from Aline and myself.

Cordially,

Clarence S. Stein

1. Albert Mayer, "New Towns and Defense," *Survey* 87 (February 1951): 64–65. Mayer wrote several articles for the *Survey* during this period after it absorbed the *Survey Graphic* in 1948. See esp. Albert Mayer, "Our Side Is Well in the Lead," *Survey* 86 (May 1950): 243–44, which responds to New York City attempts to stop public housing after the enactment of the Housing Act of 1949. Albert Mayer, "A New Towns Program," *Journal of the AIA* 15, no. 1 (1953): 5–10. The entire issue is devoted to "New Towns for American Defense," with articles by William Wheaton, David Greer, Roger Creighton, and others. Albert Mayer, "Editorial: A Call to the Planners," *Journal of the American Institute of Planners* 16, no. 4 (1950): 61–62.

---

416   To Catherine Bauer Wurster

[New York City]   May 21, 1951

Dear Catherine:

Yesterday I had a long phone talk with Carl Feiss regarding yours of the 17th. [He said that] he had not seen your telegram but probably did. Carl knows in general what our proposed state law is.[1]

He says that the legal boys (I almost slipped into saying legalistic bastards) are softening somewhat in regard to putting development before redevelopment. But they can find no way of getting more than loans—no subsidies. In regard to the housing bill, he says we should get after the congressmen—the Senate will continue [to stall].

I told him that we must fight this out on three levels: (1) Congress, (2) state legislatures, and (3) those who will make use of proper legislation to go ahead with . . . development.

Tomorrow I am going out to Nassau to see the CIO crowd.[2] They seem ready to go ahead, but I can't see just how they can do [anything] at the proper scale unless we have both the federal and state legislation. So I will try to get them on the warpath.

Now, as to Stanford. Last week I heard from Brandin, the business manager. He said he had been away but would take the matter up with the president of the university and the committee in charge. However, I question whether he goes at the matter with enthusiasm. Therefore, if Mr. Gunst is interested, he can be of great help. Will you talk to him? Also, Bill said he knew someone else who might help. Now is the time. Do let me know if anything can be started.

Affectionate greetings from Aline and Clarence to you all.

1. The RDCA had written a model state law for urban redevelopment, which included development of housing on vacant land.
2. Bauer was active in securing labor union support for urban development legislation.

---

417   To Aluminum Company of Canada Limited

[Stanford, California]   July 27, 1951

Attention of Mr. Eric F. West

Gentlemen:

I appreciate the opportunity to offer my services as consultant in connection with the planning of the proposed town at Kitimat. As consultant, I believe my experience can be of most value to the Aluminum Company of Canada in the comprehensive coordination of the various physical and functional elements of the development so as to produce a town completely organized and equipped for efficient operation from the time the houses are ready for occupation.

I propose that as consultant I be responsible for:

I. Outlining Basic Requirements for Comprehensive Development and Operation for purpose of giving maximum livability at minimum long-term operating cost.

Then, after this overall conception of a completed functioning town has been broken down into its various component fields of activity—

II. Formulating Programs for Each Special Field, including
   A. Local Government
   B. Housing Agency, for creating, marketing, and operating residential and related development
   C. Community Organization and Facilities
   D. Education and Child Care
   E. Recreation
   F. Health
   G. Utilities and other public services, including transit and transportation
   H. Protection
   I. Shopping Centers

The Program in each field will include recommendation as to basic policy; organization and administration; relations to other governmental, public, and private agencies and services; financial policy and budget of operating costs and probably returns; outline description of building and equipment required to make each service function.

Programming, as far as possible, will be scheduled for various stages of development.

These special studies are to be carried out by authorities in each field, as suggested below.

III. Coordinating These Special Programs into a Comprehensive Overall Program and Schedule.

The above is merely a skeleton outline of the study that I would like to make for the Aluminum Company of Canada. I would be glad to explain it in more detail, if you desire. As to the manner of carrying out the work, let me say a word about my organization.

My Organization

The service I have to offer is based on my experience, investigations, and observation over the past quarter of a century in connection with the planned development and the operation of various types of communities. This experience is in part described in my book *Toward New Towns for America,* which has just been published. I am attaching to this letter a summary of my principal housing and community planning work.

This is in the main a personal service that I propose. My organization for carrying it out will be limited in size. My principal assistant will be Roger Willcox, who will devote all of his time to this job. A short description of his past experience is attached. In addition, I will use research workers, draftsmen, secretaries, or other assistants when needed.

Studies, analyses, and consultation in the various fields indicated above . . . will be made by experienced specialists and authorities, most of whom have worked with me in the past. They will be employed only when required for a specific job. I suggest that they be appointed on my recommendation and that they be paid directly by the company. I am not including the list of specialists that I have in mind, as there has not been time to discuss the matter with them. If you desire, I will be glad to find out whether their professional services are now available and approximately what the cost would be.

This proposed service of developing a comprehensive related town entity in which all activities will be functionally as well as structurally ready for operation when required is somewhat different from what is generally called a Master Plan. Both are needed. The services I propose to give will complement and help to guide the development of the Master Plan for the physical development of the town.

The fundamental need of a planned development that is far broader and more all-inclusive than a physical plan is apparent in the experience of so many new communities that have been inadequately prepared for operation. A physical plan is not enough. There must be a complete plan for living. Here, it must work from the beginning.

In the case of the proposed town at Kitimat, there are greater reasons than usual that the plan for living and the means of making it function be completed before and certainly not after the physical plan.

1. The success of the proposed aluminum plant depends on securing required workers from the beginning and in holding them.

2. Because of its distance from other developments, it is essential that prospective workers be confident from the beginning that they are going to move into a community with all of the accustomed facilities—or better—for education and modern good living.

3. The reputation of being a well-operated town where one can live an unusually complete and good life at a moderate cost should be permanent, so that other industry may be drawn to the town.

4. Your company is rightly determined that Kitimat shall not be a "company town." However, the fact that the corporation will be heavily involved financially and that the success of your enterprise is greatly dependent on the prosperity of the town means that there must be from the beginning local government and community organization that will be democratic but at the same time will not be antagonistic to the Aluminum Company.

5. The town must pay its way. That is, it must be set up so that operation-maintenance cost of both housing corporation and government are fully and regularly covered by receipts, even if the original investment is in part accepted as an industrial investment.

The charge for my services and my personal organization would be Twenty-five Thousand Dollars ($25,000) for six months. I would devote myself to this job during that time, and Roger Willcox would give all his time to it. At the end of that period, we would be better able to judge what time would be required thereafter, so that we could determine the charges that should be justly made for the remainder of the work.

These charges are exclusive of traveling and living expenses while traveling and of long-distance telephone and telegraph charges. As I have explained they do not include the recompense of the specialists that would be chosen later, if you desire to have me undertake this work.

If there is any additional information that you desire in regard to the services that I would give you as Coordinating Consultant, please let me know. Should you decide to employ me and my organization, we could start at the beginning of September or possibly even earlier.

Clarence S. Stein

418 To Eric F. West[1]

[Palo Alto, California]   July 27, 1951

Dear Mr. West:

This is a personal note which I am writing you so as to be sure there is no mis-understanding in regard to the matters in connection with the proposed town of Kitimat that we have discussed of late. Although it covers the same subject that I have just discussed in the letter sent you as representative of the Aluminum Company of Canada, it covers a few matters that seem to me would make the letter to the company too lengthy.

Let me first thank you for the time that you have given to this matter, and for your patience. I can very well understand your original difficulty in comprehending the somewhat different approach that I desire to make to the study of the require-ments of the New Town. I admit that it is an unusual approach, but to my mind it is the only one that has any common sense and has the possibility of leading to suc-cess from the beginning—and it is the beginning in a New Town that counts most.

So as to clarify the method of procedure, I would like to make, if I can find the time, a more detailed outline for the president and other officials of the company during my next week or two in California.

I had intended to include a list of the specialists in various fields of which I spoke in my letter to the company. I finally decided it was better not to do so because I had not had an opportunity to discuss the matter with them. Although I believe most of them would be greatly interested, they might not be available at the present time. Here, off the record, are the names of some of those whom I would like to ask to assist me, if approved. (See attached list [omitted here].) I have shown you re-ports that have been made by a number of the people mentioned, and have spoken to you about others.

As I told you yesterday, I would be delighted to have an opportunity to talk to the president of the company, Mr. R. E. Powell, at Vancouver, if he has time to see me. I believe you said he would be returning somewhere around the 15th. Is that right? If he desired to see me any time before the end of the month in Montreal, it would necessitate quite a lengthy trip. Of course, I would make it if the matter were urgent.

You spoke of the possibility of Mr. Edward Mejia going to California during the month of August, after a trip to the site of the proposed plant. I would be glad to see him in San Francisco or Los Angeles, if that could be worked out. My present plans are to be in Palo Alto from August 1 to August 20.

Kindest regards.

Yours cordially,
Clarence S. Stein

1. West was a vice president of the Aluminum Company of Canada, which was facing the problem of housing and community services for the large number of workers they would need for their proposed large aluminum smelter in British Columbia. One possibility was a New Town, and so ALCAN had contacted a number of potential planning consultants.

---

419   To A. W. Whitaker, Jr.[1]

[New York City]   October 5, 1951

Dear Mr. Whitaker:

I am to direct and coordinate all physical and functional planning for the development of the town of Kitimat and surrounding areas. In doing this, I am to be responsible for:

I. *Outlining basic requirements for the comprehensive development and operation* for the purpose of giving maximum livability at minimum long-term operating cost.

II. *Formulating and outlining the program for each of the component fields of activity.* In this connection I am to recommend to ALCAN for its approval and retention consultants in these various fields to carry out in detail these programs under my direction. The resulting studies in each field will include recommendations as to basic policy; organization and administration relationships to other governmental, public, and private agencies and services; financial policy and budget of operating cost and estimated returns; outline or diagrammatic description of building and equipment required to make each service function efficiently.

The functional and physical fields to be studied will include the following:

A. Local government
B. Housing and housing agency, for creating, marketing, and operating residential and related development
C. Community organization and facilities
D. Education and child care
E. Recreation
F. Health
G. Protection
H. Commercial and business facilities
I. Problems having to do with surrounding area:
   1. Control of water and flood dangers
   2. Land use as affecting plant and town
   3. Transportation
   4. Regional recreation program
J. Other related fields for which programs or plans be required.

III. *Coordinating these special programs into a comprehensive, overall program and schedule,* including definite recommendations for the physical master plan and the operation of the ultimate town at various stages of development.

Clarence S. Stein

1. This letter served as Stein's contract with ALCAN for his work as director of planning for Kitimat.

---

420   To Aline Stein

On the *Princess Nora* between Kitimat and Vancouver
October 23, 1951

Aline dear:

That is somewhat the way it looks near Kitimat, where they are cutting a power-house inside the mountain—like the caves of Ellora. This is a wonderful two-day voyage—ever-changing views, with the two shores close to you, excepting the short trip in the open sea in Queen Charlotte sound. Choppy enough there on the trip up to induce me to lie down.

Not a bad boat our *Princess Nora.* Plentiful means and good roast beef rare couple of times a day. Eric and I have what the waiter cabin boy calls a "super de-lux" cabin—real beds, bathroom, good view of the snowy heights. You will like it next

spring. Coming up, we were too late to get such luxurious quarters and had to be content crowded three in a cabin. But the great out-of-doors was roomy enough, and there is a parlor, smoking room, and an all-windowed room with comfortable chairs with footrests lined up to take in the changing view.

It was a restful trip up Saturday and Sunday, but not all loafing by any means. The chief engineer in charge for ALCAN was along, also a number of the chiefs of Kitimat constructors who are doing the building, including the new head of the Kitimat job. We had two long sessions to determine a building program for the next two years—the building of the first neighborhood.

[Clarence]

---

421   To Arthur Glikson[1]

[New York City]   December 16, 1951

Dear Arthur Glikson:

I was delighted to have a talk with Arieh Sharon.[2] I am sorry that we could not be together longer, but there was time for me to appreciate his devotion to the cause for which he is working and his quite apparent ability as a leader. I was glad to see him further because he brought news from you.

I hope that somehow or other Mrs. Stein and I will have an opportunity of visiting Israel in the not-too-distant future [to] see the work that you and [Arieh] Sharon are doing. But it is impossible to make any definite plans at the present time.

One of the principal reasons that I do not know when we could even consider going away is the fact that I am devoting all of my time to the most fascinating planning problem. The Aluminum Company of Canada proposes to build a new plant for the purpose of producing aluminum in British Columbia some four hundred miles north of Vancouver. This is rugged, mountainous country, real wilderness. It is one of the few places in that mountainous area that has land flat enough to permit the building of colossal industrial works and also a town for the workers and service employees of the town, as well as their families. The town will start with about 6,000 population, when the first section of the plant is to be completed. The town will grow along with the aluminum plant until there is some 35 to 50 thousand population.

My present job is to coordinate the various elements of planning, not only physical but functional, including education, health, government, etc. I needn't tell you that it is an extremely interesting job and that it fills all of my time. This explains why I have not answered your letter sooner.

Do let me know what you are doing when you have time to write. Thanks for your card of Christmas greetings. Here are my best wishes to you for the coming year.

Cordially yours,
Clarence S. Stein

1. Arthur Glikson was active in planning in Israel.
2. Sharon's best-known work in planning was his plan for Tel Aviv. He also planned a number of university campuses and university buildings in Israel and Africa.

422   To Gordon Stephenson

[New York City]   December 16, 1951

Dear Gordon:

At last, a more or less peaceful Sunday at home, in which to try to catch up with my personal life. My weekdays are filled with the British Columbia job, and I generally carry the problems along with me to the country when I happen to be at this end of the continent. . . .

By the way, I had word of you last week. After a number of attempts to get in touch with [Anthony] Minoprio,[1] we did have a leisurely luncheon together. Strange I had not met him before. He told me that he had been out to Liverpool to see you a short time before [and] that you were very busy. He also said that he had been very much interested to know that you had used something like a Radburn Plan in Wrexham. However, he said that you did not show him the plans. On the other hand, either you or Holliday had shown him the Stevenage Center, about which he seemed very enthusiastic. I wish he or someone could get some sense into Bennett's head in regard to this affair. . . .

As to Wrexham, I am very anxious to see just what you have done. I am glad that you are going to send me some drawings within a month or so. You are right, it certainly does take an enormous amount of energy to move people from their orthodox views. That is something I am going to have to do all over again in connection with this Canadian job. You never know just how it is going to come out, you lose again and again, but the continued struggle, I assure you, is worthwhile just for the few times you get people to see clearly and to start on the way to building new forms. . . .

Now, as to the [*Town Planning*] *Review.* I have reminded Albert Mayer that you expected an article on the capital of East Punjab. He, as usual, is working at altogether too many things, and so I can make no promises for him. There is, in addition, I believe, a great mental difficulty in getting down to this subject. I have asked him to write merely about *his* plan, but of course it is very difficult for him to close his mind to the fact that what is being built is a compromise with Corbusier, if such a thing as compromising with Corbusier is possible. . . .[2]

In regard to Fresh Meadows, I am not at all certain whether Ralph Walker is the one either to explain Fresh Meadows or to give a judgment upon it. . . . It brings up, among other subjects, the relation of the very tall apartment house to the development of low houses. Lewis Mumford, as you probably know, wrote an article or two on Fresh Meadows for the *New Yorker.*[3] They were good, but I do feel that perhaps Lewis was overenthusiastic due to the fact that there are so few housing developments that are worthy of enthusiasm. . . .

You say we should publish our articles on Paris and Venice. Let me remind you that they were not sent to you for that purpose. What I wanted was your criticism, not in detail, of course, but as to the point of view, etc. I feel that they are incomplete. I wish I could spend another month in Paris going over things once more before finishing that article. The [article on] Venice, I think, is better, mainly because the point of view is simpler and more closely related to works of my own experience, but there also I should do a little more studying, either on the spot or in the libraries here. . . .[4]

At present, I am giving all my time and myself to the work in connection with Kitimat, the new city for the Aluminum Company in Canada. . . . It is proposed that ultimately it will be a city of some 35 to 50 thousand population, but it will grow with the main industrial plant, which is intended to produce aluminum. The first section, which will open in the beginning of 1954, will require a town of some 6,000 population. Then, as each section of the industrial plant is opened, there will be an added 7,000 or so population, until we reach 20,000. . . . Then there may be a pause until additional electric power has been produced. After that, it will be possible to develop the plant and, as a result, the city to at least 35 thousand population. Anyhow, the physical plans, which are being done in the office of Mayer and Whittlesey, are in preparation for a development at that point. . . . My job is to coordinate all of the different types of physical and functional planning—health, education, government, commercial, and all that. . . .

Now, as to my book—I was in Chicago a couple of weeks ago and saw the chief for publications. He reported a steady demand, no great sale but enough to have used up over half of their supply. There would be, unquestionably, a greater sale if nonprofessional people had the slightest idea how they could easily purchase a copy. . . . Getting the material together, working with you, and finally having it all in such a goodly book has been worth it all.

Our affectionate Christmas and New Year's greetings to Flora and you and all the girls.

Cordially,
Clarence S. Stein

1. Minoprio was the architect and planner for a housing group at the New Town of Crawley, England, which incorporated Radburn ideas, as had Gordon Stephenson's earlier plans for new housing at Wrexham.

2. The decision to replace Mayer and Whittlesey with Le Corbusier seems to have been chiefly political. Before Le Corbusier was brought in, Mayer published "The New Capital of Punjab" in his *Journal of the AIA* (October 1950). Its illustrations of the Mayer, Whittlesey, Glass, Stein, Nowicki plan and of plans for neighborhoods and superblocks with green open space in their centers show how clearly they followed the Radburn and Baldwin Hills prototypes.

3. "Skyline," reprinted as Lewis Mumford, "From Utopia Parkway Turn East" and "Fresh Meadows, Fresh Plans," in *From the Ground Up* (New York: Harcourt Brace and Co. Harvest Book, 1956).

4. The unpublished manuscripts of Stein's articles on Paris and Venice are in the Clarence Stein Papers of the Cornell University Archives (CSP/CUA).

423 To Steen Rasmussen

[New York City]   December 23, 1951

Dear Steen:

Your book has arrived.[1] I don't know how to tell you how much pleasure it has already given me. To begin with, it is, as you know, a subject that is close to my heart, and I find so little that has been written about cities in the spirit in which you explore them. Then the setup of the book is such a splendid architectural work—by that, I mean it is so well planned. For instance, the notes running along the side of the page are convenient and yet do not call one's attention from the text. Besides, the illustrations not only illustrate, but are located in the proper relation to the subject matter. Again, the plans are simple, straightforward, and above all they are in comparable scales. It is a truly beautiful book.

I think I told you, when we were together in Holland, that I had an opportunity while visiting Gordon Stephenson to read the proofs of the sections on Peking and the Paris of the Musketeers. I found them quite as delightful in the re-reading. What you have to say about Peking brings back to the Steins one of the most pleasant periods in our travels in the Orient. As to the rest of the book, I have skipped from section to section, and I have found much to delight me. But, until I have read the book as a whole, I will not attempt to comment further. . . .

I am particularly anxious that the book become well known so that I may use it when I make another effort to get some of the universities interested in inviting you to America.

Cordially,
Clarence S. Stein

1. Steen Rasmussen, *Towns and Building* (Cambridge: Harvard Univ. Press, 1951).

424 To Aline Stein

[New York City]   February 3, 1952

Aline dear:

. . . The dreary weather has returned. But we have little time to think of it—plenty of pleasant work. Yesterday was a good day in the history of Kitimat; at least, it promises to go down to history as such. Larry Smith, our hard-boiled shopping center advisor, was here. We discussed in meeting with Radley, Dudley, and others of the company Julian's plans of the marketplace and Larry's report and finally got down to [the] basic question of control and ownership. ALCAN fears the stigma of "company town" and "company store," but says Larry: "The increased value of land in commercial areas, when the city of Kitimat has reached its growth to 35 to 50,000 people with some 10 million dollars every year, there can be an immense return to the owner of the underlying land. Rather than handing this over to commercial entrepreneurs, it would seem wise to retain those values for the good of the community—the people of Kitimat."

And there developed out of our talk the idea of a "Kitimat Foundation," a nonprofit organization that would operate all commercial property. The income would be used for grants to schools, hospital, recreation, etc., at Kitimat.

Not a word of this, Aline. Perhaps it was a dream. Anyhow, it will have to be carefully handled if it is to get ALCAN's approval.

I love you,
Clarence

---

425 To Paul Oppermann

[New York City]   February 17, 1952

Dear Paul:

It is some time since we have discussed the Stanford matter. I am particularly interested at this moment because I have been considering a trip to California. . . .

I have been looking over old letters, and I find that way back in November I was congratulating Alf E. Brandin on having taken charge of the development of some 6,000 acres of Stanford. Even earlier than that, in August, it began to appear that Caldwell-Banker was taking command and that Welton Becket would probably be the architect for the Emporium in connection with the shopping center. As you will remember, it was my idea that the university should hold on to all the underlying property to be used as a main shopping center and that that would form a strong basis for the financial success of the 11 square miles.

I would appreciate very much your writing me as soon as you receive this, telling me how things are going and if you think there is any possibility of our assisting in developing the affair in the manner that I originally proposed. . . .

Cordially,
Clarence S. Stein

---

426 To Gordon Stephenson

[New York City]   February 28, 1952

Dear Gordon:

It is over a month since I wrote you, and much has happened in connection with the planning of our New Town since then. Of that I will speak briefly later. But first let me write about the various matters of mutual interest mentioned in your letter of January 24.

First, in regard to Robert Alexander writing an article for the review of his work in India, I telephoned him while passing through Los Angeles. He was away, but Mrs. Alexander seemed very much interested and said that she would talk to Bob as soon as he got back from Guam, where he is apparently planning, along with Neutra, some large works for the United States Government. . . .

You wrote that you have mislaid the articles on Venice and Paris. I think we have an extra copy. If so, it will be sent you. Do let me know if they turn up. But let me emphasize again that I do not look upon these as finished articles ready for publication. They are first drafts, and I want to get your criticism of them so that, when I find time to visit the cities or study the subjects further, I can complete them.

I will talk to Ralph Walker about the article concerning Fresh Meadows. It has occurred to me that someone in Canada should write an article on the subject of company towns. Possibly the best person for this would be Alan H. Armstrong, Executive Director, Community Planning Association of Canada, 169 Somerset W., Ottawa. If not, he will know who should do it. As you probably know, there have been a great many single-industry towns created in connection with lumber or other industries. There is a great consciousness in Canada of the difficulties that grow out of ownership of town and plant by the same company. The Aluminum Company of Canada has had a great deal of experience in building and is determined that Kitimat should not be a "closed town." I am, of course, enthusiastically in agreement, but, as you well understand, this leads to many problems that we are doing our best to solve. . . .

I cannot recollect whether I have told you just what I have been trying to do there, but let me try to put it in a few words. The idea is to see if functional planning can set the pace for physical planning. That is to say, I am attempting to determine as far as is possible just how the city will operate as a good but economical place in which to live, the various stages of its growth, and then to mold the physical planning to fit these needs. The difficulty in following this program has naturally been the fact that, to keep pace with the building of the industrial plant, we had to start construction at an early date. In fact, in spite of the heavy snows last winter, the main roads leading up to the site to be developed this summer are being cleared now. So I have been forced to compromise by having the functional plans developed at the same time as the physical plans. This has meant careful direction so that, in determining the location and the size of all community facilities at various stages of development, we never lost sight of our general program of operation.

In the development of the programs and requirements in government, commerce, property management, health, leisure time activities (including recreation), etc., I have chosen as advisers not only people of wide experience but those who are sympathetic with the general objectives. All of the consultants have kept closely in touch with Mayer and Whittlesey, who are preparing a physical plan.

I have also (on my trips to British Columbia) kept in as close touch as possible with the deputy ministers and other officials of the provincial departments and found that, especially in education and health, their point of view was very progressive. The responsibility of the state, or rather the province, is, of course, much greater in a pioneering area such as British Columbia than in our more developed states.

The splendid series of master drawings of Mayer and Whittlesey are nearing completion. On my last trip we started to bring the local architects into the work of actually planning the development in detail. I think they are going to make a really good contribution. A modern architectural style is developing in British Columbia, particularly in Vancouver, that unites the younger practitioners there and in many ways is quite different from what one finds in other parts of Canada.

More of this in my next.

Affectionate greetings to the family from Aline and

Clarence

---

427   To Benton MacKaye

[New York City]   February 29, 1952

Dear Ben:

Just received your letter of February 28. I am glad to hear that everything is OK in Washington.

Here's another thought in regard to Kitimat—or at least the beginnings of an idea. On the plans of the Civic Center of Kitimat is indicated a museum. It seems to me that, if we gave a little thought to the matter, we might develop an institution there that would be of real value to the people of the community. It could, if properly designed, tell folks in a very simple way about the wilderness that surrounds them and how it came about—in short, the story of geology and all that. Then it might go on to deal with the natural elements that led to location of the plant for manufacturing bauxite from South America into aluminum at this northern plant—first, electric power and how it is to be harnessed and carried over the mountain to Kitimat; then, how bauxite is made into alumina before being transported to Kitimat; after that, the problems of transportation; then, the explanation of manufacturing of aluminum in the industrial plant, which forms the economic basis of Kitimat.

A whole section might be devoted to the development of the plans or, if you will, the discovery of the plan. That will deal with the influences of the river, the dangers of flood, and what Ken is doing to keep us out of the way of the water. It will also show how the climate, including winds, have affected the location of housing.[1] It will naturally deal also with the ocean currents' effect on weather and the necessity of care in forestry to prevent increased danger of flood.

There should, of course, also be a very important section devoted to [the] history of man's past use of the Kitimat area. This would deal in the main with the Indian. I believe the Museum of Natural History here in New York has, in addition to the great amount of material that it has on exhibit in the big hall devoted to the Alaskan Indian, a great many things that are stored away for lack of space. If that is so, they might be glad to lend or give some to Kitimat. . . .

It is whispered that you are about to have another birthday. How young are you this time?

Our very best wishes to you.

As ever,
Clarence

1. Stein, in consultation with MacKaye, had advised his ALCAN clients at Kitimat to reevaluate the danger of flooding from the river, which divided the most buildable area of the town site. His recommendation that they build only above the 100-year flood line was accepted after a flood of nearly that magnitude occurred during the planning process.

---

428 To J. B. White

[New York City]   March 15, 1952

Mr. J. B. White, Vice President
Aluminum Company of Canada, Ltd.

Dear Mr. White:

This is to confirm my conversation with you and Mr. Whitaker, Jr., at Montreal on March 12th relative to the continuation of my professional services as Coordinator and Director of Planning for Kitimat, British Columbia.

I am to continue my work as outlined in my letter of October 5th, 1951, to Mr. Whitaker, which has served as an agreement until March 6th, 1952. Thereafter, I am to devote approximately one-third of my working time until the end of 1953, an equivalent of six months' working time during twenty months.

During the period March 6th to May 6th, I will devote myself to the planning functions listed in the letter of October 5th, 1951. I then expect to travel abroad for the next two months. Upon my return I will complete the studies as soon as practicable. At all times I shall be prepared, whenever required by ALCAN, to advise, carry out studies, or to recommend and direct specialists in any of the fields of physical and functional planning in connection with Kitimat or other similar developments by ALCAN.

As compensation I am to receive $2,500 per month for the two months ending May 6th, 1952. After that I am to receive $1,100 per month for approximately twenty months, which is until December 31st, 1953.

If this proposal is in accordance with your understanding, kindly authorize it by issuing the proper order.

Cordially yours,

Clarence S. Stein

---

429   To Benjamin Kizer

[New York City]   May 10, 1952

Dear Ben:

Your letter about my book gave me a glowing feeling. Such wonderful praise—and from you—means much to me. But what is important to me is that you and I see things so much in the same way. I feel that my objectives and yours are practically the same, and that makes me feel very proud.

I have been on this Kitimat job for a steady eight months. It has been a wonderful experience. It seems that all my life's work and all the experience that I tried to write about in *Toward New Towns* finally came to a head in the development of plans for Kitimat. Here has been a chance to work out a good, worthwhile, well-rounded urban life in an industrial environment that will support it and yet in close touch with unspoiled nature. We have tried to see the thing whole, to work out the details of operating government, the schools, the care of health, the use of leisure time so that they will make a complete and united pattern. These last couple of weeks have been devoted to finishing up a series of reports and recommendations on the functional plans of the various elements, including commerce, recreation, education, and all the rest.

Working with Albert, of course, has added much to the interest of the Kitimat job. He is off in India again now, as you may have heard. . . .

This is an eventful day. It is my last day of work for some time to come. Tomorrow we close the book for a while. Aline and I are taking a plane straight to Stockholm. We have had our usual good luck. A friend of mine, Yngve Larsson, who is interested in much the same things that you and I are, has been good enough to find us a little house. It is out in the Royal Park in Stockholm and, I understand, overlooks the waters through which the boats enter the port.

We have no plans as yet, but I think it is very likely I will spend some time getting well acquainted with the work of the big central housing cooperatives.[1] It seems to me that the time has come for us to turn to cooperation as a means of securing housing, at least for the lower middle classes—that is, a great many of the workers in this country. We are forming an organization in New York now for [the] purpose of doing something of the kind that they have done so successfully in the Scandinavian countries.

But I am not going over for the purpose of studying anything in particular. It is just that Aline and I find it good to get away now and then. We expect to make short trips around Sweden, Denmark, and perhaps Norway, then to England, and possibly a short stop in Holland. We will be back about the middle of July, I think. I hope it will not be long after that before I go west again, at which time I hope we can see each other.

Aline joins me in affectionate greetings to you all.

Cordially,

[Clarence Stein]

1. Stein visited several housing cooperatives in Denmark and Sweden and spent much time learning about the process of developing suburban satellite New Towns around Stockholm. His article "Vällingby, a Satellite Town," which made extensive use of the Radburn concept, appeared in the *Proceedings* of the October 1952 annual meeting of the American Society of Planning Officials (ASPO), *Planning, 1952*.

---

430   To Arthur Glikson

[New York City]   May 10, 1952

Dear Arthur Glikson:

Your long and interesting letters contain so much that I would like to discuss with you that I keep on putting it off! It has been a very busy eight months or so for me.

I have been working steadily at plans for the new city in British Columbia. It has been a great opportunity to see the varied problems of urban environment as a whole and to try to form a pattern of development over a period of growth from a town of 6 to 7 thousand to a city of 35 to 50 thousand. It has been particularly interesting because we are setting this new city right in the wilderness. There are no other communities of any importance near enough to it to affect the development of Kitimat. One cannot say, "Oh, well, we need not bother about a complete hospital or having sufficient stores; it will be taken care of in one of the nearby cities." . . .

There will be a dominant—we hope not a single—industry in this town, so we can pretty well tell just what number of workers will be needed at such period of development of the town. That will follow a pattern that can be fairly well predicted, in size if not exactly in time. The great aluminum works that will be the main source of employment will be built in a series of units, each requiring 1,000 to 1,100 workers. Taking this as a basis, we have worked out what the need would be of non-industrial workers to operate the municipality. Thus, we have been able to prophesy the population at the various major periods of growth. [On this basis] we have developed a series of functional plans . . . in the fields of education, health, government, leisure time activities, commerce, etc., and [have projected] them through various periods of growth.

On the basis of this and paralleling it in development, Mayer and Whittlesey have created a splendid master plan. It makes good use of the elements that I attempted to describe in *Toward New Towns* and relates them superbly to the varied setting of flat plateaus and deep gullies separated by steep, wooded land, backed by great, snow-clad mountains. If you are interested I will see if I can't send you some of the physical plans and reports on programming of the functional or operational processes.

Now I am leaving all this to take a vacation. . . . I hope to spend two weeks in England on my way back, and on the way, if possible, we will stop off at Holland. I will have your article on regional planning with me, and if I go there I will study it well in advance.

Kindest regards, yours cordially,

Clarence S. Stein

---

431   To Eric Carlson

[New York City]   July 3, 1952

Dear Eric:

Your note of 23rd June, containing Winslow Carlton's memo of 10th June, caught up with me here. I am glad that you are writing to Nasstrom, and I am sure that he will take care of the corrections of your manuscript. In fact, when I saw him last he had already started to do so.[1]

I am returning here with the section devoted to Denmark. I did not have time enough in Copenhagen to find a proper person to correct this section. However, I did get pretty well acquainted with the work of one of the organizations, Dansk Almennyttict Boligselkab. This is a young organization—it has been active for only ten years, but it has, in my opinion, all of the advantages of youth; that is to say, a good deal of the work is being done by young people, and they are very much alive and ready to try out new ideas. I visited all four of their developments. Each one of them has a different character. One can see how their ideas grow and develop; for instance, in one of the small . . . developments, the houses for old folks were massed together. In the next community, they decided to distribute them among the other houses.

One of the most interesting ventures is that of the collective house. This is a type of apartment that takes care of working individuals or families; by *working families,* I mean those in which both parents work. Here they have tried out all sorts and kinds of common services, including nursery, creche, dining room, stores, etc., etc. Of all this I will tell you when I get back.

The important thing that impressed me, as far as it concerns your article for the [United Nations], is that the Dansk Almennyttict Boligselkab is *not* really a cooperative. It is a public service association. In describing the collective house, the Ministry of Housing says: "The residents take no part in the operation or the financial management of the house." The organization, therefore, comes much closer to our limited dividend corporations than to being a cooperative. Its purpose is to supply housing as efficiently and economically as possible. It is distinguished from what we call the "normal" method of housing by the fact that it is for people rather than for profit. I noted in my earlier letter to you that in Sweden the H.S.B.[2] is doing a number of large jobs on the same basis—that is to say, they are designing, building, and operating groups of houses that are rented and not owned cooperatively by the tenants. This, of course, is only at the present time a sideline with them, as they continue to do their regular cooperative work. There is a strong tendency in that direction, as I told you.

It seems to me that you should, in your U.N. article, carefully distinguish between these two types of operation—the limited or nonprofit rental and the tenant-owned cooperative.

Our Cooperative Housing Foundation will also want to consider whether the CHF Company should not carry on both kinds of work,[3] that is to say, cooperative and limited-profit rental. You, Winslow, and I and the others should discuss this when I get back. By the way, my return has now been postponed to 22nd July. You can reach me here until the 21st—that is to say: c/o Unwin, Wyldes, North End, London, N.W. 3. . . .

With kindest regards,
Cordially,
Clarence

1. Carlson was writing an article on cooperative housing for a U.N. publication.

2. Hyresgästernas Sparkasse och Byggnadsforening, or HSB (Renters Investment and Building Association), was a large company begun in Stockholm in 1923 as a cooperative building organization selling its apartments to its members or to prospective members. HSB developed into a very large Swedish company that finances and builds cooperative housing, rental apartments, and complete districts of housing. The group also manufactures and sells building materials and prefabricated building components. It is owned by the people who rent or buy houses it plans and builds.

3. Stein was one of the founders, with Willcox and others, of the Cooperative Housing Foundation, an organization that built several communities in the United States. In the 1970s and 1980s, it was active in building housing in Central America.

---

432   To Philip Klutznick[1]

[New York City]   November 11, 1952

Dear Phil:

Last time I was in Park Forest, I missed seeing you. That was some time ago. I hope I am going to have an opportunity before long to talk with you about certain of the problems that you have been helping to solve there and which I am faced with from time to time.

One of these is the multiple use of movie theaters. It comes to mind because, [at] the end of the morning in which I was last in Park Forest, I noticed that a large group, perhaps all of the schoolchildren, were marching into the movie theater. I have been wondering to what extent you have been able to use the theater for educational purposes. How often do they have pictures for the school? Does the school board pay the proprietor of the movie theater for its use? Or does he give it to them, so as to keep in good relations with the public?

I would appreciate it if you would let me have this information just as soon as possible.

Cordially,

Clarence S. Stein

1. Philip Klutznick was the developer of the privately financed New Town of Park Forest south of Chicago.

---

433   To Aline Stein

[New York City]   January 22, 1953

Aline dear:

Let me follow your outline, but a little more fully.[1]

Work—fair today, but with some assistance from Roger.

Sociability this evening—Ben and I visit the Arthur Geddes, at whose house we enjoyed ourselves in Edinburgh yesterday. Sociability was entirely in the family. [I] am with Arthur and Benton . . . later in the evening. Lillie returned from her meetings which she has been attending all week. Ben and I even were guests of Charlotte's at noon. It was Elsie's day out.

P. was pastel this morning—a very rapid impression of the rising sun—not too good.

H. Physical—good, as always.

Mental health much better today. Zabriskie ordered another shock treatment, which took place night before last. Today his general estimate over the telephone based on my report of a good night's sleep was all right. I will see him tomorrow.[2]

I put off reporting until today to you, dear, because it is so difficult to know immediately how much improvement there is. Today I think it is very apparent. Certainly nothing to worry about. Z. says there are always ups and downs, and you say take it slower.

A fine letter came from Leo about his and Al's visit with you and Jennie Mac; also, he made the whole relations with the insurance co. clear. We certainly are lucky to have Leo to take care of this for the family.

Eric West phoned enthusiastically that the silver cup, etc., had come. It had been miscarried and had just arrived.

Ben continues to set a noble example of calm and content. I will try to follow his lead. He is taking good care of me.

My very best to our dear Jennie, and all my love to you, darling.

Clarence

1. Early in January Clarence had had another serious episode of mental breakdown. Aline was trying to monitor his reduced schedule from California.

2. Stein continued to experience bouts of depression in the early 1950s, but he seemed to have worked out methods for reducing their effects on his life, hence the reports to Aline on "Work, Sociability, Play, Health, and Mental Health."

---

434   To J. E. Dudley

[New York City]   January 26, 1953

MEMO   To Mr. J. E. Dudley, Aluminum Company of Canada, Ltd.

You have asked for my opinion on regulating [development in] the Kitimat Valley as proposed and whether the scope is proper and sufficient.

The basic idea is sound. In fact, I believe it to be essential—essential to the very success of the Kitimat community. The two, the municipality and the surrounding area, are interdependent. This is true both in regard to protection and development of the natural terrain and to ensure decent and economic human settlement.

The proper development of the valley will be of value to the future residents of the entire area. For instance, control of sanitation and stream pollution affects the welfare of everybody living in the valley. Improper sanitation anywhere in the valley can become a grave health menace to the people of the municipality.

The Kitimat municipality, for its own economic protection, must prevent settlements just outside its borders that cannot pay their way. Otherwise, it will ultimately have to assist in their children's education and also in their fire and health protection.

The area proposed by Mr. Henderson goes far enough to the north. It is high enough up the slopes on either side of the valley for all purposes other than complete flood control. This area to be regulated is ample with respect to the agricultural and rural development of the region being opened. For purposes of sustained yield forest management, the belt would stand widening, and for flood control it would, of course, have to include the whole Kitimat watershed.

Full and orderly regional development of the valley and its relation to the municipality will eventually require a positive program as well as the regulatory one now proposed. This need is illustrated in your comment to Mr. Henderson: "Provision should be made for construction of dams, levees, or dikes with proper approval." It also is indicated by Mr. Henderson's suggestion that some day a complete community should be planned south of Lakelse Lake.

The Kitimat Regulated Area should be established as soon as possible. The request for such establishment should come, as you say, from the Kitimat Municipality, that is, if this can be accomplished within six months. Otherwise, ALCAN ought to take the initiative.

In sum, the proposal is excellent as a protective measure. It will eliminate substandard, uncontrolled development. It will prevent major deterioration of natural conditions pending development of more constructive measures. This is essential because a full and positive regional program for the constructive development of the watershed will eventually be needed.

Clarence S. Stein

435   To Aline Stein

[New York City]   February 3, 1953

Aline dear:

This morning I visited our good Dr. Z. He came out finally, as you have, in favor of leaving the Kitimat job—resigning from it. I am not in condition for carrying it through just now.

And so I am planning to give up the work, to resign, though I must admit it is somewhat hard to do. It means so much to us. It's what all this past work has been leading up to, and there are many other arguments for it.

But these problems must be put aside at present. They are or seem too great. This is the time to turn to other things.

I hope that we will be together again soon—in the joyful life we have known so often in the past, in Sweden and California, in Westchester, everywhere.

I was not able to get an opinion from Dr. Z. this morning. It seemed enough to get one thing decided.

Your fine letter of advice was so helpful. I am sure it is all going to work out.

All my love,
Clarence

---

436   To J. B. White

[New York City]   February 5, 1953

Dear Mr. White:

My doctor advises me that I should discontinue any further work at this time. It is therefore with deep regret that I must ask ALCAN to relieve me of further duties under our agreement of March 15, 1952.

I will continue to be vitally interested in the great Kitimat undertaking. I feel confident of its success and shall always be proud of having my name connected with it.

When I am again well, my services will be at the disposal of the company, if desired.

Sincerely,
Clarence S. Stein

---

437   To Aline Stein[1]

[A Thousand Years, Yorktown, N.Y.]   February 22, 1953

Darling:

And now it is Monday morning. A beautiful, clear, but cold morning. And I have spent the night in this, the most beautiful room, or at least my favorite room. I hope we are going to spend a good part of our time out here at the farm just as soon as the weather is steady. I hope it will fit with your plans.

I am preparing to make a try at another book. Back in 1949–51, I was working from time to time on what I called "The Regional City," so I took the material I had started in those days out here with me. I have re-read most of it and find it good. All this happened before I gave my whole self to ALCAN.

I had forgotten in the year and more that has passed how much good there was in my conception. The fact is that the outline for the Kitimat study seems to have been very much influenced by [the] "Regional City" study, and now I think I am ready to return to it.

This morning, for the first time since Benton joined me, I got up early enough to make our first coffee. The old days are coming back. Now all I need is Aline back again.

Next Saturday or Sunday? . . . By rail or air? If by rail, shall I meet you here? Some good news about the farm: (1) Walter Smith will take care of the fruit trees. (2) Donald Richard would like to move near us. And I love you no end.

Clarence

1. Aline had been in Los Angeles working on *The Eddie Cantor Story* since early January 1953. This was not one of her best films.

---

438   To Catherine Bauer Wurster

[New York City]   February 23, 1953

Dear Catherine:

I have postponed writing to you about Gordon Stephenson's *Town Planning Review* because I thought there was a chance that I might see you in California. Aline has been out in Los Angeles doing a movie for the past six weeks, and I had intended to join her. But now we have changed our plans; she is returning and I am staying here.

I presume that you and Bill have noticed the extent to which the *Town Planning Review* has decreased in size and also is of somewhat poorer quality than it was a year or so ago—particularly as to illustrations and variety of articles. This is to a large extent due to the fact that the University of Liverpool has lately withdrawn its annual subsidy of about £1,000, which made it possible to sell the magazine here in America for a dollar a number. I think it is of the utmost importance that we find some way to replace that support . . . until that time when we are able to build up adequate subscriptions to get support from advertisement.

There is need of a planning magazine in America in the broadest sense. It should, as the TPR has attempted to do, cover various angles of the subject, including these that have interested our own RDCA: relation to natural setting, governmental aspects, detailed physical planning, as well as the archeological subjects that have been so well handled by Gordon's magazine.

I think it is impossible to bring out such a magazine here in America, fully enough illustrated, for the price of say a dollar a number. Such reproduction seems to be much easier in England than elsewhere. . . . The subsidy, however, it seems to me, must for the time being come mainly from this country. . . .[1]

I am interested to see whether we can get something started before Gordon Stephenson passes through America on his way back from Australia. My understanding is that he is going to visit Berkeley to see Kent, you, and Bill somewhere around April 12. He is then coming East. . . .

The middle of last week I made a start to see if I could not collect something. I had lunch with Ralph Walker and Albert Mayer. They will each give comparatively good contributions, and I will give what little I can. . . .

When are you coming East again?

Affectionate greetings to you, Sadie, and Bill.

Cordially yours,
Clarence S. Stein

1. Clarence seems to have recovered sufficiently from his mental illness to take on a fund-raising project for the *Town Planning Review*.

---

439   To J. B. White

[New York City]   February 27, 1953

My dear Mr. White:

. . . In spite of the fact that I am no longer under contract with the Aluminum Company of Canada, I hope you will understand that my interest in the Kitimat job is in no way lessened. I hope you will call on me at any time when I can be of service.

During the last two weeks, I have begun to feel like by old self, and I will be very happy in the near future to look up records or give you my personal opinion on anything in connection with the big job. I hope that you will tell Jim Dudley when he gets back that he should feel free to call upon me any time that he wishes.

This morning I was over to see Julian Whittlesey again. He is still unable to leave his apartment but moves from bed to wheelchair.[1] But mentally he is very much alive, and his interests are centered on the work at Kitimat. Once he gets started telling me about the work, it is difficult to stop him—but luckily I enjoy nothing better.

I do hope you will let me know the next time you come to New York so that Mrs. Stein and I can entertain you. She is on her way back from California now and expects to arrive here on Saturday.

With kindest regards to you and my other friends in the Montreal office.

Cordially yours,
Clarence S. Stein

1. Whittlesey had been seriously injured in a skiing accident in Vancouver, British Columbia, during the previous month. After he returned to New York, he continued to work at home on the plans for Kitimat.

---

440   To Paul Oppermann

[New York City]   March 12, 1953

Dear Paul:

. . . I am very glad you are going to find out what you can about the Stanford affair. I am not at all hopeful in regard to it. From what I can see, they have lost a great opportunity of doing an outstanding job of planning development and education in regard to new communities for America. I still think, as I have said in the past, that the decision in regard to the shopping center is of primary importance.[1] That decision should have been made as part of the basic economic, social, and physical plan of the whole 11 square miles. I doubt whether they have had the advice of the right person in regard to that.

I hope, of course, that I am mistaken in regard to this and that there is still an opportunity to do a really fine job in regional development. Do let me know what information you gather from Brandon or Ted Spencer. . . .

Very best wishes from Aline and myself to all the Oppermanns.

Cordially,

Clarence S. Stein

1. The shopping mall built on the northeastern corner of the Stanford University property was very successful. It contained seven major department stores. Governor Stanford's gift of land to the university prohibited sale of the land in fee simple, so the leased land produced a very large annual income for the university.

---

441   To Gordon Stephenson

[New York City]   April 22, 1953

Dear Gordon:

Yesterday I sent you a copy of a brief memorandum in regard to what we did in relation to the TPR while you were here. Please let me know if there are any corrections to be made.

I have been up to my neck in certain work in connection with Kitimat since you departed.[1] This explains why I have not written earlier to say how much Aline and I enjoyed having you with us. All we have to say about it is that it was too short. . . .

If a special number is devoted to Kitimat, I am of the opinion that it may be valuable to follow this in the next number with a lengthy article or series of articles on the subject of the U.S. Steel Corporation's large industrial plant being built in

Bucks County, Pa., and its affect on the development of housing and communities for workers and others. The problem there in certain ways is a parallel to that of the Aluminum Co. of Canada and has been handled in an entirely different manner.[2] I phoned yesterday to Bob Mitchell and asked whether anything could be done about this if the TPR was interested. He tells me that they (I presume he means himself and students) have been making a study of the subject for some branch of the U.S. government. He is of the opinion that the government will permit the release of a good deal of this material. What do you think of the idea? I could go to Philadelphia in a couple of weeks to talk it over with Mitchell, if you desire.

Last night I met the Lloyd Rodwins at Paul Weiner's house. She is charming. I expect to see more of Lloyd at meetings at Cambridge at the end of next week.[3]

[Clarence S. Stein]

1. Stein was back on the job at Kitimat.

2. The Levitt brothers built one of their Levittowns in Bucks County to meet some of the need for housing generated by the new steel plant.

3. Lloyd Rodwin's conclusions about the failure of the British New Towns program were published in *The British New Towns Policy* (Cambridge: Harvard Univ. Press, 1956). Clarence Stein could neither agree with nor understand Rodwin's argument. Stein was a true believer in the efficacy of the British New Towns program.

---

442 A Note on Letchworth

[New York City]   June 22, 1953

"THE INFLUENCE OF LETCHWORTH IN AMERICA":
NOTES BY CLARENCE S. STEIN

The influence of Letchworth in this country was not direct, as far as I know. It came to us as part of the Garden City Idea and as the creation of men who were an inspiration to us here in our work—work, however, which we did in our own way, or rather to meet our own needs.

Henry Wright and I were certainly greatly influenced in that manner. Soon after we started planning Sunnyside, but with our thoughts on the future American Garden City that we intended to create with Alexander Bing, we went to England. We visited Ebenezer Howard in Welwyn and Raymond Unwin at Wyldes. We got acquainted with them, talked things over with them, and saw how their ideas were realized. I remember walking about Welwyn with old Ebenezer and how alive he was to the way his conceptions developed and changed in practice: "Some people like to work in gardens, but others don't. So we have learned to lay out different types of lots to fit their varied desires." Of Unwin's work we were most impressed by Hampstead Garden Suburb—the wonderful feeling that he and his partner [and] brother-in-law, Barry Parker, had for the relation of buildings to the form of the land, to

each other, and to the background of foliage. I know nothing finer of that romantic age before life and cities were molded to serve the requirements of speeding autos rather than humans.

Perhaps we saw more of Hampstead than of Letchworth because it was more
convenient. In fact, I have no very definite recollection of the buildings of Letchworth as we saw them then. In the long talks, on our return ocean trip, about what
we had learned and might apply in our future work in America, I cannot now
remember what was said about them. We dealt mainly with the idea of the Garden
City and how it was applied in the two great experiments, Letchworth and Welwyn.

I must confess that my impression of the underlying plan of Letchworth is that
it did not altogether work. People and vehicles just didn't seem to move from railroad station to houses and elsewhere as they should have. I wonder if the center has
not been somewhat stranded, as it definitely is at Hampstead Garden Suburb. Perhaps that was what Parker and Unwin wanted. And probably these impressions of
mine come mainly from later visits to Letchworth after new problems of the auto
age had changed the requirements.

The important point, as far as I am concerned, is that Ebenezer Howard and
Raymond Unwin were among the great influences on my thinking and working in
those days when we were planning and building Sunnyside, Radburn, Chatham
Village, and ever since. Perhaps there is more apparent reflection of English Garden
City architectural form and particularly site planning in Chatham Village than in
the others. But, as a whole, I do not think that Henry Wright and I really borrowed
form and arrangement, not intentionally so, anyhow. It was the inspiration of two
great human beings who loved their fellow men and who had so much to give them
that counted most.

I am thankful that I was able to keep in touch with both of them from time to
time. Ebenezer Howard lived at our home when he was here to preside at the meetings of the International Association, in 1926, I think it was. Raymond Unwin visited Radburn with Henry and me when it was being built, probably 1929, and gave
us very sound advice—which the dark depression prevented our using. I visited
both of them on various later trips to Europe. Finally, thanks to Columbia University, we all had an opportunity to see much of Sir Raymond during his final stay in
America. Carl Feiss was particularly lucky in working directly with him.

It was Raymond Unwin's talks and writing and his presence that brought us
quite indirectly but still closely to what he had expressed in building and planning
at Letchworth. And, in the same way, the great ideas of Sir Ebenezer, which took
form first at Letchworth, have been and will be passed on through the works of
others to form part of America's future cities.

443   To Henry Klaber

[New York City]   September 18, 1953

Dear Henry:

I am very glad that I am going to see you here in New York on the 30th. Let's make it one o'clock lunch. I suggest that you phone me here when you arrive, so we can decide definitely where to meet.

In regard to the matter of the East Punjab Capital, of which Le Corbusier has taken possession, I feel quite as strongly on this matter as you do. I have considered writing something on the subject ever since I saw the publication of the CIAM called *The Heart of the City*.[1] In this, Le Corbusier completely forgets to mention Mayer and Whittlesey. A similar mistake was made in an article in *Town and Country Planning*, the latter quite apparently through ignorance of the matter. I postponed doing anything about it because I wanted to see whether Albert wanted a controversy started, and he was away in India.[2]

I talked the matter over with him on the telephone this morning and told him of your letter. I think that he would prefer not have a public discussion on the matter. I have asked Albert to lunch with us on the 30th, and he will try to keep the time open. We will then have a chance to talk on this and other things.

Aline's away on a trip in Europe.[3] Otherwise, she would join in affectionate greetings to you and Dorette.

As always,

Clarence S. Stein

1. The addresses of the Congress Internationaux d'Architecture Moderne (CIAM), or the International Congresses for Modern Architecture, were published in 1952: Jacqueline Tyrwhitt, L. Sert, and Erneste N. Rogers, eds., *The Heart of the City: Toward the Humanization of Urban Life* (London: Lund Humphries, 1952).

2. Le Corbusier's short summary of Chandigarh's core notes his British collaborator Maxwell Fry and his French partner Pierre Jeanneret, but leaves out mention of the earlier works of Albert Mayer and Matthew Nowicki and Le Corbusier's other British associate, Jane Drew. For a balanced evaluation of the roles of Le Corbusier, Mayer, and Nowicki in the planning of Chandigarh and of Stein's role as consultant, see Chandigarh Research Group, Delhi University of Technology, *Chandigarh Forty Years after Le Corbusier* (Amsterdam: ANQ, 1988).

3. Aline was acting in a British film being made in London.

---

444   To Chloethiel Smith[1]

[New York City]   November 8, 1953

Dear Chloethiel:

Your letter and the material in regard to the Southwest Washington Project arrived on Friday afternoon, just when I needed it. I don't know how I can thank you sufficiently for your promptness, the material you sent, and the spirit in which the work was carried out! It is difficult to tell you how I appreciate it, so I will just say much thanks. It is going to help me no end.

The meeting with Ralph Walker for Saturday morning did not come off because of the storm. It was just as well. What he wanted was advice from a few of us so-called planners in regard to the work he will do in connection with the President's Advisory Committee to determine policy for the present government concerning urban redevelopment, etc. I am glad to have a little more time to think this whole thing up in simpler, clearer terms. I refer to the part the national government shall take in the future in regard to the rebuilding of our cities, including assistance to be given to local authorities for housing or slum clearance, etc.

To judge what should be done, one should know much more than I do in regard to what has happened during the national government's short experience in rede-velopment, etc., since Title I Housing Act of 1949 was passed. Perhaps it is just as well that I have followed only a few examples of the work planned under it. I think I can still see the main objectives with a certain clarity and simplicity.

Your experience on the development of the Southwest Redevelopment Project is of immense aid in seeing this matter with clarity, this both in regard to technical possibilities and in terms of so-called practical reality. Here was a splendid oppor-tunity to develop an ideal balanced neighborhood as a part of a great city—where it would be of more influence to the rest of the nation than anywhere else. Result: a forward-looking plan negated by local authorities.

What is most needed now nationally is:

1. clarity of purpose, simplicity and directness of procedure
2. definite decision to move forward toward that objective.

Progress may have to be taken slowly, step by step. But direction must be clear, and there must be no compromises between the welfare of the people, com-munities, nation, and any temporary monetary profit.

I do not think Ralph Walker will play any part in determining how Southwest Development Project will be planned, certainly not now.[2] His opportunity will be in preventing backsliding as to general policy in regard to redevelopment, slum clearance, etc. Also in helping to develop a clearer and more forward-looking objec-tive for national participation or assistance in making new neighborhoods, cities, and related regions that are part of a contemporary America in such a way as to keep parallel with our future's needs and capacities.

[page 2 of letter missing from Stein Papers]

1. Smith had been one of the students in Henry Wright's housing design school in New Jersey during the mid-1930s.

2. Walker, president of the American Institute of Architects, was active in lobbying for changes in the Housing Act of 1949.

445   To Gordon Stephenson

[New York City]   November 27/December 12, 1953

Dear Gordon:

Your letter of November 16 gave me great pleasure in many ways. The official acceptance of the Radburn Plan [for the Stevenage Town Center] by the government is really great news. There is no question that it is in large part due to your professional as well as editorial work.

Although I have not read the October number of the *Review* in detail, it looks very good to me, and I am delighted that you feel as you do about it. . . .

Cordially,

Clarence S. Stein

446   To Lewis Mumford

[London, England]   July 4, 1954

Dear Lewis:

. . . Your letter of some time ago suggested that we visit Bath and Oxford. We were at both places last time. We surely expect to return to Oxford this trip. I want to spend a number of days rambling around some of the campuses. My heart, however, is in Cambridge. That, it has seemed to me, has more to offer than any other place I know.[1] We are postponing the Oxford trip so as to see a play there, in which a friend of our's participates.

The Radburn Plan is gradually taking a hold here, although generally with very incomplete understanding of its possibility. For example, yesterday morning I spent with Hart, the General Manager of Hemel-Hempstead, discussing his problem and then driving around some portion of the New Town. It is quite commonplace, most of it, with houses facing on through streets, many of which are used by buses. After lunch he told me that the boys in the drafting room would like to meet me, as they were planning an area on the edge of the town according to the Radburn scheme. Sure enough, they were! Gordon's Wrexham Scheme was their model, although they spoke knowingly of Baldwin Hills. They had the apparent . . . tightness of most of the house groups at W. but had neglected an equivalent of the open spaces in the sloping ground. I could not resist the temptation of asking for a piece of tracing paper and taking off my coat. I noted that their land was just about the size of Baldwin [Hills Village]—1,100 × 3,000 feet, so I suggested a single superblock. I roughly indicated a series of large greens passing through the Center and connecting with exterior woods and other open areas near by: thus quite different than B.H. Perhaps something may come of it.

More soon.

Affectionate greetings to you and Sophia from Aline and

Clarence

1. Stein wrote a long article on Cambridge University, which was never published. The manuscript is in the Clarence Stein Papers at Cornell University Archives. It praises the spatial qualities of Cambridge and the relationships of the colleges to the open gardens of the Cam River.

---

447   To Douglas Haskell

[London, England]   July 30, 1954

Dear Doug:

From Lewis Mumford I heard that the Kitimat story was out.[1] He was so enthusiastic about your editorial that I decided I must see it at once. I ultimately borrowed a copy of [*Architectural Forum*] at the Swanky Life-Time headquarters.

The article is beautifully and concisely presented. It is foolish to comment on it in detail until I have a chance to go over it carefully. But I hasten to tell you how deeply I appreciate your friendly understanding. Fact is, I am a bit overwhelmed.

You know, Doug, although the aim of an explorer is naturally to reach his goal, his real joy is the search. Next to this is the satisfaction of having sympathetic friends who understand where he is going. Thanks for expressing it so clearly and affectionately.

I am spending most of my time here finding out to what extent the British experience in creating New Towns can help us in our somewhat different problems of building a new United States.

Our best to you.

[Clarence Stein]

1. See "Industry Builds Kitimat: First Complete New Town in North America," *Architectural Forum* 101 (July 1954): 128–47 and 102 (August 1954): 158–61.

---

448   To Charles Lewis[1]

[New York City]   January 7, 1955

Dear Charles:

The *Architectural Record* has asked me to write another article about Chatham Village. Their chief editor, John Knox Shear, I think was formerly in charge of the school at Carnegie Tech. Anyhow, he had a number of friends in Chatham Village, and he is very enthusiastic about it. Although I am deep in the writing of another book and hate for that reason to take on anything else, I do think that I will make an attempt to write about the Village again, if I can have your assistance. The reason I want to do it is that I believe that the younger men in the profession can learn as much from Chatham Village as any development that I have had any experience with. An architect, when he first goes into housing work, is likely to be awed by a successful promoter-client, who is generally insistent on doing more of whatever is selling in his locality. For this reason there is little chance to fully analyze a problem and to explore possibilities of new approaches, as was done at Chatham Village.

I would like to show in as simple a manner as possible how Chatham Village's great success is due in large part to the fact that it had just the opposite attitude to the typical commercial client. I would like to illustrate not only with photographs and diagrams but with facts and figures how the charm and the good living in the Village, as well as its economic success, [are] due in large part to the fact that it negated many of the common real estate practices.

I think if we can make this clear the fact will have strong educational value, not only for the younger community architects but also for their clients and the general public. I hope you agree because, if I am to do this, I want to ask your help, not only in making material available to me, but in helping me to analyze just what has happened during the last quarter of a century in Chatham Village. Do let me know whether you think this is worth doing.

Best wishes for the coming year,

Cordially,

Clarence S. Stein

1. Lewis was the director of the Buhl Foundation in Pittsburgh, which had been the developer of Chatham Village during the early 1930s.

---

449   To Peter Blake[1]

[New York City]   August 19, 1955

Dear Peter Blake:

I am delighted that you are attacking the basic problem of housing—that is, land use. You asked me for suggestions of what to stress in the series.

Here are just two problems that grow out of a strong point that you make in your first article: that is, that the equivalent of all the waste land that is saved by using row instead of freestanding houses be put together for communal use. The suggestion is fine: green commons of that kind dispersed throughout cities and towns as a basic need. But I fear this may not look practical to the builder, who wants to get out quickly without any unusual problems to explain to purchasers. He will ask: Will they pay for that land no individual will own? And by whom and how are the greens going to be maintained? Has this idea sold houses somewhere else, and how did it work out in the long run?

These questions lead to the two subjects I want to suggest for a future article:

1. Where to place the common land.
2. How to conserve and operate it to maximum advantage and at least cost to those concerned.

The *Locational advantages* of the Center rather than the perimeter of blocks or Green Commons should be easy to explain. Henry Wright in *Rehousing Urban America* developed this theory thoroughly. Examples of its use in practice at Sunnyside, Radburn, Greenbelt, Baldwin Hills, and elsewhere appear in my *Toward New Towns for America*.

Some of the apparent advantages of block-center location are:

1. *Cost* is less because of saving in perimeter main highways and utilities.
2. *Usefulness* is greater, as it is closer to most homes, easier to reach, and can be watched from their homes by mothers whose children are playing there.
3. *Safety* against dangers of automobiles is [better] in the developments with built-in greens or parks.
4. *The Beauty* and attraction of a natural green oasis in the monotony of a housing development is far more striking if it is located where it can best be seen and enjoyed. The rocky hill in the center of Easter Hill, which you illustrated, is an example.

The *conservation and useful operation* of the central greens is the basic problem, but it can and has been met again and again in a practical way.

Your term "communal county club" sounds good to me. But it may seem a little fancy and difficult to sell to the hard-headed builder. It can be carried out with great satisfaction to the surrounding homeowners by use of deed restrictions (which builders use for much less valuable purposes). Radburn and Sunnyside exemplify this. At Radburn it was comparatively easy to explain the need of it as part of a new and unusual plan pattern. But at Sunnyside the commons were placed in the center of ordinary checkerboard blocks. The Sunnyside deed restrictions were for forty years. Yet, as I remember, the houses sold rapidly. For thirty years . . . the shading trees and the restful greens have been conserved thanks to the deed restrictions.

I will be glad to discuss this further with you when I get back to New York end of September. Now I want to congratulate you on the presentation of Vernon De-Mars's Easter Hill. Vernon took me out to see it the last time I was here. What a relief after the prisonlike monotony of most public housing. Vernon has a sense of adventure. He is an explorer. As a result some of his discoveries may seem at first sight somewhat crude and unfinished. But you are aware at Easter Hill of his glowing, joyful sense of rhythm, dance, and song in relation to color and form, as in the dance and music of the American Indians.

My best wishes.

Cordially,
Clarence S. Stein

1. Blake was editor of *Architectural Forum*.

---

450   To Stanley Rough

[New York City]   October 12, 1955

Dear Stanley Rough:

Your letter reached me this morning. I am delighted that the copies of the pamphlet "Kitimat: A New City" were found and distributed. No matter how good a city is planned or built, it will never do its job unless the people who live in it understand its unique qualities, for the people are the city. All we planners can offer is a stage that will best fit modern acting and give the performers the maximum freedom to live as full a contemporary life as individuals and as a community as is possible. That's what we tried to do.

I only hope that everyone in Kitimat will have a pride in his town when he reads [in] the foremost architectural journal in America of Kitimat as the first complete twentieth-century "New Town," completely new, completely modern in North America.

If all those who live there decide to make it so, I believe that it can be made so. But that means that they must understand how and why Kitimat differs from most other communities and what those differences can mean in opportunities for good, tranquil, safe living and in a lot of other ways. The articles from the *Architectural Forum* tell the story, but it would be a fine thing if the publications in Kitimat continuously called attention to specific qualities in the plan that can be brought to life if the people want and will it.

What luck has the town had in finding a community head?

Best wishes to you and your wife and to my other friends at Kitimat.

Cordially,
Clarence S. Stein

---

451   To Carl Feiss

[New York City]   [October 1955]

DRAFT MEMORANDUM ON PLANNING EDUCATION AT MIT

President Killian in his letter to us said: "Planning . . . covers many fields of action and, for that reason, any given curriculum may suffer from lack of focus. It seems to us also that a satisfactory program for education in Planning must take stock of the special resources and personnel available at M.I.T." There is great wisdom in limiting the field of study of any specialized school and of integrating it as fully as possible into the institution of which it forms a part.

Planning is practiced in two quite different ways. Both propose to determine the physical setting for community life. But they go about it in diametrically different ways. Therefore, these two professions require different kinds of training. One of these, and that is the one in which specialized education has been altogether too limited in this country, is closely related to architecture. I believe it is, in fact, architecture, but architecture dealing with a broader and broadening field.

Therefore, it seems logical that the curriculum at MIT *focus* on the constructive rather than the administrative or regulatory field, *deal primarily with city building* and particularly the functions of the designer in the creation of a community, SPECIALIZE in preparing students to be *community architects*. MIT might well, and I think wisely, limit its training in the field of broader planning to the preparation of students for participation in planned city building or in community and regional development. It should deal with the design of any community, be it a small group of related buildings, a neighborhood, a town, a city, a region, or a state, in the same manner as a realistic contemporary architectural office would handle an architectural project.

The practice of community architect (or city or town architect, if you prefer) is quite different from that which is generally called *city planning*. The latter is concerned with the outline of a city, with its framework for circulation and its subdivisions into blocks and lots; thus, the detailed form of a city is not determined or designed but is merely limited or regulated. The preparation and administration of restrictions and other limitations of use, height, and bulk is an important part of the city planners' activities. Although this type of work is at present an essential requirement, it is quite different from designing a city or any other community that is to be predetermined in form and mass as well as in plan: that is, to be molded in three dimensions, with all its elements related to each other as designed.

City planning in practice generally deals with two-dimensional diagramming. Its specifications are negative regulations and generalized limitations instead of positive, specific, constructive requirements for a particular accomplishment.

The architect's work is a dynamic activity that is aimed at a special goal. Each individual job requires a unique solution. This is to be reached by predetermined structural accomplishment for a definite purpose, use, occupation; it [specifies] which activities can be carried out according to definite requirements of functional procedure, but with adequate leeway for flexible change and growth.

Architecture deals with production of a structure or group of structures. Design and the other activities of an architect's office are futile unless they lead directly a solid, three-dimensional attainment. Architectural planning is an essential step, not only toward the construction, but toward the practical use of a building for specific purposes and functional operations.

The attitude required for planning New Towns or other contemporary communities parallels that of the regular practice of really contemporary architectural offices. This is illustrated in the development of a school, or better a high school, from the coordination of the specialists' requirements by a partnership of administrator and architect through the harmonizing and unifying of these in the three-dimensional design to the ultimate goal of realization and operation. All this is similar to the type of city planned development that we will require more and more in the near future. It is the approach that will be required in building New Towns to care for dispersement or in broad redevelopment of existing cities and the planned development of regions. It is the method we followed at Kitimat, to the best of our abilities.

All this points to the need of at least one "city planning" division of an architectural school in America that will deal solely with the creation of communities according to the contemporary method of architectural design. Such a school will turn out not "city planners" but community architects.

There are many reasons why a school that will specialize in the preparation for the practice of the profession of *Community Architecture* should be first set up at MIT. Community building and the work of the Community Architect is much more closely allied to construction, engineering, and particularly to architecture than it is to city planning as it is generally practiced. Therefore, the special resources and personnel available at MIT, of which President Killian wrote, will be of special value. This is true of various divisions of the institute, but particularly of the Architectural Department. MIT has the further advantage of its location close to the special schools of Harvard and other technical institutions [and of] the fact that so many of the leading architectural practitioners in broad planning are on the East Coast and might conveniently be called in as lecturers, critics, or advisors.

The School of Community Architecture should be a continuation of the School of Architecture. The same approach should carry through the two schools as though they were one. The effect on the Architecture might be quite as valuable as on the graduate school.

It might be possible to integrate into the whole architectural school the broader planning approach requiring relation of every building to its environment, to nearby buildings, to site conditions, to background, both natural and manmade. If the architectural student studies each project as a part of the development of neighborhood and town for more effective and pleasanter conditions for living, working, and loafing [and] if, from the beginning, he thinks of every building he designs as an essential, related part of a community, functionally and visually, he will be prepared to continue his studies and experience in the broadening fields of city and regional planned development, if he so desires. The architecture of buildings will flow naturally into that of the architecture of communities; there will be no strange obstacle or bridge to cross. It will be merely another step in the student's architectural exploration, with larger areas to conquer and integrate and more elements to harmonize and coordinate in design. But the method of approach, as well as the basic purpose and objective, is similar, whether the problem is a house or a city: the goal is the creation of an effective physical setting for contemporary life, labor, and leisure.

---

452   To Gordon Stephenson

[New York City]   November 22, 1955

Dear Gordon:

I spent all last Tuesday at meetings up at Massachusetts Institute of Technology. . . . Meanwhile, I am putting in what time I can on the second book. It is crawling along.

My visit to Cambridge last week had to do with a meeting of a committee of five which the President of Tech., J. R. Killian, Jr., had appointed to help them develop a policy and a program in connection with the future of the School of Planning. I presume that our presence would not have been needed if they had succeeded in getting you to head up things. Anyhow, there was a general expression of regret at your not being there from [President] Killian, Pietro Belluschi, and other members of the staff.

Our committee consisted of Jack Kent; Carl Feiss; Arthur McVoy, director of planning in Baltimore; Joseph Fisher, associate director of Resources for the Future, Inc. (a branch of the Ford Foundation); myself; and Dr. Burdell, president of Cooper Union, who was chairman.

It was a long and busy day. We talked with the president and provost, as well as the various members of the staff. This limited very much the time in which the members of the committee could each express his point of view. Dr. Burdell is now trying to put it all together, as a tentative report. I don't know just how anyone can gather together in a single bundle all our different approaches to the problem, but Burdell is very clever.

I am enclosing a copy of a memorandum I had prepared for the meeting. This, as you will understand, as well as what I said about our meeting, is confidential for the time being. But I would like to get a quick impression from you in regard to my idea of the kind of school that I think is badly needed now and will be even more urgently required when we try to meet the problem of New Towns. That time I feel sure will come before most of the boys now in school are long in practice. I don't claim that this is the only kind of planning school that is needed, but we should have, it seems to me, at least one school that specializes in turning out Community Architects, or whatever you want to call them.

I have noted down suggestions for a curriculum for such a school, but I am not going to burden you with that now. The educational method of carrying out the work you understand much better than I do. What I would like is to get your immediate reaction to my proposal. It will help me in reconsidering the whole matter when I get the preliminary report from Burdell. Naturally, I will not refer to you in connection with this unless you wish.

Of course, if fate had decided that you were to have run the school, there would have been no need of our going through all this. For the first time since I saw you in Toronto, I felt a little sorry that fate, or Washington, had interfered. I judge from all I heard that they certainly would have given you every opportunity possible. But I think you are going to have that in Toronto. I hope so, for their sake as well as your own.[1]

Aline joins me in affectionate greetings to you all.

Cordially,

Clarence S. Stein

1. Stephenson's inability to assume the MIT professorship and department chairmanship was a result of the McCarthy era American spasm of rejection of anyone who had known a Communist Party member or had close relations with people associated with the Soviet Union. He described the experience in his autobiography: Gordon Stephenson, *On a Human Scale: A Life in City Design* (South Fremantle, Western Australia: Fremantle Arts Centre Press, 1992). Chapter 17, "An Encounter with McCarthyism" (pages 154–71), deals with his 1954 decision to leave Liverpool University to work temporarily in Western Australia and at the University of California, Berkeley, and then to "take up a permanent appointment as professor of City and Regional Planning at MIT" in 1955.

While at Perth, his application for a visa to immigrate was denied by the American consul under section 212(a),27 of the Immigration and Nationality Act of 1952. An FBI investigator had discovered that Stephenson had belonged to the Liverpool Relief Committee for the Victims of German Fascism. The committee had included a Communist Party member and had occasionally had a communist speaker. President Killian of MIT, Pietro Belluschi, dean of Architecture and Planning, Ralph Walker, later president of the AIA, Clarence Stein, and many other friends wrote to the State Department and Walker directly interceded with Secretary of State Dulles, all to no effect.

Stephenson accepted a faculty position at the University of Toronto, where a new program in city and regional planning was being started. He became an active participant in Toronto city planning activities and continued to teach at the university until 1960, when he left Canada for Australia. There, in addition to teaching at the University of Western Australia at Perth, he was very active in university campus planning and numerous other urban design consulting assignments.

---

453   To Pietro Belluschi[1]

[New York City]   November 22, 1955

Dear Pietro:

It was good to see you yesterday evening. I am glad that you agree with me that I should make a clear statement covering the point of view that we discussed at breakfast the day of the meeting up at Tech. if, of course, I find that it has been lost in Burdell's preliminary report. I have no objection to a great center of planning studies being set up at Tech., or somewhere close by. In fact, the results of a broad-gauge research are needed to form a background for a school which will center primarily on production of practical planners of really modern communities. But I hope that the adequate preparation of City Architects is not going to be lost in a department or school devoted to innumerable other objectives.

Perhaps it has all been worked out in the Chairman's Preliminary Report, so I am looking forward to seeing it.

Do let me know when next you come to New York. Kindest regards to you and your wife.

Cordially,
Clarence S. Stein

1. Pietro Belluschi was dean of the School of Architecture and Planning at MIT.

---

454   To John Ross

[New York City]   November 23, 1955

Dear John:

. . . In regard to Chandigarh, I am going to have a lot of questions to ask you. I hope you spent plenty of time walking around, and I take for granted you saw it from the sky! I am particularly curious about the residential superblocks, whether they seem too large, if the central greens seem too crowded with schools, market, and all that, and a lot of other things. You say that you doubt if I am in accord with Chandigarh because there seem to be obvious departures from the plans that we first made. On the contrary, I feel that the basic principle, which all of us excepting Corbusier now call the Radburn idea, and which he calls "*my* idea," is there in Chandigarh, on a big scale.[1] I want to know how well it works and what can be done better the next time. So prepare yourself for many questions. . . .

Our best to you,
Clarence S. Stein

1. Stein seemed to be aware of the fact that Le Corbusier's plans had incorporated many of the features of the Mayer, Whittlesey, Nowicki plan, for which Stein had served as a major consultant in 1950.

---

455   To Carl Feiss

[New York City]   January 28, 1956

Dear Carl:

You seem to be running a campaign for CSS and doing it single-handed.[1] Thanks very much.

Is there anything that I ought to do about it? I note that, in the letter from one of the regional directors, he asked for more material in regard to me. I am not quite sure just what was finally sent to Washington. Henry Churchill, I believe, put certain of the material that I forwarded him into one or two binders. Perhaps if you think that there is reason for doing anything further I should look over what has been sent. As there are a number of other things I have to do in Washington, I might be able to go there in a week or so. Do you think it is worthwhile? Meanwhile, you might ask the AIA secretary.

How have things been with you? It seemed to me that the MIT Report came out pretty well, finally. You fellows must have worked pretty hard to cut out some of the wordiness of the draft that Ed Burdell submitted. There is only one thing that worries me about it, the question of the choice of director of the center. A really tremendous job could be done in this field if we had an outstanding man of big caliber, not only in what we call planning but in the field of public affairs and human relations. Perhaps I don't know either of the candidates quite well enough to be sure we have chosen rightly. Anyhow, I wish some of us could think of someone else to add to the list.

> Cordially,
> Clarence S. Stein

1. Feiss and Henry Churchill had nominated Stein for the Gold Medal of the American Institute of Architects.

---

456   To Albert Mayer

[New York City]   February 3, 1956

Dear Albert:

I presume, if you are not back yet, that you will be in New York shortly. I hope I will have a chance to see you soon. Meanwhile, I want to congratulate you on the excellent article on New Towns in the [*New York*] *Times* magazine section. It is very clear and factual. And besides, it is good reading. It should be an immense help in getting the big idea over to Americans, including industrialists and members of labor unions.

Just one paragraph that seems to me to give a wrong impression: that is the one in which you say pedestrian and motor traffic are in general insulated from each other. I found quite the contrary to be in general characteristic of the New Towns; in fact, separation for any but very short distances exists only in exceptional places. It is only now, since the war, . . . as a result of the gradual[ly] increased production of automobiles, that the Radburn principle is being accepted in England. Note mention of this in (among other places) the January number of *Town and Country*

Planning in L. E. White's article on the "New Ideas in Harlow," in which he says that they have discovered already the hard fact that we must come to terms with the motor era.[1] Very little that I remember of Harlow really did this. Certainly the first Town Center that they built was originally arranged in such a way as to make crossing from store to store anything but safe.

In spite of this small criticism, I am delighted with what you had to say and the way you said it.

Cordially,

Clarence S. Stein

1. L. E. White, "New Ideas in Harlow," *Town and Country Planning* 24 (January 1956): 19–22. The entire issue is devoted to New Towns and is entitled "New Towns and British Prestige."

---

457   To Walter Creese

[New York City]   February 6, 1956

Dear Mr. Creese:

I am very much interested in your proposal to study the development of the English Garden City. From your outline I get the impression that you are setting yourself a tremendous task of research. I am wondering whether you could not serve your purpose just as well by cutting down on or eliminating a number of elements or examples. I should think, for instance, that most of the section on the country house might be eliminated. Also, the first section on industrialism might very well be kept as compact as possible, as the subject has been covered so often. I am delighted that you seem to have the same interest and enthusiasm in Cotswold and particularly Chipping Camden. So have I, and I hope you will be able to show its relation to the work of Raymond Unwin and the others of his day.

I think also that it would be impossible to do justice to so many examples of Garden Cities and Suburbs unless you intend to do no more than mention the greater part of them. The same is probably true also of your *Section E,* which gives so many examples in various countries.[1]

In spite of the four major reasons which you give for your proposed study of Garden Cities, I am not altogether clear in regard to your approach. As I understand it, your purpose is to take up architecture and planning. Therefore, your interest is not, I presume, in history, but in the application of the work of the past to the quite different world in which we now live. I have had the experience a number of times in the last few years of returning to cities which I had known very well in my student days from the point of view of the architectural quality and historical background of individual buildings. I have tried to see cities such as Paris, Venice, and others purely from the point of view of what ideas there were that could be applied to the planning and building of truly modern cities. I wonder if it would be of value to you to think through this whole subject you have chosen with that approach. That would mean that you would take the Garden Cities and their descendants, the New Towns, and see what are the suggestions that they have to offer to us as architect-planners of this age of auto traffic and ever-increasing leisure time. . . .

Henry Wright and I, when we were starting out work on Radburn, visited the Garden Cities. That was just after Welwyn had been started, and it was immensely interesting to walk around that New Town with Ebenezer Howard. I am sorry that you have not had the opportunity to meet those pioneers of the Garden Cities—Howard, Unwin, Parker. However, Mrs. Parker is still alive and is just as deeply interested in the Garden City ideas as ever. She lives at Letchworth, and I feel certain that she would be glad to see you if you told her of your interest in the work of her husband. You will find a great deal of valuable material in the files of the magazine *Town and Country Planning*, both in regard to Garden Cities and the New Towns. . . .

As you know, both Henry Wright and I have written about Radburn and related communities in America. Wright's book *Rehousing Urban America* (publisher Columbia University) should be of particular value to you.

If you go to Stockholm, I think you will be particularly interested in Vällingby, which is the latest of the new communities that is complete or approaching completion. . . .

I do hope that some of my suggestions may be of help to you. Best wishes!

Yours cordially,
Clarence S. Stein

1. Creese's book was published ten years later as *The Search for Environment: The Garden City Before and After* (New Haven: Yale University Press, 1966) and in an expanded edition by the Johns Hopkins University Press in 1992.

---

458   To Lewis Mumford

[New York City]   February 14, 1956

Dear Lewis:

I spent the greater part of last week down in Washington with Ben at the Cosmos Club. Ben is in really very good condition, excepting that he moves and thinks a little bit more slowly.[1] He has really started writing descriptions of his diagram. He didn't show me any of it, but I am glad that it is under way. He spoke of going north again at the beginning of March. That, I think, would be a great mistake. He should stay in Washington at least two weeks longer. He is comfortable at the Cosmos Club, and he seems to find the library there an ideal quiet place for work. I have just written to him telling him that I hope he will change his mind and decide to stay there somewhat longer.

I found much to interest me in and around Washington. As a result of the *Architectural Forum*'s big story about the national capital in its January number, I have been thinking and reading and writing about the possibility of really sending enough of the office workers out of the city to set up a circle of New Towns. I think I told you that that was taking me back to our studies and ideas of 1950.

I happened to meet Douglas Haskell in Washington my first day there. I told him he had some very good ideas beautifully presented in his story of the national capital. There was only one trouble—they completely missed the essential point; that the only way we are going to be able to enjoy the spacious beauty of Washington in the future [is] to clear out some of the workers, along with their automobiles that are packed in all of the open spaces.

I spent a couple of long mornings traveling around the outskirts of the capital district, going out almost 30 miles into Montgomery County, Maryland, and some distance up the river in Virginia in search of sites to which it is proposed to disperse certain of the federal agencies. But they are really beginning to move out![2] At that distant point in Maryland, the AEC [Atomic Energy Commission] is going to set up its executive offices, but, they say, not their laboratories. I was delighted to find how open and attractive the country is out that way. The same was true near the location of the Central Intelligence Agency, which is only about 7 air-miles from the center of Washington on the Potomac. They are proposing to move some 10,000 workers out there. As far as I can make out, there are not plans for housing them. It seems to me that the time should come soon when we will be able to get something started in the way of dispersed communities around the capital. Washington is really the best place to start, not only because there is such wonderful open country fairly close in but because it is *The* place that all the younger folks visit. . . .

I did see a lot of old friends down there that were, as usual, holding a housing planning conference of some kind, the best part of it being with Ben.

Aline joins me in affectionate greetings to Sophie and to you. Our best to Alison.

Clarence S. Stein

1. Benton was seventy-seven. He had been born in Stanford, Conn., in 1879, but until he was nine he had lived in Manhattan with his actor-playwright father, Steele MacKaye.

2. Stein's efforts to persuade Washington dispersal planners in 1950–51 seem to have had an indirect effect on the planners of Montgomery County, Md., through Frederick Gutheim. The county's development regulations were used in the 1960s to shape the development of new subdivisions, laws about planned unit developments (PUDs), the county park program, and so forth, to provide some of the elements of a New Town in the sense Stein understood this term (greenways, pedestrian ways, etc.).

459   To Lewis Mumford

[New York City]   April 2, 1956

Dear Lewis:

Benton just arrived. He looks fine but seems a little older. . . .

I was glad to learn from your letter that *From the Ground Up* is such a big success.

I certainly did notice Osborn's comment on your criticism of New Towns in *Town and Country Planning.*[1] He surely has a well-trained mind that travels along a familiar rut.

You ask me for the density of Baldwin Hills Village. There are 7.8 houses per acre there. How unimportant this game of numbers is is apparent from the air views which appeared in my book. They contrasted the open development of Baldwin Hills Village with the surrounding real estate subdivisions, which have 3-1/2 to 4 houses to the acre.

Osborn does not as yet fully understand what Unwin meant by "Nothing gained by Overcrowding." If he did he would know the cost of land for housing is not so much in the land itself but in its development with utilities and roads. Therefore, if you are using raw land the number of houses per acre is much less important than how the houses are grouped and related to parks and means of access. That is, of course, where the superblock and the Radburn scheme come in as far as economy is concerned. As Henry Wright used to say, the parks are like the hole in the middle of the doughnut, you don't have to pay anything for it. . . .

England has at last, as you know, recognized the Radburn Plan and permits separation of path and road. I think you saw the development that Gordon Stephenson did in Wales. That seemed to me, although it had certain charm, altogether too tight. Other developments by a couple of the county councils in England, which appeared in the *Town Planning Review* a year or so ago, seemed to me freer.[2]

As the production of automobiles in Great Britain increases, as it is bound to, some form of the Radburn scheme will become regular practice, in spite of all Osborn may say. But let's hope that you can make him understand just what it is all about, and tell him he can have his private gardens as well as a safe common in the center of the block that he won't have to pay a shilling more for.

When are you coming down this way again? I hope before long. I expect to go out to California before the end of the month to help judge a competition, and then I'll probably stay on till May 17th, when the AIA is going to give me the Gold Medal. This news is just for you and Sophie for the moment.

Affectionate greetings to you both from Aline and

Clarence

1. Lewis Mumford, "Opinions on the New Towns," *Town and Country Planning* 24, no. 141 (1956): 161–64.

2. Gordan Stephenson, "The Wrexham Experiment—the Queens Park South Estate," *Town Planning Review* 24, no. 4 (1954): 271–96, is a detailed account of Stephenson's work with J. M. Davies, the borough surveyor, engineer, and architect of Wrexham, North Wales, on housing area designs that make use of a modified Radburn Plan. In its 1953 supplement the 1949 *Housing Manual,* the British Ministry of Housing and Local Government had supported the use of the "Radburn system" in local authority housing layouts. See also Kermit C. Parsons, "British and American Community Design: Clarence Stein's Manhattan Transfer, 1924–47," *Planning Perspectives* 7 (1992): 181–210.

---

460   To Carl Feiss

[New York City]   April 10, 1956

Dear Carl:

. . . Luck was with the Steins, as Aline is to do a picture on the coast. She leaves for Hollywood tomorrow. The job will last three or four weeks, and, as you see, it will just fit in with the AIA convention. The picture is a wild and woolly westerner, so part of it will be made at Tucson, which, as you know, is pretty well surrounded by Indians.[1] Possibly I may take a short trip to Mexico City. Eric Carlson tells me that a number of architects are beginning to do work based on the Radburn idea. I'd like to see just what they are doing.

What I wanted to talk to you about particularly before I went out to the coast is this: In the talk that I am to make, among other things I am tempted to say some not-too-complimentary things about urban redevelopment and urban renewal, the point being that their design is too restrained by obsolete street pattern; that they have not in most cases broken away completely from the framework and mass that make our cities so uninhabitable. It is because I feared that my impression of the general trend of the work might be unfair that I wanted to go over some of the past work with you and see to what extent they are really turning out contemporary areas of a large-enough scale to adequately affect living and working conditions in American cities. Perhaps you can refer me to examples that really show a complete break with the past. The Detroit Redevelopment of Mies van der Rohe [Gratiot], which I have just seen in the last *Architectural Forum,* is possibly an example of what I am looking for. . . .

Best wishes to you and Alleen.

Cordially,

Clarence S. Stein

1. The film was *The Man from Laramie,* a highly rated Western in which Aline appeared with James Stewart, Arthur Kennedy, Donald Crisp, and Wallace Ford.

461 To Lewis Mumford

[Palo Alto, California] July [29], 1956

Dear Lewis:

I am sorry I missed seeing you in New York. It must have been less than a week after we left that you were there. I look forward to seeing your report about Pittsburgh. I don't know if I told you that I did try my hand at developing hillsides, just outside of that city, some years after we did Chatham Village.[1] One of them would have been a guide to future public housing,[2] if it had not been for insanely misplaced economies on the part of the Washington authorities. I think that there is more to be learned from Chatham's 25 years of success. I believe I will write an article for the *Architectural Record* on "Chatham Village Revisited" to explain how it was possible to do all the things that were "impossible" in Pittsburgh: row housing for rental, autos separated from homes, Radburn type plans facing commons, greenbelts, and all.

We are enjoying university life, or perhaps it is the climate, the beauty of the setting (which the builders of Stanford have so far neglected), and the delightful people. . . .

When I came here, I expected to spend my time writing my book. I have been writing and studying, true, but it is not just the subject I expected. But it may fit it or help mold it. The last three weeks I have been devoting myself to Santa Clara County. . . .

Our affectionate greetings to Sophie and to you.

Clarence

1. These are the Pittsburgh/Allegheny County Housing Authority's defense housing projects in Shaler and Stowe Townships.

2. Probably Stein was referring to the Clariton Township project (his third in Pittsburgh), which was not built.

---

462 Excerpts from AIA Gold Medalist acceptance speech, 1956

[Los Angeles] [July 1956]

"COMMUNITIES FOR THE GOOD LIFE"[1]

In the contemporary city the green openness will go far beyond the parks, flowing through and connecting the superblocks. Not only will every building open on views of fine old trees or distant hills, but broad greenbelts will be close by for agriculture or forests, for great sport fields or hiking, boating, fishing, swimming, skating, or just for solitude in the peaceful valleys or the wilds.

This is the kind of beautiful and healthful city that can be built in various parts of the United States if we start from the ground up. Such communities cannot be secured by the ordinary piecemeal process of city planning. A beautiful and livable urban environment cannot be boxed into cubbyholes bounded by fixed and dominating streets and lot lines. It must be created as an entity, embracing the site, the mass of buildings, and their relation to each other and to the natural setting—in short, to all the visual surroundings.

You may say that this is not a problem of architecture, it is a question of securing adequate land and planning it for leisure-time use where it is needed. But the fact is [that] the two must go hand in hand, the design of buildings and outdoor spaces for the new life and the allocation of adequate and proper land where and when it is needed.

What we need is an architectural attack on problems much more comprehensive than the individual building. The architect must deal with the whole environment in which his building is set, of which it forms a part. In short, he must become a *community architect.*

Note that I suggest *community architecture,* not *city planning,* as a fitting, an essential practice for our profession. The two fields are basically different.

City planning deals with two-dimensional diagramming, with a city's framework for circulation and its subdivision into blocks and lots. Its specifications are negative regulations and generalized limitations, such as zoning. They are not positive, specific, constructive requirements, as those for a particular building. Thus, the detailed form and mass of a city is not designed but is merely limited.

The architect's work is a dynamic activity that forms part of the realistic production of a structure or group of structures. Design and other activities of an architect's office are futile unless they lead directly to solid, three-dimensional attainment. Architectural planning is an essential step not only toward the construction but toward the practical use of a building for specific purposes and functional operations.

I recognize and admire the able, public-spirited work that city planning administrators are doing. It is essential under present limitations, but these make it impossible to accomplish the purpose of the constructive rebuilding of America that we need so badly. What is called *city planning* does not create solid realities; it outlines phantom cities. It does not determine the bulk, the solid body of a city. It produces skeletons, framework for marketable lots, not vibrant communities of homes and working places for realistic and pleasant living and doing here and now in the twentieth century. That shape and appearance of these cities is a chaotic accident. It is the summation of the haphazard, antagonistic whims of many self-centered, ill-advised individuals. Under these conditions people have little freedom of choice. They can fit their buildings into one of the cubbyholes outlined by a plot plan or fit their family's life into the monotonous, repetitive patterns stamped out by the builder's machine. Look at Los Angeles!

It shows, as do most American metropolitan areas, that the only way to get modern cities and to keep them modern is by all-inclusive, architecturally planned city building, followed by permanent dynamic administration to keep their purpose and form alive. That zoning or similar restrictive methods will not serve this purpose is apparent in the present development of the San Fernando Valley. The City Planning Department of Los Angeles made a farsighted plan to prevent the continuous sprawl of population over the 212 square miles of the valley. They separated the moderate-size communities from each other by greenbelts zoned as agricultural open areas. This has come to naught. The practical house developers have had the greenbelts erased where most needed, that is, between the growing communities. Zoning is only a temporary barrier or protection. It cannot stand up against the flood of monotonous commonplace or greed of land subdividers. To permanently preserve greenbelts and keep modern green towns green and modern requires constructive, purposeful development and operation. Positive action must replace negative regulation for cities as well as building. That is why I am convinced that architects must be community architects.

In the development of a new culture, certain physical expressions of a civilization are affected much more slowly by technical, social, and economic change. For example, our cities have lagged far behind our buildings. The technological revolution has given us a fresh, contemporary architecture. Architects are throwing off the chains that tied them to the past. They are free to mold their works to express their purpose and their feelings. Free—yes, free of restriction of past rules and clichés.

But our architecture is by no means fully free, for in our cities our buildings have nowhere to go. The golden period of American architecture will have to wait until our lagging cities recognize that this is the mid-twentieth century.

Modern architecture demands a modern setting, a place where it can be properly viewed and enjoyed, a site where it can open up and stretch and change. As community architects we must create cities and buildings as a single entity, completely interrelated in design and structures. These new communities should remain continuously youthful. Therefore, they must be both spacious and flexible enough to take new form with changing ways of living, laboring, and loafing. We must replace dying cities with communities that fit and foster the activities and aspirations of the present. We must build new cities as a stage—a joyful setting for the good life here and now.

1. This article, "Communities for the Good Life," was excerpted by Clarence Stein from his address to the 1956 AIA convention. *Journal of the AIA* 26 (July 1956): 11–18.

463   To Robert Alexander

[New York City]   September 5, 1956

Dear Bob:

. . . I did my best a couple of weeks ago to telephone to you. I was at the Los Angeles airport and tried to get you just before my plane to New York arrived, but I had no luck. We had been spending a couple of months at Stanford University. Aline, as "artist-in-residence," was acting with the students in the School of Drama. She has done this a couple of times in the past and enjoys it very much.

Meanwhile, I was making a study of Santa Clara County. In part I was trying to see if there was any way to protect that fertile valley from the ruthless destruction resulting from the unorganized invasion of industry and housing. It is apparent to me that something much more drastic than zoning is required. I hope you and I will have a chance to talk about this together before long. If there is any chance of your coming to New York on a visit, . . . do let me know in advance.

Aline joins me in affectionate greetings to you and Mary.

Cordially,
Clarence S. Stein

464   To Henry Klaber

[New York City]   December 5, 1956

Dear Henry:

. . . Now as to the big question that you bring up in the body of your letter. I agree with you that New Towns of 60,000 population or so are not adequate to serve all the varied requirements of present-day living. They can't do it just by themselves. True, we must plan and build on a much bigger scale. But these greater cities should be broken up into smaller, integrated units by greenbelts or wedges closely accessible to all homes and working places.

The limited-sized community will be an important, in fact, an essential element in the organic development of the great cities built on a regional basis, no matter how large their scale may be. Such integrated small communities have much to offer that is crowded out of a metropolis. We need the close community grassroots relation that grows up in a limited-sized town. They foster an interest and pride in public affairs in which the individual participates, which is missing in most metropolitan cities. We must have proximity to large open places and to neighborly centers of culture, education, and everyday affairs, such as marketing and local association.

Yes, we must have moderate-sized, well-balanced communities, New Towns in a sense. On the other hand, there is need of planned development and administration on a large-enough scale to make possible all the central facilities to which you refer and the varied opportunities and occupations which only a great city can afford or support. This combination of the "grassroots" community and of the Big City is what I have aimed for in my proposal of a Regional City.

The enclosed outline description of the idea I think you have already seen. An important thing is that a Regional City can take many different forms—and that the smaller communities of which it is composed can have endless variety and individuality. They each will be self-dependent as far as local affairs are concerned. So each will, or should, develop in an individual form and manner. The Regional City will therefore offer a variety of choices to people who seek different ways of living. It will permit like and different people to get together easily and participate in community affairs or to be just lonely if they prefer.

A Regional City will consist of a series of communities of different sizes, within larger and larger communities with ever-increasing functions. Thus, each of us will be part of a number of communities. Each will have its own center and its own defined boundaries. A small group of families may gather round a nursery or common workshop; a larger community, say 800 families, might have as center an elementary school; a neighborhood twice that size would be related to a supermarket, health center, and community meeting places; a Junior and Senior High School with their related buildings and grounds will form the gathering places for culture, education, sports, and so on for communities of ten to thirty thousand population. These Junior and Senior Districts are playing a more and more important part in the life of cities such as Seattle.

The diagrams which I went over with you the last time we were together are an attempt to relate these organic communities, which fit one within the other, to a simple work pattern of traffic, convenient open spaces, and various community centers.

It is difficult to squeeze all this into a few paragraphs.[1] It is so much better if we can sit down and talk it over at greater length. So I hope you will be in New York again soon after you return from the West. Meanwhile, Aline and I hope you will have the best of times out there.

Affectionately,
Clarence S. Stein

1. This may be Stein's best short description of his and the RPAA's idealistic Regional City idea.

465   To Paul Oppermann

[New York City]   January 9, 1957

Dear Paul:

Thanks for your letter of January 3. I am delighted that you agree with my suggestion in regard to the preservation of the agricultural land in Santa Clara Valley. You are right in saying that we might as well advocate the real remedies "as the educational and political action tasks never become any less difficult." To a good many people it may seem a radical solution, but I am convinced, as you seem to be, that in the long run something of the type that I have suggested is essential and will be accepted. Zoning, even Belser's "A" Zone, will ultimately fall down unless the method of developing agricultural land is permanently limited.[1]

I hope that you will keep me posted on the progress that is made by your California Legislative Committee in regard to this or related legislation. When the matter does come up, what is most needed, it seems to me, is to show that the solution is not altogether novel or radical. We should rather get together solutions of other parallel problems that deprived property owners of certain of their customary privileges. If I remember rightly you spoke of a number of examples when we first discussed this matter during our short ride from San Francisco to Palo Alto. One very apparent example that comes to my mind is that of redevelopment, which takes private land and then resells it with limitations of its use. There must be a good many other similar parallels.

The more I read of conditions in the Santa Clara County and the crazy patchwork of diminutive cities, the more strongly I feel that there should be a radical change in the relation of the small incorporated cities and the country. At present, the municipality, no matter how small or technically ill-equipped, seems to be more powerful than the county. This is particularly apparent in their freedom to annex outlying areas. As far as I could observe, the problems being dealt with are mainly large areas or regional in nature. What would fit the needs of Santa Clara is to make it into a Regional City of the kind I have tried to describe. The first move in that direction, I should say, would be to increase the powers of the county in relation to the small incorporated cities. . . .

Best wishes for the coming year to you all.

Cordially,

Clarence S. Stein

1. Agricultural and open-space land preservation has come a long way since Stein's 1957 criticism of the Santa Clara County agricultural zoning regulations. The purchase of easements and development rights, outright purchase, the use of land trusts, and more sustainable agricultural zoning have become relatively common in the outer rings of some metropolitan areas.

466   To Lewis Mumford

[New York City]   February 13, 1957

Dear Lewis:

There still is hope that we may see each other before one or the other of us finally gets started on a trip. Ours has been postponed for the time being. Among other reasons is my desire to see the [new edition of the] book *Toward New Towns* really completed before we leave. There is still a little of the proof I have not finally looked over, although the text was finally checked some time ago. Reinhold reports that the first parts of the book are being printed. They still hope to get it out as a February book. So you will be able to see it before you leave. It is quite different in appearance from the first edition and includes a number of additional illustrations. My impression is that they are making a very good job of it. But you will be able to judge that for yourself before long. . . .

Affectionate greetings from the Steins to you and Sophie,

Clarence S. Stein

467   To Charles Abrams

[New York City]   May 8, 1957

Dear Charles:

The evening that you were at our house some weeks ago we spoke of my suggestion in regard to conservation of agricultural land in Santa Clara County, California. I am enclosing the memo that I mentioned in regard to it.

Perhaps it should be noted that at present one of the great difficulties of protecting land in Santa Clara from undesirable development is the right of the small, so-called "cities" to annex outlying land. This is carried out generally by taking over narrow strips or shoestrings of land, often highways. It is apparent that the dominant authority should be lodged in the County, if not in the Bay Area or State.

I would be glad to have your comments on the memorandum, particularly on the suggestions in regard to the purchase or taking of development rights.

Cordially yours,
Clarence S. Stein

468   To Lewis Mumford

[New York City]   July 2, 1957

Dear Lewis:

It was good to have your letter from Welwyn. The mention of Hitchin[1] brings up delightful recollections. Aline spent as much of her time there as she could while I was going over the problems of Stevenage Center. It is certainly an excellent point from which to explore Letchworth and Stevenage.

It is too bad that so little came of our effort at Stevenage. I will be interested to hear from you just what was finally done to preserve the separation of pedestrian mall and highways and parking areas. The town as a whole, which Gordon Stephenson planned to make an example and inspiration to the other towns that were to follow, is certainly one of the most dismal failures.[2]

I saw the *New York Times* report of your talk at The Hague. What you had to say about the little motor cars may not have been the most important part, but it made quite an impression on a number of people with whom I discussed the article.

During the last week or so, I have been roughly outlining what might turn into a book. In it I am trying to restrict myself to the limited field of what I called the Radburn idea. I want to show what its influence has been and can be, not only in residential communities but as the basis of other developments. To do that I will want to build up its family tree of precedents on which it grew and then go on to try to predict its possible future influence, both here and abroad. The Venice story, of course, is part of this. I don't know whether it will work out in the simple way in which I would like to present the subject or whether it will get confused in its relation to the other important changes that must be made in our city and regional development.

Perhaps nothing will come of it! . . .[3]

Affectionate greetings from both of us to both of you.

Clarence S. Stein

. . .

1. Hitchen is an old village just south of the Garden City of Letchworth.

2. Stein's work with Stephenson to plan a pedestrian-oriented town center at Stevenage would be vindicated during the following year, when the Stevenage Town Council would insist on implementing a pedestrian-oriented town center plan over the objections of the Stevenage Development Corporation and the Ministry of Town and Country Planning. Its pedestrianization would have an influence on later British New Town centers, including Cumbernauld in Scotland.

3. In June 1957 Stein was seventy-five and still going strong.

469   To Steen Rasmussen

[New York City]   August 7, 1957

Dear Steen Eiler:

Both Aline and I were delighted with your short article in the last number of *Town and Country Planning* about Hampstead Garden Suburb and Raymond Unwin. You made him alive again for us. What an inspiring person he was! To us it was wonderful to return again to Hampstead and Wyldes with you.

I don't remember whether you met Albert Mayer when you were here. As you know, he and I worked together on Kitimat, British Columbia. Since the war he has done a good deal of very interesting work in the East, particularly in India.[1] He has helped Nehru in replanning and giving a new life to the small towns of Northern India. His whole approach to the problem has been very practical and at the same time very human. He is at present organizing the redevelopment of Delhi and New Delhi, as well as acting as consultant for a new port town for Israel. I am writing to you now because he expects to visit Copenhagen later this month or the beginning of September. He looks forward to seeing you and will write to you in advance to tell you when he will be there. I am sure you will have much to talk about and that you can be of great help to him in getting acquainted with Copenhagen.

I hope you will show the work that has been done in connection with the neighborhood that you are building which you call "Gygemosen." I don't remember whether I have written to you to tell you how much I was interested in the arrangement of the plan and the apparent completeness of the community facilities. How are they working? Are the people really making good use of the facilities? I am also interested to know how the proportion and scale of the open spaces works out, both the enclosed courts and the central green. But the development is probably not far enough advanced yet to judge the latter.

Aline and I recollect with great pleasure the visit of the Rasmussens. Our very best wishes to your wife and to the two girls.

Kindest regards,
Cordially,
Clarence S. Stein

1. Mayer described his village development planning in Uttar Pradesh, India, in detail in long letters to his friends. Many are in the Clarence S. Stein Papers in the Cornell University Archives. An excellent account of the work is provided in Albert Mayer and Associates, *Pilot Project India* (Berkeley: University of California Press, 1958).

470   To Lewis Mumford

[New York City]   September 23, 1957

Dear Lewis:

On my return from a short trip to Canada, I found your letter awaiting me. I am very glad to have your article on "A New Approach to Workers' Housing." I have just glanced at it so far, but I look forward to reading it very soon.

I was tempted away from the Frederick Law Olmsted book. What a wonderful character! I have been having a good time going through the birth of the Radburn idea a century ago. I came on many interesting notes. One in particular you may not remember. It seems that Olmsted was asked by what driving route one would see the park to best advantage. He answered: "The Central Park was laid out with a view to giving the greatest satisfaction when seen in driving northward on the west side, southward on the east side." The map at the end of the book is splendid. I am going to do a certain amount of exploring to see what changes have been made in the northern end of the park. I hope you are not in a great hurry to get the book back, as otherwise I will go through it leisurely.

My trip to Canada was at the suggestion of Gordon Stephenson. He wanted me to attend the meeting of the Planning Institute of Canada, which took place near a little lake just outside of Quebec. The principal subject was *New Towns*. Cyril Henderson, the municipal manager of Kitimat, who by the way is also a town planner, spoke about Kitimat. The weather was delightful, and we were able to have a good part of the meeting out of doors, surrounded by autumnal colors, which have arrived there quite a bit in advance of Westchester's.

With Flora Stephenson I took a trip to and around the older portions of Quebec. It is still a romantic spot, although it is becoming a little too much of a tourist center.

I was particularly happy to be at the conference because it gave me an opportunity to see the Stephensons again. Gordon is accepting the fact that he is to be a Canadian and not a citizen of the U.S. with a good deal of grace, which I think is growing into satisfaction. He is beginning to see, as Albert Mayer and I have already recognized, that there is a great opportunity in the Canada of the future. . . .[1] I observed that he plays a very important part in the institute, and I presume that in time he will be of great influence in the University and in Toronto, if not in Canada as a whole.

I hope that you and Sophie have found the new house comfortable. Best wishes to her and to you.

As always,

Clarence S. Stein

1. The development of metropolitan Toronto did indeed make major use of the satellite New Towns as an instrument of regional development policy.

471   To Eric Carlson

[New York City]   October 15, 1958

Dear Eric:

Although I have given a great deal of thought [to] and seen a number of people in connection with the problem of the Banco Obrero in Caracas which you outlined in your letter of October 2, I am not ready yet to send you a full opinion on the subject as a whole.[1] In fact, I am waiting to hear from you in more detail. However, the notes that follow in regard to references may, I think, be of value to you.

Lewis Mumford's article on Fresh Meadows, which originally appeared in the *New Yorker*, is reprinted in his book *From the Ground Up*, published by Harvest Books. He also wrote an article for "Skyline" in the *New Yorker* on May 6, 1950, in regard to the work of the [New York City] Housing Authority [NYCHA]. This he called "The Red Brick Beehive." I think possibly there may be a certain parallel in the work that is being done here and that which you are studying in Caracas.

In regard to living in the NYCHA developments, Elizabeth Wood, as you probably know, has written some interesting articles and reports for the CHPC [Citizen's Housing and Planning Council]. You may want to write her, as she had a great deal of experience in connection with tall apartments when she was directing the work of the Housing Board in Chicago. You can address her care of the CHPC.

My last letter mentioned articles in *Town and Country Planning* in regard to comparative costs and advantages of tall and low building for residential purposes. I have just come on one of these, which may have some suggestions for you. It is in the July 1958 number and is called "High Density or More Dispersal: A Note on Some Relative Costs."

Last weekend I again ran through Henry Wright's *Rehousing Urban America*. Although it was written some years ago, much of it is pertinent at present. I think you would find it well worth looking at again, if you haven't done so. His methods of analysis are well worth studying. Among others is that of the Housing Study Guild, on p. 144. But the important thing to remember in all these analyses is that building costs are only one factor to be considered. Among others, there is the cost of improvement, and operation-maintenance costs, and the life of the building, based on the approved standards that will be required as time goes on.

[Clarence]

1. Carlson had inquired about density as a factor in housing design policy for Brazil.

472 Draft of a Speech of Acceptance: American Institute of Planners Honorary Members Award

Washington, D.C.   October 29, 1958

Much of that for which I am being honored this evening was the cooperative work of a number of us, but one I must particularly mention in connection with Sunnyside and Radburn. That was my fine associate and planning genius, Henry Wright.

I only wish he were here to share this tribute. Henry Wright was a stimulating associate. He bubbled over with ideas. He was never content with past solutions (not even his own). He was ever finding more logical and more livable ways of relating buildings to each other, to the land, and to good living. He was the greatest site planner I have known, excepting possibly Raymond Unwin.

His conceptions were sometimes revolutionary, but they grew out of practical, logical analysis of reality. Henry was a simple, unpretentious person, but a great thinker with down-to-earth conceptions—a real genius.

The spirit in which we worked together and in which I have worked since was that of pioneers. From Sunnyside to Baldwin Hills Village, the communities were conceived, planned, [and] developed in the spirit of exploration. We have sought ways, economical ways, practical ways of bringing safe and peaceful life in spacious green surroundings to ordinary people without the necessity of long, tiresome auto trips.

When we worked together [there was a] period of hope for a better world [and an] opportunity to create a new environment for a new community life. War was over. [There were] new problems and opportunities and events created by the automobile and increased industrialization. [The] urban flood was already apparent.

We foresaw the explosion of the metropolis and overspill—the flooding of the open spaces, agricultural, recreational, or wilderness between our cities. There were two movements in regard to meeting this.

1. Accept the inevitable; we must serve it, but make it as orderly as possible.
2. Prevent it by creating permanent green open spaces.

Dispersal of people [should incorporate] work and leisure occupations in moderate-sized communities, planned and built to serve the future. [We could limit] the need of going to distant places by preserving nearby open spaces and by bringing work, markets, and leisure-time occupations close to homes.

Highways would not be the primary factor in remolding the U.S.A. physically. Contemporary communities, their location and creation in relation to the land would dominate. Emphasis [would not be] on movement, but on good living in communities built for an age of ever-increasing leisure, with the good and useful things for which we travel so far dispersed or preserved close to home, work, markets, leisure-time occupations.

These modern, safe, green communities might be New Towns. They might result from the rebuilding of obsolete urban neighborhoods, revising the street and block pattern, opening up the center of the superblocks as a park, surrounding the neighborhood with a greenbelt. . . .

This should be the time for developing contemporary communities in America as we are creating contemporary architecture. In fact, the trouble with our modern, functional buildings is that they have nowhere to go. Our city street patterns and subdivision layouts are (most of them) obsolete. . . . Modern architecture demands a modern setting—a spacious setting with light, air, views of trees, and well-grouped buildings and outdoor space for the inhabitants to enjoy their leisure time. This might be the period of great opportunity for the young-minded community planners of neighborhoods, cities, regions.

There is a growing public interest in planned development that relates to present living, working, and loafing. Look at *Fortune* and other magazines.

The federal, state, and municipal governments are aiding in the large-scale redevelopment of our cities by subsidizing the cost of land—the artificial values of which blocked open, contemporary neighborhood building.

Our gigantic national [and] state highway program should open up the most desirable locations for new communities; it should protect existing neighborhoods and essential greenbelts. It would do this if practical community and regional planners determine the framework of the plan and thus . . . the location of the throughways to be developed by the highway engineers.

In short, we need vision and statesmanship to make it possible for the planning profession to take constructive leadership in the contemporary rebuilding of the [cities of America].

---

473   To Gordon Stephenson

[New York City]   December 17, 1958

Dear Gordon:

. . . Of late I have been trying to get a clear view of what is really happening to our great cities and their surroundings. Also, I have been wondering whether I should take some different line than in the past in my search for a sane and practical solution of the relation of city and countryside. Your "Thoughts on Planning of Metropolitan Regions," which I have read a number of times, has been inspiring.

Two particular things that I have been actively interested in of late have to do with state development and the possibilities of urban renewal. I have long felt that one of the most important responsibilities of the governor of New York State is the continuous physical development of the state in harmony with changing needs. To carry out this work effectively, he should have a staff advisor in the Executive Department to help him in forming development policy and to see that the work of the various state agencies [is] harmonized in realizing these policies. In other words, we need what might be called a development coordinator. I have suggested something of this kind to a number of past governors since 1926, when our State Commission of Housing and Regional Planning brought out its report on the basis of a plan for New York State. The idea, I think, should appeal to Governor-elect Rockefeller. We will see.

Another thing that I have been actively interested in is one of the proposed urban renewal projects here in New York. I have, as you know, in the past felt I could be of more use in working in fresh ground, where the development of new street and open air patterns had a minimum of restrictions. But I am tempted for the moment to see to what extent it is possible and practicable to revise the gridiron layout so as to serve present-day good living and urban traffic without destroying too many of the old buildings.

Perhaps I should put all this aside before long and try to get back to the reconsideration of the Regional City. This and many other things I hope to be able to discuss with you before so very long. . . .

We both send you, Flora and the children, our affectionate best wishes for Christmas and a joyful 1959.

As always,

Clarence S. Stein

---

474 To Gordon Stephenson

[New York City]   April 22, 1959

Dear Gordon:

Your letter in regard to your proposed research and book reached here just before I arrived home from our trip to Iran and Israel. It was one of our great experiences. I will not try to tell you about it now—it is too much of a story. . . .

I want to write to Mr. Gilpatric or meet him to tell him why I think you are the person to do this study and why the clarification of the subject is so essential now, during this period of mad, misdirected urban growth. For this, I wish you would send me a short summary of your connection with the development of the New Towns while you were in the Ministry and before and after. Also, what part you played in the Abercrombie London plan. A short biographical summary might help. . . .

I said I was not going to talk about our trip. But just one thing, because it relates to your subject, although quite differently than in connection with London. This is the regional and national planning of Israel. A group of enthusiastic architects induced the government to create a Planning Department in the beginning of the republic some 11 years ago. A number of them were appointed to run this national-regional planning agency under the dynamic leadership of the architect Arieh Sharon. In the 4-1/2 years they were in power, they laid the foundation for the rebuilding of Israel, with New Towns, as many as [were built in] England, I believe. What is more, the basic plan is being broadly realized. I know nothing to equal it in national planned development, excepting in Holland.

Our affectionate greetings to Flora and you.

Cordially,

Clarence S. Stein

---

475   To Arieh Sharon

[New York City]   April 29, 1959

Dear Sharon:

My visit to Israel was all too short. But it was long enough to leave me with a supreme enthusiasm for the way Israel is being recreated to meet the needs of the future. I know of no other country where national and regional planned development is being carried out on such a magnificent scale and with such broad-minded understanding and consideration of the state as a whole and the interrelation of the various regions and local rural and urban parts. The difficulties of finance, unpredictable mass immigration, and nature may sometimes have limited the extent to which the detailed finish can be realized. But it seemed to me that the form of the future has been determined with broad vision. This must be due primarily to the vision of the group of architects that formed the first Planning Department and particularly to the leadership.

It was good to be with you and to have your guidance in our first view of the inspiring work that you and your associate planners have realized. Aline joins me in gratitude for your and Mrs. Sharon's cordial hospitality and your endless help in becoming acquainted with Israel and the people that are creating it.

Since my return I have been trying to make a unified picture of all that we saw on our travels in Israel. I have also been studying what I could of the past geotechnical history. I started with Walter Clay Lowdermild's "Palestine, Land of Promise" and am now going on with the reports of plans and attainments that I have. I wonder if you have not written something about the history, the objectives, and the work of your first Planning Department. If so, can you send me a copy? (I have your *Planning in Israel,* reprinted from "Israel and Middle East.")

Benton MacKaye has suggested an interesting type of museum for Kitimat, which is in his report on that subject.

The Study of Commercial Facilities [at Kitimat] was made by Larry Smith, perhaps the leading, and one of the most practical, man in the field in America. He has set the requirements for a great many of the large shopping centers that are being built throughout the United States. I'll send you copies of his complete report covering the distribution of facilities in the main center of the neighborhood, etc., or else the shorter articles on the approach to the problem in our Kitimat Town Site Report. I hope these will reach you soon enough to be of use to you.

I am also sending you a copy of *Pilot Project, India,* which is the story of Albert Mayer's great work in rural development in India.

Again I want to tell you how much both Aline and I appreciate all the help that you gave us and our great pleasure at having been with you.

With gratitude and best wishes,

Cordially,

Clarence S. Stein

---

476   To Karl Belser

[New York City]   May 16, 1959

Dear Karl:

Thanks for the *Plan for Parks, Recreation and Open Space.* You have presented the subject superbly. The illustrations, colored photographs, plan and perspective sketches, and paintings could not be better.

The only thing that troubled me was the graphic presentation of the plan at the end. This because it shows the vast extent to which the Northern Valley is being taken over by urban communities. If there was only more green and less dark brown! I certainly hope that you ultimately succeed in holding as much of the area of the southern valley for agriculture as you have shown.

On a trip that Mrs. Stein and I have just made to the Middle East, I was reminded of the problem of Santa Clara County and your fine struggle to preserve the uniquely rich lowlands as far as possible for orchards and farms. In Israel we visited a similar fertile valley lying between hills. Bordering on this valley the small ancient town of Nazareth is situated. A much larger urban community of a New Nazareth is required and is being constructed to act as commercial, cultural, and industrial center of the region. This New Town has been located on the hill above old Nazareth. The plateau at the top is kept open for recreation and schools. The houses step down the slope in a very picturesque as well as practical manner. At other places, apartment houses are entered on an upper floor by a bridge from the road on the hilltop.

No part of the New Nazareth will be allowed to spread over the valley. This will be conserved entirely for agricultural purposes. In fact, the preservation and intensive cultivation of all the best flat land for farms and orchards I found not only here but throughout all of Israel that I visited. The housing is restricted to the small villages of agricultural workers. The size of the New Towns or the old cities has been limited. I saw no chaotic, disorderly overspill.

All this was the result of a broad, comprehensive, national planned development that is really being carried out. The Development Plan is not only a series of separate plans for the growth of each New Town or old city or drainage basin. It included all these, but it is national in scope.

I know of no other nation that is actually being developed so thoroughly according to a comprehensive interrelated national plan for the use and development of its land, water, and other natural resources, for the distribution of population in rural, service, and urban centers, for the limitation of the growth of these, for the location of agriculture and reforestation. . . .

I hope that before long we will have a chance to see each other. Meanwhile, do write me in regard to legislation and public opinion concerning your plans for the Santa Clara Valley.

With best wishes,

Cordially
Clarence S. Stein

---

477   To Yngve and Elin Larsson

[New York City]   June [5], 1959

Dear Yngve and Elin:

. . . This spring Aline and I finally saw a portion of the world we had long dreamed about—the Near East. . . . It was a great and delightful experience. This is in spite of the fact that our time was short, as Aline had to return to start rehearsals in the middle of April.

Except for short stops on our way out and back at Rome, Istanbul, and Paris, we devoted ourselves to Iran and Israel. What an astounding contrast! Iran still lives mainly in the past, a rich and beautiful past, many of the splendid buildings and open places of which are still there. Israel is the present and the future. What that small nation is doing is the most remarkable thing I have seen in the re-creation of a country through comprehensive planned development.

This development plan for Israel had its beginning eleven years ago, when the new independent nation was formed. It was the conception of a group of far-sighted enthusiasts. They were mainly architects-planners, I am proud to say. They induced the government to set up a Planning Department with real power. From their ranks were chosen much of the staff of that body, under the direction of the architect, Arieh Sharon. In the first four and a half years, they worked out the national and regional plans that have been basically followed. I had the opportunity of meeting with a number of the authors of this great plan and, with some of them that are helping carry it out, we visited certain parts of it that [are] now being realized. . . .[1]

We visited a New Town that had a population of a few thousand when the national plan was made. That is Beersheba, which is to be the center for the Negev—culturally, socially, as well as for trade and industry connected with the minerals and chemicals that will come from the Negev and the Dead Sea. Beersheba already has some 40 thousand population. It has a large regional hospital, as well as a concert hall. The plan of the residential areas follows the neighborhood, superblock scheme [of] Vällingby and Radburn in general, as do most of the New Towns I saw. They are not as finished as your work around Stockholm. The tremendous flow of immigration and the limited resources of the nation [have led] to economy. . . . The Housing Department of the Labor Ministry, which created these towns, could learn much about coordinated preparation of plans from your organization in Stockholm, but that requires time, and they have so far always been rushed by the unexpected floods of immigration.

Our affectionate greetings,
Clarence

1. In a later, much longer, and somewhat more critical letter to Sharon written in the fall of 1959, Stein asked his advice on a talk about Israel's national planning he was to give in New York at the Technion Club.

---

478   To Benton MacKaye

[Stratford, Canada]   August 8, 1959

Dear Ben:

I am strongly in favor of separating what you intended as one book into a number of volumes.[1] Readers are not often tempted to get a book that is too thick, nor to purchase a series until they have been interested in what the writer has to say and how. Your "New Exploration" was quite long enough—perhaps a little more, 50,000 words at the most.

I think your idea of finishing the Conservers (under another title) first is the thing to do. You took part in what you describe and personally knew many of the principal characters of your story. You are one of the authorities on the subject.

I question publishing it as part of a series. That might scare some readers away. They might think they would have to wait for the two earlier books or that it would all be too much to undertake. After they have read "The Conservers," they should be waiting for more.

However, I think you might consider an introduction or first chapter that would outline the history of the settlers and path builders as far as that is essential to the understanding of the conservers. There you might suggest that you perhaps would write further on that subject at some future time.

Another suggestion: perhaps in your last chapter you might want to indicate the job that the conservers left for the regionalists in taking what they had preserved into the building of the nation and its regions. . . .

Best from
Clarence

1. MacKaye's projected book, like Stein's proposed Regional Cities book, was intractable. Neither was published. Perhaps they had already said what they had to say, but we will never know because neither of these two old pioneers was lucky enough to secure an editor who could help him make his manuscript concise, orderly, and clear.

---

479   To Frederic Osborn

[New York City]   September 23, 1959

Dear F.J.:

I can't tell you what great pleasure your letter gave me. I am deeply honored by the action of the executive of the Town and Country Planning Association in choosing me to receive the Ebenezer Howard Memorial Medal. Please thank them for me.

I feel that it will bind me still more closely to Ebenezer Howard, for whom I always had such a strong affection and admiration.

You asked me when I am likely to be in England to receive the medal. I am sorry there is no possibility of my being there next month, at the time of the 60th Year Celebrations. I do not know as yet about next spring. Might I suggest that I write to you at a later time whether it is possible for me to be at the annual meeting of the association?

Otherwise, although of course I would prefer to be with you and [the] association in person, someone else might formally receive the medal for me.

With kindest regards,
Yours cordially,
Clarence S. Stein

480   To Aline Stein

[New York City]   November 30, 1959

Aline dear:

There were a number of things that I was going to write about, but they seem un-important compared with the fact that Al Bing is gone. He was so much alive the other night when we were with him and finding so much in life that pleased him (including much from Africa, I hear you say). Well, it's good that he has had these years of his own since Florence went. He's made good use of them.

It was Stanley Isaacs that told me about it (early this morning). I hadn't seen that section of the *Times* as yet. I called up Stanley because I was so thrilled by his ap-pearance on television last night—such clear vision as to public purpose in govern-ing New York. I felt the urge to tell him that I admired him—real fun stuff. Stanley told me that Al's trouble was some form of cancer and that if he had lived he would have not been his old self. Perhaps he's right, and so it would be better this way.

Now to return to the weekend of which we have spoken with you both at Jen-nie's and Tucson (so happy you like it there). Ralph [Walker] told me that he was one of those who was being considered by the Ford Foundation to develop an ar-chitectural conception for the American Theatre. . . .[1]

All my love,
Clarence

1. Stein, a student of theater design and writer on the subject, had yet to design a theater.

106. Stein writing a report on Kitimat (c. 1950).

107. From left: Steen Eiler Rasmussen, Danish architect; Edmund Bacon, planning director of Philadelphia; Clarence Stein; and an unknown person in Philadelphia (c. 1952).

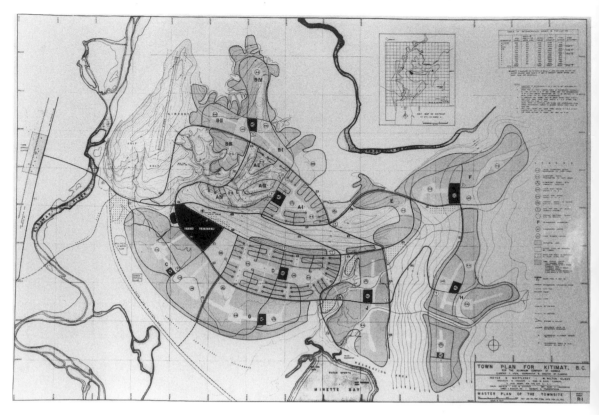

108. Master plan for Kitimat, British Columbia (1952).

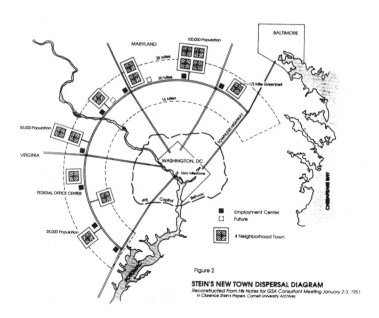

109. Stein's and Augur's dispersal diagram for New Towns and federal government offices in the Washington, D.C., area (1951).

110. Diagram of dispersed employment centers and New Towns by Augur and Stein, part of a decentralization plan of the Washington, D.C., area (1951).

111. Stein receiving the Gold Medal of the American Institute of Architects (1956).

8

Satisfaction
1960–1968

Clarence Stein, the inveterate, constant admirer of sunrises from the Steins' apartment nest atop One West Sixty-fourth Street, New York City, also enjoyed the sunset of his life. We sense this from his serious, yet warm and amused letters of the 1960s. He was impressed by the work of Milton Breivogel and Karl Belser in shaping new urban growth in southern California. He took pleasure in the possibility that Nelson Rockefeller, as governor of New York, had established an effective state planning and development process. Clarence, now in his mid-eighties, had urged at least five New York governors to do so. He also responded positively to Edmund Bacon's creative ideas for green pedestrian ways in Center City Philadelphia and North Philadelphia's new residential areas. Stein wrote paeans of praise for New York State's new development plan, especially for its regional development organization. He continued to observe Washington's fitful planning for the dispersion of federal employment in the Washington region, and he admired the Copenhagen "finger plan, [which] inspired" the Washington *Plan for the Year 2000*. He was pleased with the private sector entrepreneurial New Town efforts of Robert Simon at Reston, Virginia, and James Rouse at Columbia, Maryland. On the other hand, he complained that the well-intentioned but weak federal New Communities legislation of 1968 was doomed to failure because it did not provide for sufficient public intervention in the urban development process, a way to acquire land for New Towns through state and regional development organizations, or assistance for the basic infrastructure needed to establish New Towns on a solid fiscal basis.

At the opening of the decade, Stein made a commitment to his future work: "I must concentrate," he wrote to Albert Mayer, "on a few related subjects. . . . I intend to deal with New Towns and the open regions of which they form a part, not with the redevelopment or patching of built-up cities." Clarence Stein was nothing if not true to the New Town idea in most of his work throughout his long life. Fifty years before, in 1909, he had glimpsed in Bournville "model village" the solution to the problem of the festering metropolis, and he had written of it to his brother. In the 1960s he wrote an affirmation to his friend and associate, Albert Mayer.

In the 1960s Clarence continued to travel with Aline: to California to see their friends, to revisit his West Coast projects, and to observe the continuing sprawl of Los Angeles; to Sweden to wonder at the efficient and beautiful expansion of Stockholm, his favorite city in all the world; and to Venice, which he admired greatly, especially its total commitment to the pedestrian. He wrote to his friends about what he saw and what it meant to him. The experiences confirmed his lifelong belief in the need for strong public intervention in region-shaping design and implementation of programs for new communities. Early in the 1960s Stein was hopeful that the "next president and his advisors [would] have vision enough to see the primary importance of a national policy in regard to the dispersal and the creation of modern communities and that the states and regions [would] follow with . . . constructive action." Stein saw hope for better national urban policy in the pronouncements of John F. Kennedy, the new "forward-looking president [with] the enthusiasm of youth . . . and the astounding wisdom of . . . choice of those who are to advise and aid him."[1] Stein liked the "talk of a new Department of Urban and Housing Affairs."

As he began his eightieth decade, Stein once again decided to "get down to real work on the Regional City book," and he was "getting involved with various problems of development . . . in New York [City]." His letters were, as ever, attacks against the "bad" (Victor Gruen's proposed "city within a city" on Welfare Island) and full of praise for the "good" (San Diego's plan by Robert Alexander for a "university city" on 10,000 acres of open land). Stein was also proud of others' approval of the ideas of his group, for example, the inclusion by the American Institute of Planners of "Lewis, Catherine, and CSS" among nine individuals cited for special awards for planning. "Three out of nine, not a bad performance," wrote Stein of this recognition of the tiny Regional Planning Association of America. The association may have meant as much to him as his many architectural and planning achievements. It surely was one of his most important intellectual children. He had tended to its rearing. He had been its founder, host, convener, and agenda maker. Mumford, on the other hand, believed that *Toward New Towns for America* was a

1. Clarence S. Stein to Yngve Larsson, 3 February 1961, Clarence S. Stein Papers, Collection 2600, Cornell University Archives, Kroch Library.

more important achievement than the RPAA because, "though [Clarence] was not such a creative mind as Olmsted . . . , [he would] probably have greater impact on later generations because what he did know and do is available in his book."[2]

Stein's letters of the 1960s reveal as much about his personality as *Toward New Towns for America* informs us about what he knew and did. His letters confirm Osborn's conclusions about his sustained optimism in the face of disappointment: "He is much less conscious of other men's thinking . . . than I am, yet he seems to scorn nobody. If he is a bit self-centered, it isn't through common egoism, but because [of an] almost unconscious sense of creative power—of a mission—and . . . of partial disappointment that he will not allow to grow into a grievance. His mind, always looking for things to appreciate, obliterates bores but doesn't recognize enemies." Osborn thought that "Clarence was a noble person."[3] Stein's later correspondence displays his generous, kindly qualities, as well as the creativity, high ideals, and stubborn purpose they clothed.

2. Lewis Mumford to Frederic J. Osborn, 26 October 1962, in Michael Hughes, *The Letters of Lewis Mumford and Frederic Osborn: A Transatlantic Dialogue, 1938–1970* (New York: Praeger, 1971), 330.

3. Frederic J. Osborn to Lewis Mumford, 25 October 1950, in Hughes, *Letters of Lewis Mumford,* 284.

---

481 To Albert Mayer

[Los Angeles, California]   January 30, 1960

Dear Albert:

In your last letter you quoted me, "It is good to have time to look back and look forward and try to decide what is most worth doing," and you asked me for my conclusions. I see clearly that I must concentrate on a few related subjects [within] the framework that led to my goal. . . .

This is limited and so is my energy. Looking backward, it seems to me that my most valuable contributions were made when I worked freshly from the ground up. That is either in developing conceptions of communities that fit contemporary living, their relation to each other and to open areas, or in realizing these, at least sufficiently to indicate the direction in which we should continue our search.

So, of this I am clear. In the future I intend to deal with New Towns and the open regions of which they form a part, not with the redevelopment or patching of built-up cities. I find the odds against a clean-cut solution too great where the basic street pattern is inflexible, the land costs speculative, the legal restrictions obsolete. There are plenty of others to work on the problem of redevelopment, renewal, or public housing on expensive land. That eliminates for the future many of the activities that have filled my time and kept me on the go for the last year or so without bringing me closer to my goal.

The need of a new approach to the development of open or slightly urbanized areas is nowhere more apparent in the U.S.A. than here in California. The setting for new contemporary communities is superb. The West Coast has the great advantage not only of climate but of a comparatively narrow coastal plain backed by a series of hills and mountains enclosing fertile valleys. Large parts of the highlands are national forests or otherwise in public ownership. Here is a beautiful background for good living, an ideal setting for use of leisure time.

Both Breivogel and Belser are able planners. They have ideas, ideals, experience, and devotion to their jobs. But they and the county governments lack adequate power to realize large-scale regional development of these areas that are dominated by competitive "cities," land subdividers, and small-scale tract developers.

So it is apparent that the field to which I have limited myself, the practical creation of groups of New Towns in relation to open country, is anything but limited. It requires the reconsideration of many subjects in a fresh way for conceptions and plans are naturally meaningless, unless they can be realized.

This means reorientations in regard to land policy, organization for production, or the basis of planned development. Government and operation—this includes a balance between grassroot, regional, and state administration. Of all this, more at some later time, perhaps at our next breakfast conference. Meanwhile, I hope I will hear from you. I don't know just how much longer we will be here—at least for a week, probably more.

Best to you from Aline and
Clarence

---

482 To William Wurster

[New York City] June 15, 1960

Dear Bill:

When I was in Stockholm a couple of weeks ago,[1] Sven Markelius told me that he was coming over to lecture at MIT next April. I asked him if he was going out to California. He gave me the impression that he wished he could. I thought you might be interested.

I am so enthusiastic about Markelius and his big-scale, realistic development of Stockholm as head of the Planning Department, as well as the fine work he is now creating in his private practice, that I might write at length about it.[2] But you know him as well as I do. So this is just to let you know that he is coming over.

There is much we have to tell you and Catherine about our latest adventures in London, Greece, and Scandinavia. But that will have to wait.

Aline joins me in affectionate greetings to you both.

Clarence S. Stein

1. Clarence and Aline Stein spent May 1960 in Europe visiting London, Stockholm, and Athens. In Athens they met Lewis Mumford, who had not previously visited the city. They met Sven Markelius during their stay in Stockholm, and Clarence collected information on the city and its regional plans for suburban satellite New Town expansion.

2. Stein did not follow up on his impulse to write about Markelius's architectural and city planning work. A discussion of the work Stein most admired is found in an excellent English translation of Eva Rudberg's *Sven Markelius, Architect,* trans. Roger Tanner (Stockholm: Arkitecture Forlag, 1989).

---

483 To Lewis Mumford

[New York City] June 15, 1960

Dear Lewis:

The silver moon was full a few nights ago. From what Ben calls our sky parlor, we saw the last rays of the sun turn the windows across the park to glittering gold in contrast with the silver moon. But our thoughts turned to that memorable evening on the Parthenon, just a month before, the day you and Sophie arrived in Athens, and then, of course, to the following noon with the family Doxiadis and their glorious panorama of Athens.

How I wish Athens, as one views it on the ground, lived up to its promise from those heights. I am glad I have at last seen it, but I feel no need of returning. Delphi, on the other hand, calls us back sometime when we can stay long enough to make the mysterious majesty of the valley part of our being. . . .

Now a word about our Scandinavian adventures. At Copenhagen, your suggestion that I get in touch with Ole Thommason was just what I needed. He spent a good deal of the three days we were there taking me to see the principal new housing communities. The Danes are doing some good work, but it does not hang together as a related large-scale metropolitan development as does the planned additions to Stockholm. However, the famous finger plan for the Copenhagen area has been actually followed. It keeps adequate open spaces close to urban development by restricting the large wedges between the railroad lines [to] rural use.

The Regional Plan, developed by Peter Bredsdorff, has functioned . . . since 1949. But the open land is held only by national restrictive laws, not public ownership, as in Stockholm. Market value of the rural area is beginning to rise, which indicates that the owners expect Parliament to loosen the restrictions. The municipal planners are seeking a new program for regional development. But they recognize that it is more than a physical conception and diagram that is required. "What we need to realize our plans is a politician (he meant 'statesman') like Dr. Yngve Larsson," said Thommason.[1]

At Stockholm we saw much of the Larssons. With him I revisited Vällingby and the other nearby communities. These the municipality is willing into being according to a broad, related plan. Stockholm has learnt, more than any metropolis that I know, that city development must be a constructive process on the part of the government, that it cannot succeed on the basis of restrictions and planning generalities. They know that, as a practical basis, the public ownership of land is essential. In Stockholm they see the problem of building communities as a related whole. True, sometimes the design of the buildings is not all that it might be, for economy or other reasons. But the structure belongs; they grow out of the form of the land; the rocks and the principal trees are preserved and protected.

They have developed an organization for city building that is second only to that of the London County Council. But it differs from that in having a broader, more complete goal and ideal. This has been due I think largely to Yngve Larsson's statesmanship; also to his sympathetic understanding with Markelius and Seidenbladh as architect-planners, and with Holger Blom (an architect, too), who makes the parks throughout Stockholm rich with blooming color.

Stockholm we love. It is a magnificent city: a port where the streams, bays, lakes are always in sight or close by. The city seems to grow out of the water. Aline and I have awarded it first place, with Peking second, as the most beautiful city that we know. But perhaps that is because we have not been to Paris or Rome of late. We look forward to hearing of your and Sophie's adventures in Greece and Venice.

When will you return?

Affectionate greetings to you both, as well as to Bill and Marjorie.

Clarence S. Stein

P.S. Sunday we lunched with John Hitchcock, Peggy's son. He is studying planning at North Carolina. He is going to England and will call on Bill Holford for advice. Poor Bill! Everyone calls on him, but I thought that he would consider the grandson of Raymond Unwin an exception. John may ask for you also. He is a fine young man.

1. Larsson was a major force in political decisions that affected the growth of Sweden's capital. In an October 1960 letter, Stein thanked Larsson for his hospitality in Stockholm and for additional information on the planning of Stockholm. He also noted his interest in Baronbackarna, which he thought carried out the Radburn concept in a thoroughly interesting and attractive manner.

---

484   To Milton Breivogel[1]

[New York City]   June 30, 1960

Dear Milton Breivogel:

I am sending you Sven Markelius's article, of which I wrote to you in Stockholm. It . . . shows one can organize the development of raw land not merely so as to house people, but so as to form good communities, and, above all, that we can keep open space for the future where it will be needed. All we have to do is to be clear as to our objectives, develop a program for carrying them out, and be persistent in spite of the organized interests against change. I am sure in the long run the people can be made to see the advantage and will give their backing.

With Markelius's article are illustrations showing what Stockholm has done and is doing. I think the folded map opposite page 62, of the Vällingby group, is particularly interesting. It shows how one-quarter of the four square miles allotted to the development has been preserved as a great natural recreation area, facing Lake Malaren.

Sven Markelius, who was head of the Planning Office that developed this plan, told me that he [will be] coming over to America next April to lecture at MIT. I wonder if it would not be a good thing to get him out to California to tell people how Stockholm not only planned but carried out large-scale additions to the city.

I hope it will not be long before we seen each other again. There is much to talk about.

With best wishes to you and Mrs. Breivogel,

Cordially,
Clarence S. Stein

1. Breivogel was director of planning for Los Angeles.

485   To Peter Mayer[1]

[New York City]   June 30, 1960

Dear Pete:

It gives me much joy to receive your letter. Thanks for your congratulations.[2] I also wish that I could see Mexico again with you. The last visit was altogether too hasty. Nonetheless, it was very enjoyable.

This spring we had one of the best trips yet, and that's saying a great deal. First we spent three weeks in and around London. I saw something of the new work they have done in building New Towns since I was last there. As a whole it is a fine job. Too bad we don't follow their example, making real planned developments outside of our big cities, where we can work as well as live and be in close touch with the open country. But it will come!

The month in Greece was delightful. The spring flowers covered the whole countryside.

From there we flew directly up to Denmark. It is wonderful, the speed with which the jet planes take you from one world to another. We spent only four days in Copenhagen but, with the help of some of the younger fellows in the Planning Office, I saw a great deal of the work they have been doing since I was last there some eight or ten years ago.

Then our last three weeks we were in Stockholm. That was particularly delightful, not only because Stockholm is one of the most delightful cities in all the world, but because we have so many friends there. And now that we are home, I am trying to work out what we in America can learn—to build complete new communities as they do, around Stockholm and London. Let's hope that it will come before we have used up all the land that is still open around our big cities.

Delighted to hear of the delightful place you found to live in. I only hope that the job is just around the corner.

Best of luck to you, Pete, and love from Aline and

Clarence S. Stein

1. Peter Mayer was Clarence's nephew, the son of Lillie and Arthur Mayer.
2. The congratulations were on Clarence Stein's seventy-eighth birthday.

486   To Benton MacKaye

[New York City]   July 6, 1960

Dear Ben:

Yesterday morning we returned from the country, and tomorrow morning we will be on our way back there. What a wonderful weekend it was! Perfect weather, and

I can't remember when the surroundings of the little old house were more beautiful.

I started painting again, which I have neglected for a long time. I find it good fun once I get down to it. But in large part I was occupied in the pursuit of an idea, or rather how best to make it understandable. It came about this way:

A couple of weeks ago, Albert Mayer, at one of our breakfasts, had the notion that it might be possible to get the New Town idea into the democratic platform.[1] Next day he departed for a long conference on India that Catherine Bauer had arranged at the University of California in Berkeley. So I started to search for a way of expressing the dispersal idea in a few sentences, so that it would appeal to a large public as just what they wanted. There didn't seem to be an apparent link between what people seek to escape in our Dinosaurus Metropolis and what the New Town has to offer. One may make it apparent in a volume but not in a compact paragraph.

Wilma looked through the files to see what we had done before. She found the ammunition for a couple of campaigns for New Towns that had slipped my memory until I saw them again.

In 1948, when the Congress was formulating legislation for redevelopment, we argued for development of new communities on open land first. Argument: scarcity of dwellings so don't pull down any existing ones until new ones have been built where none exist. Then in 1950–51, when the atom bomb had taken the center of the stage and congressional committees were struggling with locating government offices out of reach of a big one dropped on or near the Pentagon, we pointed out that the dispersed offices would be of little use if the bombing of Washington after dark would wipe out the workers themselves. Moral: build New Towns for both working and living.

That security argument doesn't make sense any longer. The world has changed so in a decade that you just can't get far enough away from a target like Washington or New York. As Lewis says, "Next time it will not be war but extinction."

Well, I searched for other links. [It was a] waste of time, money, and energy going places instead of enjoying places and other truths that most city and suburban folks should recognize from their own sad experience. But I found it all took too much explaining. A lot more cultivating has to be done before we can expect our seed to give us flowers. We must make the new realities obvious, so that people react.

[On] Sunday Hugh Pomeroy came to breakfast up at 1,000 Years. We had a good three-hour-long talk about this and kindred subjects, and we agreed that all we could do in a campaign was to open up the way for a future frontal attack. There is a growing awakening to the need of preserving open spaces, through [linear green spaces] and [as greenbelts] around our own cities. The public is at last awakening to some of your and the RPAA ideas of the twenties. Let's see if we can get open spaces not only for parks, recreation, and agriculture, but to give sound form and structure to our urban areas, says Hugh. It's a long shot, but we may find a way to keep large enough open space for the future, until we can more clearly get the facts of life understood in this crazy world.

Meanwhile, we are enjoying some of the most beautiful summer days ever, both here in the sky parlor and out at Thousand Years.

And how are things in your Empire?

Best to you from Aline and

Clarence S. Stein

1. Although a New Town policy was not made a part of the 1960 Democratic party platform, President Kennedy did achieve the formation of an urban development department called the Department of Housing and Urban Development (HUD) in the executive branch. His advisors laid the groundwork for the Lyndon Johnson Housing Act of 1966, which provided for a private enterprise approach to the development of New Towns, with federal guarantees of loans to finance them. Lack of sufficient funding for infrastructure and high local taxes, as well as local governments' tenacious hold on land development decisions and the opposition of many private developers, assured the failure of this, the first American New Towns program since FDR's Greenbelt Towns of 1935.

---

487   To Vernon DeMars

[New York City]   August 3, 1960

Dear Vernon:

. . . We enjoyed Copenhagen, but we must admit our favorite city is still Stockholm. There they have found a way to preserve the beauty of the past in the old city while creating a new center and surrounding the whole with a ring of New Towns growing out of contemporary life and the natural setting.

Vällingby, now practically completed, is a great accomplishment. There urban meets natural countryside, in fact, almost wilderness. Of the four square miles of the land allotted to the development, one-quarter has been preserved as a great forest park on Malaren Lake.

The farsighted job that Sven Markelius did at Vällingby and elsewhere as director of the Planning Department was one of the reasons I wrote to Bill Wurster that he was coming over to America in April, as I understood. Markelius's work, now that he has returned to private practice, shows the same sense of relating his buildings to their surroundings and the general development of the city as did his city planning. That is apparent in the Folkes Hus, the great Union Headquarters, and in the proposed municipal theater. That ingenious solution of multiform and multisized theater I am sure would interest you.

By the way, what progress has there been toward building your fine University Theatre?

There is much more to tell you of our adventures in England, Greece, Denmark, and Sweden. But that will wait until we see you and Betty. We hope that will be soon and here.

Affectionate greetings to you both from Aline and

Clarence

---

488 To F. J. Osborn

[New York City]   August 27, 1960

Dear F.J.:

Hugh Pomeroy showed me these delightful photographs of you, which he took on the day that you were 75. I told him that I was about to write you and asked him to let me enclose the pictures. I did this to give me an excuse to congratulate you at this late date.

Much thanks for your two letters regarding employment and greenbelts in the New Towns. They will be of great help to me.

In regard to the adequacy and permanency of the greenbelts, I am particularly impressed by your statement that they are "being safeguarded by the county planning control, now firmly established in national policy and supported strongly by public opinion and all the political parties." This is a tremendous step in progress and is probably due to the perseverance of you and your associates in large part.

I would like to ask a few questions in regard to this manner of permanent control of open land. This so we can see to what extent it can be applied to law and practice in the U.S.A. What is the national legislative basis of the county planning control that will keep greenbelts permanently open? How and when did this become firmly established in national policy?

I ask this because here, as you know, public controls are arrived at differently than in England. Zoning, for instance, is anything but a permanent protection. Zoning never can withstand the pressure groups, such as the land speculators, subdividers, and the mass house builders.

In regard to employment I am glad that you are going to ask some of the New Towns for an estimate of the composition of the local working population. Even if they have not taken a detailed census, those directors that have followed conditions for a number of years should be able to give a close figure of the number employed in nonindustrial occupations. They should also be able to estimate how many come from nearby country or villages and the extent to which they are still commuters to or from London or other metropolitan centers.

I am confident from past talks with D.C. directors and with officials of the Ministry that "most of the employed population in all the New Towns live in the towns or within cycling distance," but I am trying to get official figures as far as possible.

This so that I can convince Americans and first of all planners and municipal administrators that the conception of Sir Ebenezer Howard and the objectives of the New Town Law are being realized [and] that the New Towns are a success in Britain. . . . There are ways in which they might be improved, but basically they are doing their job. You need more of them, as you point out, and they will come. They should serve as inspiration for the future here in America. Our New Towns will be different, but with the fundamental conception the basic policy should be the same. Much thanks for your help.

Very best wishes to you and Margaret from Aline and

Clarence

---

489   To Carl Feiss

[New York City]   October 11, 1960

Dear Carl:

I have postponed answering your letter asking me to write on "The Architect's Responsibility in Designing Urban America" because I have been so busy with other things. The subject unquestionably is of great interest to me, and just as soon as I get a chance I will let you know whether I can find time to write about it.

I have wanted also to tell you that I felt that the [AIA] Committee on Community Planning had made a great mistake in taking a new title.[1] I think that most people would get an impression that it was their intention to limit the field to purely urban problems. In my opinion the urban and rural must go hand in hand. There is no solution to the difficulties of our cities without a regional background. There is no approach to the problems of our cities that can be successful excepting as part of a region. I think the title of the committee should indicate this.

I have the same feeling in regard to the proposed U.S. Dept. of Urban Affairs.

I look forward to seeing you soon.

Cordially,
Clarence S. Stein

1. The committee had been renamed the Committee on Urban Design.

---

490   To Sir Frederic J. Osborn

[New York City]   November 8, 1960

Dear FJO:

At the annual conference of the American Institute of Planners two weeks ago, there was a panel devoted to "What Happened to the New Town Concept?" The discussion was led by Holmes Perkins as chairman, followed by Lewis Mumford, Professor Charles Haar of Harvard Law School, Professor Anthony Adamson of the University of Toronto, and myself. I think you know them all, with the possible exception of Adamson. He was the only one of us that did not speak favorably, if not enthusiastically, about the New Town concept and attainments. He based his feelings apparently on observation in the Toronto area. There was a very warm debate between him and Lewis. This was what primarily interested the large audience.

Most of those present seemed to have a very limited knowledge of what [had] happened in Great Britain since Ebenezer Howard and particularly since the New Towns Law was passed. This is indicated by the title of the discussion, "What Happened to the New Town Concept?" as though there was a possibility that nothing had resulted. I am afraid that the ten or twelve minutes that we each had to introduce the subject was too little to make clear what those concepts were and to what remarkable extent they have been realized.

It is apparent that a great deal more background is required here before there will be an adequate understanding of the vital need of large-scale regional New Towns programs in the U.S.A. and the resulting action that is needed. This is true even of the professions that should be the leaders. . . .

The best effect of this meeting, as far as I was concerned, was the preparation for it. That is, the fact that it induced me to make a review of what led up to the New Towns and a broad study of what the results have been, that is, the extent to which, in their realization, they have carried out the conception of Sir Ebenezer Howard and the policy and program of the New Towns Committee and the law of 1946. Your letters were of great help to me in getting at the real facts and in clarifying my own mind. For them, much thanks.

As a result of my study, I am more than ever enthusiastic about what has been done in Britain. There is much that can be criticized about the manner in which the New Towns have been carried out. But those are details. The great thing is that so much has been accomplished in a field of real pioneering. There should be more New Towns, but the fact that so much has been done in the difficult financial period after the war is astounding. . . .

This is Election Day. Let us hope that our next president or his advisors will have vision enough to see the primary importance of a national policy in regard to dispersal and the creation of modern communities and that the states and regions will follow with really constructive action.

Aline joins me in cordial best wishes to you and Margaret.

As always,
Clarence S. Stein

491   To Catherine Bauer

[New York City]   January 5, 1961

Dear Catherine:

The joyful picture of you, Bill, and Sadie has delighted us. It is one of the few Christmas cards that we prize and will not throw into the fire. What an attractive daughter you have!

Your "Framework for an Urban Society" is a masterpiece.[1] It forms a sound basis for the broad approach to the problem of our urban physical environment that is needed so badly at present. You have covered an immense field concisely and clearly, and your program is positive without the pretense of being final. You are right—there are other packages, but yours is one that holds together. Any worthwhile criticism must judge it as a whole framework. It shows clearly that housing must be developed in relation to location of work and markets, to the highway program and transportation, to open spaces, to clear air and clean water, to the form and administration of government, and to a multitude of other things. All are interrelated, and they must be attacked on a regional basis. That seems to me the most important conclusion that one gets from your article.

I am delighted that you have indicated the need of continued exploration and discovery through research and open-minded experience and experiment.

You have painted the picture with broad strokes. You have left room for others to fill in the details, that is, unless you find time in the near future to cover more fully at least some of the fields. I hope you will.

One of the things that I think, at first reading, could be more fully covered is what you mean by "a regional network of strong cities, old and new." Perhaps you mean to contrast these with the British New Towns. I do not think that is necessary. Our old as well as our new cities should be large enough to support all or most of the opportunities and facilities of the great cities. The Regional City would do just that. It would be a cluster of towns or moderate size districts, separated by green open spaces in easy reach of all inhabitants, but tied closely enough together by "townless highways" to put all the convenience of a metropolis in easy reach of everyone by auto or bus. In fact, if we were wise we would start on a program of breaking up the old cities into districts separated by continuous park belts.

As I read the "Framework" over again, I may have some more criticisms or questions, but now I have only enthusiasm at the skill and the broad-minded vision and understanding with which you have united the various objectives into a united goal.

You probably are as pleased as I am that the president-elect has chosen Robert Weaver as chief of housing, which may lead, as the *New York Times* suggests, to his heading the new federal department dealing with cities, etc., if there is one. Your article indicates continuously the need of making it a Department of Urban and Regional Development. To keep ahead of growth of our metropolitan areas and to protect essential agriculture, wilderness, and other open spaces and all that, it must be regional in scope. I hope Dr. Weaver has studied, or will, your "Framework [for an Urban] Society" carefully.

We wish you both, and Sadie, a joyful 1961.

Cordially,

Clarence S. Stein

1. Catherine Bauer, "Framework for an Urban Society," in *Goals for Americans: Report of the U.S. President's Commission on National Goals* (New York: Prentice-Hall, 1960).

---

492   To Carl Feiss

[New York City]   January 17, 1961

Dear Carl:

I received your memo in regard to the relations between the AIA [American Institute of Architects] and the AIP [American Institute of Planners], as to who is going to do what. I can't for the life of me see why architects should not take part in city planning. In fact, some of the best planners I have met were architects: Sven Markelius, Sir Patrick Abercrombie, Bill Holford, Henry Wright, Albert Mayer, just to mention a few.

There is no use writing to you at length about this, as I hope to be in Washington next week and we can have a long talk about it.

Now I remember that I did give my opinion on the subject of the difference between a community architect and the city planner when I addressed the institute at the convention of 1956. You may still have a copy of that talk. I feel very much as I did at that time in regard to the function that the architect can serve in creating new cities and recreating old ones.

Best to you and Aline.

Cordially,

Clarence S. Stein

---

493   To Lewis Mumford

[New York City]   January 17, 1961

Dear Lewis:

Somehow or other I missed what interested me most in the *New York Times* last Thursday: QUEEN HAILS MUMFORD! Even a queen can use common sense when she is advised by those who know that the essential of architecture, as of broad planning, is not drawings and details, but conceptions of the relation of building to people and to communities and life today and tomorrow. She is right, you are one of the few great leaders in molding a contemporary environment to fit not only the present, but spacious and flexible enough to serve the future.

I was again convinced of this when I read your "Social Function of Open Spaces" in the new *Landscape* last evening. My congratulations on both the medal and the article.

I am looking forward with pleasure to the forthcoming book,[1] even though the final stage has caused such endless misery to both you and Sophie. I am delighted that you are going to escape to Amenia for a whole month of rest.

Aline has been busy the last couple of months acting in *All the Way Home,* first in tryout in New Haven, where I had a chance to get acquainted with the rambling campus of Yale with a busy city highway cutting it in two; then at Boston, where Benton met me for a few days, and we revisited his past around the Harvard yard. Finally, the play opened in New York and, in spite of enthusiastic reviews in the *Times* and *Herald,* the producers gave notice that advance sale of tickets was so small they would close in a few days. There was an immediate reaction from the part of the New York public that welcomed a serious modern play. They have kept the play going six weeks so far.[2]

I am going to Washington next week with Ken Ross to visit Ben. At the same time I want to see if I can find any way to prevent the proposed new federal department being called Urban Affairs or, worse, Department of Housing and Urban Affairs. How can we make anything out of our cities without developing them as an integral part of a region? Your article in *Landscape* shows that clearly. So does Catherine's chapter in *Goals for America,* which treats all factors of our urban environment and its surroundings as an interrelated whole.

I would like to see a Department of Regional Development or, as a probably necessary compromise, Urban and Regional Development. What difference does a name make? I remember that when Governor Al Smith asked me to be chairman of the proposed Housing Commission, I said I would gladly do so on condition that it was called Commission of Housing and Regional Planning. The legislature didn't know what regional planning was, so I had my way. Result: I was able to employ Ben and then Henry Wright and publish his brilliant *Basis for a Plan of the State of New York.*[3]

Aline sends affectionate greetings to you and Sophie.

As ever,

Clarence S. Stein

1. Lewis Mumford, *The City in History* (New York: Harcourt, Brace and World, Inc., 1962).
2. At the same time, Aline was playing the role of a doctor in the film *The Young Doctors.*

3. The section of the *Report of the Commission of Housing and Regional Planning* (Albany: The Commission, 1926) that dealt with proposals was titled "The Structure and Resources of the State Suggest a Basic Plan for the Future" (pages 75–82).

---

494   To Yngve Larsson

[New York City]   February 3, 1961

Dear Yngve:

. . . These are exciting days here with all eyes turned toward Washington. It is like the First Hundred Days of F. D. Roosevelt. Things are happening. A forward-looking president is trying to see the hard facts of this changing world in realistic manner and do something about them. President Kennedy has the enthusiasm of youth, but with it he seems to have astounding wisdom in his choice of those who are to advise and aid him in carrying out the colossal job for which the president of the U.S.A. is responsible. He has a broad knowledge of the innumerable problems, internal and foreign, that face our country after these eight years of a genial, beloved president whose conception of an executive was that of passing responsibilities and even decisions on to his staff and their subordinates. President Kennedy also has charm, but he is aware that in our unique form of government all responsibility of decision and execution is that of the president. We have great hopes for the future, just as we did in those difficult hundred first days of Roosevelt.

I spent much of the last week in Washington. I wanted to visit my good friend Benton MacKaye, but at the same time I hoped to see if it were not possible to broaden the attitude of the federal government toward the problems of our gigantic cities. The U.S.A. aids states and cities with vast subsidies for housing, redevelopment, highways, and community facilities. But it seems to me there is lacking any basic conception of the kind of community, city, or region that they are or should be creating. There is talk of a new Department of Urban and Housing Affairs. What is needed, it seems to me, is some division of the government that would give leadership and assistance in broad regional development. I did not have a chance to see anyone in the legislative or executive departments. Everyone was occupied those first few days of the new administration and the new Congress. However, I learned much of the complication of a big government and the difficulty of change. So now I am back to try to think it out again. Probably nothing will come of it. We will see.

Aline joins me in affectionate greetings to Elin and to you.

Cordially,

Clarence S. Stein

---

495 To Sir Frederic J. Osborn

[New York City] February 13, 1961

Dear F.J.:

This has been an exciting winter here—a really snowy winter. It was superbly beautiful from our "sky parlor," looking over the vast, open, sparkling white park to the gray, crowded skyscrapers beyond. The succession of storms crippled activities in the big city. Many suburbanites were snowed in; others found the railroad trains hours late. After the last storm, which closed many of the New York streets, the mayor refused entrance to the city by private autos. Their owners were forced to leave them at the city's borders and shoved themselves into already crowded buses and trains. However, the only mistake the mayor made was in not keeping most of the private machines out permanently! Schools were closed. (In fact, when I was in Washington a couple of weeks ago, just before the second storm arrived, all government workers were ordered to go home at noon.)

To return to New York: we have had a number of other indications of how easily the working of the giant metropolis is arrested. The strike of the railroad ferry workers held up the arrival of food. More important, these strikers picketed the entrance to the railroad stations of the New York Central and New York–New Haven Railroads, and these lines were closed. Thus, employees in New York living in Westchester or New England were forced to come in on overcrowded buses, subways, their own cars, or to stay at home, which many preferred. It was about that time, or perhaps a little before, that a water main burst and flooded one of our principal subways. Three cheers for better and above all bigger cities! Some day we all may be able to stay at home! . . .

That brings me to something in your last letter, which I have long wanted to discuss with you. That is "the suitability of the Radburn type of layout to English conditions," which you question. I am wondering if the great increase in personal autos is not beginning to change British conditions. In fact, my observation in a couple of New Towns, and my discussions with architects and town managers, and my reading of technical magazines since lead me to believe that quietly a revolution is just starting in English planned housing developments. Change in transportation is trending toward revision of urban plans, even in New Towns.[1]

The greatest change I noted in England since my visit six years before was the recognition of the automobile and the effect on town planning. I had time to see only three of the New Towns. In the newer residential sections of both Basildon and Stevenage, the architects and general managers called my attention to the fact that they were being inspired by the Radburn idea in their grouping of housing. By that, they meant particularly that they were as far as possible separating the roads for auto's access and for garages from the pedestrian ways.

The Lee Chapel North Neighborhood in Basildon exemplified this. Most of its 2,650 dwellings have (or will have) entrances from paths and roads at opposite sides of the houses. The main pedestrian routes leading to the Neighborhood Center are planned to pass under the main highways and the walkways from the Center to the future stadium and playing field will bridge the principal highway.

It is true that the centers of the blocks are not large greens or playgrounds, as at Radburn or Greenbelt. But that may well come in future developments. The first and most important step has been taken in segregating vehicular and pedestrian access. Anthony B. Davies, the chief architect-planner, told me that they are providing garages for 50% to 80% of the houses. That is quite a change since 1954, when I was last in England. Some of the courts around which the houses were placed were charming. They were open only to those on foot, like the courts of Oxford and Cambridge.

The new section of Stevenage was not far enough advanced when I saw it for me to be able to judge it very fully. But I am sure from talks with the architect-planner L. G. Vincent and with Mr. R. S. McDougall that the intention is to follow the Radburn idea.

I am particularly sorry that I did not have the time to see the work my friend Arthur Ling has been doing in Coventry, particularly at Willenhall Woods. On the basis of plans he has sent me, I judge that it is charming. That is true particularly of the varied views of house groups and trees, as one walks through the development. He has apparently completely separated people on foot and in machines. Ling says it is the "Radburn" of Coventry. His interpretation of the Radburn idea differs from ours mainly because he has placed the autos in the center of the house blocks and has located his large open spaces along the edge, instead of the center, of superblocks.

This reminds me that you say that "there is a great dislike in England of public pathways behind home gardens." Arthur Ling has located the garages and cul-de-sacs between the deep gardens and the house. The paths are on the other side, which he calls the front. I note that, at Harlow, Frederic Gibberd has done the same thing in a more formal manner in the Radburn Close.

There are a number of other more or less Radburn types of development throughout Great Britain that have been tried out since Gordon Stephenson made his plans for Wrexham over ten years ago. There he separated walks and vehicles completely, as I remember. However, my impression when I saw it in 1954 was that Gordon had been required to crowd his housing into too small an area.

I am convinced, as I know you are, that there must be plenty of open space near homes in this age of ever-increasing leisure time. I think [the open space] should be placed where children and other folks can walk to it easily, quickly, and above all safely. That, I have found, for everyday activities is best in the center of superblocks. You or others may prefer it elsewhere. However, in making a comparison, I do not think the play space and the park in the center of the block should be included in determining the number of houses per net acre, any more than you would include a playground at a distance or across a street.

I hope that there may be something to report in U.S.A. concerning a change of policy in regard to the broader problems of community development and interrelation. But such things take time, as we both know. Our new government may be too busy building dwellings, rather than creating new communities. We will see.

We just came on your New Year card with the good-natured dragon of Teotihuacan by the side of Margaret.[2] Aline joins me in greetings to her and to you.

As always,

Clarence S. Stein

1. The British sociologist and critic, Paul Ritter, wrote a series of nine articles published in the *Architects Journal* from November 1960 to February 1961; these articles provide a detailed assessment of Radburn planning in Britain. See also Kermit C. Parsons, "British and American Community Design: Clarence Stein's Manhattan Transfer," *Planning Perspectives* 7, no. 2 (1992): 181–210.

2. Teotihuacan, the central city of a pre-Aztec civilization (c. 400 A.D.), was first being excavated extensively during the 1960s.

---

496 To Benton MacKaye

[New York City]   April 19, 1961

Dear Ben:

Here is the memorandum on the proposed new department, of which we spoke when I was last in Washington. I have tried to boil it down as far as possible.[1]

As you probably noticed in the paper this morning, Senator Clark proposed a bill for a Department of Urban and Housing Affairs. I do not know whether there will be any very close relation between our two ideas. I hope to talk the matter over with the senator soon after he gets back from a trip abroad. He already has a copy of the outline which I am sending you. I do not know just what can be done to change things, but as you know I am a great believer in the impossible! . . .

When you go back [to Shirley Center], will you stop off in New York, as in the past? I hope so, so that we will have a chance to go up to the farm and see the wilderness once more.

You may have noticed in the *Times* this morning that Aline's play received the Drama Critics' Award as best American play of the season.

How is the book coming?

Best from Aline and

Clarence S. Stein

1. The most radical part of Stein's outline was his proposal that the Bureau of Public Roads be transferred from the Commerce Department to the proposed Department of Housing and Urban Development. Stein met with Senator Joseph Clark late in April 1961 about the bill establishing HUD.

---

497   To Lewis Mumford

[New York City]   April 19, 1961

Dear Lewis:

Enclosed is the memorandum that I prepared for *The Resources of the Future,* of which we spoke when we were together here. I thought there were things in it that might interest you, particularly the indication of the similarities and differences between the New Towns encircling London and the so-called Town Districts around Stockholm.

You will note in my suggestions for speakers that I have not yet found the right person for Greater London.[1] Osborn has so taken possession of the problem that he seems to have left others in the shadow. One thought that I have had is of quite a different kind of person, W. Eric Adams. He was general manager of Harlow from the beginning up to a short time ago. When I spent some time visiting the various towns and their managers some years ago, I found that he gave the most analytic description of the practical creation of the town and its organization as a living community. At the present time he is in charge of the building of a community in the Toronto metropolitan area, so that it would be very easy to get in touch with him. . . .

I am also enclosing the final draft of my outline of suggestions for the Control and Design of Metropolitan Growth and Development. I have sent a copy to Senator Clark of Pennsylvania, who presented the bill that was drawn up by the president's office. However, I don't think there is any similarity between my suggestion and the bill in its first form. Ed Bacon, who served under Clark when he was mayor of Philadelphia, has a very high opinion of him. Among other things to his credit, he says that he has read Lewis Mumford's books on cities! I will try to see Senator Clark in a couple of weeks, after he returns from a trip abroad. Just what the next step after that will be, I don't know.

Best to you and Sophie.

Clarence S. Stein

1. Stein and Mumford were trying to organize and finance a major national conference on metropolitan regional planning.

498 To Eric Carlson

[New York City]   May 10, 1961

Dear Eric:

. . . In my last letter I mentioned the fact that the president has sent to Congress a bill proposing a new Executive Department of Urban and Housing Affairs. If passed, this will broaden the responsibility of the development of our cities. However, in my opinion, it could be very much improved. For instance, I cannot see how we can solve the principal problems of growth and design of our metropolitan areas unless the highway functions of the federal government are adequately coordinated with the land and building plan.

I am enclosing a copy of my proposal for a Federal Department of Urban and Regional Development. There is just a slight possibility that this might have an influence in broadening the legislation. . . .

Last night I had an opportunity to look through, though not too thoroughly read, your article in the *Town Planning Review* of last October. That is the one in regard to Caracas. You certainly did a very thorough job.

Aline's play is still running. In fact, it received the Pulitzer Prize and the Drama Critics Award.

Best wishes from both of us.

Clarence S. Stein

499 To Arthur Glikson

[New York City]   May 10, 1961

Dear Arthur Glikson:

Thanks for the reprint from *Landscape*. I have read your article on the design of new lands with much pleasure. It is beautifully written and is based on keen observation and understanding.

Your description of Holland made me want to return there again and to stay there long enough to really become acquainted with those who have taken God's place in creating so much of Holland. Certainly, Israel and the Netherlands are the two little giants, so far as international planned development goes.

Lewis and Sophie Mumford are going to London before the end of the month. You have heard, of course, that Lewis is to receive the Gold Medal of the British Institute of Architects this year. I am delighted that his great work is being recognized in this way.

Both Lewis and Sir William Holford spoke at the annual meeting of the AIA a couple of weeks ago. Both talks were excellent. Lewis is relaxed now that his book is out. I wonder whether you have seen it: *The City in History.* I feel certain that you will enjoy it just as much as I do.

I hope to hear from you in the near future. Kindest regards.

Cordially,

Clarence S. Stein

---

500   To Gordon Stephenson

[New York City]   May 31, 1961

Dear Gordon:

This letter has been postponed from week to week in hopes that our program for the coming summer and autumn might take more definite form. We still are looking forward to a voyage to Japan again, to be followed, if possible, by a visit with Flora and you in Perth. . . . Our indecision about travel has been due in large part to the unforeseen success of Aline's play [*All the Way Home* by Tad Mozel]. It won the Critics' Award as Best Play of the Year, followed by the Pulitzer Prize to the author. That has built up the audience during the past month. So there is no telling when it will close, though it is doubtful if a serious show will be popular during the summer. Aline is fatigued after six months of the same part eight times a week. She wants more than anything else to just settle down in our lovely wilderness in Westchester. . . .

Much of my time these past months has been devoted to an attempt to guide public policy toward a broader vision regarding planned physical development. First, nationally the president has proposed a new Federal Department of Urban Affairs and Housing, and I have been trying to broaden the scope so that it will be Regional and Community, and not limited to residential and city details. . . .

How far I will get in realizing . . . these attempts I can't say as yet. But my own ideas on the subjects have been further clarified and simplified as a result of my studies. This is an important step toward making the ultimately desirable possible in the not too distant future.

Now I want to put aside all the limitations of political expediency and the public's hazy misunderstanding our our metropolitan problems. I would like to concentrate as far as possible on a simple statement of the real problem and a solution or at least an escape from the maze in which we are floundering. I want to return to the Regional City idea again, test it out by my observation during the past ten or more years and the endless surveys that have been made by others, then think it through once more. Finally, I must state it in the simplest, most understandable, convincing words, diagrams, illustrations. At least I will make a try.

The convention of the AIA this year was devoted to the subject of cities instead of buildings. It was held in Philadelphia, where the architects had something to show of their leadership in city building.

A number of our friends were there: Bill Holford and Lewis Mumford both gave splendid talks. Bill looked tired. He had been down to South Africa, then took Marjorie, who is still ill, on a short trip to Israel before he flew over for a few days just to give the keynote speech. Bill quite apparently needs a good rest. He was doing too much with his various jobs and the school and then came the presidency of the RIBA [Royal Institute of British Architects] and the chairmanship of the convention. He had no repose at Philadelphia. His spare moments were filled with radio and television discussions and a lecture or two at the university. Poor Bill!

The Mumfords looked relaxed and content, for the big book [is] done and at last published. Have you seen it, *The City in History,* as yet? It seems to me, as far as I have gone, to be the best of Lewis's long books. I am delighted that his contribution to the profession is being recognized in the award of the RIBA gold medal. He and Sophie have just left for London, where they will be staying in the Holford's house.

I am delighted that you and Flora are going to analyze the problems of university development and point the way to a broader approach for the future. You asked me for some advice. It is a subject I have not studied very deeply. But rather hasty visits to Harvard, MIT, Yale, Pennsylvania, and Columbia, since Aline opened in New Haven last November, have given me a few impressions in regard to the relation of university and city. I was going to speak about that here, but this letter is already too long. I will try to send you a few notes on the subject later, when I see it all somewhat more clearly.

Aline joins me in affectionate good wishes. We were both delighted with [your] square house surrounded by endless porches. We hope that we will see you and Flora before long.

Yours,

Clarence S. Stein

---

501   To Benton MacKaye

[New York City]   June 10, 1961

Dear Benton:

Just a few words to tell you that both Aline and I are enjoying life in spite of the fact that the heat of summer is coming at last. Aline's play is still drawing fairly good audiences after six months of playing. Of course, that is nothing compared to the records that your father made, but Aline could quite well stand a rest or a change of part.

We do go up to Thousand Years, leaving here Sunday morning and returning Monday afternoon in time for the evening performance. It makes a short but delightful relief from the city. I am trying to get down to real work on the Regional City book, but I find myself getting involved in various problems of development here in New York.[1] There is in the first place the proposed new charter. I am trying to induce them to broaden the scope of the planning department and really make it a department for development of the city, instead of one for making drawings and passing capital budgets. I now have the New York Chapter of the AIA backing me, but I don't know just how far I will get with the politicians.

A proposal is now being made that one of the few large pieces of land the city owns, Welfare Island in the East River, between Manhattan and Queens, be made into an enormous residential community for some 50,000 people, most of them living in towers 40 to 50 stories high. Albert Mayer and I are going to see what we can do to arouse an interest in turning Welfare Island and the other two islands in the East River into areas largely green, another Central Park. No telling how far we will get with this, but anyhow it is worth trying. My hope is that it will not take too much of my time because I feel about the city of the future as you and I see it. . . .

> Best from Aline and
> Clarence

1. Clarence had been working on some version of this book for ten years. He was almost eighty years old and never gave up.

---

502   To Lewis Mumford

[New York City]   June 23, 1961

Dear Lewis:

Just as I was about to write to tell you what joy and inspiration your book is giving me, I received a letter from Ingve Larsson, to whom I had sent [your book]. As his feelings and impressions are in so many ways like mine and as he expresses them so much better, I am going to quote what he says about it.

"Lewis Mumford's mighty book, *The City in History*, his magnum opus, summarizes his lifework, I presume. It is a most valuable book; his knowledge of the subject is immense, based not only on his wide reading, but on his own experience and observations. Reading Mumford you are always reminded of truths an architect, a planner, never may forget: a city is a community, interwoven with countless human connections; it is, or ought to be, the best possible expression of the life, the culture of the community. That's why planning isn't a specialty for the experts; there is too much at stake. I am reading the book slowly, beginning with the first and the last hundred pages and then re-reading it, chapter by chapter, just like the Bible. The best you can say of a book: you are compelled to think things over, once again, to re-examine what you have done, to doubt it, to ask if you haven't forgotten essential things in order to get immediate results. . . . You know, if you can't sleep at night you are visited by ideas of that kind."

Last week while I was drafting a memo for the [New York] chapter of the AIA, attacking Victor Gruen's proposed "City within a City," with 70,000 population, to be perched on Welfare Island, our electric power quit, along with five square miles of Manhattan, as well as Welfare Island. I thought, what a fitting climax for Lewis's story or better, perhaps, an introduction for "Regional Cities," if I ever get to it.

All our mechanical servants walked out for 4-1/2 hours. [There was] no water, no cooking, no TV or radio. The elevator quit. Luckily it was 5 o'clock, so we could do without the lights till near the end of the siege. Aline was able to walk down 12 flights and dash in a taxi to the theater, in spite of the fact that traffic lights didn't function. We were comparatively lucky.

The office workers, particularly in the sealed, air-conditioned buildings, were glad to escape. Most of them had an endless walk down to the street. Some were trapped in elevators between floors, one chap for four hours. And then the IND subway broke down.[1] Jammed cars were stalled between stations. All this at the peak hour on New York's hottest day for years.

If Victor Gruen's dream city had been in existence, imagine the homecoming of the 20,000 working in Manhattan, for whose benefit it is proposed to be built. If they had been among the lucky ones packed in the subway and if they hadn't been in the train stalled under the East River, they would have found the elevators were stalled. As at least half would be housed in 50-story apartment towers, I guess they would have camped out if they could have found room enough.

The matter of [reprinting] Raymond Unwin's *Town Planning in Practice* has come up again. Jane wrote to Carl Feiss about it. He thought it impractical, as we did. He wrote to Peggy Hitchcock, suggesting a biography and that he thought it better that Peggy write it. She answered: "I quite agree with your feeling about *Town Planning in Practice.* Mother talked several times to Curtice about the possibilities of reissue, and we always had to be discouraging. . . . I wish there were someone who could do a good life and times of my father, but it is a job that would require familiarity with the planning profession and the times in England and good writing."

You will remember, Lewis, that you had a very constructive suggestion when Jane wrote to you and that I agree with you. It was that parts of the book that apply particularly to the present day be published with the addition of "Nothing Gained by Overcrowding" and others of the shorter articles that are as pertinent now as they were half a century ago. You said, if I am not mistaken, you would help with advice or in editing.

As to biography, I think it should be an introduction to the articles and that some illustrations of Hampstead Garden Suburb and others of his works should be included.

It would be a fine thing if you would have a talk with Jane. I think she is being badly advised, possibly by her neighbor, Nikolaus Pevsner. She needs some sensible guidance, and you can give it to her about this matter better than anyone else. She's still living at Wyldes.

Our heartfelt congratulations for the great occasion on the 27th. I long have had a deep admiration for the keen understanding and the common sense of the British. Now that they have chosen you to receive the Royal Gold Medal of the British Institute, I know I am right.

Aline joins me in affectionate greetings to Sophie, also to Bill and Marjorie, and of course to you.

As always,

Clarence S. Stein

1. The Independent Subway (IND), which was located under Park Avenue West and Eighth Avenue, served the Bronx and extended to Long Island City in Queens and to Brooklyn. It opened in 1933 and was city owned and operated. All New York City subway systems were consolidated in 1939 and turned over to the Transit Authority in 1953.

---

503   To Paul Oppermann

[New York City]   August 2, 1961

Dear Paul:

I have been thinking a good deal of you of late. I have been taking a journey into your past—the period in the [late 1940s and early 1950s] when we started a campaign for New Towns. Your notes [and mine] on the conferences, and your minutes, and the programs we drew up brought it all back to my mind. First, you remember, there was that inspiring meeting with Osborn up in our Westchester wilderness, December 12, 1947. Then came our discussions with General P. B. Fleming and James W. Follen.

It did look as though the early days of the atomic bomb might lead to dispersal of federal offices. You really seemed to have General Fleming ready for action, prepared to take the first step toward balanced satellite towns. But nothing happened because of the complete lack of interest and understanding of Commissioners Reynolds of PBA [Public Buildings Administration] and MacDonald of PHA [Public Housing Administration].

Perhaps it is just as well we were not rushed into a hasty building of . . . New Towns then. I, for one, have learned a good deal in these 13 years, through Kitimat and studies of new communities in Great Britain, Sweden, and Israel. Basically I feel just as you and I did back in 1947. But I no longer think that a New Town is going to be enough to prove the case for dispersal. A small city of 50 or even 100 thousand may have the advantages of bringing work and plenty of open spaces convenient to homes. But, as I have seen in the British New Towns, they are too small to afford the varied cultural advantages of a metropolitan city or gathering with special groups of people of all kinds to discuss or develop ideas or to do things.

But a Regional City such as I have talked of for many years could have a million population in ten or more New Towns. They could be tied together by Townless Thruways, so that the time-distance to any one of them would be less than the typical journey to work in a metropolis. That it is practical and would work I am convinced. But where could it be created? Of course, first we have to convince others. One of the first questions is where [there is] a large enough piece of land that is well enough located. A Regional City for a million people or so in towns of fifty to one hundred thousand, or perhaps more, when I diagrammed it in 1954, was to take 1,000 square miles, mainly open country for agriculture, forest, recreation. Probably 500 square miles would do it, with plenty of open country between in agriculture, etc.

There are areas of that size probably in California, in the Central Valley, or possibly elsewhere. I am leaving tomorrow for a month's stay in California and will keep thinking about it. Are there any large areas that might be considered in the region of northeastern Illinois or thereabouts? I don't mean uninhabited. Better that there are some small or moderate-sized communities that can be redeveloped later or made part of a neighborhood or district of a future community, as is being done with most of the British New Towns.

I wish we could see each other again before long and talk about this and many other things. But, meanwhile, I look forward to hearing from you when you have time. . . .

Best wishes to you and Kay.

Cordially,

Clarence S. Stein

---

504 To Gordon Stephenson

[New York City]   September 27, 1961

Dear Gordon:

. . . We spent our last week in California in San Francisco. What a delight to be again in that unique, characterful, American city. We always think that it is unsurpassed in urban beauty—anyhow, as seen from the top of the Mark Hopkins. However, I must admit that, the night when we reached home and stepped out on the balcony, we felt that at least one view of New York competes with it.

But to return to San Francisco. The Mumfords arrived a few days before we left. We all dined together at the Wursters: Lewis and Sophie, Catherine and Bill, Aline and I. Lewis had much to tell us about London. In fact, we all had a great deal to tell each other, it was so long since we had been together. I only wish you and Flora had been with us.

I will send Lewis "Planning for Reconstruction" (to look at, not to keep). I wanted to read it once more, which I did last night. It is fine—what enthusiasm and clarity! Those were great days for you, who helped plan for the future Britain. And much has come from it. New Towns are only a beginning, it's true, but they are on the way.

Our nearest parallel to that period is the twenties, when our little Regional Planning Association of America explored the possibilities of a better world and took some first steps toward creating it. Just this last week I have been going over the minutes and records of the RPAA. I am quite aware that we have a long, long way to go.

In California, particularly around Los Angeles, anyone but an everlasting optimist might give up hope. I was in search of proposed New Towns there. I had heard of various "new cities," but when I examined the designs, in Victor Gruen's or other offices, they turned out to be particularly large housing developments or communities. But hopelessly lacking in a balance of industry and homes.

There was one exception. In San Diego I found that there was a community being designed for 90 to 100 thousand population, which would center around the daily work of its inhabitants—the work being education. It is spoken of as University City or Community. It is about to be built to serve a new [campus of the] University [of] California . . . : teaching, learning, and servicing the university will be the prime occupations of its inhabitants. . . .

The regents of the University of California, with the approval of the legislature, in 1958 decided that sites be found and studied to make two additional campuses in southern California, each to have an ultimate 25,000 students. There was a lengthy study to find the most desirable site . . . in the San Diego area. The location chosen is situated along and above the ocean, and from my airplane looked like rough terrain. But the report says that it is "a relatively flat mesa irregularly cut by deep, steep sided canyons." These canyons help preserve at least narrow greenbelts or subdividers or neighborhoods. The area of the property for "University City" is about 10,000 acres, of which 1,000 acres [are] to be used for the future campus.[1]

I discussed the plan with the designer in charge, Frazier Armbruster. He frankly admitted that the Master Plan is a study proposed to explain the general intention. There is much further study required. But, at least, here is a real attempt to study the requirements for growth of a university and the community that will grow around it.

Since you wrote me about your and Flora's intention of making a broad study of universities, I have been observing those that I visited. Most of them, in spite of their charm or other quality, are too congested. They have preserved utterly inadequate area for future growth. They lack flexible space for inevitable growth and change. Columbia is an outstanding example. It also exemplifies a second cardinal defect, lack of relation with or control of the development of the surrounding area. Much of its surroundings is becoming a so-called depressed area, if not a slum. I am told that the same is true of the University of Chicago.

It seems to me that the outstanding feature of the proposal and plan for the San Diego State University is that its authors face these facts, as far as they can judge from past experience.

We are sorry that we could not start across the Pacific this summer. But if we do not get to South Australia before too long, we must plan to meet somewhere between here and there.

Aline joins me in affectionate greetings to you both.

Clarence S. Stein

1. The campus and community plan were the work of Robert Alexander, who had been associated with Stein in the planning of Baldwin Hills Village in Los Angeles during the late 1930s.

---

505   To Benton MacKaye

[New York City]   November 9, 1961

Dear Ben:

"The Living Wilderness" has arrived and we have enjoyed your article immensely. They ought to hear more often from the Honorary President.

Last week Aline and I took a trip to Washington. It was queer being there and not on a visit to you at the Cosmos Club. Instead, we went to the old Hay-Adams. I don't know how many years [have passed] since I stopped there. In the old days, back in the '20s and perhaps the early '30s, Robert Kohn and I and others made that our headquarters. Nonetheless, when I came in, the chap who took our bags said, "How are you, Mr. Stein?" He had been through the war and whatnot since last we met.

Aline had a lot of theater folks and others to see, and I had a couple of jobs that took up the daytime. I spent the first day trying to get more information on the job that I have been studying—your job, Regional Decentralization. I had a good talk with Ed Graham about what they're doing in the Agricultural Department and a long spiel with Fritz Gutheim, who always knows what's happening everywhere.

I have told you, haven't I, that I got back to the subject that you and Lewis covered so thoroughly in 1951, with the result that the matter is coming up in a hearing in the House, and Congressman Reuss, who is proposing a bill for decentralization throughout the country, instead of merely dispersing around the capital, had asked me to appear. As I told you, I have been trying to bring myself up to date for a number of weeks. I finally came to the conclusion that I hadn't had time to find out enough of what had been happening since 1951 . . . to be prepared to tell the Congress of the USA just what they should do. If you remember, you spent four months on your investigation, and a great deal has happened since then, but it was good to look the matter over again. I feel more convinced than ever that there should be pretty complete reorganization on a regional basis. The only thing is I do not think I have enough facts to convince the boys up on the hill.

My two other days were spent at the Octagon discussing housing and urban planning.[1] I met a number of old friends there: Henry Churchill, Fred Bigger, Carl Feiss, and so on. A pleasant occasion, even though I did have to get into a number of arguments. Why do they always want to take the middle road?

Evenings Aline and I had a good time dining with old friends. The only thing we missed was Ben!

Our best to you,
Clarence S. Stein

1. The Octagon (1798), former Washington, D.C., home of John Tayloe, had been purchased and adapted for use as the headquarters of the American Institute of Architects. It was designed by William Thornton, first designer of the Capitol. The editorial offices of the *Journal of the American Institute of Architects* had also been located there when Clarence Stein served as associate editor for community planning in the 1920s.

---

506   To Fritz Gutheim

[New York City]   November 27, 1961

Dear Fritz:

I was glad to have your letter of November 20. It is quite true that Aline is to play in *The Madwoman of Chaillot* at the Arena Theatre. That will mean that we will be in Washington a good part of December and January.

Soon after I get there, I will look forward to seeing you. We will then have a chance to talk further about the proposed talks on Control and Design of Metropolitan Growth and Development. I am glad you are interested in it.

I think a series of that kind, properly carried out, would be particularly valuable at this time in Washington. It would show people that there is more than one practical way of attacking and possibly solving the problems so urgent in Washington at the present time.

I have made notes on what they are doing or propose to do in a number of other places, including Oslo and the ring of cities in Holland that are trending toward a single conurbation.

Cordially,
Clarence S. Stein

507   To Benton MacKaye

[New York City]   December 13, 1961

Dear Ben:

Your letter of the 4th reached me in Washington. I am looking forward to seeing you on or about December 28. I will have no trouble in finding room 305 at the Cosmos, if you are not seated in your office in front of the fireplace! We will have the greater part of a month in which to talk things over.

Although we arrived in Washington Monday, the fourth, I didn't get to the club until the end of the week, when I had lunch with Carl Feiss. It is a good trip from our new home in the Southwest.[1] Besides, I am not yet a member. However, I note that I was about 4th or 5th in the line to be considered, and as the gentleman who gives his residence as the White House, and occupation, president of the U.S., is much further down the line, I don't feel so badly about it.

I am here in New York for just a few days, so that I can induce Wilma to do the heavy work of writing letters and telling me where things are kept. I also want to see what progress is taking place in planning and the general development of the city. I suspect there has been some trouble between the mayor and Jack Felt, who is the head of the Planning Department. The mayor, I imagine, feels that he is really grown up, now that he has been re-elected. I hope he has sense enough to let Felt take care of the development of the city, including the preservation of old Blackwell's [Welfare] Island as a park instead of a 50-story apartment site.[2]

In Washington we were very lucky in getting an apartment in one of the new buildings that are going up in what was said to be a slum, that has been cleared. It is far from being a slum now. The building we are in turns out to be one of which Chloethiel Woodard Smith was architect. She has done a fine job, and we, with our usual luck, have a little apartment on the top floor, which is the eighth, where I can see the sun rise at almost the same angle as here. In other words, we face pretty squarely to the east. The foreground below is great garden spaces, then some small houses, also designed by Chloethiel, and then beyond them, open spaces waiting for new building. From our bed we get a full view of the dome of the Capitol, which is now flooded with light until midnight.

Aline has been rehearsing daily. It is a wonderful play, which she enjoys no end. As I think I told you, she has already performed in it twice, in different places in California.

I am keeping busy enough, seeing friends and visiting old familiar places. I have been particularly interested in getting up to date on what has happened in Greenbelt since the government sold it to a cooperative. All that I will tell you when we meet in Washington.

Your letter to Lewis was fine. I am sure he will not stop off at Washington to see us. I gather from a letter that I had from him that he wants more than anything else to get back to Amenia. As far as I heard, he has done a fine job in California, particularly in his attempt to give the students and others some idea of the truth in regard to the present worldwide emergency. But there is nothing he wants more than to escape the crowd. . . .

Very best from Aline and

Clarence S. Stein

1. During Aline's performance at the Arena Theatre, Clarence and Aline Stein were living in one of the new apartments that had been designed by Chloethiel Smith in the Southwest Washington Urban Renewal Area.

2. Welfare Island in the East River, parallel to Manhattan, was to be converted to a "New Town in Town" and renamed "Roosevelt Island."

---

508   To Eric Carlson

[New York City]   September 17, 1962

Dear Eric:

. . . I can't remember just when I last wrote you. So here [are] just a few words about our travels.

After our stay in Hawaii in March and part of April, we went to London, where Aline did another picture.[1] She flew directly from Los Angeles; I came back here for a week or so. Although our headquarters were in London for 12 weeks, we took short trips to Paris and Stockholm.[2] On my way back from Sweden, I stopped a few days at Copenhagen.

I was particularly impressed in Britain, as well as in Scandinavia, to see how the mass invasion of the auto was affecting planning. When they built Vällingby outside of Stockholm some 12 years ago, there was altogether too little thought given to parking around the central shopping center. Now that they are constructing Farsta, the center of another group of new communities, the second big district to be added to Stockholm, it is quite another story. In fact, the three branch department stores are drawing trade from the neighborhood stores.

In Cumbernauld, the New Town that is being constructed in Scotland, practically all commercial facilities are to be centered under one roof of a building almost a half a mile long. They propose to have only shops for occasional buying in the neighborhood, for essential daily buying. Paths will be laid directly to the big center from practically all parts of the town, with 50 minutes or less walk. These paths, as far as I can see, never collided with a road. There, as elsewhere in the British New Towns, architects, planners, and managers wanted to talk about how they were carrying our the Radburn idea. There is no question but that it is having an immensely greater influence there, as well as in Stockholm and Copenhagen, that it has had for many years in the U.S.A. Stevenage is planning a whole neighborhood in which there will be complete separation of machines and pedestrians.

Of course, in Farsta, as in Vällingby, the Radburn idea is taken for granted as a planning principle. And now in Copenhagen, the younger architects are developing new ways of using it.

The important news about Copenhagen is that they are developing a new plan to take the place of, or rather carry on, the Finger Plan, in a new fashion. They are proposing New Towns, or rather new districts, in outlying parts of the city, which will have a population each of 250,000. This is quite a jump from Ebenezer Howard's proposal for Garden Cities of 30,000 and the New Towns, which started with about 50,000 and ultimately ran up to 80,000 or so, as you remember. But in England they are already beginning to talk of increasing the size of Stevenage, Harlow, and some others.

But there is no use trying to tell you now about the various changed points of view in realizing planned development that I found. We will talk of this, if it interests you, when I see you. Above all, I look forward to hearing much more about the work that you are doing in Caracas.

Aline sends her very best wishes to you all. So does

Clarence S. Stein

1. In London, Aline acted in the film *I Could Go on Singing,* with Judy Garland.

2. In Paris, Clarence and Aline lived in the Latin Quarter not far from the place where he had lived when he studied architecture in Paris from 1905 to 1911.

---

509   To Lewis Mumford

[New York City]   November 14, 1962

Dear Lewis:

On Monday, Roy Lubove spent the whole day here. He copied large portions of the minutes [of the RPAA], 1923–33. These included the description of the discussions in two of our meetings at the Hudson Guild Farm. As a result he should have a clearer idea of what it is all about. I think he has, but we will have to wait until he has corrected his manuscript. As I wrote you, I had hopes that the result would be a complete rewriting. I don't think he will go as far as that, but we will just have to wait and see what are the results.

We found that we have additional copies of the greater part of the minutes and programs between 1923–33. I am enclosing these, as I am not sure whether you have kept the records during that period. There are missing the minutes of Feb. 5, 1925, and the discussion at the Hudson Guild Farm Oct. 17–19, 1930. It seems to me that at this meeting we covered our ideas of regional development more closely than at any other. . . .

Best wishes to you both.

Cordially,

Clarence S. Stein

---

510   To Stuart Chase

[New York City]   January 3, 1963

Dear Stuart:

. . . I look forward to receiving the *Reader's Digest* article on Town Planning Commissions. But far more I hope that I will see you again before the New Year is much older. There is much I want to hear about your adventures. Besides, I might tell you something of my last year's travels and discoveries for 1962 was for me a great year of exploration. There were two months in Hawaii, where they were trying out a new scheme of broad state zoning: just dividing the island into Agriculture, Urban, and Conservation Zones.

Soon after, for about 2-1/2 months, we were in London. That meant re-exploration of New Towns in Scotland and England, where new forms of planned development are at last appearing. Above all, now that the mass invasion of autos has at last overtaken Britain, the builders of the New Towns are making the "Radburn idea" a must.

From London we took short trips to Paris, Copenhagen, and to our beloved Stockholm. . . . Stockholm is to us the most attractive of all the great cities. That is partially because so much of the natural beauty has been preserved in water and rocky hills as [the] setting for the urban structures. But perhaps mainly we love to get back to Stockholm because there are so many old friends there who are creating new communities: architects, town planners, landscape architects, and administrators. What is most heartening is that the direction in which they are traveling in city and regional development is in so many ways that in which I think we should be going.

In October Aline started doing a picture, *All the Way Home,* down in Knoxville. So I spent a week in the Tennessee Valley, getting more acquainted with the big job that TVA has done. It is the greatest thing that has happened to the U.S.A. in our lifetime.

I hope we will have a chance to get together and talk of our adventures and explorations and all that before long.

Aline joins me in greetings for 1963 to Marian and to you.

As always,

Clarence S. Stein

511 To Gordon Stephenson

[New York City] April 26, 1963

Dear Gordon:

I was delighted to read your "Planning in the Metropolitan Region" that *Canada Plan* sent me.[1] It is fine. You have stated the case for the Regional City as basis for the development of metropolitan areas with remarkable clarity as well as sanity. Above all, in your conclusions you place first things first.

It is that which I feel [is] lacking always in the work of the [New York] Regional Planning Association. Of late I have thought they were changing their attitude and that their policy was coming to be more constructive, rather than that of following the guide of past tendencies.

The RPA has been publicizing its latest studies over television. These have been particularly aimed at small discussion groups they have organized throughout the metropolitan area. The subject has been "Goals for the Region." This was good educational work, but it was only in the last of the five of these talks that they got down to the basic conception: "Policies that will solve the problem." And they deal most strongly with the importance of easy, quick, face-to-face contact in the core of the region. That means, of course, an emphasis on new means of travel. It is true they have made a splendid study of open spaces around New York. They are carrying on a campaign now to get them. Also they have dealt with the need of more compact community development in their earlier television programs.

However, I think that your article contrasts with their final approach in leaving no doubt as to the fact that planned, balanced communities, surrounded by open spaces, should dominate as objective, over the means of speedy movement. . . .

This summer—May, June, and July—we expect to have our headquarters in Paris and to travel from there to various parts of Europe. The next time we must turn our faces east. . . .

Our very affectionate greetings to you both.

As always,
Clarence S. Stein

1. Gordon Stephenson, "Planning the Metropolitan Region," *Plan Canada* 3, no. 3 (1963): 113–18.

512 To Sir Frederic J. Osborn

[New York City] May 8, 1963

Dear F.J.:

Last weekend in Boston I had a long talk with Peggy Hitchcock regarding the best way to celebrate her father's centennial. Since then I have discussed the matter with

Lewis Mumford. We agree in the following proposal, which we hope you will approve:

The story of Sir Raymond's unique personality and work should be published in a periodical that reaches those who are particularly interested in the field in which Unwin worked. There should be a few articles written by those who knew him well or have made a thorough study of his life and times. The articles should not attempt to form a full biography. Professor Walter Creese's book or some future study will cover the detailed story.[1]

The most fitting periodical is your *Town and Country Planning*. It deals with the broad field and objectives that formed the background of Raymond Unwin's activities. Other magazines, such as the Liverpool *Town Planning Review,* are devoted to a more limited technical approach. It is of course you who must decide whether the November number of . . . *Town and Country Planning* can give adequate space or can be slightly enlarged to make an Unwin memorial number. We hope the idea will appeal to you and you will find it practical to carry it out.

Our suggestions for principal contributors are Professor Walter Creese, Lewis Mumford, [and] Steen Eiler Rasmussen. An additional proposal was Dr. Ernst May. In our choice we considered mainly the knowledge of or acquaintance with Sir Raymond and the ability to tell the story fully but concisely. Also, because of the limited time and lack of financing, it seemed important to choose those who were prepared to write without undue additional research. Walter Creese can draw upon the material he has gathered in preparation for his book. Lewis Mumford proposed to give a lecture about Unwin at Pennsylvania University in November. I will give him some few notes of my recollections, but Lewis is the best one to write the story.

Steen Eiler Rasmussen, during the period of his youth, when he wrote his great book, *London: The Unique City,* often visited Wyldes. He was inspired by Unwin, to whom he dedicated his book. In fact, at Runsted, outside Copenhagen, the form of the living room in his home was greatly influenced by his memories of the living room at Wyldes. There I believe Raymond did much of his writing, and, I am delighted to say, I finished my book there.

Ernst May was suggested by Peggy Hitchcock and also Lewis Mumford. Although I knew May back in the twenties and saw him again last summer in London, I do not know about his acquaintance with Sir Raymond. Jane Unwin can probably best tell you about that.

As I go over the names I have mentioned, I find that none are British. Of course, we hope that you will write at least an introductory editorial note. Besides, we feel there should also be an article by some outstanding professional architectural planner. I propose Sir William Holford; I do this in spite of the fact that I am sure he is very, very busy.

Now just a few words as to other suggestions that have been made and why we favor that which I have described:

1. The republishing of Raymond Unwin's *Town Planning in Practice* . . . would require much editing to bring this great book up to date. It would be difficult to get a publisher because its sale would be very limited.

2. Republishing of some of his shorter articles, such as "Nothing Gained by Overcrowding" and possibly parts of his Columbia lectures . . . might be considered later. There is not time to do it before November. By the way, I believe the lectures, as well as other papers from Columbia, that were returned to Wyldes, are now in the library of the RIBA.

3. A memorial volume—we do not know how this would be financed, even if there were time to publish it before November.

Our proposal is closely related to the memoir which you suggested on March 30. It seems to me to have these advantages:

1. It would not require a separate publication and advertising and sale of a book, for which, I am told, there is too little time.

2. It would not contain Raymond Unwin's writings, which would take time and expense to choose and collect. These could be left for future publications, which would probably have greater success if the memoir of his centennial appeared in November in the proper periodical.

3. It would have the best possible audience if you found it desirable and practical to publish the proposed articles in *Town and Country Planning*.

We hope that this will appeal to you and that you will ask those whom we have suggested, or others, to prepare articles under your leadership.

Cordially,

Clarence S. Stein

1. In addition to Creese's book *The Legacy: A Human Pattern for Planning* (Cambridge: MIT Press, 1967), there are now two recent biographies of Unwin: Frank Jackson, *Sir Raymond Unwin, Architect, Planner and Visionary* (London: A. Zwemmer, 1985), and Mervyn Miller, *Raymond Unwin: Garden Cities and Town Planning* (Leicester, England: Leicester Univ. Press, 1992).

513   To Lewis Mumford

[New York City]   December 10, 1963

Dear Lewis:

. . . I don't remember that you asked me to write out a full synopsis of my life. I think it is a very good idea to go over it year by year as you suggest, but I don't know just how much of the earlier parts I can put together. I will try to make a start first by collecting what we have of a general synopsis and then gradually looking up the work that I did in my architectural practice and in connection with the state government and various organizations in the institute, etc. Of course, a great deal of the architectural work, as far as it has to do with housing and city development, is covered in my book. I don't know just when I will be able to [do] the job, but I will make a start as soon as I get an opportunity. . . .[1]

Cordially,

Clarence S. Stein

1. Clarence was 81 and feeling his mortality, but he would live another decade. Sadly for our knowledge of his life, he seemed to have done little to follow up on Mumford's suggestion.

---

514 To Percy Johnson-Marshall

[New York City]   January 6, 1964

Dear Percy:

. . . I have been postponing for a long time telling you how welcome your last letter was. Also I wanted to let you know something about the great interest that is at last developing in regard to New Towns for America. The various divisions in Washington that have to do with housing have been making studies on the future growth of the capital. *The Plan for the Year 2000* is very similar to the old Finger Plan of Copenhagen, with numerous small communities tied to the capital. Of this, I will try to write you more before long. . . .

Cordially,

Clarence S. Stein

---

515 To Frederick Gutheim

[New York City]   April 2, 1964

Dear Fritz:

Thanks for the information about Paul Ritter's book.[1] I have written for it.

Did you see Robert Weaver's excellent talk at the University of Illinois? He sees the problem clearly enough, but I fear he will miss the mark if he depends on the private developers as the agents to carry out the complicated job of realizing a New Town. The progressive and imaginative private developers, of whom the president's message speaks, are rarities, particularly if they have to see a complicated, long-drawn-out, social-economic-civic project made a living reality. This is particularly true if the housing is to include all income and racial groups. If government (federal, state, or some type of regional government) is not going to take a constructive lead in the development, then demonstration New Towns will be required. The Washington area is a good, if not the best, place for leadership. So I am delighted that you are going to emphasize its value.

But we will need others built under the auspice of nonprofit organizations, following the lead of Tapiola, Finland. Here the larger unions' housing cooperatives indicate a possible agency. But they will need much and varied technical assistance and leadership.

Cordially,

Clarence S. Stein

1. Paul Ritter, *Planning for Man and Motor* (New York: Pergamon Press, 1964), deals in elaborate detail with one of Stein's major concerns, planning cities for pedestrians so that residential open spaces and pathways are separated from trafficways. Ritter devotes several pages to the design of Radburn (pp. 319–21) and a longer section to the evaluation of applications of the Radburn pattern to residential areas in British New Towns (pp. 227–57).

---

516 To Mr. and Mrs. Edward Ames

[New York City]   May 23, 1964

Dear Edward and Muriel Ames:

Your letter was very welcome. I am delighted that the Kitimat article is taking form. I am sure that it is going to be an outstanding work. We have had so little experience with New Towns here in America that the observation of those who have lived in them and taken an active part in operating one of them will be of particular value, especially now, because of the president's proposal to Congress.[1] Frankly, I hope that you will bring out the inadequacies of the Kitimat setup (one industry, etc.), as well as advantages of the type of living it made possible.

Now as to the proposal for the federally aided New Towns in the Housing Bill. I am glad it has so strongly brought the subject to public attention. But, although the objective is outstanding, the means are inadequate to attain the goals. Among other things, it would put the job in the wrong hands, those of the typical speculative housing developer.

So I am strongly opposed to the president's New Town proposal, but for quite different reasons than those who will in all probability prevent its passage. Albert Mayer and Lewis Mumford are of the same opinion. I am glad that, based on your experience and observation, you see its defects. The program is inadequate. It is much better to wait and to work for a policy and a program of action that would serve our needs.

Our basic requirements are the same as those in Great Britain. It took time for them to build a foundation in land control and distribution of industry that made it possible for them to develop a national policy of New Towns and their regional distribution. That you, of course, know. But you may be interested in a book that has just been published that covers the subject thoroughly. It is *The New Towns: The Answer to Megalopolis,* by Sir Frederic Osborn, the authority on the subject . . .[2]

Cordially, with best wishes from Mrs. Stein and,

Clarence S. Stein

1. Lyndon B. Johnson's proposal for a U.S. New Towns program had been inherited from the Kennedy administration. It was implemented by passage of the New Communities Act in 1968.

2. Frederic J. Osborn and Arnold Whittick, *The New Towns: The Answer to Megalopolis* (London: Leonard Hill, 1963). A second edition, completely revised and reset, was published in 1969.

---

517   To Benton MacKaye

[Yorktown Heights, New York]   [c. June 1964]

Dear Ben:

. . . Now as to the big news, which you probably saw in yesterday's (Monday, 29th) *New York Times.* Governor Rockefeller has had a basic plan for the State of New York worked out during the past two years by his Office of Regional Development. I was invited to the gathering of reporters at which it was released to them. That was because the basic plan follows that which our H. & R. P. [Housing and Regional Planning] Commission developed with the help and genius of Henry Wright, as well as of Ben MacKaye.

So you see that those who have laid out this basic program for development of the state of New York have been greatly influenced by Geddes and MacKaye, as well as Henry Wright's brilliant study of forty years ago in which you took an active part. . . .

Take good care of yourself, Ben. Our very best to you.

Clarence

---

518   To Benton MacKaye

[New York City]   July 8, 1964

Dear Ben:

. . . You said you wanted more information about the rebirth of interest in the Plan of the State of New York. I am enclosing a copy of the article and editorial that appeared in the *New York Times* on June 29. I thought that you might have seen [it] at the club. I enclose a copy of what I have written to a number of my planning friends here and abroad.

Ben, I have waited some 40 years for this to happen. (The report of my commission is dated 1926 but, as you remember, you probably started work on it before Henry Wright, a year or two before that.) Now that a development plan is to be realized, I naturally am deeply interested in having it follow as far as possible the idea that means so much to you and Lewis and to me: that is to say, the old RPAA. So I am glad that in the tentative plan they show a number of New Towns and even new cities, and in some places they are grouped together so they might very well become Regional Cities. I will have to find some way of getting those who will develop the plan to really understand the advantage of creating Regional Cities in the Hudson and Mohawk Valleys and possibly along the lakes and the St. Lawrence River. Also, when the time comes, you and the Wilderness Society should recommend that large parts of the vast areas in the mountains and hills, that they hope to conserve for forest and recreation, should become real wildernesses. . . .

Aline joins me in good wishes to the Johnsons. And our very best to Ben.

Clarence S. Stein

---

519   Extract of letter to friends

[New York City]   [c. July 1964]

The main news I have about my own work concerns something that started forty years ago. Just at the end of June, I had a thrilling experience when Governor Rockefeller proposed a broad program for the development of the State of New York. In doing so, he called attention to the fact that it followed the basic principles and form of the program plan that my Commission of Housing and Regional Planning prepared for Governor Alfred Smith forty years ago.

I think you know our report, prepared by Henry Wright, in which we followed the development of the state from its early settlement to see how its natural form and resources have served and affected the location and activities of the people through the various stages of economic, industrial, and cultural development. All this was to serve as a guide as well as a warning for the future.

The final program plan that we, as well as the one that the present governor's State Development Office presented is a policy program, illustrated by a basic plan that indicates broadly the location and form of major urban and rural and conservation areas. The cities new and old are located—or rather, located themselves—in the flat lands along our great waterways and particularly along the Hudson and Mohawk Rivers and the Erie Canal, by which the Great Lakes commerce flowed to the port of New York, which consequently became the foremost city of the East Coast. The mountains or highlands are to be—many of them are already—vast forest areas to protect the source of our rivers and serve as great recreation areas and will, I hope, become largely wilderness areas. I am glad to find that the new program proposed ultimately that the state should have even greater green conservation areas than we had asked for.

All of this is only the basic outline of a plan growing out of the dictates of nature and man's changing activities. The comprehensive, although flexible, plan is now to be developed. This will be done on a regional basis. The state will plan each of the ten regions into which it has been divided for this purpose, with the cooperation of local authorities and regional councils.

520 To Benton MacKaye

[Yorktown Heights, New York]   [c. July 1964]

Dear Ben:

Here I am on the porch, surrounded by all the glories, sights, and sounds of the nearby wilderness. There is a refreshing breeze. The air is dry—quite different than yesterday, when the outdoor heat kept us indoors.

The governor's proposal to realize our program for the plan of the state has led me back forty years. I have been trying to recollect not only those days of Al Smith, when the search for a plan was made by the Commission of Housing and Regional Planning. Also, I have been retracing my efforts since Henry Wright's brilliant report to get various governors to set up an agency in his department to carry on the development of the state along the lines we had indicated. I find records of my proposals to Governor FDR, to Dewey, and also to Governor Rockefeller (although I cannot remember sending the latter—he seems somehow to have followed the conception I had in 1958). I am particularly glad that he used the title Development instead of Planning. I hope it will mean action and not merely research, reports, and diagrams—Dynamic Development, not Static Planning.

Henry Wright's work is recorded in the report of 1926 and his article in the Regional Planning number of *Survey Graphic*. But there is nothing regarding the beginnings that you made—that was in 1924, was it not? What do you recollect or what have you in your diary or elsewhere? There is such a strong basis of geotechnics in the program that I suspect that there was a certain directional guidance [from] Benton that remained after your departure. Anyhow, see if you can recollect anything about your work and thoughts connected with that historic conception and the early study.

But don't waste too much time on this. The book comes first. How is it coming? . . .

Clarence

P.S. I just came on your memo of November 23, 1958, regarding a proposal for State Development Coordinator which I was then drafting.

521 To Walter Creese

[New York City]   September 9, 1964

Dear Walter Creese:

This is in answer to questions you asked me in your letter of August 10 about the International Town Planning Conference in 1925. It was a particularly interesting meeting. Among other things, the proposed plan program for the State of New York, as well as the studies of the Regional Survey of New York and Environs, were discussed. The period after the First World War certainly was an exciting time, full of adventure and discovery in the field of planning and development.

Barry Parker attended this Congress and also the weekend party Alexander Bing and I organized at Hudson Guild Farm, to which we invited a small group of our foreign delegates. It was of this party I wrote in my note on Raymond Unwin, but Barry Parker did not join in the folk dancing.

By all means, use the story of Raymond Unwin joining the folk dancing. I told it at the meeting of the Town and Country Planning Association in London, when I received the Ebenezer Howard Medal, in 1960.

I have not heard that Constable lived in Hampstead Garden Suburb. Mrs. Jane Unwin might know.

You speak of what looks like a Radburn pedestrian underpass in the report on Wythenshaw of 1927. I do not see how it could be influenced by Radburn, which we started in 1928. Underpasses had been used before, of course (in Central Park, for instance, designed by Frederick Law Olmsted in 1858).

I will be very glad to see your article on "The Planning Theories of Raymond Unwin" in the AIP journal.

Best wishes.

Cordially,
Clarence S. Stein

---

522   To Carl Feiss

[New York City]   February 2, 1965

Dear Carl:

Thanks for copies of your correspondence with F. J. Osborn. You have done a valuable service, and a fine job, in keeping him up to date in regard to the American situation in the fields of community development and New Towns.

In regard to the New Towns, I feel that the most difficult thing we have to face in this country is the land problem. Unless we can get rid of speculation in land, we never will solve the problem of keeping the lower-income workers in the towns.

I have been in California lately, and from what I have heard of the New Towns there I have the impression that many, if not most, of them are a large-scale approach to speculation in land and building.

Any governmental assistance must insist on community or cooperative ownership of land. Otherwise, government subsidy would be absurd.

After the Greenbelt Towns were made cooperatives, Congress passed legislation giving the individual cooperators the right to own their own homes at prices commensurate with the low rentals they paid. It was well-intentioned legislation. But it led to the sale of property by many of the former tenants at a speculative profit. As I remember, Senator Douglas of Illinois was responsible for the legislation; if so, I probably was a party to the blunder, as I had been his consultant when the cooperative scheme was first developed.

I hope that sometime in the spring I will be going to Washington and that we will have an opportunity to discuss the whole question of a sound, workable policy for New Town legislation again.

Cordially,
Clarence S. Stein

---

523   To Gorän Sidenbladh

[New York City]   February 2, 1965

Dear Goran Sidenbladh:

. . . In most American cities there is plenty of planning, but too little coordinated development. The private ownership and speculation in land and building, of course, has much to do with this.

But there are exceptional cities. Philadelphia illustrates how much can be done under our limitations (so many of which you may have read of in the articles by Albert Mayer which I sent you). Under the leadership of Ed Bacon, Philadelphia has been developed in a masterly way. Bacon has a fine and broad conception of the city of the future, not only physically as a great work of community architecture, but also socially and economically. He also has been able to lead the municipal officials and the general public to accept his basic conception. He is a great architect-planner who knows how to express his objectives and the form and nature of the city that [are] required to realize them. I am sure there is no need of speaking further about him, as I believe you saw him when you were in America, and he told me that he had lately been to Stockholm.

Both Mrs. Stein and I long to visit Stockholm again. We have fond memories of the charm of the city. But, even more, we want to see our good friends once more. We both send cordial greetings to you and Mrs. Sidenbladh.

Sincerely,
Clarence S. Stein

524   To Lewis Mumford

[New York City]   September 21, 1966

Dear Lewis:

Last night my original purpose in phoning you was to talk to you about your Geddes article in *Encounter,* and I spoke to you about everything else. The rest of us accepted [Patrick] Geddes on the basis of what we took to be your attitude toward him. And now I find that even you questioned the perfection of the self-elected prophet of planning!

I remember the last time I saw him. It was at Montpelier. We had spent the day before trailing after him through the long corridors of the university and listening to his ceaseless explanation of all we saw in the surrounding countryside. We couldn't take more of that. We decided that the next day we would escape to Paris.

So, early in the morning, we called to say our final farewell. It was a difficult task, but we succeeded, and we got away. And that is the last I saw of Geddes.

Our best to you and Sophie. Have a fine time in Cambridge.

As always,

Clarence S. Stein

525   To Lewis Mumford

[New York City]   March 13, 1967

Dear Lewis:

It was good to talk to you last week. We hope Sophie is feeling much better. Really, you should move to the city in the winter for health's sake, even if you have to keep the fact more or less secret so that you can devote yourself to your writing. I know it would be difficult because of the many requests for lectures, meetings, and so on. But you should try some way to escape the hard winter of country living.

The Australian [subdivision] plan based on the Radburn idea, that you sent me,[1] is just another of the many that have been tried. This one has good points. The green park, although narrow, runs through the whole plan, with access on all the cul-de-sacs. The greenbelt runs around a large portion of the boundary, but it should be much wider. The Civic Center seems to include all or at least most of the essential structures.

I know that there is an increasing interest in the Radburn idea in Australia. In the first place, as you know, Gordon Stephenson is working and teaching there. His home for some years has been in Perth, where he is planning, as well as teaching at the University of Western Australia. He and Flora are now on a long trip, apparently around the world. They are to be in the United States (Philadelphia) in late March, and I presume in New York.

The present architect-planner in charge of the development of the capital city of Canberra, Peter Harrison, was here last year, and we had a good talk. He called my attention to the fact that my definition of the Regional City was just what they were creating at Canberra. This is "a constellation of moderate-sized communities, separated by great open areas, but bound closely together by townless highways."

I hope we will be able to see each other soon. Our affectionate greetings to you and Sophie.

Clarence S. Stein

1. This was the plan for large subdivision outside Adelaide, Australia.

---

526   To Benton MacKaye

[New York City]   August 14, 1967

Dear Ben:

I find a series of notes here. I don't know whether I phoned you about all of them, so I am writing them to you now that Wilma's here. I want to thank you for your many letters, and for the Greenbelt article.

Aline returned from Los Angeles last Tuesday. Since then we have been looking forward to visiting the farm, as we have not been able to do so for some time. We now expect to go tomorrow. The weather earlier was very hot and has been better the last couple of days, more like September than August.

Albert Mayer's book is out at last. In case you didn't get a notice, it's called *The Urgent Future: People—Housing—City—Region.*[1] I'm sending you a copy.

It's a splendid book. After a bird's-eye view of the present disorderly growth, it offers a program not only for building New Towns, but [for] relating them to the development of districts and regions and to the great green background of forest and field and wilderness. I hope that one of the universities may put it out in paperback soon, so that students can buy it more easily.[2]

I think that all other news of interest we covered in our phone talks.

Please give my best wishes to Mr. and Mrs. Barnes.

As ever,
Clarence S. Stein

1. Albert Mayer, *The Urgent Future: People—Housing—City—Region* (New York: McGraw-Hill, 1967).

2. At eighty-five Stein was still alert and engaged. (MacKaye was almost ninety.)

527 To Benton MacKaye

[New York City]   October 12, 1967

Dear Ben:

There was a meeting of the AIP at Washington last week, which I did not attend. On the last day they gave special Fiftieth Anniversary Awards. There were nine individuals so honored. One-third of them were members of our little association with the big name the Regional Planning Association of America: Lewis [Mumford], Catherine Bauer, and CSS. Not so bad for an organization that never had more than 16 members—in fact, many less than that who were active! I enclose a copy of my citation.

Your many letters with their detailed description of your writing and doings are fascinating reading. I am keeping them all, so I have quite a history of your doings over all these years since Charlie Whitaker brought us together at the Hudson Guild Farm.

Aline yesterday started rehearsing again at Lincoln Center. The first play in which she will act is to be in the small theater which is below the Vivian Beaumont, where she performed last year. She is enjoying it, although the rehearsals are long.

I have spent the day going over the minutes of our old Regional Planning Association of America, dating back to March 1923. Lots of pleasant recollections of old friends among others of our first meeting at the Hudson Guild Farm.

Albert Mayer comes here once a week, and we have a good hour's talk about planned development and that sort of thing. He is very active, largely as consultant, although he is also planning a New Town—no end of energy. This means he is traveling a good part of the week, all over the United States and in Puerto Rico. He is doing a fine and very useful job.

Aline joins me in affectionate greetings. Our best wishes to Lucy.

As ever,

Clarence S. Stein

528 To Lewis Mumford

[New York City]   October 22, 1967

Dear Lewis:

I am delighted that you are going to give a talk on the future of the American city. This is the time to speak, and no one can do it better or with more authority than you. It will be of immense value, just at this particular time. I want to review and rethink my own present ideas and put them in condensed form, and then if I come on anything of possible new value I will send it to you.

One suggestion (which I am sure is not necessary): emphasize above all the fact that the land must be owned by and continued in the ownership of the community; but what community? District? City? County? The more I think of the subject the more I feel that *no speculation* is the primary essential. Cities must set population limit; but how? As long as land is in private ownership, it is impossible. So the basic requirement is that which Ebenezer Howard recommended: all land MUST be community land, with long-term leases, but no sale, and so no speculation. (I return your clipping with thanks.)

Al Mansfeld, the able and brilliant architect of Israel, sent me a magazine devoted to his work in Israel, particularly in Jerusalem and Haifa. It has great strength and character. I wish I could go there again to see how the city has changed since I last visited.

Mansfeld's museum in Jerusalem is on the heights above the main part of the city. It consists of a group of small structures connected with each other, so that one gets some relief from endless series of exhibit halls. Years ago I made a lengthy study of museum design, in search of something that would be less exhausting than the long tramp through the Metropolitan and the like. I came to the conclusion that what we needed was to break the museum down into groups of modest-sized units with connecting arcades through outdoor gardens. . . . [Later] I found that they had built just that at Copenhagen.

Fond greetings to you and Sophie from Aline and

Clarence S. Stein

---

529   To Lewis Mumford

[New York City]   January 2, 1968

Dear Lewis:

Thanks for introducing me to Stewart Udall's *Agenda for Tomorrow.* Udall would have been a splendid addition to the RPAA as we were in the 1920s, while we were still a compact group, small enough in number to each offer an individual contribution to our outlook on the future.

You united our individual plans for the future into the farsighted report of the AIA Committee on Community Planning.

Cordially,
Clarence S. Stein

530 To Aline Stein

[New York City]   [Late 1968][1]

Aline dear:

Your many letters are delightful. They have given me much joy. That Jennie Mac could make such a long trip is wonderful. She is ageless. My love and admiration to her.

This is one these "typical" New York summer days—hot, hot, hot. But here in 12A it is pleasant, even without turning on the air [conditioning].

Your letters and the colored photos give me some idea of the brilliant flags of Betty [DeMars]. They are superb and I believe unique. The building by Vernon was roughly there when I was last in California. But it needed the glowing colors that the DeMars have contributed. My affectionate admiration to them. I will write to them.

This evening I am dining with Arthur and Lillie. Tomorrow I will invite them and Gertrude. Otherwise, I have not been very social, even though Thursday I expect to lunch with Robert Simon, who lost his control of [the New Town of] Reston to a money-making insurance company. John Morgan, who lives there, is full of admiration for Simon and his devotion to Reston and all he did for its inhabitants.

And now I must take a nap—so Mrs. James tells me. She is now preparing for all my needs. More like an Englishman's man than anyone I have known.

So that she can mail this when she goes, I will stop here.

All my love

Clarence

1. Stein's letters and notes, especially to Lewis Mumford, continued well into the early 1970s, when he entered his tenth decade. They dealt mostly with personal matters. His lifelong written commentary on matters urban and architectural came to a quiet close in the late 1960s.

112. Clarence Stein and Albert Mayer
at A Thousand Years (c. 1961).

113. Clarence Stein from his apartment overlooking Central Park
(1965).

APPENDIXES

APPENDIX A

Chronology

---

19 June 1882   Clarence Samuel Stein was born in Rochester, N.Y., the third child of Leo Samuel and Rose Rosenblatt Stein. His father, Samuel Stein, was an officer in the National Casket Company, the second generation in this business. His mother, originally from New York City, was active in educational and community activities. His brothers were William and Herbert; his sisters were Clara (d. at sixteen months), Gertrude, and Lillian.

1890   The Stein family moves to New York City, West Side, Thirty-second St. (Chelsea), where Clarence is enrolled as a tuition-paying day student in the Workingman's School of Felix Adler's Ethical Culture Society.

1897+   Summer vacation at Margaretville, N.Y.

1900–1902   Clarence works in the National Casket Company, where his father is now president.

1903   During a summer trip to Europe with his father, they visit Italy, Switzerland, Germany, France, and England.

1903–5   Active member of the Young Men's Municipal Club, a reform group organized by John Elliott of the Ethical Culture Society.

1904–5   While a student for one year at the School of Architecture at Columbia University, Clarence decides to study interior decoration at the École des Beaux Arts in Paris. His father agrees to pay for professional education.

July 1905   Arrives in Paris to prepare for entering the École. Fails first entrance exam in December 1905.

1906   Begins classes in French and architectural history and continues separate lessons in drawing and modeling.

1907   Passes entrance exam with Eli Jacques Kahn, who had arrived in Paris that summer after graduating from the Columbia School of Architecture. Clarence enters the atelier of M. Laloux.

1907–11   Many sketching trips with Henry Klaber (his roommate in Paris) and Eli Jacques Kahn to France, Germany, England, Italy, and Spain.

1910   Decides not to complete work for the diploma of the École, but to continue to study architectural design at an advanced level.

1911   Returns to New York City and in September joins the firm of Goodhue, Cram, and Ferguson, working in Bertram Goodhue's office in New York City. Takes up civic reform work again with Elliott at the Hudson Guild in Chelsea.

1912–18   In the office of Bertram Grosvenor Goodhue; projects include the San Diego Exposition and the copper mining New Town of Tyrone, New Mexico. Clarence Stein writes an essay on designs of the San Diego Exposition and St. Bartholomew's and St. Thomas churches (New York City). Continues work with City Club "reform" projects.

1915–19   Secretary, City Planning Committee of the City Club of New York City. Active in city politics. Supports candidacy of Al Smith for city and state offices. Continues to write for the *Journal of the American Institute of Architects.* Participates with Henry Klaber in survey of Chelsea district.

1918   Leaves office of Bertram Grosvenor Goodhue to serve briefly as a lieutenant in the Army Corps of Engineers. Nearly fails the medical examination because "underweight." First discusses with Charles Whitaker a model housing law and writes an article on postwar reconstruction for the *AIA Journal.*

1919   Joins Robert D. Kohn, Charles Butler, and Frank Vitolo as "Architects Associates," a cooperative architectural practice. Stein is listed as especially experienced in industrial housing, village planning, ecclesiastical work, and decoration. Serves on Governor Smith's Reconstruction Committee of the State of New York and as secretary of its Housing Subcommittee.

1920   Candidate for vice president on the Independent ticket with Alfred Smith as the presidential candidate. Designs Hudson Guild Farm and dining hall at Netcong, N.J., for the Ethical Culture Society.

1921   Introduced to Benton MacKaye by Charles Whitaker. Writes introduction for MacKaye's article in the AIA journal calling for the creation of the Appalachian Trail. Appointed associate editor of the *Journal of the American Institute of Architects* and chairman of the Community Planning Committee of the AIA. Designs the White Plains Meeting House of the Ethical Culture Society.

1922   First meets Aline MacMahon, New York City actress, and the young literary social critic, Lewis Mumford. Marks his fortieth birthday and, in the summer, takes a trip to Holland. Studies housing policies and projects with Ernest Gruensfeldt and works with Charles Whitaker as assistant editor of the *Journal of the American Institute of Architects*. On the return voyage, Stein outlines a proposal for a "city planning atelier": meetings, membership, purpose, projects. Designs residence for Paul Rie with Ernest Gruensfeldt. Stein begins to write a book on New York City (fiction); finishes two chapters and a sketch of a play based on the story.

1923   The Regional Planning Association of America is formed with twelve charter members: Alexander Bing (chairman), Clarence Stein (treasurer), Robert Kohn, Charles Whitaker, Lewis Mumford, Benton MacKaye, Stuart Chase, Henry Wright, and New York architects John Bright and Sullivan Jones. Patrick Geddes visits the United States to meet with Lewis Mumford and Clarence Stein at the New School; spends weekends at Hudson Guild Farm in Netcong, N.J., with RPAA members to discuss regional planning. Stein is appointed chairman of the New York State Housing and Regional Planning Commission by Governor Al Smith; Stein, Wright, and Bing complete the pre-Sunnyside report, "A Proposed Garden Community in the New York City Region."

1924   With Henry Wright, visits Letchworth and Welwyn Garden Cities and their founder Ebenezer Howard in England and Raymond Unwin at Hampstead Garden Suburb. Bing establishes the City Housing Corporation, which purchases land in the Bronx and starts construction of Sunnyside Gardens, an experimental low-density project of twelve hundred houses with shared inner courtyards designed by Stein and Wright.

1925   Elected vice president of the International Garden City Planning Federation, predecessor of the International Federation of Housing and Town Planning (IFHTP), which holds its first U.S. meeting in New York City. IFHTP tour includes first houses at Sunnyside. Howard, Unwin, and others participate in a weekend "extra session" at the Hudson Guild Farm. Mumford, Chase, Stein, Wright, Bing, and MacKaye write a special issue on cities and regional planning for the *Survey Graphic*.

1926   Travels to Mexico, continues work on Sunnyside, and begins his serious courtship of Aline MacMahon. He and Henry Wright, with editorial help from Lewis Mumford, prepare and publish the landmark study of regional planning for New York State. It includes a "sketch plan" for future state development, which applies the idea of the "regional city of the RPAA to the state."

1927   Performs extensive nonhousing architectural work. The most important commissions are a library and classroom building for the California Institute of Technology and the first building of the Fieldston School, the Ethical Culture Society's new school in Riverdale, N.Y. Travels to Turkey and Russia to study community and regional planning and starts studies with Wright and Ackerman and Ralph Eberlin for building an American community of twenty-five thousand on a site purchased in the Saddle River Valley at Fairlawn, N.J.

1928   On March 27, Aline MacMahon and Clarence Stein marry. He had first proposed to her in 1925, shortly after his sisters introduced them. The Sunnyside project is completed and rented. It is a commercial and urban planning success of great importance. Stein, Wright, Ackerman, and Bing work on a detailed layout and housing plans for Radburn, N.J., intended to be the first large-scale Garden City in the United States, but Bing does not secure all of the land needed for a full New Town, in spite of the urging of his associates. Clarence Stein starts work, with Robert Kohn and Charles Butler, on designs for Temple Emanu-El, to be built at Park Avenue and Seventy-first Street.

1929   On 29 May, Radburn's first occupants move in (five months before the Wall Street Crash in October). Stein, Wright, and Ackerman continue work on site plans and house plans for new sections of Radburn and start their first work designs for a Pittsburgh housing project for the Buell Foundation—housing for "clerical workers," soon to be named Chatham Village.

1930   Work on site planning and housing layout for Chatham continues, as does design work for Radburn houses with Ackerman and Wright.

1931   Designs Phipps Garden Apartments with Henry Wright; construction begins. Does consulting work at Chatham Village with Henry Wright. Stein and Mumford organize and produce a summer Institute on Regionalism at the University of Virginia; FDR is present, and the concept of the TVA is discussed. Aline Stein moves to Hollywood to work on films with Warner Brothers; Mother Stein dies in spring; Aline's father dies in September. Catherine Bauer focuses the RPAA as its executive secretary.

1932   Clarence Stein designs Wasser House at a cost estimated at $25,000; makes plans for the Princeton University Museum. Aline Stein takes "The Casa," a house in California, and acts in the films *The Mouthpiece* and *Week End Marriage.* Clarence Stein meets Archibald MacLeish in April and discusses Neutra House.

1933   Clarence Stein's office receives a $15,000 retainer for the Hillside Homes project in the Bronx.

1935   Works on designs for Wichita Art Institute, Rose Walter Cottage, and Hillside Homes; continues plans for Princeton University Museum; planning consultant for Greenbelt, Md., Greendale, Wis., and Greenhills, Ohio. Travels to China from December 1935 through July 1936.

1936   Designs house for sister Gertrude. First serious bout with depression; hospitalized for several months.

1937 Steins purchase "A Thousand Years," summer retreat on Journey's End Road, Yorktown, N.Y., in Westchester County.

1938 Becomes president of Civic Films, Inc.; first meetings with Robert Alexander, Reginald Johnson, Wilson, and Merrill as consultant on Baldwin Hills community housing in September and in California again in December as consultant on public housing designs in Los Angeles at Long Beach; designs Asian style house at "A Thousand Years" for Aline's birthday present.

1939 Civic Films produces *The City*, with music by Aaron Copland and a script by Lewis Mumford. Father Stein dies.

1941 Works on Baldwin Hills Village and Harbor Hills defense housing (Los Angeles), three defense housing projects in Pittsburgh, and the Museum of Costume Art; Gold Medal from New York Chapter of the American Institute of Architects for apartment housing; award for distinguished work with low-cost housing.

1942 Moves to Silver Hill sanatorium to recover from depression; then to a guest ranch in Tucson, Ariz., with his sister Lillie Mayer.

1947 Travels to Sweden with Aline. Meets Sven Markelius, Yngve Larsson, J. H. Martin, and Gorän Sidenbladh.

1948 Reorganizes RPAA; becomes president of the Regional Development Council of America (RDCA).

1949 Plans with Nowicki for Columbus Circle, New York City. Travels to England and Germany.

1950 Travels to Europe with Aline.

1951 Publishes *Toward New Towns for America;* is planning director and coordinator for the New Town, Kitimat, British Columbia, for Aluminum Company of North American (ALCAN); *Town Planning Review* articles (through 1952).

1955 Receives award for *Toward New Towns for America* from American Society of Planning Officials.

1956 Receives Gold Medal of the American Institute of Architects.

1959 Visits Nazareth, New Town in Israel; travels to Paris, Rome, Athens, Istanbul, Tehran, Shiraz, Isfahan, Tel-Aviv, Beer Sheeba, Nazareth, and Haifa.

1960 Receives Ebenezer Howard Memorial Award; travels to London, Athens, Marosi, Rhodes, Crete, Delphi, Copenhagen, and Stockholm.

1962 Travels to Scotland, London, Paris, Denmark, and Sweden.

1963 Travels to Paris and Arnheim for International Federation of Housing and Planning.

1965   Receives Distinguished Service Award from New York Home Builders Association.

1966   Travels to Geneva and Ireland.

1967   Receives Andrew J. Thomas Award from the New York Chapter of the American Institute of Architects and the 50th Anniversary Design Award (for design of Sunnyside and Radburn) from the AIA. Travels to Paris, Brussels, and London.

1968   Plans to give his papers to Cornell University. Travels to San Francisco.

1969   Travels to London, Switzerland, and Los Angeles.

1970   Travels to Paris and Spain.

1975   Dies on 7 February.

APPENDIX B

Architectural, Planning, and Housing Projects

Date	Project Name	Place	Associates
1921	White Plains Meeting House	White Plains, N.Y.	None
1921–23	Hudson Guild Farm camp buildings	Netcong, N.J.	None
1922–24	National Casket Company (office & facility design & renovation)	New York City, Brooklyn, Newark, White Plains, Long Island City	None
1922	William Pollack House	Netcong, N.J.	None
1922	Paul A. Rie House	Port Washington, Long Island	Ernest Gruensfeldt, Architect
1923	Edwin Wasser House	Riverdale on Hudson, N.Y.	
1924	Sunnyside Gardens (community design, block layouts, & housing design)	Long Island City, N.Y.	Henry Wright, Architect; Frederick L. Ackerman, Architect

COMPLETED PROJECTS

Date	Project Name	Place	Associates
1926	Park West Hospital	New York City	Charles Butler, Architect
1926–28 & 1932	Fieldston High & Lower School	Riverdale, N.Y.	Robert D. Kohn, Architect
1926–28	Old People's Home	New York City	None
1927–29	California Institute of Technology, Chemistry Building Annex	Pasadena, Calif.	Mayers, Murray & Phillips, Architects
1927	Lavanburg Homes	Goerck Street, New York City	Stein, Planning Consultant Charles Butler, Architect; Frank E. Vitolo, Architect
1928	Midtown Hospital	New York City	
1929	Michigan Boulevard Garden Apartments	Chicago, Ill.	Stein, Consultant in Association with Henry Wright
1929	Radburn (town design, housing	Fairlawn, N.J.	Henry Wright; Frederick Ackerman; Andrew J. Thomas; James Renwick Thomson; Marjorie Sewell Cautley, Landscape Architect
1930	Temple Emanu-El	New York City	Robert D. Kohn; Charles Butler
1931	Hudson Guild Farm	Netcong, N.J.	None
1931 & 1936	Phipps Garden Apartments	Long Island City, N.Y.	Marjorie Sewell Cautley, Landscape Architect
1932–35	Chatham Village (community & layout)	Pittsburgh, Pa.	Henry Wright, Consultant; Ingham & Boyd, Architects
1935	Hillside Homes	Bronx, N.Y.	Marjorie Sewell Cautley, Landscape Architect
1935	Wichita Art Institute	Wichita, Kans.	None

COMPLETED PROJECTS

Date	Project Name	Place	Associates
1935–38	Greenbelt New Community	Maryland	Stein, Consultant to Resettlement Administration; Douglas D. Ellington, Architect; R. J. Wadsworth, Architect; Hale Walker, Town Planner
1938	Hill House at "1,000 Years"	Croton, N.Y.	None
1939	Carmelitos Housing Project	North Long Beach, Calif.	Stein, Architectural and Site Planning Consultant
1939	Temple of Religion, New York World's Fair	New York City	Alfred E. Poor, Architect; Oliver Reagan, Architect
1940	Harbor Hills Housing Project	San Pedro, Calif.	Stein, Architectural and Site Planning Consultant
1941	Baldwin Hills	Los Angeles, Calif.	Stein, Architectural and Site Layout Consultant; Reginald D. Johnson, Wilson, Merrill, & Alexander Architects
1941	Fort Green Houses (Public Housing)	Brooklyn, N.Y.	Clarence Stein, Chief Architect; Charles Butler, Architect; Henry S. Churchill Architect; Robert D. Kohn, Architect
1941	Indian Head Prototype Defense Housing	Maryland	None
1941	Shaler Township Defense Housing	Allegheny County, Pa.	Charles & Edward Stotz, Architects
1941	Stowe Township Defense Housing	Allegheny County, Pa.	Charles & Edward Stotz, Architects

COMPLETED PROJECTS

Date	Project Name	Place	Associates
1950	Stevenage Town Center	Stevenage, England	Stein, Consultant; Gordon Stephenson, Town Planner
1951	Kitimat New Town	British Columbia, Canada	Stein, Coordinator & Director of Planning; Albert Mayer, Architect; Julian Whittlesey, Town Planner
Unknown	Jefferson Trust Company	Hoboken, N.J.	None

PROPOSED PROJECTS NOT BUILT

Date	Project Name	Place	Associates
1923	Spuyten Duyvil Housing Development	New York City	None
1927–35	Pasadena Art Institute	Pasadena, Calif.	None
1930–35	Princeton Museum	Princeton, N.J.	None
1933	Housing Development Planning	Milwaukee, Wis.	None
1933	San Francisco Housing Surveys	San Francisco, Calif.	None
1933	Valley Stream Housing	Long Island, N.Y.	Frank Vitolo, Architect
1941	Clariton Defense Housing	Allegheny County, Pa.	Charles & Edward Stotz, Architects
1943	Maplewood Housing Project	Lake Charles, La.	None
1944	Fresh Meadows Park	Long Island, N.Y.	None
1944	Gary Land Company	Gary, Ind.	None

PROPOSED PROJECTS NOT BUILT

Date	Project Name	Place	Associates
1949	Columbus Circle	New York City	Matthew Nowicki, Architect
1949	Temple Beth-El	Rochester, N.Y.	None
1950	Chandigarh: New Provincial Capital	Chandigarh, Punjab, India	Stein, Town Planning Consultant; Albert Mayer, Town Planner; Matthew Nowicki, Architect; built to plans of Le Corbusier and Pierre Jeanneret
1951–52	Stanford University	Stanford, Calif.	None
1954–55	Oakland Housing	Near Pontiac, Mich.	Mayer & Whittlesey, Architects

PROJECTS DIRECTED BY BERTRAM G. GOODHUE

Date	Project Name	Place
1911–18	California State Building	San Diego, Calif.
1911–18	Plan for the San Diego Exposition	San Diego, Calif.
1911–18	George Washington Hotel	Colon, Panama
1911–18	St. Bartholomew's Church	New York, N.Y.
1914–18	Town of Tyrone, for Phelps-Dodge Corporation	New Mexico
1917	Marine Corps Base	San Diego, Calif.
1917	Naval Air Base	San Diego, Calif.

Sir (Leslie) Patrick Abercrombie (1879–1957). British architect and town planner. University of Liverpool, lecturer and studio instructor (1915–35); University College, London, professor of town planning (1935–46). Editor, *Town Planning Review.* Architect, London County Council; Minister of Works (1942–52). Prepared post–World War II schemes for rebuilding London with J. H. Foreshaw: *The County of London Plan* (1943) and *The Greater London Plan* (1944) proposed the construction of satellite towns as part of the policy for planned dispersion of London's population and rebuilding of the inner city. Prepared plans for many British cities, including Plymouth and Hull. C. S. Stein and his friend Lewis Mumford were keen observers and friendly critics of the *Greater London Plan.*

Frederick Lee Ackerman (1878–1950). Architect. Born in upstate New York and educated at Cornell University (B.Arch. 1909). One of the first architects to recognize fully the social responsibilities and economic factors in architecture. Worked in Washington during World War I with Robert Kohn, designing and building housing for shipyard workers. Proposed an expanded program of federal construction of workers' housing after World War I known as the Ackerman Program. Collaborated with Charles Whitaker to write on European housing in the *Journal of the American Institute of Architects* (September 1917 to February 1918). A follower of the ideas of Thorstein Veblen and active in the technocracy movement in the early 1930s. With Stuart Chase, Charles Whitaker, and others, Ackerman founded the discussion group Technical Alliance, a precursor of Stein's Regional Planning Association of America. Architectural practice, New York City (1910–50). Chair of the New York City Housing Authority (1933–38). Close friend of C. S. Stein and architect of many housing units at Sunnyside and Radburn.

Thomas Adams (1871–1940). Pragmatic conservative British, Canadian, and American town planner. Born in Edinburgh. Educated at Daniel Stewart's College. Chairman, Young Scots Society. Journalist. First Secretary of the Garden City Association (1901–6). Secretary, First Garden City Company (1903–6). Planning consultant: British Garden City Suburbs associated with Mawson and Lutyens (1906–14). An organizer and first president of the British Town Planning Institute (1913–14). Town Planning advisor to Canada's Commission on Conservation (1914–20). Consultant, Advisory Group of Planners, Regional Plan of New York 1921–23; General Director of Plans and Surveys, RPNY, 1923–39. An organizer of the Town Planning Institute of Canada. With John Nolen, Frederick Law Olmsted, Jr., George B. Ford, and Nelson Lewis, Adams organized the American City Planning Institute (1917), which became the American Institute of Planners (1938). Editor and principal author, *Regional Plan of New York and Its Environs* (1929), which included a general satellite New Town proposal and noted Radburn as an exemplar; consultant to the Regional Plan of New York (1930–33); faculty member, School of Planning, Harvard University; lecturer in civic design, Massachusetts Institute of Technology (1930–38). Author: *Rural Planning and Development* (1917), *Recent Advances in Town Planning* (1932), *Outline of Town and City Planning* (1935).

Felix Adler (1851–1933). Religious leader and educator. Born in Alzey in the Rhineland. Received undergraduate degree at Columbia College and a Ph.D. in Berlin and Heidelberg. Founded the Society for Ethical Culture (1876) and the Workingman's School of the Ethical Culture Society (1878), where art, crafts, and moral instruction were valued and where Clarence Stein was a student from 1890 to 1901. Established the first kindergarten in New York City and several secular New York community organizations, including the Hudson Guild Settlement House and the City Club. Active in the New York City reform movement and in housing reform. Author: *An Ethical Philosophy of Life* (1918) and *The Reconstruction of the Spiritual Ideal* (1924).

Robert Evans Alexander (1907–92). Architect and city planner. Born in southern California. Educated at Cornell University (B.Arch. 1929). Associate of Richard Neutra in the mid-1930s, worked with Clarence Stein on the FHA-insured rental project Baldwin Hills Village (1938–42). Architectural practice in California (1930–90): defense housing, Los Angeles Hall of Records, and Bunker Hill Residential Towers, Los Angeles. Active in Los Angeles City Planning Department (1946–70). Prepared master plan for the campus of the University of California, San Diego (1951).

Charles Stern Ascher (1899–1978). Lawyer and public administrator. Born in New York City and educated at the Ethical Culture School and Columbia University. Employed by Alexander Bing in 1924 to develop covenants for the open space and community associations of Sunnyside and Radburn and to acquire land for Radburn. Junior member of the RPAA (1924–33). Secretary and general counsel for City Housing Corporation, New York City. Executive director for National Housing Agency. Professor of political science, Brooklyn College, City University of New York (CUNY) (1948–69). Director of Citizen's Housing and Planning Council in New York City. Author of *Better Cities, Better America* (1942); co-author of *Urban Redevelopment: Problems and Practices* (1953).

Tracy Baldwin Augur (1896–1974). Landscape architect and city planner. Studied at Cornell (B.L.A. 1917) and Harvard (M.L.A. 1921). Planning consultant, New York City (1922–23). Practice in landscape architecture, Detroit (1928–33). Principal planner for the Tennessee Valley Authority (1933–48). U.S. National Security Resources Board (1949–52). Developed plans for dispersion of essential federal government workers from Washington, D.C. Planner in the Urban Renewal Administration of the Housing and Home Finance Agency (1953–64).

Edward Murray Bassett (1863–1948). Lawyer and zoning consultant. Born in Brooklyn, New York. Educated at Amherst College, Columbia University, Hamilton College, and Harvard University. Practiced law in Buffalo and New York City. Chaired New York City Commission on Building Districts and Restrictions, which prepared the first zoning ordinance (1916). Appointed by Secretary Hoover as a member of the Advisory Committee on Zoning, Department of Commerce. President of the National Conference on City Planning (1928–29). Author of *Zoning* (1936) and *The Master Plan* (1938). C. S. Stein and his associates were opposed to Bassett's conservative, strictly regulatory approach to city planning and zoning.

Catherine Krouse Bauer. See Catherine Bauer Wurster

Walter Curt Behrendt (1884–1945). Architect and author. Born in Metz and educated at the Technische Hochschule at Berlin-Charlottenburg and at the Universities of Berlin and Munich. Architectural advisor to minister of finance in Prussia. Wrote articles on German town planning for Whitaker's *Journal of the AIA* in the 1920s. Came to the United States in 1934 under sponsorship of C. S. Stein and Lewis Mumford. Held position as the technical director of the City Planning Association of Buffalo, New York. Lecturer at Dartmouth College. Professor of city planning and housing at the University of Buffalo. Author of *Modern Building* (1937)

Aline Bernstein (1882–1955). Scenic and costume designer and author. Born in New York City and educated at Hunter College and the New York School for Applied Design. Set designer of many Broadway plays and musicals. Taught costume and set design at Hunter College and Vassar. Set and costume designer, Henry Street Settlement House and Neighborhood Playhouse. Helped organize and became first female member of the Scene Designers' Union. Co-founder of the Museum of Costume Art (1937) and president after 1946, when it became the Costume Institute of the Metropolitan Museum of Art. Now and then friend, companion, and patron of novelist Thomas Wolfe from 1925 to 1935. Close friend of Aline MacMahon Stein and C. S. Stein.

Frederick Bigger (1880–1963). Architect, town planner. Born in Pittsburgh, Pennsylvania. Educated at University of Pennsylvania. Practiced architecture in Seattle (1908–11); city planning and housing in Philadelphia (1911–13); consultant on public housing projects, Cleveland, Ohio, and Pittsburgh, Pennsylvania (1918–35). Chief of planning staff, suburban division, Resettlement Administration (1935–36). Worked with C. S. Stein as consultant on Greenbelt Town planning and design (1935). Urban planning advisor to Federal Housing

Administration (1945–50). Principal author: *Handbook on Urban Redevelopment* (1941). Member and chairman, Pittsburgh City Planning Commission; staff, National Capital Planning Commission.

Alexander Bing (1878–1959). Lawyer, real estate. Born in New York City and educated in the Ethical Culture Schools (classmate of Stein's) and Columbia University. Developer with his brother, Leo Bing; Bing and Bing developed major apartment and hotel projects on Fifth Avenue in New York City (1908–17). Negotiator, U.S. Department of Labor (1917–19). Founder and chief executive officer of the City Housing Corporation, which built Sunnyside, Queens, and Radburn, New Jersey (1922–36).

Russell Van Nest Black (1893–1969). Planner, landscape architect, environmentalist, civil engineer. Graduated from Cornell University (B.L.A. 1916). Director of Bay Counties (San Francisco) Regional Plan (1923). Director of plans and surveys, Philadelphia Regional Plan (1925–29). Vice president and president of the American Institute of Planners (1933–37). Consultant to the New York, New Jersey, Pennsylvania, and Virginia state planning boards. Pioneer in state and metropolitan planning.

Ernest Bohn (1901–75). Lawyer, liberal Republican politician, and university lecturer. Born in Austria-Hungary and educated at Adelbert College and Western Reserve University. Member of Cleveland City Council, active in development of city, state, and regional planning and housing legislation, including the Ohio Housing Authority Law (1933). Organized the Regional Association of Cleveland (1934–65). Active in national housing legislation as the first president of the National Association of Housing Officials; major lobbyist for the Housing Act of 1937 and subsequent national housing and urban redevelopment legislation (Housing Acts of 1949 and 1954). Director, Cleveland Metropolitan Housing Authority (1937–62). With Clarence Stein and Catherine Bauer, effectively lobbied Congress to prevent federal government from selling FDR's three Greenbelt Towns to speculative buyers. Taught planning and housing at Case-Western Reserve University (1963–73).

D. Knickerbacker Boyd (1872–1944). Architect. Born in Philadelphia and educated at the Academy of Fine Arts, Spring Garden Institute (Philadelphia), and the University of Pennsylvania. With Ingram, architectural practice in Pittsburgh (1920–50). Designed houses at Chatham Village, where Stein and Henry Wright consulted on site layout. Designer of many Carnegie Library buildings, schools, and suburban homes. Served as a consultant on housing and labor relations for the U.S. Public Housing Administration.

Louis Brownlow (1879–1963). Journalist and public administrator. Born in Buffalo, Missouri, and educated at American University and Syracuse University. City manager for Petersburg, Virginia, and Knoxville, Tennessee. Visiting professor at the University of Chicago, Washington University, and Syracuse University. Author of *The President and the Presidency* (1949), *Passion for Politics* (1955), and *A Passion for Anonymity* (1958). Associated with C. S. Stein and Alexander Bing as municipal government consultant for planning of Radburn, New Jersey.

Charles Butler (1871–1953). Architect. Educated at the École des Beaux Arts in Paris. Worked in the Shipping Board's housing division with Frederick Ackerman, Henry Wright, and Robert Kohn. Worked in architectural practice in New York City in association with Clarence Stein and Robert Kohn (1919–53). Designed Department of the Interior, Washington, D.C. (1928); Temple Beth-El, New York City (with Kohn and Stein, 1920), and Ethical Culture Society, New York City (with Kohn, 1922).

George Cadbury (1839–1922). British chocolate manufacturer and social reformer. Builder of Bournville, one of the first modern British Garden City suburbs, outside Birmingham in 1880. C. S. Stein visited and admired Bournville in 1911 when he was a student at the École des Beaux Arts. Cadbury actively supported national legislation for old age pensions and worked to eliminate bad working conditions.

Marjorie S. Cautley (1891–1954). Landscape architect. Educated at Cornell (B.L.A. 1922). Prepared landscape plans (working with Clarence Stein) for Sunnyside (1925), Radburn (1928–30), Hillside Homes (1932), and Phipps Garden Apartments (1931). Author of *Building a House in Sweden* (1931) and *Garden Design* (1935).

Stuart Chase (1888–1977). Accountant-economist, writer. "Junior" member of New Deal Brain Trust (1933–40). Studied at MIT and Harvard (B.A. 1910). Investigated meat packing industry in Chicago and Washington for Federal Trade Commission (1917–20). Research economist, Labor Bureau, New York City (1922–39). Associated with Regional Planning Association of America. Consultant to Resettlement Administration (1935), Rexford Tugwell (1935–40), Securities Exchange Commission (1939), TVA (1940–41). Author: *A Tragedy of Waste* (1925), *Man and Machines* (1929), *Soviet Russia in the Second Decade* (1928), *Mexico: A Study of Two Americas* (1931), *A New Deal* (1932) (which outlined a progressive economic policy that drew extensively on the theories of John Maynard Keynes), *Rich Land, Poor Land* (1936), *The Road We Are Traveling* (1941), *The Proper Study of Mankind* (1948).

Henry Stern Churchill (1893–1962). City planner and architect. Born in Chicago and educated at Cornell University (B.Arch. 1916). Architectural practice in New York City (1918–53). Worked with Henry Wright, Alan Kamstra, and Albert Mayer under Tugwell's New Deal Resettlement Administration (1935) on the Greenbelt Town project of Greenbrook, New Jersey (not built). Practiced architecture and planning in New York City. Helped Henry Wright and Catherine Bauer organize the Housing Study Guild (1934). Lecturer at Columbia, MIT, and Harvard. Author of *The City Is the People* (1945).

Miles Lanier Colean (1898–1980). Economist and consultant. Born in Peoria, Illinois, and educated at University of Wisconsin and Columbia University. Interested in the financial and economic aspects of housing and planning. Editorial adviser for *Architectural Forum, House and Home,* and *House Beautiful* magazines. Author: *Can America Build Houses?* (1938), *Stabilizing the Construction Industry* (1945), *Renewing Our Cities* (1953), and *A Backward Glance, an Oral History: The Growth of Government Housing Policy in the United States* (1978).

Le Corbusier, pseudonym of **Charles Édouard Jeanneret** (1887–1965). Architect, architectural and planning theorist. Born in France and educated at Federal Polytechnique in Zurich. Designed many seminal buildings in the development of the International Style. Plans for cities of Buenos Aires, Stockholm, Antwerp, Algiers, Nemours, Chandigarh, and others. Consultant for city planning to numerous governments. Author: *Toward a New Architecture* (1922) and many others.

Vernon DeMars (1920–   ). Architect and professor at School of Architecture, University of California, Berkeley. Authority on row-house design and design of row-house communities. Architect of farm workers' housing for Resettlement Administration (1935–40), Easter Hill planned unit development (1955).

Earle Sumner Draper, Sr. (1893–1993). City planner. B.S. in landscape architecture, Massachusetts State College (1915). Worked with city planner John Nolen as southern representative, where he planned Kingsport, Tennessee. Planner of industrial towns, parks, universities, schools, private estates, golf courses, land subdivisions. Planning director for the Tennessee Valley Authority (1933–39); planning and construction of the town of Norris, rural freeways, powerhouses, and dams; worked with Benton MacKaye on TVA's regional planning program. Assistant administrator of Federal Housing Administration (1940), later deputy commissioner.

Ralph Eberlin. Civil engineer. Longtime friend and associate of Stein's. Worked with Stein and Wright on Sunnyside Homes and Radburn (1925–30). Administrator in the Federal Public Housing Administration. Assisted by Stein at Federal Works Administration (FWA) on program of defense housing (1941–43).

Otto Mark Eidlitz (1860–1928). Architect, builder. Born in New York and educated at Cornell University. Involved in housing issues in Washington, D.C. Served as chairman of the World War I Committee on Housing for Industrial War Workers and as director of the Bureau of Housing and Transportation for the Department of Labor.

Sergei Eisenstein (1898–1948). Film director. Born in Riga, Latvia. Studied engineering and architecture at Riga and Japanese at Moscow University. Pioneer in cinematography; completed six films. In 1930, he directed *Que Viva Mexico!* in Mexico and Hollywood. Upton Sinclair backed this film, which was never released. Taught at the Institute of Cinematography. Developed a body of theory relating to the creative process and film aesthetics. Loyal to the idea of a new society. Films include *Strike* (1924), *Potemkin* (1925), *October* (1928), *Alexander Nevsky* (1938).

John Lovejoy Elliott (1868–1942). Ethical Culture Society leader and social worker. Born in Princeton, Illinois. Undergraduate education at Cornell University (B.A. 1892) and Ph.D. at the University of Halle in Germany (1894). Assistant to Felix Adler and innovative teacher at the Ethical Culture Society's Workingman's School (1894–1932). Stein valued his association with Elliott as his teacher and as a fellow student of reform politics in New York City. A pioneer in New York City settlement work, Elliott founded the Hudson Guild, a settlement house in the Chelsea district of Manhattan's west side. Its purpose was to develop the latent social power in working-class men and women. Was co-founder of the City Club. Leader of the Society for Ethical Culture after Adler's death in 1933.

Carl Feiss (1907–). Educator, city planner, and consultant on historic preservation. Born in Cleveland, Ohio. Bachelor of Fine Arts from the University of Pennsylvania (1931); Master of City Planning, Massachusetts Institute of Technology (1938). Studied at the Cranbrook Academy of Art under Eliel Saarinen (1932–35). Taught city planning at Columbia University with Raymond Unwin (1936–38). U.S. Housing Agency (1938–39). Consultant, National Resources Planning Board; Virginia State Planning Board (1940–41). Dean of the College of Architecture, University of Colorado at Denver (1939–43). Director of City Planning Commission, Denver, Colorado (1942–44). Chief of Planning and Engineering Branch, Division of Slum Clearance and Urban Renewal, Housing and Home Finance Agency (1950–55). Consultant, urban redevelopment, housing and historic preservation planning (1954–72). Professor of urban and regional planning and department chair, University of Florida, Gainesville (1971–83). Author and technical editor, *With a Heritage So Rich* (1966); co-author: *Historic Savannah* (1968).

George Burdett Ford (1879–1930). Architect and city planner. Born in Clinton, Massachusetts, and educated at Harvard University, MIT, and the École des Beaux Arts. A leading figure in the early "city planning movement" in the United States. Served as a consultant to the American, French, and Philippine governments. Head of the Reconstruction Bureau of the American Red Cross for the United States. In France in 1917. Founded the magazine *City Planning*. Columbia University lecturer; Harvard instructor in social ethics. Advocated architectural control for all new buildings. Director of the New York Regional Plan (1928). Author: *The Housing Problem* (1911); *Out of the Ruins* (1919); *Urbanisme en Practique* (1920); *Building Height, Bulk and Form* (1931).

Patrick Geddes (1854–1932). Scottish biologist, sociologist, regionalist, and town planner. Born in Perth, Scotland. Student of Huxley and "Lewis Mumford's master." Professor, University College, Dundee. Stressed the use of diagnostic survey in regional planning. Organizer of the "Cities Exhibition" (1896–1914). Founding father of city and regional planning and environmentalism. Established the Outlook Tower at Edinburgh's Castle Hill as an instrument for regional survey; practiced "conservative surgery" on the slums of old Edinburgh. Valued field work and civic action. Held the Chair of Civics and Sociology at Bombay University. Prepared city plans for Dunfirmline, Scotland; Dublin; Hebrew University, Jerusalem; and many Indian towns. Author: *City Development* (1904); *Cities in Evolution* (1915).

Henry George (1839–97). Economist and founder of the single-tax movement. Born in Philadelphia. Developed the theory that the existence and growth of a community made land valuable but benefited only a few individuals who owned land; that "a single tax on land would reduce the negative effects of the resulting unearned increment in land value." *Our Land and Land Policy* (1871) and *Progress and Poverty* (1879) presented his theories and had a wide readership. Moved to New York (1880); lectured, wrote, and entered politics. As Reform candidate for mayor (1886), ran ahead of Republican Theodore Roosevelt. Influenced local property tax policy in Australia, New Zealand, Canada, and the United States. Influenced the ideas of many intellectuals, reformers, and politicians, including Ebenezer Howard, Clarence Stein, and the RPAA.

Arthur Glikson (1911–66). Architect. Born in Königsberg. Educated at Technische Hochschule at Berlin-Charlottenburg. Emigrated to Israel in 1935. Served as the director of the Planning Department of the Housing Division, Ministry of Labour of Israel, and was a senior (guest) lecturer on national and regional planning at the Hebrew Institute of Technology at Haifa. Dealt with problems of settlement and consolidation after colonization and during intense periods of immigration. Interested in the tensions between economic and physical planning. Supervised regional and New Town planning and settlement policy for Israel. Intellectual correspondent with Stein.

Bertram Grosvenor Goodhue (1869–1924). Architect. Born in Pomfret, Connecticut. Studied under James Renwick in New York. Worked with Ralph Adam Cram (1890–91). Best known for his church design and residential work. Developed a style that was Gothic yet in a modern form. Buildings at West Point Military Academy; St. Thomas Church; St. Bartholomew; San Diego Exposition (1913); National Academy of Sciences, Washington, D.C.; State Capitol, Lincoln, Nebraska (1924). Stein worked as chief draftsman for Goodhue (1911–18).

Ralph Griswold (1894–1991). Landscape architect. Born in Warren, Ohio, and educated at Cornell University (B.L.A. 1924) and the American Academy in Rome. Practiced landscape architecture in Pittsburgh, Cleveland, and New York City. Worked with Henry Wright and C. S. Stein on Chatham Village.

Ernest Gruensfeldt. Architect. Educated at the École des Beaux Arts (1906–10) with Stein. Architectural practice in Chicago (1911–50). Work included the Michigan Boulevard Garden Apartments in collaboration with Eugene Klaber.

Moss Hart (1904–61). Pulitzer Prize–winning playwright. Born in New York City. Studied at Columbia University. First important play was *Once in a Lifetime* with George Kaufman (1930); Aline MacMahon starred in the film version in 1932. With Kaufman, Hart wrote very successful plays and musicals, including *You Can't Take It with You* (1937), *The Man Who Came to Dinner, Winged Victory, Face the Music, As Thousands Cheer,* and *Lady in the Dark.* Author of *Act One: An Autobiography* (1959).

Douglas Haskell (1899–1979). Editor. Born in Monastir, Turkey, and educated at Oberlin College. Associated with *Creative Art Magazine, Architectural Record,* and *Architectural Forum.* Professor, Columbia School of Architecture. Vice chairman of the architectural advisory committee of the Public Housing Administration. Editor: *Rehousing Urban America* (Henry Wright, 1935); *Building USA* (1957).

Sir William Holford (1907–75). British architect, city planner, and civil engineer. Born in Johannesburg and educated at Liverpool University. Worked in Ministry of Town and Country Planning. Plans for rebuilding bombed area north of St. Paul's, London (1950), and several British New Towns.

Raymond Mathewson Hood (1881–1934). Architect. Born in Pawtucket, Rhode Island, and educated at Brown University, MIT, Architecte Diplomé par le Gouvernement Français, and École des Beaux Arts. Practiced architecture in New York City. Specialized in office buildings; won Tribune Tower (Chicago) competition (1922, completed 1925), *New York Daily News* building, buildings at Rockefeller Center (1932), Chicago Century of Progress Exposition (1933).

Ebenezer Howard (1850–1928). English town planning theorist who developed a satellite town theory of planned urban decentralization as a means of restructuring and rebuilding modern urban regions. Born in London. No formal postsecondary education. Court reporter; inventor of an early typewriter. Visited Chicago (1872). Author: *A Peaceful Path to Real Reform* (1898), published as *Garden Cities of Tomorrow* (1902). Garden City innovator. Initiated the development of the first satellite Garden City in England, Letchworth (1903), and also participated in the planning and development of Welwyn Garden City (1922).

Harold L. Ickes (1874–1952). Lawyer, politician, public official. Born in Pennsylvania. Studied at the University of Chicago, Washington and Jefferson College, and Northwestern University. Newspaper reporter active in municipal reform politics in Chicago. Member of Theodore Roosevelt's Progressive Bull Moose Party (1912–14). Organized "Western Republicans" for FDR (1932). U.S. Secretary of the Interior (1933–46). Head of Public Works Administration (PWA) under Franklin D. Roosevelt and Harry Truman. Appointed Robert Kohn, close associate of C. S. Stein, to head the Housing Division of the PWA (1934). Author: *The New Democracy* (1934), *Autobiography of a Curmudgeon* (1943), *My Twelve Years with FDR* (1948), and *The Secret Diary of Harold L. Ickes: The First Thousand Days, 1933–1936* (1953–54).

Stanley Myer Isaacs (1882–1962). City official. Born in New York City and educated at Columbia College, Columbia Law School, New York Law School, and Hebrew Union College. Became involved in city politics in 1938. Sat on various committees dealing with housing and social work. Received many prestigious awards for his work.

Reginald D. Johnson (1882–1952). Architect. Born in Westchester, New York, and educated at Williams College and MIT. Worked with Stein in Goodhue's office (1911–18) and later on buildings for the California Institute of Technology (1925) and on the public housing project of the Carmelitos California Housing Commission of the City of Los Angeles in the late 1930s and early 1940s. Also worked with Stein on the Los Angeles project "A Thousand Gardens" (Baldwin Hills Village).

Sullivan Jones (1878–1955). Architect. Born in New York City and educated at MIT. State architect for New York (1923–25). Housing projects in New York City (1920s). Chairman of the National Construction Planning and Adjustment board. Consultant for postwar housing program in California.

Ely Jacques Kahn (1884–1972). Architect. Born in New York City and educated at Columbia University and the École des Beaux Arts. C. S. Stein's companion in Paris. Taught at Columbia University, Cornell University, and New York University. Innovator in office building design. Architect for many Art Deco buildings in New York City. Author: *Design and Art in Industry* (1935).

Frederick P. Keppel (1875–1943). Executive secretary, Regional Planning Association of New York (1921–23). Foundation executive, Carnegie Corporation, and official of the Russell Sage Foundation (Regional Plan of New York). Provided funding for Henry Wright's school in New Jersey and the graduate programs in city and regional planning at Harvard, MIT (1930), and Cornell University (1935).

Eugene Henry Klaber (1883–1971). Architect. Born in New York City and educated in the Ethical Culture School with Stein and at Columbia University and the École des Beaux Arts when Stein was a student in Paris. Worked with Stein in surveying the Chelsea neighborhood in 1911 in support of the Hudson Guild's efforts to preserve the neighborhood. Worked for several decades in federal housing agencies. Practiced architecture in New York City and Chicago. Director of architecture for rental housing for the Federal Housing Authority. Director of Planning and Housing Division of the School of Architecture at Columbia University. Author: *Housing Design* (1954).

Robert David Kohn (1870–1953). Architect. Born in Manhattan, New York, and educated at Columbia and École des Beaux Arts. Director of the Shipping Board Housing Corporation during World War I and head of housing production of the Emergency Fleet Corporation, Division of Housing, during World War I. Architect of the *New York Evening Post* building, the Ethical Culture Meeting House, Macy's department store, and Temple Emanu-El (all in New York City). Director of housing division of Public Works Administration (1933–34). Longtime friend and associate of C. S. Stein.

Fiorello H. LaGuardia (1882–1947). Lawyer, politician. Born in New York City and educated at New York University, St. Lawrence University, and Washington and Jefferson College. U.S. Air Force during World War I (1916–18). Deputy attorney general of New York. Four-term U.S. congressman; mayor of New York City (1934–45). Major reformer of New York City courts, reducing corruption, modernizing the city, and introducing slum clearance projects; one of New York City's most colorful mayors.

Victor Laloux (1850–1937). French architect and master of architectural design atelier in the École des Beaux Arts. Born in Tours, France. Educated at the École des Beaux Arts (enrolled 1869). Won the Grand Prize of Rome (1878). Architect of Cour de Cessation and the École National des Mines; Inspector General des Batment Civil et Palais National. A favorite instructor for American architecture students; C. S. Stein studied in his atelier. Honorary fellow to the American Institute of Architects (1920). Laloux's most famous project was the Gare du Quay d'Orsay in Paris (1898–1900).

Lee Lawrie (1877–1961). American sculptor. Born in Rixdorf, Germany, and studied with Augustus St. Gaudens at the St. Vincent de Paul School, Yale, and Washington College. Instructor in sculpture at the Yale School of Fine Arts. Specialized in architectural sculpture and was a consultant to the architect of the U.S. Capitol and to the American Battle Monuments Commission. Designed the sculptures for most of the buildings designed by Bertram Grosvenor Goodhue at West Point and for St. Thomas, New York City, as well as the Nebraska Capitol building and Stein's Wichita, Kansas, Art Museum (1931).

Le Corbusier, alphabetized under Corbusier

William Lescaze (1896–1969). Architect. Born in Geneva and educated at the College de Geneve and the École Polytechnique Federal, Zurich, Switzerland. Worked in devastated areas of France after World War II. Established architectural practice in New York City. Principal works include the Philadelphia Savings Fund Society Building, Longfellow Building in Washington, and Spinney Hill Homes, Manhasset, Long Island.

Sinclair Lewis (1885–1951). American novelist. Born Saik Center, Minnesota. Journalist in Washington, D.C. (1918), where he met Stuart Chase. First successful novel: *Main Street* (1920). Wrote about small-town life in the Midwest in *Babbitt* (1922) and about medical doctors in *Arrowsmith* (1928); received the first American Nobel Prize for Literature in 1930. Later novels included *It Can't Happen Here* (1935) and *Kingsblood Royal* (1948).

Liang Ssu-ch'eng (1901–72). Chinese architectural historian. Born in Tokyo, where his father was a temporary political refugee. Educated at Tsing Hua University and the University of Pennsylvania, Department of Architecture (1924–27). Pioneer in the study of Chinese architectural history. Founder of two departments of architectural education at a northeastern university at Shenyang in Lianing Province (1928) and Tsing Hua University (1946). Active in city planning and conservation in Beijing. Liang and his wife, Phyllis, became good friends of the Steins on their trip to China in 1935. Member of international group of architects for U.N. Headquarters, New York City (1947). Author: *A Pictorial History of Chinese Architecture* and many treatises and books on architecture.

Pere Lorenz (1905–72). American documentary filmmaker. Born in West Virginia. His films *The Plow That Broke the Plains* (1932) and especially *The River* (1938) inspired Stein to produce a film, *The City*. Lorenz wrote the shooting script and made the film. Lewis Mumford narrated. Lorenz's images of industrial Pittsburgh, small-town Shirley Center, Massachusetts, and the New Towns of Radburn, New Jersey, and Greenbelt, Maryland, make a classic documentary of city planning. The film's musical score is by Aaron Copland.

Roy Lubove (1934–   ). Urban social historian. Born in New York City. Educated at Columbia University (B.A. 1956) and Cornell University (Ph.D. 1960). Author: *Community Plan-*

ning in the 1920s: The Contribution of the Regional Planning Association of America (1963), *The Progressives and the Slums—Tenement House Reform in New York City* (1963).

Benton MacKaye (1879–1975). Conservationist and forester. Born in New York City and educated at Harvard. Associate of Gifford Pinchot. Conceptualized the Appalachian Trail in 1922 and worked to implement the idea through the Appalachian Trail Association. Founding member of the RPAA (1923). TVA Land Planning Division (1933–40). Helped draft the bill for the conservation of natural resources of Alaska. Author: *The New Exploration* (1928).

Archibald MacLeish (1892–1982). American writer and poet. Librarian of Congress (1939–44). Assistant Secretary of State (1939–48). Born in Glencoe, Illinois, and educated at Yale and Harvard (L.L.B. 1919). Taught at Johns Hopkins University, University of California, Queens University, Carleton College, and Amherst College. Poems include "The Hamlet of A. MacLeish" (1928), "Frescoes for Mr. Rockefeller's City" (1933) "The Fall of the City" (1937). Strong supporter of FDR and the New Deal. Briefly associated with C. S. Stein, Lewis Mumford, and Catherine Bauer on writing projects in the mid-1930s. Principal author of *Housing in America* by the editors of *Fortune* (1932). Worked with Henry Wright, Catherine Bauer, and Lewis Mumford on their *Fortune* articles on European housing policy and projects. Harvard faculty (1949–82). Author: verse-drama *J.B.* (1958).

Aline MacMahon (1899–1992). Actress on Broadway stage and in motion pictures. Born in McKeesport, Pennsylvania. Educated at Barnard College. MacMahon began acting at Barnard and at the Hudson Guild in 1916, where she met Clarence Stein, whom she married in 1928. MacMahon began acting in Broadway plays in 1921, and during her career she appeared in such productions as *Artists and Models, The Eve of St. Marks*, and *All the Way Home*. MacMahon's career began to shift toward motion pictures in 1931, when she appeared in the West Coast company of Moss Hart's stage play, *Once in a Lifetime*. She had played the leading role in the play's pre-Broadway trial run in 1930. Soon after she arrived in Los Angeles, she took a screen test and signed a contract with Warner Brothers. MacMahon's performance in the 1944 film *Dragon Seed* earned her an Oscar nomination. MacMahon's screen credits include *Five Star Final* (1931), *The Heart of New York, The Mouthpiece, Life Begins, One Way Passage, Once in a Lifetime* (1932), *Gold Diggers of 1933, Heroes for Sale, The Life of Jimmy Dolan, The World Changes* (1933), *Heat Lightning, Side Streets, Big-Hearted Herbert, Babbitt* (1934), *I Live My Life, Kind Lady, Ah Wilderness!* (1935), *When You're in Love* (1937), *Back Door to Heaven* (1939), *Out of the Fog* (1941), *The Lady is Willing* (1942), *Dragon Seed, Guest in the House* (1944), *The Mighty McGurk* (1947), *The Search* (1948), *Roseanna McCoy* (1949), *The Flame and the Arrow* (1950), *The Eddie Cantor Story* (1953), *The Young Doctors* (1961), *Diamond Head, All the Way Home* (1963).

Albert Mayer (1897–1981). Civil engineer and environmental planner. Born and grew up in New York City. Mayer studied at Columbia University (B.A. 1917) and Massachusetts Institute of Technology (B.C.E. 1918). Engineering practice, New York City (1918–34); worked in the office of Clarence S. Stein (1934–39). During the early 1930s, wrote several articles on housing and urban policy, including some on Stein's housing developments, Phipps Garden

Apartments and Hillside Homes. Served in the Army Engineers in India during World War II (1942–45), where he met many of India's future leaders, including Jawaharlal Nehru and Pandit Pant. After the war Mayer continued to work in India and in his New York City–based practice in architecture and planning with Julian Whittlesey and Milton Glass. Planning and development advisor to the government of Uttar Pradesh (1948–60). Town planner, Chandigarh, Calcutta, New Delhi. Author: *Pilot Project, India* (1958), *The Urgent Future: People, Housing, City, Region* (1967).

Arthur Mayer (1886–1981). President, Mayer-Burstyn Corporation (film company). Director of publicity and advertising, Paramount Pictures (1930–33). Stein's brother-in-law. Commissioned Stein to build a movie house in the late 1930s. Helped Stein with his distribution of documentary film *The City*.

John Raymond McCarl (1879–1940). Comptroller General of the United States. Born near Des Moines, Iowa, and educated at the University of Nebraska. Member of the law firm Cordeal & McCarl, McCook. Private secretary to U.S. Senator George W. Norris, executive secretary of the National Republican Congressional Committee. As Comptroller General, McCarl's negative decisions on the legality of New Deal appropriations for PWA housing and the Greenbelt Towns program slowed the pace of government investment in housing construction during the early 1930s.

Belle Israels Moskowitz (1877–1933). Social worker and politician. Born in New York City and educated at Teachers College. Worked closely with Governor Al Smith of New York State. Wrote many of Smith's speeches in the 1920s and early 1930s. Secretary of the Governor's Labor Board, the Educational Council, the Port of New York Authority, and the Mayor's Committee of Women on National Defense. Secretary of the New York State Reconstruction Committee, where she worked with Clarence Stein on housing policy.

Lewis Mumford (1895–1990). Author and social philosopher. Born in Flushing, Long Island, and educated at Columbia, New York University, and the New School for Social Research. Editor of *The Dial* (1919) and RPAA issues of *Survey Graphic* (1925). Longtime friend and close associate of Benton MacKaye and Clarence Stein in the RPAA's projects in regional planning and community building (1923–73). Studied European housing with Catherine Bauer (1931–33). Professor of humanities and city and regional planning at Stanford, University of Pennsylvania, University of California at Berkeley, and Wesleyan University. Author of many books, including *The Story of Utopias* (1922), *Technics and Civilization* (1934), *The Culture of Cities* (1938), *The South in Architecture* (1941), *From the Ground Up* (1956), *The City in History* (1961), and *The Pentagon of Power* (1970).

Frederick V. Murphy (1879–1958). Architect. Born in Fond du Lac, Wisconsin, and educated at Columbia (now George Washington) University and the École des Beaux Arts, where he studied architecture with Clarence Stein. Practiced architecture in Washington, D.C., and taught at Catholic University.

Richard Neutra (1892–1970). Architect. Born in Vienna, Austria, and educated at Vienna's Technischehochschule. Influenced by Gustav Amman, landscape architect of Switzerland in early 1900s, and by Eric Mendelsohn, a Berlin architect. Immigrated to the United States in 1923. Worked in New York City, Chicago, and Los Angeles. Most celebrated for his design of Los Angeles houses, which contained his trademark clearly articulated post-and-beam structure. Author of *Survival through Design* (1954).

Isamu Noguchi (1904–88). American sculptor. Studied in Paris with Brancusi. Known for his abstract sculpture but did occasional portrait heads, including one of Aline MacMahon. Work in Mexico and at Rockefeller Center; stone garden for UNESCO in Paris.

John Nolen (1869–1937). City planner and landscape architect. Born in Philadelphia, Pennsylvania, and educated at Girard College (1884), University of Pennsylvania (B.Phil. 1893), University of Munich, and Harvard (Landscape Architecture, 1905). Extensive national consulting practice in city planning and landscape architecture (1900–35). Prepared city plans in San Diego (1908); Madison, Wisconsin (1909); and especially in Tennessee, New Jersey, and Florida in the 1920s. Member of the advisory housing committee of the Emergency Fleet Corporation. Consultant to the National Park Service, the Housing Division of the PWA, and the Resettlement Administration. Author: *Replanning Small Cities* (1911), *New Ideals in the Planning of Cities, Towns and Villages* (1919), *New Towns for Old* (1927).

Matthew Nowicki (1910–50). Polish architect and town planner. Born in China, near the Siberian border. Educated at Warsaw Polytechnic. Designs for the reconstruction of Warsaw, soon after its liberation in 1945. Member of the international team of architects (with Markelius, Le Corbusier, and others) who designed the United Nations Headquarters in New York City. There he met C. S. Stein. They collaborated on several designs, including the early plan for Chandigarh under Albert Mayer. Taught at School of Architecture, North Carolina State College in Raleigh.

Frederick Law Olmsted (1822–1903). American landscape architect. Born in Hartford, Connecticut, and informally educated. Traveled and wrote about the South in the 1850s. Author: *A Journey to the Seabound Slave States* (1856). Inspired to study landscape design by a visit to Italy in 1856. Appointed architect in chief of Central Park, New York City (1858). Appointed superintendent of the New Central Park in New York City (1859). Strove to make this early American park not only a work of art, but also a successful municipal enterprise and an instrument for social and cultural change. Subsequently designed major parks and park systems in many American cities including Chicago, Montreal, Boston, and Buffalo. Supported development of state and national parks and city planning.

Frederick Law Olmsted, Jr. (1870–1957). Educated at Harvard University (B.A. 1894). Studied landscape architecture under his father. Landscape architect of the Metropolitan Park System of Boston (1898–1920). Designer of many public parks and subdivisions, including Forest Hills Gardens on Long Island, New York (1912–16) and Roland Park outside Baltimore, Maryland (1891–1910). Manager of the Town Planning Division of the U.S. Housing

673

Corporation (1918–19). Director of Planning, National Capital Park and Planning Commission, Washington, D.C. (1929–54).

Sir Frederic J. Osborn (1885–1978). Born in London. Attended Council Schools and was self-educated. Fabian Society (1905). Associated with the Webbs, George Bernard Shaw, and H. G. Wells. Secretary, Welwyn Garden City (1919–36). Played a major role in shaping British post–World War II urban dispersal policy as secretary of the British Town and Country Planning Association (New Towns Act of 1946). Honorary Secretary, Garden Cities and Town Planning Association, later the Town and Country Planning Association. Editor: *Town and Country Planning* (1938–66).

Francis Perkins (1881–1965). Secretary of Labor in FDR's administration (1933–45). Born in Boston. Educated at Mt. Holyoke College (B.A. 1902) and Columbia (M.A. 1910); graduate study in economics with Simon Patten. Worked at Hull House in Chicago, New York Consumers League (1910–12), and New York State Factory Commission investigating industrial safety. Member of New York State Industrial Board (1923–29) in Smith's administration. First woman in U.S. cabinet. Major achievements in insurance for old age and unemployment and legislation on the minimum wage and social security. Author: *The Roosevelt I Know* (1946).

Nelson Aldrich Rockefeller (1908–79). New York governor (1959–73); U.S. vice president (1974–77). Born in Bar Harbor, Maine, and educated at Dartmouth. One of the directors of the Museum of Modern Art when Clarence Stein developed the museum's building program. At various times, director, president, and chairman of the Rockefeller Center, Inc. Author: *The Future of Federalism* (1962), *Unity, Freedom and Peace* (1968), and *Our Environment Can Be Saved* (1970).

Eleanor Roosevelt (1884–1962). Humanitarian and international official. Born in New York City and educated at finishing schools in England and France. Daughter of Elliott Roosevelt and niece of Theodore Roosevelt. Active in social causes during the early twentieth century. Wife of Franklin D. Roosevelt. Took an interest in the New York City reform movement and in philanthropy. Served on the board of directors of Alexander Bing's City Housing Corporation (1924–34). Active in national women's organizations. Informal advisor to FDR, often through members of his Brain Trust (Rexford Tugwell and Samuel Rosenman) and through Harry Hopkins, Louis Howe, and Francis Perkins). Newspaper column, "My Day," beginning in 1935. U.S. delegate to the United Nations (1945–53 and 1961–62). Books include *I Remember* (1949), *On My Own* (1958), and *Autobiography* (1961).

Franklin Delano Roosevelt (1882–1945). Thirty-second president of the United States. Born in Hyde Park, New York, and educated at Harvard and Columbia Law School. Wilson's assistant secretary of the Navy (1913–20). Governor of New York (1928–32). Defeated Al Smith for presidential nomination at Democratic Convention of 1932. FDR's New Deal was formulated with the help of many advisors, including the Brain Trust (Samuel Rosenman, Rexford Tugwell, Raymond Moley, Adolph Berle). Continued the social, financial, and economic reforms started during the administrations of Theodore Roosevelt and Woodrow Wilson to foster the development of domestic policies in social security, employment, housing, and social services. Two of FDR's advisors, Stuart Chase and Rexford Tugwell, were conversant with RPAA policy proposals and introduced them into discussions of domestic policy. In 1934 Marriner Eccles was recruited by Chase to work for Tugwell and drafted the Housing Act of 1934, which established the FHA-insured mortgage. Roosevelt established the Resettlement Administration in 1935, which developed a housing and community development program designed to build suburban satellite New Towns (Greenbelt Towns). Clarence Stein's associates were involved in several of FDR's New Deal programs: Stein in PWA housing, the Greenbelt Towns, and defense and public housing; Benton MacKaye in the TVA; and Catherine Bauer in national public housing and slum clearance legislation. During FDR's second term, the most radical RPAA ideas were dropped or modified.

Charlotte Rumbold (1895–1960). Housing reformer, city planning advocate. Cleveland City Planning Commissioner (1930–50). Educated at the University of Missouri. Did housing studies for St. Louis and Cleveland. Assistant secretary of the City Planning Committee of Cleveland, Ohio. Founder with Ernest Bohn of the Ohio Planning Conference and officer of OPC (1919–43). Active in developing state and local legislation on housing and planning.

Eliel Saarinen (1873–1950). Finnish-American architect. Born in Helsingors, Finland, and studied at various Finnish and German universities. Practiced architecture both in Finland and in the United States. His most important Finnish works were the Helsinki Railroad Station and the National Museum, Helsingors. After taking second prize in the Tribune Tower competition, he practiced architecture in the United States and taught urban design at the Cranbrook Academy of Art (1928–43), where he also designed several of the school's buildings and its art museum, as well as the buildings of the Cranbrook Boys School and the Cranbrook School. Many of his students became leaders in American architecture and city planning. In the United States, Saarinen also designed the Kleinhans Music Hall in Buffalo, New York; the Tabernacle Christian Chapel in Columbus, Ohio; and numerous university and commercial buildings.

Lee Simonson (1888–1967). Theater set designer and art critic. Born in New York City and educated at Ethical Culture School, Harvard University, and École des Beaux Arts, where he studied when C. S. Stein was resident in Paris. Founder and director of the Theatre Guild Inc., the Garrick Theatre, and the Guild Theatre. Also lectured and wrote about the stage and related subjects. Close friend of Clarence Stein and Aline MacMahon Stein.

Alfred E. Smith (1873–1944). American politician. Four-term governor of New York (elected 1918, 1922, 1924, 1926). Born in New York City's lower East Side. No formal higher education beyond secondary school. Led New York City and State Democratic progressive reform movement, including legislation on state housing measures. Stein worked for and with Smith to promote the agenda of the Progressive Era, serving as secretary of the Housing Committee of the New York State Reconstruction Commission (1919–20) and chairman of Al Smith's New York State Housing Commission (1926). Francis Perkins, later FDR's secretary of labor, served in Smith's cabinet, as did Robert Moses. Nominated for president in 1928 with FDR's help. Left politics after FDR's nomination for president in 1932.

Chloethiel Woodward Smith (1911–93). Architect and urban planner. Born in Peoria, Illinois. Smith graduated from the University of Oregon and received a master's degree in architecture and urban planning from Washington University in St. Louis. New York architectural practice and Henry Wright's "housing school" (1933–34). Chief of research and planning for the Federal Housing Administration (1935). Private practice, Washington, D.C. (1940). Founding partner in the firm of Keyes Smith Satterlee and Lethbridge. Later formed a partnership with Satterlee and in 1963 created own firm, Chloethiel Woodward Smith and Associates. Work includes Capitol Park apartments, Harbor Square town houses in southwest Washington, National Airport Metro station, Consolidated Federal Law Enforcement Training Center in Beltsville, Blake Building, Washington Square, 1100 Connecticut Avenue, Lafayette Park Office Building, F Street pedestrian promenade, and Southwest Freeway. Served on the Washington, D.C., Fine Arts Commission (1967–76).

Joel Elias Spingarn (1875–1939). Author and literary critic. Born in New York City and educated at Columbia and Harvard. A founder and literary adviser to the publishers Harcourt, Brace & Co. (1919–32), where he became Lewis Mumford's editor and close friend. Founded the movement for rural cooperative recreation. Officer in the National Association for the Advancement of Colored People (NAACP). Author: *A History of Literary Criticism in the Renaissance* (1899), *Poetry and Religion* (1924), *Henry Winthrop Sargent and the Early History of Landscape Gardening and Ornamental Horticulture in Dutchess County, NY* (1937). Editor of many collections of essays and creative criticism.

Liang Ssu-ch'eng, alphabetized under Liang

Gordon Stephenson (1908–   ). British, Canadian, and Australian town planning consultant and architect. Born in Liverpool. Educated at Liverpool Institute, University of Liverpool, University of Paris (B.Arch. 1932), Massachusetts Institute of Technology (M.C.P. 1938). Studio master, Architectural Association School of Architecture, London (1939–40). First chief planning officer of the Ministry of Town and Country Planning, London (1942–47). Lever professor of civic design, University of Liverpool (1948–53). Professor of town and regional planning, University of Toronto (1955–60). Professor of architecture, University of Toronto (1955–60) and University of Western Australia (1960–72). Transplanted the Radburn idea to influence the design of British housing projects and New Towns and Australian suburban community plans, including one in Canberra. Editor of the British planning journal, *Town Planning Review* (1948–54).

Oscar Stonorov (1905–70). Architect. Born in Frankfurt-am-Main, Germany, and educated at the University of Florence, Italy, and École Polytechnique Federale, Zurich, Switzerland. Came to the United States and began general practice of architecture with a special interest in public housing and city planning. Employed Catherine Bauer (1933–34). Was associated with various housing and planning organizations. Author: *Le Corbusier: His Work* (1929), *You and Your Neighborhood* (with L. I. Kahn, 1945).

Nathan Straus (1889–1961). Government official and journalist. Born in New York City; son of New York philanthropist Nathan Straus. Member of the New York State legislature (1921–26); director of the U.S. Housing Authority (1937–42). Author: *Seven Myths of Housing* (1944) and *Two Thirds of a Nation* (1952). The site Clarence Stein selected for his prototype mid-density housing project, Hillside Homes, in the Bronx was owned by Straus. Became the developer and head of the limited dividend corporation that developed this project in 1933–34 with PWA funding.

Harry S. Truman (1884–1972). Thirty-third president of the United States. Born near Lamar, Missouri. Truman had a high school education. Managed his father's farm at Grandview, Missouri (1906–17). When Truman's National Guard regiment mobilized in 1917, he left the United States as a lieutenant, and he returned a major in 1919. Elected county judge for Jackson County (1922); served two nonsuccessive terms in this capacity. Elected U.S. senator on the Democratic ticket (1934). A firm supporter of the New Deal. In 1944, nominated and elected vice president as a member of the Democratic Party. After the death of Franklin D. Roosevelt on 12 April 1945, Truman was sworn in as president. Crucial decisions on use of atomic bomb in Japan, European peace (Potsdam Conference), European Recovery Program (Marshall Plan). Followed FDR's policies on social welfare and civil rights. Progress on social security, minimum wage, public housing. Developed plan for shelters for atomic war defense in Washington, D.C. (1951–52). C. S. Stein was consultant on New Town proposals for dispersal of D.C. federal government workforce.

Rexford Tugwell (1891–1979). Economist, political scientist, and planning educator. Born in Sinclaire, New York, and educated at the University of Pennsylvania (B.S. 1915; Ph.D. 1922) and the University of New Mexico. Taught economics at Columbia University (1920–37). Member of the Brain Trust of the early New Deal (1932–36). Assistant secretary of the Department of Agriculture. Administrator of the Resettlement Administration (1935–36), for which C. S. Stein served as programming and design consultant. Chairman and head of New York City Planning Department (1937–41). Governor of Puerto Rico (1941–45). Head of the Graduate Program in Planning, University of Chicago (1946–57). Author: *The Economic Basis of Public Interest* (1922), *The Place of Planning in Society* (1954), *The Democratic Roosevelt* (1957), *The Light of Other Days: An Autobiography* (1962), *The Brains Trust* (1968), *Tugwell's Thoughts on Planning* (1975).

Sir Raymond Unwin (1863–1940). City planner, architect, and teacher. Born in Whiston, England. Educated at Oxford (B.A. 1877, M.A. 1881). Knew Ruskin and Morris as a student. Also influenced by the radical ideas of Edward Carpenter. Active in development of Socialist and Labor Party ideas in connection with architecture, town planning, and housing. An active leader in the development of the Garden City movement. Partnership with Barry Parker (1896–1914): workers' housing and community planning and housing design for New

Earswick, York, with Rowntree (1902). Worked with Ebenezer Howard on town plan of Letchworth (1906) and designed Hampstead Garden Suburb working for Henrietta Barnett (1904–6). Town plans in Dublin (1916) with Patrick Geddes (1916). Chief architect for British Munitions Department, World War I (1915–19). War workers' housing. Major force in shaping the evolution of local council housing in Great Britain (1920–28). Technical advisor to the Greater London Regional Planning Committee (1929–33). Developed a plan for the greater London region that advanced Greenbelt and New Towns concepts. Advisor on U.S. housing policy and legislation to several organizations early in the New Deal era, including the PWA and the National Housing Association (1933–1934). Taught in graduate program in city planning at Columbia University (1936–40). Author: *Town Planning in Practice* (1909), *Nothing Gained by Overcrowding* (1912), and *The Art of Building a Home* (with Barry Parker, 1901–14). Unwin's approach to residential design significantly influenced Stein's housing design work in the 1920s and 1930s, and they were good friends.

Joseph Maria Urban (1872–1933). American architect and stage set designer. Born in Vienna, Austria, and educated at Art Academy and Polytechnicum, Vienna. Practiced architecture in Leningrad (1900). Moved to New York City (1911). Practiced in New York City and Palm Beach, Florida. Set designer for the Zeigfeld Follies and the N.Y. Metropolitan Opera. Designed the main building of the New School in New York City (1930).

Thorstein B. Veblen (1857–1929). Radical economist, teacher, author. Born in Wisconsin and educated at Carleton College, John Hopkins, Yale (Ph.D. 1884). Taught at Cornell University, University of Chicago, Stanford University, and New School of Research. Developer of the field of institutional Economics. Author: *The Theory of the Leisure Class* (1899), *The Theory of Business Enterprise* (1904), *The Instinct of Workmanship* (1914), *The Place of Science in Modern Civilization and Other Papers* (1920), *Engineers and the Price System* (1925). His ideas influenced several members of Stein's 1920s group, the Regional Planning Association of America, especially Charles Whitaker, Frederick Ackerman, Lewis Mumford, and Benton MacKaye, whose short-lived organization, the Technical Alliance, was a precursor of the RPAA.

Warren Jay Vinton (1889–1969). Government official and city planner. Born in Detroit, Michigan, and educated at the University of Michigan and Columbia University. Under the Resettlement Administration Vinton was chief of research for the Division of Suburban Resettlement in charge of economic and sociological studies for Greenbelt Towns. Field research supervisor with the Federal Housing Administration, where he developed the research techniques used in the first housing census by the Census Bureau in 1940. Served as first assistant commissioner of the Public Housing Administration (1937–57). Close friend of Catherine Bauer and rival for her affections with Lewis Mumford and Jacob Crane in the 1930s.

Ralph Walker (1889–1973). Architect. Born in Waterbury, Connecticut, and educated at MIT and Syracuse University. Practiced architecture in New York City. Architect planner for New York Life after World War II. Public housing and middle-income housing in New York City. Designed public and private projects in the United States, South America, and Europe.

Charles Whitaker (1872–1938). Architectural editor and critic. Born in Woonsocket, Rhode Island. Received no formal architectural training. The radical editor of the *Journal of the American Institute of Architects* (1913–27) worked to change the editorial policy of the journal to introduce more articles on architectural education, urban development, housing, and national policy affecting these subjects. Fought against "pork barrel" appropriations for public buildings and advocated post–World War I government construction of housing. Introduced the later members of the Regional Planning Association to each other. Co-author of *The Housing Problem in War and Peace* (1918). Author of *The Joke about Housing* (1920), *From Rameses to Rockefeller: The Story of Architecture* (1934).

Julian Whittlesey (1905–95). Architect and city planner. Born in Greenwich, Connecticut. Educated at Yale (B.S.C.E. 1927; B.F.A. 1930) and Fountainbleu School of Fine Arts. Worked in the firm Howe and Lescaze (1931–32). Housing Study Guild student with Henry Wright, Stein, and Albert Mayer (1932–33). For the Resettlement Administration, worked with Albert Mayer on planning the Greenbelt Town of Greenbrook, New Jersey (1935). Associate to RA Research Director Vinton (1936–38). Chief architect, Project Planning Division, U.S. Housing Authority (1938–39). Partner, Mayer and Whittlesey (1939–78): Manhattan House Apartments in New York (also with Skidmore, Owings, and Merrill) (1951); Calcutta Master Plan; New Town of Reston, Virginia; Kitimat, B.C. Worked in association with Stein on the Chandigarh, Punjab's new capital city (1948–50), and on Kitimat, British Columbia, the New Town project for the Aluminium Corporation of Canada (ALCAN) (1950–52), for which Stein was director of planning.

Carleton M. Winslow (1876–1946). Architect. Studied at the Art Institute in Chicago and the Atelier Pascal and Atelier Chifflot Frères at the École des Beaux Arts. Practiced architecture with Bertram Grosvenor Goodhue in San Diego, Los Angeles, and Santa Barbara. Designed several buildings at the San Diego World Fair and a number of residences and churches in California. Author: *Architecture and the Gardens of the San Diego Exposition* (1916), *Small House Designs* (1924).

Edith Elmer Wood (1871–1945). Housing reformer. Born in Portsmouth, New Hampshire. Received her undergraduate education at Smith College and her Ph.D. from Columbia University. One of the earliest serious researchers in the housing field. Author: *Recent Trends in American Housing* (1931), *Slums and Blighted Areas in the United States* (1935); co-author of *The Housing Problem in War and Peace* (1918). Wood was an active participant in the housing policy discussions of the Regional Planning Association of America.

Coleman Woodbury (1902–82). Economist, housing official. Born in Sandwich, Illinois, and educated at Northwestern University. Assistant professor of economics and research with his mentor, land economist Richard Ely (1927–32). Executive secretary, Illinois State Housing Board (1932–34); first executive director of the National Association of Housing Officials (1934–42); National Resources Committee (1935); Federal Housing Administration (1936). Director, Urban Redevelopment Study (1948–51). Author and editor: *The Future of Cities and Urban Development* (1953), *Urban Redevelopment: Problem and Practices* (1953).

Henry Wright (1878–1936). Architect, landscape architect, community planner, teacher. Born in Lawrence, Kansas, and educated at the University of Pennsylvania (B.Arch. 1902). Worked with Kessler on site planning, Kansas City and St. Louis housing subdivisions (1903–1917). Community planning in Emergency Fleet Housing Corporation (1917–19). Helped organize St. Louis City Planning Association (1920–22). In 1923 became associated with C. S. Stein on the plans for Sunnyside Gardens, Queens; Radburn, New Jersey; and Chatham Village, Pittsburgh. With Stein and Benton MacKaye, Wright wrote the Regional Plan for New York State (1926). Organized Housing Study Guild (1932) with Albert Mayer, Henry Churchill, and Catherine Bauer. Developed much-used analytical methods for housing layout and subdivision design. Their research and training activities greatly influenced U.S. large-scale housing project design. Organized and taught in his own housing design school at New Jersey. Studio teacher of city planning, graduate program in city planning at Columbia (1932–36). Developed town plans for Greenbrook, New Jersey, the fifth (unbuilt) Resettlement Administration Greenbelt Town. A founding member of the RPAA. Author of *Rehousing Urban America* (1935); co-author of *Urban Blight and Slums* (1938).

Catherine Bauer Wurster (1906–64). City planner and housing expert. Born in Elizabeth, New Jersey. Educated at Vassar College (B.A. 1926). Briefly studied architecture at Cornell University during her junior year. Editorial work at Harcourt Brace (1927–30), where she met Lewis Mumford. Executive secretary, Regional Planning Association of America (1931–33). After her studies of European housing policy and design, became a major figure in U.S. housing and urban policy analysis. Worked with Clarence Stein on housing and community facility research (1932–34). Helped organize the American Federation of Labor Housing Conference (LHC) and was a major lobbyist for the proposed 1936 housing legislation and the Wagner-Steagall Housing Act of 1937. Director of Research for the U.S. Housing Authority (1937–39). Married architect William Wurster and joined the faculty of city planning at the University of California at Berkeley (1940). Moved to MIT with Wurster (1943–50). Bauer, Stein, and Lewis Mumford revived the then-dormant RPAA as the Regional Development Council of America to address post–World War II urban policy issues (1947–53). Worked with Stein and Ernest Bohn lobbying Congress on appropriate sale of FDR's Greenbelt Towns by the federal government (1948). Founding member and vice president of the National Housing Conference (1936–60). Professor of city and regional planning and associate dean of the College of Environmental Design at the University of California, Berkeley (1950–64). Author: *Modern Housing* (1934), *A Citizens Guide to Public Housing* (1940), *Social Issues in Housing and Town Planning* (1952), "Redevelopment: A Misfit in the Fifties" in *The Future of Cities and Urban Redevelopment* (1955), *Modern Architecture in England* (1957).

Bibliography

Works by Clarence S. Stein

"A Triumph of the Spanish-Colonial Style." In *The Architecture and the Gardens of the San Diego Exposition,* edited by Carleton Monroe Winslow, 10–18. San Francisco: P. Elder and Co., 1916.

"Transportation or Housing." *Journal of the American Institute of Architects* 6, no. 6 (July 1918): 363.

"Housing and Reconstruction." *Journal of the American Institute of Architects* 6, no. 10 (October 1918): 469–72.

"The Housing Crisis in New York City," *Journal of the American Institute of Architects* 5 (May 1919): 220.

"Competition for the Remodeling of a Block of Old Tenements in New York City." *Journal of the American Institute of Architects* 8, no. 3 (March 1920): 135–36.

Interview. "To Solve the Housing Problem, This Expert Says the State Should Have the Power to Hold Land and Develop It for Homes." *New York World,* 20 June 1920.

Interview. "The Housing Crisis in New York." *Survey* (1 September 1920): 659–62.

Interview. "Men, Money, Material Needed to Solve Housing Problem." *Better Times* 1, no. 8 (October 1920): 20–22.

Interview. "What the Legislature Did to Solve the Housing Problem." *Better Times* 1, no. 9 (21 November 1920): 16–17.

"Cooperation: The Ultimate Solution to the Housing Problem." *Better Times* 2, no. 1 (January 1921): 1.

"Community Planning Recommendations." *Journal of the American Institute of Architects* 9, no. 12 (December 1921): 399–400.[1]

1. As associate editor for community planning and housing for the Journal of the AIA from 1921 to 1924, Clarence Stein commissioned articles from Henry Wright, Lewis Mumford, and Nils Hammerstrand: Wright

"The Professor Proves That There Was No Housing Emergency." *Journal of the American Institute of Architects* 10, no. 1 (January 1922): 19–20.

"Community Planning and Housing: Milwaukee Squarely Faces the Housing Problem." *Journal of the American Institute of Architects* 10, no. 1 (January 1922): 21–22.

"Community Planning and Housing: Current Notes." *Journal of the American Institute of Architects* 10, no. 2 (February 1922): 52–54.

"Community Planning and Housing." *Journal of the American Institute of Architects* 10, no. 3 (March 1922): 82–85.

"Community Planning and Housing." *Journal of the American Institute of Architects* 10, no. 4 (April 1922): 126–28.

"The Housing Shortage." *Survey* 48 (15 April 1922): 80–81.

"Town Planning and Housing." *Journal of the American Institute of Architects* 10, no. 5 (May 1922): 165–67.

"Community Planning and Housing." *Journal of the American Institute of Architects* 10, no. 6 (June 1922): 203–5.

"Community Planning and Housing." *Journal of the American Institute of Architects* 10, no. 9 (September 1922): 298–99.

"Community Planning and Housing." *Journal of the American Institute of Architects* 10, no. 10 (October 1922): 334–36.

"Amsterdam Old and New." *Journal of the American Institute of Architects* 10, no. 10 (October 1922): 310–28.

"Community Planning and Housing." With Niles Hammerstrand. *Journal of the American Institute of Architects* 10, no. 11 (November 1922): 366–67.

"The Housing Crisis in Old and New Amsterdam: A Comparison of Methods Used to Meet Situation." *New York Times,* 5 November 1922, 117–22.

"Community Planning and Housing: The Future of Big Cities." *Journal of the American Institute of Architects* 11, no. 1 (January 1923): 24–27.

"Community Planning and Housing—Notes: The Regional Planning Association of America." *Journal of the American Institute of Architects* 11, no. 7 (July 1923): 292–93.

"Housing New York's Two-thirds." *Survey* 51 (15 February 1924): 509–10.

"Housing and Community Planning: The New York Puzzle." *Journal of the American Institute of Architects* 12, no. 5 (February 1924): 84.

"Post War Housing at Ruislip Northwood." *Journal of the American Institute of Architects* 12, no. 5 (May 1924): 225–29.

"Report of the Committee on Community Planning to the Fifty-seventh Annual Convention, April 3, 1924." *Journal of the American Institute of Architects* 12, no. 5 (May 1924) (6-page insert).

"Co-operative Housing from the Architect's Standpoint." In *Proceedings of a Conference on Cooperation in the US,* 117–22. Fifth session, 7 November 1924, Dr. John Elliott, chairman. New York: Cooperative League of America, 1924.

"Suggestions for the Demolition of Slums in New York City." *New York Times,* 23 January 1925, sec. 10, p. 6.

---

and Mumford on "Housing Progress" (December 1923), Mumford on "A Democratic Regional Planning Scheme: Abercrombie's London Plan" (October 1923), and Nils Hammerstrand on "Swedish Housing" (1924).

"New Ventures in Housing." *American City* 32 (March 1925): 277–81.

"A Plan for the State of New York." In *International Town Planning Conference, New York, 1925 Report,* 282–86. London: International Federation for Town and Country Planning and Garden Cities, 1925.

"Dinosaur Cities." *Survey Graphic* 54 (1 May 1925): 134–38.

"Cooperative Housing: The Architect's Viewpoint." *Brotherhood of Locomotive Firemen and Enginemen's Magazine* (August 1925): 117–22.

"City House That Has the Quality of a Feudal Castle." *Arts and Decoration* 23 (September 1925): 34–37.

"The Savings and Loan Association and Its Relation to the Housing Problem." *Bulletin of the New York State League of Savings and Loan Associations* (November 1925).

"Wanted: A Place to Play." *Playground* 19 (25 November 1925): 52.

"Community Planning of Homes." *American Federationist* 33 (March 1926): 340–47.

"Housing the People." *Nation* 122 (10 March 1926): 246.

"Nobody's Business." *Standard* 12 (March 1926): 209.

"Sunnyside, Long Island City, New York." *Architectural Record* 63, no. 3 (May 1928): 238.

"A Tenement House Law for the Rich." *Survey* (15 January 1929): 495–97.

"A Building on the Board: The Wichita Art Institute." *Pencil Points* 10, no. 8 (August 1929): 535–44.

"The Art Museum of Tomorrow." *Architectural Record* 67, no. 1 (January 1930): 5–12.

"The Problem of the Temple and Its Solution." *Architectural Forum* 52, no. 2 (February 1930): 55.

"Home Owners Have Stake in Neighbor's Houses." *New York Herald Tribune,* August 1930.

"Building Homes as Unit Project Gives Harmony." *New York Herald Tribune,* 14 September 1930, sec. 2, p. 15.

"The President's Housing Conference: A Challenging Opportunity." *American City* 43 (November–December 1930): 141–43.

"Radburn and Sunnyside." *Architectural Forum* 56 (March 1932): 239–52.

"An Outline for Community Housing Procedure." *Architectural Forum* (March, April, May 1932): 221–28, 393–400, 505–14.

"Housing and Common Sense." *Nation* 134 (11 May 1932): 541–44.

"Making Museums Function." *Architectural Forum* 56, no. 6 (June 1932): 609–16.

"Slums, Large Scale Housing and Decentralization: President's Conference on Home Building and Home Ownership."

"A Comparison of Two Ways of Housing 5000 People." *Architectural Forum* 58, no. 2 (February 1933): 126.

"Destructive Housing vs Constructive Housing." *Architectural Record* (May 1933).

"Housing and the Depression." *Octagon. A Journal of the American Institute of Architects* 5, no. 6 (June 1933): 3–5.

"A Housing Policy for the Government." *Octagon: A Journal of the American Institute of Architects* 5, no. 6 (June 1933): 6–7.

"Slums as Economic Blight." *New York Times,* 16 July 1933, sec. 10, p. 2.

"Community Planning and Architecture." *New York Times,* 23 July 1933, sec. 10, p. 2.

"New Towns for the Needs of a New Age." *New York Times Magazine,* 8 October 1933, sec. 6, pp. 6–7, 13.

"Store Building and Neighborhood Shopping Centers." With Catherine Bauer. *Architectural Record* 75 (February 1934): 175–87.

"Hillside Housing Development, Bronx, New York City." *Architectural Forum* 60, no. 2 (February 1934): 124–25.

"The Price of Slum Clearance." With Catherine Bauer. *Architectural Forum* 60 (February 1934): 154–57.

"Form and Function of the Modern Museum." *Museum News* (15 October 1935): 6–8.

"Hillside Homes." *American Architect* 148 (February 1936): 16–33.

"A Garden Homes Development by the Bruhl Foundation, Pittsburgh, Pennsylvania." *American Architect* 150 (February 1937): 63–66.

"The Wagner-Steagall Housing Act of 1937." With Coleman Woodbury, Langdon Post, and Albert Mayer. *American Architect and Architecture* 151 (November 1937): 35–38.

"The Gardens of Sochow." *Pencil Points* (July 1938): 427–30.

"The Case for New Towns." *Planners Journal* 5, no. 2 (March–June 1939): 39–41.

"Investment Housing Pays." *Survey Graphic* (February 1940): 75–77.

"Harbor Hills Housing." *Pencil Points* 2, no. 11 (November 1941): 677–83.

"Housing for Defense." *Common Sense* (April 1941).

"City Patterns . . . Past and Future." *New Pencil Points* 23, no. 6 (June 1942): 52–56.

"Preparedness for Post-war Urban Redevelopment." *American City* 57 (February 1942): 67–69.

"Planning Technique and the London Plan." *Architectural Review* 96, no. 573 (September 1944): 79–80.

"Education and the Evolving City." *American School and University* 17 (1945): 40.

"Theatre in a Revolution." *Theatre Arts* 29 (July 1945): 390–97.

"The City of the Future: A City of Neighborhoods." *American City* 60 (November 1945): 123–25.

"Baldwin Hills Village." *Journal of the American Institute of Architects* 7, no. 2 (February 1947): 76.

"Greendale and the Future." *American City* (June 1948).

"Toward New Towns for America." *Town Planning Review* 20, no. 3 (October 1949): 205–82.

"Toward New Towns for America." *Town Planning Review* 20, no. 4 (January 1950): 319–418.

Toward New Towns for America. Liverpool: University Press of Liverpool, 1951.

"Dynamic Cities." *Journal of the American Institute of Architects* 15 (January and June 1951): 235.

"The Pros and Cons of Architecture for Civil Defense." With fifteen other authors. *Progressive Architecture* 32, no. 9 (September 1951): 63.

"Stockholm Builds a New Town." *Planning Proceedings of the American Society of Planning Officials Conference 1952*, pp. 57–64.

"Communities for the Good Life." *Journal of the American Institute of Architects* 26 (July 1956): 11–18. Same article in *Architectural Record* 120 (August 1956): 175–77.

"Chatham Village Revisited." *Architectural Forum* 112 (May 1960): 118–21.

"Communities for the Good Life." *Journal of the American Institute of Architects* 35 (March 1961): 31+.

"New Towns and Fresh In-City Communities." With Albert Mayer. *Architectural Record* (August 1964): 129–38.

"Regional Patterns for Dispersal." *Architectural Record* 136 (September 1964): 205–6.

Works about Clarence S. Stein and the Regional Planning Association of America

"AIA Gold Medal for Clarence Stein Salutes Planning Attuned to People." *Architectural Forum* 104 (May 1956): 21+.

"Apartment House Development: Critique." *Beaux Arts Institute of Design Bulletin* 11 (December 1934): 7–10.

"Architecture of Urban Housing in the United States during the Early 1930s." *Journal of the Society of Architectural Historians* 37, no. 4 (December 1978): 235–64.

Augur, Tracy. "Radburn, the Challenge of a New Town." *Michigan Municipal Reader* 4 (February–March 1931): 39–41.

"Awarded Medal." *Architect and Engineer* 144 (March 1941): 62.

"Baldwin Hills Village." *Architect and Engineer* 168 (March 1947): 24–26.

"Baldwin Hills Village, 1941." *Architectural Design* 51, no. 10–11 (1981): 87.

Bauer, Catherine. "Baldwin Hills Village." *Pencil Points* 25 (September 1944): 44–60.

Baughman, Marjie. "A Prophet Honored More Abroad, Even More Than at Home." *Journal of the American Institute of Architects* 65, no. 12 (December 1976): 30–31.

Bing, Alexander. "Community Planning in the Motor Age." *National Association of Real Estate Boards Bulletin* (March 1929).

Birch, Eugenie. "Radburn and the American Planning Movement: The Persistence of an Idea." *Journal of the American Planning Association* 46 (October 1980).

Brownlow, Louis. "Radburn, a New Town Planned for the Motor Age." *International Housing and Town Planning Bulletin* (February 1930).

"Building on the Board: Wichita Art Institute, Wichita, Kansas." *Pencil Points* 10 (August 1929): 535–44.

"Clarence Stein Remembered." Special issue of the *Journal of the American Institute of Architects* 65 (December 1976): 17–33.

Clute, Eugene. "A New Craftsmanship in Cast Stone: Wichita Art Institute." *Architecture* 72 (November 1935): 241–46.

Dal Co, Francesco. "From Parks to Gardens." In *The American City from the Civil War to the New Deal,* edited by Giorgio Ciucci, Francesco Dal Co, Mario Manieri-Elia, and Manfredo Tafuri, 143–291. Cambridge: MIT Press, 1979.

Eckardt, Wolf Von. "New Towns: Humane Oases." *Washington Post,* 27 November 1976, p. C1+.

———. "Architect Left Humanist Monuments." *Los Angeles Times,* 9 December 1976, pt. 7, p. 8.

Ferretti, Fred. "Radburn, 'Town for Motor Age,' Is Still Running Smoothly: Longtime Residency Mark of Its Success." *New York Times,* 19 April 1979, p. B1.

Filler, Martin. "Planning for a Better World: The Lasting Legacy of Clarence Stein." *Architectural Record* 170 (August 1982): 122–27.

Goldberger, Paul. "Radburn, 'Town for Motor Age,' Is Still Running Smoothly: Model Designed on Dreams of Utopia." *New York Times,* 19 April 1979, p. B1.

Gutheim, Frederik Albert. "Stein as Catalyst of the Regional Planning Movement." *Journal of the American Institute of Architects* 65 (December 1976): 52–54.

Haskell, Douglas. "A Practitioner of Architecture as the Art of Human Settings." *Journal of the American Institute of Architects* 65 (December 1976): 32–33.

"Hillside Homes, New York City, PWA's First Limited Dividend Housing Project; C.S. Stein, Architect." *American Architect and Architecture* 148 (February 1936): 17–33.

"Hillside Housing Development in the Bronx, New York; C. S. Stein, Architect." *Architecture New York* 71 (May 1935): 245–52.

Hinman, Albert G., and G. Coleman Woodbury. "Landscape Architecture's Role in Modern Housing Projects." *Landscape Architecture* (October 1929): 9–15.

"Honors Bestowed on Two Well Known Planners." *American City* 70 (December 1955): 22.

Hunt, William Dudley. 1980. *Encyclopedia of American Architecture,* 503–6. New York: McGraw Hill.

Huxtable, Ada Louise. "Stein's Sunnyside Left a Permanent Imprint." *New York Times,* 25 June 1972, sec. 8, p. 1.

———. "Clarence Stein: The Champion of the Neighborhood." *New York Times,* 16 January 1977, p. 23+.

———. "Forgotten Prophet: Clarence Stein." In *Architecture Anyone?* New York: Random House, 1986.

"Industry Builds Kitimat—First Complete New Town in North America." *Architectural Forum* 101 (July 1954): 128–47. Article continued in *Architectural Forum* 102 (August 1954): 158–61.

"Institute's Gold Medal for 1956." *Journal of the American Institute of Architects* 25 (May 1956): 169–73.

Lewis, Charles F. "A Moderate Rental Housing Project in Pittsburgh." *Architectural Record* 70 (October 1931): 217–34.

Lubove, Roy. *Community Planning in the 1920s: The Contributions of the Regional Planning Association of America.* Pittsburgh: University of Pittsburgh Press, 1963.

———. *The Urban Community: Housing and Planning in the Progressive Era.* Englewood Cliffs, N.J.: Prentice-Hall, 1967.

Mumford, Lewis. *Roots of Contemporary American Architecture,* 430–31. New York: Reinhold Publishing Corp., 1952.

———. "A Modest Man's Enduring Contributions to Urban and Regional Planning." *Journal of the American Association of Architects* 65, no. 12 (December 1976): 19–28.

———. "Regional and Dramatic Sallies." Chapter 4 of *Sketches from Life: The Autobiography of Lewis Mumford—The Early Years.* New York: Dial Press, 1982, 333–51.

"New Art Museum Designed to Symbolize the Southwest; C. S. Stein, Architect." *Art Digest* 10 (15 October 1935): 14.

Parsons, K. C. "Shaping the Regional City, 1950–1990: The Plans of Tracy Augur and Clarence Stein for Dispersing Federal Workers from Washington, DC." In *Proceedings of the Third National Conference on American Planning History,* 649–91. Cincinnati: Society for American City and Regional Planning History, 1989.

———. "American Influence on Stockholm's Post World War II Suburban Expansion." *Planning History—The Bulletin of the Planning History Group* 12, no. 1 (1990): 3–14.

———. "Clarence Stein and the Greenbelt Towns." *Journal of the American Planning Association* 56, no. 2 (Spring 1990): 161–83.

———. "British and American Community Design: Clarence Stein's Manhattan Transfer, 1924–74." *Planning Perspectives* 7 (1992): 181–210.

———. "Clarence Stein's Middle Years: The Transition from Greenbelt Consultant to Urban Statesman." In *Proceedings of the Fifth Biennial Conference on the History of American City and Regional Planning.* Columbus, Ohio: Society of American City and Regional Planning History, 1994.

————. "Collaborative Genius: The Regional Planning Association of America." *Journal of the American Planning Association* 90 (autumn 1994): 462–82.

————. "Financing Affordable Housing: Lessons from Alexander Bing's Innovations at Sunnyside and Radburn in the 1920s" (paper presented at the Annual Conference of the Association of Collegiate Schools of Planning, Tempe, Arizona, 6 November 1994).

————. "The Regional Planning Ideas of the Regional Planning Association of America, 1925–1965" (paper presented at the Sixth National Conference on American Planning History of the Society for American City and Regional Planning History, Knoxville, Tennessee, 13 October 1995.

————. "Benton MacKaye's Collaboration with the Regional Planning Association of America: Its Influence on the Appalachian Trail and Regional Planning (1921–1931)" (paper presented at the One-Day Public Conference on Benton MacKaye and the Appalachian Trail, Albany, New York, 22 November 1996).

Parsons, K. C., and Bonnie MacDougall. "Chandigarh's Romantic/Rational Reputation Reconsidered" (paper presented at the Seventh International Conference of the International Planning History Society, Thessaloniki, Greece, 19 October 1996.

"Peaceful Retreat in the Automobile Age (Baldwin Hills Village, Los Angeles Residential Development)." *Journal of the American Institute of Architects* 58 (July 1972): 26–27.

"Planning for Art Museum Services." *Museum News* 16 (1 January 1939): 5–12.

"Planning for a Better World." *Architectural Record* 170, no. 10 (August 1982): 122–27.

"Planning Techniques and London Plan." *Architectural Review* 96 (September 1944): 79–80.

"Project: City History Museums." *Beaux Arts Institute of Design Bulletin* 10 (February 1934): 4–6.

Rosenfeld, Isadore. "Birthday Tribute to Clarence S. Stein." *Journal of the American Institute of Architects* 58 (October 1972): 64–65.

Schaffer, Daniel. *Garden Cities for America: The Radburn Experience.* Philadelphia: Temple University Press, 1982.

"Shaler Township Defense Houses: C. Stein, Architect." *Architectural Forum* 75 (October 1941): 232–33.

Smith, Geddes. "A Town for the Motor Age." *Survey Graphic* (March 1930).

Spann, Edward. *Designing Modern America: The Regional Planning Association of America and Its Members.* Columbus: Ohio State Univ. Press, 1996.

"Stowe Township Houses: C. S. Stein, Architect; Views, Plan and Construction Outline." *Architectural Forum* 77 (July 1942): 83–84.

"Study Storage: Theory and Practice." *Museum News* 22 (15 December 1944): 9–12.

"Sunnyside Gardens." *Metropolis* 10, no. 10 (June 1991): 15–19.

"Sunnyside Gardens: A Walking Tour." *Sites* 16–17 (1986): 81–89.

"Sunnyside Gardens Renewed." *Progressive Architecture* 67, no. 11 (November 1986): 47.

Sussman, Carl. *Planning the Fourth Migration: The Neglected Vision of the Regional Planning Association of America.* Cambridge: MIT Press, 1976.

"A Vision for the Town: Radburn." *Architecture New Jersey* 27, no. 4 (1991): 9, 21.

Wright, Henry. "The Autobiography of Another Idea." *Western Architect* 39 (September 1930): 137–41.

Wright, Henry Niccolls. "Radburn Revisited." *Architectural Forum* 135 (July 1971): 52–57.

Index

Abercrombie, Leslie Patrick, 447, 462, 584, 609, 660

Abercrombie Plan, 446–47, 451, 462, 584, 660

Abrams, Charles, 577

Ackerman, Frederick Lee, 91n1, 174, 180, 193, 215, 244, 267, 277, 295, 376, 408, 413, 425, 470, 515, 664; and AIA, 80, 105; biography of, 660; CSS on, xxvii, 187; and CSS's projects, 259, 655, 656; and New Deal, 253, 266, 269; and New York Housing Authority, 282, 283, 285, 306; and RPAA, xix, xxiv, 120n1, 156, 207, 210, 471; and Technical Alliance, 678; technocracy and, 188n1, 237, 239, 243, 246, 255, 374, 379, 380n; on TVA, 248

Ackerman Program, 78, 92, 660

Adams, Thomas, xxiv, 115, 156, 192, 209, 210, 224, 236; biography of, 661

Adams, W. Eric, 615

Adamson, Anthony, 607

Adler, Felix, 29, 38, 97n1; biography of, 661; and Elliott, 77, 665, 666; and Ethical Culture Society, 1, 2, 4, 111n, 416; visit to CSS, 4, 34–35; and Workingman's School, xxi, 6

affordable housing, xviii, xix, 108, 139n2; Constitutional Amendment for, 112; Labor Party on, 144–48; in New Towns, 105, 175, 326; and rent legislation, 120–22; and RPAA, 109, 245n2; and slum clearance, 132–35, 177, 277n2; tax exemptions for, 142n1

agriculture: and Garden Cities, 128–29; in Israel, 586–87; and New Deal policy, 259, 262; in New York state, 127, 193, 195–96, 198, 200; preservation of, 576, 577; and regional cities, 481–82, 622; in Russia, 141, 142

airfield housing projects, 177, 266, 267, 268, 301n3, 305n2b

Alexander, Robert Evans, 362, 390, 459, 459n3, 491n1, 537, 574, 596, 624, 661

Algonquin Club, 107–8

Allegheny County Housing Authority (Pa.), 414n1, 419–20, 451n, 497

Aluminum Company of Canada (ALCAN), xxxi, 504, 526–32, 539, 546,

Aluminum Company of Canada (ALCAN) (*cont.*) 547; and land ownership, 535–36, 537. *See also* Kitimat New Town

Amenia (N.Y.), 232, 263–64, 296n1, 363, 445

American City Planning Institute, 85n2, 123, 244, 661

American Federation of Labor, 91, 680

American Institute of Architects (AIA), 92, 104, 616, 618; and Ackerman Program, 78; and Appalachian Trail, 113, 117, 118; Community Planning Committee of, xxiv, 91n1, 104, 105, 113, 114, 117, 118, 124n2, 135, 643; Gold Medal from, xvii, xxii, 76n4, 409, 505, 565n, 569, 571, 593; on housing policy, 123, 124n2; New York Chapter of, 187, 201, 283, 619, 620; public information committee of, 80–81; Urban Design Committee of, 606

American Institute of Planners (AIP), xvii, 237, 596, 606–7, 609, 661, 663; awards of, 505, 582, 642

American Society of Planning Officials (ASPO), 475

Amiens (France), 36

Anderson, Maxwell, 400

Antwerp (Belgium), 88, 665

Appalachian Trail, xix, xxiii, xxiv, 91n1, 104, 105, 107, 112–19, 166, 175, 224n, 671

Appalachian Trail Club, 433

Architectural Forum, xxviii, 191n2, 570, 664, 667; CSS's articles for, 216n1, 222n4, 361; on Kitimat, 556, 559; on Washington, D.C., 568

Architectural League, 187, 247, 425; 1933 exhibit of, 243n3

architecture: and acting, 314–15; CSS on design, xxi, 22, 25; design pranks in, 201, 202; International Style of, 248n1, 665; limitations on, 135–37; modern, 248n1, 372n, 573, 583; Whitaker on, 273–74. *See also* community architecture

Architecture magazine, 265, 373, 670, 673, 679, 680

Arensburg, Walter, 362, 385, 486

Armbruster, Frazier, 623

Armenger, Oscar, 246n1, 302

Armstrong, Alan H., 537

Army Corps of Engineers, 78, 90, 92

Aronovici, Carol, 207, 208, 210, 224, 225, 226, 231, 290

art deco style, 164, 177, 669

art nouveau, 39, 284n1, 372n

arts and crafts style, 103, 159, 160, 161

Ascher, Charles Stern, 189, 204, 237, 255, 289, 290, 291n2, 303n2a, 366; biography of, 661; and CSS's projects, 106n, 107, 443; and New Deal, 292, 302; and RPAA, xix, 106

Astaire, Fred, 261

ateliers, 3, 10–11, 16, 17, 23–24, 26n, 49–60; of Besson, 38; of Bruel, 12, 14; of Chifflot Frères, 12, 679; of CSS (RPAA), 104–5, 120n1; of Umbdenstock, 3, 23, 24, 25, 38, 70. *See also* Laloux, Victor

Augur, Tracy Baldwin, xxx, 205, 263n3, 503, 514n1, 524, 524n1; biography of, 662; and dispersal plan, 512n, 515, 592, 593; on Radburn, 152n

Australia, 176n4, 617, 667, 676; regional cities in, 640–41

automobiles, xvii, xxv, 195, 387, 486, 552, 558, 582; AMS's purchase of, 367; and defense housing, 427, 429; and New Towns, 565–66, 567, 612, 613, 627, 629; and Radburn, 150–51, 152n, 185n2, 501, 569. *See also* highways; streets; townless highways

Bacon, Edmund, xxxi, 595, 615, 639; photograph of, 591

Baco Obrero (Caracas, Venezuela), 581

Baerwald, Emile, 276

Baerwald, Jennie, 260, 261n1, 275–76, 276n1

Baerwald, Paul, 261n1

Baldwin Hills (Los Angeles, Calif.), xxix, 106, 362, 558, 657; associates on, 582, 624n, 661, 668; CSS on, 401, 464, 486, 488, 491, 492; density of, 569; expansion of, 458–59; footpaths in, 510–11; influence of, 534n2, 555; photographs and plan of, 396

Bali, xxviii, 179, 359, 444

Barbizon (France), 20–23, 34–35

Barnard, Margaret W., 494

Baronbackarna (Sweden), 601n1a

Basildon (England), 612–13

Bassett, Edward Murray, 85, 237, 238, 662

Bauer, Catherine Krouse. *See* Wurster, Catherine Bauer

Beacontree Estate (London County Council), 229, 230n1

Becket, Welton, 536

Beersheba (Israel), 588

Behrendt, Lydia, 228, 283, 294, 368, 369, 370, 411

Behrendt, Walter Curt, 91n1, 228, 283, 368, 369, 370, 373, 460, 461; biography of, 662; CSS on, 372; at Dartmouth, 284n1, 294

Bell, Elliott V., 459, 460n1

Belluschi, Pietro, 562, 563

Belser, Karl, xxxi, 576, 586, 595, 598

Benchley, Robert, 107

Berlage, 284n1

Berlin (Germany), 148; City Planning Exhibition in, 183n4, 189, 195n1, 225, 342

Bernstein, Aline, xxvii, 174, 223, 264, 281, 314, 315, 316n1, 430; biography of, 662; and costume museum, 360, 369–70; photograph of, 397; suicide attempt of, 315, 316n1

Bernstein, Ethel, 183, 250, 282, 432

Bernstein, Teddy, 316n2

Bernstein, Theodore, 223, 264, 314, 315, 316n2, 430, 432

Bigger, Frederick, 236, 318n1, 320, 324, 326, 327, 368–69, 409, 470, 471, 625; biography of, 662; and Greenbelt (Md.), 364–65; and RA, 369

Bing, Alexander M., 144, 243, 290, 294; biography of, 663; and CHC, xxvi, 105–6, 139n3, 153, 193, 674; and CSS's projects, xxiv, 107, 152, 174, 189–90, 192, 194, 259n1, 551, 661; death of, 590; on De-

pression, 218; photographs of, 169, 334; and RPAA, xix, xxiii, 120n1, 209, 638

Bing, Florence, 194, 218, 243, 370, 590

Bing, Leo, 663

Birch, Eugenie L., 152

Black, Russell Van Nest, 205, 207, 208n5, 210, 237, 244, 365, 366; biography of, 663; and Kohn, 266, 269; and RPAA, 156, 182, 257

Blackham, Louise, 443, 446n3, 510

Bliven, Bruce, 210, 224, 225

Boden, S. F., 517

Bohn, Ernest, 446, 675; biography of, 663; CSS's correspondence with, 483–84; and NAHO, 290, 291n2; and sale of Greenbelt Towns, xxix, 401, 680

Bournville village (England), 52–53, 131, 596, 664

Boyd, D. Knickerbacker, 211, 663

Brandin, Alf E., 525, 536, 550

Branford, Victor, 123

Bredsdorff, Peter, 600

Breivogel, Milton, 595, 598, 601

Britain. *See* England

British New Towns, 493, 508, 556, 585, 602, 605–6; automobiles in, 612, 613; Bournville village, 52–53, 131, 596; Crawley, 534n1; and CSS, 401, 487, 491, 501–2, 505, 508, 551n3, 602, 621, 622; employment in, 605; Garden Cities, xxiii, 96, 120n1, 130n, 131, 465, 466, 467; Garden Suburbs, 131, 146, 664; Hampstead Garden Suburb, 105, 120n1, 130, 131, 502, 579; Harlow, 566, 615; Hemel-Hempstead, 555; Radburn Plan in, 152n, 176n1, 555, 565–66, 612, 629, 634n; and regional cities, 608; Stevenage, 402, 501, 521, 533, 555, 578n2, 612, 613, 658; superblocks in, 555, 613; Welwyn Garden City, xxiii, 120n1, 128, 129, 130, 467, 668; Wythenshawe, 376. *See also* Letchworth

Bronx (N.Y.), 96, 216, 240, 292. *See also* Hillside Homes

Brooklyn (N.Y.), 96, 216, 276

Broome, Harvey, 271

Brownlow, Louis, 262, 285; biography of,

Brownlow, Louis (*cont.*)
663; CSS on, 236–37; and Radburn, 152, 219; and RPAA conference, 156, 193, 200, 204, 205n1, 206
Bruere, Paul, 269
Bruere, Robert, 156, 210, 266
Buck, Pearl, xxviii, 178, 290n1, 400, 446, 461
Buck Hills Falls meetings, 310n3, 312–13
Buhl Foundation, 175, 184, 194, 211n3, 236, 557n
Burdell, Ed, 562, 563, 565
Bureau of Indian Affairs, 257n1, 259n2, 263n1
Butler, Charles, 174, 189, 190, 259, 267, 283, 294; biography of, 664; collaboration with CSS, 103, 186n1, 310, 656, 657; CSS on, 253; photograph of, 496
Buttenheim, Harold, 181, 417, 440, 442, 460, 463, 515, 516

Cadbury, George, 53, 54, 664
California, xviii, 502, 595, 598, 638; Carmelitos, 362, 387–88, 423, 657, 668; defense housing in, 106, 440; Harbor Hills, 362, 389, 423, 657; housing authorities in, 362, 383–86, 423; military bases in, xxii, 76, 189n2, 659; Palos Verdes, 303, 305n1b, 384–85; Pasadena Art Institute, 164, 165, 307, 320n1, 658; San Francisco, xxx, xxxi, 622, 658, 663; Santa Clara County, 571, 574, 576, 577, 586; University of, xxxi, 474, 623, 624, 661. *See also* Baldwin Hills; Los Angeles; San Diego World's Fair; Stanford University
California Building (San Diego World's Fair), 76, 80n2, 100, 101, 189n2, 659
California Institute of Technology (Pasadena, Calif.), 138, 144n, 162, 163, 207, 308n2, 656, 668
Cambridge University (England), 555
Canada, 537, 580, 607, 667. *See also* Kitimat New Town
capitalism: CSS on, xxvi, 246, 282, 300, 422; and democracy, 404, 418; and metropolitanism, 374

Caracas (Venezuela), 581, 616, 628
Carlson, Eric, 513, 542, 570, 581, 616, 627
Carmelitos Housing Project (North Long Beach, Calif.), 362, 387–88, 423, 657, 668
Carmody, John, 406, 407, 408, 409, 415, 419
Cautley, Marjorie S., 219, 298, 300, 303, 656, 664
Central Park (New York City), 174, 183n1, 580, 638, 673
Chamberlain, Allen, 114
Chandigarh (East Punjab, India), xxx, 106, 510–11, 533, 553, 659, 665, 672, 673, 679; and Radburn Plan, 504, 534n2, 564
Chase, Stuart, xxviii, 174, 192, 199, 244n1, 670; biography of, 664; CSS's correspondence with, 470, 629; and New Deal, 257n1, 675; and RPAA, xix, 116, 119, 120, 471; and RPAA conference, 156, 204, 205n1; and Russian Reconstruction Farms, 141, 144; and Technical Alliance, 242, 243n1, 660
Château of Chaumont (France), 35
Chatham Village (Pittsburgh, Pa.), xviii, xxvii, 106, 173, 175, 269, 656; CSS on, xxix, 189, 236, 369, 401, 486, 488, 490, 556–57, 571; CSS's work on, 185n1a, 186, 211, 361; gentrification of, 237n2; photographs of, 344; plans of, 343
Chelsea district (New York City), xxii; Chelsea Park, 83–85, 96; and CSS, xx, xxi, xxvi, 1, 2, 77–78, 81–85; survey of, 94–97, 669
Chicago (Ill.), 81, 88, 624, 656, 675; Century of Progress Exposition (1933), 191, 270, 668; Housing Authority of, 214n
Childs, Dick, 463, 464
China, 445, 462; CSS on, 179, 289, 431, 523, 600; Peking, 431, 535, 600; Steins' visits to, xxviii, 179, 254n2, 313, 332n, 359, 391–93, 670
church design, 79, 667
Churchill, Henry Stern, xix, 191, 294, 325n1b, 406, 625, 657; biography of,

664; on CSS, xxii, 565n; and Housing Study Guild, 216, 289, 303n1a, 680

cities: CSS on, 86, 105, 124–27, 438–39; CSS's love of, xxxii; and highways, 93–94, 150, 151, 175, 294; land purchase by, 112, 147; linear, 109; vertical and horizontal, 187. *See also* city planning; Garden Cities; regional cities

Citizen's Housing and Planning Committee (CHPC; New York City), 581, 661

The City (documentary film), xxviii, 362–63, 377–78, 380, 389, 403n2, 515, 516; collaborators on, 381, 670, 672

City and Suburban Homes Company, 455

City Club (Ethical Culture Society), 77, 78, 80, 95n1, 111n, 161, 246; City Planning Committee of, 84, 95, 97, 110–11; founders of, 661, 666

City Housing Corporation (CHC), xxiv–xxv, 130n, 149; and Bing, xxvi, 105–6, 139n3, 153, 169, 193, 209, 663; financial problems of, 174, 193–94, 342; and Radburn, 152n, 153, 219n2, 259n1; staff of, 429, 661; and Sunnyside, 184n2, 443

city planning, xvii, xix, xxii, xxiii, 666; and community architecture, 560, 572–73, 609; CSS on, xxx, 77–78, 80–81, 85–89, 135; economics of, 131, 133; neighborhood in, 81–85, 228n2, 467n2a; and regional planning, 124–27. *See also* urban development; urban redevelopment

Civic Films, 515, 516

Clark, Frederick P., 447

Clark, Joseph, 614, 615, 615n1

Cleveland (Ohio), 247, 296n2a, 446; Housing Authority of, xxix, 291n1a, 401, 484, 663; housing projects in, 251, 253, 259, 263, 265n1a, 280, 281n1a; Regional Association of, 291n1a, 663

Cloud Club (Chrysler Building, New York City), 213–14

Colean, Miles Lanier, 301, 405, 664

Columbia (Md.), xviii, xxx, 174, 595

Columbia River Basin development, 474–75, 522

Columbia University, xxxi, 366n2b, 624, 669; CSS at, xxi, 3, 4, 14n, 22, 44n1, 292, 295n, 368

Columbia Valley (N.J.), 118

Columbus Circle (New York City), 659

commercial facilities, 80, 321–22, 586, 627; at Hillside, 216n1, 222n4, 494n

Commission on Rural Housing, 207

Committee on Un-American Activities, 476

Common Sense magazine, 272, 420

community architecture: and city planning, 560, 572–73, 609; and CSS, xvii, xx, xxi, 2, 362–63, 505, 571–73; and New Towns, 560–61, 562

community equipment, xxxii, 16–17n, 514, 519

community planning: for automobiles, 486, 567, 612, 613, 627; and CSS, 76, 77–78, 103, 139n2, 452–53; economics of, 136, 329–30, 405, 408, 455–56; and Garden Cities, 127–30; and health facilities, 493–94; and house plots, 136, 137; and housing projects, 223n3; and leisure, 249; and management, 453, 457; for mixed economic groups, 454–55; and nature of communities, 106, 442–46; postwar, 400–401, 434, 452; and RPAA, xxiii, 105; and transportation for workers, 85n4, 87–89, 95–97. *See also* city planning; regional planning

Congress, U.S.: and dispersal policy, 503, 512n, 514n, 524–25; and Greenbelt Towns, 482, 483, 485, 486; housing legislation from, 508; and New Towns, 480, 603; and regional decentralization, 624–25; and urban redevelopment, 525–26

Connecticut, 113, 115, 150n, 375

Connecticut River survey, 390

constitutional amendments, 112, 147

cooperative housing, 540, 542–43

Copenhagen (Denmark), 595, 600, 627–28, 629, 633, 643

Copland, Aaron, 363, 516, 670

Le Corbusier (Charles Édouard Jeanneret),

Le Corbusier (*cont.*)
670, 677; biography of, 665; and Chandigarh, 504, 511, 533, 534, 553, 564, 659, 673
Cornell University, xx, xxxi, 139n4, 188n1, 195n3, 219n1b, 279, 295n, 296n2a
Costume Museum project, 360, 369–70
Cotswolds (England), 195, 416, 566
County of London Plan (Abercrombie and Forshaw), 447n2, 660
Coventry (England), 613
Cram, Goodhue, and Ferguson (architectural firm), 75–76, 79
Crane, Jacob, 447, 678
Creese, Walter, 566, 631, 637
Cret, Paul Philippe, 304
cummings, e. e., xxvii

Dahir, James, 466
Dal Co, Francesco, xix, 120
Davies, Anthony B., 613
Davies, J. M., 570
Davies, Joseph E., 269, 270n2
decentralization, 207, 442, 447; of industry, 196, 249, 477, 478, 518; and New Deal housing policy, 260, 262; regional, 624–25. *See also* dispersal policy
deed restrictions, 85n3, 106, 303n2a, 558, 661
defense housing, 412, 428, 665; in California, 106, 440; and CSS, 399, 400, 406–7, 410, 571, 675; day-care facilities in, 427, 429, 440; and dispersal policy, 514–15; experiments with, 137; and industry, 518–20; in Maryland, 400, 407–11, 419, 657; in Pennsylvania, 106, 400, 415–20, 424n1, 497, 571, 657; photographs of, 497; policy on, xxix, 208n6, 430n2; and transportation, 427, 429, 519; in Washington, D.C., 106, 400
Delano, Frederick, 199
DeMars, Vernon, 514, 558, 604, 644, 665
Democratic Party, 78, 603, 604n
Denmark, xviii, 541n, 579, 602, 604, 643; AMS's work in, 402; CSS's influence in, 502, 627–28; Finger Plan in, 595, 600,

628, 633; New Towns, 628; Steins' visits to, 401–2, 487, 489, 490–91, 541, 627, 629
Department of Housing and Urban Development (HUD), 503, 596, 604n, 611, 617; creation of, 608–9; CSS on, 610, 614, 615, 616
Depression, xxvi, xxvii, 173–75, 190n, 195, 443; bank holiday in, 250–51, 253; CSS on, 218, 235, 237; unemployment in, 220, 246, 291, 300, 306, 307
Detroit (Mich.), 429, 570
Dewey, Thomas E., 440–41, 442, 447, 637
"Dinosaur Cities" (Stein), 105
dispersal policy, 660, 662; CSS's work on, 522–23; and defense housing, 514–15; and GSA, 503, 514n; and industry, 108, 514–15, 519–20; and New Towns, 503–4, 512n, 514n, 603, 621–22, 677; and RDCA, 513, 517, 524–25; RPAA on, 519–20; and U.S. Congress, 503, 512n, 514n, 524–25; for Washington, D.C., 503, 568, 592, 593, 595
Dixon, Jean, 183
Double U Ranch (Tucson, Ariz.), 435–38
Douglas, Paul M., 485, 639
Dozier, Melville, 386, 422
Draper, Earl, 263n2, 266n2, 268, 420, 421n2, 665
Drew, Jane, 553n2
Dublin (Ireland), 666, 678
Dudley, Jim, 535, 549

Easter Hill, 558, 665
Ebenezer Howard Memorial Medal, 589
Eberlin, Ralph, 325, 330, 373, 400, 416, 417, 443, 452, 457, 665
Eccles, Marriner, 260, 675
École des Beaux Arts, xvii, xxi–xxiii, 3–6, 11, 16n, 28, 79, 135, 310n2; ateliers of, 49–60; CSS's admission to, 43–48; entrance examinations for, 4, 9, 12n, 13–14, 20–21, 22–23, 33; graduates of, 32, 33n; students of, 664, 666, 667, 668, 669, 672, 675, 679; teachers at, 669–70
Edelman, Kate, 510

education: architectural, 104; about city planning, 80–81; about housing policy, 91, 147, 231; in planning, 233n3, 295, 366, 559–65

Egan, Jack, 473, 479, 482, 484

Eidlitz, Otto Mark, 92, 665

Eisenhower, Dwight D., 503, 512, 512n, 611

Eisenstein, Sergei, 208, 209, 665

Eken, Andrew J., 216, 218, 241, 264, 378–79; collaboration with CSS, 225, 230n2, 231, 232, 235, 238, 239, 259, 266, 274, 278, 282, 287, 300; and Straus, 292n2, 293, 304

Ellington, Douglas D., 329, 657

Elliott, John Lovejoy, xxi, xxiii, 29, 38, 83, 84, 97n1, 416; biography of, 665–66; influence of, 2, 77; Sunday Clubs of, 54n1; visit to CSS, 4, 34–35

Elliott, Walter, 182, 229

Ely, Richard, 679

Emergency Fleet Housing Corporation, 669, 673, 680

Emerson (dean at MIT), 295, 366

Emma (cook), 213, 214

Emmerich, Herbert, 188, 207, 208n6, 377, 427; and FPHA, 426, 429; and New Deal, 285, 287, 410; photographs of, 334, 351; and Radburn, 184, 185n2, 258, 268; and RPAA, 257

Empire State Building, 203, 274n3

England, xviii, xxxi, 72, 555, 613, 660; AMS's work in, 402, 553n3; automobiles in, 627, 629; building costs in, 129, 131; and CSS, xxix, xxxi, 4, 52, 115n2, 401, 404, 502; housing in, 105, 133, 228n3; planning in, 81, 463n2, 465–66, 668; Radburn's influence in, 152n, 492, 555, 569; Steins' visits to, 153n, 332n, 391, 487, 489, 491, 501–2, 506, 542, 555. *See also* British New Towns; Letchworth; London

environment, natural, xx, 75, 108; and forestry, 180, 193, 195, 481–82; and MacKaye, 671; and national forests, 119, 254; and national parks, 224, 250, 673; in New Towns, 127, 311, 604; in regional planning, 127, 137, 512, 666; and urban development, 447–48; wilderness, 641; of wilderness areas, xviii, 250, 582, 636, 641

Ernst, Morice, 191, 208

Ethical Culture Society, 77–78, 140n, 161; and CSS, xxi, xxii, 1–2, 27, 194; Fieldston School of, 2, 104, 144n1, 162, 186, 231, 656; leaders of, 34–35, 661, 665–66; meetinghouse of, 115n2, 664, 669. *See also* Adler, Felix; City Club; Workingman's School

Europe, xviii; CSS in, xxi, xxiii, 3; housing in, 111n, 133, 212, 225n2, 248; influences in, xxix, 174, 284n1; New Towns in, xxiii; planning in, 117, 222. *See also particular countries*

Farsta (Sweden), 500, 502, 627, 628

Federal government, U.S.: and dispersal policy, 503, 515, 519–20; financing from, 224–25, 226, 230; housing policies of, 174, 218, 220, 307, 362, 399, 401, 664; and housing reform, 90, 92; and New Towns, 308, 477, 478–79, 484, 604n, 633, 634; and regional planning, 119, 126, 199, 611; and urban development, 178, 554, 583, 625

Federal Housing Administration (FHA), 292, 293, 514; advisors to, 662–63; and Baldwin Hills, 362; and community planning, 409; loans from, 293n1, 456, 478, 675; staff of, 665, 669, 676, 678, 679

Federal Public Housing Administration (FPHA): CSS's work for, 400, 426n1, 431n1, 441n1; and Greenbelt Towns, 465; staff of, 429, 665

Federal Works Administration (FWA), 408, 665; CSS's work for, 418, 419, 426n1

Feiss, Carl, xxx, xxxi, 296n2a, 462n, 525, 565n, 625, 626; biography of, 666; CSS's correspondence with, 517, 559, 564, 570, 606, 609, 638; and dispersal policy, 515; and HHFA, 503; and MIT, 562; and Unwin, 366n2b, 390, 552, 620

Felt, Jack, 626

Ferris, Hugh, 425

Fields, W. C., 285

Fieldston School (Ethical Culture Society; Riverdale, N.Y.), 2, 104, 144n1, 162, 186, 231, 656

financing: of CSS's projects, 177, 229–30, 266–67, 300–301, 458; of dispersal policy, 520; federal, 224–25, 226, 230; for housing, xxiv–xxv, 96, 98, 110–11, 112, 122, 221, 240n2; and housing shortages, 146–47; for New Towns, 307n1a, 477, 479, 604n; for research, 225n2; and RFC, 222n2; of RPAA projects, 106; state, 122, 134, 147

Finger Plan (Copenhagen, Denmark), 595, 600, 628, 633

Finland, 402, 634, 675

Firth, Cedric, 14, 486

Fleming, P. B., 480, 621

Florence (Italy), 41, 523

Floyd Bennett Field (Long Island, N.Y.), 267n1b, 349

Foley (Egan's superior), 473, 479, 480, 482, 484, 494

Ford, George Burdett, 123, 661, 666

Ford, Henry, 137, 200, 367

Foreshaw, J. H., 447, 660

Fort Green Houses (Brooklyn, N.Y.), 657

Fortune magazine, xxviii, 221, 228, 449, 583; Bauer's articles for, 203, 216n1; MacLeish's articles in, 278, 671; Mumford's articles in, 212, 215

France, xviii, 37, 81; CSS on, 404; CSS's influence in, 402; people of, 17, 18, 24, 30–31; Radburn's influence in, 152n; Steins' visits to, 391, 506, 523, 627, 629, 630. *See also* Paris

French, F. F., 245, 246

Fresh Meadows Park (Long Island, N.Y.), 455n2, 499, 533, 537, 581, 658

Froebel, Friedrich, xxi, 2

Fry, Maxwell, 511, 553n2

Fulmer, Kline, 406, 419, 445, 446

Gallo, Luillio, 385

Garden Cities: concept of, xxv, 89; CSS on, 127–30, 137; in England, xxiii, 54n, 120n1, 130n, 131, 465, 466, 467, 677; and industry, 421; influence of, xxiii, 551–52; limitations of, 113; modernization of, 376n; and New Towns, 567; originators of, 661, 668, 677–78; and regional cities, 144, 149; and regional planning, 117; and RPAA, xxiii, 116, 513; size of, 628; studies of, 566–67; and transportation, 146; in U.S., 83

Garden Cities and Regional Planning Association of America, xxiii, 116. *See also* Regional Planning Association of America

Garden Suburbs, 131, 146, 664. *See also* Hampstead Garden Suburb

Garner-Wagner Bill, 230

Gaus, John M., 206, 446, 447, 480, 482

Geddes, Patrick, 139n4, 678; biography of, 666; and CSS, 77; CSS on, 225, 640; influence of, 183n5, 635; and Mumford, 123n, 226n4; and RPAA, xxiii, 109, 117, 120n2

General Services Administration (GSA), xxx, 503, 514n, 523, 524n

George, Henry, 188, 666

Germany, 4, 227, 370; AMS's work in, 402; architecture in, 372n; Bauer in, 203, 221, 222; Berlin City Planning Exhibition in, 183n4, 189, 195n1, 225, 342; housing in, 190, 194, 212, 225, 228n3; Jews in Nazi, 174, 261n1a, 275–76, 284n1, 370; planning in, 493, 662; prejudice against people of, 56; Radburn's influence in, 152n, 182; Steins' visits to, 148, 203, 508

Gibherd, Frederic, 613

Glass, Milton, 672

Glikson, Arthur, xxxi, 532, 541, 616, 667

The Good Earth (film), xxviii, 178, 289, 298, 299, 318, 328, 332, 371

Goodhue, Bertram Grosvenor, 124n4, 139n1, 189n2, 362, 412n3, 668, 679; biography of, 667; buildings of, 207n2, 239, 304, 670; CSS's work for, xxii, xxiii,

75–77, 79, 103, 308n2, 310n2b, 659; in-
fluence of, 163, 164
Goodrich, Ernest P., 203, 204, 205
Gove, George, 210, 226, 228, 290, 302, 443,
455
Grant, Cary, 359, 365n2
Gratiot (Mies van der Rohe), 570
Greater London Plan (Abercrombie and
Forshaw), 447n2, 660
Greece, 599–600, 602
Greeley, W. Roger, 156, 182, 470, 472
Greely, Roland, 207, 208n
Greenbelt (Md.), xx, xxviii, 177, 317n1b,
326n1, 327, 481, 657; and *The City*, 363,
381, 670; CSS on, 364–65; CSS's influence on, 178, 329n, 331n2, 355, 361,
412n1; footpaths in, 510–11; photographs
of, 356, 357; plan of, 355; proposed sale
of, 465–66, 482–83, 484–85; sale of, xxix
Greenbelt Towns, 106, 191n1, 219n3; appropriations for, 672; in Britain, 678; as
communities, 445; consultants on, 662;
CSS on, xxix, 320–22, 326, 401, 467,
486, 488, 490, 491; CSS's role in, xviii,
xx, xxvii, xxviii, 177–78, 313, 317–20,
324–31, 412n1, 430n2; design of, 319n;
land ownership in, 638–39; and postwar
planning, 468; proposed sale of, 401,
473, 479–80, 482–83, 484–85, 486, 487,
663, 680; and RA, 304–5, 308n1, 675,
678; and RPAA, 199n2, 501
Greenbrook (N.J.), 325, 664, 679, 680
Greendale (N.J.), 191n1, 473, 479–80, 482,
483
Greenhills (Ohio), 479, 482, 484
Gries, John M., 180, 181
Griswold, Ralph E., 175, 211, 212, 417, 667
Gruen, Victor, 596, 620, 623
Gruensfeldt, Ernest, 27, 115, 214, 655, 667
Guadalupe (Mexico), 139–40
Gutheim, Frederick, 255, 256, 262, 263, 515,
568n2, 624, 625, 633
Gygemosen (Denmark), 579

Haar, Charles, 607
Hall, Gus, 366

Hallett, George, 460
Hamilton Fish Park (New York City), 8
Hampstead Garden Suburb (England), 579,
621, 638, 678; CSS on, 131, 551–52; CSS's
visits to, 105, 120n1, 491–93, 501–2;
transportation in, 130
Harbor Hills House Project (San Pedro,
Calif.), 362, 389, 423, 657
Harbor Square town houses, 676
Harlow (England), 566, 615, 628
Harrison, Wallace, 369, 468, 469
Hart, Moss, xxvii, 174, 183, 217, 308, 317,
324, 667, 671
Haskell, Douglas, 191, 556, 568, 667
Haussmann, Baron, 13
Hawaii, 381, 627, 629
Hegemann, Werner, 245n2, 292
Henderson, Cyril, 545, 546, 580
Henry Street Settlement Playhouse, xxvi
Henry Wright Library (Columbia Univer-
sity), 375
highways, 182n, 615n1a; and cities, 93–94,
150, 151, 175, 294; CSS on, 582, 583; and
federal government, 236, 263, 611, 616;
and land values, 154–55; and New
Towns, 153, 477, 485; and parkways,
180n, 182n; in wilderness areas, 224n,
250. *See also* automobiles; streets; townless highways
Hillside Homes (Bronx, N.Y.), 173, 176–77,
656; approval of, 238, 266, 273n1a, 274,
275; closed streets at, 229, 303, 304, 312,
347; and community facilities, 216n1,
222n4, 494n; construction of, 277, 290,
291, 294; contract for, 282, 284; CSS on,
xxix, 315, 368, 401, 453–54, 486, 488;
CSS's work on, xviii, xxvii, 106, 361;
dedication of, 311–12; design of, 226n3,
278, 279, 280, 288; financing of, 214–15,
222n2, 233–34; income from, 296; influence of, 223n3, 492–93; and Kohn,
244–45; landscaping of, 298, 664;
models of, 241; and New Deal, 259,
260n, 287; photograph of, 348; plans of,
347; problems with, 246, 247, 285, 286;
reactions to, xxxii, 315–16, 318, 672; rents

Hillside Homes (*cont.*)
  at, 220, 347, 456; site of, 226–27; and
  State Housing Board, 232, 234, 235; and
  Straus, 174, 230n2, 231, 292, 293, 376,
  677; tenants' association at, 443; visits
  to, 291n2, 300, 315
Hitchcock, Peggy, 153, 424, 601, 620, 630,
  631
Holford, Marjorie, 618
Holford, William, 502, 601, 609, 616, 618,
  631, 668
Hollywood blacklist, xxxi, 475n2
Honolulu (Hawaii), 381
Hood, Raymond Mathewson, xxvii, 187,
  191, 668
Hoover, Herbert, 220, 240n2, 260, 662;
  housing policies of, 181, 230, 279n1
Hopkins, Harry, 307, 674
Housatonic Valley Conference, 420, 421
housing: cooperative, 540, 542–43; density
  of, 106, 181n3, 569, 581, 613–14; detached, 136; freestanding, 181, 186, 386;
  legislation on, 131, 132, 142, 221, 226, 231,
  508; local boards for, 111–12, 197, 221;
  municipal, 111, 122; postwar, 139, 400–
  401, 410, 413, 434, 438–42, 447–49, 452,
  465, 468–70, 477–78; public, 408–9; as
  public utility, 145; reform of, 90, 92, 103,
  239n, 360; and regional planning,
  124–27; relocation, 134n; shortages of,
  146; speculation in, 110–11, 146; statistics
  on, 204, 239n, 323–24; subsidized, 98n,
  133–34, 399, 477, 611, 638. *See also* affordable housing; housing authorities;
  housing costs; housing policies
Housing Acts: of 1934, 260n, 288n, 675; of
  1936, 199n2; of 1937 (Wagner-Steagall-
  Taft-Ellender Bill), 231n1, 361, 362,
  373n1, 377n4, 399, 663, 680; of 1949,
  296n2a, 479n, 554, 663; of 1954, 663; of
  1966, 604n
Housing and Home Finance Agency
  (HHFA), 296n2a, 494n, 503, 520, 662,
  666
housing authorities: in California, 362,
  383–86, 423; in Chicago, 214n; idea of,

247; in Ohio, xxix, 291n1a, 401, 484,
  663; in Pennsylvania, 414n1, 419–20,
  451n, 497; in St. Louis, 223n3; in Washington, D.C., 484. *See also* New York
  City Housing Authority
Housing Authority, U.S., 377n1, 389, 677,
  679; Bauer at, 363, 680; and Los Angeles
  projects, 386, 387–88
Housing Corporation, U.S., 137, 181n2,
  188n1, 519, 674
housing costs, 112, 222, 225; and architects,
  135–36; and density, 106, 181n3; in
  Greenbelt Towns, 321, 324, 326, 327,
  329–30; at Hillside, 220, 347, 456; and
  Los Angeles projects, 386, 387–88; and
  slum clearance, 132–34
Housing Exhibition (1933), 247–48
housing policies, 228, 583; AIA on, 123,
  124n2; and defense, 430n2; and Depression, 220; education about, 91, 147, 231;
  in Europe, 115n2; of FDR, 174, 177–78,
  210, 231n1, 410n1b; federal, 174, 218,
  220, 307, 362, 399, 401, 664; of Hoover,
  181, 230, 279n1; New Deal, 177, 260,
  260n, 261, 262, 278, 281; in New York,
  xxii, xxiii, 104, 122, 210, 399; and RPAA,
  xxiii, 105; state, 399; of Truman, 426n2,
  677; of TVA, 291n2
Housing Study Guild (Philadelphia),
  216n1, 289, 303n1a, 581, 664, 679, 680
Howard, Ebenezer, 207, 326, 364, 474, 475,
  607, 667, 678; biography of, 668; CSS's
  visit with, xxiii, 120n1, 130, 567; Garden
  Cities of, 128, 144, 181n3, 467, 606, 628,
  643; and Garden City movement, 54n;
  influence of, xxv, 89, 551–52
Howard, Jack, 296
Howe, Louis, 674
HSB (Hyresgästernas Sparkasse och Byggnadsforening), 543
Hudson Guild, 77, 78, 84, 669; AMS at,
  671; library of, 59; Settlement House of,
  xxi, xxii, xxiii, 97n2, 159, 160, 661, 666;
  theater of, 19, 140n, 397, 415–16
Hudson Guild Farm (Netcong, N.J.), 113,
  153–54, 229, 656; buildings at, 103, 655;

meetings at, 109, 117, 139n4, 166, 181n1; photograph of, 159; RPAA at, 628–29, 642

Hughes, Charles Evans, 38, 39

Hunter (Eken's partner), 278, 282, 304, 317

Ickes, Harold, xxvii, 277n1, 289–90, 319n, 320n1a; biography of, 668; and FDR's housing policy, 199n2, 260n; and Hillside, 177, 286n1b, 292, 293; and Kohn, 245n3, 274, 281n1b, 288; MacLeish on, 278n

India, xxx, xxxi, 452, 603, 679; Albert Mayer in, 462, 540, 579, 586, 672; Steins' visits to, 173, 391. *See also* Chandigarh

Indian Head Prototype Defense Housing (Md.), 400, 407–11, 419, 657

Indonesia, 179, 254n2, 332n, 359, 391

industry: and agriculture, 141; decentralization of, 196, 249, 477, 478, 518; and defense housing, 518–20; and dispersal policy, 108, 514–15, 519–20; in FDR's land policy, 195–96, 198, 200; and housing costs, 133–34, 245n2; at Kitimat, 528, 541, 634; in New Towns, 245n2, 421, 486; in New York City, 95–97, 196; and regional planning, 93, 125–26, 127; and workers, 82–83, 85n4, 88–89, 97, 112–13, 137, 222, 605

Ingram and Boyd (architectural firm), 175, 185, 195, 211, 656

interior decorating, xxi, 3, 12, 25, 76

International Federation for Housing and Town Planning, xxiv, 195n1, 376

International Town Planning Conference (1925), 637–38

Iran, 506, 584, 586

Isaacs, Stanley Myer, 218, 288, 590, 668

Israel, xxxi, 579, 643; CSS on, 616; New Towns in, 585, 621, 667; regional planning in, 532, 586–88, 643; Steins' visits to, 506, 584, 585, 586

Italy, 4, 7, 41, 61–62, 69, 73, 402; Steins' visits to, 332n, 506, 523

Jacobs, Jane, xxxii

Jamison, Kay Redfield, xxviiin19, 360n4

Japan, 462; Steins' visits to, 179, 254, 268, 391, 617

Jeanneret, Charles Édouard. *See* Le Corbusier

Jennie Mac. *See* MacMahon, Jennie Simons

Jews, xxxi, 8, 418; in Nazi Germany, 174, 261n1a, 275–76, 284n1, 370

Johnson, Lee, 480, 483, 514

Johnson, Lyndon B., 604n, 635n1

Johnson, Philip C., 202, 248n1, 508

Johnson, Reginald D., 212, 308n1, 362, 383, 385, 459, 491n1, 657, 668; CSS's correspondence with, 382, 389

Johnson, Wilson, Merrill, and Alexander (architectural firm), 362, 382

Jones, Sullivan, 123, 302, 668

Journal of the American Institute of Architects (JAIA), 114, 124n2, 188n1, 625n, 679; Ackerman's articles in, 660; and Appalachian Trail, 105, 113, 166; Behrendt's articles in, 294n, 662; CSS as associate editor of, xxiv, 78, 104, 115n2; CSS's letters to, xxii, 90–91; Mayer's articles in, 524; Mumford's articles in, 123n

Justiment, Louis, 523, 524n1

Kahn, Ely Jacques, 309, 310; biography of, 669; travels with CSS, 4, 43, 44, 47, 54, 56, 59, 60–62, 76, 79

Kahn, Ernest, 290, 291

Kamstra, Alan, 191, 233, 242, 254, 288, 325, 664

Kansas City Art Museum, 163

Kaufman, George, 183

Kennedy, John F., 596, 604, 611, 635; CSS on, 596, 607, 611, 614; and HUD, 604n, 608–9

Kent, Jack, 474, 482, 549, 562

Keppel, Frederick P., 669

Keppel, John, 363, 377, 378n12

Kern, Jerome, 425

Kessler, George, 680

Keyserling, Leon, 479, 481

Killian, J. R., Jr., 559, 561, 562, 563

Kitimat New Town (British Columbia, Canada), xx, xxxi, 106, 504, 525–34, 580, 658; architects on, 579, 679; commercial facilities in, 586; as community architecture, 561; CSS on, 541–42, 545–46, 548, 549, 559, 621; CSS's work on, 537–40, 547, 550; flood control at, 538–39, 545–46; land ownership in, 535–36, 537; museum in, 538–39, 586; plan of, 592; reactions to, 556, 634

Kizer, Benjamin H., xxxi, 461, 462, 462n1, 474, 521–22, 540–41

Klaber, Eugene Henry, 231, 237, 286, 667; biography of, 669; with CSS in Arizona, 436, 437, 438n; with CSS in Paris, 4, 26, 27, 29, 34, 39, 43, 47, 53, 54, 58; CSS's correspondence with, 470, 553, 574; and Kohn, 266, 269, 285; and New Deal, 287–88, 292, 301, 427n1; and RPAA, 120n1, 471; survey of Chelsea by, 95–97

Klutznick, Philip, 543, 544n1

Knickerbocker Village community association (N.Y.), 443

Kohn, Estelle, 253, 273, 281, 283, 286

Kohn, Robert David, xxvii, 174, 180, 181n2, 188n1, 194, 207, 225, 237, 239, 253, 263n1, 270, 285, 286, 295, 317, 467, 624; biography of, 669; and *The City*, 377, 515; and CSS, 5, 103–4, 186, 248, 272–73, 282, 283, 290, 656, 657; and Hillside, 244–46; and housing legislation, 226, 228, 231; and Ickes, 245n3, 274, 281n1b, 288, 668; and MacKaye, 424; MacLeish on, 278n; and MIT, 295; and New Deal, 254, 257, 259, 260, 261, 262; photograph of, 496; at PWA, 265, 266, 267; resignation of, 277, 281, 285–86; and Rockefeller Foundation, 229n; and RPAA, xix, 120n1, 470, 471; at Shipping Board, 78, 92, 660, 664; and Henry Wright, 270, 375

Labor Party: England, 677; New York, 144–48

labor unions, 91, 413n2, 680; and CSS, 90–91, 404, 413n2; and housing, 239,

289, 428; and urban development, 455, 456, 525

La Follette, Robert, 206

LaGuardia, Fiorello H., xxvii, 308–9, 312, 669

Laloux, Victor, xxi, xxiii, 4, 49–51, 59; biography of, 669–70; picture of, 70

land: development of, 129; and eminent domain, 147, 221, 226n1, 477, 479; for New Towns, 478–79, 595; ownership of, 112, 187, 188n2, 204, 255, 256n3, 535–36, 537, 600, 638–39, 643; purchase of, 110, 477; for regional cities, 622; use of, 572–73

landscape architecture, 662, 664, 673–74; at Chatham Village, 175, 211n2, 667; CSS on, 258; at Hillside, 300, 303; at Radburn, 219n1b; at Sunnyside, 171; in TVA, 262

Landscape magazine, 610, 616

land values: and architecture, 137; in FDR's land policy, 195; and Garden Cities, 128; and height of buildings, 187; and highways, 154–55; and housing costs, 124, 125, 134, 147; and planning, 377, 583; and slum clearance, 177, 234

Lanham Act, 465

Lansill, John, 178, 323–26, 328, 330, 364; CSS's correspondence with, 329

Larsson, Yngve, xxxi, 502, 507, 509, 540, 600, 601, 619; CSS's correspondence with, 587, 611

Lawrie, Lee O., 207, 298, 298n1, 670

legislation: and dispersal policy, 515; housing, 98n, 104, 216n1; on model housing, 90; on New Towns, 595, 604n, 639; on open space, 605. *See also* Congress, U.S.; Housing Acts

Lehman, Herbert, 250, 251n2, 267, 275

Lescaze, William, 290, 670

Letchworth (England), 467, 567; and Howard, 89, 668; influence of, xxiii, 105, 551–52; as model, 83, 128, 130, 131; and Unwin, 678

Lewis, Charles F., 175, 185, 194, 211, 556

Lewison, Irene, 369–70

Liang, Phyllis, 179, 393, 467

Liang Ssu-ch'eng, 179, 381, 393, 467, 469n1, 670

limited dividend corporations, 134, 221, 223, 226n1, 227, 543; and federal subsidies, 399; and Greenbelt Towns, 485, 487; tax exemptions for, 142n1

Ling, Arthur, 613

Lin Yutang, 382, 431

Loeb, Sophie, 309

Logue, Edward, 442n3

London (England), 134, 180, 296, 615, 660; City Council of, 600; County Council of, 229; development plans for, 446–47, 447n2, 451, 462, 584, 660; Steins' visits to, 523, 599, 627

Long Beach Housing Authority (Calif.), 383–85

Loos, Peter Beherenns, 284n1

Lorenz, Pere, 362, 363, 370, 381, 382, 670

Los Angeles (Calif.): architecture in, 673; CSS on, 384n3, 463, 572–73, 596, 601; housing authorities in, 362, 383–86, 423

Lowe, Frank, 443, 446

lower East Side (New York City), 276–77, 298–99, 405, 454

Lubove, Roy, xix, 120, 628, 670

Mac, Jennic. *See* MacMahon, Jennie Simons

MacKaye, Benton, xxvii, xxxi, 103, 150, 173, 174, 232, 236, 244, 246, 252, 259, 266, 299, 330, 331, 372, 377, 379, 408, 441, 461, 466, 544, 548, 567–68, 611, 665, 672, 675, 678, 680; and Albany museum, 389; and Appalachian Trail, xxii–xxiii, 91n1, 112–13, 115, 118–19, 120n3, 166, 433; biography of, 671; Boston by-pass of, 193; and Bureau of Indian Affairs, 257n1, 259n2, 263n1; and *The City*, 363, 380; Connecticut River survey by, 150n, 390; and CSS, 104, 107; CSS on, 567, 569; CSS's correspondence with, 114, 116, 141, 142, 144, 148, 149, 152, 153, 154, 180, 181, 192, 199, 203, 206, 224, 228, 235, 238, 256, 257, 258, 261, 265,

271, 275, 370, 371, 373, 375, 380, 389, 390, 401, 405, 406, 420, 423, 424, 428, 433, 437, 439, 442, 451, 470, 491, 511, 538, 588, 602, 614, 618, 624, 626, 637, 641, 642; and CSS's illness, 360, 361, 370, 371, 373; and CSS's mental illness, 499; in Forestry Department, 381; and Henry Wright library, 375; illness of, 271–72; and Kitimat, 539n, 586; and Kohn, 424; and Mumford, 175; on national forests, 254; and National Park Service, 224; and New Deal, 236n; on New York State Housing and Regional Planning Commission, 610; and 1926 *Report*, 635, 637; photographs of, 166, 352, 499; and RDCA, xxviii, 516; and regional cities, xviii, 375; and RPAA, xix, xxiv, 105, 156, 205n1, 471; on skyline highways, 250n; and Technical Alliance, 242, 243n1; on townless highway, 182n, 204; and TVA, 257n2, 275, 295, 665, 675; writings of, 149, 215, 489, 588–89

MacKaye, Hazel, 149, 153

MacKaye, Jessie, 104

MacKaye, Steele, 568

Mackesey, Thomas W., 296n2

MacLeish, Archibald, xxvii, 212, 278, 671

MacMahon, Aline. *See* Stein, Aline MacMahon

MacMahon, Jennie Simons (mother-in-law), 140n, 283, 284n2, 309n3, 368, 382–84, 405, 407–9, 416n1b, 417, 430, 434–36, 451, 476, 502, 544, 644; photograph of, 499

Manning, Eleanor, 92

Marin City community association, 442–43

Marine Corps Base (San Diego, Calif.), xxii, 76, 189n2, 659

Markelius, Sven, 469, 500, 502, 507, 509, 510, 599, 600, 601, 604, 609, 673

Mars, Vernon de, 466

Marx, Karl, 246

Maryland, xviii, xxx, 174, 568n2, 595, 674; defense housing in, 400, 407–11, 419, 657. *See also* Greenbelt

Massachusetts, 91, 92, 193, 673–74; and Ap-

Massachusetts (*cont.*)
 palachian Trail, 113, 119. *See also* Shirley
 Center
Massachusetts Institute of Technology
 (MIT), xxxi; CSS's teaching at, 295,
 379; planning department at, 559–64,
 565
May, Ernst, 631
May, Stacey, 297
Maybury, 378
Mayer, Albert (architect), 174, 233, 248n2,
 290, 294, 330, 332, 480, 516, 549, 580,
 596, 639; biography of, 671–72; and
 Chandigarh, 504, 511n, 533, 534n2, 553,
 564, 659, 673; and CSS, 242, 254n1, 288;
 CSS on, 299, 609, 641, 642; CSS's correspondence with, 510, 565, 598; and defense housing, 406; on dispersal policy,
 517, 524, 525n; and Hillside, 315; on
 Housing Act of 1937, 373n2; and Housing Study Guild, 680; in India, xxx,
 462, 540, 579, 586, 672; and Kitimat,
 538, 540, 542, 658; on New Deal housing, 279; on New Towns proposal, 603,
 634; photographs of, 645; and RA,
 191n1, 318n, 325n1b, 664, 679; and
 RDCA, xxviii, 503, 513; and RPAA, xix,
 257; on slum clearance, 276, 277n2; and
 Welfare Island, 619
Mayer, Albert (builder), 239, 248n2, 671
Mayer, Arthur (brother-in-law), 187, 213,
 253, 411, 435, 462, 602, 644; biography
 of, 672; and *The City*, 363, 377; movie
 theater plans for, 359
Mayer, Margaret (niece), 229, 275, 285, 290
Mayer, Michael (nephew), 275, 368, 368n1,
 434
Mayer, Peter (nephew), 602
McCarthy, Joseph, 482, 483
McCarthyism, 475n2, 563n
McCormack, Walter, 281n1
McDonald, Charles, 483, 510, 511, 621
McLaren, Wallace, 156
McVoy, Arthur, 562
Messenger Lectures (Cornell University),
 472n

Metropolitan Life Housing program,
 378–79, 443, 446, 455
Mexico, 209n1, 570, 614, 664; CSS on,
 139–40; film of, 208, 209, 665; Steins'
 visits to, 297, 299
Midtown Hospital (New York City), 192,
 656
Miller, Donald, xxvi
Miller, Mervyn, 376
Ministry of Town and Country Planning
 (England), 668, 676
Minoprio, Anthony, 533, 534n1
Mitchell, Grant, 240n1
Mitchell, Robert, 233n3, 551
Montgomery, Roger, 223
Moore, Grace, 359, 365n2
Morewood Gardens (Pittsburgh, Pa.),
 416n1b
Morgan, Arthur E., 257, 257n1, 258, 262,
 263n4, 266
Morgan, Keith, 269, 270n2
Morris, D. H., 253
Morris, Miss (secretary), 242, 250, 282, 305,
 332
Moses, Robert, 111, 284n3, 441, 454, 676;
 CSS on, 283–84, 465; and New York
 City roads, 294; and RFC, 244, 245n1,
 246
Moskowitz, Belle Israels, 191, 192, 233, 235,
 241, 284, 285n1, 309, 412, 672
Moskowitz, Henry, 191, 192, 233
Moskowitz, Joseph Israels, 191, 241
Mozel, Tad, 617
Mumford, Allison, 461
Mumford, Geddes, 232
Mumford, Lewis, xxxi, xxxii, 103, 141, 148,
 173, 191, 218, 236, 246, 251, 258, 263, 267,
 281, 410, 506, 556, 623, 644n, 662, 666,
 680; AMS on, 272; articles by, xxiv,
 xxviii, 105, 212, 215, 240, 534n3; awards
 of, 596, 609–10, 616, 618; and Bauer,
 194, 202, 212, 214, 216n1, 255, 368n1,
 449, 678; and Behrendt, 284n1; and
 Berlin City Planning Exhibit, 183n4; biography of, 672; books by, 263n5, 382;
 and *The City*, 363, 380, 381, 389, 670; on

city of future, 420–21; on communities, 445; and CSS, 91n1, 232, 263–64, 360, 370, 490, 492–93; on CSS, xxvi–xxvii, 3, 243, 271n, 325n1a, 504, 521; CSS on, 248, 626–27; and CSS's books, xxix, 399, 522, 619–20; CSS's correspondence with, 123, 138, 180, 204, 224, 229, 272, 363, 364, 372, 374, 375, 380, 381, 401, 438, 440, 460, 461, 463, 464, 466, 472, 474, 490, 492, 518, 555, 567, 571, 577, 578, 580, 599, 609, 615, 619, 628, 632, 640, 642, 643; and dispersal policy, 513, 524, 624; in Europe, 230n1, 463; on European housing, 226n2, 228n3; and FDR, 199, 207, 235, 238, 242, 250n; on Fresh Meadows, 533, 581; and Geddes, xxiii, 120n2, 226n4, 640; and Greenbelt Towns, 501; and Henry Wright Library, 375; on housing, 181n3, 279, 406; and London Plan, 447n2, 462, 660; and MacKaye, 149, 152–53, 175, 489; and MacLeish, 671; and New Communities Act, 634, 635; on New Towns, 376n, 569, 607; on nuclear war, 603; photographs of, 166, 169; and Radburn, 152n; and RDCA, 503, 516; and regional cities, xviii, 144; on *Regional Plan of New York and Its Environs*, 209, 210, 225n1; and RPAA, xix, 116, 119, 156, 174, 192, 203, 205n1, 256, 257, 471; and Spingarn, 296, 676; on subways, 237n3; on transportation, 154, 578; on Unwin, 631; and U.S. École des Beaux Arts, 184; on Wisconsin land use policy, 206

Mumford, Sophie, 141, 153, 212, 380, 516, 610, 616, 618, 623, 640; CSS on, 232, 263, 264, 421, 438

Murphy, Frederick V., 32, 33, 672

Museum of Modern Art, 248n1, 508–9, 674; CSS's work on, 360, 362, 378

Myrdal, Alva, 509

Nathan, Alan, 421

National Association of Housing Officials (NAHO), 291n2, 663, 679

National Capital Housing Authority, 484

National Capital Park and Planning Commission, 484, 523, 663, 674

National Casket Company, 1, 173, 655

National Federation of Settlements, 114

National Housing Corporation, 305n2b, 349

National Resources Planning Board, 199n2, 441n2, 666

National Security Resources Board, 478, 514n, 520, 662

Naval Air Base (San Diego, Calif.), xxii, 76, 189n2, 659

Netherlands, 79, 222, 227, 585, 616, 625; housing in, 105, 115n2, 133; Steins' visits to, 332n, 542

Neutra, Richard, 362, 390, 537, 661, 673

New Communities Act (1968), 595, 635n1

New Deal, xix, xxvi, 244n1, 257n1, 278n, 678; Brain Trust of, 664, 675, 677; and CSS, 255, 269–70, 325n1a; housing policy of, 177, 260n, 271–72, 281; and RPAA, 199n2

New England, 113, 115, 118, 141, 149, 153, 182

The New Exploration (MacKaye), 118, 148, 671

New Hampshire, 113, 118, 119

New Nazareth (Israel), 586–87

New Republic magazine, xxviii, 107, 180, 193, 206, 433; debate with Adams in, 224, 225n1; Mumford's articles in, 209n2, 210, 279

New School (New York City), 139n4, 191, 209n1; buildings of, 183, 678

New Towns: and CSS, xviii, xxiii, xxv, xxx, 77, 596, 598; CSS on, 421, 468, 469–70, 477–78, 490, 582–83; health facilities in, 493–94; history of, 606–7, 621; Radburn's influence on, 174; requirements for, 128; and RPAA, 467n2b, 470–73, 501; site planning at, 508. *See also* British New Towns; Garden Cities; Greenbelt Towns

New Towns Act of 1946, 674

New York Central Railroad, 82, 83, 84, 88, 95

New York City: changes in, 86–87; and *The*

New York City (*cont.*)

City, 363; city planning in, 81; CSS in, xx, xxi, 1–3, 7, 9, 75, 77–78, 174; CSS on, xxxii, 7–9, 16, 40, 49, 201, 360n3, 596, 612; CSS's homes in, 1, 2, 36, 174, 595; and federal government, 261n1b, 309; highways in, 294; housing in, 97, 124, 210, 279n1, 289n1a, 517; industry in, 196; and New Deal, 284n3; in 1920s, 107–8; planning in, 80–81, 619, 626; population congestion in, 126; port of, 93, 127; postwar, 438–39, 440, 447, 465; redevelopment plans for, 454; reform movement in, 661, 665, 674, 675; rents in, 185; and RPAA, 174; schools in, 445; slums in, 132, 298–99; surveys of, 93–94

New York City Housing Authority, 273, 276, 283, 285, 315, 581, 660; appointment of, 279; CSS on, 441; and Hillside, 287; and Valley Stream project, 306

New York City Planning Commission, 377

New York Regional Planning Association (RPA), 630

New York state: and Appalachian Trail, 113, 116, 118, 119; CSS's plan for, xix, 183n5; development plans for, 449, 635–36; Division of Planned Development for, 447–49, 459–60; Housing Board of, 246, 273, 275, 441; housing in, xxii, xxiii, xxv, 90, 104, 122–23, 144–48, 210, 226n1, 399; land survey of, 193; New Towns in, 635; redevelopment of, 440–41, 442, 447–49; reforestation in, 250; and regional planning, 104, 126–27, 180, 182, 584, 595, 669; Reorganization Commission of, 143; and RPAA, 174; urbanization of, 108; water for, 116

New York State Commission of Housing and Regional Planning, xxv, 120–27, 136, 610, 635; 1926 *Report* of, 108–9, 120n1, 142n2, 143, 168, 183n5, 196, 361, 389, 441, 442, 460, 584, 611n, 635, 636, 637, 638

New York State Reconstruction Commission, 672; Housing Committee of, xxii, 97–98, 110, 111–12, 121, 122, 675

New York Urban Development Corporation, 442n3

New York World's Fair (1939), 360, 361, 369, 370n, 378n1b

Niagara Falls, 127

Niagara Frontier regional planning board, 143

Niemeyer, Oscar, 468

Noguchi, Isamu, 299, 309, 310n3, 673

Nolen, John, 141, 156, 256, 263n2, 366, 484, 486n1, 661, 665, 673

Norris (Tenn.), 263n3, 665

Northeastern Trail Conference, 113, 114n1

Nowicki, Matthew, 409, 468, 469n1, 489, 504, 511, 553, 564, 659, 673

Nugent, Elliott, 213n2

Oakland Housing (Pontiac, Mich.), 659

Octagon, 90, 625n

Odum, Floyd, 204, 205, 206

Old People's Home (New York City), 656

Olmsted, Frederick Law, xx, 580, 597, 638, 673

Olmsted, Frederick Law, Jr., 661, 673

Once in a Lifetime (play), xxvii, 183, 184, 186, 189, 192, 206, 220, 222, 228, 230, 233, 667, 671

O'Neill, Eugene, xxvi

O'Neill, George, 251

open space, xviii, xx, xxx, 557–58, 630; at Carmelitos, 387; at Chatham Village, 211; in community architecture, 571, 573; covenants for, 85n3, 303n2a, 661; CSS on, 582–83; and dispersal policy, 512, 515; in Paris, 16–17n; preservation of, 576n, 603–4, 605; at Radburn, xxv, 106, 152n, 501; and regional cities, 481–82, 608; and residents' associations, 106; and superblocks, 613–14

Oppermann, Paul, xxx, xxxi, 473; CSS's correspondence with, 536, 550, 576, 621

Orton, Lawrence, 515

Osborn, Frederic J., xxxi, 401, 502, 621, 634, 635n2, 638; biography of, 674; on CSS, xxxii, 504, 506, 597; CSS on, 465, 467, 569, 615; CSS's correspondence with, 524, 589, 605, 606, 612, 630; and RPAA, 463, 466

Palmer, Frank L., 414, 450, 451, 453
Palos Verdes (Calif.), 303, 305n1b, 384–85
Panama-California Exposition (San Diego), 100, 101
Paris (France): boulevards in, 13n, 40n1; CSS in, xxi–xxii, 3–6, 9–61, 148; CSS on, xxxii, 16, 18, 49, 533–34, 537, 566, 600; CSS's home in, 27–30, 38, 60, 61, 67; Latin Quarter of, 9, 29, 628n2; modern, 40n1; parks in, 30–31, 39; Pres aux Clercs, 31–32, 34, 38, 43, 45, 188; walls of, 40
Parkchester development (Metropolitan Insurance Co.), 443, 446, 455
Parker, Barry, 376, 551, 552, 567, 638, 677–78
Parker, Dorothy, 107, 108
Park Forest (Ill.), 544
parks, 87, 89, 113, 129, 150, 229; and regional planning, 125, 127
Pasadena Art Institute (Pasadena, Calif.), 164, 165, 307, 320n1, 658
Paul A. Rie House (Port Washington, Long Island), 115n2, 655
Peck, Graham, 523
Peets, Elbert, 245n2
Pencil Points (journal), 413, 413n1, 423, 458
Pennsylvania, 119, 416n1b, 551; defense housing in, 106, 400, 415–20, 424n1, 497, 571, 657; housing authorities in, 414n1, 419 20, 451n, 497; University of, 233n3. *See also* Chatham Village; Philadelphia; Pittsburgh
Perkins, Francis, 254, 284, 285, 285n2, 674, 675
Perkins, Holmes, 607
Perry, Clarence, 228
Philadelphia (Pa.), xxxi, 92, 595, 639
Phillips, Hardie, 406, 412n3
Phipps, Henry, 184
Phipps East River Apartments, 307, 308n1
Phipps Garden Apartments (Long Island City, N.Y.), xviii, xxvii, xxix, 173, 656;

addition to, 176, 293–94, 296–97, 298, 303, 306; articles on, 671–72; costs of, 220, 222, 225; CSS on, 219n1a, 314–15, 317; CSS's work on, 184, 186, 188–89, 361; defense of, 237; designers of, 188n3; as housing project, 223n3; improvements in, 226n3; landscape architect for, 664; photographs of, 345; plans of, 344, 346; visitors to, 214, 217
Pinchot, Gifford, 116, 671
Pink, Louis H., 279, 279n2, 454
Pittsburgh (Pa.), 236; and *The City*, 363, 670; defense housing projects in, 106, 415–20, 424n1; Housing Authority of, 414n1
Planned Development Agency, 448–49
planning boards, 111–12, 197, 198n, 200
playgrounds, 85, 87, 89, 126, 222, 227, 230; in Carmelitos project, 387; in Chelsea, 83–84; at Sunnyside, 171
Pollack houses, 160, 655
Pomeroy, Hugh, 513, 603, 605
Poor, Alfred E., 314n2, 657
population congestion, 124–26, 136, 137, 146, 177, 187, 469–70
population distribution, 222
Port Authority (New York City), xxiii
Portuguese Synagogue (New York City), 202
Post, Langdon, 276, 277n1, 279, 298, 299, 373
Powell, R. E., 529
President's Conference on Home Building and Home Ownership, 180
Princeton Museum project (Princeton, N.J.), 302, 320n1, 658
Progressive Era, xvii, xxi, 39, 78, 675
Public Buildings Administration (PBA), 408–9, 411, 415, 503, 621
Public Housing Administration, 621, 663, 667, 678
publicity, 80–81, 138, 235, 241n
Public Service Commission, 261
Public Works Administration (PWA): appropriations for, 307n1a, 672; CSS in, 675; and Hillside, 273n1a, 274n2,

Public Works Administration (PWA) (*cont.*)
286n1b, 287, 347, 677; of Hoover,
279n1; Housing Division of, 177, 235n,
245n3, 265, 362, 673; and Red Hook
project, 315; and RPAA, 199n2; staff of,
262, 668, 669; and Unwin, 678; and
Wichita Art Institute, 289–90

Purdom, C. B., 462

Purdy, Lawson, 90, 91

Radburn (Fairlawn, N.J.), xviii, xix, xx,
xxiv, xxvii, xxix, 103, 144n1, 656; apartments in, 258, 261, 266; associates on,
185n2, 188nn2&3, 660, 663, 664, 665; in
Berlin exhibition, 182, 195n1; and Bing,
169; and Chatham Village, 211; and
CHC, 663; and *The City,* 363, 381, 670;
construction of, 105, 106; CSS on, 184,
248, 268, 401, 467, 486, 487, 488, 490,
491, 492, 507; CSS on photographs of,
490, 492, 507; CSS's work on, 361; Emmerich at, 429; facilities at, 155, 321, 445;
financial problems of, xxvi, 173, 174,
190n, 194; footpaths in, 510–11; and
Garden Cities, 567; and height of buildings, 187; and Hillside, 453; influence of,
107, 152n, 174, 175, 176, 502; influences
on, 552; later development of, 219, 369;
map of, 333; and New Deal, 259; open
space at, xxv, 106, 303n2a, 558, 661; photographs of, 337, 338, 339, 340; planning
of, 130n, 150–52, 153, 189–90, 192; plans
of, 334, 335, 341, 342; and postwar planning, 468; reactions to, xxxii, 222, 634n;
in *Regional Plan of New York and Its Environs,* 661; tenants' association at,
443–44; and TVA, 249; and Unwin, 153;
visits to, 291n2, 325, 351; and Henry
Wright, 176, 582, 680

Radburn Plan, xx, xxviii, 176n4; and 1939
World's Fair, 370n; and Baldwin Hills,
362; CSS on, 578; density of, 569; and
Greenbelt Towns, 329n, 331n2; influence
of, 408, 410n2, 492, 500, 501, 533, 534n2,
541n, 555, 564, 565–66, 588, 601n1a, 612,
627–28, 629, 640; and Norris (Tenn.),

263n3; and Olmstead, 580; and Stevan-
age, 555; and Valley Stream, 267n1b,
268n2, 349

Radio City (New York City), 270

railroads, 53, 88, 129, 130; in New York, 82,
83, 84, 88, 95

Rasmussen, Steen Eiler, 502, 535, 579, 631;
photograph of, 591

Ratensky, Sam, 331

Reagan, Oliver, 657

Reconstruction Finance Corporation
(RFC), 221, 235n, 244–45, 259n1, 260n,
279n1; and Hillside, 233–34, 236, 246,
274n2, 286n1b

recreation, in New Towns, 134, 153, 521, 544

Red Hook Project Associated Architects,
313, 314n2, 315–16

regional cities, xviii, 109, 142n2; in Australia, 640–41; Bauer on, 608–9; concept of, 376; criticisms of, 462; CSS on,
401, 481–82, 505, 547–48, 574–75, 584,
596, 617, 619, 620; and dispersal policy,
512; and Garden Cities, 144, 149; and
highways, 175; and New Towns, 401,
622; and New York state, 635–36; in
Santa Clara County, 576; Stephenson
on, 630

Regional Development Council of America
(RDCA), xxviii, 480, 482, 503, 513–14,
516; and dispersal policy, 524–25; and
federal policy, 504; and *Town Planning
Review,* 548–49; on urban redevelopment, 525–26; and Washington Regional Planning Council, 511–12

regional planning, xvii, xix, 117, 137, 512,
606; and Appalachian Trail, 116–19, 119;
and city planning, 124–27; and community architecture, 561; conferences
on, 155–57, 615; and conservationists,
589; and CSS, 139n2, 505; CSS on,
440–41; and dispersal policy, 514–15,
520; and economic development, 272n2;
education in, 233n3, 295, 366, 559–65;
and housing costs, 134; and HUD, 610,
617; at MIT, 560; and RDCA, 513; and
RPAA, xxiii, 105, 471n1a; and state gov-

ernments, 142–43, 440–41, 441n2; surveys for, 666; upbuilding technique of, 118

Regional Planning Association of America (RPAA), xviii–xix, xx, xxiv, xxvi, 623, 643; and Thomas Adams, 192n3; and Algonquin Club, 107–8; and Appalachian Trail, 116–19; and *The City*, 363; conferences of, 155–57; and CSS, 174, 363, 596; and FDR, 199n1, 236n, 238; founding of, xxiii, 104–5, 120n1, 671, 680; and Geddes, 139n4; housing legislation, 221, 479n; influence of, xxix, xxx, 108–9, 120n1, 463n2, 603; influences on, 667, 678; and International Federation for Housing and Town Planning, 376; meetings of, 166, 181–82, 207, 628–29; members of, 149, 169, 208nn4–7, 242, 642, 661, 664, 679, 680; objectives of, 513; and *Regional Plan of New York and Its Environs*, 209, 638; and PWA, 265, 266, 269; and regional cities, 574–75; on relocation housing, 134n; revival of, 401, 467n2b, 470–73, 474, 475, 501, 503, 680; and Russian Reconstruction Farms, 142; and slum clearance, 277n2; and *Survey Graphic*, 672; and Technical Alliance, 243n1, 660; Ten-Year Program of, 181–82

Regional Plan of New York and Its Environs (1929), xxiv, 91n3, 115n1, 126, 192n3, 209, 638; Association, 480; contributors to, 661, 666; CSS on, 441, 474; Mumford on, 209–210, 225n1

Rehousing Urban America (Wright, Henry), 271, 281, 558, 567, 581, 667, 680

Reid, Kenneth, 413

Reimersholme (Sweden), 509

rents, 145, 146, 185, 456; legislation on, 120–22. *See also* Baldwin Hills

Renwick, James, 656, 667

Resettlement Administration (RA), 177–78, 191n1; Bigger on, 369; consultants to, 664, 673; and CSS, 317n1b, 318n1, 320–22, 324–25; funding for, 307n1a, 319n; and Greenbelt Towns, 304–5,

325n1b, 326n2, 328n2, 680; and New Towns, 178, 301n2, 675; photograph of drafting room, 354; and RPAA, 199n2; staff of, 662, 665, 677, 678, 679; and Valley Stream project, 301n1

Reston (Va.), xviii, xxx, 174, 233n3, 595, 644, 679

Reuss, Henry, 624

Richard, Donald, 548

Richards, E.C.M., 275

Ritter, Paul, 633

Rivera, Diego, xxvii, 208, 209

Robertson, Ella, 435

Rochester (N.Y.), 1, 121

Rockefeller, John D., xxiv, 297

Rockefeller, Nelson Aldrich, 360, 378, 464, 595; biography of, 674; and CSS, 362, 637; CSS on, 378, 595; and New York Urban Development Corporation, 442n3; and regional planning, 584, 635–36

Rockefeller Center, 208n1, 668

Rockefeller Foundation, 291n2, 351; and Bauer, 255; and Behrendt, 294; and *The City*, 363; funding from, 229n, 281, 297, 299

Rodwin, Lloyd, 551

Rome (Italy), 7, 61–62, 600; ancient, 86

Roosevelt, Eleanor, 419, 674

Roosevelt, Franklin Delano (FDR), 240n2, 244n1, 306, 674–75; Brain Trust of, 413n1a, 674, 677; and CSS, 195–97, 269–70, 325n1a, 637; CSS on, 206–7, 211n2, 228–29, 235–36, 250, 251, 253, 260, 282, 366, 418, 611; CSS's correspondence with, 195, 249; CSS's interview with, 198–200; as governor, 273, 412; housing policy of, xxvii, 174, 177–78, 207, 208n6, 210, 231n1, 291n2, 301n1, 351, 400, 407n1, 410n1b; and Ickes, 668; and Kohn, 245n3; MacLeish on, 278n; and Robert Moses, 284n3; photograph of, 355; Recovery Act of, 260–62, 272n2; and regional planning, 193; and RPAA, xix, 238, 241–42, 243, 244, 249–50, 256n2; U.S. Housing Authority of, 363, 377n1; at Virginia Conference, 156n, 199, 205n1

Roosevelt, Theodore, 667, 668, 674, 675
Rosenman, Samuel I., 413, 674, 675
Rosoff, Sam, 216–17
Ross, John, 564
Ross, Ken, 610
Rouen (France), 71
Rough, Stanley, 559
Rouse, James, 595
Royal Institute of British Architects
    (RIBA), 616, 618
Rumbold, Charlotte, 675
Russia, xxx, 198, 288; CSS in, 148–49, 167;
    CSS on, 251; and dispersal policy, 503;
    housing in, 212, 428; regional planning
    in, 182, 204
Russian Reconstruction Farms, 141, 142,
    144, 148–49

Saarinen, Eliel, xxvii, 283, 366, 666, 675
Sage Foundation, 225n1, 480, 669
Saint-Cloud (France), 30, 31
Samuel, Alice, 290, 291, 351
San Diego World's Fair, xxii, 79, 163, 596,
    659, 667, 679; California Building at,
    76, 80n2, 100, 101, 189n2, 659; Spanish-
    colonial style of, 308n2; use of color in,
    310n2
satellite communities, 190, 426, 599n1, 660,
    668
Sawyer, Donald H., 265
Schaffer, Daniel, 120, 152
Schilling, Cecil, 386, 387, 388
schools, 222, 227, 445; in Greenbelt Towns,
    322; at Hillside, 229; and neighborhood
    unit concept, 228n2; at Radburn, 151,
    153
Scondal (Sweden), 500
Scotland, 627, 666
sculpture, 207, 670; and CSS, 76, 79, 80n2,
    299; on Wichita Art Institute, 298, 353
Seattle (Wash.), 575
Shaler Township Defense Housing (Alle-
    gheny County, Pa.), 400, 417n1, 419–20,
    571, 657
Sharon, Arieh, xxxi, 532, 585, 588, 588n1
Shaw, George Bernard, 217, 674

Shear, John Knox, 556
Shipping Board, U.S., 92, 137, 664, 669
Shirley Center (Mass.), 204, 242, 352, 370,
    371, 373, 465; in *The City*, 363, 380, 670
Shreve, Harold, xxvii, 274, 290, 379
Shurtleff, Favel, 123
Siam (Thailand), 179, 332n, 391
Sidenbladh, Gorän, xxxi, 502, 510, 600, 639
Silver Hill Sanitarium (Conn.), 360,
    371–73, 400, 431–34, 461
Simon, Robert, xxiv, 595, 644
Simonson, Caroline, 208, 251, 264, 412
Simonson, Lee, xxvii, 5, 54, 185, 186, 203,
    208, 251–52, 264, 410; biography of, 675;
    CSS on, 56, 187–88, 191, 192; mental ill-
    ness of, 412
Sinclair, Upton, 209, 665
Skidmore, Owings, and Merrill (architec-
    tural firm), 503, 679
slum clearance, 132–35; and affordable
    housing, 177; and Bauer, 675; in Chi-
    cago, 214n; CSS's projects, 266; and fed-
    eral government, 554; financing for, 221;
    and Hillside, 247; and housing costs,
    234; and LaGuardia, 312, 669; and New
    Towns, 477, 479; in New York City,
    266, 276, 298–99; RPAA on, 245n2; and
    urban redevelopment, 517–18
slums, 77, 110, 121
Smith, Alfred E., 3, 90, 91n4, 116, 240,
    279n2, 674; biography of, 675–76; and
    CSS, xxii, xxv, xxvi, 78, 104, 111n, 198n,
    442, 460, 610, 636, 637; CSS's corre-
    spondence with, 142; housing policy of,
    121, 122; and Belle Moskowitz, 233, 284,
    309, 672
Smith, Chloethiel Woodward, xxxi, 233,
    554, 626, 627, 676; CSS's correspond-
    ence with, 553
Smith, Geddes, 152, 210
Smith, Larry, 535, 586
Sochow (Suzhou, China), 179, 431
socialism, 203, 246n, 278n
Socialist Party, 185n, 289n1a, 677
Soviet Union. *See* Russia
Spain, 4, 76, 79

Spanish-Colonial style, 76, 79, 163, 308n2

Sparkman (Ala. senator), 479

speculative development, 110–11, 131, 137, 146, 249; and Garden Cities, 130; and housing shortages, 145, 146; and New Towns, 633

Spingarn, Joel Elias, 296n1, 676

Springfield Museum (Springfield, Mass.), 182, 185, 186

St. Bartholomew's Church (New York City), xxii, 76, 310n2, 659, 667

Stanford University (Stanford, Calif.): CSS's work with, 525–26; land development projects of, xxx, 502–3, 536, 550, 659; Steins at, 502, 571, 574

Starrett Brothers Construction Company, 235n

state governments: and community planning, 538; and dispersal policy, 515; financing from, 122, 134; and housing, 90, 92, 133, 146, 221, 228, 399; and industry, 222n3; and land, 147, 577; and limited dividend corporations, 223; and New Towns, 598; planning boards of, 221, 440–41; and regional planning, 118, 119, 126, 142–43, 195–97, 198, 199, 200; and urban redevelopment, 441n2, 525–26, 583

Staten Island (N.Y.), 94, 126

Steichen, Edward, 417

Stein, Aline MacMahon (wife), xxv–xxvi; awards of, 614, 616, 617; biography of, 671; cooking of, 451; CSS on career of, 314–15; and CSS's depression, 285n1b, 286n1a, 360, 361; death of, 183n1; in Europe, 402; film career of, xxvii, 183n2, 186n3, 201n, 208n3, 220n1, 221, 222, 230, 240n1, 362, 382, 502; films of, 178, 213, 268, 359, 365n2, 368n2, 400, 414n3a, 414n3b, 418, 548, 553n3, 570, 610n2, 628n1, 629, 667; and *The Good Earth*, 289, 298, 318, 328, 332; illnesses of, 438, 439; income of, 184n1; marriage of, 153n; on Mumford, 272; Noguchi bust of, 309–10, 353; in *Once in a Lifetime*, 667; photographs of, 358, 391, 394, 397; plays

of, 107, 206, 385n1a, 400, 432n, 433, 434, 436, 437, 438, 462n, 474, 489, 490–91, 508, 610, 617, 618, 625, 626, 642; plays produced by, 461; political activities of, 475n2; separation from CSS, 192, 193n, 200–201, 234, 360; social life of, 174; at Stanford, 502; wartime organizational work of, 424, 425n1a, 437

Stein, Clarence Samuel: achievements of, xvii; aesthetics of, xxxii–xxxiii, 2, 76, 506; on air travel, xxviii, 269, 412, 413; appearance of, 107; as architect, xviii, xix, xxi, xxii, 138, 139n2; Asian influences on, 363; autobiographical writing of, 632–33; awards of, 505, 571–73, 642; birthdays of, 308; and cities, xxxii, 85–89, 377, 420–21; and *The City*, 362–63; on community planning, 323; as consultant, 399, 400–401, 450–51, 452, 453–55, 456–58; creativity of, 280; death of, xxxii, 183n1; decorative work of, 76, 186n1, 290n3, 352; on the Depression, 252; discouragement of, 463; draftsmanship of, 33; on film and architecture, 314–15; and Goodhue, 75–76, 79; handwriting of, 361, 364n1, 427n2; income of, 173n, 189, 417, 418; influence of, 503–4; lack of work, 320n1, 359; on law, 85; leadership of, xxvi–xxvii, 504; lifestyle of, xxvii, xxxii; marriage of, xxv–xxvi; mental illness of, xxviii, 285n1b, 286n1a, 287n, 305n3, 306, 360–61, 366n1a, 370–73, 400, 401, 405–6, 411–12, 414n2, 423, 424n1, 430–38, 435–36, 437, 461n, 498, 499, 504, 544–48; on museum design, 353, 360, 385, 391, 643; New York apartment of, 183n1, 497; and New York City, xxvii, 1–3, 32, 75; organizational skills of, 76, 176, 504; on own work, 268, 467n1b; in Paris, xxi–xxii, 3–6, 9–61, 26–27; partial blindness of, xxi, 2; personal characteristics of, xxvii, xxxii–xxxiii; photographs of, 63, 65, 99, 165, 167, 334, 351, 352, 354, 358, 391–93, 394, 395, 397, 496, 498, 591, 593, 645; as planner, xviii, xix; political activities of,

Stein, Clarence Samuel (*cont.*)
77–78, 90–91, 142–43, 174, 210; political
views of, 175, 185n, 204, 322, 366; on
postwar planning, 440–41, 442, 447–49,
464; on Prohibition, end of, 273; on racism, 425; as reformer, xxii, xxvi, 77–78,
138, 139n2; and RPAA, xviii–xix, xxiii–
xxiv, 108, 120n1; separation from AMS,
192, 193n, 200–201; sketches by, 66, 69,
71, 72, 73; social life of, 174; travels of,
xxvii–xxviii, 325, 332; use of color by, 76,
310, 310n2, 314; and World War II, xxii,
417; and Henry Wright, 264, 270–71;
writing of, 242, 243, 251, 254, 307, 359,
360, 365, 367, 399, 401, 468, 504–5, 534,
547–48, 578. See also *Toward New Towns
for America*
Stein, Gertrude (sister), 1, 60, 244, 260,
275, 368, 370, 375, 411, 415, 438, 644;
and Aline, 140n; CSS's correspondence
with, 16; house for, 359, 365, 395, 412;
photographs of, 73, 165
Stein, Herbert (brother), xxi, 3, 5, 7, 50, 51,
59, 229, 285; CSS's correspondence with,
26, 48, 52; photographs of, 65, 165
Stein, Leo (father), xxi, 1, 7, 50, 229, 259,
275, 285, 296, 308, 312, 313, 367, 369,
370, 544, 620; CSS's correspondence
with, 9, 10, 11, 12, 13, 17, 18, 19, 20, 21,
23, 25, 27, 31, 33, 34, 35, 36, 38, 39, 41, 43,
44, 46, 50, 55, 57, 58, 59, 60, 61; photographs of, 63, 65, 73, 165, 395
Stein, Lillie (sister), 19, 140, 140n, 187, 203,
218, 253, 261, 275, 377, 411, 544, 644;
with CSS in Arizona, 435–37; photographs of, 73, 165, 498
Stein, Rose Rosenblatt (mother), xxi, 1, 19,
33, 60; CSS's correspondence with, 7, 9,
10, 11, 12, 17, 18, 19, 20, 23, 27, 29, 31, 34,
35, 36, 38, 39, 41, 43, 44, 46, 50, 54, 55,
57, 58, 59, 60, 61; death of, 202; photographs of, 63, 73, 165
Stein, Samuel (grandfather), 65
Stein, William (brother), xxi, 3, 61, 187,
207, 285; and CSS, 207n1; CSS's corre-

spondence with, 56; photographs of, 65,
165
Steiner, Richard, 381
Stephenson, Flora, 487, 580, 617, 623
Stephenson, Gordon, 401, 502, 522, 535, 548,
549, 640–41; biography of, 676; CSS's
articles for, xxix, 402, 487n1, 489, 490,
492, 493, 501; CSS's correspondence
with, 486, 487, 488, 521, 533, 536, 550,
555, 562, 583, 584, 617, 622, 630; and
McCarthyism, 563n, 580; projects of,
534n1, 569, 570n2, 578, 613, 658
Sterling, Henry, 91
Stern, Alfred, 214, 241, 274, 288
Stern, Carl, 181, 218, 226, 228, 417, 430, 465
Stern, Maurice, 9
Stevenage Town Center (Stevenage, Eng-
land), 402, 501, 521, 533, 658; pedestrianization of, 578n2; and Radburn Plan, 555,
612, 613, 628
Stockholm (Sweden), 615, 665; CSS on, 600,
604, 629, 639; Steins' visits to, 602, 627
Stone, Is, 424n2
Stonorov, Oscar, 212, 216, 263, 264, 289,
289n2, 406, 676
Stotz, Charles, 657, 658
Stotz, Edward, 657, 658
Stowe Township Defense Housing (Allegheny County, Pa.), 400, 416, 417n1,
419–20, 421, 497, 571n2, 657, 658
Straus, Nathan, xxvii, 177, 300, 312, 384,
454; and Eken, 292n2, 293, 304; and
Hillside, 174, 230n2, 231, 235n, 237,
238n2, 239, 240, 274, 277, 292, 293, 376,
677; and Los Angeles projects, 386; on
U.S. Housing Authority, 377n1
streets, 87, 136, 137, 521; in Hillside, 229, 312,
347; inflexible pattern of, 136, 187, 486,
584, 598; separation from footpaths,
510–11, 565–66, 569, 578, 595, 612, 613,
627–28, 634n. See also automobiles;
highways; townless highways
Stuyvesant Town (Metropolitan Life Housing program), 379n2
subsidies, 98n, 133–34, 477, 638; federal,
399, 611; state, 133

suburbs, 88, 89, 94, 126, 136, 150, 469–70;
Garden, 131, 146, 664
subways, 236, 237n3, 241, 620
Sullivan, Louis, 284, 372, 509
Sunday Clubs, 27, 54n1
Sunnyside Gardens (Long Island City,
N.Y.), xviii, xx, xxiv, xxix, 107, 153, 655;
associates on, 188nn2&3, 660, 664, 665;
and Bing, 169; construction of, 106, 107;
CSS on, 138, 139n3, 248, 401, 486, 488,
490, 492; CSS's work on, 141, 144, 361;
financial problems of, xxvi; legal problems of, 218; and Letchworth, 551, 552;
maintenance of, 466; open space at, xxv,
106, 303n2a, 558, 661; and Phipps apartments, 184n2; photographs of, 171–72;
planning of, 130n; playgrounds in, 227;
search for photographs of, 376; site plan
for, 170; tenants' association at, 443; and
Henry Wright, 176, 582, 680
superblock system, 571; at Baldwin Hills,
458; in British New Towns, 555, 613; at
Chandigarh, 504, 564; at Chatham Village, 175; cost savings of, 330; CSS on,
583; and density, 569; at Hillside, 176,
230; in Israel, 588; at Radburn, 486, 501;
at Valley Stream, 177
Survey Graphic magazine, 105, 107, 120n1,
156, 524, 637; CSS's articles in, 361; and
MacKaye, 489; and RPAA, 672
surveys: block, 121–22; of Chelsea, 94–97,
669; of Connecticut River, 390; CSS's
advocacy of, 77; land, 193, 195, 197, 199;
of Newark Bay region, 94; of New York
City, 93–94; regional, 93, 118–19, 121–22;
for regional planning, 666; of San Francisco, 658; of Staten Island, 94
Sussman, Carl, xix, 120
Swarthe, Hilda, 191
Sweden, xviii; automobiles in, 627; community planning in, 599, 600, 601; cooperative housing in, 517, 543; CSS's influence in, xxix, xxxi, 401, 502; New
Towns in, 493, 500, 502, 505, 508–10,
588, 604, 621; Radburn's influence in,

152n, 492; Steins' visits to, 487, 491, 502,
507, 540, 596, 599
Swope, Gerard, xxvii, 265, 436, 523

Taft, Charles (senator), 484
Taft-Ellender Wagner Bill (Housing Act of
1937), 231n1, 361, 362, 373n1, 377n4, 399,
663
Tapiola (Finland), 634
Taut, Bruno, 372
tax exemptions, 142n1, 226n1, 238, 456
Technical Alliance, 242, 380n, 660, 678;
and RPAA, 243n1
technocracy movement, 188n1, 237, 239,
243, 246, 255, 374, 379, 380n, 660
Temple Emanu-El (New York City), 103,
164, 186n1, 202, 656, 669
Temple of Religion, New York World's Fair
(New York City), 657
tenant leagues, 146
tenements: censuses of, 94; in Chelsea, 83,
95, 96; CSS on, 86, 87; in England, 52;
in France, 36; and housing reform, 134;
and interest rates, 136; laws on, 96, 122;
New York City Commission on, 94, 232,
276, 279; and population congestion,
124; and rent legislation, 121, 122; Edith
Elmer Wood on, 239n
Tennessee Valley Authority (TVA), xxx,
243, 248, 291n2, 415, 425, 664; CSS on,
268, 629; and MacKaye, 271, 275, 671,
675; and New Towns, 249; and RPAA,
199n2, 249–50, 255–58, 262, 263n4, 266;
staff of, 662, 665
Teotihuacan (Mexico), 614
Thailand (Siam), 179, 332n, 391
theater, 26, 107; and community, 444, 445;
and CSS, 174, 217; design for, 5, 54n1,
590, 604; in Paris, 26, 30, 44, 50
Theatre Guild, 251, 675
Thomas, Andrew J., 133, 297n1, 656
Thomas, Miss (secretary), 215, 216
Thomas, Norman, 185, 366
Thommason, Ole, 600
A Thousand Gardens project (Los Angeles),

A Thousand Gardens project (*cont.*)
362, 382, 383, 385, 390. *See also* Baldwin
Hills

A Thousand Years (Steins' summer home),
331, 363, 389, 390, 391, 403, 619; Hill
House at, 394, 657; photographs of, 495,
496; in World War II, 400

Toronto (Canada), 580, 607

Torry, Raymond, 116

Toward New Towns for America (Stein), xix,
xxx, xxxii, 189, 330, 487, 493, 527; on
green commons, 558; and Kitimat, 542;
Kizer on, 540; Mumford on, 596–97;
new edition of, 577

Town and Country Planning, 553, 565–66,
579, 581; editors of, 674; on New Towns,
567, 569; Unwin memorial issue, 630–32

Town and Country Planning Association,
589, 638, 674

townless highways, xviii, 142n2, 154, 180,
182, 204, 249, 263; in Australia, 641; and
regional cities, 175, 608, 622. *See also* automobiles; highways; streets

Town Planning Review, xxix, xxxi, 152n,
360n3, 401, 402, 508, 616, 631; CSS on,
555, 631; CSS's articles for, 359n1,
467n1b, 486, 487, 488, 489, 490, 491,
492, 493, 501, 507; and CSS's book, 521,
522; editors of, 660, 676; fund raising
for, 548–49; Mayer's articles for, 533; on
New Towns, 569

transportation: and agricultural belts, 129;
and agriculture, 141; and city planning,
80; collapse of, 105; commuting, 85n4,
87–89, 95–97, 127; and defense housing,
429, 519; and dispersal policy, 515, 520;
in England, 53; in Garden Cities, 127,
128, 130, 146; and housing costs, 134;
improvement of, 108; and industry,
82–83, 85n4, 88–89, 97, 112–13, 137, 222,
605; and New Towns, 469–70; and population congestion, 125, 126; in regional
surveys, 93; and RPA, 630; street railroads, 53; subways, 96; surveys of, 93;
and TVA, 249; and urban congestion,
xxiv; for workers, 85n4, 87–89, 95–97

Truman, Harry S., xxix, xxx, 424n2, 479,
514, 520, 668, 677; CSS on, 476; and
dispersal policy, 503, 512n; housing policy of, 426n2; on New Towns, 479n

Tugwell, Rexford, 243, 244n1a, 413n1a, 664,
674, 675; biography of, 677; and CSS,
300, 301n1, 313, 314n1, 317–20, 325n1a,
327, 411; and Greenbelt Towns, xviii,
xxvii, 313; and highways, 262–63; and
Housing Act of 1934, 260n; photograph
of, 355; and RA, 178, 307n1a, 308–10;
and RPAA, 156n, 199n2

Turner, Albert N., 115, 141

Tyrone, Town of (Phelps–Dodge Corporation, N.Mex.), xxii, 76, 659; photograph
and plan of, 102

Udall, Stewart, 643

United Nations: headquarters of, 393,
463–64, 468, 469n1, 500, 670, 673; and
Eleanor Roosevelt, 674

university development, 618, 623–24

University of California: at Berkeley, xxxi,
474; at San Diego, 623, 624, 661

Untermeyer, Louis, 251

Unwin, Jane, 620, 621, 638

Unwin, Lady (Mrs. Raymond), 424

Unwin, Raymond, xxxii, 180, 230, 375,
376n, 566, 567, 569, 579, 601, 666; biography of, 677–78; at Columbia, 366n2b,
390n1b; CSS on, 492, 493, 582; CSS's
visits to, 105, 120n1, 130, 153, 501–2;
Hampstead home of, 489, 491, 508; influence of, 551–52; and RPAA conference, 156n, 157; *Town and Country Planning* memorial issue for, 630–32; visits
to U.S., 290, 291n2, 389, 638; writings
of, 620–21

Urban, Joseph Maria, 183, 247, 678

Urban Affairs, U.S. Department of, 606

urban development, xix, 104; and CSS, 441,
442, 454, 584; and dispersal policy, 512;
and federal government, xxvi, xxxi, 625;
and insurance companies, 454; management skills for, xxv; and natural environment, 447–48; and New Towns, 477,

478–79; postwar planning of, 469–70; and regional planning, 512, 606; and RPAA, xxiv, 221, 222n1

urban redevelopment, 222n1; CSS on, 570, 583–84, 596, 598; CSS's use of term, 441, 442; and dispersal policy, 515; federal subsidies for, 611; in India, 579; postwar, 450; RDCA on, 525–26; and slum clearance, 517 18; urban renewal programs, 296n2a

Urban Renewal Administration. *See* Housing and Home Finance Agency

Valley Stream project (Long Island, N.Y.), 177, 178, 267n1b, 268n2, 300–301, 303, 308n1, 313, 658; loss of, 320n1; and New York Housing Authority, 306; plans for, 349, 350; problems with, 305

Vällingby (Sweden), 500, 502, 567, 588, 601, 604; automobiles in, 627; CSS on, 541n; Radburn Plan in, 628

Vanderlip, Frank A., 239, 240n2, 267n1

Van de Velde, Henry, 284n1

Van Tassel, Gretchen, 507

Veblen, Thorstein B., 188, 243, 380, 660, 678

Venice (Italy): CSS on, xxxii, 41–42, 533–34, 537, 566, 578, 596; sketch of, 73

Versailles (France), 31, 34, 54

Villier, Lawrence, 239n1

Vinton, Warren Jay, 318, 320, 320n1, 326, 473, 678

Viollet-le-Duc, 37

Virginia, 119, 205

Virginia Conference, 192–93, 199, 200, 204–5, 206; FDR at, 229; program for, 203

Vitolo, Frank, 216, 217, 253, 261, 267n1a, 269, 270, 273, 303, 304, 317, 379, 656, 658; and Hillside, 237, 287, 291, 292, 312

Vladeck, B. Charney, 288, 289n1

Vladeck Homes (lower East Side, New York City), 289n1a

Von Eckardt, Wolfe, 152

Voorhees, Walker, and Smith, 201, 231, 302

Wadsworth, R. J., 329, 657

Wagner, Robert F., 221n1, 225, 254n3, 281n2, 285

Wagner-Steagall (Taft-Ellender) Bill (Housing Act of 1937), 220, 221, 224, 226, 227, 231n1, 281n2b, 361, 362, 373nn1&2, 377n4, 399, 663, 680

Walker, Hale, 329n, 657

Walker, John O., 219, 223, 323, 325, 443, 449, 453, 456

Walker, Ralph, 231, 417, 430, 462, 468, 549, 554, 563, 590; biography of, 678; and Fresh Meadows, 533, 537; and Greenbelt Towns, 364, 365; Irving Trust building of, 201, 202n1a; on vertical city, 187, 533

Wallace, Henry, 260, 262, 476

Wallender, Sven, 509

Walter Pollack house (Morristown, N.J.), 160

Wank, Roland, 415, 425, 455

Ware, Harold, 141, 142, 148

Ware, Jessica, 141, 148

Washington, D.C., xxx, xxxi, 676; defense housing in, 106, 400; dispersal plan for, 503, 592, 593, 595; New Towns near, 524n, 568, 592, 593; Southwest Urban Renewal Area, 233n3, 553–54, 626

Washington Regional Planning Council, 512

Wasser House (Riverdale on Hudson, N.Y.), 104, 161, 655

Weaver, Robert, 608, 609, 633

Webb, Beatrice, 674

Webb, Sidney, 674

Weber, Max, 428

Welfare Island (New York City), 596, 619, 620, 626

Welwyn Garden City (England), xxiii, 120n1, 129, 467, 567, 578, 674; agricultural belt of, 128; CSS on, 551; and Howard, 668; transportation in, 130

West, Eric F., 526, 529, 545

West Side Improvement (New York City), 82

Whitaker, A. W., Jr., 530

Whitaker, Charles, xxvii, 114, 116, 123,

Whitaker, Charles (*cont.*)
124n4, 257n1, 283, 642, 660, 662, 678;
on architecture, 273–74; and Behrendt,
284n1, 294n; biography of, 679; CSS's
correspondence with, 90, 93; as editor
of *JAIA,* xxii, 78, 92, 104; and RPAA,
xix, 120n1; and Technical Alliance, 243

Whitaker (of ALCAN), 539

White, J. B., 539, 547, 549

White, L. E., 566

Whittlesey, Julian, xxx, 504, 511, 535, 549,
550, 658, 672, 679; CSS's correspondence with, 510

Wichita Art Institute (Kans.), 289–90, 310,
656; CSS on, 314; decorative elements
in, 290n3, 352, 353; drawing of, 352; ornament on, 298; photograph of, 353;
sculpture on, 670

Wilderness Society, 512, 636

Willcox, Roger, 504, 513, 515, 527, 528,
543n3, 544

Williamsburg, colonial, 205

Wilson (brother of Lewis Wilson), 459

Wilson, Edmund, 175

Wilson, Lewis, 458, 459n3, 491, 491n1

Wilson, Woodrow, 433, 675

Winston, Oliver, 466

Wolfe, Thomas, 316, 662

Wollett, R. M., 213, 214, 215n1, 216, 217,
231, 232

Wood, Edith Elmer, xix, 210, 239, 239n,
257, 266, 269, 679

Wood, Elizabeth, 581

Woodbury, Coleman, 302, 373, 679

Woodlands (Tex.), xviii, 174

Workingman's School (Ethical Culture Society), xxi, 1–2, 4, 5, 104; influence of,
77, 78; photograph of, 64; students at,
661, 663, 669, 675; teachers at, 665

World War I, xxii, 81, 90, 92, 519

World War II, xxxi, 131, 399, 429, 519; CSS
on, 404, 418, 433

Wrexham (North Wales), 533, 555, 569,
570n2, 613

Wright, Eleanor, 364

Wright, Frank Lloyd, 2, 190, 191, 284, 372n,
372n1

Wright, Henry, 105, 144, 174, 189, 210, 239,
253, 285, 290; architectural school of,
229, 230, 233, 280, 554n1, 669, 676, 680;
articles by, 265, 279; and Baldwin Hills,
582; and Berlin Exhibit, 182; biography
of, 680; book by, 216, 265, 281n2a, 581;
and British Garden Cities, 120n1, 130n;
and Chatham Village, xxvii, 175, 184,
185n1a, 186, 194, 195n2, 211, 663; at Columbia University, 188n3, 292n1, 364n2,
366n2b; at conferences, 156, 203, 237;
CSS on, 365, 582, 609; CSS's breakup
with, 176, 264, 265n1a, 270–71; CSS's
collaboration with, xviii, xxiv, xxv, xxvi,
106, 208n6, 655, 656, 665; death of, 360,
364; European housing trip of,
225–26n2, 248, 249; and *Fortune,* 215,
228, 671; and Greenbelt Towns, 191n1,
318n, 324, 325, 326; on green commons,
558; on horizontal cities, 187; and Housing Study Guild, 303n1a, 664, 679; and
Kohn, 266, 267, 269; and Letchworth,
551, 552; library dedicated to, 375; and
MacKaye, 259, 261, 263n1; and model
housing law, 231; and 1926 *Report,* 109,
142, 183n5, 610, 611n3, 635, 636, 637; on
parks, 569; photographs of, 168, 351; and
Radburn, 107, 151–52n, 153, 190, 567; on
reforestation, 180; and RPAA, xix, 207,
257; site planning of, 492, 493; on slum
clearance, 245n2, 265n1a, 280, 281n1a;
and Sunnyside, 138, 139n3, 141

Wright, Richard, 425

Wurster, Catherine Bauer, xxx, xxxi, 174,
194, 210, 230, 244, 261, 483n, 623; articles by, 206n, 449, 671; awards to, 596,
642; and Berlin Exhibit, 183n4; biography of, 680; books by, 255, 295; on community facilities, 222n4, 321, 322,
493–94, 494n1; conferences of, 603; as
consultant, 317; at Cornell University,
195n3, 472n; and CSS, 241–42, 254n1,
401; CSS on, xxvii, 202–3, 368n1; CSS's
correspondence with, 190, 215, 221, 227,

241, 255, 289, 295, 373, 376, 446, 449, 470, 471, 479, 482, 493, 516, 525, 548, 608; defense housing work of, 407; on European housing, 226n2, 228n1; and Greenbelt Towns, xxix, 318n1, 320, 323, 325n1a, 326, 484, 485, 501, 663; at Hillside, 216n1, 222n4, 494n; and Housing Act of 1937, 373n1; and Housing Study Guild, 289, 302, 303n1a, 664, 680; influence of, xix; and London Plan, 446–47; on Milwaukee, 269; at MIT, 481n; and Mumford, 194, 202, 212, 214, 216n1, 246, 255, 368n1, 449, 672, 678; on New York planning, 480; photograph of, 495; on postwar planning, 449; and proposal to FDR, 250n; and RDCA, 482, 503, 516–17; on redevelopment, 134n, 525–26; on regional planning, 608, 610; and RPAA, xix, 207, 257, 471; on slum clearance, 279n1, 675; and Stonorov, 676; and *Town Planning Review*, 548–49; at U.S. Housing Authority, 363,

377n4; and Vinton, 678; and Henry Wright, 680
Wurster, Sadie, 495, 608
Wurster, William, xxxi, 384, 446, 447, 482, 483, 486, 517, 526, 549, 604, 608, 623, 680; CSS's correspondence with, 484, 599; photograph of, 495
Wyldes (Hampstead Garden Suburb), 491–92, 502, 508, 551, 579, 621, 631
Wythenshawe (Manchester, England), 376, 638

Yale University, 202, 610

Zon, Raphael, 256, 257n1
zoning regulations, 82, 85n2, 108, 111; agricultural, 576; and architects, 135; developers of, 662; in Hawaii, 629; limitations of, 572, 573, 574, 605; in New York City, 87; and regional planning, 125; and rent legislation, 121

Division of Rare and Manuscript Collections, Cornell University Library, Clarence S. Stein Papers / Title page illustration, illustrations 1–3, 5–11, 13–17, 23–34, 36–37, 40, 42–46, 49, 51, 59, 62, 64–66, 69–77, 82, 84–99, 101, 102–104, 106–108, 111–112. Photographs by: Richard Southall Grant, ill. 27; Bachrach, ills. 33, 37; Kenneth Clark, ill. 45; Brown Brothers, ill. 49; Kornovski, ill. 52; Peter Shannon, ill. 62; Gottscho-Schleisner, ill. 65; Palmer Shannon, ill. 76; G. Kline Fulmer, ill. 82; Lewis H. Dryer, ill. 103.

Division of Rare and Manuscript Collections, Cornell University Library, Clarence S. Stein Papers, Gretchen VanTassel Collection / Illustrations 54–58

Division of Rare and Manuscript Collections, Cornell University Library, Justin R. Hartzog Papers / Illustration 80

Division of Rare and Manuscript Collections, Cornell University Library, Housing Study Guild Collection / Illustration 38

Ethical Culture Society Archives / Illustration 4

Photograph Collection, Library of Congress / Illustrations 79, 81, 83. Photograph by Carl Mydans, ill. 79.

Drawings by Paul Daniel Marriott / Illustrations 109–110

Monthly Labor Review 7, no. 3 (September 1918) / Illustrations 21, 22. Photographs by Leifur Magnuson.

The New Exploration: A Philosophy of Regional Planning, by Benton MacKaye (New York: Harcourt Brace and Co., 1928), 119 / Illustration 35

New York Herald Tribune, June 1965 / Illustration 113. Photograph by Warman.

New York City Housing Authority (1946), "Construction Cost Analysis, 1945," vol. 1 / Illustration 68

1926 Report of the New York State Commission of Housing and Regional Planning, p. 81 / Illustration 39

Kermit C. Parsons, private collection / Illustrations 48, 63, 78, 100. Photographs by Parsons, ill. 63, 78, 101.

Pencil Points 18, no. 10 (October 1937), 625 / Illustration 12

Phipps Garden Apartment Archives / Illustration 67

Radburn Association Archives / Illustrations 47, 50, 52, 53, 60

Rehousing Urban America, by Henry Wright (New York: Columbia University Press, 1935), 48 / Illustration 61

San Diego Historical Society Research Archives / Illustrations 18–20

A General Plan of Stockholm—1952, 329 / Illustration 105

The Survey 59, no. 11 (1 March 1928) / Illustration 41

ABOUT THE EDITOR

Kermit Carlyle Parsons is a city planner and professor of city planning in the Department of City and Regional Planning, College of Architecture, Art and Planning, at Cornell University in Ithaca, New York. He has taught, practiced, and conducted research in urban planning, the urban development process, and urban planning history since 1957. He was chairman of the department from 1964 to 1971, dean of the college from 1971 to 1980, and director of the Cornell in Washington Public Policy program during the mid-1980s. He is the author of *The Cornell Campus: A History of Its Planning and Development* (Cornell University Press, 1968), *Public Land Acquisition for New Communities: Alternative Strategies* (New York: Center for Urban Development Research, 1977), and many professional articles on city planning and its history. He has also served as a consultant in city planning, urban renewal planning, and college and university planning in numerous cities, in Puerto Rico, Africa, the Philippines, South Korea, and Mexico. He was a founding member and the first president (1966–68) of the Society for College and University Planning. Since 1983 he has been editing the letters and papers of Clarence S. Stein for publication. During that period, he has written a dozen articles and papers about Stein's work and influence on American and European community planning. He is currently completing a biography of Clarence S. Stein and writing a history of the controversies over urban interstate freeway design in Baltimore, Maryland, during the 1960s.

LIBRARY OF CONGRESS CATALOGING-IN-PUBLICATION DATA

Stein, Clarence S.

   The writings of Clarence S. Stein : architect of the planned community / edited by Kermit Carlyle Parsons.

     p.   cm.

   Includes bibliographical references and index.

   ISBN 0-8018-5756-2 (alk. paper)

   1. City planning—United States—History—20th century. 2. Architecture, Modern—20th century—United States. 3. Stein, Clarence S. 4. Architects—United States—Biography. I. Parsons, Kermit C. (Kermit Carlyle), 1927– . II. Title.

NA9108.S83   1998

711'.45—DC21

97-44457

CIP

I Complete Separation of auto & ped

II. View of all stores from auto

from roads. Show line
change Supers above stores

III. Parking at front of Store
do not hide front of stores

IV. Additional parking and

V. Pedestrian walk next to

VI. ___ at no pt. Crosses